The Global Intercultural Communication Reader

The field of intercultural communication seeks to understand the process of communicating across cultural boundaries with an aim toward promoting positive relations between different cultures and nations. *The Global Intercultural Communication Reader* is the first comprehensive anthology to take a distinctly non-Eurocentric approach to analyze and appreciate the diverse ways of communicating in different cultures, incorporating African and Asian as well as Western perspectives. The volume's international scope aims to expand and enlarge the field by promoting greater engagement with the closely related field of international communication.

Featuring twenty readings by important intercultural and international communication scholars, *The Global Intercultural Communication Reader* is edited by Molefi Kete Asante, one of the founders of the field of intercultural communication, along with international scholars Yoshitaka Miike and Jing Yin. The volume is ideal for undergraduate and graduate courses in intercultural communication, particularly those with an international focus.

Molefi Kete Asante is Professor of African American Studies at Temple University. A prolific author of more than sixty books, Asante is largely credited with founding the field of intercultural communication with the publication of his book *The Handbook of Intercultural Communication* (Sage, 1979).

Yoshitaka Miike is Assistant Professor in the Department of Communication at the University of Hawai'i, Hilo.

Jing Yin is Assistant Professor in the Department of Communication at the University of Hawai'i, Hilo.

The Global Intercultural Communication Reader

Molefi Kete Asante, Yoshitaka Miike,
& Jing Yin

EDITORS

Routledge
Taylor & Francis Group

NEW YORK AND LONDON

First published 2008
by Routledge
270 Madison Ave, New York, NY 10016

Simultaneously published in the UK
by Routledge
2 Park Square, Milton Park, Abingdon, Oxon OX14 4RN

Routledge is an imprint of the Taylor & Francis Group, an informa business

© 2008 Taylor and Francis Group

Typeset in Minion by RefineCatch Limited, Bungay, Suffolk
Printed and bound in the United States of America on acid-free paper by Edwards Brothers, Inc.,
Lillington, NC

Library of Congress Cataloging in Publication Data
The global intercultural communication reader / (edited by) Molefi Kete Asante,
Yoshitaka Miike, and Jing Yin.
  p. cm.
  Includes bibliographical references and index.
  1. Intercultural communication.   I. Asante, Molefi K., 1942–.   II. Miike, Yoshitaka.
III. Yin, Jing, 1974–
  HM1211.G56 2008
  303.48′2—dc22

                                                                           2007027865

ISBN10: 0–415–95812–1 (hbk)
ISBN10: 0–415–95813–X (pbk)
ISBN10: 0–203–93498–9 (ebk)

ISBN13: 978–0–415–95812–7 (hbk)
ISBN13: 978–0–415–95813–4 (pbk)
ISBN13: 978–0–203–93498–2 (ebk)

Contents

Dedication
In Honor of Dr. Everett M. Rogers (1931–2004)

Molefi Kete Asante, Yoshitaka Miike, & Jing Yin

On October 21, 2004, Dr. Everett M. Rogers, Distinguished Professor Emeritus in the Department of Communication and Journalism at the University of New Mexico, passed away peacefully at his home in Albuquerque after a prolonged battle with kidney cancer. It is to his memory that we dedicate this collection of essays written on the theory and practice of intercultural communication. Ev remains monumental in his influence, inspiration, and philosophy in the study of culture and communication. Although there are areas in which we disagreed with him, it is impossible to ignore his profound impact on the way we think about communication across national borders and cultural boundaries. Ev was certainly not alone in advancing the field of intercultural communication (see Rogers and Steinfatt, 1999), but none spoke or wrote with any more clarity of purpose or in such earnestness as Ev.

While he was trained as a rural sociologist, Ev followed in the footsteps of the late Dr. Wilbur Schramm—whom he admired and called "the founder of the field of communication study" (Rogers, 1994, p. 446)—and became a pioneer in the discipline of communication in the United States. For nearly half a century, his book *Diffusion of Innovations* (first published in 1962 and now in its 5th edition in 2003) has been a provocative and catalytic work adding to the understanding of how a new idea, practice, or object is disseminated, accepted, or resisted in a given cultural context. In the years after its publication, it was translated into over fifteen languages and helped to inspire an entire generation of communicationists and culturalists. He was a lightning rod for some and a magnet for others. Subsequent to its publication, Ev distinguished himself as an icon of international scholarship in the philosophy of development and the politics of social change. From his theory of diffusion have come scores of dissertations and numerous books, both scholarly and popular. He became within a few years of the first publication of *Diffusion of Innovations* a significant presence in the field of communication. During his 47-year scholarly career, he wrote more than thirty books and five hundred articles.

Ev was born in Carroll, Iowa, on March 6, 1931. Growing up on a family farm, he was puzzled and frustrated by farmers in his home community, including his father, for their delay in adopting agricultural innovations such as the new hybrid seed corn that could have benefited them. After serving as an Air Force officer during the Korean War for two years, he returned to Iowa State University, where he received a bachelor's degree in agriculture (1952), for graduate work. He earned an M.A. (1955) and a Ph.D. (1957) both in rural sociology there. It was his ambition then to learn something about how innovations spread (see Rogers, 2003, pp. xv–xxi for his detailed personal account). What caused some agricultural ideas to be adopted and others rejected? In the course of this worthwhile endeavor, he discovered, among other things, the value of culture and the sustaining power of cultural agency in the transmitting of all messages. He concluded that diffusion is "a special type of communication concerned with the spread of messages that are perceived as new ideas" (Rogers, 2003, p. 35).

While we aptly and eagerly use the ideas and concepts first suggested by Ev as if they were natural, they are indeed ideas that we have inherited from his genius. We are aware of the fact that many marketers and Wharton school graduates do not know that notions of adopters, early or late, majorities, early or late, are Rogerian. Today, we speak of the diffusion of innovations (Rogers, 2003), communication and development (Rogers, 1976), international communication (Rogers, 2002), communication technology (Rogers, 1986), and homophily and heterophily (Rogers & Bhowmik, 1970/1971) with ease, although when Ev began to write these ideas, if they existed, were in the specialized vocabularies of a few enlightened ones in the communication discipline. In the sense that he gave so much of his intellectual energy and moral vision to the problem of human interaction across cultures, he becomes for us one of the enduring symbols of intercultural communication.

Ev's distinction is that he developed his own special approach to international issues and demonstrated by the evolution of his intellectual interest what ought to be the trajectory of the scholar. The incredible beauty of his work, in an aesthetic form, is that it covered so many areas of communication with the same gentle narration of our common humanity (see Singhal & Dearing, 2006). He is indeed a champion for humanity. Scholars found in his work something of value if they were interested in diffusion theory, a history of communication study, how media communicated the dangers of volcanoes to the public, systems theory, computer-mediated communication, especially the Internet, information theory, cybernetics, intercultural communication, health communication, and terrorism communication. How can one scholar touch so many lives and be read so broadly?

There was nothing in communication under the sun that did not interest Ev. Sometimes when we heard him talk it was like he knew something about communication everywhere. If one asked him about Africa and the Internet he was ready with an answer that the lack of strong infrastructures contributed to the lack of Internet access. It was impossible to have strong Internet access without reliable systems like consistent telephones and so forth. If one asked him about Asia, he would say that it was expanding its capacity at a rapid rate and would be the area of greatest growth in the next few years. In classrooms, Ev often shared the mistakes that he had made and the lessons that he had learned in other cultures (sometimes the "hard way" as he put it): dining etiquettes and wedding rituals in India, the importance of facework in Indonesia, and the practice of *nemawashi* in Japan, for example.

When he wrote *Diffusion of Innovations* in 1962, Ev did not know the route he would take or be taken by his academic interests. He held faculty positions at Ohio State University (1957–63), Michigan State University (1964–73), and the University of Michigan (1973–75). He was the Janet M. Peck Professor of International Communication at Stanford University (1975–85) and the Walter H. Annenberg Professor and Associate Dean for Doctoral Studies in the Annenberg School for Communication at the University of Southern California (1985–93). He also taught at the National University of Colombia (Bogotá), the University of Paris (France), the University of Bayreuth (Germany), Nanyang Technological University (Singapore), and Johns Hopkins University.

At the end of his life, however, Ev had come to believe in the need for intercultural communication so strongly that he had devoted his last years to creating and sustaining a doctoral program at the University of New Mexico (UNM). He chaired the UNM Department of Communication and Journalism from 1993 to 1997 (see Hart, 1998). As his role model Schramm founded the first doctoral program in "communication," he founded the first doctoral program in "intercultural communication" after he successfully gained a total of sixteen approvals from various administrative authorities. He was instrumental in writing a program overview, developing a curriculum, and securing funds. During New Mexico days, he also focused some of his intensive energy on intercultural communication, especially its intellectual histories (Rogers, 1999, 2000; Rogers & Hart, 2002; Rogers, et al., 2002; Rogers & Steinfatt, 1999). He was a giant scholar and wonderful teacher. But, above all, he was an excellent mentor. Throughout his career, he directed over seventy dissertations and about fifty M.A. theses.

Ev was open to new ideas and different perspectives. He liked "a healthy critical stance" as he often put it. He wrote at the end of his Preface in the 5th edition of *Diffusion of Innovations*: "We do not need more-of-the-same diffusion research. The challenge for diffusion scholars of the future is to move beyond the proven methods and models of the past, to recognize their shortcomings and limitations, and to broaden their conceptions of the diffusion of innovations" (p. xxi). Echoing his message as it applies to the field of intercultural communication, we present this volume in the hope that we will take future academic pursuits in culture and communication studies with such a challenging mind. Then, it is to his memory that we will carry forward the spirit of humanity along with diversity that he taught us.

References

Hart, W. B. (1998). An interview with Everett M. Rogers: On the past and future of intercultural relations study. *The Edge: The E-Journal of Intercultural Relations, 1*(3). Available: http://www. interculturalrelations.com/v1i3Summer1998/sum98hartrogers.htm.

Rogers, E. M. (Ed.). (1976). *Communication and development: Critical perspectives.* Beverly Hills, CA: Sage.

Rogers, E. M. (1986). *Communication technology: The new media in society.* New York: Free Press.

Rogers, E. M. (1994). *A history of communication study: A biographical approach.* New York: Free Press.

Rogers, E. M. (1999). Georg Simmel's concept of stranger and intercultural communication research. *Communication Theory, 9*(1), 58–74.

Rogers, E. M. (2000). The extensions of men: The correspondence of Marshall McLuhan and Edward T. Hall. *Mass Communication and Society, 3*(1), 117–135.

Rogers, E. M. (2002). Funding international communication research. *Journal of Applied Communication Research, 30*(4), 341–349.

Rogers, E. M. (2003). *Diffusion of innovations* (5th ed.). New York: Free Press.

Rogers, E. M., & Bhowmik, D. K. (1970/1971). Homophily–heterophily: Relational concepts for communication research. *Public Opinion Quarterly, 34*(4), 523–538.

Rogers, E. M., & Steinfatt, T. M. (1999). *Intercultural communication.* Prospect Heights, IL: Waveland Press.

Rogers, E. M., & Hart, W. B. (2002). The histories of intercultural, international, and development communication. In W. B. Gudykunst & B. Mody (Eds.), *Handbook of international and intercultural communication* (2nd ed., pp. 1–18). Thousand Oaks, CA: Sage.

Rogers, E. M., Hart, W. B., & Miike, Y. (2002). Edward T. Hall and the history of intercultural communication: The United States and Japan. *Keio Communication Review, 24*, 3–26.

Singhal, A., & Dearing, J. W. (Eds.). (2006). *Communication of innovations: A journey with Ev Rogers.* New Delhi: Sage.

Notes on Contributors

Molefi Kete Asante (Ph.D., University of California at Los Angeles, 1968) is Professor in the Department of African American Studies at Temple University. Dr. Asante has published more than sixty scholarly books and three hundred journal and magazine articles. Among the most recent books are *Erasing Racism: The Survival of the American Nation, The History of Africa: The Quest for Eternal Harmony*, and *Race, Rhetoric, and Identity: The Architecton of Soul*. He has published more scholarly books than any contemporary African author and has recently been recognized as one of the ten most widely cited African Americans. He created the first Ph.D. program in African American Studies and has directed over 125 Ph.D. dissertations. Dr. Asante is the founding theorist of Afrocentricity. His books, *Afrocentricity: The Theory of Social Change, The Afrocentric Idea*, and *Kemet, Afrocentricity and Knowledge* are the key works in his field. He has been or is presently a consultant for more than twelve school districts for rewriting curricula. Dr. Asante has received numerous awards and honorary doctorates including the 2002 Douglas W. Ehninger Distinguished Rhetorical Scholar Award from the National Communication Association. He is the founding editor of the *Journal of Black Studies*.

Anantha Sudhaker Babbili (Ph.D., University of Iowa, 1981) is Dean of the College of Mass Communication at the Middle Tennessee State University. Dr. Babbili also taught at Texas Christian University and the University of Western Ontario in Canada. He has published his research in several books including *Communication Ethics and Universal Values, Critical Issues in Media, Bosnia by Television, Mass Media in the Middle East*, and *The Press and the State*. His articles have appeared in *Media, Culture & Society, Journal of Communication Inquiry, Newspaper Research Journal*, and *International Third World Studies Journal*. Dr. Babbili is the editor of *Journalism & Communication Monographs* and serves on the editorial boards of the *Journal of Mass Media Ethics* and *Journalism Studies*. He received the Barry Bingham Award from the National Conference of Editorial Writers. The Carnegie Foundation and the Council for the Advancement and Support of Teaching named Dr. Babbili the Texas Professor of the Year.

Hui-Ching Chang (Ph.D., University of Illinois at Urbana-Champaign, 1994) is Associate Professor of Communication at the University of Illinois at Chicago, where she served as Graduate Director from 1996 to 2001. She also served as President of the Association for Chinese Communication Studies (1995–1996) and was Visiting Scholar to the Graduate Institute of Communication Studies at National Chiao Tung University (2001), Graduate Institute of Journalism at National Taiwan University (2003–4), and Department of Communication Studies at Hong

Kong Baptist University (2007). Her research focuses on interpersonal and intercultural communication, and she has received several grants and top paper awards for her research. Her publications have appeared in *Discourse Studies*, *Research on Language and Social Interaction*, *Journal of Language and Social Psychology*, *Journal of Asian Pacific Communication*, and *International and Intercultural Communication Annuals*.

Guo-Ming Chen (Ph.D., Kent State University, 1987) is Professor of Communication at the University of Rhode Island. He received the 1987 outstanding dissertation award presented by the Speech Communication Association International and Intercultural Communication Division. Dr. Chen is the founding president of the Association for Chinese Communication Studies. He served as chair of the Eastern Communication Association Intercultural Communication Interest Group and the co-editor of the *International and Intercultural Communication Annual* (2003–5). In addition to serving as an editorial board member of several professional journals, Dr. Chen presently is the co-editor of *China Media Research* and *Intercultural Communication Studies*. His primary research interests are in intercultural/organizational communication, including the areas of Chinese communication, global communication, communication competence, and conflict management and negotiations. Dr. Chen has published numerous articles, books, chapters, and essays. Those books include *Foundations of Intercultural Communication*, *Communication and Global Society*, *Chinese Conflict Management and Resolution*, and *Theories and Principles of Chinese Communication*.

Sarah Amira De la Garza (formerly María Cristina González) (Ph.D., University of Texas at Austin, 1982) is Associate Professor in the Hugh Downs School of Human Communication at Arizona State University, where she serves as associate director of the North American Center of Transborder Studies. Her research explores borderlands identities, emphasizing postcolonial ethnographic methodology, and she received special commendation by the National Communication Association's Ethnography Division for her influence on the field's scholarship in 2003. Her book, *Maria Speaks: Journeys into the Mysteries of the Mother in My Life as a Chicana*, explores the influence of Mexican religious, cultural, and historical feminine icons on the self-expression of women, developing a methodology for autoethnographic data generation. She has held two Fulbright scholarships to Mexico. Also an affiliate faculty member of the Women and Gender Studies and Transborder Chicana/o and Latina/o Studies departments, she holds the additional degree of D.Min., and her current work explores ethnicity, memory, and trauma in the negotiation of narrative confusion.

Rona Tamiko Halualani (Ph.D., Arizona State University, 1998) is Associate Professor of Language, Culture, and Intercultural Communication in the Communication Studies Department at San Jose State University. Her research interests include race relations, intercultural contact, diversity, prejudice, critical intercultural communication studies, identity and cultural politics, diasporic identity, and Hawaiians/Pacific Islanders. Dr. Halualani possesses expertise in qualitative and critical research methods. For the last three years, she has focused on examining intercultural contact and race relations among university students. She teaches courses on intercultural communication, racial/ethnic identity, cultural studies, diasporic and global movements in relation to culture, quantitative and qualitative research methodology, and gender communication.

Nkonko M. Kamwangamalu (Ph.D., University of Illinois at Urbana-Champaign, 1989) is Professor of Linguistics and English at Howard University in Washington, D.C. He has taught linguistics at the National University of Singapore, the University of Swaziland, and the University of Natal in Durban, South Africa, where he was professor and director of the Linguistics

Program. He has also received a Fulbright award. His research interests include multilingualism, codeswitching, language policy and planning, language and identity, new Englishes, and African linguistics. He has published widely in most of these and related areas. Currently, Dr. Kamwangamalu is researching in the area of language and the economy, with a focus on Africa.

William Kelly (Ph.D., University of New Mexico, 2000) currently teaches in the Communication Studies departments at the University of California, Los Angeles, and California State University, Northridge. He also taught at Sagami Women's University (1986), Sanno Junior College (1987–96), and Aoyama Gakuin Graduate School (1995–96) in Japan. His articles appeared in the *Speaking of Japan, Japan Strategic Management Journal, Sanno Junior College Bulletin, Public Relations Review*, and *China Media Research*. He regularly reviewed books for *The Japan Times* and played a leading role in the development of the Society for Intercultural Education, Training, and Research (Japan). His research interests include dialogue between different regions of the world, nonviolent communication, communicating for peace, and postcolonialism.

Judith N. Martin (Ph.D., Pennsylvania State University, 1980) is currently Professor of Communication in the Hugh Downs School of Human Communication at Arizona State University. She has also taught at the University of Minnesota and the University of New Mexico. Her scholarship focuses on the role of communication in overseas sojourns, issues of ethnicity, race and communication, and culture and new communication technologies. She has co-authored several textbooks in intercultural communication, as well as numerous research articles.

Yoshitaka Miike (Ph.D., University of New Mexico, 2004) is Assistant Professor in the Department of Communication at the University of Hawai'i, Hilo. Inspired by Dr. Molefi Kete Asante's Afrocentric idea, Dr. Miike has proposed the metatheory of Asiacentricity as an alternative paradigm for the study of Asian cultures and communication. He received a 2004 Distinguished Scholarship Award from the International and Intercultural Communication Division of the National Communication Association for the "Outstanding Article" published in 2003. Dr. Miike co-edited journal special issues on *Asian Approaches to Human Communication* and *Asian Contributions to Communication Theory*. His articles have appeared in *China Media Research, Communication Monographs, Human Communication, Intercultural Communication Studies*, the *International and Intercultural Communication Annual, Keio Communication Review*, and the *Review of Communication*. Dr. Miike was elected as the 3rd vice president of the Pacific and Asian Communication Association for 2006–8. He currently reviews manuscripts for several professional journals.

Dreama G. Moon (Ph.D., Arizona State University, 1997) is Chair and Associate Professor in the Communication Department at California State University, San Marcos. She holds an M.A. in Human Relations and Organizational Development, and a B.A. in Criminal Justice. In her scholarly work, she is interested in the social construction of domination and the ways in which both dominant and non-dominant group members negotiate, acquiesce to, and oppose domination. Her research broadly focuses on how ideologies of domination, such as white supremacy, classism, and sexism, are reproduced in and by communication as well as how they are contested, disrupted, and resisted.

Hamid Mowlana (Ph.D., Northwestern University, 1963) is Professor in the School of International Service at American University. Dr. Mowlana served as the founding director of the International Communication Program from 1968 to 2005. He has been a visiting professor at universities in Europe, the Middle East, Latin America, and Africa and has worked for UNESCO in Paris. Among his many books are *Defeat or Victory? Essays on the American Invasion of Iraq*,

Civil Society: A Critique, The Pattern (Model) of Islamic Press and Media, The Rise and Fall of Modernity, Global Communication in Transition: The End of Diversity? and *Global Information and World Communication: New Frontiers in International Relations.* Dr. Mowlana was president of the International Association for Media and Communication Research from 1994 to 1998. He has won numerous national and international awards for outstanding scholarship, research, and other professional contributions including the International Studies Association's Distinguished Senior Scholar Award.

Thomas K. Nakayama (Ph.D., University of Iowa, 1988) is currently Professor in the Hugh Downs School of Human Communication and founding director of Asian Pacific American Studies at Arizona State University. His research is focused on developing critical approaches to intercultural communication and public communication. He has written on whiteness, dialectical approaches to intercultural communication and Asian American studies. He is a fellow of the International Academy of Intercultural Research, a former Fulbrighter at the Université de Mons-Hainaut in Belgium, Libra Professor at the University of Maine, and he served on the Board of Directors of the Arizona Humanities Council.

Humphrey A. Regis (Ph.D., Howard University, 1983) is Professor in the Department of Journalism and Mass Communication, and Director of the Program in Liberal Studies, at the North Carolina A&T State University in Greensboro, North Carolina, USA. He has been a teacher, print journalist, and radio journalist in Saint Lucia and in the United States for more than thirty years. He studies the relationships between mass communication and cultural domination by re-importation/re-exportation, orientation to reference groups, and location in global social space. He also studies the relationships between the long history of the ancient World African Community and the current realities and imperatives in the lives of People of African Descent in the Caribbean.

Edward W. Said (Ph.D., Harvard University, 1964) was University Professor of English and Comparative Literature at Columbia University. He was also a visiting professor at Harvard University, Johns Hopkins University, the University of Toronto, and Yale University. Dr. Said is regarded as a founding theorist in postcolonial studies. He is the author of more than twenty books, which have been translated into thirty-five languages, including the highly acclaimed *Orientalism, Culture and Imperialism,* and *Reflections on Exile and Other Essays.* Dr. Said won several prestigious awards for his memoir, *Out of Place.* He was a sought-after commentator on Middle Eastern politics and regularly wrote for *The Guardian* of London, *Le Monde Diplomatique,* the Arab-language daily *al-Hayat,* and the *Nation.*

Robert Shuter (Ph.D., Northwestern University, 1973) is Professor and Chair of the Department of Communication Studies at Marquette University. He has authored multiple books and scores of articles that have appeared in leading journals including *Communication Monographs, Journal of Communication, Journal of Social Psychology,* and *Management Communication Quarterly.* Dr. Shuter has served on the editorial boards of many journals and is an associate editor of the *Journal of International and Intercultural Communication,* the NCA's new quarterly journal on intercultural communication. Committed to intercultural education for over thirty years, Dr. Shuter is a past president of the National Communication Association's Intercultural Communication Division and has served on numerous intercultural programs, panels, commissions, and committees. A proponent of intracultural theory and research, he has attempted through his work to return "culture" to preeminence in intercultural investigations.

Lise M. Sparrow (Ed.D., University of Massachusetts at Amherst, 2005) has spent her life involved in intercultural work. Her interest in identity stems from her cross-cultural experiences with life and language in Europe, Latin America, and Africa. She received her Master's in English as a Second Language and Spanish from the School for International Training and her Doctorate in Culture, Language, and Literacy from the University of Massachusetts at Amherst. She taught for more than twenty-five years at the School for Intercultural Training in Vermont, focusing on issues of intercultural communication, identity, and diversity. More recently, she has been involved, both overseas and in Vermont, with issues of identity and religious diversity.

William J. Starosta (Ph.D., Indiana University, 1973) is Graduate Professor of Rhetoric and Intercultural Communication at Howard University. He is founding editor of the *Howard Journal of Communications*. His most recent research concerns Gandhian *Satyagraha*, coverage of interethnic conflict, double emic criticism, intercultural listening, and third culture building. His work appears in *International Philosophical Quarterly*, *Political Communication and Persuasion*, *International and International Communication Annual*, *World Communication*, *International Journal of Intercultural Relations*, *Journal of Black Studies*, *Educational Communication and Technology Journal*, *Quarterly Journal of Speech*, and in other speech communication journals.

Dolores Valencia Tanno (Ph.D., University of Southern California, 1990) is currently Associate Dean of the Honors College at the University of Nevada, Las Vegas. Before taking on an administrative role, she was a professor of Communication specializing in intercultural communication and ethics of communication research. Dr. Tanno has been a visiting professor at Arizona State University (1996) and at Roskilde University in Denmark (2002). She has been invited to give presentations in Poland, Denmark, Mexico, New Zealand, and Costa Rica, as well as across the United States. Dr. Tanno has published three books and many articles in national, interdisciplinary, and international journals.

Yukio Tsuda (Ph.D., Southern Illinois University at Carbondale, 1985) is currently Professor at the Doctoral Program in Modern Cultures and Public Policies in the Graduate School of Humanities and Social Sciences at the University of Tsukuba in Japan. His major academic interests include global language policy, critique of the hegemony of English, international communication and English language teaching. He has published a number of books including *Language Inequality and Distortion in Intercultural Communication: A Critical Theory Approach* (1986), *Eigo Shihaino Kouzou* [*The Structure of the Hegemony of English*] (1990), *Eigo Shihaieno Iron* [*Objections to the Hegemony of English*] (1993), *Eigo Shihaitoha Nanika* [*What is the Hegemony of English?*] (2003), and *Eigo Shihaito Kotobano Byoudou* [*The Hegemony of English and Linguistic Equality*] (2006).

Tu Weiming (Ph.D., Harvard University, 1968) is Professor in the Department of East Asian Languages and Civilizations at Harvard University and Director of the Harvard-Yenching Institute. He is the first professor of Confucian studies at any English-language university, a position awarded to him in 1999. Dr. Tu has also taught at Princeton University, the University of California at Berkeley, Peking University, Taiwan University, the Chinese University of Hong Kong, and Ecole des Haute Etudes in Paris. He was invited by the United Nations as a member of the Group of Eminent Persons to facilitate the Dialogue among Civilizations in 2001 and gave a presentation on civilizational dialogue to the Executive Board of UNESCO in 2004. Dr. Tu has published over a dozen books in English including *Confucian Thought: Selfhood as Creative Transformation* and *Confucian Traditions in East Asian Modernity*. His five-volume collected works were published in China in 2001. He is currently studying the modern transformation of Confucian humanism in East Asia and tapping Confucian spiritual resources for human flourishing in the global community.

Jing Yin (Ph.D., Pennsylvania State University, 2003) is Assistant Professor in the Department of Communication at the University of Hawai'i, Hilo. Dr. Yin's research interests include the impact of globalization, media discourse and representation, and non-Western feminist discourse. She has published in such journals as *China Media Research, Critical Discourse Studies, Discourse Processes,* the *Howard Journal of Communications,* the *Journal of the Association of University Technology Managers,* the *Review of Communication,* and *Technovation.* Her works have also appeared in several scholarly books including *Chinese Communication Studies: Contexts and Comparisons* and *Systems and Policies for the Globalized Learning Economy.* Dr. Yin translated several theoretical essays on culture and communication into Chinese, which were published in *Intercultural Communication* and *Theories and Principles of Chinese Communication.* She is a member of the editorial board of *Human Communication: A Journal of the Pacific and Asian Communication Association.* She won a top paper award from the International and Intercultural Communication Division of the National Communication Association.

Acknowledgments

We would like to extend our sincere appreciation to Matthew Brynie, senior editor in media and cultural studies, and Mr. Stan Spring, editorial assistant, at Routledge, for their advice and guidance. We are also indebted to Dr. Michael L. Hecht at Pennsylvania State University, Dr. Rona Tamiko Halualani at San José State University, and the other anonymous reviewers for their comments and criticisms and to all the authors of the present volume for their works that broaden and deepen our understanding of the processes and politics of intercultural communication. We wish to express our heartfelt thanks to the Department of African American Studies at Temple University and to the Department of Communication at the University of Hawai'i, Hilo, for their timely support and ready cooperation. Finally, we are grateful to Ms. Ana Yenenga for always being caring and considerate as we made progress toward the completion of this book and to Dr. Corinne L. Shefner-Rogers for providing us with accurate information about the life and work of Dr. Everett M. Rogers.

Introduction
Issues and Challenges in Intercultural Communication Scholarship

Molefi Kete Asante, Yoshitaka Miike, & Jing Yin

The intercultural communication enterprise has been driven by an emphasis on the relationships between the modern European world, as expressed by the dominant cultures of North America and Europe, and various native peoples of America, Asia, and Africa. From the outset, the field's academic emphasis, following general commercial and trade interests, has been on interpreting "other" cultures in search of the most productive pathways to the consumers of those societies. This strategic alterity has proven significant in theoretical and methodological developments in the field. Indeed, it is the basis for the work of many contemporary scholars in intercultural communication. As globalization and localization intensify in every corner of the world, however, the field is increasingly confronted by more fundamental issues of identity, community, and humanity. In effect, intercultural communication is the only way to mitigate identity politics, social disintegration, religious conflicts, and ecological vulnerability in the global village. Human survival and flourishing depends on our ability to communicate successfully across differences.

In response to this worldwide sense of urgency, the intellectual nature and scope of the intercultural communication field are evolving and transforming. Intercultural communication studies are at a crossroads today. Certainly, the field has gone through many changes toward methodological pluralism and refinements and has reached the turning point of thinking dialectically about culture and communication. But the question still awaits an answer: Is the intercultural field truly intercultural? One may wonder if "the topics we pursue, the theories we build, the methods we employ, and the materials we read adequately reflect and respond to the diversity of our communicative experiences in a globalizing world" (Miike, 2003, pp. 243–244). If the field is in ferment, as Starosta and Chen (2003) noted, it is imperative for intercultural communication researchers to further formulate critical reflections on established theories and proven methods, and to contemplate on past achievements and future directions.

Our aim in this volume, then, is to present the best works of some of the principal scholars on the subject of intercultural communication in order to provide an impetus for the field's future. Most of the essays selected for this collection are fugitive pieces scattered across different journals and books. They are essential readings that deserve due attention in the current intercultural communication literature. For the present anthology, we strived to cover a wide range of continents, countries, and cultures. However, we did not include the essays published in major intercultural outlets such as the *International and Intercultural Communication Annual* (e.g., Tanno & González, 1997, 1998, 1999; Chen & Starosta, 2004; Collier, 2000, 2001, 2002; Orbe et al., 2006; Starosta & Chen, 2003, 2005) as they are readily available. This edited reader is designed primarily for graduate seminars and upper division undergraduate courses related to the study of culture and communication.

Issues and Challenges in the Field

In selecting readings for this compilation, we focused specifically on three unresolved issues in the field of intercultural communication: (1) Eurocentric intellectual imperialism in cross-cultural communication research; (2) the neglect of indigenous perspectives in culture and communication inquiries; and (3) communication equality and mutuality in intercultural contexts. The fact that these three long-standing issues in the field remain unresolved has little to do with the methodological expertise of communication researchers.

The first issue is Eurocentric intellectual imperialism in cross-cultural communication research. The field has produced some of the most outstanding contemporary intellectuals. Their work is used in sociology, social work, political science, history, literature, and anthropology. Nevertheless, there is a lacuna in the literature about the impact of communication imperialism on the communicative situation itself. There seems to be a presumption in most cases that the communication scholars have found the truth and the only thing left is the application of that truth to various cultures of the world. They "would simply pack their tools from Western organizational or interpersonal theory, make camp at the intercultural interaction, and unpack the same instruments for work" (Asante & Vora, 1983, p. 294). It is like saying that your mother's cooking is the best cooking without ever tasting anyone else's food. Therefore, we believe that these issues should be resolved openly and with the objective of creating a synergy of relationships that extend beyond the imposition of one system on the other.

In 1979, the *Handbook of Intercultural Communication* was produced with Molefi Kete Asante, Eileen Newmark, and Cecil A. Blake as editors. This book was the first attempt to explain communication between cultures in a coherent manner. The editors were interested in calling into question some of the old habits in the discipline of communication. The work was a success in that it set the intercultural field on a more theoretical path. However, by the time the second *Handbook of International and Intercultural Communication* edited by Asante and William B. Gudykunst appeared in 1989, the field's character had changed, becoming far more interested in socio-psychological dimensions. Books that concentrated on cultural learning, particularly as it related to Asian societies, were popular. In one sense, communication interaction may be said to have followed commercial interaction. While recent readers (Chen & Starosta, 2000; Gonzalez et al., 2004; Fong & Chuang, 2004; Jackson, 2004; Jackson & Richardson, 2003; Jandt, 2004; Leeds-Hurwitz, 2005; Lengel, 2005; Lustig & Koester, 2006; Martin et al., 2002; Milhouse et al., 2001; Samovar et al., 2006; Shuter, 1990; Sitaram & Prosser, 1998) enrich the discourse by bringing together a number of outstanding scholars to examine various aspects of intercultural communication, Eurocentric intellectual imperialism is still pervasive in the field. We must end a Eurocentric era of the intercultural field and begin a multicultural era of the intercultural field (Miike, 2003).

The second issue is the neglect of indigenous perspectives in culture and communication inquiries. One only has to point to the numerous articles and books that have sought to provide the Western reader with an understanding of the East or the South. As the late Edward W. Said (1993, p. xi) once said, what is striking about these discourses is the prevalence of such terms as "the Asian or African mind," "mysterious China," and "force as the best measures for some of these people." Thus, the theoretical and methodological plinth retains some of the more naive perspectives that one would find during the era of Western imperialism. We "must not impose Western categories, otherwise we make the mystification of the intercultural encounter insoluble because we operate in a cultural closet. By misunderstanding the complexity of the intercultural questions, we short-circuit all reasonable answers" (Asante & Vora, 1983, pp. 293–294). We should be alert to the fact that "The cultural values of the scholars who study intercultural communication affect what they investigate, with what methods, what they find, and how they interpret the findings" (Rogers & Steinfatt, 1999, p. 74).

It should not be expected, in the first case, that all the writers from non-Western cultures have been untouched by the phenomenon of defining their own cultures by the boundaries set by the West. Too often, they have failed to utilize the experiences of their own cultures to add to the discourse on communication. This failure has produced a troubling deficit in theoretical developments from those cultures because some scholars have been eager to demonstrate that they, too, have been able to see through the same eyes as those European and American scholars who have pioneered in this field. One of the dangers often discussed by the late Everett M. Rogers was that students arriving from Africa or Asia would accept the given molds of communication rather than bring to the forefront the gifts that they have from their own cultures. As Ev and others have understood it, this acceptance would be the rational response to cultural or communication imperialism, not a rejection of the platform that had been established, but an enlarging, re-mixing, and re-creation of it to include ideas, concepts, theories, and methods that may have prevented the communication scholar of the past from examining other ways of creating and maintaining communication.

Asante (1998, p. 71) stated that "Any interpretation of African culture must begin at once to dispense with the notion that, in all things, Europe is teacher and Africa is pupil." He used the teacher–student metaphor to refer to the issue of "culture as text and culture as theory" that Miike (2004) pinpointed. There has been an implicit tendency to approach Western cultures from a student's perspective and non-Western cultures from a teacher's perspective in the study of culture and communication. In fact, much intercultural communication research deals with non-Western cultures as targets for analysis and critique, but not as resources for theoretical insight. Even critical intercultural communication studies often fail to approach non-Western cultures from a student's perspective and see cultures as texts for deconstruction rather than theories for reconstruction. Therefore, it also promotes a teacher's perspective on non-Western cultures, which decenters and dislocates non-Western people. We cannot appreciate cultures when we always analyze and critique them. We can appreciate cultures when we learn from them (Miike, 2006). The time is long overdue for intercultural communication professionals to challenge and change this problematic structure of culture learning.

The third issue is communication equality and mutuality in intercultural contexts. It is impossible to have communication equality, that is, an appreciation of the nuances, philosophies, and bases of communication without confronting communication imperialism (Asante, 2005; Miike, 2007). It is essential for humans to attempt to "feel" into the other culture if we are to be abundant communicators in intercultural contexts. Of course, feeling into is not enough. We must seek to know the way individuals think and the nature of communities' philosophies of life if we are to be satisfied that our messages have been adequately delivered and received. It is one thing to deliver a message to someone; it is another thing for that message to be received, and yet another for it to be received as you intended it.

Understandably, communication scholars trying to appreciate the varieties of cultural differences become subscribers to the most elaborate and complex theories about human relationship. If one examines the early works in intercultural communication, what is clear is the singularity of their progressive agenda, to construct a world of human cultures, without hierarchy, in the best tradition of communication scholarship. Since the late 1970s, we have seen an explosion of intercultural work. Scores of articles and manuscripts have been produced. Unfortunately, we have often become victims of provincial and narrow attitudes about world cultures and therefore have produced a plethora of papers that detail ways to influence at a pragmatic level without the necessary emphasis on substance in communication.

In particular, the impact of power on communication equality and mutuality has not been scrutinized in many intercultural communication studies. Asante (1980, p. 402) expounded on the nature and role of power in communication across cultures as follows:

Indeed, as propounded by Eurocentric social scientists, the idea of interaction may be the principal instrument of the transubstantiation of privilege and power into accepted reality. It legitimizes the values of a Eurocentric theoretical perspective on human communication and makes it possible for the strengthening of the established power relations by obscuring the power relations as power relations.... The dominated culture legitimizes its own domination by participating in the world view of the dominating culture.... As long as the legitimizing concepts are acceptable to the "illegitimates," the dominated, then there is no need for the dominating culture to introduce brute reinforcement for the perception and domination of its views because to do so would be to disturb the accepted balance of power and creates an awakening in the "illegitimates" toward the true nature of the communication interaction.

One of the formidable challenges that interculturalists are facing today is to find a way to properly account for complex issues of power and privilege embedded in communication itself because, as Asante (1983, p. 9) tersely put, "Intercultural communication as a harmonious endeavor seeks to create the sharing of power."

In one way or another, the chapters that follow in the present anthology challenge Eurocentric intellectual imperialism in cross-cultural communication research, provide indigenous insights into the intersection of culture and communication, and address equality and mutuality in intercultural communication contexts. We hope to remind scholars and students in the intercultural field of the openness that Asante and Vora (1983, p. 298) emphasized:

The opportunities for creative research into non-Western perspectives are numerous. Collaborating with scholars from different cultural backgrounds, tapping international students, living in a different culture for a relatively long period of time, researching with persons from different but related disciplines in other cultures, and other approaches provide tremendous exciting avenues for broad intercultural studies. We have the intellectual capability to advance on this new frontier through the acceptance of openness toward non-Western ideas, perspectives, and philosophies.

Overview of the Book

This edited volume is divided into six parts. Part I, Perspectives on Culture in Theory and Research, is comprised of three reflexive reviews of literature, which critically examine the history of intercultural communication scholarship in light of its conceptualizations of culture. In chapter 1, Dreama G. Moon interrogates how the notions of culture have been constructed and changed in the intercultural communication literature over the years. In chapter 2, Dolores Valencia Tanno challenges the often-employed "comparative approach," which implicitly treats one culture as the standard to judge another culture, and offers ethical guidelines for multicultural research. In chapter 3, Robert Shuter argues that culture should not merely serve as a laboratory for theory validation research and proposes an intracultural imperative as a new research agenda that returns culture to preeminence.

Part II, Metatheoretical Frameworks for Future Directions, includes three thought-provoking pieces that guide future theoretical development and methodological refinement in culture and communication research. In chapter 4, Molefi Kete Asante asserts that power, ideology, economics, politics, and symbols have been neglected in the intercultural communication field and suggests that theoretical postures based on African cultural heritages should be formulated in future research on African communication. In chapter 5, Yoshitaka Miike propounds a communication metatheory of Asiacentricity by envisioning its research objectives, content dimensions, and methodological considerations. In chapter 6, Judith N. Martin and Thomas K. Nakayama map out four contemporary approaches to the study of culture and communication and delineate six dialectics of intercultural communication practices that may be able to integrate the field's metatheoretical diversity.

Part III, Contextual Approaches to Culture and Communication, assembles four culture-specific inquiries. These emic studies take a careful look at cultural discourses in context and proffer some theoretical and methodological insights into communication practices in particular communities. In chapter 7, Hui-Ching Chang explicates the what and why of verbal communication among East Asians from a Confucian perspective and urges the importance of understanding Asian philosophical thought to appreciate Asian styles of communication. In chapter 8, Nkonko M. Kamwangamalu defines and delimits the pan-African concept of *ubuntu* and its ethical implications for communication in local and global contexts. In chapter 9, Jing Yin analyzes the construction of Chinese culture in the film, *The Joy Luck Club*, and maintains that the self–other dichotomy is achieved through selective representation, attribution, and subsumption of class and gender to culture. In chapter 10, Amira De la Garza explores the intersection of ontology and methodology and proposes the Four Seasons of Ethnography as a context-sensitive, co-creative method of inquiry.

Part IV, Impact of Globalization on Intercultural Communication, presents three critical interrogations about cultural exchange and change in the wave of globalization. In chapter 11, Yukio Tsuda problematizes the frequent use of English in intercultural interactions as a form of hegemony, which, in his opinion, is linked with globalization as Anglo-Americanization, transnationalization, and commercialization. In chapter 12, Rona Tamiko Halualani scrutinizes Asian mail-order bride catalogs as hegemonic constructions that subjugate Pilipina females to commodities, sexual objects, and racial others. Such cultural texts, she posits, sustains and reproduces the dominant Anglo patriarchal ideology and the inequitable racial and gender relations. In chapter 13, Humphrey A. Regis examines re-importing and re-exporting issues in global communication by analyzing how cultural practices and artifacts originated in Caribbean African communities are transported to, and modified in, Europe and the United States and then re-imported to Africans in the Caribbean region.

Part V, Identity and Intercultural Communication Competence, consists of three essays that synthesize and challenge past conceptualizations of multicultural identity and intercultural communication competence. In chapter 14, Guo-Ming Chen and William J. Starosta outline six approaches to the study of intercultural communication competence and propose a model of affective intercultural sensitivity, cognitive intercultural awareness, and behavioral intercultural adroitness. In chapter 15, Lise M. Sparrow challenges Peter Adler's model of "multicultural man" and questions if "marginality," "in-betweenness," and "uniqueness" are indeed essential characteristics of multicultural identity. In chapter 16, William Kelly applies a critical approach to interpersonal communication between White U.S. Americans and the Japanese and then presents his own personal narratives to illustrate alternative visions of intercultural identity and competence.

Part VI, Ethical Considerations in Intercultural Communication, collects four well thought-out writings for the future of the global society. They concern themselves with ethical issues in local and global communication. In chapter 17, Hamid Mowlana offers an Islamic perspective on ethical communication by highlighting the theory of *tawhid*, the doctrine of *tabligh*, the concept of *ummah*, the principle of *taqwa*, and the meaning of *amanat*. In chapter 18, Anantha Sudhaker Babbili addresses the contours and complexities of communication ethics in postcolonial India by historicizing the nation's colonial experiences and detailing her religious foundations. In chapter 19, Edward W. Said provides a vivid personal account of the question of Palestine and suggests that the pieties, exuberance, and triumphalism of wars should be re-examined. This edited reader concludes with chapter 20, where Tu Weiming poses some critical questions about global ethics and convincingly argues that mutual referencing and learning is vital to human flourishing and social development in the global community.

Toward Harmonious Coexistence

Consciousness expands with time and experience. Scholars working in intercultural communication have seen the tremendous advances made possible by expanded consciousness. What those living in the West know about the civilizations of Africa, Asia, and South America is far more than was known just a few years ago. Connected to vast regions of the world by the Internet, we have all become organically linked to information. No one needs to declare provinciality anymore. We are truly the world, and more immediate and contemporary images can replace the old worn-out ones that we may have once had about others or ourselves. In this regard, a form of globalization has already taken place. We can never be naive again about our own place in the world. We are not just who we think we are; we are also who others think we are. Somewhere in the convergence of the two perceptions, we discover always the meaning of our existence.

So what are the implications for intercultural communication in this type of new world? Implied in all of the selections in this collection is the idea that the people of the world can communicate. There is a sense that we are against conflict and in support of the harmonious coexistence of humans. One does not become involved in communication at the interactive level without some optimistic perspective in mind. The aim of the scholar as much as the communicator in an ordinary interactive situation is to create a way to engage in harmony. This is no pipe dream; it is in actuality the only reason why we communicate, that is, to make ourselves understood in ways that produce harmony.

No one believes that harmony will occur all the time, but we do believe that it is essential that the communicative doors are open to the possibilities of useful human coexistence. Once the doors are closed to communication, one cannot have dialogue or discourse; the attitude of the communicator in this new world should include an openness to the great varieties of human creativity. The fact of the matter is that Jerusalem is no more sacred than Mecca, or Benares, or Kyoto, or Ile-Ife to those who see their connections in those places. But neither are any other places more sacred than Jerusalem. An enormous human creativity sits at the very gate of our communication process. Until we are able to establish this type of consciousness in the literature, we will not create it in the commonplaces of ordinary conversation.

To claim that there is something of Tokyo in every city and something of Lagos in every city is to make a claim for international connectedness based on the exchange of ideas, thoughts, myth, and goods. We are participants in a world running full speed toward a common language transmuted, but not because it becomes a language embedded with world ideas rather than those of a single culture. Of course, this is a new view, but an essential one in the sense that we are determined to demonstrate by the present volume a variety of ways that we can approach human communication in a global manner. Global cannot mean the prosecution of a single cultural reality as if it is global; it must mean the acceptance of an integrative global system where those who communicate are able to bring into consideration the *yuan-fen* and *nkrabea* as well as Western concepts.

Our work as scholars is to assist in mapping where we have been and where we are going as human beings. However, only a radical reassessment of our traditional patterns in communication can provide us with a model, a scheme, an understanding of our future (Asante, 2005). As simple patterns of Western communication universalized to resemble a world system, the communication models of the past have brought us to the brink of chaos. There is general agreement that we cannot order and generalize about the nature of the human reality without assembling more information from other than Western cultures. This is our challenge, and it is one that we must confront fully if we are to appreciate causal relationships among phenomena in different cultures and nations. Our map, therefore, is not simple; it is complicated, and the work of the scholars we present in these pages is difficult but rewarding for those who wish to enter the world of the complex which, after all, is the world we live in.

References

Asante, M. K. (1980). Intercultural communication: An inquiry into research directions. In D. Nimmo (Ed.), *Communication yearbook* (Vol. 4, pp. 401–410). News Brunswick, NJ: Transaction.

Asante, M. K. (1983). The ideological significance of Afrocentricity in intercultural communication. *Journal of Black Studies, 14*(1), 3–19.

Asante, M. K. (1998). *The Afrocentric idea* (Rev. ed.). Philadelphia, PA: Temple University Press.

Asante, M. K. (2005). *Race, rhetoric, and identity: The architecton of soul.* Amherst, NY: Humanity Books.

Asante, M. K., & Vora, E. (1983). Toward multiple philosophical approaches. In W. B. Gudykunst (Ed.), *Intercultural communication theory: Current perspectives* (pp. 293–298). Beverly Hills, CA: Sage.

Asante, M. K., & Gudykunst, W. B. (Eds.). (1989). *Handbook of international and intercultural communication.* Newbury Park, CA: Sage.

Asante, M. K., Newmark, E., & Blake, C. A. (Eds.). (1979). *Handbook of intercultural communication.* Beverly Hills, CA: Sage.

Chen, G.-M., & Starosta, W. J. (Eds.). (2000). *Communication and global society.* New York: Peter Lang.

Chen, G.-M., & Starosta, W. J. (Eds.). (2004). *Dialogue among diversities* [*International and Intercultural Communication Annual,* Vol. 27]. Washington, DC: National Communication Association.

Collier, M. J. (Ed.). (2000). *Constituting cultural difference through discourse* [*International and Intercultural Communication Annual,* Vol. 23]. Thousand Oaks, CA: Sage.

Collier, M. J. (Ed.). (2001). *Transforming communication about culture: Critical new directions* [*International and Intercultural Communication Annual,* Vol. 24]. Thousand Oaks, CA: Sage.

Collier, M. J. (Ed.). (2002). *Intercultural alliances: Critical transformation* [*International and Intercultural Communication Annual,* Vol. 25]. Thousand Oaks, CA: Sage.

Fong, M., & Chuang, R. (Eds.). (2004). *Communicating ethnic and cultural identity.* Lanham, MD: Rowman & Littlefield.

Gonzalez, A., Houston, M., & Chen, V. (Eds.). (2004). *Our voices: Essays in culture, ethnicity, and communication* (4th ed.). Los Angeles, CA: Roxbury.

Jackson, R. L. (Ed.). (2004). *African American communication and identities: Essential readings.* Thousands Oaks, CA: Sage.

Jackson, R. L., & Richardson, E. B. (Eds.). (2003). *Understanding African American rhetoric: Classical origins to contemporary innovations.* New York: Routledge.

Jandt, F. E. (Ed.). (2004). *Intercultural communication: A global reader.* Thousand Oaks, CA: Sage.

Leeds-Hurwitz, W. (Ed.). (2005). *From generation to generation: Maintaining cultural identity over time.* Cresskill, NJ: Hampton Press.

Lengel, L. B. (Ed.). (2005). *Intercultural communication and creative practice: Music, dance, and women's cultural identity.* Westport, CT: Praeger.

Lustig, M. W., & Koester, J. (Eds.). (2006). *AmongUS: Essays on identity, belonging, and intercultural competence* (2nd ed.). Boston, MA: Allyn & Bacon.

Martin, J. N., Nakayama, T. K., & Flores, L. A. (Eds.). (2002). *Readings in intercultural communication: Experiences and contexts* (2nd ed.). New York: McGraw-Hill.

Miike, Y. (2003). Beyond Eurocentrism in the intercultural field: Searching for an Asiacentric paradigm. In W. J. Starosta & G.-M. Chen (Eds.), *Ferment in the intercultural field: Axiology/value/praxis* (pp. 243–276). Thousand Oaks, CA: Sage.

Miike, Y. (2004). Rethinking humanity, culture, and communication: Asiacentric critiques and contributions. *Human Communication: A Journal of the Pacific and Asian Communication Association, 7*(1), 67–82.

Miike, Y. (2006). Non-Western theory in Western research? An Asiacentric agenda for Asian communication studies. *Review of Communication, 6*(1/2), 4–31.

Miike, Y. (2007). An Asiacentric reflection on Eurocentric bias in communication theory. *Communication Monographs, 74*(2), 272–278.

Milhouse, V. H., Asante, M. K., & Nwosu, P. O. (Eds.). (2001). *Transcultural realities: Interdisciplinary perspectives on cross-cultural relations.* Thousand Oaks, CA: Sage.

Orbe, M. P., Allen, B. J., & Flores, L. A. (Eds.). (2006). *The same and different: Acknowledging the diversity within and between cultural groups* [*International and Intercultural Communication Annual*, Vol. 29]. Washington, DC: National Communication Association.

Rogers, E. M., & Steinfatt, T. M. (1999). *Intercultural communication*. Prospect Heights, IL: Waveland Press.

Said, E. W. (1993). *Culture and imperialism*. New York: Vintage.

Samovar, L. A., Porter, R. E., & McDaniel, E. R. (Eds.). (2006). *Intercultural communication: A reader* (11th ed.). Belmont, CA: Wadsworth.

Shuter, R. (1990). Patterns of intracultural communication [Special issue]. *Southern Communication Journal*, *55*(3), 237–328.

Sitaram, K. S., & Prosser, M. H. (Eds.). (1998). *Civic discourse: Multiculturalism, cultural diversity, and global communication*. Stamford, CT: Ablex.

Starosta, W. J., & Chen, G.-M. (Eds.). (2003). *Ferment in the intercultural field: Axiology/value/praxis* [*International and Intercultural Communication Annual*, Vol. 26]. Thousand Oaks, CA: Sage.

Starosta, W. J., & Chen, G.-M. (Eds.). (2005). *Taking stock in intercultural communication: Where to now?* [*International and Intercultural Communication Annual*, Vol. 28]. Washington, DC: National Communication Association.

Tanno, D. V., & González, A. (Eds.). (1997). *Politics, communication, and culture* [*International and Intercultural Communication Annual*, Vol. 20]. Thousand Oaks, CA: Sage.

Tanno, D. V., & González, A. (Eds.). (1998). *Communication and identity across cultures* [*International and Intercultural Communication Annual*, Vol. 21]. Thousand Oaks, CA: Sage.

Tanno, D. V., & González, A. (Eds.). (1999). *Rhetoric in intercultural contexts* [*International and Intercultural Communication Annual*, Vol. 22]. Thousand Oaks, CA: Sage.

Part I
Perspectives on Culture in Theory and Research

1

Concepts of "Culture"
Implications for Intercultural Communication Research

Dreama G. Moon

A discursive formation can be seen as a system of statements that "set the context in which constitutive statements are held to . . . be 'true'" (Rice, 1992, p. 339). For Foucault, "truth" is an "ensemble of rules . . . [and] a system of ordered procedures for the production, regulation, distribution, and operation of statements" (1980, pp. 132–133). In essence, a Foucaultian genealogical inquiry seeks to trace the "descent" and "emergence" of new discursive formations and to chart a discourse's lineage across the path of contradictions and logical discontinuities, particularly the "accidents, chance, passion, petty malice, surprises . . . and power" (Davidson, 1986, p. 224) that foster discursive formations (Rice, 1992).

In this Foucaultian sense, I interrogate the historical emergence of intercultural communication as a field of inquiry and the subsequent impact this has had on intercultural communication scholarship. In addition, I examine how the configuration of the field affects the ability of scholars to engage in current theoretical debates. If it is true that disciplines as a group "constitute systems of control in the production of discourse" (Foucault, 1972, p. 222), inquiry into the formation of intercultural communication discourse should serve to create a vision of not only where we have been, but where we are and where next we might want to go as intercultural communication scholars.

The task is to highlight a historical moment in the formation of intercultural communication discourse in which particular statements came to be taken as "truth" within the field. In course, I briefly revisit the era encompassing the work of Edward T. Hall at the Foreign Service Institute (FSI), review a sample of intercultural communication scholarship published in communication journals during the 1970s, and then discuss current theoretical debates and their impact—or lack of—on intercultural communication scholarship. From a Foucaultian frame of power and knowledge, I then examine the construction of the discipline of intercultural communication and how certain statements became hegemonic and defining while others did not.

In the course of developing the above argument, I pay particular attention to the text of Leeds-Hurwitz (1990) as it attempts to provide the definitive history of the field. I deconstruct that text to show the absence of alternative readings of culture. Next, I examine published work in the 1970s and 1980s, when the discipline of intercultural communication becomes crystallized. Finally, I end by examining contemporary work in the field and indicating some contributions that critical feminist theory can make to a broader intercultural communication inquiry.

A Genealogy of Intercultural Communication

Employing a dialectic of continuity and discontinuity, Foucault (1980) argues that "historical breaks always include some overlapping, interaction, and echoes between the old and the new" (p. 361). Through examining such ruptures, one can begin to "grasp historical events in their real complexity" (Best & Kellner, 1991, p. 46). One such "break" with respect to intercultural communication encompasses the creation of the Foreign Service Institute (FSI) and the role played there by anthropologist Edward T. Hall. Indeed, this era is often marked as the "beginning" of the field of intercultural communication (Leeds-Hurwitz, 1990); its importance to the development and formation of intercultural communication as a field has been documented (e.g., Harman & Briggs, 1991; Leeds-Hurwitz, 1990). However, according to Leeds-Hurwitz (1990), Hall's work "was shaped by the specific context of the FSI" (p. 260). More to the point, his vision of and approach to the study of "culture" was substantially altered by his experiences at the FSI. Though acknowledged by Leeds-Hurwitz (1990), the implications of Hall's transformative experience at the FSI remain unexamined. In light of this, I revisit the development of the FSI and Hall's experience there, paying particular attention to the connection between power and knowledge.

Dis/abling legacy?: Edward T. Hall and the FSI

The Foreign Service Institute was formally established in 1947 to provide career-long inservice training to Foreign Service officials. In 1951, Edward T. Hall joined the staff (Leeds-Hurwitz, 1990). It should be noted that the duties of Service officers were not limited to diplomatic ones in the strictest sense of the word. Much of their role included feeding important information regarding their countries of assignment back to the U.S. government. If Foreign Service personnel were to be the "eyes and ears" of the government, however, they would require a variety of specialized cultural training.

The training that Hall and his associates offered to foreign service personnel consisted of "beginning instruction in the language of the country of assignment, orientation to the mission and its philosophy, limited study of the country and area," as well as limited anthropological and linguistic conceptualizations of "culture" (Leeds-Hurwitz, 1990, p. 267). However, many of the FSI students found the anthropological concept of culture as a shared historically transmitted system of codes—or in Hall and Hall's (1989) words, "shared information along with shared methods of coding, storing, and retrieving that information" (pp. xiii–xiv)—difficult to understand and irrelevant, preferring more specific and concrete information. The trainees' limited perceptions and emphasis on goal achievement complicated the training task for Hall and his associates. Hall (1956) writes:

> The younger officers . . . because of the emphasis on "political" reporting, often were left with the idea that there was nothing of importance to be learned from the foreigner as a member of his culture, and that if they could just get to the "right person," in the political sense, the cold dope on any given situation could be obtained.
>
> (p. 7)

This attitude reflected what Hall (1956) called the "self-evident truths" of the trainees—unquestioned, unexamined, taken-for-granted beliefs assumed to be "true" and "common sensical"—against and with which Hall struggled. Two of these taken-for-granted beliefs were particularly problematic: the first being the old saw that "people are the same wherever you go" and the other being "the best way to learn is through personal experience" (Hall, 1956). The training situation was further complicated by other problems including bureaucratic red tape, disrespect for academics in general and anthropologists in particular, and the view that training was unneeded and unimportant (Hall, 1956).

Unable to overcome these obstacles, Hall and his colleagues were forced to abandon an anthropological view of "culture" and to treat "culture" in a pragmatic, goal-oriented manner. According to Leeds-Hurwitz (1990), this decision set the agenda for intercultural communication as a field of inquiry. She summarizes the connections between Hall's work and current intercultural communication research in the following ways: (1) comparison of (national) cultures rather than focus on a single culture, (2) a move from macroanalysis (i.e., culture in general) to microanalysis (i.e., smaller cultural units such as tone of voice, gestures, time and spatial relations), (3) a focus on interaction between members of different cultures (i.e., dyadic emphasis), (4) communication as patterned, learned, and analyzable, (5) use of "real life" intercultural experiences as teaching tools, (6) use of descriptive linguistics, and (7) an expanded audience for intercultural training (i.e., international business) (pp. 263–264). In short, when taken together, these statements comprise the current discursive rules of inquiry within the field of intercultural communication. As such, they set the conditions of possibility for producing, regulating, and distributing knowledge about intercultural communication discourse.

While it is clear that political interests of the time dictated how the notion of "culture" was configured at the FSI, it is not clear why or under what circumstances this notion of "culture" was later adopted by intercultural communication scholars. In fact, there is evidence that at least during the decade of the seventies, what was defined as "culture" and as "intercultural communication" was less constrained.

The "Habeas Corpus" of the 1970s

In this section I focus on intercultural communication articles found in journals published within the discipline of communication and identified as such in the *Index to Journals in Communication Studies Through 1990* (Matlon, 1992)—the so-called Matlon Index.[1] As Matlon's *Index* is published by the field's national professional association (Speech Communication Association), it serves as an indicator of what is formally understood as "intercultural communication" research within the field. Publication in journals such as those listed in Matlon's *Index* have an impact on tenure and other career achievements made by communication scholars. With only three articles published during the 1950s and six in the 1960s, Matlon (1992) cites 52 additional intercultural communication articles published in the following communication scholarly journals during the 1970s: *Journal of Communication* (28), *Communication Quarterly* (5), *Southern States Communication Journal* (2), *Communication Monographs* (3), *Communication Research* (5), *The Quarterly Journal of Speech* (3), *Journalism Quarterly* (2), *Western Journal of Communication* (1), *Central States Speech Journal* (2), and *Communication Education* (1).[2] Several trends are noted in this literature. These trends are discussed in turn.

Most significant in this body of work is the diverse ways in which "culture" is defined. Although a series of articles dealing with the global impact of media define "culture" in terms of nation-state (e.g., Pipe, 1979; Porat, 1978; Righter, 1979), most others conceptualize "culture" in terms of race, social class, and gender identity. For instance, Daniel (1970a, 1970b) argues that communication between the poor and the affluent should be viewed as a case of cross-cultural communication. Whiting (1971) and Whiting and Hitt (1972) examine code-restrictedness and problem-solving communication among lower and middle class black and white teenagers. Philipsen (1975, 1976) examines how talk is used by working class white men. Rich (1971) investigates interracial communication in the classroom between Black, Chicano, Anglo, Native, and Japanese American students. Chesebro (1973) juxtaposes the goals and beliefs of "establishment" and "counter" cultures that result in rhetorical conflicts.

While many of the studies cited above compare two or more cultures, a number of other studies are concerned with the explication of one culture. For instance, Dubner (1972) examines nonverbal aspects of Black English. Daniel and Smitherman (1976) explicate the Traditional African Worldview and argue for its significance in understanding African American communication. Shuter (1979) investigates the use of the "dap" in the military—a handshake used by African American soldiers to express solidarity.

Also of note are the variety of methods employed in studying intercultural communication. Philipsen (1975, 1976) utilizes ethnographic methods. Rich (1971) employs case studies. Whiting and Hitt (1972) use a quasi-experimental design, and Dubner (1972) conducts a textual analysis of film, previous research, and popular literature.

Evident too in this body of research is a concern for and an involvement with social debates of the 1970s. Gregg, McCormack, and Pedersen (1970), Daniel (1970a, 1970b), Rich (1971), Dubner (1972), Lumsden, Brown, Lumsden, and Hill (1974), Daniel and Smitherman (1976), Colquit (1977), Sayer (1979), and Shuter (1979) in various ways attempt to come to terms with or offer insight into the ways in which communicative differences play into the social problems between Anglo and African Americans. In a similar vein, Daniel (1970a, 1970b), Whiting and Hitt (1972), and Philipsen (1975, 1976) attempt to highlight how social class differences negatively affect communication. Indeed, a 1977 special issue *of Journal of Communication* entitled "When Cultures Clash" is devoted to the examination of the effects of new technologies, products, and systems of communication on "authentic" or traditional cultures (e.g., Katz, 1977; Lomax, 1977). In addition, a number of articles address the effects of the "New World Information Order" on developing countries (e.g., Grossberg, 1979; Nordenstrong, 1979; Righter, 1979).

Lastly, a number of articles call into question some of the underlying assumptions of communication inquiry. For instance, in a study of communication competence across social class, Whiting (1971) suggests that as most researchers are middle class and insensitive to working class communication strategies, scholarly investigations of "competence" may be class-biased. In a similar vein, Colquit (1977) argues that definitions of "competence" are race-biased and privilege the communicative style of middle class white Americans. Dubner (1972) argues that many of the communication problems between African Americans and Anglo Americans are largely due to (faulty) interpretations of the behaviors of "Others" by dominant group members. Shuter (1977) finds that Edward Hall's assumptions about nonverbal forms of communication (i.e., proxemics and haptics) do not bear out when the gender of the participants is taken into account. Noting the ethnocentrism of American communication scholarship and its isolation from European thought (e.g., Marxism, structuralism), Carey (1975) asks: Where, if anywhere, does ideology leave off and science begin?

In examining the articles published in the 1970s, some patterns emerge. Up until about 1977, "culture" is conceptualized in a variety of ways (i.e., race, social class, gender, and nation), diverse analytical methods are utilized, and there is deep interest in how intersections between various nodes of cultural identity both play out in, and are constructed by, communication. Starting about 1978, "culture" comes to be conceived almost entirely in terms of "nation-state" and by 1980, "culture" is predominantly configured as a variable in positivist research projects (see Appendix for a chronological listing of published articles throughout the eighties). As shown below, this view of "culture" becomes further entrenched throughout the decade of the eighties.

Into the eighties

The first article published in the decade of the eighties (Jin, 1980) is an empirical test of acculturation. By 1983, the intercultural communication literature begins to be dominated by Gudykunst and associates and cross cultural tests of uncertainty reduction theory (e.g., Gudykunst, 1985; Gudykunst & Hammer, 1988; Gudykunst, Seung-Mock, & Nishida, 1985; Gudykunst,

Sodetani, & Sonoda, 1987). Working out of a positivist tradition, the studies of Gudykunst and associates account for almost one-half of the articles published during the 1980s—12 out of the 29 published works. The conceptualization of "culture" as nation-state, comparison of cultures, a focus on dyadic interaction between members of different cultures, and microanalysis characterize much of the work published during this decade. Furthermore, Gudykunst and Nishida (1989) outline their "objectivist" approach to the study of intercultural communication which strikingly corresponds to the discursive rules for intercultural communication scholarship as laid out by Leeds-Hurwitz (1990) and attributed to Hall.

Clearly, the year of 1980 represents a "disjuncture" in the study of intercultural communication. It is during this time that a heterogeneous notion of "culture" gets displaced. Foucault (1972) observes that such "breaks" or "ruptures" are so radical that an entire way of knowing a phenomenon is altered irrevocably. This certainly appears to be the case in regards to what was published from the 1970s to the 1980s in the field of intercultural communication. It is of more than passing interest that this disjuncture occurs in conjunction with other ruptures, in particular the rise of Reaganomics in the United States and Thatcherism in Great Britain.

How is this "disjuncture" to be accounted for, and what are the ramifications for the study of intercultural communication? Casmir and Asuncion-Lande (1990) offer some insight into these issues. Toward the end of the 1970s, many studies were published that addressed the diffusion of innovations from one culture to another, particularly so in the *Journal of Communication*. Indeed, a special issue of the *Journal of Communication* was devoted to this topic in 1977 and diffusion studies dominated in both the 1978 and 1979 issues of the journal as well (see Appendix for a chronological listing). Casmir and Asuncion-Lande (1990) suggest that the impact of these studies on the field of intercultural communication was in "moving the locus of communication research from the United States to various cultures in which communication concepts, structures, styles, and functions [were] not similar to our own" (p. 288). In other words, the emphasis on defining "culture" as nation-state is attributed to the international interest created by these diffusion studies.

In addition, the late 1970s witnessed dissent within the field regarding the status of the discipline of intercultural communication itself. Following the social sciences and eschewing the "faddism" of the seventies, intercultural communication scholars extolled "methodological rigor" as a means of transforming the discipline into one that would be taken seriously both within and outside the academy (Casmir & Asuncion-Lande, 1990, p. 282). Not surprisingly, "methodological rigor" involved the "careful application of statistical and mathematical models" (Gudykunst, 1983a) and placed a priority on theory development and testing (Gudykunst, 1983b). Shuter (1990) observes that:

> Intercultural studies in national and regional speech communication journals are neither of an etic or emic nature; they are products of a nomothetic model developed in psychology that drives communication research and aims at identifying laws of human interaction rather than describing cultural patterns.
>
> (p. 239)

Shuter goes on to argue that much intercultural communication research is concerned with refining existent communication theories (i.e., uncertainty reduction) wherein "culture" serves principally as a "research laboratory for testing the validity of communication paradigms" (p. 238). Although Shuter argues for the importance of "culture" in intercultural communication inquiry, he does not question the conceptualization of "culture" in terms of national boundaries. In fact, his above remarks are located in an introductory essay of a 1990 special issue of the *Southern Communication Journal* dealing with intracultural communication within and across national boundaries.

In summary, it appears that the "disjuncture" that occurred around 1980 within the field of intercultural communication had its roots in a variety of influences, including the political and capitalist interests of the United States, the impact of diffusion studies, and the felt need to establish disciplinary status through the adoption of social scientific approaches. What so often gets lost in the traditional rhetoric of historical accounts is the interplay of power relations. This is the single issue that intercultural communication research published in the 1970s speaks to most clearly and one that the majority of the work in the 1980s obscures. By conceptualizing "culture" in a variety of ways and challenging dominant definitions of taken-for-granted communication concepts such as that of "competence," these scholars brought into question hegemonic assumptions about the nature of "culture" and often "centered" the voices of the less powerful (e.g., Daniel's 1970 discussion of communication from the perspective of the poor). Diverse readings of "culture" encourage the inclusion of a power analytic in the study of intercultural communication and contest the notion of "culture" as unproblematically shared.

A plurality of perspectives also encourages debate. For example, Colquit (1977) challenges definitions of "competence" that privilege the communicative style of middle class white Americans, while, in vehement disagreement, Sayer (1979) claims that mastery of a "socially superior" (dominant) language is not racist. These and similar debates in much of the work published in the 1970s show evidence for the inherently contested nature of "culture." As Dirks, Eley, and Ortner (1994) remind us, "culture [may be seen] as multiple discourses, occasionally coming together in large systemic configurations, but more often coexisting within dynamic fields of interaction and conflict" (p. 4). This contested nature of "culture" often gets lost in homogenizing views of "culture as nationality" where dominant cultural voices are often the only ones heard, where the "preferred" reading of "culture" is the only reading. This certainly seems the case in most of the intercultural communication work published in the eighties. As we have seen, in many of these studies the experiences and self-reports of privileged members of the United States and Japan represent "culture" for all cultural members.

Discussion

From my reading of the intercultural communication scholarship published in the 1970s, it is clear that this body of literature deviates—often dramatically so—from the discursive rules that, according to Leeds-Hurwitz (1990) now define intercultural communication scholarship. Indeed, according to Leeds-Hurwitz, this body of work is clearly *not* intercultural communication and is therefore absent in her account of intercultural scholarship. How might intercultural communication scholars recover the seventies in order to create a broader intercultural communication in the 1990s? Rumblings of this move to recover are already being heard within the field.

This essay calls for the insertion of more complex notions of "culture" into intercultural communication scholarship. Such reconceptualizations would entail substantive rethinking of the field and attendant goals, desires, needs, and visions of our work. We must again, as in the 1970s, seriously consider whose interests are served by continuing to construct "culture" primarily in terms of national boundaries and by maintaining the current focus on the development of "intercultural cookbooks" for interaction. This re-visioning needs to be a collective effort by a community of scholars. I would like to offer some possible directions as suggested by critical/feminist theoretical perspectives.

Most immediately, insights derived by critical/feminist scholars have the potential to expand the predominant conceptualizations of "culture" currently accepted in intercultural communication inquiry. As a rule, intercultural communication scholars are not interested in the idea of "culture" per se, but use operationalized notions of cultural variation (e.g., individualism/collectivism) as one among many independent variables that affect the dependent variable (i.e., communicative phenomena such as uncertainty reduction, Gudykunst & Nishida, 1989). "Culture," at this level, is most often defined as nationality, and the constructedness of this position and its intersection with other positions such as gender and social class is not considered. The outcome is that diverse groups are treated as homogeneous, differences within national boundaries, ethnic groups, genders, and races are obscured, and hegemonic notions of "culture" are presented as "shared" by all cultural members. Moreover, intercultural communication of this sort is most often studied within dyads wherein two disembodied, ahistorical beings communicate across cultures.

The utilization of critical/feminist perspectives would allow intercultural communication scholars to employ more sophisticated and politicized analyses of cultural identity in general and to examine how these identities are constructed in communication, as well as how they affect communication. For instance, feminist scholars such as Marsha Houston (1992), Patricia Hill Collins (1993), and bell hooks (1989) argue that inquiry must address interlocking and overlapping nodes of identity (i.e., race, class, and gender) rather than focus on any one node alone. Wood (1994) reminds us that notions of femininity and masculinity, constructed differently across lines of race, class, nation, inform the communication process. Cultural feminists such as Johnson (1989) argue that women are culturally different from men and that "woman's culture" should be treated as analytically distinct from that of men.

Regarding the notion of "culture" as shared, Dirks et al. (1994) asks "By whom? In what ways? and Under what conditions?" (p. 3). Such insights have major implications for intercultural communication scholarship. For instance, in light of the fact that Shuter (1977) discovered that commonly accepted ideas about nonverbal communication across and within cultures derived from the work of Edward T. Hall do not pertain when gender is taken into account, the exclusion of this aspect of cultural identity in intercultural communication inquiry is difficult to understand or justify.

Another critical/feminist notion that intercultural communication scholars could find useful is Alcoffs (1988) idea of "positionality," as it directs attention to the *context* in which subjects are situated rather than focusing on the individual characteristics of the person. In this way, subjects become embodied, contextualized, historicized—a site of contradiction rather than one that is static, unitary, stable, fixed, and thereby indifferent to context and history. Assuming a different positional perspective has interesting implications for intercultural communication research. For instance, research employing a construction of "culture-as-nationality" could include an examination of interactants' positions within their own social structures in relation to gender, social class, status group, ethnicity, religion, and so forth, and could explore how this positionality affects and/or is constructed in intercultural interactions. In short, if "culture" signifies the intersection of various subject positions within any given society, then ways of studying intercultural communication that acknowledge this multi-facetedness are needed.

These approaches would require a vastly deeper understanding of intracultural communication than is currently available. Without a sense of how communication is patterned within groups, we can have little understanding of how that communication differs from or resembles communication between groups (Shuter, 1990). All too often intercultural communication scholars focus their research efforts on privileged Anglo American and Japanese college students. The result has been the formation of what van Dijk (1987) calls "elite" discourse and what I call "colonizer" discourse. In short, we know quite a bit about the communication patterns of social elites in this and other countries, but little or nothing about those of "Others." In part, our lack of knowledge stems from the imposition of dominant definitions and constructs onto the communication of "Others," with the resulting comparison of their communication to that of the dominant group(s) in the language of dominance.

Nakayama's (1994) "Other/wise" reading of texts offers an alternative approach to colonizer/ing discourse. In Nakayama's (1994) terms, an "Other" is called up—essentialized and centered—in order to view social relations and communication from an "Other" place. This strategy enables insights and perspectives usually ignored or marginalized. What would intercultural communication look like when viewed from these "Other" places? Would uncertainty reduction theory "hold water" when viewed through the lens of Collins's (1993) Afrocentric feminist epistemology which assumes that making connections is a primary motive in human interaction rather than the reduction of uncertainty? How would understandings of intercultural communication be enriched if the reduction of uncertainty/anxiety was assumed to be a Western rather than a global concern? What could be learned if notions such as intercultural communication competence were studied "Other/wise?" How would theories of intercultural communication be enriched or expanded by taking such positions?

In this decade, we are seeing more scholarly work that takes communication within cultural groups as a primary focus which, in turn, allows us to gain insight into intracultural communication patterns (e.g., Collier, Ribeau, & Hecht, 1986; Collier, 1988; Hecht, Ribeau, & Alberts, 1989; Hecht, Larkey, Johnson, & Reinard, 1992). This work allows us to understand communication patterns within groups in their own terms without the distraction of comparisons with dominant group patterns. However, much of this research remains limited to cultural groups within the United States.

In writing about ethnography, Kauffman (1992) makes several points from which intercultural communication researchers can benefit. Kauffman argues that the positionality of the researcher is implicit in every research effort, thus rendering research an explicitly political act. This brings to mind Houston's (1992) metaphor of "multiple jeopardy" in that not only are our subjects infused with multiple, interlocking identities, but so are researchers. When researchers perceive themselves as positioned and embodied beings—gendered, racial, sexual, and social class—we can begin to acknowledge how these particularities shape our research. We can affect what gets constituted as a "problem" worthy of study, whose reality/knowledge will be constructed as "answers," and what findings will be selected or reported as "facts" (Kauffman, 1992, p. 192).

Cultural studies, with its focus on popular culture, provides another alternative frame. Hall (1981) argues that the media produce "representations of the social world, images, descriptions, explanations, and frames for understanding how the world is and why it works as it is said and shown to work" (p. 35). In a similar vein, van Dijk (1987) claims that most of what white Americans know about "Others" is gleaned from mass media. If we are to agree with Hall (1981), then much of how we understand ourselves as cultural members and our interactions with "Others" is too impacted by media representations. By examining these discourses, we can better understand these processes and how they affect and are played out in intercultural interactions.

With its emphasis on popular culture, feminist cultural studies suggests an alternative to the study of intercultural communication that moves away from focusing on dyadic intercultural encounters to popular representations of intercultural communication. In an age when media images abound in "first, second, and third worlds" and keeping in mind van Dijk's (1987) claim that much of what we know about "others" we learn from media, what we can learn from analyses of popular cultural forms of intercultural communication and their audiences seem especially promising. For example, one could argue that intercultural communication scholarship should rightly include studies of the impact of foreign media communication on cultural members. If one envisions the interaction between text and audience as another case of communication, then one's watching of an Italian film as a white American woman is a form of intercultural communication. Indeed, cultural norms, values, and beliefs are communicated in media which are actively constructed and deconstructed by audience members. This is worthy of intense study.

Into the Nineties: A Note in Closure

Matlon's *Index* (1992) indicates twelve articles classified as intercultural communication published in communication journals in the first year of the decade of the nineties. The first such work is a historical piece by Leeds-Hurwitz (1990) which lays out the discursive rules of the field attributed to Hall. In a 1990 special issue of the *Southern Speech Communication Journal* devoted to intracultural communication, Shuter (1990) calls for the reinsertion of "culture" into intercultural communication scholarship. He argues that the development of intracultural communication theory is critical for three reasons:

> First, it provides a conceptual framework for analyzing interaction within a society and world region. Second, intracultural theories demonstrate the inextricable linkage between communication patterns and sociocultural forces. And, lastly, it provides a conceptual basis for making intercultural communication comparisons between dissimilar societies.
>
> (p. 243)

The articles in this special issue describe patterns of intercultural communication in groups as diverse as the Yoruba of Nigeria (Asante, 1990), Greeks (Broome, 1990), Mexicans and Mexican Americans (Gonzalez, 1990), the North Yemini (Frye, 1990), Chinese and Americans (Ma, 1990), and Japanese (Di Mare, 1990). Interestingly, these research efforts do not "qualify" as intercultural communication scholarship under the discursive rules laid out in Leeds-Hurwitz (1990). As discussed earlier, the late 1980s and early 1990s also exhibit a turn to the intracultural in terms of domestic cultures within the United States (e.g., Hecht, Ribeau, & Alberts, 1989). These are hopeful signs. These efforts alone, however, are insufficient to move the field of intercultural communication to include an analytic that recognizes the contested and power-infused nature of "culture" within intercultural communication.

In this essay, I have examined how the field of intercultural communication has been constructed and how certain definitions have become hegemonic, thereby reading others out. I have paid attention to Leeds-Hurwitz's historical account of the field and have shown how this account leaves out the prolific intercultural communication scholarship published in communication journals during the 1970s. Moreover, I have traced the emergence of the discipline identifying the disjuncture at which current conceptualizations of intercultural communication inquiry became hegemonic. Lastly, I suggest how critical/feminist insights might contribute to a broader intercultural communication inquiry.

Notes

1. Matlon's *Index* is utilized as an external indicator of what is considered as "intercultural communication" research within the field of communication. It is published by the Speech Communication Association, the discipline's national professional and academic association. Since Matlon's as yet has not published an index covering the years 1992–1995, the intercultural communication articles published in the field's journals during these years could not be considered here.
2. The Appendix provides a chronological listing of these research articles so that the reader may see the foci of these inquiries as they evolved during the decade of the seventies. In addition, all of the published works termed as "intercultural communication" by Matlon are contained in the Appendix in chronological order by decade as well.

References

Alcoff, L. (1988). Cultural feminism versus post-structuralism: The identity crisis in feminist theory. *Signs: Journal of Women in Culture and Society, 13*, 405–436.

Asante, M. K. (1990). The tradition of advocacy in the Yoruba courts. *Southern Speech Communication Journal, 55*, 250–259.

Best, S., & Kellner, D. (1991). *Postmodern theory: Critical interrogations.* NY: The Guilford Press.

Broome, B. J. (1990). "Palevone": Foundations of struggle and conflict in Greek interpersonal communication. *Southern Speech Communication Journal, 55,* 260–275.

Carey, J. W. (1975. Communication and culture. *Communication Research, 2,* 173–191.

Casmir, F. I., & Asuncion-Lande, N. C. (1990). Intercultural communication revisited: Conceptualization, paradigm building, and methodological approaches. In James A. Anderson (Ed.), *Communication Yearbook 12* (pp. 278–309). Newbury Park, CA: Sage.

Chesebro, J. W. (1973). Cultures in conflict—a generic and axiological view. *Communication Quarterly, 21,* 11–20.

Collier, M. J. (1988). A comparison of conversations among and between domestic groups: How intra- and intercultural competencies vary. *Communication Quarterly, 36,* 122–144.

Collier, M. J., Ribeau, S., & Hecht, M. L. (1986). Intracultural communication rules and outcomes with three domestic cultures. *International Journal of Intercultural Relations, 10,* 434–457.

Collins, P. H. (1993). *Black feminist thought: Knowledge, consciousness, and the politics of empowerment.* New York: Routledge.

Colquit, J. L. (1977). The student's right to his own language: A viable model or empty rhetoric? *Communication Quarterly, 25,* 17–20.

Daniel, J. (1970a). The facilitation of white-black communication. *Journal of Communication, 20,* 134–141.

Daniel, J. (1970b). The poor: Aliens in an affluent society: Cross-cultural communication. *Communication Quarterly, 18,* 15–21.

Daniel, J. L., & Smitherman, G. (1976). How I got over: Communication dynamics in the Black community. *Quarterly Journal of Speech, 62,* 26–39.

Davidson, A. (1986). Archaeology, genealogy, ethics. In D. C. Hoy (Ed.), *Foucault: A critical reader* (pp. 221–233). New York: Basil Blackwell.

Di Mare, L. (1990). *Ma* and Japan. *Southern Speech Communication Journal, 55,* 319–328.

Dirks, N. B., Eley, G., & Ortner, S. B. (1994). Introduction. In N. B. Dirks, G. Eley & S. B. Ortner (Eds.), *Culture/power/history: A reader in contemporary social theory* (pp. 3–45) Princeton, NJ: Princeton University Press.

Dubner, F. S. (1972). Nonverbal aspects of Black english. *Southern Speech Communication Journal, 37,* 361–374.

Foucault, M. (1972). *The archaeology of knowledge.* New York: Pantheon Books.

Foucault, M. (1980). *The history of sexuality.* New York: Vintage Books.

Frye, P. A. (1990). Form and function of North Yemeni Qat sessions. *Southern Speech Communication Journal, 55,* 292–304.

Gonzalez, A. (1990). Mexican "otherness" in the rhetoric of Mexican Americans. *Southern Speech Communication Journal, 55,* 276–291.

Gregg, R., McCormack, A. J., & Pedersen, D. (1970). A description of the interaction between black youth and white teachers in a ghetto speech class. *Communication Education, 19,* 1–8.

Grossberg, L. (1979). Interpreting the "crisis" of culture in communication theory. *Journal of Communication, 29,* 56–68.

Gudykunst, W. B. (1983a). Intercultural communication theory, current perspectives. In W. B. Gudykunst (Ed.), *International and intercultural communication annual* 7 (pp. 13–20). Beverly Hills: Sage.

Gudykunst, W. B. (1983b). Toward a typology of stranger-host relationships. *International Journal of Intercultural Relations, 7,* 401–413.

Gudykunst, W. B. (1985). The influence of cultural similarity, type of relationship, and self-monitoring on uncertainty reduction processes. *Communication Monographs, 52,* 203–217.

Gudykunst, W. B., & Hammer, M. R. (1988). The influence of social identity and intimacy of interethnic relationships on uncertainty reduction processes. *Human Communication Research, 14,* 569–601.

Gudykunst, W. B., & Nishida, T. (1989). Theoretical perspectives for studying intercultural communication. In M. F. Asante, & W. B. Gudykunst (Eds.), *Handbook of international and intercultural communication* (pp. 17–46). Newbury Park, CA: Sage.

Gudykunst, W. B., Seung-Mock, Y., & Nishida, T. (1985). A cross-cultural test of uncertainty reduction theory: Comparisons of acquaintances, friends, and dating relationships in Japan, Korea, and the U. S. *Human Communication Research, 11,* 407–455.

Gudykunst, W. B., Sodetani, L. L., & Sonoda, K. T. (1987). Uncertainty reduction in Japanese-American/ Caucasian relationships in Hawaii. *Western Journal of Communication, 51,* 256–278.

Hall, E. T. (1956). Orientation and training in government for work overseas. *Human Organization, 15,* 4–10.

Hall, E. T., & Hall, M. R. (1989). *Understanding cultural differences.* Yarmouth, ME: Intercultural Press.

Hall, S. (1981). The whites of their eyes. In G. Bridges & Rosalind Brunt (Eds.), *Silver linings: Some strategies for the eighties* (pp. 28–52). London: Lawrence and Wishart.

Harman, R. C., & Briggs, N. E. (1991). SIETAR survey: Perceived contributions of the social sciences to intercultural communication. *International Journal of Intercultural Relations, 15,* 19–28.

Hecht, M. L., Larkey, L., Johnson, J., & Reinard, J. C. (1992). African American and European American perceptions of problematic issues in interethnic communication effectiveness. *Human Communication Research, 19,* 209–236.

Hecht, M. L., Ribeau, S., & Alberts, J. K. (1989). An Afro-American perspective on interethnic communication. *Communication Monographs, 56,* 385–410.

hooks, b. (1989). *Talking back: Thinking feminist, thinking black.* Boston: South End Press.

Houston, M. (1992). The politics of difference: Race, class and women's communication. In L. F. Rakow (Ed.), *Women making meaning* (pp. 45–59). New York: Routledge.

Jin, K. (1980). Explaining acculturation in a communication framework: An empirical test. *Communication Monographs, 47,* 155–179.

Johnson, F. L. (1989). Women's culture and communication: An analytical perspective. In C. M. Lont & S. A. Friedley (Eds.), *Beyond boundaries: Sex and gender diversity in communication* (pp. 301–316). Fairfax, VA: George Mason University Press.

Katz, E. (1977). Can authentic cultures survive new media? *Journal of Communication, 27,* 113–121.

Kauffman, B. J. (1992). Feminist facts: Interview strategies and political subjects in ethnography. *Communication Theory, 2,* 187–206.

Leeds-Hurwitz, W. (1990). Notes on the history of intercultural communication: The Foreign Service Institute and the mandate for intercultural training. *Quarterly Journal of Speech, 76,* 262–281.

Lomax, A. (1977). Appeal for cultural equity. *Journal of Communication, 27,* 125–138.

Lumsden, G., Brown, D. R., Lumsden, D., & Hill, T. A. (1974). An investigation of differences in verbal behavior between Black and white informal peer group. *Communication Quarterly, 22,* 31–36.

Ma, R. (1990). An exploratory study of discontented responses in American and Chinese relationships. *Southern Speech Communication Journal, 55,* 305–318.

Matlon, R. J. (Ed.). (1992). *Index to journals in communication studies through 1990.* Annandale, VA: Speech Communication Association.

Nakayama, T. K. (1994). Show/down time: "Race," gender, sexuality, and popular culture. *Critical Studies in Mass Communication, 11,* 162–179.

Nordenstrong, K. (1979). Behind the semantics—a strategic design. *Journal of Communication, 29,* 195–198.

Philipsen, G. (1975). Speaking like a "man" in Teamsterville: Cultural patterns of role enactment in an urban neighborhood. *Quarterly Journal of Speech, 61,* 13–22.

Philipsen, G. (1976). Places for speaking in Teamsterville. *Quarterly Journal of Speech, 62,* 15–25.

Pipe, R. (1979). National policies, international debates. *Journal of Communication, 29,* 114–123.

Porat, M. U. (1978). Global implications of the information society. *Journal of Communication, 28,* 70–80.

Rice, J. S. (1992). Discursive formation, life stories, and the emergence of co-dependency: "Power/knowledge" and the search for identity. *The Sociological Quarterly, 33,* 337–364.

Rich, A. L. (1971). Some problems in interracial communication. *Central States Speech Journal, 22,* 228–235.

Righter, R. (1979). Who won? *Journal of Communication, 29,* 192–194.

Sayer, J. E. (1979). The student's right to his own language: A response to Colquit. *Communication Quarterly, 27,* 44–46.

Shuter, R. (1977). A field study of nonverbal communication in Germany, Italy, and the United States. *Communication Monographs, 44,* 298–305.

Shuter, R. (1979). The dap in the military: Hand-to-hand communication. *Journal of Communication, 29,* 136–142.

Shuter, R. (1990). The centrality of culture. *The Southern Communication Journal, 55,* 231–249.

van Dijk, T. A. (1987). *Communicating racism: Ethnic prejudice in thought and talk.* Newbury Park, CA: Sage.

Whiting, G. C. (1971). Code restrictedness and opportunities for change in developing countries. *Journal of Communication, 21,* 36–57.

Whiting, G. C. & Hitt, W. C. (1972). Code-restrictedness and communication dependent problem solving: An exploratory study. *Communication Monographs, 39,* 68–73.

Wood, J. T. (1994). *Gendered lives: Communication, gender, and culture.* Belmont, CA: Wadsworth.

Appendix

Decade of the 1950s

1951 November	Campa, A. L. Language barriers in intercultural relations. *Journal of Communication, 7,* 41–46.
1952 May	Knode, D. P. The Iron Curtain refugee in a new world. *Journal of Communication, 2,* 1–5.
1958 Spring	Bakonyi, S. Divergence and convergence in culture and communication. *Journal of Communication, 3,* 24–30.

Decade of the 1960s

1963 June	Keller, P. W. The study of face-to-face international decision-making. *Journal of Communication, 8,* 67–76.
1964 Autumn	Chu, G. C. Problems of cross-cultural communication research. *Journalism Quarterly, 61,* 557–562.
1966 December	Wedge, B. Nationality and social perception. *Journal of Communication, 16,* 278–282.
1966 December	Flack, M. J. Communicable and uncommunicable aspects in personal international relationships. *Journal of Communication, 16,* 283–290.
1966 December	Stewart, E. C. The simulation of cultural differences. *Journal of Communication, 16,* 291–304.
1968 December	Lorimar, E. S., & Dunn, S. W. Reference groups, congruity theory, and cross-cultural persuasion. *Journal of Communication, 18,* 354–368.

Decade of the 1970s

1970 January	Gregg, R., McCormack, A. J., & Pedersen, D. A description of the interaction between black youth and white teachers in a ghetto speech class. *Communication Education, 29,* 1–8.
1970 Spring	Bostian, L. R. The two-step flow theory: Cross-cultural implications. *Journalism Quarterly, 67,* 109–117.
1970 June	Daniel, J. The facilitation of white-black communication. *Journal of Communication, 20,* 134–141.
1970 Winter	Daniel, J. The poor: Aliens in an affluent society: Cross-cultural communication. *Communication Quarterly, 18,* 15–21.
1971 March	Whiting, G. C. Code restrictedness and opportunities for change in developing countries. *Journal of Communication, 21,* 36–57.
1971 Winter	Rich, A. L. Some problems in interracial communication. *Central States Speech Journal, 22,* 228–235.
1972 March	Whiting, G. C. & Hitt, W. C. Code-restrictedness and communication dependent problem solving: An exploratory study. *Communication Monographs, 39,* 68–73.
1972 Summer	Dubner, F. S. Nonverbal aspects of Black english. *Southern Speech Communication Journal, 37,* 361–374.
1973 Spring	Chesebro, J. W. Cultures in conflict—a generic and axiological view. *Communication Quarterly, 21,* 11–20.
1974 Fall	Lumsden, G., Brown, D. R., Lumsden, D., & Hill, T. A. An investigation of differences in verbal behavior between black and white informal peer group. *Communication Quarterly, 22,* 31–36.

1975 February	Philipsen, G. Speaking like a "man" in Teamsterville: Cultural patterns of role enactment in an urban neighborhood. *Quarterly Journal of Speech, 41,* 13–22.
1975 March	Miller, D. T. The effect of dialect and ethnicity on communication effectiveness. *Communication Monographs, 62,* 69–74.
1975 April	Carey, J. W. Communication and culture. *Communication Research, 2,* 173–191.
1975 Winter	Woodward, G. C. Mystification in the rhetoric of cultural dominance and colonial control. *Central States Speech Journal, 26,* 298–303.
1976 February	Philipsen, G. Places for speaking in Teamsterville. *Quarterly Journal of Speech, 62,* 15–25.
1976 February	Daniel, J. L., & Smitherman, G. How I got over: Communication dynamics in the Black community. *Quarterly Journal of Speech, 62,* 26–39.
1976 Summer	Fine, G. A. Obscene joking across cultures. *Journal of Communication, 26,* 134–140.
1977 January	Stevenson, R. L. Studying communications across cultures. *Communication Research, 4,* 113–128.
1977 Spring	Katz, E. Can authentic cultures survive new media? *Journal of Communication, 27,* 113–121.
1977 Spring	Dissanayake, W. New wine in old bottles: Can folk media convey modern messages? *Journal of Communication, 27,* 122–124.
1977 Spring	Lomax, A. Appeal for cultural equity. *Journal of Communication, 27,* 125–138.
1977 Spring	Pool, I. del Sola. The changing flow of television. *Journal of Communication, 27,* 139–149.
1977 Spring	O'Brien, R. C. Professionalism in broadcasting in developing countries. *Journal of Communication, 27,* 150–153.
1977 Spring	Cassirer, H. R. Radio as the people's medium. *Journal of Communication, 27,* 154–157.
1977 Spring	Martin, T. H., Byrne, R. B., & Wedemeyer, D. J. Balance: An aspect to the right to communicate. *Journal of Communication, 27,* 158–162.
1977 Autumn	Kent, K. E. M., & Rush, R. R. International communication as a field: A study of Journalism Quarterly citations. *Journalism Quarterly, 54,* 580–583.
1977 Fall	Colquit, J. L. The student's right to his own language: A viable model or empty rhetoric? *Communication Quarterly, 25,* 17–20.
1977 November	Shuter, R. A field study of nonverbal communication in Germany, Italy, and the United States. *Communication Monographs, 44,* 298–305.
1977 Winter	Goodyear, F. H., & West, A. An organizational framework for cross-cultural communication. *Southern Speech Communication Journal, 42,* 178–190.
1978 July	Kreiling, A. Toward a cultural studies approach for the sociology of popular culture. *Communication Research, 5,* 240–263.
1978 July	Leed, E. J. Communications revolutions and the enactment of culture. *Communication Research, 5,* 305–319.
1978 July	Golding, P., & Murdock, G. Theories of communication and theories of society. *Communication Research, 5,* 339–356.
1978 Winter	Rogers, E. M. The rise and fall of the dominant paradigm. *Journal of Communication, 28,* 64–69.
1978 Winter	Porat, M. U. Global implications of the information society. *Journal of Communication, 28,* 70–80.
1978 Winter	Parker, E. B. An information-based hypothesis. *Journal of Communication, 28,* 81–83.

1978 Winter   McAnany, E. G. Does information really work? *Journal of Communication, 28*, 84–90.

1979 Spring   Masmoudi, M. The new world information order. *Journal of Communication, 29*, 172–185.

1979 Spring   Androunas, E., & Zassoursky, Y. Protecting the sovereignty of information. *Journal of Communication, 29*, 186–191.

1979 Spring   Righter, R. Who won? *Journal of Communication, 29*, 192–194.

1979 Spring   Nordonstrong, K. Behind the semantics—a strategic design. *Journal of Communication, 29*, 195–198.

1979 Summer   Pipe, R. National policies, international debates. *Journal of Communication, 29*, 114–123.

1979 Summer   Eger, J. M. U. S. proposal for progress through negotiations. *Journal of Communication, 29*, 124–128.

1979 Summer   Heintz, A. The dangers of regulation. *Journal of Communication, 29*, 129–134.

1979 Summer   Freese, J. The dangers of non-regulation. *Journal of Communication, 29*, 135–137.

1979 Summer   Saur, R. A. C. Protection without protectionism. *Journal of Communication, 29*, 138–140.

1979 Summer   Mendelsohn, H. Delusions of technology. *Journal of Communication, 29*, 142–143.

1979 Summer   Hamelink, C. J. Informatics: Third world call for new order. *Journal of Communication, 29*, 144–148.

1979 Summer   Jacobson, R. E. The hidden issues: What kind of order? *Journal of Communication, 29*, 149–155.

1979 Fall   Starosta, W. Roots for an older rhetoric: On rhetorical effectiveness in the Third World. *Western Journal of Speech Communication, 43*, 278–287.

1979 Winter   Grossberg, L. Interpreting the "crisis" of culture in communication theory. *Journal of Communication, 29*, 56–68.

1979 Winter   Sayer, J. E. The student's right to his own language: A response to Colquit. *Communication Quarterly, 27*, 44–46.

1979 Winter   Shuter, R. The dap in the military: Hand-to-hand communication. *Journal of Communication, 24*, 136–142.

Decade of the 1980s

1980 August   Jin, K. Explaining acculturation in a communication framework: An empirical test. *Communication Monographs, 47*, 155–179.

1980 Winter   Jain, H. C, Kanungo, R. N., & Goldhaber, G. M. Attitudes toward a communication system: A comparison of Anglophone and Francophone hospital employees. *Human Communication Research, 6*, 178–184.

1981 February   Stanback, M. H., & Pearce, W. B. Talking to "the man": Some communication strategies used by members of "subordinate" social groups. *Quarterly Journal of Speech, 68*, 21–30.

1981 April   Mansell, M. Transcultural experience and expressive response. *Communication Education, 30*, 93–108.

1982 Fall   Chesebro, J. W. Illness as a rhetorical act: A cross-cultural perspective. *Communication Quarterly, 30*, 321–331.

1982 Winter   Yum, J. O. Communication diversity and information acquisition among Korean immigrants in Hawaii. *Human Communication Research, 8*, 154–169.

1983 Summer   Wolfson, K., & Pearce, W. B. A cross-cultural comparison of the implications of self-disclosures in conversational logics. *Communication Quarterly, 31,* 249–256.

1983 Fall   Gudykunst, W. B. Similarities and differences in perceptions of initial intra-cultural and intercultural encounters: An exploratory investigation. *Southern Speech Communication Journal, 49,* 49–65.

1983 Winter   Korzenny, F., Neuendorf, K., Burgoon, M., Burgoon, J. K., & Greenberg, B. S. Cultural identification as predictor of content preferences of Hispanics. *Journalism Quarterly, 60,* 677–685.

1984 March   Gudykunst, W. B., & Nishida, T. Individual and cultural influences on uncertainty reduction. *Communication Monographs, 51,* 23–36.

1985 Spring   Gudykunst, W. B., Seung-Mock, Y., & Nishida, T. A cross-cultural test of uncertainty reduction theory: Comparisons of acquaintances, friends, and dating relationships in Japan, Korea, and the U.S. *Human Communication Research, 11,* 407–455.

1985 September   Gudykunst, W. B. The influence of cultural similarity, type of relationship, and self-monitoring on uncertainty reduction processes. *Communication Monographs, 52,* 203–217.

1985 Fall   Gudykunst, W. B. An exploratory comparison of close intracultural and intercultural friendships. *Communication Quarterly, 33,* 270–283.

1985 Winter   Johnson, J. D., & Tums, A. R. Communication factors related to closer international ties. *Human Communication Research, 12,* 259–273.

1986 March   Wheeless, L. R., Erickson, K. V., & Behrens, J. S. Cultural differences in disclosiveness as a function of locus of control. *Communication Monographs, 53,* 36–46.

1986 Spring   Choe, J. H., Wilcox, G. B., & Hardy, A. P. Facial expressions in magazine ads: A cross-cultural comparison. *Journalism Quarterly, 63,* 122–126.

1986 September   Stewart, L. P., Gudykunst, W. B., Ting-Toomey, S., & Nishida, T. The effects of decision-making style on openness and satisfaction within Japanese organizations. *Communication Monographs, 53,* 236–251.

1986 Winter   Gudykunst, W. B., & Nishida, T. The influence of cultural variability on perceptions of communication behavior associated with relationship terms. *Human Communication Research, 13,* 147–166.

1987 February   Gudykunst, W. B., Yang, S. M., & Nishida, T. Cultural differences in self-consciousness and self-monitoring. *Communication Research, 14,* 7–34.

1987 Summer   Gudykunst, W. B., Sodetani, L. L., & Sonoda, K. T. Uncertainty reduction in Japanese-American/Caucasian relationships in Hawaii. *Western Journal of Communication, 51,* 256–278.

1987 Fall   Foeman, A., & Pressley, G. Ethnic culture and corporate culture: Using Black styles in organizations. *Communication Quarterly, 35,* 293–307.

1988 Spring   Collier, M. J. A comparison of conversations among and between domestic culture groups: How inter and intracultural competencies vary. *Communication Quarterly, 36,* 122–144.

1988 Spring   Ting-Toomey, S. Rhetorical sensitivity style in three cultures: France, Japan, and the United States. *Central States Speech Journal, 39,* 28–36.

1988 Summer   Gudykunst, W. B., & Hammer, M. R. The influence of social identity and intimacy of interethnic relationships on uncertainty reduction processes. *Human Communication Research, 14,* 569–601.

1988 December   Yum, J. O. The impact of Confucianism on interpersonal relationships and communication. *Communication Monographs, 55,* 374–388.

1989 Spring Chen, G. M. Relationships of the dimensions of intercultural communication competence. *Communication Quarterly, 37,* 118–133.

1989 Fall Gonzalez, A. "Participation" at WMEX-FM. *Western Journal of Communication, 53,* 385–410.

1989 December Hecht, M. L., Ribeau, S., & Alberts, J. K. An Afro-american perspective on interethnic communication. *Communication Monographs, 55,* 385–410.

1989 Winter Gudykunst, W. B., Nishida, T., & Schmidt, K. L. The influence of cultural, relational, and personality factors in uncertainty reduction processes. *Western Journal of Speech Communication, 53,* 13–29.

The year of 1990

1990 February Leeds-Hurwitz, W. Notes on the history of intercultural communication: The Foreign Service Institute and the mandate for intercultural training. *Quarterly Journal of Speech, 76,* 262–281.

1990 Spring McCroskey, J. C, Burroughs, N. F., Daun, A., & Richmond, V. P. Correlates of quietness: Swedish and American perspectives. *Communication Quarterly, 38,* 127–137.

1990 Spring Shuter, R. The centrality of culture. *Southern Speech Communication Journal, 55,* 231–249.

1990 Spring Asante, M. K. The tradition of advocacy in the Yoruba courts. *Southern Speech Communication Journal, 55,* 250–259.

1990 Spring Broome, B. J. "Palevone": Foundations of struggle and conflict in Greek interpersonal communication. *Southern Speech Communication Journal, 55,* 260–275.

1990 Spring Gonzalez, A. Mexican "otherness" in the rhetoric of Mexican Americans. *Southern Speech Communication Journal, 55,* 276–291.

1990 Spring Frye, P. A. Form and function of North Yemeni Qat sessions. *Southern Speech Communication Journal, 55,* 292–304.

1990 Spring Ma, R. An exploratory study of discontented responses in American and Chinese relationships. *Southern Speech Communication Journal, 55,* 305–318.

1990 Spring Di Mare, L. *Ma* and Japan. *Southern Speech Communication Journal, 55,* 319–328.

1990 Fall Andersen, P. A., Lustig, M. W., & Andersen, J. F. Changes in latitude, changes in attitude: The relationship between climate and interpersonal communication predispositions. *Communication Quarterly, 38,* 291–311.

1990 Fall Collier, M. J., & Powell, R. Ethnicity, instructional communication, and classroom systems. *Communication Quarterly, 38,* 334–349.

1990 Fall McCroskey, J. C. & Richmond, V. P. Willingness to communicate differing cultural perspectives. *Southern Speech Communication Journal, 56,* 72–77.

2

Ethical Implications of the Ethnic "Text" in Multicultural Communication Studies

Dolores Valencia Tanno

Understanding the role of communication in multicultural communities continues to gain importance in our discipline. Our increased awareness of a diverse society has helped make the context of "culture" seem less strange alongside other communication contexts such as the interpersonal, organizational, political, and so on.

Within a multicultural context, communication acts are enriched as they are informed by a variety of value systems, philosophies, traditions, and histories. A multicultural discursive community results form an interplay between a specific culture's values and philosophies and those of the society at large as they play out in language. In some cultural communities, bilinguality adds a third dimension to this interplay. These dimensions manifest themselves in "thick" communication (Geertz, 1973), suggesting not layers of communication but rather an intertwining, so that it becomes difficult to know where one dimension ends and another begins. Any knowledge about multicultural communication, therefore, must account for the often indistinguishable interdependence among these dimensions of communication.

Both the complexity and the relative newness of the multicultural communication context in our discipline calls for what Bazerman (1992) has described as the "reflexive rhetorical turn" that focuses attention on language and its impact. The "reflexive rhetorical turn" in this chapter focuses on the multicultural communication research process, paying particular attention to the language of multicultural research, its relationship to knowledge gained through comparison rather than dialogue, some ethical imperatives arising therefrom, and what these may imply for researchers. The ethnic "text" is the pivotal point around which this examination takes place.

Introduction

An explanation about my use of the terms "multicultural," "ethics," and ethnic "text" is appropriate at this point. I use the term "multicultural" to describe all the contexts (variously known as intercultural, cross-cultural, intracultural, international, etc.) within which communication between, among, and within cultural communities take place. At the same time that the term "multicultural" captures the diversity of cultural communities and contexts, it is also a reminder of the multitude of cultural voices waiting to be engaged in empowering dialogue.

The issue of empowerment is embodied in the term "ethics" as one ties it conceptually to choice. Choice is one part of the essence of ethical communication, the other part being responsibility for the impact of our communication. In 1968, Winterowd captured this dual essence of ethical communication when he defined language as "perhaps the only human and humane act" by which "we can literally talk ourselves to death" (p. 14).

When using the term "text" in relation to the word "ethnic" I follow Bazerman's lead in "The Interpretation of Disciplinary Writing" (1992). Arguing that his study of social scientific texts "reverses" traditional hermeneutic assumptions, Bazerman (1992) writes: "When looking at a text in isolation, I look at how the text reaches out beyond the page, what connections it makes with the reader, the ambient natural world, the ambient social world. I look at how a text defines or reorders relationships and defines activities" (p. 35). This "rhetorical self-consciousness" (Bazerman, 1992, p. 37) begins with a keen awareness of language use and its relationship to knowledge. Within critical and social scientific multicultural studies, our language choices for definitions, identifying labels, interpretations, and conclusions have the potential to leap "beyond the page" and impact groups of people in ways we never intended nor imagines. Furthermore, the language of our studies composes the knowledge base of multicultural understanding. I will argue that the term "ethnic" becomes an exemplar of a specific "text" in multicultural studies that extends into society, creating a particular and not always accurate perception about members of cultural groups.

Currently, much of our understanding of multicultural communication is based on the pursuit of *comparative* knowledge. We gather information and evaluate it by comparing it to often unconsciously assumed a priori norms or by comparing it to consciously developed frames of reference. One result of this is an attribution of relative worth of one norm over another. Discussing genres of discourse, Hariman (1986) argued that "the act of comparing discourses implies both manifest definitions of substance and latent attributions of status for each genre" (p. 38).

In and of itself, comparison is not an unproductive approach for pursuing knowledge and understanding. In the context of multicultural communication research, however, the act of comparing communication practices between and among cultures has the potential for the same consequences of the attribution of greater or lesser status that Hariman speaks about. As an example of how this might happen, I offer a brief glimpse of the passage through time the word "ethnic."

The Ethnic "Text," Then and Now

In 1975, Glazer and Moynihan provided a short history of the word "ethnicity," indicating that, in its sense of describing the "character or quality of an ethnic group," it was first used in 1953 by David Riesman in his essay "Some Observations on Intellectual Freedom" (p. 1). In 1986, Werner Sollors provided a more comprehensive examination of the use of "ethnicity," tracing it back again to Riesman, but reporting that the "apparently first occurrences" of this term were found in W. Lloyd Warner's (1945) study of a Massachusetts city (p. 23). In fact, the root word "ethnic" can be traced back to Greek times. It derived from *ethnikos*, the Greek word for nation, and the Ecclesiastical Late Greek word for heathen or pagan; thus to be ethnic was to be a member of a heathen nation. This meaning survived relatively intact through the eighteenth century.

Ethnic as heathen or pagan

Examples of "ethnic" as it relates to paganism are found in social, philosophical, and historical treaties as well as in poetry. In 1588, in *An Admonition to the Nobility*, William Allen warned: "This I faie, yf he obeie not, or heare not the churche, let him be taken for an ethnike" (p. xxxvii). In *Leviathan*, published in 1651, Hobbes addresses the apostles' efforts to warn converts about "their then Ethnique Princes" (p. 338). In his *A Complete History of Algiers*, Morgan (1731) describes those he perceives as barbarous as "the blindest and most wretched of all *heathens, Ethnikes, Pagans,* and *Idolaters*" (p. 77). The English traveler Thomas Coryate (1611) carries through on this theme of barbarity; observing visitors to St. Mark's square in Venice, he note: "here you may both see all manner of fashions of attire, and heare all the languages of christendom, besides those that are spoken by the barbaripus [*sic*] Ethnicikes (p. 177). Writing about John Sterling, Thomas Carlyle (1851) describes Sterling's break with the church "as good as altogether Ethnic, Greekish" (p. 51).

In its sense of heathen or pagan, "ethnic" is also found in poetry. Longfellow's "Drinking Song" reflects this meaning: "These are ancient ethnic revels / of a faith since forsaken / Now the Satyrs, changed to devils / Frighten mortals wine-o'ertaken."

Ethnic as empirically inferior

During the Age of Enlightenment, the meaning of the word "ethnic" changed. This period marked the shift from pietism to scientism and from faith to fact, so it is not surprising that ethnicity was no longer defined on the basis of religious difference. Instead, ethnicity was defined on the basis of observable and verifiable physical features. One who documents this state of affairs with great insight and completeness is Charles Rosenberg (1976) in *No Other Gods: On Science and American Social Thought.* Rosenberg addresses how the scientific community resorted to "facts" to prove the inferiority of women and to argue for the value of eugenics by comparing the "grading" racial traits. As an example, Rosenberg reports that Charles Davenport, the father of eugenics, argued that skin color was directly correlated to superiority—the lighter the color, the more superior the individual.

In *The Inequality of Human Races* (1915), Arthur de Gobineau defined as superior those races more prone toward civilization and defined the civilized as those "compelled, either by war or peaceful measures, to draw their neighbors within their sphere of influence" (p. 28). Gobineau "scientifically" rank-ordered the superior, civilized races according to skin color, with the "ethnics," or dark-skinned, relegated to the most inferior positions.

In 1914, Edward Alsworth Ross (*The Old World in the New: The Significance of Past and Present Immigration to the American People*) referred to African, Chinese, Japanese, Greeks, and others as the "lesser ethnics" (p. 168), and went on to state: "to the practiced eye, the physiognomy of certain groups unmistakably proclaims inferiority of type" (p. 286), particularly the "hirsute, low-browed, big-faced persons of obviously low mentality" (p. 285). In 1939, C. S. Coon attempted to understand differences in height, shape of face, size of head, and nose structure, but appeared to reserve the term "ethnic" to describe only the Jewish population.

In and of itself, the focus on differences in observable and empirically verifiable physical features might be granted some respectability. But it was the value judgments placed on those differences that effectively set the standard for the pursuit of scientifically based comparative knowledge. The aforementioned Edward Alsworth Ross (1914) concluded that differences in facial features were correlated with "ethical endowments": "That the Mediterranean people are morally below the races of northern Europe is as certain as any social fact. . . . The Northerners seem to surpass the southern Europeans in innate ethnical endowments" (p. 239). The relating of ethnicity and morality was still occurring in the 1950s and 1960s when Lawrence Kohlberg discussed the relationship between complex societies and high moral reasoning. As Anthony Cortese (1990) argues in his book *Ethnic Ethics,* Kohlberg's moral development theory is based on the placement of societies "on a continuum from simple to complex," but then is extended to relate complexity to moral superiority and simplicity to moral retardation (p. 147). As Cortese describes it, Kohlberg's measurement of the relative simplicity or complexity of societies occurs through the comparative process whereby he examines the relative sophistication of social and political infrastructures. But like Edward Alsworth Ross before him, Kohlberg proceeded to place a value judgment on the relative worth of "simple" societies by designating them as morally inferior.

Ethnic/white ethnic as foreign or exotic

In the early-to-mid twentieth century, the influx of immigrants to the United States gave a new meaning to the word "ethnic." Captured in this word were the styles, rituals, traditions, and value systems of the Irish, Italians, Dutch, Jews, Poles, Russians and others. Indeed, during this period, the word "ethnic" and the phrase "white ethnic" were used interchangeably, indicating how differences in rituals, traditions, and language identified the outsider. Julian Huxley and A. C. Haddon (1935), although addressing the issue of ethnicity in Europe rather than in America, nevertheless offer one of the most enlightening treatises on the issue of ethnicity. Huxley and Haddon use the term ethnic "to signify the complexity of such factors as language, ritual, and tradition as defining factors of a group" (p. 30), and argue for the relative importance of *socialization* process over *biological* factors.

As a result of a study conducted between 1930 and 1935, Warner and Srole (1945) examined the adjustment to the United States of "the ethnic groups [of] the Irish, French, Canadians, Jews, Italians, Armenians, Greeks, Poles, and Russians" (p. 1) and described these groups as "foreign" in the sense of strange or unfamiliar rather than in the sense of coming from another land (p. 283). S. M. Miller (1964) addressed the political and economic issues of "the white ethnics— first the Irish, later the Jews, and still more recently the Italian" (p. 297). In a 1979 *Journal of Communication* article, Jeffries and Hur define "white ethnic groups" as, among others, Irish, Italians, Poles, Slavs, and in a departure from the norm, the Puerto Rican/Chicano (p. 116).

Using "ethnic" and "white ethnic" interchangeably suggests that differences in cultural behaviors and language, rather than a skin color, served to identify groups of people. The stigma of inferiority prevailed, however. In the *Times Literary Supplement* of November 17, 1961, a book review critique describes "the former 'ethnics,' a polite terms for Jews, Italians, and other lesser breeds just inside the law" ("Eggheads," p. 823).

Ethnic as "people of color"

As our cultural consciousness has matured, we have attempted to find other words or phrases that we think move us away from implications of value. "People of color" is such a phrase. Today, "ethnic" largely means to be a person of color. Ethnicity as a function of language, rituals, and so on, has not been dismissed; but increasingly it appears it is *only* the languages, rituals, and traditions of people of color that undergo intellectual scrutiny. Although African Americans, Latino/as, Asian Americans, and Native Americans have always constituted a part of the American population, they were rarely mentioned in connection with American ethnicity studies done before the 1950s and 1960s. This changed with the Civil Rights Movement, the Chicano Movement, and the American Indian Movement. Protesting their invisibility, members of these cultural groups worked to be seen and heard by proclaiming their respective black, brown, and red power movements. The strategy of choosing a color as an identifying label cannot have been accidental, and it served to set the stage for the eventual change of meaning for the word "ethnic." In the introduction to *Interethnic Communication: Current Research*, Kim (1986) provides a definition of ethnicity as the combination of the "objective . . . symbolic markers [such] as race, religion, language, national origin" and the " 'subjective' identification of individuals with an ethnic group" (p. 10). The compelling aspect of this definition is that it does not limit ethnicity as a descriptor only of people of color; it encompasses all ethnic groups, including "white" ethnics. It is revealing, however, that the greater number of articles comprising this anthology focus exclusively on people of color—Eskimos, Hispanics, and blacks—so although

Kim's definition is encompassing, studies continue to define ethnics as "people of color." Within that same volume, ethnicity is sometimes defined even more narrowly: "ethnicity (black versus white)" (p. 205), or ethnicity as "the social demands of being, for instance, a black, or a Mexican-American" (p. 102).

There are two themes running through these various definitions of "ethnic." The first theme is marginalization; like the groups of people it defines, "ethnic" has historically been used as an exclusionary rather than a merely descriptive label. Our pursuit of knowledge about ethnics began when individuals or communities were identified as being outside the defined standards of religious practices, physical appearances, traditions, or skin colors. Thus the label "ethnic" encapsulated assumptions, conscious or otherwise, about cultural others. The studies described above serve as representative cases illustrating how language choices reinforced marginalization through the use of "scientific" studies. The relationship between language and knowledge points to the second themes cutting across the various definitions of "ethnics," one that is essentially the foundation for marginalization, that is, comparison followed by value judgment. Clearly, marginalization happens whenever one group is compared to another and found "deficient" in some way or another. As stated earlier, comparison is not a bad approach to the pursuit of knowledge, especially when what is being compared is devoid of cognition or emotion. Furthermore, were the process to stop at comparison, we could have understanding—and perhaps appreciation—of difference.

Limits of Comparative Knowledge

But the comparison technique is fundamentally grounded in what Woelfel and Napoli (1984) have described as a "standard reference frame" (p. 118). When applied to sentient beings, unexamined standards of reference have the potential for great harm because a set of values is embedded in any definition of the "standard." As examples, we have only to recall the standards revealed in the different meanings of "ethnic" that led to value judgments about the *worth* of the differences observed. Thus religious difference could be projected to mean "irreligious" or "unenlightened," shapes of noses could mean "moral bankruptcy," varying rituals could mean "alien," and skin color could relegate groups of people to "subcultures." In 1965, Edwin Black wrote: "the aims of a man [woman] will display their symptoms in what he [she] says and how he [she] says it" (p. 17). This is as true of the individual who engages in public discourse about political and socioeconomic issues as it is of researchers who engage in the discourse of cultural discovery and understanding. Words—labels—convey volumes about assumptions and perceptions, as do conclusions of studies that generalize to an entire community on the basis of a single identifying label, in this case the label "ethnic." The language of multicultural ethnic studies creates a "text" that often serves as the only knowledge connection among researchers and between researchers and the cultural communities they attempt to study and define.

A recent debate illustrates how "texts" are often created. Published in volumes 14, 17, and 18 of the *International Journal of Intercultural Relations* (Hecht et al., 1990, 1993; Mirandé & Tanno, 1993a, 1993b; Delgado, 1994), the debate centers around issues of researcher perspectives, contextual validation, and ethnic labeling in the study of multicultural communication in the Latino community. Researcher perspective addresses the value of etic or emic approaches to the study of cultural communities. The argument for contextual validation through dialogue is grounded in the idea that a richer and deeper understanding of multicultural communication would occur if we allowed "members of the cultures an opportunity to literally 'talk back' to the researcher" (Mirandé & Tanno, 1993a, p. 154). But it is the issue of labeling that lies at the heart of both researcher perspective and contextual validation. By inventing the multiple labels by which they wish to be identified, members of cultural groups are communicating a very important fact about their heterogeneity. When researchers choose to use data only from participants who use a particular label (e.g., Mexican American), reject data from those who self-identify differently (e.g., Chicana, Latino, Mexican, etc.), and then generalize to an entire cultural community, they are communicating homogeneity. This inaccurate perception of cultural homogeneity finds its way into print and becomes the knowledge base or "text" of the Latino community that is read by other researchers. This "text" of cultural homogeneity may also become the frame of reference for subsequent studies.

If frames of reference are to be used, they should be constructed from within the culture being studied, with the help of members of that particular cultural community. Geertz's (1973) suggestion that the study of cultures should be to seek meaning rather than laws provides a powerful rationale for the co-construction of frames of reference that will eventually lead to co-constructed texts. Fisher's (1987) concept of narrative as the process by which we give meaning and order to our lives offers a strategy for gaining insight into different cultural "texts" or stories created by the cultural members themselves. Understanding the different meanings of communication in multicultural contexts is bound to be enriched when the values and assumptions underlying selected frames of reference are commensurate with the values and assumptions of the particular culture being studied.

An ethnic "text" based on lack of rhetorical sensitivity about labels and frames of reference serves to marginalize groups, even if such is not the conscious intent of researchers. As Starosta (1984) argued, it matters little "that one attempts to 'empathize' with native conditions; one maintains the change emphasis of the rhetorician. And identificationist-extractionist distinctions dissolve into mattes of strategy, not substance. Both aim to create that 'frame of reference' within which things or new ideas can take root" (p. 234).

Foucault's (1972) argument that inequality is the product of a standard discourse of a cultural and Starosta's comment about the researcher as change agent ring true in the context of multicultural communication studies. Tafoya (1984) reinforces the idea of discourse as a force of marginalization and inequality when she argues that, "One of the paradoxes found in some cross-cultural texts and studies is that their authors, while claiming to adhere to process notions defining a culture as something that is constantly evolving or changing, somehow fell confident that they can label or identify particular or specific characteristics or behaviors of members of the culture(s) reviewed. It is distressing to see so few qualifier when so much is dynamic and diffuse" (p. 48). Foucault's insights speak to the power of discourse generally and Tafoya's insight speaks to the particular power of multicultural research studies and conclusions. There insights also illuminate what has been, until recently, the monologic characteristic of the ethnic "text" in multicultural studies, a characteristic rooted in what Robert Bellah (1975) has described as the American "rational, technical, utilitarian, ideology" that has given us much information, but little wisdom (p. xiv).

Research-as-Dialogue

Bellah (1975) also has argued that "the first step toward . . . wisdom is humility" (p. xv). In a research context, wisdom may come when researchers are able to participate in authentic dialogue with members of cultural communities and thus co-create a richer "text." Walter Fisher (1992) has argued that "genuine communication cannot be the usual forms of monologic discourse . . . whether in debate [or] in conversations" (p. 201), or, it could be argued, in multicultural research studies.

This idea of dialogue as a means of gaining knowledge (and wisdom) is not peculiar to multicultural communication studies. It is, for example, at the core of current debates in higher education and visual communication.

With regard to higher education, dialogue has been addressed by several individuals (for example, Boyer, 1990; Christensen et al., 1991; Arnett, 1992). Arnett (1992) provides the grounding for dialogue: a willingness to be open, a commitment to affirmation, and a desire to ask value questions about the application of knowledge (p. 10). While Arnett (1992) focuses on dialogue between teacher and student, his observation about "viewing dialogue as reaching out to the other in an authentic fashion, [and being] willing to try to meet and follow the unpredictable consequences of the exchange" applies equally to the interaction between research and participant (p. 11).

In the context of visual communication, Ruby (1991) argues: "While most documentaries are Vertovian, that is, the filmmakers/'authors' present us with their vision, some documentarians have aspired to replicate the subject's view of the world. . . . The documentary is assumed to give a 'voice to the voiceless,' that is, portray the political, social and economic realities of oppressed minorities and others *previously* denied access to the means of producing their own image. From this perspective, the documentary is not only an art form, it is a social service and a political act" (p. 51). The documentary is thus created through dialogue that give forces also to the image of the "documented" where before it gave force only to the image of the documentarian. In addition, integrating the possibility of social service and political empowerment serves to give equal force to the discourse of the participant in higher education, in visual communication, and in multicultural research. But research-as-dialogue demands that some ethical imperatives be in place.

Ethnical Imperatives for Multicultural Studies

In *A Short History of Ethics*, Alasdair MacIntyre (1966) helps us understand how ethical analysis can "insulate itself from correction": "In ethics it can happen in the following way. A certain unsystematically selected class of moral concepts and judgments is made the subject of attention. From the study of these it is concluded that specifically moral discourse possesses certain characteristics. When counter-examples are adduced to show that this is not always so, these counterexamples are dismissed as irrelevant, because [they are] not examples of moral discourse; and they are shown to be nonmoral by exhibiting their lack of the necessary characteristics" (p. 4).

In similar fashion, we can "insulate" ourselves against the process of re-examining how we go about gaining understanding about multicultural communication. We do this by accepting, without constant reassessment, certain methodological characteristics and certain language choices. If we are truly to gain rich understanding of the communication patterns of difference cultural groups, it seems to me that the overarching ethical imperatives are first, a keen awareness about and concern for the language we use in our studies and critical analysis, and second, an emphasis on dialogues in the research process.

Geertz (1973) described the study of culture as "not an experimental science in search of law but an interpretive one in search of meaning" (p. 5). Rhetorical sensitivity and dialogue will allow the creation of shared meanings, the co-writing of a cultural "text." As researchers/critics we must be concerned about language we use insofar as it affects how we describe, prescribe, or otherwise rhetorically characterize cultural groups. We can address this concern about language in three ways.

First, *whatever label we anticipate applying to groups of others, we must first apply to ourselves.* What does the label mean when I apply it to myself? How would I feel if it were frequently used to describe me? As an example, let me use the label which gave rise to this essay. In spite of the current practice of defining it narrowing as "people of color," ethnic in its broadest meaning refers to groups with a common cultural heritage. If we accept that, all of us can be so labeled, and yet many of us would not think to use that word as a self-descriptor. Why? In the process of pursuing answers, we may unearth those assumptions behind the label with which we are most comfortable or uncomfortable and in that way come closer to understanding the moral consequences of applying that—or any similar—label to others exclusive of oneself. Krippendorf (1989) referred to this process as the "self-referential imperative," which admonishes us to "include yourself as a constituent of your own constructions" (p. 83).

Second, *the language of our studies should reflect the relationship between diversity and universality*. While the form of communication may differ from culture to culture, it may be that the purpose behind the communication may be universal. As Lu and Frank (1993) argue: "A multicultural perspective of rhetoric should assume cultural diversity and universality. . . . we should seek out and learn from the differences in cultural expressions. . . . However, this diversity may be connected by a culturally invariant recognition of the role played by speech in human affairs" (p. 461). All cultures have been influenced by philosophic ideas, by events that tear people apart, and by traditions and rituals that keep them together. These influences manifest themselves in a diversity of *patterns* of language. But as Lu and Frank (1993) rightly point out, language itself is a universal endeavor, and the surest way of not losing sight of this important insight is by assiduously avoiding making value judgments about the various patterns of discourse.

Third, *the language of our studies should promote the relationship between social enhancement and research*. In general, the use of language entails moral responsibility. But in multicultural studies specifically, moral responsibility requires that we incorporate into the study and analysis process the answer to several question: Does this knowledge enhance the lives of the cultural groups we are studying? How does the language of our studies serve to empower them? Does our language minimize isolation or marginalization? Does it promote acceptance? For example, in assessing how ancient Eastern and Western religions provide us with a rich source of guidelines for communication ethics, Jensen (1992) concludes that ancient religions "go beyond the three fundamental purposes of rhetoric . . . to inform, to persuade, and to please—and add a fourth, to edify" (p. 65). Does the language of the conclusions of our various studies uplift members of cultural group morally, spiritually, and politically? Arguably, this question suggests the possibility that while knowledge in and of itself is a necessary motive, it may no longer be a sufficient motive for conducting multicultural communication research.

One of the means by which we, as researchers/critics, can enhance our sensitivity about language choice is by emphasizing dialogue as part of the research process. Elsewhere in this chapter I have addressed the relationship between language and knowledge and between dialogue and wisdom. *The relationship between language and wisdom may be enhanced by seeking knowledge through genuine dialogue with the participants of multicultural studies.* In his book *Dialogic Education*, Arnett (1992) writes: "Dialogic education asks the question, what will be the impact on others when information is implemented?" (p. 9). This question applies equally well to multicultural studies, and we cannot hope to gain answers to it until and unless we incorporate dialogue into the research process.

General Implications for Multicultural Researchers/Critics

The major implication of research-as-dialogue is essentially one of re-visioning our role in the research process. In the pursuit of multicultural understanding, we need to see ourselves more as participants in the co-construction of meaning and less as autonomous experts seeking generalizable laws to explain what are, in essence, groups with great internal diversity. We need also to see ourselves as potential persuaders and possible change agents, since our studies do "define" cultural groups and in that sense impact general as well as particular perceptions of them.

The re-visioning process requires commitment and time, and if we are successful, it means that the research process itself will become more time consuming, The results of the process, however, cannot but yield a truer, richer body of knowledge.

Summary

Tracing the label "ethnic" as it has been used over time, addressing the limits of comparative knowledge as it affects perceptions of marginalization, and arguing for dialogue as a necessary part of the research process constitute an attempt at "rhetorical self-consciousness" (Bazerman, 1992) that culminated in what I consider to be the ethical imperatives of multicultural communication research and the implications for researchers/critics. This self-consciousness represents a beginning, and it is communicated in the hope that it will engender a dialogue about research-as-dialogue and its impact on the language and process of inquiry.

Considering that multicultural communication studies have the potential to create ethnic texts with a potential for negatively impacting cultural groups, the ethical imperatives of research in this context are ones that we should take to mind and to heart.

References

Allen, W. (1588/1971). *An Admonition to the nobility*. Yorkshire, England: Scolar Press.

Arnett, R. (1992). *Dialogic education: Conversation about ideas and between persons*. Carbondale, IL: Southern Illinois University Press.

Bazerman, C. (1992). The interpretation of disciplinary writing. In R. H. Brown (Ed.), *Writing the social text: Poetics in social science discourse* (pp. 31–38). New York: Aldine de Gruyter.

Bellah, R. (1975). *The broken covenant: American civil religion in time of trial*. New York: Seabury Press.

Black, E. (1965). *Rhetorical criticism: A study in method*. Madison, WI: University of Wisconsin Press.

Boyer, E. (1990). *Scholarship reconsidered: Priorities of the Professoriate*. Princeton, NJ: Carnegie Foundation for the Advancement of Teaching.

Carlyle, T. (1851/1903). *The life of John Sterling*. New York: Scribner's.

Christensen, C. R., Garvin, D., & Sweet, A. (Eds.). (1991). *Education for judgment: The artistry of discussion leadership*. Boston: Harvard Business School Press.

Coon, C. S. (1939). *The races of Europe*. Westport, CT: Greenwood Press.

Cortese, A. (1990). *Ethnic ethics: The reconstruction of moral theory*. Albany, NY: State University of New York Press.

Coryate, T. (1611). *Coryats crudities*. London: Scolar Press.

Delgado, F. (1994). The complexity of Mexican American identities: A reply to Hecht, Sedano, and Ribeau and Mirande and Tanno. *International Journal of Intercultural Relations, 18*, 77–84.

Eggheads and floating voters. (1961, November 17). *Times Literary Supplement*, p. 823.

Fisher, W. (1987). *Human communication as narration: Toward a philosophy of reason, value, and action*. Columbia, SC: University of South Carolina Press.

Fisher, W. (1992). Narration, reason, and community. In R. H. Brown (Ed.), *Writing the social text* (pp. 199–217). New York: Aldine de Gruyter.

Foucault, M. (1972). *The archaeology of knowledge and the discourse on language*. (A. M. Sheridan Smith Trans.). New York: Pantheon Books.

Geertz, C. (1973). *The interpretation of cultures*. New York: Basic Books.

Glazer, N., & Moynihan, D. P. (Eds.). (1975). *Ethnicity: Theory and experience*. Cambridge, MA: Harvard University Press.

de Gobineau, A. (1915). *The inequality of human races*. (Adrian Collins, Trans.). New York: Putman and Sons.

Hariman, R. (1996). Status, marginality, and rhetorical theory. *Quarterly Journal of Speech, 73*, 38–54.

Hecht, M., Ribeau, S., & Sedano, M. (1990). A Mexican American perspective on interethnic communication. *International Journal of Intercultural Relations, 14*, 31–55.

Hecht, M., Sedano, M., & Ribeau, S. (1993). Understanding culture, communication, and research: Application to Chicanos and Mexican Americans. *International Journal of Intercultural Relations, 17*, 157–165.

Hobbes, T. (1651/1946). *Leviathan; or, The matter, forme, and power of a commonwealth ecclesiastical and civil*. Oxford: Basil Blackwell.

Huxley, J. S., & Haddon, A. C. (1935). *We Europeans: A survey of "racial" problems*. London: Jonathan Cape.

Jeffries, L. W., & Hur, K. K. (1979). White ethnics and their media images. *Journal of Communication, 29*, 116–122.

Jensen, J. V. (1992). Ancient Eastern and Western religions as guides for contemporary communication ethics. In J. A. Jaksa (Ed.), *Proceedings of the Second National Communication Ethics Conference* (pp. 58–67). Annandale, VA: Speech Communication Association.

Kim, Y. Y. (1986). Introduction: A Communication approach to interethnic relations. In Y. Y. Kim (Ed.), *Interethnic communication: Current research* (pp. 9–18). Newbury Park, CA: Sage.

Krippendorf, K. (1989). On the ethics of constructing communication. In B. Dervin, L. Grossberg, B. O'Keefe & E. Wartella (Eds.), *Rethinking communication: Vol. 1 Paradigm issues* (pp. 66–96). Newbury Park, CA: Sage.

Longfellow, H. W. (1893). *The complete poetical works of Henry Wadsworth Longfellow.* Boston: Houghton, Mifflin.

Lu. X., & Frank, D. A. (1993). On the study of Ancient Chinese rhetoric/bian. *Western Journal of Communication, 57,* 445–463.

MacIntyre, A. (1966). *A short history of ethics.* New York: Macmillan.

Miller, S. M. (1964). Poverty, race, and politics. In I. L. Horowitz (Ed.), *The new sociology: Essays in social science and social theory* (pp. 290–312). New York: Oxford University Press.

Mirandé, A., & Tanno, D. (1993a). Labels, researcher perspective, and contextual validation: A Commentary. *International Journal of Intercultural Relations, 17,* 149–155.

Mirandé, A., & Tanno, D. (1993b). Understanding interethnic communication and research: "A rose by any other name would smell as sweet." *International Journal of Intercultural Relations, 17,* 381–388.

Morgan, J. (1731/1970). *A complete history of Algiers.* New York: Negro University Press.

Riesman, D. (1953/1954). Some observations on intellectual freedom. *American Scholar, 23,* 9–25.

Ross, E. A. (1914). *The old world in the new: The significance of past and present immigration to the American people.* New York: Century Co.

Rosenberg, C. (1976). *No other gods: On science and American social thought.* Baltimore, MA: Johns Hopkins University Press.

Ruby, J. (1991). Speaking for, speaking about, speaking with or speaking alongside. *Visual Anthropology Review, 7,* 50–67.

Sollars, W. (1986). *Beyond ethnicity: Consent and descent in American culture.* New York: Oxford University Press.

Starosta, W. J. (1984). On intercultural rhetoric. In W. B. Gudykunst & Y. Y. Kim (Eds.), *Methods for intercultural communication research* (pp. 229–238). Beverly Hills, CA: Sage.

Tafoya, D. W. (1984). Research and cultural phenomena. In W. B. Gudykunst & Y. Y. Kim (Eds.), *Methods for intercultural communication research* (pp. 47–65). Beverly Hills, CA: Sage.

Warner, W. L., & Srole, L. (1945). *The social system of American ethnic groups* (Vol. 3 of Yankee City Series). New Haven, CT: Yale University Press.

Winterowd, W. R. (1968). *Rhetoric: A synthesis.* New York: Holt, Rinehart, and Winston.

Woelfel, J., & Napoli, N. R. (1984). Measuring human emotion: Proposed standards. In W. B. Gudykunst & Y. Y. Kim (Eds.), *Methods for intercultural communication research* (pp. 117–127). Beverly Hills, CA: Sage.

3

The Centrality of Culture

Robert Shuter

Intercultural communication has been examined for many years by communication scholars with the terms first appearing in Edward Hall's *Silent Language* published in 1959. Edward Hall is an anthropologist with a keen interest in human interaction. His early writings on culture and communication influenced many disciplines including speech communication where they spawned a new field of inquiry: intercultural communication.

Edward Hall's (1959, 1966, 1976) research reflects the regimen and passion of an anthropologist: a deep regard for culture explored principally by descriptive, qualitative methods. A theoretician as well, Hall (1976) developed communication theories like high context/low context cultures which he used to categorize societies and explain communication in which particular cultural groups engage. His theories are intracultural in nature; that is, they are generated from an understanding of shared values and interaction patterns *within* similar societies. However, he applies these theories interculturally to explain communication issues between dissimilar national cultures.

Unlike Hall, researchers in communication who conduct intercultural research do not generally exhibit in their published studies a passion for culture, an interest in descriptive research, or a desire to generate intracultural theories of communication. Instead, much of the published research in intercultural communication, particularly in the national and regional speech communication journals, is conducted to refine existing communication theories: culture serves principally as a research laboratory for testing the validity of communication paradigms.[1]

While this research agenda has produced significant insights on selected communication theories, it has virtually ignored the heart and soul of intercultural research: culture. As a result, intercultural researchers, as documented in the following section, have produced few published investigations of global regions, scattered examinations of communication in particular societies, and scant intracultural communication theories that can be applied interculturally. The challenge for intercultural communication in the 1990s, as argued in this essay, is to develop a research direction and teaching agenda that returns culture to preeminence and reflects the roots of the field as represented in Edward Hall's early research.

Research on Intercultural Communication: A Ten-Year Overview

Since 1980, there have been 51 intercultural communication studies published in the national and regional speech-communication journals, and the overwhelming majority of these articles are theory validation studies not cultural research. Theory validation research conducted interculturally is aimed at testing the validity and generalizability of extant communication theories like uncertainty reduction (Gudykunst, 1988; Gudykunst, Chua, & Gray, 1987; Gudykunst & Nishida, 1984; Gudykunst, Yang, & Nishida, 1985), initial interaction (Gudykunst & Hammer, 1987; Nakanishi, 1986; Shuter, 1982), intercultural communication competence (Hammer, 1984; Hwang, Chase, & Kelly, 1980; Nishida, 1985), communication apprehension (McCrosky, Fayer, & Richmond, 1985; Watson, Monroe, & Atterson, 1989), intercultural adaptation (Kim, 1987; 1988), and relationship development (Cronen & Shuter, 1983; Gudykunst, 1983, 1985)—the theories most frequently examined in intercultural research over the last decade. While theory validation is often classified as etic research, it is not, at least according to John Pike's (1966) original discussion of etic and emic ". . . as standpoints for the description of behavior" (p. 37).

For Pike, a linguist and anthropologist, etic researchers use predetermined analytical categories for investigating language behavior within particular societies with the principle aim of describing cultural patterns. While these cultural descriptions may help generate unified theories of human behavior, the etic researcher is first and foremost interested in cultural description, much like the emic investigator who also describes cultural patterns without being guided by external predetermined analytical categories and schemes.

Etic and emic similarities and differences are best stated, writes Pike (1966), ". . . in the words of Sapir who anticipated this position years ago: (p. 39).

> It is impossible to say what an individual is doing unless we have tacitly accepted the arbitrary modes of interpretation that social tradition is constantly suggesting to us from the very moment of our birth. Let anyone who doubts this try the experiment of making a painstaking report (an etic one) of the action of a group of natives engaged in some activity, say religious, to which he has not the cultural key (i.e., a knowledge of the emic system). If he is a skillful writer, he may succeed in giving a picturesque account of what he sees and hears or thinks he sees and hears, but the chances of his being able to give an accurate picture of what happens in terms of what would be intelligible and acceptable to the natives are practically nil. He will be guilty of all manner of distortion.
>
> (Pike, 1966, p. 39)

Intercultural studies in national and regional speech-communication journals are neither of an etic or emic nature: they are products of a nomothetic model developed in psychology that drives communication research and aims at identifying laws of human interaction rather than describing cultural patterns (Shuter, 1985a). Since the nomothetic model relegates culture to a laboratory for refining theory and generating laws, it is not surprising that a ten-year review of national and regional journals did not uncover a series of studies dedicated to a global region or a line of research on a particular culture except Japan.

For example, in the last decade not a single study had been published in the national or regional speech-communication journals on Africa, South and Central American, or Southeast Asia. European investigations include just four studies scattered among Sweden (Watson, Monron, & Atterstrom, 1989), U.S.S.R. (Corcoran, 1983), Britain (Bass, 1989), and France (Ting-Toomey, 1988). In East Asian, one study examines the region (Yum, 1988b), and the remaining investigations focus on Japan and Korea (Gudykunst & Nishida, 1984; Gudykunst, Sodetani, & Sonada, 1987; Gudykunst, Yang, & Nishida, 1985; Stewart, Gudykunst, Ting-Toomey, & Nishida, 1986; Gudykunst, Sodetani, & Sonada, 1987; Yum, 1982). Taiwan and People's Republic of China are not examined in separate studies. There are a few studies on the Middle East principally investigating Israel (Frank, 1981; Katriel, 1987) and Iran (Heisey & Trebing, 1983), and one additional investigation on South Asia (Carlson, 1986).

It is possible that the nomothetic bias of the discipline serves as an obstacle for accepting etic or emic intercultural investigations in national or regional journals. This may be the case;

however, after examining the published studies over the last ten years in the *International and Intercultural Communication Annual*—the only speech-communication journal dedicated to intercultural studies—one finds publishing patterns similar to those found in the national and regional speech-communication journals. First, there is not a line of research on any global region, and only East Asia (Cushman & King, 1985; Kume, 1985, Okabe, 1983; Yum, 1988a, 1988b), Europe (Hopper & Doany, 1989; Magiste, 1988; Punetha, Giles, & Young, 1988), and the Middle East (Griefat & Katriel, 1989; Hopper & Doany, 1989) are examined in more than one investigation. Africa, South and Central America, and Southeast Asia are not explored in the studies published in the annual since 1980.

Moreover, the emphasis of communication studies in the annual has been on communication theory validation and the development of intercultural communication theory. While the annual has made significant contribution to the discipline, its dedication to theory development has resulted in a paucity of research on world regions and single cultures.

Not surprisingly, the last ten years has also resulted in few studies of an intracultural nature in national and regional speech-communication journals except for scattered investigations on selected U.S. and European co-cultures (i.e., ethnic groups and races within a particular society) (Booth-Butterfield & Jordan, 1989; Campbell, 1986; Gudykunst & Kim, 1986; Hammerback & Jensen, 1980; Jensen & Hammerback, 1980; Lake, 1983; Stanback & Pearce, 1981). Since intracultural investigations tend to focus on a particular society, they are not perceived as being easily translated into intercultural communication theory. For this reason, researchers may tend to avoid conducting intracultural studies and, instead, execute comparative intercultural investigations.

In summary, intercultural communication research since 1980 has provided important validation studies of communication paradigms and significant breakthroughs in the development of intercultural communication theory. However, the decade's published research has neglected people, context, and national culture. As a result, interculturalists have provided precious few data based insights into how *specific* societies, world regions, and ethnic groups communicate. It is time for a change in direction.

Intercultural Communication in the 1990s: A Cultural Imperative

Culture is the single most important global communication issue in the 1990s. New cultural coalitions and alliances are redefining global relationships. Western Europe, for example, struggles with the development in 1992 of the European Economic Community, which strives to unify European trading regulations within the Common Market without dismantling national cultural traditions that provide the historical and contemporary identity of each member county (Bruce, 1988; Montet, 1989). While Western Europe evolves into a unified marketplace, North America wonders about the development of "fortress" Europe—a monolithic cultural bloc that may prevent North American products and communication from successfully penetrating the European community (Reimer, 1989; Rosenbaum, 1989).

As Western Europe attempts to harmonize cultural differences to achieve trade unification, Eastern European countries proclaim their cultural independence by changing their political systems and celebrating age-old cultural values, traditions, and communication patterns (Berend, 1988). With the diminution of Soviet control of Eastern Europe, there is a resurgence of national cultures in countries that have traditionally surrendered a significant degree of cultural and political independence to Soviet control.

Culture dominates the Pacific Basin as well, with Japan reordering its relationships with East and Southeast Asian countries to develop what some have described as the Pacific equivalent to the European community (Yahuda, 1988; Yang, 1989). As Japan, Korea, Taiwan, Hong Kong, and Singapore develop sustained and cooperative trading relationships, these countries, at the same time, retain distinct cultural identities that are carefully preserved but sometimes cause cultural rifts between them (Pearce, 1988; Tank, 1987).

Culture is also the central theme in Africa, the Middle East, South Asia, and Central and South America. These diverse cultural regions struggle with maintaining traditional cultural systems while developing technological and communications infrastructures that may threaten cultural and religious values and national identities (Kelly, 1988; Kwarteng, 1988; Shamsuddin, 1988).

Culture is also the dominant issue *within* global societies (Rosen and Weissbrodt, 1988). In the U.S., for example, cultural tensions are the result of long-standing conflicts between co-cultures as well as more recent communication issues posed by immigration into North America (Roberts, 1988). Countries in Africa, Latin America, the Middle East, and South Asian struggle with co-cultural tensions and confrontations fueled by racial divisions, religious and cultural differences, and tribal identifications (Kelly, 1988; Rupesinghe, 1988; Weissbrodt, 1988). Societies within Eastern and Western Europe are also coping with serious intracultural communication issues that have evolved from age-old ethnic divisions and more recently changes in immigration patterns (Armstrong, 1988).

Compelling global conditions require intercultural researchers to alter their research agenda and return culture to preeminence in their studies. This can be accomplished by examining intracultural patterns of interaction within societies and world regions.

An Intracultural Communication Research Agenda for the 1990s

Intracultural research identifies and examines communication patterns endemic to a particular country or co-culture within a society. This type of research generates cultural data that not only increases understanding of a society, but also serves as a springboard for developing intracultural communication theory.

Unlike intercultural theory, an intracultural perspective marries culture and communication theory and, hence, produces communication paradigms about a co-culture, country, or world region. This approach to theory development is best exemplified in Kincaid's (1987) *Communication Theory: Eastern and Western Perspectives*, which identifies differences and similarities between Korean, Chinese, Japanese, and Indian communication theories. While Kincaid's book stops short of identifying different Western communication theories—French versus British communication theory for example—it is a most significant contribution in intracultural communication theory development.

Intracultural communication theory is critically important for several reasons. First, it provides a conceptual framework for analyzing interaction within a society and world region. Second, intracultural theories demonstrate the inextricable linkage between communication patterns and sociocultural forces. And lastly, it provides a conceptual basis for making intercultural communication comparisons between dissimilar societies.

With an intracultural perspective, researchers can concentrate on developing a line of research on a society or world region. This approach should produce comprehensive communication data on countries and world regions as well as establishing the foundation for developing culture specialists—researchers and teachers who are experts on a particular country and world region. Culture specialists in communication are vital if global and co-cultural conflicts are to be understood and ameliorated.

An intracultural perspective also has implications for teaching intercultural communication. With comprehensive intracultural data, teachers should be able to design multiple courses in intercultural communication that focus on interaction within a society and world region—a marked improvement over many intercultural curricula that currently consist of a single course offering called Intercultural Communication. For example, with sufficient intracultural data, a series of communication classes could be offered on Africa, East Asia, or South Asia with seminars also available on specific countries within these regions. Currently, this type of curriculum is not easily developed because intercultural researchers have devoted limited attention to intracultural communication. Without an expanded intercultural curriculum, it will be difficult to develop students and teachers who are culture specialists in communication.

Conclusion: Back to the Future

The goal of this essay is to set a new intracultural agenda for scholars and teachers of intercultural communication. An intracultural perspective examines patterns of intracultural communication "those common, unstated experiences which members of a given culture share, communicate without knowing, and which form the backdrop against which all other events are judged" (Hall, 1966, p. 4). They are, according to Ruth Benedict (1934), the cultural forms and processes that are an integral part of every society. When cultural patterns are linked to communication, the terms refer to shared, recurring, and culturally derived ways of interacting that are manifested in the ebb and flow of human transactions within a society.

Pattern research tends to be descriptive in nature: it details the form and function of communicative behavior within a society. Methodologically, it can be conducted either quantitatively or qualitatively in a research laboratory, field study, or rhetorical analysis of primary or secondary sources. Because pattern research is not bound to a particular methodology, it can enhance our understanding of intracultural nuances, producing fresh understanding of cultural mindsets and dispositions. In fact, pattern research has the promise of unearthing hidden dimensions of culture and communication that Edward Hall so eloquently described decades ago—the treasures of human interaction that remain buried unless mined by the intraculturalist. In fact, our modern age cries out for intraculturalists—communication teachers, researchers and professionals with a deep understanding of specific co-cultures, countries, and world regions. Hopefully, this essay is small step towards achieving this goal.

Note

1. For this essay, the speech-communication journals reviewed for intercultural communication research included: *Central States Speech Journal, Communication Monographs, Communication Quarterly, Human Communication Research, Quarterly Journal of Speech, Southern Communication Journal,* and *Western Journal of Speech Communication.*

References

Armstrong, J. (1988). Toward a framework for considering nationalism in East Europe. *Eastern Europe Politics and Societies, 2,* 280–305.

Bass, J. (1989). An efficient humanitarianism: The British slave trade debates, 1791–1792. *Quarterly Journal of Speech, 75,* 152–165.

Benedict, R. (1934). *Patterns of culture.* Boston: Houghton Mifflin.

Berend, I. (1988). Crisis and reform in East-Central Europe. *Studia Diplomatica, 41,* 257–267.

Booth-Butterfield, M. & Jordan, F. (1989). Communication adaptation among racially homogeneous and heterogeneous groups. *Southern Communication Journal, 54,* 253–272.

Bruce, L. (1988). Where adversaries converge. *International Management, 43,* 70–73.

Campbell, K. (1986). Style and content in the rhetoric of early Afro-American feminists. *Quarterly Journal of Speech, 72,* 434–445.

Carlson, C. (1986). Gandhi and the comic frame: Ad Belum Purificandum. *Quarterly Journal of Speech, 72,* 446–455.

Condon, J. C. (1984). *With respect to the Japanese: A guide for Americans.* Yarmouth, ME: Intercultural Press.

Corcoran, F. (1983). The bear in the backyard: Myth, ideology, and victimage ritual in Soviet funerals. *Communication Monographs, 50,* 305–320.

Cronen, V. E., & Shuter, R. (1983). Forming intercultural bonds. In W. B. Gudykunst (Ed.), *Intercultural communication theory: Current perspectives* (pp. 89–118). Beverly Hills, CA: Sage.

Cushman, D., & King, S. (1985). National and organizational cultures in conflict resolution: Japan, the United States, and Yugoslavia. *International and Intercultural Communication Annual, 9,* 114–133.

Frank, D. (1981). Shalom Achshave: Rituals of the Israeli peace movement. *Communication Monographs, 48,* 165–182.

Griefat, Y., & Katriel, T. (1989). Life demands *Musayara:* Communication and culture among Arabs in Israel. *International and Intercultural Communication Annual, 13,* 121–138.

Gudykunst, W. B. (1983). Similarities and differences in perceptions of initial intracultural and intercultural encounters: An exploratory investigation. *Southern Communication Journal, 27,* 49–65.

Gudykunst, W. B. (1985). An exploratory comparison of close intracultural and intercultural friendships. *Communication Quarterly, 33,* 270–283.

Gudykunst, W. B. (1988). Uncertainty and anxiety. In Y. Y. Kim & W. B. Gudykunst (Eds.), *Theories in intercultural communication* (pp. 123–156). Newbury Park, CA: Sage.

Gudykusnt, W. B., Chua, E., & Gray, A. (1987). Cultural dissimilarities and uncertainty reduction processes. In M. McLaughlin (Ed.), *Communication yearbook* (Vol. 10, pp. 456–469). New Brunswick, NJ: Transaction.

Gudykunst, W. B., & Hammer, M. (1987). The effects of ethnicity, gender, and dyadic composition on uncertainty reduction in initial interaction. *Journal of Black Studies, 18,* 191–214.

Gudykunst, W. B., & Kim, Y. Y. (Eds.). (1986). *Interethnic communication.* Newbury Park, CA: Sage.

Gudykunst, W. B., & Nishida, T. (1984). Individual and cultural influences on uncertainty reduction. *Communication Monographs, 51,* 23–36.

Gudykunst, W. B., Sodetani, L., & Sonada, K. (1987). Uncertainty reduction in Japanese-American and Caucasian relationships in Hawaii. *Western Journal of Speech Communication, 51,* 256–278.

Gudykunst, W. B., Yang, S. M., & Nishida, T. (1985). A cross-cultural test of uncertainty reduction theory. *Human Communication Research, 11,* 407–454.

Hall, E. T. (1959). *The silent culture.* Garden City, NY: Doubleday.

Hall, E. T. (1966). *The hidden dimension.* Garden City, NY: Doubleday.

Hall, E. T. (1976). *Beyond culture.* Garden City, NY: Doubleday.

Hammer, M. (1984). The effects of an intercultural communication workshop on participants' intercultural communication competence. *Communication Quarterly, 32,* 352–362.

Hammerback, J., & Jensen, R. (1980). The rhetorical worlds of Cesar Chavez and Reises Tijerina. *Western Journal of Speech Communication, 44,* 166–176.

Heisey, R., & Trebing, D. (1983). A comparison of the rhetorical visions and strategies of the Shah's White Revolution and the Ayatollah's Islamic Revolution. *Communication Monographs, 50,* 158–174.

Hopper, R., & Doany, N. (1989). Telephone openings and conversational universals: A study in three languages. *International and Intercultural Communication Annual, 13,* 157–179.

Hwang, J. Chase, L., & Kelly, C. (1980). An intercultural examination of communication competence. *Communication, 9,* 70–79.

Jensen, R., & Hammerback, J. (1980). Radical nationalism among Chicanos: The rhetoric of Jose Angel Gutierrez. *Western Journal of Speech Communication, 44,* 191–202.

Katriel, T. (1986). *Talking straight: Dugri speech in Israeli Sabra culture.* Cambridge: Cambridge University Press.

Katriel, T. (1987). Rhetoric in flames: Fire inscriptions in Israeli youth movement ceremonials. *Quarterly Journal of Speech, 73,* 444–459.

Kelly, J. (1980). Class conflict of ethnic oppression? The cost of being Indian in rural Bolivia. *Rural Sociology, 53,* 399–420.

Kim, Y. Y. (1987). Facilitating immigration adaptation: The role of communication. In T. C. Albrecht, M. B. Adelman et al. (Eds.), *Communicating social support* (pp. 192–211). Newbury Park, CA: Sage.

Kim, Y. Y. (1988). *Communication and cross-cultural adaptation: An integrative theory.* Clevedon, England: Multilingual Matters.

Kincaid, D. L. (Ed.). (1987). *Communication theory: Eastern and Western perspectives.* San Diego, CA: Academic Press.

Kume, T. (1985). Managerial attitudes toward decision-making: North America and Japan. *International and Intercultural Communication Annual, 9,* 231–252.

Kwarterg, C. (1988). Difficulties in economic integration: The case of ECOWAS. *Transafrica Forum, 5,* 17–25.

Lake, R. (1986). Enacting red power: The consummatory function in Native American protest rhetoric. *Quarterly Journal of Speech, 72,* 434–445.

Magiste, E. (1988). Changes in the Lateralization pattern of two immigrant groups in Sweden. *International and Intercultural Communication Annual, 9,* 233–251.

McCroskey, J. C., Fayer, J. M., & Richmond, V. (1985). Don't speak to me in English: Communication apprehension in Puerto Rico. *Communication Quarterly, 33,* 185–192.

Montet, M. (1989). Europe's spiritual organs. *International Management, 44*, 38–39.

Nakanishi, M. (1986). Perceptions of self-disclosure in initial interaction: A Japanese sample. *Human Communication Research, 13*, 176–190.

Nishida, H. (1985). Japanese intercultural communication competence and cross-cultural adjustment. *International Journal of Intercultural Relations, 9*, 247–269.

Okabe, R. (1983). Cultural assumptions of East and West: Japan and the United States. *International and Intercultural Communication Annual, 7*, 21–41.

Pearce, J. (1988). Free port, no trade restrictions, mark Singapore development. *Business Japan, 33*, 31–32.

Philipsen, G. (1975). Speaking "like a man" in Teamsterville. *Quarterly Journal of Speech, 61*, 13–22.

Pike, J. (1966). *Language in relation to a unified theory of the structure of human behavior.* The Hague, The Netherlands: Mouton.

Punetha, D., Giles, H., & Young, L. (1988). Interethnic perceptions and relative deprivation: British data. *International and Intercultural Communication Annual, 9*, 252–266.

Reimer, B. (1999, March 27). Europe may slap a quota on *General Hospital. Business Week*, pp. 46–47.

Roberts, A. (1988). Racism sent and received: Americans an Vietnamese view one another. *Research in Race and Ethnic Relations, 5*, 75–97.

Rosen, S., & Weissbrodt, D. (1988). The 39th session of the UN Sub-Commission on Prevention of Discrimination and Protection of Minorities. *Human Rights Quarterly, 10*, 487–508.

Rosenhaum, A. (1989). Fortress or façade? A unified EC is far from finished. *Industry Week, 238*, 54–55.

Rupesinghe, K. (1988). Ethnic conflicts in South Asia. *Journal of Peace Research, 25*, 337–350.

Shamsuddin, M. (1988). UNSCO and the flow of information: A case study. *Pakistan Horizon, 41*, 31–49.

Shuter, R. (1979). The Dap in the military: Hand-to-hand communication. *Journal of Communication, 29*, 136–142.

Shuter, R. (1982). Initial interaction of American Blacks and Whites in interracial and intraracial dyads. *Journal of Social Psychology, 117*, 45–52.

Shuter, R. (1985a). The Hmong of Laos: Orality, communication, and acculturation. In L. A. Samovar & R. E. Porter (Eds.), *Intercultural communication: A reader* (4th ed., pp. 102–108). Belmont, CA: Wadsworth.

Shuter, R. (1985b). *Nomothetic and ideographic approaches to developing an intercultural communication curriculum.* Paper presented at the annual meeting of the Speech Communication Association, Chicago, IL.

Stanback, M. & Pearce, W. B. (1981). Talking to "The Man": Some communication strategies used by members of subordinate social groups. *Quarterly Journal of Speech, 67*, 21–30.

Tank, A. (1987, April). Korea's Japanese jinx. *Management Today*, pp. 88–90.

Ting-Toomey, S. (1988). Rhetorical sensitivity style in three cultures: France, Japan, and the United States. *Central States Speech Journal, 39*, 28–36.

Watson, A. K., Monroe, E., & Atterstrom, H. (2989). Comparison of communication apprehension across cultures: American and Swedish children. *Communication Quarterly, 37*, 67–76.

Weissbrodt, D. (1988). Country related and thematic developments at the 1988 Sessions of the UN Commission on Human Rights. *Human Rights Quarterly, 10*, 544–558.

Yahuda, M. (1988). The Pacific Community: Not yet. *Pacific Review, 1*, 119–127.

Yang, D. J. (1989, April 10). Japan builds a new power base: Its emerging clout in East Asia could come at America's expense. *Business Week*, pp. 42–45.

Yum, J. O. (1982). Communication diversity and information acquisition among Korean immigrants in Hawaii. *Human Communication Research, 8*, 154–159.

Yum, J. O. (1988a). Locus of control and communication patterns of immigrants. *International and Intercultural Communication Annual, 9*, 191–211.

Yum, J. O. (1988b). The impact of Confucianism on interpersonal relationships and communication patterns in East Asia. *Communication Monographs, 55*, 374–388.

Part II
Metatheoretical Frameworks for Future Directions

4

The Ideological Significance of Afrocentricity in Intercultural Communication

Molefi Kete Asante

At the Bellagio Conference on African Communication I advanced the position that there were three broad views of cultural reality: Afrocentric, Eurocentric, and Asiocentric (Asante, 1980a). Although it is possible to make more precise delineations, the basic tenets of my position have been enhanced by the work of Ruch and Anyanwu (1981). The philosopher Anyanwu argues correctly that Afrocentricity makes no sharp distinction between the ego and the world, subject and object. He says, "In the conflict between the self and the world, African culture makes the self the center of the world. Since the African world is centered on the self, every experience and reality itself is personal." Not only has my position been substantiated by other fields, it has become even more self-evident that the cultural differences we face in the world are rooted in different views of reality.

The African world shares a common approach to phenomena.[1] Even a term like "person" or "human" means something different to a European and Asian than it does to an African. In this sense all definitions are contextual and grow out of a people's cultural heritage. For example, while the European seeks to conquer nature, to subdue it, the Asian flees from the illusions of the world, and the African finds coexistence with nature and a harmonious relationship with all of the elements of the universe. Diop (1978) has understood this as the Two Cradle theory of human civilization: Europe and Africa, where Asia becomes a combination of the two cradles. Actually for Diop the African Cradle predates the European but the special characteristics of the European Cradle are associated with the glaciers, particularly as they relate to fire and ice, the dual gods of Westerners. In *Iceman Inheritance* (1978) Bradley extends Diop's position, contending that Europeans carry within them the enduring myth of Ragnarok. There is a sense in which Europe is still trying to resolve ice and fire according to Bradley's thesis. There needs to be further intensive work on European mythology and psychology.

What we are witnessing in the development of intercultural communication as a field of inquiry is the creation of theoretical postures from which to survey the whole of human interaction between cultures. What obtains in such circumstance is how power is defined and used, that is, the question becomes the focus of the problem. How do Shona communicate with British? Or how does a Kikuyu communicate with an Arab? What description can we give to the intercultural communication between Yoruba and Portuguese? All of these questions are at their fundamental level questions of status power, perceived or real.

Power

I emphasize that intercultural communication at the international or national level is a matter of power.[2] The proper discussion of intercultural communication seems to reside in the examination of power relationship between people. In societies where cultural differences exist and are the bases for misunderstandings, the control problem is an imbalance of power. Ruling ideas do rest with ruling classes; this is a historical fact. Where Africans have interacted with Europeans with difficulty, that difficulty has been the result of perceived power and status. Thus we cannot achieve intercultural communication which is mature and effective until we address the material conditions of the people. Power relationships dictate so much of what is right, correct, logical, and reasonable. The limits are drawn by those who wield the economic, political, and cultural power.

Consequently, my concern has turned more and more toward the ideological significance of communication and Afrocentricity, the logical philosophical heir to Negritude. Social science in the West is imperialistic, the disciplinary justification for expansion. Richards (1980) is clear on this point. In her brilliantly provocative essay on the European mythology of domination she has exposed the European obsession with filling up space in the name of progress. Richards is not alone in this interpretation of the European use of social science; indeed Herbert Marcuse (1968) and Michael Bradley (1978) have provided ample demonstration of positivism as the pillar upon which operationalism manages to expand. Communication is a Western field of inquiry, much like other analytical forms, seeking to analyze audiences, examine data, and theorize about how humans are persuaded, in order to aid the persuaders, not the audience. In this respect, communication as a science becomes another thrust into the belly of non-Westerners.

My aim, therefore, is to clarify how Afrocentricity serves in an ideological fashion to enhance the opportunity for effective interaction between Africans and non-Africans. The assumption I make is simple; effective intercultural communication must be based upon the equality of the interactants because the sharing of meaning is the fundamental prerequisite of communicative understanding. A development of the Afrocentric view with regards to objective conditions for the liberation of African minds demands a wholistic philosophy. Even rhetorical discourse among Africans in the Western world is polluted, distorted and dismembered by the onslaught of European images and symbols.[3] Sharing of images is reasonable, valuable, and positive; image domination, however, is the same as other colonial conquests, vile, repressive, and negative. Thus, my aim is to develop a metatheory out of which theories will emerge to explain intercultural interactions.

Ideology and Economics

The discussion of a comprehensive approach, including communication, to the theory of African liberation, both continental and diasporan, has been fraught with historically divergent, partly dissociated, politically conflicting, and conceptually incongruent patterns among our leading thinkers (DuBois, 1961; Garvey, 1969; Diop, 1978; Karenga, 1978; Cruse, 1968; Cabral, 1973; Fanon, 1967; Nkrumah, 1970; and Nyerere, 1974).[4] They have argued different positions, debating from their own ideological reference points, yet they have all sought to explain the African relationship to the European in historical and contemporary times. This analytical similarity, that is, as it refers to the relationship of African peoples to European peoples, has not meant a congruent approach to the nature of cultural liberation. Numerous varieties exist in our political orientations as well as in our understanding of the objective conditions of our lives. Perhaps it is the differences perceived in the objective conditions that give rise to the great diversity in ideological approaches. One issue is settled among these scholars: no one can define for us how we will behave in intercultural encounters. They recognize the need for a people to define their own power vis-à-vis another.

Afrocentricity is the ideological centerpiece of human regeneration, systematizing our history and experience with our own culture at the core of existence (Asante, 1980a). In its epistemic dimensions it is also a methodology for discovering the truth about intercultural communication. We have needed more culturally sensitive treatments for our analysis of reality. Indeed the principal theoretical analyses by Africans of the African political economy on the continent and wherever it is substantial in the diaspora have often been enmeshed in reactionary thought. Those analyses which have not been rigidly reactionary have often turned to Marxist referents. Although both the capitalist and the Marxist positions are European and consequently derive from European exeriences, that is no reason in and of itself to reject them wholeheartedly. A more serious charge is that both theoretical positions encapsulate the interests and aspirations of the masses of Africans, subsuming African interests to the dominant interests of Europe (Rodney, 1980; Marable, 1982).

It is therefore necessary for us to explore alternatives in order to at least know what is possible from an African cultural perspective. Wey and Osagie (1977) have proposed the integratism inherent in all markets as the basis for Nigerian economic development and ultimately an approach to all African economic development. The principal factor in Wey and Osagie's system is the cultural heritage of the people. The modifying and systematizing of this cultural heritage along more successful economic lines becomes the major change element in ending the capitalist/socialist struggle. Although I am not an apologist for the past, I do believe that we can build upon the foundations firmly entrenched in our culture. The afrologist must begin to explore all economic analysis which must be seen as contributing to our symbolic system. But the relationship between economics and communication remains one of a definition of power. The gates of world power are kept by guardians who conference among themselves to secure their places and to thwart African communication or economic maturity, on the continent and in the diaspora. A market system which seeks profits correlates with a view of intercultural communication which seeks to use people. DeBeers Consolidated Diamonds controls the bulk of the diamonds sold in the world through a distribution system open to 300 European diamond dealers. Thus, through this arrangement only a select number of gem diamonds are placed on the world market. This happens while the major diamond producing area of the world remains Africa. In order for an African on the continent or in the diaspora to participate in the process of securing gem diamonds, he or she must submit to the Europeans whose native lands produce almost no gem diamonds. In no other continent and among no other peoples have outside influences so thoroughly dominated economic life. Our battle is intense, the struggle we wage for status power is serious and we cannot *communicate* as equals when our economic position is that of servants.

Changes in the Western markets will tend to be toward more monopolistic vertical integration which allows transnational companies to own and control the sources of their raw materials. Walter Rodney, in his awesome work *How Europe Underdeveloped Africa*, showed the negative character of the social, political, and economic consequences of European exploitation. In Rodney's view the viciousness of the colonial system with respect to African social services was stunning. Colonized African populations were severely maltreated in health, education, and welfare. In fact, Rodney's thesis on colonized people deepened our understanding of the brutality of race exploitation underscored by the fact that the colonists owned and controlled the raw materials which gave them enormous surplus and allowed them to ship massive amounts to the various metropoles without returning equal profits to the Africans who made it all possible. For example, John Cadbury chaired the West African Cocoa Board and used this position to amass wealth and to exploit the African cocoa farmers, becoming one of the richest chocolate manufacturers in the world. Almost every African colony had its white settlers or businessmen who controlled vast areas of the country's natural resources. In too many examples, those settlers were the most violent supporters of racism against Africans.

Politics and Symbols

Politics is the struggle for symbols, that is, the endeavor to secure some predetermined objective. Power is the ability to see those symbols materialized and the objective realized. On a basic level the forces of SWAPO possess a vision for Namibia which they intend to implement; the implementation of that vision will be an indication of power. Theoretically, a person may have a vision about securing assent to some philosophical position. The marshalling of evidence, data, and arguments to obtain acceptance of that theory reveals intellectual power.

Intercultural communication as a harmonious endeavor seeks to create the sharing of power. In the exchange, the interchange, we find the source of creative understanding. For the African scholar the principal audience is African and from that audience one makes contact with the universal audience.

I am a Diopian in terms of philosophy and analysis, believing that no method is adequate if it cannot explain the possibility of harmony. Every topic, economics, law, communication, science, religion, history, literature, and sociology must be reviewed through Afrocentric eyes. When I met Cheikh Anta Diop at IFAN, University of Dakar, in December 1980, and spoke to him about symbols and culture, he emphasized the need to expand the understanding of African culture, not defend it. In the mind of this outstanding scholar the future of African scholarship rested with those scholars who would explore every subject afrocentrically. We must examine the African invasions of Europe, African influences on the court systems of Europe as it emerged from the White Ages, and the African American origin of American science. The afrocentric line is not an easy line, it is a difficult analytical method, fraught with pitfalls, detours, and intellectual seductresses and seducers. Yet it is a worthwhile method, perhaps the only valid method, for a proper understanding of our objective reality. Otherwise intercultural communication becomes a mere pipe dream unrealized and unrealizable because Europeans and Africans have such limited understanding of each other's essential mythologies and motifs.

Eurocentric Aggression

McWorter (1980) has seen that the methods and conclusions of afrocentric scholars are often diametrically opposed to European intellectual traditions and this objective fact means that many scholars of African descent are not published in eurocentric journals. The opposition of the two world views derives from the concept of origin. Michael Bradley's (1978) thesis is that the rise of Europeans must be seen in the caves of Europe during the time of the glaciers. Their use and worship of fire arose in the same period. This led to a fear of strangers, xenophobia, and an aggressive behavior, all for the protection of one's fire. According to Bradley, the European's aggressiveness constitutes the single most important factor in his expansion throughout the world. It was not only spatial but intellectual. As with geography what they saw they attempted to fill, even though there were other people or ideas in those places. Concomitant with the European colonization of Africa was the European colonization of information about Africa. It would be a mistake for any African theorist or philosopher to underestimate the extent of white aggressiveness in the communication process. Since aggression is the primary reason for white expansion (Richards, 1980; Bradley, 1978) in other spheres, Schiller (1976: 82) correctly sees the struggle for domination over communication as essentially a creation of the capitalist ethos of white western industrialized societies. According to Schiller (1976: 55), "western technology is not only an integral part of an exploitative system of production but extends and deepens that exploitation." My own view is that Marxist technology also seeks to impose itself on Africa. In communication, as in other fields, the aim of the eurocentric aggression is to dominate through the subjection of nature and people. Ultimately, this quest for domination is a quest for salvation which Europeans find only in the acquisition of more and more. The Hobbesian analysis of European "man" that he desires and desires and there is no end to his desire seems as accurate now as it was in the seventeenth century. Acquisition was often made a reality by changing the names of things, places and even people and then treating them as if they were what Europeans said they were, in effect, objects.

The Europeans imposed themselves and gave new names to mountains, rivers, and villages. Monopotapa existed long before there was any Rhodes or Rhodesia; Victoria Falls is an imposition on the ancient water falls called Musi-wa-tunya, and New York and Baltimore are recent names to the geography of North America. In the world of ideas, Europeans imposed new histories, new sciences, and new interpretations which disregarded the sacred histories and sciences of the ancients. They were like children playing in the garden of adults. Progress became a term for an antihuman thrust of racial vanity. Bradley (1978) is perhaps one of the few white writers who correctly understands this penchant for progress as a "symptom of undisplaced aggression resulting from Caucasoid psychosexual maladaptation." What other races have viewed as civilization is puzzling to whites who view progress as civilization (Bradley, 1978; Richards, 1980).

African scholars can never hope to achieve intellectual, cultural, or political liberation by following in eurocentric footsteps; this is the exacting truth of history. The foundations of eurocentric thought makes Africans anti-African. Neither can we expect to communicate if we refuse to use our own voice. Our own voice is the source of effective interaction with others. While anthropology, sociology, history, and economics exist as reasonable categories for studying the world, it is in the development, analysis, and criticism of those disciplines that we will find our differences with eurocentric writers. We should not abandon the principal disciplines, nor must we relinquish excellence, intellectual integrity, methodological clarity, and productivity. If it should become necessary to challenge the so-called Western disciplines, we must do so from an afrocentric perspective using intellectual integrity which is comprised of an absolute commitment to the discovery of truth. And truth is never against the people; it can only support the best traditions because it is in harmony with nature. For example, if one is asked to discuss anthropology, one must understand its racist origin. Classification of humans was initially done for racist reasons: to try to show white supremacy and the inferiority of every other people. Thus when the white person spoke to the African or Asian he or she spoke with the perceptions of white superiority. Many nonwhites, educated in white studies, assumed their own inferiority and accepted the superiority of white culture as promulgated by white studies. The communication between such a person and a white person is superficial and often meaningless.

Criticism and Knowledge

The bulk of what Africans have written has added to the body of European literature. Even our criticism has been criticism from a European posture, that is, when we have been critical we have used foreign critical categories. Our research often begins with a review of the European literature on our subjects. What we need is a method to prevent the invisibility of our own scholars and history. The afrocentric approach to research permits a *specific* and a *general* survey in search for African writers who have studied the topic on them. This is done to prevent provincialism and racism. These two levels of inquiry will always reveal an African who has understood or developed a perspective on an issue. If you are talking about systems theory, then explore the question from the specific survey level. How does system theory work? What is its relationship to society in the large? What significance does it have to Africans? These questions should give the researcher enough information to find an African who has written on the subject. If not, then proceed to the next level, the general survey. What are the methodological approaches to this topic? What mythological bases exist in African culture? When the answer is found we can say, perhaps, that Marcus Garvey advanced systems theory long before von Bertanlanfy ever dreamed of the concept. Garvey demonstrated the wholistic nature, the unitary nature of the racist system. Moreover, at the general survey level one discovers that Ogotemmeli's exposition on Dogon philosophy and works in Zulu and Yoruba philosophy show the interconnectedness of the world. Even in *umbanda,* myalism, voodoo, and Rasta one has to understand the elements of input-output equations, entropy, and leading force. So if we are to be truly afrocentric in our research we will need to understand that our work must add to the body of information related to our perspective; otherwise we are Africans doing eurocentric research. This is difficult because it causes us to thinks about the topics we tackle but more importantly how we tackle them. It is too easy to disregard the communication research of African scholars; that is why it is necessary to make a special effort.

Collective worldview means that we have a common vision for our research; it does not mean that all of our research must be on the same topics. Afrologists need three professional qualities: competence, clarity of perspective, and understanding of the research object (Asante, 1980a). The afrocentric method makes afrological study. So one may study any subject and be an afrologist so long as the subject is studied afrocentrically. Everything is in relation to Africa, not Africa in mere geographic terms but Africa as vision, ideal, and promontory.

History and tradition teach us that cultural power is the fundamental basis of economic power. John Henrik Clarke is correct to observe that a major clothing industry among African Americans could have been created if Dr. Martin Luther King, Jr., had refused to wear any clothes but those manufactured by Africans. Chopsticks will not be replaced in China by forks and spoons, not even in the Westernization period, because whole villages are engaged in the manufacturing of chopsticks; they are cultural and economic. Our economics is a symbol system, what we wear and what we buy are symbols to those who see us.

Afrologists, as guiding theorists, can create the foundations for economic victory, but we have to be willing to propose bold research plans which will redound to the image of a nation; indeed, this is true imagination. Such an Ogunic thrust into the future is what we need to prepare ourselves and our children for economic independence. This means that they look to create rather than to join with the oppressor. Architects should build edifices which reflect African values and symbols. Scientists should examine the African secrets and mysteries related to herbs. Linguisticians must decipher the Meroitic texts. Historians should write unifying histories of the continent. Psychologists should examine white people, particularly as such examination into racist behavior will make for interracial understanding, and report their findings in journals of Black Studies and African research. My point is that ideology is essential to cultural action and afrocentricity is the ideological posture which allows us to act creatively.

Afrocentric Counterbalance

Afrocentricity provides us with a counterbalance to the penetration of eurocentric ideology in communication. Most doctrines of communication developed in the Western world are meant to protect the status of the exploiter, the dominator or if they were not so intended have become the reality. Free flow of information, for example, strengthens the exploiter and keeps the weak nations weak. As a concept, free flow of information rises with American imperial expansion and global hegemony. Freedom for capital expansion was therefore appreciated as freedom for movement of information. My contention is that this view of the world haunts our theoretical positions on intercultural communication. In fact, what I (1980b) have called temporary communication estrangement or TCE occurs regularly in the interactions of Africans with Europeans. The receiver who fails to interrupt an incorrect view in order to achieve some other purpose causes a communication problem. Thus, most creative solutions to the intercultural communication estrangement are in our hands.

We are creatures of our history, and the brilliance of any liberation paradigm must be found in that history. When we know, truly know, that the Isonghee of Zaire invented the first mathematical calculator 8000 years ago or that DuBois's bibliography lists 2377 articles and books, or that Ifa with its 256 major odus covers more ethical material than either the Bible or Koran, or that Tubman was a socialist and a revolutionary nationalist, or that geometrical principles were used by the Africans of the Olduvai Gorge a million years ago, we can analyze contemporary situations more accurately. I do not mean to make this too simple by citing only a few examples because afrocentricity is a difficult theoretical philosophy to perfect, yet it is the most historically correct philosophy of scholarship and life for the African scholar. Our history is one of struggle and victory; this knowledge is necessary as we attempt to reconstruct and mobilize. There are two important attributes of the afrocentric person: (1) African symbolization and (2) culture creation. We have no way of living but in culture; rituals and ceremonies organize our culture for us. Without rituals and ceremonies we are a rudderless people floating in an abstract sea of materialism. To symbolize is to find representatives for our thoughts, ideas, values, and attitudes that teach us how to create and to enhance our creativity.

In the diaspora our cultural scientists must give more attention to rites of passage for our children.[5] These rites, like all previous rites, must grow out of history. Karenga, more than any of our contemporary scientists, has understood the creative and victorious value of cultural nationalism. To the degree that Karenga has seen the need for us to have rites, ceremonies, and holidays that reflect our values, he has opened the possibility for cultural stamina in the tradition of Garvey and Elija Muhammad. Kariamu has created the *mfundalai* rite for young children. In this rite there is the passing from childhood to adulthood. At thirteen years of age the girl or the boy must learn to recite from THE WAY, the book of Njia, interpret the recitation, and apply it to situations in their lives. This rite is held in the presence of friends and family who listen to the child's recitation of the deeds, events, and personalities in our history. If the child is not successful, she must repeat the rite at the age of fourteen. We say rhythm is the primary fact of life, participate in the rhythm of the universe and sense happiness. A discipline which expands our rites, organizes our sciences, and enhances our cultural development is highly desirable.

Nuclearism, the highest form of the Viking religion, the worship of weapon as deity, has become the main obsession of Europeans. They even speak in apocalyptic terms about the beauty of the weapon, the security it provides, and its awesome power. Since nuclearism has become the god of the Europeans and they are poised for a violent Ragnarok, it is very essential that our scholars, afrologists, not divorce ideology from science. We have been captured too long by the notion that we cannot make value judgments in criticism, history, art, economics, law, communication, anthropology, political science, and psychology. Yet our own experiences have taught us or should have taught us that we must remain vigilant in our attack on dehumanization. Communication theory derived from afrocentricity must be open to human development. Awareness, therefore, is a relevant issue in cultural understanding and cultural nationalism. The word "awareness" is derived from two aspects, namely, *wariness* and *illumination*. We must be wary of psychic numbness and assume a mission of rescue for African culture by not separating knowledge from feeling.

All cultural research must have dynamic symbolism.[6] The afrologist is engaged in an intense, persistent, and ideological struggle to see a vision of the world realized. Surrounded by hostile forces, even within the race, we cannot withdraw from creative theory tested by practice. Whole courses should be taught on afrocentricity, Kawaida, the theories of Cheikh Anta Diop, DuBois, ancestralism, Karenga, King, and Garvey. Our literature and political theories are rich and varied. Afrologists who study communication must view African Studies wholistically where

Africans are joined politically, culturally, and economically. We must read the works of Soyinka, Guillen, Obenga, Ravell, Nascimento, Roumain, Osagie, Diop, Aboaba, Wey, Anyanwu, Vandi, Ikpewho, Nhiwatiwa among others from the continent, South America, and the Caribbean.[7] We shall win the victory, that much is inexorable and so we call upon the spirit of our children and their children to witness what we have done and who we are, to learn strength from us and truth from us and be not afraid as we are not afraid and to come forth for you have been counted. It is done!

Notes

1. This has been demonstrated by the new research coming out of the Buffalo School of African Communication. A whole list of scholars: Boadu, Harrison, Appiah, Abarry, Vandi, Aboaba, Nhiwatiwa, Hunter, Grant, and Holmes, have shown the unity of African culture. More explicitly, I have advanced the position that Africans are united by *ancestralism, extended kinship, rhythmic ritualism,* and a *Supreme Deity.* These concepts cross most boundaries of Africans.
2. There has not been a full power analysis of interpersonal communication. I believe that the status studies and the hierarchical studies engaged in by traditional white communicationists skirt the principal contradiction of power relationships among people.
3. African Americans have frequently adopted the language of the oppressor in order to achieve liberation. Frantz Fanon predicted this behavior for all colonized people. It is necessary to reject symbols of victimage in order to free our minds. Leachim Semaj's work on race and identity in children of the African diaspora is important on this point (see *Studia Africana,* Fall 1981).
4. I see all discussions of science as discussions of human liberation. Thus in speaking of intercultural communication I must address the issue of the liberation of the mind, the freeing of the soul, and the personality, otherwise we participate in the worst kind of impractical research.
5. This is a concern of mine that has its origin in the doctrine of Kawaida which I recognize as a peculiarly brilliant gift to mankind. A full appreciation of the African contact with the marauding Europeans, especially in the middle passage and so-called new world, remains to be done. Rites are necessarily the results of historical experience.
6. To be able to employ one's own myths intelligently in conversation is to educate both those that hear and oneself. I am convinced that only a practice of this sort will elevate our intercultural interactions.
7. Intercultural communication between Yoruba and Ibo, Kikuyu and Luo, Mashona and Matebele, African American and Jamaican, Ashanti, and Ewe must be based upon knowledge and humility. All intercultural relations begin with the perception of self and then extend outward; but to be meaningful it must be knowledgeable.

References

Asante, M. (1980a). *Afrocentricity: The theory of social change.* Buffalo, NY: Amulefi Publishing Company.
—— (1980b). Intercultural communication: an Afrocentric inquiry into encounter. In B. E. Williams & O. L. Taylor (Eds.). *International Conference on Black Communication: A Bellagio Conference, August 6–9, 1979* (pp. 1–18). New York: Rockefeller Foundation.
Bradley, M. (1978). *Iceman inheritance.* Toronto: Dorset.
Cabral, A. (1973). *Return to the source.* New York: Monthly Review Press.
Cruse, H. (1968). *Rebellion or revolution.* New York: William Morrow.
Diop, C. A. (1978). *Cultural unity of Black Africa.* Chicago: Third World Press.
Dubois, W.E.B. (1961). *The souls of Black folk.* New York: Fawcett World Library.
Fanon, F. (1967). *The wretched of the earth.* New York: Grove Press.
Garvey, A. (1969). *The philosophy and opinions of Marcus Garvey.* New York: Antheneum.
Karenga, M. (1978). *Essays in struggle.* San Diego: Kawaida.
Marable, M. (1982). *How capitalism underdeveloped Black America.* Chicago: Southend Press.
Marcuse, H. (1968). *One dimensional man.* Boston: Beacon Press.
McWorter, G. (1980). *Guide to Black scholarly publications.* Urbana, IL: University of Illinois Afro American Research Institute.
Nkrumah, K. (1970). *Class struggle in Africa.* New York: International Publishers.
Nyerere, J. (1974). *Freedom and development.* New York: Oxford University Press.

Richards, D. (1980). European mythology: The ideology of "progress". In M. K. Asante and A. S. Vandi (Eds.). *Contemporary Black thought: Alternative analyses in the social and behavioral sciences* (pp. 59–79). Beverly Hills, CA: Sage.

Rodney, W. (1980). *How Europe underdeveloped Africa.* Washington, DC: Howard University Press.

Ruch, E. A. & Anyanwu, K. C. (1981). *African philosophy.* Rome: Catholic Book Agency.

Schiller, H. (1976). *Communication and cultural domination.* White Plains, NY: Sharpe.

Wey, S. O. & Osagie, E. (1977). *An ideology for social development.* Lagos: Academy Press.

5

Toward an Alternative Metatheory of Human Communication

An Asiacentric Vision*

Yoshitaka Miike

> A metatheory or paradigm is a conception that includes a multiplicity of theories; as such, it allows us to develop better interpretations, fuller under-standings, and more effective articulations of the meaning of human goals and interactions. A metatheory suggests the character and content of theories by prescribing what a theory should explain . . . and what analytical tools are required for revealing and establishing concepts. . . . A metatheory, then, is the product of decision rather than discovery, and it is justified by the theories that are consonant to it.
>
> Molefi Kete Asante (1998, p. 45)

To theorize about Asia is not the same as to theorize from the Asian perspective. One can address and appraise Asian people and phenomena without reference to Asian languages, religions/philosophies, and histories. Such an intellectual orientation is, however, fundamentally unsound if one wishes to see the Asian world through Asian eyes because Asians think and speak in Asian languages, believe in Asian religions/philosophies, and struggle to live in Asian historical experiences. In order to truly understand and appreciate Asian thought and action, therefore, one must successfully explore and examine the cultural agency of Asians in the linguistic, religious/philosophical, and historical contexts of Asia. To theorize from the vantage point of Asians as centered is thus to theorize from Asian everyday languages, religious-philosophical traditions, and historical experiences as vital resources.

European intellectual imperialism, which results in the intellectual dislocation of non-Europeans, has been increasingly problematized and challenged across disciplines in recent years (Asante, 1992, 1998, 2002, 2003). The field of communication cannot escape from this inter-disciplinary intellectual movement. Many researchers, Asian and non-Asian alike, in the field have assumed the universal applicability of the metatheory and methodology of Eurocentric communication scholarship. In the case of knowledge production about Asian communication practices, they have done extensive research through analytical tools grounded in European intellectual traditions. Although some of their findings are insightful and useful, such Eurocentric studies of Asian communication have often dislocated Asians out of their cultural context and have thereby denied the centrality of Asians in the communication process.

One of the urgent tasks of Asian communication scholars at this critical juncture is to conduct Asiacentric studies of Asian communication. They are now prodded to engage in human communication scholarship whose concepts, models, and principles are derived from

Asian cultures as resources for theory building. In an attempt to propound an alternative metatheory that guides such Asiacentric inquiries into Asian communication, the present essay stipulates its research objectives, content dimensions, and methodological considerations. These three components of the metatheory specify why, how, and what kind of communicative knowledge from Asia ought to be pursued. Along with the theoretical assumptions outlined elsewhere (Miike, 2002, 2003ab), they envision the contours of an Asiacentric communication paradigm.[1]

Asiacentric Research Objectives

In this first section, I wish to address *why* (or *for what purpose*) knowledge should be produced in Asiacentric communication scholarship. There are five Asiacentric research objectives that I would like to discuss herein: (1) to critique misleading Eurocentric studies of Asian communication behaviors; (2) to preserve Asian cultural values and modes of communication; (3) to explore spiritual liberation through communication; (4) to depict multiple visions of harmony among complex relationships; and (5) to examine (inter)cultural communication needs and problems seen through Asian eyes. These interrelated research goals are designed to systematically advance the Asiacentric knowledge of human communication.

The first Asiacentric research objective is to critique misleading Eurocentric studies of Asian communication behaviors. Asiacentric critics need to evaluate Eurocentric representations of Asian cultures and communication from at least two angles: (1) questions of consequence; and (2) questions of foundation. Theoretical perspectives and research findings, whether intended or unintended, often have negative impacts on the researched community. They are also knowingly and unknowingly misapplied to misrepresent the theorized people. It is the role of Asiacentric communication critics to elaborate on how certain Eurocentric representations have come to do harm to Asians. If such representations foster stereotyping, for example, they ought to elucidate what kind of representation becomes a stereotype and why.

When Eurocentric social scientists use such constructs as interdependent self-construal, collectivism, and high-context to characterize Asian individuals and cultures, do these characterizations promote the complex understanding and deep appreciation of Asian selves and cultures? When Eurocentric interpretive observers describe Asian modesty simply as an interaction tactic for a relational concern, does such an observation encourage non-Asians to practice Asian communication styles? When Eurocentric critical interrogators scorn Confucianism as a cult of oppression, do they really acknowledge the cultural agency of Asians and empower them? These are questions of scholarly consequence.

Asiacentric communication critics must also address questions of scholarly foundation. If Eurocentric theoretical frameworks and research methods are comprehensive and inclusive, Asiacentric communicologists should be able to answer how elements of Thai or Filipino culture substantially contributed to the conceptualization of the individualism-collectivism dimension, how the observation criteria of the ethnography of speaking took the unique cultural context and condition of Tibet into account, and how critical theorists learned from Hinduism in the process of theory building. These questions should be posed not to completely dismiss the usefulness or applicability of Eurocentric theory and research but to be aware of their limitations and culture-boundness.

Asiacentric communication researchers ought to reflect on what kind of inherent bias may exist in Eurocentric theoretical origins, how inappropriate Eurocentric data collection and analysis procedures may be to the conditions of doing research in Asia, and even how differently Eurocentric research findings can be interpreted from Asiacentric perspectives. They need to carefully reconsider who theorists are, how they develop theories for whom, and how they standardize research processes and evaluations in Eurocentric communication scholarship, and why their applications are possible or impossible in Asia.

The second Asiacentric research objective is to preserve Asian cultural values and modes of communication. There have been debates and controversies over "Asian values" in political discourse since Singapore's Senior Minister Lee Yuan Yew challenged the Eurocentric universalistic position that the Western version of democracy is ideal for the rest of the world (Zakaria, 1994; Kim, 1994; McCarthy, 1998). Asianness, however defined, has been condemned by many Westerners without careful considerations. There is also a growing concern in Asia that positive aspects of Asian cultures are being lost. Given these circumstances, the question of Asian values is worthy of pursuit among Asiacentric communication professionals especially in light of cultural preservation and protection.

Koh (1999) states that there is no agreement among Asian intellectuals as to whether or not there is such a thing as "Asian values." There is probably no absolute Asianness that can represent the cultural values of all Asians. But it is not necessary to answer such an either-or question because, in any case, the searching process for Asian values itself is of immense value. Whether Asian values are partially similar to, or different from, Western values is a secondary question. The most important question is what are the cultural values that have shaped Asian communicative life.

In seeking answers to this question, Asiacentric scholars also ought to examine their positive and negative impacts on human communication. If Asian cultural values and communicative modes are changing, they must try to understand why they are changing and evaluate such changes. If they believe that those changes are not desirable, they have to argue convincingly why certain cultural values and communicative modes should be preserved in the future. Furthermore, it is possible for Asiacentrists to estimate what are the costs and compensations of Asian values and modes of communication rather than to absolutely determine which are good and which are bad.

For example, Chen and Chung (2000) lay out communication costs and compensations in Confucianism-influenced organizations. They isolate six costs: (1) the rule-learning cost; (2) the long-term interaction cost; (3) the out-group exclusion cost; (4) the intermediary cost; (5) the personal contact cost; and (6) the education cost. According to Chen and Chung (2000), these communication costs are respectively paid off by the following six compensations: (1) reduced guesswork and uncertainty; (2) reduced apprehension and increased liking and mutual respect; (3) easier motivation; (4) reduced conflict; (5) loyalty and commitment; and (6) reduced misunderstanding and clarification efforts. This type of assessment merits increasing scholarly attention.

The third Asiacentric research objective is to explore spiritual liberation through communication. Asante (1980) characterizes Afrocentric personalism, Asiacentric spiritualism, and Eurocentric materialism as three "broad" views of reality. According to him, the Afrocentric viewpoint holds that "all modalities and realities are united and move in one grand manner. There can be no separation of material and spiritual" (p. 405). The Asiacentric viewpoint holds that "the material is an illusion; that the real only comes from the spiritual. Therefore Asian philosophical concepts are enamored with spirit-over-matter notions" (p. 405). The Eurocentric viewpoint holds that "the material, the experiential, is real and that the spiritual is an illusion. Everything that is not within sense experiences becomes nonsense" (p. 405). Although they are gross characterizations that border on overgeneralizations, these worldviews are manifested in Afrocentric, Asiacentric, and Eurocentric scholarship.

Whether social scientific, interpretive, or critical, Eurocentric scholarship has largely neglected spiritual dimensions of human communication due to its material emphasis. Asiacentric communication professionals should compensate for this neglect by consciously focusing on spirituality. Kincaid (1987a) points out that Western materialism and Eastern spiritualism may lead to different philosophical conceptions of self, freedom, and the role of communication:

The meaning of liberation in traditional Indian philosophy is intertwined with the related concepts of oneness, nonindividuality, and material nonattachment. Freedom is something attached when one gives up his/her individuality, renounces material things, and spiritually becomes one with something greater than oneself. Freedom, at least in the American sense, is associated with the independence to pursue one's own—often material—interests in fair competition with other individuals. In the West you *do* something to achieve whatever ends make you happy. In the East you *become one* with something greater than yourself for no other conscious purpose. Both speak of freedom.

(p. 335)

Kincaid's insightful observation implies that the Asiacentric ultimate meaning of communication is to become connected with, rather than isolated from, everyone and everything in the universe, which does not contradict the ontological assumption for an Asiacentric paradigm— everyone and everything are interrelated across space and time (Miike, 2002, 2003ab). The role of communication is then to facilitate egolessness and connection toward Asiacentric spiritual enlightenment—the oneness of the universe. Seen from this perspective, "the realization that the self is imbedded in the whole and becomes complete only when one becomes egoless becomes the basis of communication competence" (Yum, 1993, p. 6). Therefore, for example, "One of the final aims of Zen training is to get rid of ego or self and to reach the spiritual freedom of selflessness" (Tsujimura, 1987, p. 115).

Dissanayake (1990) cautions that "as we seek ways and means of cultural integration in a global age, we should not ignore the spiritual realm. As technology begins to dominate lives and secularization becomes the cherished goal, there emerges a sense of spiritual void" (p. 93). Dissanayake (1990) predicts that "as a reaction to the pervasive impersonality generated in the postindustrial society, a quest for fundamental meaning in life is likely to surface" (p. 93). It is against this background that Asiacentric scholars can warrant their theoretical contributions to spiritual aspects of human communication in an age of modernization and urbanization (see also Dissanayake, 1989).

If there are Eurocentric ego-centered theories of communication that encourage unique individuality and material freedom, should not there be Asiacentric ego-decentered theories of communication that encourage connectedness and spiritual liberation? If there are Eurocentric conceptualizations of power and privilege in view of material freedom, should not there be Asiacentric conceptualizations of them in view of spiritual liberation? If there is Eurocentric *material* development communication and the diffusion of *material* innovations, should not there be Asiacentric *spiritual* development communication and the diffusion of *spiritual* innovations?

The fourth Asiacentric research objective is to depict multiple visions of harmony among complex relationships. Harmony is one of the cardinal themes in the Asian worldview (Chen, 1993, 2002b; Dissanayake, 1983, 1989; Yum, 1987, 1993). It is the ultimate Asiacentric goal of communication. Although this prominent value has been extensively discussed in culture and communication studies, most of the past discussions are limited in the sense that they only address social harmony among humans in interpersonal, group, and organizational interactions. The axiological assumption for an Asiacentric paradigm is that harmony is vital to the survival of everyone and everything (Miike, 2002, 2003ab). Harmony in this sense is a more broad and holistic concept and refers to harmony on every level in the whole universe.

Harmony always exists in relationships. The higher level of harmony one attempts to achieve, the more complex relationships she or he needs to consider. It is therefore a challenging task for Asiacentric communication specialists to holistically theorize ideal versions of harmony on many levels among many relationships. Ishii (2001, 2003a) stresses harmonious triworld communication among the worlds of supernatural beings, natural beings, and human beings. It is imperative that Asiacentric communication experts reconsider complex relationships among these three worlds and indicate what should be their ideal relationships. Such an attempt is a formidable yet important mission of Asiacentrists in the present age of "money-oriented values, rich-poor discrepancies, wasteful lifestyles, environmental devastation, shortage of natural resources, and mass destruction" (Ishii, 2003b, pp. 1–2).

Asiacentric depictions of harmony among complex relationships should be based on the Asiacentric communicative assumption that mutual adaptation is of central importance in harmonious communication processes (Miike, 2002, 2003ab). Harmony, particularly on its higher levels, cannot be ideally achieved by control (Miike, 2003b). Controlling other human beings, natural beings, or even spiritual beings for self-interest from the progressive view of science and technology has not proved to be *the* successful strategy toward harmony in the universe. Asiacentric visions of harmony must lead one to see the importance of making herself or himself change toward a higher degree of harmony through mutual adaptation. This fourth Asiacentric research goal of depicting multiple visions of harmony among complex relationships will go hand in hand with the third Asiacentric research goal of exploring spiritual liberation through communication.

The fifth Asiacentric research objective is to examine (inter)cultural communication needs and problems seen through Asian eyes. The soil of Asia, due to its cultural diversity, has been "needed" by Western principal investigators whose primary goal is to test Western theories for establishing their universal generalizability (Sinha, 1996). It is their needs (or sometimes curiosities) that have determined the directions of investigation. As a result, the needs of Asian societies have been ignored. Such cross-cultural research, no matter how theoretically refined and methodologically sophisticated, has been irrelevant to the problems of Asia and, hence, has little utility value for local residents in Asian communities.

Asia is not free from its own unique communication needs, issues, and problems in its sociocultural milieu, which require socioculturally sensitive care, considerations, and solutions also in local contexts. If Asiacentric communication researchers strive to thoroughly identify the local needs and problems and systematically address their causes and solutions, they will pursue new research programs. Such investigations will have local relevance and consequences because they start from the researched community's needs and problems. Asiacentric communication investigators have not yet engaged in these community-based projects, especially in relation to geographical conditions, philosophical underpinnings, historical influences, political systems, economic situations, and educational practices.

Intercultural communication studies in global contexts, as well as intracultural communication studies in local contexts, can benefit greatly from this scholarly priority of Asian needs and problems. Chu (1986) points out that "Although much insight has been gained, one wonders whether the conception of intercultural communication problems might have been biased by the Western perception" (p. 4). Chu (1986) speculates that "[because] Intercultural communication involves two sides, it would be most useful if Asian communication researchers can bring their insight and cultural perception into the research problems" (p. 4). Seen through Asian eyes, then, what would be the needs and problems in intercultural communication both within and outside Asia?

Future investigations of Asian communication needs and problems in both local and global contexts can lead to an enhanced understanding of communication competence and ethics because meeting needs and solving problems are matters of effectiveness and appropriateness and matters of right and wrong. Recent literature in the intercultural field pinpoints Eurocentric biases in theorizing communication competence and ethics (Chen, 1993, 1994; Shuter, 2003; Yum, 1993, 1994). From a Korean perspective, for instance, Yum (1994) makes a sharp observation that "mutual" (in)competence instead of "individual" (in)competence should be duly emphasized. Asiacentric need/problem-centered conceptualizations of human communication competence and ethics will provide rich insights into such an important theoretical issue.

Asiacentric Content Dimensions

The communication metatheory of Asiacentricity insists on viewing Asian cultures as central sources in theorizing, not as peripheral targets in researching (see Misra and Gergen [1993] and Sinha [1996] for discussions on the place or role of culture in knowledge production). The content of theoretical knowledge in and from Asia ought to reflect the diverse and distinct cultural traditions of Asia. In this second section, I will expound on *what kind of* knowledge should be explored and theorized in Asiacentric communication scholarship. Three content dimensions that I find essential in search of the Asiacentric knowledge of human communication are (1) concepts in Asian everyday languages; (2) principles from Asian religious-philosophical traditions; and (3) struggles in Asian historical experiences.

First, *Asiacentric communication theorists should explore and establish Asian concepts in Asian everyday languages in order to reconsider and reconceptualize the nature of human communication.* Concepts are vital to any theory because "The most basic element of a theory is its concepts" (Littlejohn, 2002, p. 20). In order to construct Asiacentric theories of communication, it behooves Asiacentrists to define, delimit, and develop Asian concepts in Asian languages (Dissanayake, 1988; Miike, 2002, 2003ab; Okabe, 1991). Diffused concepts used in communication research about Asia originate in European languages, mostly in English, and hence reflect the linguistic worlds of Europeans or U.S. European Americans. Those Eurocentric imported concepts, even though they are translated into Asian languages, remain quite foreign to Asians who live in completely different linguistic worlds.

Three fundamental tasks must be undertaken to valorize Asian indigenous concepts in Asian languages as legitimate analytical tools for human communication research. The first task is to describe both synchronically and diachronically Asian words and phrases, particularly in everyday use, whose meanings are directly and indirectly related to communication. Chen (2002a), for instance, examines language expressions that were used to represent communication activities in traditional China. Such a linguistic examination has not been made to date in most Asian languages to investigate how Asians have conceptualized the nature of human interaction. It would be commendable for Asiacentric semanticists to further compare and contrast those communication-related words and phrases across time with a view to assessing their semantic continuities and changes and to speculate on the reasons behind them. Asian words and phrases can also be analyzed from the perspective of etymological origins.

As for Asian words and phrases whose meanings are indirectly linked with human communication, Asiacentrists need to make clear what kind of bearing they have on the communication process in which the creation, interpretation, and negotiation of meaning take place. They sometimes dwell on what such words and phrases signify but do not explore their implications specifically for communication inquiries. In that case, those words and phrases, no matter how conceptually rich, cannot serve as useful concepts for communication studies. Miike (2003c), for example, defines *amae* as message-expanding and message-accepting needs and discusses it in *enryo-sasshi* and assertion-acceptance communication among the Japanese.

The second task is to identify and analyze relationships among Asian concepts so as to explore cultural worldviews and values manifested in these concepts. Asiacentric theorists in communication studies have thus far focused exclusively on *one* Asian concept and detailed it in depth as it relates to cultural communication. They are prone to see that concept as *the* most important and fail to locate it in a larger picture of the culture and communication landscape.[2] They need to take another step forward to consider the connections among the concepts so that they can holistically reveal the deep structure of cultural worldviews and values manifested in the surface structure of language expressions. This line of exploration will eventually help Asiacentrists answer the question of Asian values and why certain aspects of culture and communication are difficult or slow to change.

The third task is to compare and contrast Asian concepts in different Asian languages in order to understand their culture-general and culture-specific implications for communication. Asian communication specialists have been so eager to compare Asian concepts with Western concepts but have paid little attention to how Asian concepts in Asian languages differ among Asian cultures. This is a serious mistake if Asiacentric communication experts wish to meaningfully discuss the what and why of Asian values and to attempt to collectively preserve some, though not all, aspects of Asianness. Such Asiacentric comparisons also preclude them from touching on Asian concepts simply in consistency with established Eurocentric pseudo-etic concepts. Chung et al.'s (2003) groundbreaking attempt represents this line of investigation. They compare and contrast the East Asian concept of *qi/ki/ch'i* (energy flow) in China, Japan, Korea, and Taiwan and its historical development in each country for communicative implications.

As Kincaid (1987b) articulates, "Good concepts allow us to see new things or to see old things in a new light. At the same time they divert our attention or blind us from seeing other things. Escaping from this paradoxical situation is no easy task" (p. xiv). Admittedly, Asian concepts may also create blindness to the complexities of Asianness, but at least they open up new intellectual dialogues and encourage non-Asians, especially Westerners, to learn Asian languages in which Asians construct their social realities. This seems to be a right direction to go given that "Eastern concepts are yet unknown to the vast majority of Western communication scholars, particularly those in the United States, whose pseudo-scientific prolificity has been unashamedly ethnocentric" (Gunaratne, 1991, p. 53).

Second, *Asiacentric communication thinkers should draw out fundamental principles of human interaction from Asian religious-philosophical traditions and propose new theoretical models of communication.* As Yum (1987) aptly notes, religious-philosophical traditions that have permeated Asian societies for hundreds of years are "the proper starting points to discover the fundamental patterns which influence the communication behavior of the diverse cultures of Asia, and they allow us to make cross-cultural comparisons that go beyond mere description" (p. 86). Most culture and communication studies have concentrated on *how* people behave and have overlooked *why* they do (Starosta & Chen, 2003). In-depth inquiries into Asian religious-philosophical traditions, which shape the core beliefs and values of Asian cultures, will also demystify why Asians communicate as they do and, more importantly, why they *should.*

It is extremely beneficial for Asiacentric students of communication to take advantage of religious-philosophical perspectives on human interaction (see Sitaram, 1995). By so doing, they can render even a very mundane topic refreshing. For example, the value and role of silence in Asian cultures have been extensively documented in the intercultural communication literature (e.g., Ishii, 1984; Jain & Matukumalli, 1996). Nonetheless, they have not yet been theorized rigorously in terms of Asian religious-philosophical traditions. What does Hinduism say about the forms and functions of silent communication? How and why have its teachings historically influenced contemporary Hindu speech and silence behavior? Bruneau and Ishii (1988) undertake a pioneering task of discussing communicative silences from several Asian religious-philosophical perspectives. But they shed light only on the tip of the iceberg.

Lessons have not been learned from Asian religious-philosophical traditions even about basic communication activities, namely, speaking, listening, writing, and reading. It is often said that listening is more valued than speaking in many Asian cultures. Nevertheless, no attempt has been made so far to theorize about listening, say, from Buddhist perspectives. Such Buddhist theories on listening must have a great deal to do with the vital role of communication in spiritual liberation and with harmony and peace in the universe. Except in Ishii's work (1992), Buddhist preaching has not been tapped for theorizing about rhetorical communication practices from non-Western perspectives. Asian religious-philosophical traditions also offer wisdom about what kind of channel people should use when, where, for whom, and why.

Drawing out communicative principles from Asian religious-philosophical teachings, Asia-centric scholars can reexamine Eurocentric theories of communication on every level (from intrapersonal to public) and propound Asiacentric alternatives. As a case in point, Ishii (2003b) constructs an Asiacentric model of intrapersonal communication grounded on the consciousness-only epistemology of *Mahanaya* Buddhism. He reconsiders the components and structure of Western intrapersonal communication and reconceptualizes Eastern intrapersonal communication by locating eight consciousnesses (i.e., *indriya-vijnana, mano-vijnana, manas-vijnana,* and *alaya-vijnana*). He not only systematically explicates the mechanism of mental activities but also suggests the inherent causes of mental sufferings and afflictions. Here, again, egolessness is the central theme for spiritual liberation.

Human-made Asian religious-philosophical traditions are not free from imperfections. They have positive and negative consequences on Asian contemporary lives. Thus, Asiacentrists must carefully ponder what we should (not) learn and how we should (not) apply their teachings in future lives, which is expected to fulfill the Asiacentric research goal toward the preservation of Asian cultural values and communicative modes. The preservation of traditional cultures is not the same as the uncritical acceptance of them (Nakamura, 1964). It is the discovery of the "newness" of old ideas based on the Asian circular worldview. As Sitaram (1998) remarks, "What began today as a 'brand new idea' has its origin in something that ended yesterday, and today's idea will begin a new one tomorrow" (p. 4).

Third, *Asiacentric communication historians should pay due attention to struggles in Asian historical experiences in their attempts to enrich the theoretical underpinnings of human communication problems, ethics, and competence.* Traditional researchers, either social scientific or interpretive, in Eurocentric communication scholarship have generally neglected Asian histories. Critical scholars are prone to look at Asian histories only as targets of deconstruction through their Eurocentric theoretical lenses. Consequently, there are few Asiacentric inquires in communication research that utilize the rich histories of Asia as resources for theory building. This is unfortunate because Asian historical struggles have much to offer in theorizing about communication problems, ethics, and competence through Asian eyes.

Throughout their long histories, Asians have had intercultural contacts with different people, ideas, and products from different societies that must have initially caused confusion and friction in their communities. It is highly rewarding for Asiacentric communication historians to investigate how each Asian society has historically coped with these intercultural encounters. In particular, as Lee (2001) observes, the coexistence of indigenous and foreign religions, which indicates some openness and tolerance for heterogeneous elements in Asia, can be a very important area of inquiry to theorize about how to solve intercultural problems and conflicts in human communication. In this connection, Lee (2001) goes so far as to say that "The song of the East is a song of tolerance, which can inject a new harmony into the music of the West" (p. 28). Insights can also be obtained into allocentric and integrative ways of adapting mutually toward harmonious communication (Miike, 2002, 2003a).

From an ethnohistorical perspective, for example, Toyama (1994) models what he calls "communication archetypes" of Japanese people. He theorizes about the mechanism and process of how the Japanese have eventually integrated something foreign into their indigenous culture by analyzing the 1450-year intercultural history of Japan. He directs special attention to the long-standing coexistence of the indigenous superbeings (*kami*) and the imported Buddhist deities (*hotoke*). He then applies his theoretical model to his own lifetime experiences of intercultural encounters and other short-term cases of Japanese cross-cultural adjustment.

It goes without saying that Asia has not been always successful in resolving conflicts peacefully or in respecting differences harmoniously. Indeed, as Funabashi (1993) writes, "Whenever unity seemed ascendant in the Asian world, history intervened" (p. 76). Different versions of Asian histories reveal that harmony was, and is, oftentimes a mask of oppression or a means of survival within and between Asian nations. All Asian countries have extensively experienced the aggression and dominance of Western empires. Furthermore, Japan made the fatal mistake to invade other Asian nations under the false ideology of the "Greater East Asia Coprosperity Sphere." Asiacentrists should not waste many historical pains in Asia that can serve as valuable assets in theorizing about the Asiacentric ethics and competence of global/local harmonious communication.

As brutal wars, unethical invasions, and ethnic conflicts around the globe still continue, what would be the messages of Asian histories about what is right and what is wrong in human communication in order not to repeat past mistakes? From the Tibetan experience, The 14th Dalai Lama advances two fundamental propositions toward peace communication: (1) Human problems can be solved through human understanding; and (2) All human beings seek happiness and avoid suffering (Miike, 2001). One of the possible Asiacentric historical contributions in communication studies is to envision peace communication by conceptualizing "imagination competence" (Miike, 2003b) that allows us to see the past of *human* suffering and pain. In so doing, Asian religious-philosophical perspectives can also be profitably incorporated.

Theorizing from many narratives of historical oppression in Asia will disclose our inability to understand human suffering and pain. As victims we have often been passionate in telling what has been done to us, but as oppressors we are not aware of what we have done to others. Many of us, in one way or another, are both victims and oppressors and are thus capable of sharing the suffering and pain of all human beings. Yet as oppressors we keep creating the same human suffering and pain of others by our ignorance and disinterest.

It is lamentable, for instance, that many Japanese do not want others to forget about the atomic bombing in Hiroshima and Nagasaki whereas they show little interest in what their ancestors did to other Asian nations. Both are, after all, stories of human suffering and pain. Tezuka (2002) analyzes the Japan–U.S. perception gap on the atomic bombing from the perspective of silence and silencing and concludes that "both countries have ended up being equally unbalanced and less comprehensive in their respective perceptions" (p. 79). More cooperative efforts can be made among Asiacentric communication historians to know more about human suffering and healing in intercultural interactions within Asia and with the West.

Asiacentric Methodological Considerations

It is impossible to theorize truly from Asiacentric perspectives without challenging Eurocentric methodological assumptions. Some Asian scholars harangue the cultural biases of Eurocentric theoretical assumptions and yet completely fail to question Eurocentric methodological assumptions. Nevertheless, it is not so meaningful to seek to construct Asiacentric theories of communication if they need to be ultimately tested against the Eurocentric research worldview in order to become legitimate theories. For Eurocentric methodologists can dismiss Asiacentric theories, no matter how insightful and useful, simply because they do not fit their way of theoretical validation. Thus, the methods used for building Asiacentric theories must also be Asiacentric.

It is a daunting task to challenge Eurocentric methodological assumptions, formulate Asiacentric methodological assumptions, and propose specific Asiacentric methods. In this last section, therefore, I will discuss three methodological issues as to *how* knowledge should be pursued in Asiacentric communication scholarship: (1) the issue of data and evidence; (2) the issue of validity and utility; and (3) the issue of visibility and invisibility. These issues are Asiacentric *initial* considerations and respectively concern themselves with Eurocentric methodological objectivism, empiricism, and materialism.

The first Asiacentric methodological issue is the issue of data and evidence. What is considered as "hard" data or "solid" evidence is socially constructed in the academic world. In Eurocentric scholarship, certain data and evidence have more credibility than others. There seems to be the hierarchical consciousness of data and evidence. Findings from questionnaire surveys, narratives collected through ethnographic interviews, and recorded notes in participant observations are conceived of as highly appropriate particularly by U.S. Eurocentric researchers. Many U.S. Eurocentric scholars assume that obtaining and analyzing these "first-hand" data and evidence guarantees the originality and advancement of scholarship, whether or not topics are repetitive, theories are mundane, and methods are ethical. As "second-hand" data and evidence, articles and advertisements from newspapers and magazines and, most recently, movies are popular texts especially in U.S. Eurocentric research.

With some exceptions (e.g., Sun & Starosta, 2002), little attention and credibility have been given to allegories, autobiographies, calligraphy, corporate histories, diaries, etymological origins, fables, idiomatic expressions, imageries, legends, metaphors, myths, novels, poems, preaches, proverbs, paradoxes, and songs as data and evidence despite the fact that some of them have survived for centuries. The Eurocentric hierarchical view of data and evidence appears to be based on the degree of *presumed* objectivity and publicity. But the question here is who determines what is more objective and public and what is more subjective and private. What is highly objective or private in one group can be what is highly subjective or public in another. Asiacentrists must reconsider this hierarchical view of data and evidence because Asia has rich "subjective" data and evidence that are *public* to Asians.

Another prevailing assumption regarding the issue of data and evidence in Eurocentric communication scholarship is that data and evidence should be "objectively" collected and analyzed. Even some Eurocentric interpretive and critical scholars do not accept subjectivity in the methodological worldview, although they acknowledge subjectivity (e.g., social constructivism) in the theoretical worldview. This pervasive tendency often deprives theory building of flexibility. Experienced researchers do and should know that sudden, unintentional, unplanned, and unrecorded "conversations" are sometimes much more insightful, valuable, and revealing than rigidly intentional, planned, and recorded "data and evidence." This is especially the case in Asia where people are not used to formal research and are likely to mark the researcher as an outsider and the researched as an insider.

The ability to holistically and diachronically utilize a variety of resources may be one of the sought-after qualities of a good Asiacentric communication researcher. Tsujimura's (1987) work demonstrates that, no matter how subjectively selective it is, a collection of data and evidence from multiple sources across time lines can be extremely rigorous for theory building and illustration. In order to elucidate *ishin-denshin* (meeting of the minds) in Japanese communication, he makes elegant use of *Zen mondo* (questions and answers between a master and a disciple in Zen monk training), Ryunosuke Akutagawa's 1954 short story, Yasunari Kawabata's 1952 novel, Dogen's 1004 Buddhist biography, and Eugen Herrigel's 1924–1930 personal experience of Zen in *kyudo* (Japanese archery) in Japan.

For his elaboration on social causes of taciturnity, indirectness, respect for reverberation, and *kuuki* (atmospheric constraints), Tsujimura (1987) skillfully touches on Japanese proverbs, a Japanese children's game called *nirameko* (staring contest), *ki* (energy flow)-related idiomatic expressions, and Jisaburoo Ozawa's statement at the end of World War II. Especially impressive is his content analysis of *Hyakunin Isshu* (*100 Poems by 100 Poets*), which is the 1235 anthology of *waka* (Japanese five-line poems) collected for over 600 years. His concise analysis illuminates such predominant communicative themes as life, love, human relationship, and nature among the noble Japanese from the 7th century to the 13th century (see also Tsujimura, 1988).

The second Asiacentric methodological issue is the issue of validity and utility. The above-discussed Eurocentric methodological objectivism is heavily grounded in Eurocentric methodological empiricism, which assumes that theories need to be *externally* validated, whether quantitatively or qualitatively, *outside* theorists and those who can resonate with their theories.

Eurocentric empirical researchers presume that every theory should be statistically testable or directly observable. It comes as no surprise, then, that Asiacentric innovative theorists are often reminded by Eurocentric empirical researchers that their theories are no more than "just ideas" and asked to demonstrate how to measure or observe them.

Nevertheless, what has been neglected in this Eurocentric empirical worldview is that external validity is not necessarily parallel to internal utility. Things objectively testable and observable are not always subjectively useful and heuristic. In other words, even if the external validity of a theory is high, its internal utility can be low. Furthermore, *experiential* knowledge can be much more advanced than *experimental* knowledge. In Eurocentric methodological empiricism, however, ideas cannot become theories unless they are measurable or observable, no matter how internally useful they are to consumers of theories in everyday life. To put it in another way, theories are deemed as "just ideas" unless they are *experimentally* verifiable, no matter how *experientially* verifiable they are (Sinha & Sinha, 1997).

It is high time for Asiacentric communication specialists to call this taken-for-granted Eurocentric methodological empiricism into question. Although external validity is of great value in other disciplines for legitimate reasons, Asiacentrists should rethink to what extent it is necessary and appropriate for the study of human communication—the ever-changing and dynamic process of human interaction in context. A number of U.S. Eurocentric communication scientists, Asian and non-Asian alike, are so obsessed with their validation research that they spend scores of years to validate what has been experientially known for decades. However, they forget to question to what extent and how validated theories can be useful to, and resonate with, people in real life and, more importantly, why external validity is essential to such usefulness and resonance. What obligates communication theorists to commit themselves to a true-or-false dichotomy rather than to insight? In any case, just as "the cultural is the incompletely understood" (Starosta, 1984, p. 203), so is the communicative.

Furthermore, Asiacentrists must ask themselves whether or not Eurocentric methodological empiricism fits the Asian worldview and is truly beneficial to Asiacentric communication scholarship. The epistemological assumption for an Asiacentric paradigm is that everyone and everything become meaningful in relation to others (Miike, 2002, 2003ab). This assumption is based on the Asian emphasis on the relativity of truth. According to Hindu culture, for example, "when no beliefs can be said absolutely true, no beliefs can be declared absolutely false" (Jain & Kussman, 2000, p. 89). Such a relativistic view of truth leads to the importance of "resonance" in Asian cultures and communication (St. Clair, 1998/1999). Seen from this angle, ideas without external validity can become theories as long as internal utility is expressed.

Additionally, Eurocentric methodological empiricism prevents Asiacentric theorists from fully utilizing Asian religious-philosophical traditions. Buddhism, Confucianism, Hinduism, Shintoism, and Taoism have low external validity but high internal utility. They may be mere ideas in the Eurocentric sense but insightful theories in the Asiacentric sense. In fact, they have historically shaped Asian cultural selves and values for ages. Nevertheless, the Eurocentric validity-based methodological worldview has little tolerance toward Asiacentric theorizing and researching emanating from these traditions and allows researchers to ignore them without taking them seriously. Asiacentrists must search for methodological assumptions that encourage them to be Asiacentric.

The third Asiacentric methodological issue is the issue of visibility and invisibility. The aforementioned Eurocentric methodological empiricism is further nurtured by Eurocentric methodological materialism. There is a tendency, especially among U.S. Eurocentric communication scholars, to exclude invisible and unobservable matters from targets of theorizing and researching. The idea that theorizing about what is visible ought be conducted through what can be seen characterizes much of U.S. Eurocentric communication research. Heavy reliance on material texts in rhetorical analyses, strong faith in ethnographic notes, and literal interpretations of narrative stories represent such a materialistic methodological worldview. Behind this method-ological practice, two underlying assumptions exist: (1) what is visible is what is important in human communication; and (2) much can be told from what is visible.

It is questionable, however, whether or not visible phenomena are always important in human communication. What is invisible is oftentimes far more important in communication than what is visible. Indeed, what can be seen are very limited parts of communication activities. While it is true that much can be told from visible phenomena, it is equally true that much cannot be told from them. Eurocentric methodological experts can be sometimes seriously mistaken if they start from the visible to infer about the invisible. There is the possibility that they will see completely different realities if they start from the invisible. It must not be forgotten that "Some research truths will always remain intuitable more than observable, and felt more than directly observable" (Starosta & Chen, 2003, p. 20).

Asiacentric communicologists need to radically challenge this Eurocentric deep-seated trust in visibility. Miike (2002) speculates that "Whereas Westerners have a general propensity to be more outwardly and behaviorally active in communicative interactions, Easterners are, by and large, predisposed to be more inwardly and perceptually active in communicative interactions" (pp. 10–11). If such is the case, Eurocentric methodological materialism cannot gauge the activeness of Asians in the communication process and ends up describing how passive they are. It is also not certain that dynamic mutual adaptation and its related mental activities of Asians can be conceptualized through this materialistically-oriented methodological worldview. Sensitivity, empathy, contemplation, enlightenment, and spiritual liberation particularly in the Asian sense are largely invisible because they take place *within* the communicator. Direct experi-ence, which many Asian cultural teachings value, might be a *sine qua non* for Asiacentric researchers in theorizing about invisible aspects of human communication.

One of the consequences of methodological objectivism, empiricism, and materialism in Eurocentric communication scholarship is the highly analytical mode of inquiry, which in turn has made Eurocentric researchers confine themselves to complex models of communication. These analytical models, featuring detailed categories and components, rely heavily on logic and reasoning, not on feeling and imagination. Howell (1979), who believes that alternative metaphoric models of communication are more useful to students and practitioners, contends:

> An inevitable result of our being analytical in the study of communication is the increasing complexity of paradigms and models. Extended analysis identifies more variables, and since the parts are presumed to add up to the whole, none can be left out of a diagrammatic representation. Thus modern models of the communication process are not quickly and easily memorized and used.
>
> A holistic approach to model design authorizes the designer to cluster groups of unspecified variables in ways that dramatize the point [she or] he wishes to make. This makes it possible to create simple models that say a great deal, because the model is metaphor rather than realistic or literal symbolization. Instead of supplying all the details, the metaphorical model guides the reader into a sequence of [her or] his own thoughts, opinions, and experiences. Nonwestern cultures are, incidentally, much more comfortable with the metaphoric model than with detailed, analytical representations.
>
> (p. 28)

There are not many attempts to propose metaphoric models of communication from Eastern perspectives. Yoshikawa's (1980, 1984, 1987) double-swing model of intercultural communica-tion is one of the few exceptions. Asiacentric communication theorists have thus far adhered to analytical, complex theoretical models partly because of their strategy to make their Eastern modes of communication understandable to the Western audience (e.g., Ishii, 1984; Hara, 2001,

2002; Miike, 2003c). But they can explore the possibility of constructing metaphoric, simple theoretical models that may appeal more to the ethos of Asian peoples. Asian religious-philosophical traditions are full of suggestive metaphorical symbols that can serve as models of communication. Asian linguistic forms such as Chinese characters can also be profitably utilized owing to their ideographic nature. Allowing many theoretical ideas to be presented without rigid methodological regimens may be one Asiacentric step toward more democratic scholarship.

Concluding Comments

"Vision is the art of seeing things invisible," Jonathan Swift elegantly opines.[3] Engaging in this art is not easy precisely because things are invisible. The present essay has undertaken such a difficult task of seeing what is possible in Asiacentric communication scholarship. Much thinking remains to be done for a more comprehensive and complete Asiacentric vision. The intellectual mission of the Asiacentric project is to generate theory and research that can reson-ate thoroughly with Asian experiences and to enrich human ways of being, knowing, and valuing in the universe. This unaccomplished mission parallels the promotion of universal humanity and the preservation of cultural diversity in an age of glocalization. For Asiacentric approaches can delve more deeply into, and reflect more earnestly on, both universal humanity in cultural communication and cultural diversity in human communication.

Asiacentricity is neither a hegemonic Asiacentrism nor an Asian version of ethnocentric Eurocentrism. Asiacentricity does not present the Asian worldview as the only universal frame of reference and impose it on non-Asians. The Asiacentric metatheory, which demands the place-ment of Asian ideals and interests at the center of inquiry, simply argues that the best conceptual system of analysis for comprehending or even criticizing the agency of Asians in cultural context is Asiacentric. In so doing, this alternative metatheory does not deny the value of other non-Asiacentric perspectives on Asians but rejects the hegemonic idea that non-Asiacentric theoretical standpoints are superior to Asiacentric ones and therefore can grossly neglect the latter in the discussion and discourse surrounding Asian people and phenomena.

At the dawn of the new century, Lee (2001) passionately suggests that Asians create a different kind of music. He observes that Asians "have gained confidence by winning world acclaim for our performance of Western music on Western instruments" (p. 26). Yet Lee (2001) finds it difficult to predict how Asians can "make a major contribution to the 21st century world, with its new cultural paradigm, simply by virtue of our ability to perform Western music better than Westerners" (p. 26). His suggestion is indeed timely. Asians ought to compose Asian music on Asian instruments in the new millennium. This alternative idea of cultural agency is the focal contention of the Asiacentric metatheory. With their firm belief in the East–West cultural equality (Ishii, 1995), Asian communication scholars as well must produce their own melody in the exciting opening of the new concert. With the Gandhian spirit of "I can wait 40 or 400 years" (Starosta & Chaudhary, 1993), let us dream of Asian harmonious music in full flourish.

* I owe a special debt of gratitude to Professor Guo-Ming Chen at the University of Rhode Island and Professor William J. Starosta at Howard University who have kindly served as my dialogical mentors. I am also most grateful to Professor Wimal Dissanayake at the University of Hong Kong for having been my source of insight and inspiration. Finally, my thanks go to Professor Karen A. Foss, Professor Bradford 'J' Hall, Professor Janet M. Cramer, and Professor Everett M. Rogers at the University of New Mexico and Dr. William Kelly at the University of California, Los Angeles for crystallizing my Asiacentric vision.

Notes

1. In accordance with my previous works (Miike, 2002, 2003ab), *Asia* in the present essay is geographically confined to China, India, Japan, and Korea (see Miike [2003b] for my operational definition of *Asia*). Nevertheless, the proposed Asiacentric research objectives, content dimensions, and methodological considerations might be applicable to human communication scholarship in other Asian nations and regions. As I acknowledge elsewhere (Miike, 2003b), my vision of Asiacentricity owes its intellectual debt to Dr. Molefi Kete Asante's (1992, 1998, 2003) legacy of Afrocentricity.
2. This point was made by Dr. Guo-Ming Chen in his responses to the papers presented on the panel, "East Asian Perspectives on Culture and Communication," at the 6th Asian Studies Conference Japan (sponsored by the Institute of Asian Cultural Studies at International Christian University) on the Ichigaya Campus of Sophia University in Tokyo, Japan on June 22–23, 2002.
3. This quote is printed in a picture frame given to me by my German colleague, Dr. Britta H. Limary as a sign of her encouragement of my Asiacentric critiques and contributions. I wish to take this opportunity to express my deep appreciation to her for her friendship and support at the best and worst times of our doctoral training. Dr. Limary is one of the most hardworking persons that I have met, and I know that she has never taken advantage of others.

References

Asante, M. K. (1980). Intercultural communication: An inquiry into research directions. In D. Nimmo (Ed.), *Communication yearbook 4* (pp. 401–410). News Brunswick, NJ: Transaction.

Asante, M. K. (1992). Afrocentric metatheory and disciplinary implications. *The Afrocentric Scholar, 1*(1), 98–117.

Asante, M. K. (1998). *The Afrocentric idea* (Rev. ed.). Philadelphia, PA: Temple University Press.

Asante, M. K. (2002). Intellectual dislocation: Applying analytic Afrocentricity to narratives of identity. In J. L. Daniel (Ed.), *Essays on African American communication scholarship* [Special issue]. *Howard Journal of Communications, 13*(1), 97–110.

Asante, M. K. (2003). *Afrocentricity: The theory of social change* (Rev. ed.). Chicago, IL: African American Images.

Bruneau, T., & Ishii, S. (1988). Communicative silences: East and West. *World Communication, 17*(1), 1–33.

Chen, G.-M. (1993, November). *Communication competence: A Chinese perspective.* Paper presented at the annual meeting of the Speech Communication Association, Miami Beach, FL.

Chen, G.-M. (1994, November). *A conceptualization and measurement of communication competence: A Chinese perspective.* Paper presented at the annual meeting of the Speech Communication Association, New Orleans, LA.

Chen, G.-M. (2002a). Problems and prospects of Chinese communication study. In W. Jia, X. Lu, & D. R. Heisey (Eds.), *Chinese communication theory and research: Reflections, new frontiers, and new directions* (pp. 255–268). Westport, CT: Albex.

Chen, G.-M. (2002b). The impact of harmony on Chinese conflict resolution. In G.-M. Chen, & R. Ma (Eds.), *Chinese conflict management and resolution* (pp. 3–17). Westport, CT: Albex.

Chen, G.-M., & Chung, J. (2000). The "Five Asian Dragons": Management behaviors and organizational communication. In L. A. Samovar & R. E. Porter (Eds.), *Intercultural communication: A reader* (9th ed., pp. 301–312). Belmont, CA: Wadsworth.

Chu, G. C. (1986). In search of an Asian perspective of communication theory. *Media Asia, 13*(1), 3–5.

Chung, J., Hara, K., Yang, C., & Ryu, J.-M. (2003). Contemporary *ch'i/ki* research in East Asian countries: Implications for communication theory. *Intercultural Communication Studies, 15*, 41–66.

Dissanayake, W. (1983). Peace and communication: A Buddhist point of view. *Media Development, 30*(2), 7–9.

Dissanayake, W. (1988). The need for Asian approaches to communication. In W. Dissanayake (Ed.), *Communication theory: The Asian perspective* (pp. 1–19). Singapore: Asian Mass Communication Research and Information Center.

Dissanayake, W. (1989). Modernization and the loss of self in the East. *The World and I, 4*(8), 527–541.

Dissanayake, W. (1990). Cultural integration in a global age. *The World and I, 5*(1), 83–93.

Funabashi, Y. (1993, November/December). The Asianization of Asia. *Foreign Affairs, 72*(5), 75–85.

Gunaratne, S. A. (1991). Asian approaches to communication theory. *Media Development, 38*(1), 53–55.

Hara, K. (2001). The word *is* the thing: The *kotodama* belief in Japanese communication (Part 1). *ETC: A Review of General Semantics, 58*(3), 279–291.

Hara, K. (2002). The word *is* the thing: The *kotodama* belief in Japanese communication (Part 2). *ETC: A Review of General Semantics, 58*(4), 408–419.

Howell, W. S. (1979). Theoretical directions for intercultural communication. In M. K. Asante, E. Newmark, & C. A. Blake (Eds.), *Handbook of intercultural communication* (pp. 23–41). Beverly Hills, CA: Sage.

Ishii, S. (1984). *Enryo-sasshi* communication: A key to understanding Japanese interpersonal relations. *Cross Currents, 11*(1), 49–58.

Ishii, S. (1992). Buddhist preaching: The persistent main undercurrent of Japanese traditional rhetorical communication. In D. W. Klopf (Ed.), *Communication practices in the Pacific Basin* [Special section]. *Communication Quarterly, 40*(4), 391–397.

Ishii, S. (1995). Cross-cultural/intercultural communication for a borderless world of diversity in harmony. *Journal of the Communication Association of Korea, 3,* 17–23.

Ishii, S. (2001). An emerging rationale for triworld communication studies from Buddhist perspectives. *Human Communication, 4*(1), 1–10.

Ishii, S. (2003a). Developing a Buddhist paradigm to induce innovations in Westerncentric communication studies (in Chinese, J. Yin, Trans.). In G.-M. Chen (Ed.), *Theories and principles of Chinese communication* (pp. 295–308). Taipei, Taiwan: Wunan.

Ishii, S. (2003b, November). *Proposing a Buddhist consciousness-only epistemological model for intrapersonal communication research.* Paper presented at the annual meeting of the National Communication Association, Miami Beach, FL.

Jain, N. C., & Kussman, E. D. (2000). Dominant cultural patterns of Hindus in India. In L. A. Samovar & R. E. Porter (Eds.), *Intercultural communication: A reader* (9th ed., pp. 81–90). Belmont, CA: Wadsworth.

Jain, N. C., & Matukumalli, A. (1996). The role of silence in India: Implications for intercultural communication research. *Education in Asia, 16*(2–4), 152–158.

Kim, D. J. (1994, November/December). Is culture destiny? The myth of Asia's anti-democratic values: A response to Lee Kuan Yew. *Foreign Affairs, 73*(6), 189–194.

Kincaid, D. L. (1987a). Communication East and West: Points of departure. In D. L. Kincaid (Ed.), *Communication theory: Eastern and Western perspectives* (pp. 331–340). San Diego, CA: Academic Press.

Kincaid, D. L. (1987b). Preface. In D. L. Kincaid (Ed.), *Communication theory: Eastern and Western perspectives* (pp. viii–xiv). San Diego, CA: Academic Press.

Koh, T. (1999). Differences in Asian and European values. *Asian Mass Communication Bulletin, 29*(5), 10–11.

Lee, O.-Y. (2001). The dawn of the Asian century. *Japan Echo, 28*(1), 23–28.

Littlejohn, S. W. (2002). *Theories of human communication* (7th ed.). Belmont, CA: Wadsworth.

McCarthy, T. (1998, March). In defense of "Asian values": An interview with Lee Kuan Yew. *Time, 151*(10), p. 40.

Miike, Y. (2001, November). *Implications of the 14th Dalai Lama's philosophy for intercultural communication in the 21st century.* Paper presented at the annual meeting of the National Communication Association, Atlanta, GA.

Miike, Y. (2002). Theorizing culture and communication in the Asian context: An assumptive foundation. In G.-M. Chen (Ed.), *Culture and communication: An East Asian perspective* [Special issue]. *Intercultural Communication Studies, 11*(1), 1–21.

Miike, Y. (2003a). An Asiacentric paradigm of communication theory (in Chinese, J. Yin, Trans.). In G.-M. Chen (Ed.), *Theories and principles of Chinese communication* (pp. 55–74). Taipei, Taiwan: Wunan.

Miike, Y. (2003b). Beyond Eurocentrism in the intercultural field: Searching for an Asiacentric paradigm. In W. J. Starosta & G.-M. Chen (Eds.), *Ferment in the intercultural field: Axiology/value/praxis* (pp. 243–276). Thousand Oaks, CA: Sage.

Miike, Y. (2003c). Japanese *enryo-sasshi* communication and the psychology of *amae:* Reconsideration and reconceptualization. *Keio Communication Review, 25,* 93–115.

Misra, G., & Gergen, K. (1993). On the place of culture in psychological science. *International Journal of Psychology, 28*(2), 225–243.

Nakamura, H. (1964). *Ways of thinking of Eastern peoples: India, China, Tibet, Japan* (P. P. Wiener, Trans.). Honolulu, HI: University of Hawai'i Press.

Okabe, R. (1991). Intercultural assumptions of communication and rhetorical theories: East and West. In P. G. Fendos, Jr. (Ed.), *Cross-cultural communication: East and West* (Vol. 3, pp. 71–93). Tainan, Taiwan: Department of Foreign Languages and Literature, National Cheng-Kung University.

Shuter, R. (2003). Ethics, culture, and communication: An intercultural perspective. In L. A. Samovar & R. E. Porter (Eds.), *Intercultural communication: A reader* (10th ed., pp. 449–455). Belmont, CA: Wadsworth.

Sinha, D. (1996). Culture as the target and culture as the source: A review of cross-cultural psychology in Asia. *Psychology and Developing Societies, 8*(1), 83–105.

Sinha, D., & Sinha, M. (1997). Orientations to psychology: Asian and Western. In H. S. R. Kao & D. Sinha (Eds.), *Asian perspectives on psychology* (pp. 25–39). New Delhi, India: Sage.

Sitaram, K. S. (1995). *Culture and communication: A world view.* New York: McGraw-Hill.

Sitaram, K. S. (1998). Introduction: Multiculturalism for a higher humanity. In K. S. Sitaram & M. H. Prosser (Eds.), *Civic discourse: Multiculturalism, cultural diversity, and global communication* (pp. 1–14). Stamford, CT: Ablex.

Starosta, W. J. (1984). On intercultural rhetoric. In W. B. Gudykunst & Y. Y. Kim (Eds.), *Methods for intercultural communication research* (pp. 229–238). Beverly Hills, CA: Sage.

Starosta, W. J., & Chen, G.-M. (2003). "Ferment," an ethic of caring, and the corrective power of dialogue. In W. J. Starosta & G.-M. Chen (Eds.), *Ferment in the intercultural field: Axiology/value/praxis* (pp. 3–23). Thousand Oaks, CA: Sage.

Starosta, W. J., & Chaudhary, A. G. (1993). "I can wait 40 or 400 years": Gandhian *Satyagraha* East and West. *International Philosophical Quarterly, 33*(2), 163–172.

St. Clair, R. N. (1998/1999). Cultural wisdom, communication theory, and the metaphor of resonance. *Intercultural Communication Studies, 8*(1), 79–101.

Sun, W., & Starosta, W. J. (2002). A thematic analysis of the 20th century classical Chinese fairy-tales collection: An implication for conflict management. In G.-M. Chen & R. Ma (Eds.), *Chinese conflict management and resolution* (pp. 73–84). Westport, CT: Albex.

Tezuka, C. (2002). An analysis of the Japan-U.S. perception gap regarding the atomic bombing from the perspective of silence and silencing (in Japanese). *Intercultural Communication Studies, 14*, 79–97.

Toyama, J. (1994). Japanese communication archetypes: An ethnohistorical study (in Japanese). *Intercultural Communication Studies, 7*, 25–46.

Tsujimura, A. (1987). Some characteristics of the Japanese way of communication. In D. L. Kincaid (Ed.), *Communication theory: Eastern and Western perspectives* (pp. 115–126). San Diego, CA: Academic Press.

Tsujimura, A. (1988). Contrast in "way of thinking" between East and West. In Christian Academy (Ed.), *The world community in post-industrial society: Vol. 4. Encounter between the East and the West and the creation of a global culture* (pp. 159–167). Seoul, Korea: Wooseok.

Yoshikawa, M. J. (1980). *The dialogical approach to Japanese-American intercultural encounter.* Unpublished doctoral dissertation, University of Hawai'i, Honolulu, HI.

Yoshikawa, M. J. (1984). Culture, cognition, and communication: Implications of the "paradoxical relationship" for intercultural communication. *Communication and Cognition, 17*(4), 377–385.

Yoshikawa, M. J. (1987). The double-swing model of intercultural communication between the East and the West. In D. L. Kincaid (Ed.), *Communication theory: Eastern and Western perspectives* (pp. 319–329). San Diego, CA: Academic Press.

Yum, J. O. (1987). Korean philosophy and communication. In D. L. Kincaid (Ed.), *Communication theory: Eastern and Western perspectives* (pp. 71–86). San Diego, CA: Academic Press.

Yum, J. O. (1993, November). *Communication competence: A Korean perspective.* Paper presented at the annual meeting of the Speech Communication Association, Miami Beach, FL.

Yum, J. O. (1994, November). *A conceptualization and measurement of communication competence: A Korean perspective.* Paper presented at the annual meeting of the Speech Communication Association, New Orleans, LA.

Zakaria, F. (1994, March/April). Culture is destiny: A conversation with Lee Kuan Yew. *Foreign Affairs, 73*(2), pp. 109–126.

6

Thinking Dialectically about Culture and Communication

Judith N. Martin & Thomas K. Nakayama

A survey of contemporary research reveals distinct and competing approaches to the study of culture and communication, including cross-cultural, intercultural, and intracultural communication studies (Asante & Gudykunst, 1989; Y. Y. Kim, 1984).[1] Culture and communication studies also reflect important metatheoretical differences in epistemology, ontology, assumptions about human nature, methodology, and research goals as well as differing conceptualizations of culture and communication, and the relationship between culture and communication. In addition, questions about the role of power and research application often lead to value-laden debates about right and wrong ways to conduct research. Whereas these debates signal a maturation of the field, they can be needlessly divisive when scholars use one set of paradigmatic criteria to evaluate research based on different paradigmatic assumptions (Deetz, 1996). The purpose of this essay is to focus attention on the metatheoretical issues and conceptualizations that underlie these various debates and to explore strategies for constructive interparadigmatic discussions.

In order to highlight the various metatheoretical assumptions of culture and communication research, we first identify four research paradigms based on Burrell and Morgan's (1988) framework categorizing sociological research. Although this framework has been borrowed often by communication researchers and provides a useful "map" to differentiate and legitimate theoretical research, a word of caution is in order. As Deetz (1996) notes, Burrell and Morgan's emphasis on the incommensurability of these paradigms has resulted in a tendency to reify research approaches and has led to "poorly formed conflicts and discussions" (p. 119). Therefore, we present this framework, not as a reified categorization system, but as a way to focus attention on current issues and to legitimate the various approaches.

We will first briefly describe the framework and the resulting four paradigms. For each paradigm, we identify concomitant metatheoretical assumptions and research goals, describe how research in this paradigm conceptualizes culture and the relationship between culture and communication and then give examples of current research conducted from this paradigm. It is important to note that the research examples given are illustrative and do not necessarily reflect the scope and depth of each area.

Four Paradigms

Burrell and Morgan (1988) propose two dimensions for differentiating metatheoretical assumptions of sociological research: assumptions about the nature of social science and assumptions about the nature of society. The assumptions about the nature of social science vary along a subjective–objective dimension, and these categories have been described ad nauseam in communication scholarship (Deetz, 1994). As described by Burrell and Morgan, objectivism assumes a separation of subject (researcher) and object (knowledge), a belief in an external world and human behavior that can be known, described, and predicted, and use of research methodology that maintains this subject-object separation. On the other hand, subjectivist scholarship sees the subject-object relationship not as bifurcated but in productive tension; reality is not external, but internal and "subjective," and human behavior is creative, voluntary, and discoverable by ideographic methods. Gudykunst and Nishida (1989) used this subjective-objective distinction to categorize then-current culture and communication research.

Burrell and Morgan's (1988) second and less discussed dimension describes assumptions about the nature of society—in terms of a debate over order and conflict. Research assuming societal order emphasizes stability and regulation, functional coordination and consensus. In contrast, research based on a conflict or "coercion" view of society attempts to "find explanations for radical change, deep-seated structural conflict, modes of domination and structural contradiction" (p. 17).

According to Burrell and Morgan, the intersection of these two dimensions yields for distinctive paradigms (see Figure 1). They use the term *paradigm* to mean strongly held worldviews and beliefs that undergird scholarship, using the broadest of the various Kuhnian meanings (Kuhn, 1970). They also identify several caveats: These paradigms are contiguous but separate, have some shared characteristics but different underlying assumptions, and are therefore mutually exclusive (pp. 23–25).

It is important to note that research usually adheres more or less to the assumptions of a specific paradigm. For example, as Gudykunst and Nishida (1989) point out, probably no contemporary intercultural communication research is strictly functionalist. Rather, it is more useful to think the boundaries among the four paradigms as irregular and slightly permeable, rather than rigid.

Functionalist paradigm

As discussed by many communication scholars, functionalist research has its philosophical foundations in the work of social theorists such as Auguste Comte, Herbert Spencer, and Emile Durkheim. It assumes that the social world is composed of knowable empirical facts that exist separate from the researcher and reflects the attempt to apply models and methods of the natural sciences to the study of human behavior (Burrell & Morgan, 1988; Deetz, 1994, Gudykunst & Nishida, 1989; Mumby, 1997). Research investigating culture and communication in this tradition become dominant in the 1980s and is identified by various (and related) labels: functionalist (Ting-Toomey, 1984), analytic-reductionistic-quantitative (Y. Y. Kim, 1984), positivist (Y. Y. Kim, 1988), objective (Gudykunst & Nishida, 1989), and traditional (B. J. Hall, 1992).

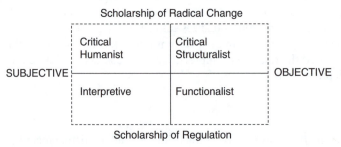

Fig. 1. Four Paradigms of Culture and Communication Research

(Adapted from Burrell & Morgan, 1988, p. 22)

As noted in Figure 2, research in this tradition builds on social science research, most notably in psychology and sociology (see Harman & Briggs, 1991). The ultimate goal is sometimes to describe, but often to predict human behavior. From this perspective, culture is often viewed as a variable, defined a priori by group membership many times on a national level (Moon, 1996), and includes an emphasis on the stable and orderly characteristics of culture. The relationship between culture and communication is frequently conceptualized as causal and deterministic. That is, group membership and the related cultural patterns (e.g., values like individualism-collectivism) can theoretically predict behavior (Hofstede, 1991; U. Kim, Triandis, Kagticibasi, Choi, & Yoon, 1994).

Research in this paradigm often focuses on extending interpersonal communication theories to intercultural contexts or discovering theoretically based cross-cultural differences in interpersonal communication (Gudykunst & Nishida, 1989; Y. Y. Kim, 1984; Shuter, 1990; Ting-Toomey & Chung, 1996), or both. Researchers have also investigated international and cross-national mediated communication (see McPhail, 1989) and development communication (see Rogers, 1995). Most functionalist research is conducted from an "etic" perspective. That is, a theoretical framework is externally imposed by the researcher and research often involves a search for universals (Brislin, 1993; Headland, Pike, & Harris, 1990; Gudykunst & Nishida, 1989).

Probably the best known and most extensively exemplars of functionalist research programs are those conducted by W. B. Gudykunst and colleagues, extending uncertainty reduction theory (recently labeled anxiety-uncertainty management) to intercultural contexts (Gudykunst, 1995), and communication accommodation theory, a combination of ethnolinguist theory and speech accommodation theory (Gallois, Franklyn-Stokes, Giles, & Coupland, 1988; Gallois, Giles, Jones, Cargile, & Ota, 1995; Gile, Coupland, Coupland 1991). See also extensions of expectancy violation theory (Burgoon, 1995) and similarity-attraction theory to intercultural contexts (H. J. Kim, 1991).

Another type of functionalist research seeks cross-cultural differences using theoretical constructs like individualism and collectivism as a basis for predicting differences (see U. Kim, Triandis, Kagitcibasi, Choi, & Yoon, 1994). For example, Stella Ting-Toomey and colleagues have conducted extensive research identifying cultural differences in face management (Ting-Toomey, 1994) and conflict style (Ting-Toomey, 1986; Ting-Toomey et al., 1991). Min-Sun Kim and colleagues have investigated cultural variations in conversational constraints and style (M.-S.

	Functional	Interpretive	Critical Humanist	Critical Structuralist
Goal of Research:	Predict	Understand	Locate oppression and strategies for resisting oppression	Locate and analyze structural oppression
Disciplinary Roots:	Psychology Sociology	Anthropology Sociolinguistics	German critical theory British cultural studies French existentialism	Russian and German Marxism
Culture:	A priori group membership	Emergent patterns	Site of struggle	Societal structures
Relationship between Culture and Communication:	Causal	Reciprocal	Contested	Contested

Fig. 2. Four Paradigmatic Approaches to the Study of Culture and Communication

Kim, 1994; M.-S. Kim & Wilson, 1994; M.-S. Kim et al., 1996). For the most recent complication of functionalist research, see Wiseman (1995).

There are a few research programs like Y. Y. Kim (1988, 1995) that do not fit neatly into one category. Although she designates her systems-based theory of cultural adaptation as distinctive from both functionalist and interpretive paradigms (Y. Y. Kim, 1988), one could argue that this theory is based primarily on functional social psychological research on cultural adaptation, and has generated primarily functionalist research (Y. Y. Kim, 1995).

Interpretive paradigm

Culture and communication research in the interpretive paradigm gained prominence in the late 1980s. As noted in Figure 2, interpretive (or "subjective") researchers are concerned with understanding the world as it is, and describing the subjective, creative communication of individuals, usually using qualitative research methods. The philosophical foundations of this tradition lie in German Idealism (e.g., Kant) and contemporary phenomenology (Merleau-Ponty, 1962), hermeneutics (Dilthey, 1976; Gadamer, 1976, 1989; Schleiermacher, 1977), and symbolic interactionism (Mead, 1934). Interpretivism emphasizes the "knowing mind as an active contributor to the constitution of knowledge" (Mumby, 1997, p. 6). Culture and communication research in this tradition has been described and labeled as interpretive (Ting-Toomey, 1984), holistic–contextual–qualitative (Y. Y. Kim, 1984), humanist (Y. Y. Kim, 1988), and subjective (Gudykunst & Nishida, 1989).

The goal of interpretive research is to understand, rather than predict, human communication behavior. Culture, in the interpretive paradigm, is generally seen as socially constructed and emergent, rather than defined a priori, and it is not limited to nation-state collectives. Similar to functionalist research, interpretivists emphasize the stable, orderly characteristics of culture, reflecting an assumption of the social world as cohesive, ordered, and integrated. Communication is often viewed as patterned codes that serve a communal, unifying function (Carbaugh, 1988a; B. J. Hall, 1992). The relationship between culture and communication is seen as more reciprocal than causal, where culture may influence communication but is also constructed and enacted through communication. Research is often conducted from an "emic" or insider perspective, where the framework and interpretations emerge from the cultural community (Headland, Pike, & Harris, 1990). The interdisciplinary foundations of this research are found in anthropology and sociolinguistics.

The sociolinguistics theory of Dell Hymes (1972) has been particularly influential on the strongest exemplar of interpretive research—ethnography of communication studies conducted by Gerry Philipsen and colleagues. They study *cultural communication* (vs. *inter* or *cross-*cultural communication). That is, their goal is generally to describe communication patterns within one speech community, for example, Philipsen's (1976) classic study of communication in "Teamsterville," Donal Carbaugh's (1988b, 1990a) numerous studies of U.S. (primarily European American) communication patterns, from "talk show communication" to more general studies.

However, some interpretive scholars are interested in intercultural communication, cross-cultural comparisons, or both. See, for example, Braithwaite's (1990) meta-analysis of the role of silence in many cultural groups, Fitch's (1994) cross-cultural comparisons of directives, and Katriel's (1986) studies of Israeli and Arab patterns of speaking, M. J. Collier's (1991, 1996) work on communication competence, as well as Barnlund and colleagues' descriptive studies of contrasts between Japanese and European American communication (Barnlund, 1975, 1996).

It should be pointed out that some interpretive research programs reflect functionalist elements. One could argue that Collier's (1991, 1996) work, Hecht and colleagues' research on ethnicity and identity (Hecht, Larkey & Johnson, 1992; Hecht, Collier, & Ribeau, 1993), and

Barnlund's (1989) research on Japanese American contrasts have produced emic, insider descriptions, but also seem to imply behavior as deterministic, sometimes linked a priori to cultural group membership. In addition, some of their studies do explicitly predict behavior, conducted from a functionalist position, but the frameworks and hypotheses are based on previous, emic research findings (e.g., Hecht, Larkey, & Johnson, 1992).

Other examples of interpretive theories are coordinated management of meaning (Cronen, Chen, & Pearce, 1988), rhetorical studies (e.g., Garner's [1994] and Hamlet's [1997] descriptions of African American communication. For recent complications of interpretive research, see Carbaugh [1990b] and González, Houston, and Chen [1997]).

Recent culture and communication research reflects a renewed interest in research issues not usually addresses by functionalist or interpretive research. These concerns of context, power, relevance, and the destabilizing aspects of culture have led to research based on the remaining two paradigms.[2] First, there seems to be a growing recognition of the importance of understanding contexts of intercultural interaction. Although functionalist researchers sometimes incorporate context as a variable (e.g., Martin, Hammer, & Bradford, 1994), and interpretive researchers address "micro" contexts, there has been little attention paid to larger, macro contexts: the historical, social, and political contexts in which intercultural encounters take place (an exception is Katriel, 1995).

Secondly, there is an increasing emphasis on the role of power in intercultural communication interaction and research, reflecting current debates among many communication scholars (Deetz, 1996; Mumby, 1997). In functionalist research, power is sometimes incorporated as a variable (see Gallois et al., 1995) and is alluded to in some interpretive research, e.g., Orbe's (1994, 1998) research on African American male communication as "muted groups communication," and notions of third-culture building (Casmir, 1993; Shuter, 1993). The recognition of the role of power is commensurate with a notion of destabilizing and conflictual characteristics of culture. Culture is seen not as stable and orderly, but as a site of struggle for various meanings by competing groups (Ono, 1998).

Scholars have also pointed out the possible consequences of power differentials between researchers and researched: How researchers' position and privilege constrain their interpretations of research finding (Crawford, 1996; González & Krizek, 1994; Moon, 1996; Rosaldo, 1989) and how voices of research participants (many times less privileged) are often not heard in the studies about them (Tanno & Jandt, 1994).

Third, there is a recognition that intercultural communication research should be more relevant to everyday lives, that theorizing and research should be firmly based in experience, and in turn, should not only be relevant to, but should facilitate, the success of everyday intercultural encounters (see Ribeau, 1997).

These issues have led to a growing body of research based on Burrell and Morgan's (1988) remaining two paradigms, radical humanist and radical structuralist, both of which stress the importance of change and conflict in society.[3] This research reflects the increasing influence of European critical theory, e.g., Bourdieu (1991), Derrida (1976), Foucault (1980), Habermas (1970, 1981), and British cultural studies, e.g., S. Hall (1977, 1985) and Hebdige (1979). These "critical" scholars have influenced communication scholarship, primarily in media studies (see Grossberg, Nelson, & Treichler, 1992; Lull, 1995) and organizational communication (e.g., Deetz, 1996; Mumby, 1988, 1997; Wert-Gary et al., 1991), but critical ideas have been less integrated into mainstream intercultural communication scholarship (some exceptions are Lee, Chung, Wang, & Hertel, 1995; Moon, 1996). So these two paradigms are less clearly defined.[4] The research goal of both paradigms is to understand the role of power and contextual constraints on communication in order ultimately to achieve a more equitable society. Research in both paradigms emphasize the conflictual and unstable aspects of culture and society.

Critical humanist paradigm

As noted in Figure 2, critical humanist research has much in common with the interpretive viewpoint, as both assume that reality is socially constructed and emphasize the voluntaristic characteristic of human behavior (Burrell & Morgan, 1988). However, critical humanist researchers conceive this voluntarism and human consciousness as dominated by ideological superstructures and material conditions that drive a wedge between them and a more liberated consciousness. Within this paradigm, the point of academic research into cultural differences is based upon a belief in the possibility of changing uneven, differential ways of constructing and understanding other cultures. Culture, then, is not just a variable, not benignly socially constructed, but a site of struggle where various communication meanings are contested (Fiske, 1987, 1989, 1993, 1994).

Founded largely upon the work by Althusser (1971), Gramsci (1971, 1978), and the Frankfurt school (Habermas, 1970, 1981, 1987; Horkheimer & Adorno, 1988; Marcuse, 1964), critical humanist scholars attempt to work toward articulating ways in which humans can transcend and reconfigure the larger social frameworks that construct cultural identities in intercultural settings. From this paradigmatic perspective, there is a rapidly developing body of literature investigating communication issues in the construction of cultural identity. Unlike interpretive identity research (e.g., Carbaugh, 1990a; Collier & Thomas, 1988), critical research assumes no "real" identity, but only the ways that individuals negotiate relations with the larger discursive frameworks (e.g., Altman & Nakayama, 1991). An example of this research is Nakayama's (1997) description of the competing and contradictory discourses that construct identity of Japanese Americans. Hegde's work (1998a, 1998b) on Asian Indian ethnicity and Lee's (1999) on Chinese also explore the contradictory and competing ways in which identity is constructed.

This scholarship often draws directly from cultural studies scholars like Stuart Hall (1985), who tells us that he is sometimes called "Black," "colored," "West Indian," "immigrant," or "Negro" in differing international contexts. There is no "real" Stuart Hall in these various ways of speaking to him, but only the ways that others place and construct who he is. His identity and his being are never to be conflated.

Other examples of research in this paradigm are critical rhetorical studies, e.g., Nakayama and Krizek's (1995) study of the rhetoric of Whiteness, and Morris's (1997) account of being caught between two contradictory and competing discourses (Native American and White). Finally, there is also a growing body of popular culture studies that explore how media and other messages are presented and interpreted (and resisted) in often conflicting ways. See, for example, Flores's (1994) analyses of Chicano/a images as represented by the media or Peck's (1994) analysis of various discourses represented in discussions of race relations on *Oprah Winfrey*. Additionally, very recent postcolonial approaches to culture and communication represent a critical humanist perspective (see Collier, 1998b). It should be noted that studies in this tradition have focused primarily on cultural meanings in textual or media messages, rather than on face-to-face intercultural interactions.

Critical structuralist

Critical structuralist research also advocates change—but from an objectivist and more deterministic standpoint:

> Whereas the radical humanists forge their perspective by focusing upon "consciousness" as the basis for a radical critique of society, the radical structuralists concentrate upon structural relationships within a realist social world.
>
> (Burrell & Morgan, 1998, p. 34)

Largely based upon the structuralist emphasis of Western Marxists (Gramsci, 1971, 1978; Lukács, 1971; Volosinov, 1973), this approach emphasizes the significance of the structures and material conditions that guide and constrain the possibilities of cultural contact, intercultural communication, and cultural exchange. Within this paradigm, the possibilities for changing intercultural relations rest largely upon the structural relations imposed by the dominant structure (Mosco, 1996). As noted in Figure 2, culture is conceptualized as societal structures. So, for example, interactions between privileged foreign students and U.S. American students cannot be seen as random, but rather are a reflection of structural (cultural) systems of privilege and economic power. These larger structural constraints are often overlooked in more traditional intercultural communication research. When power and structural variables are incorporated into functionalist research (e.g., communication accommodation theory, diffusion of innovation), they are conceptualized as somewhat static, and the goal is not to change the structures that reproduce the power relations.

The focus, like that of critical humanism, is usually on popular culture texts rather than interpersonal interactions. For this reason, this scholarship has traditionally been defined as mass communication and not intercultural communication per se (see Asante and Gudykunst's [1989] distinction between international and intercultural communication). These scholars largely examine economic aspects of industries that produce cultural products (e.g., advertising, media) and how some industries are able to dominate the cultural sphere with their products (Fejes, 1986; Meehan, 1993). An example is Frederic's (1986) study on the political and ideological justifications leading to the establishment and maintenance of *Radio Marti*, the U.S. radio presence in Cuba. Another example is Nakayama and Vachon's (1991) study of the British film industry between World War I and World War II. They compare the quality of films produced in Britain and in the United States during this time. Based on a paradigmatic assumption that economic structures constrain the kinds of texts (e.g., films) that are possible, they argue that British films were inferior during this time, due to explicit economic strategies (e.g., Lend-Lease Act) to undermine the British film industry.

We should note that postmodern approaches (Mumby, 1997) to communication studies may represent the future of culture and communication research, but at this point, it is too early to articulate the relationship between the framework outlined here and a postmodern position.

Beyond the Paradigms

Understanding these four paradigmatic perspectives allows us to locate the source of many scholarly debates, helps to legitimize and also identify strengths and limitations of contemporary approaches, and presents the possibility of interparadigmatic dialogue and collaboration. The source of debates can be clearly seen in the dramatic differences among these four perspectives (see Figure 2). How can identifying or acknowledging the existence of these traditions lead to more productive research? There are probably a variety of responses or directions one may advocate with respect to interparadigmatic research. We have identifies four positions that we think can challenge our way of thinking about culture and communication research: liberal pluralism, interparadigmatic borrowing, multiparadigmatic collaboration, and a dialectic perspective.

Liberal pluralism is probably the most common and the easiest, a live-and-let-live response. This position acknowledges the values of each paradigmatic perspective, that each contributes in some unique way to our understanding of culture and communication. One could point out that research in the functionalist paradigm has provided us with some useful snapshot images of cultural variations in communication behavior, that interpretive research has provides many insights into communication rules of various speech communities and contexts. However, one would also have to acknowledge that because cultures are largely seen as static and cultural behavior as benign in those two paradigms, the structural dynamics that support any culture are often overlooked. Critical researchers fill this gap by focusing on important structural and contextual dynamics, but provide less insight on intercultural communication on an interpersonal level.

Although the value of each paradigmatic tradition is acknowledged in this position, there is little attempt to connect the ideas from one paradigm to another, or to explore how ideas from one paradigm may enrich the understanding of research from other paradigms. This is analogous to African Americans and Whites acknowledging and respecting both Kwanzaa and Christmas traditions, but never actually talking to each other about the cultural significance of these holidays.

There is a strong belief underlying this position that the best kind of research is firmly grounded in solid paradigmatic foundations. As many have noted, paradigmatic beliefs are strong and deeply felt, a sort of faith about the way that world is and should be, and it takes extensive study and experience to become proficient in research in one paradigm (Burrell & Morgan, 1988; Deetz, 1996).

A second position is that of *interparadigmatic borrowing*. This position is also strongly committed to paradigmatic research, but recognizes potential complementary contributions from other paradigms. Researchers taking this position listen carefully to what others say, read research from other paradigms and integrate some concerns or issues into their own research. This is seen in currently functionalist and interpretive research that has been influenced by critical thinking, for example, Katriel's (1995) essay on the importance of integrating understanding of macrocontexts (historical, economic, political) in cultural communication studies, or Collier's recent essay incorporating notions of history and power differentials in ongoing studies of interethnic relationships (1998a) and cultural identity (1998b). This borrowing is analogous to a traveler abroad learning new cultural ways (e.g., learning new expressions) that they incorporate into their lives back home. However, the researcher, while borrowing, is still fundamentally committed to research within a particular paradigm.

A third position is *multiparadigmatic collaboration*. This approach is not to be undertaken lightly. It is based on the assumption that any one research paradigm is limiting, that all researchers are limited by their own experience and worldview (Deetz, 1996; Hammersly, 1992), and the different approaches each have something to contribute. Unlike the other positions, it does not privilege any one paradigm and attempts to make explicit the contributions of each in researching the same general research question. Though this sounds good, it is fraught with pitfalls. Deetz (1996) warns against "teflon-coated multiperspectivalism" that leads to shallow readings (p. 204). Others have warned against unproductive synthetic (integrative) and additive (pluralistic, supplementary) approaches (Deetz, 1996; B. J. Hall, 1992).

Although it would be nice to move across paradigms with ease, most researchers are not "multilingual." However, one could argue that culture and communication scholars are particularly well positioned for interparadigmatic dialogue and multiparadigmatic collaboration; that they, of all researchers, should have the conceptual agility to think beyond traditional paradigmatic (cultural) boundaries. In a way this approach reminds us of our interdisciplinary foundations, when anthropologists like E. T. Hall used linguistics frameworks to analyze nonverbal interaction—a daring and innovative move (Leeds-Hurwitz, 1990).

Because it is unlikely that any one researcher can negotiate various paradigms simultaneously and conduct multiperspectival research, one strategy is collaborative research in multicultural terms (Deetz, 1996; Gudykunst & Nishida, 1989). An example of this is a current investigation of Whiteness where scholars from different research traditions (a critical position, an ethnographic perspective, and a social scientific tradition) and representing ethnic and gender diversity are investigating one general research question, "What does being White mean communicatively in the United States today?" (Nakayama & Krizek, 1995; Martin, Krizek, Nakayama, & Bradford, 1996).

In this collaborative project we are conducting a series of studies using multiple questions, methods, and perspectives, but, more importantly, different paradigmatic assumptions. However, each study meets the paradigmatic criteria for one research orientation, representing what Deetz (1996) described as an ideal research program—where complementary relations among research orientations are identified, different questions at different moments are posed, but at each moment answering to specific criteria of an orientation. This multiparadigmatic orientation permits a kind of rotation among incompatible orientations and has led to new insights about the meaning of Whiteness in the U.S. today.

A fourth position is a *dialectic perspective*. Like multiparadigmatic research, this position moves beyond paradigmatic thinking, but is even more challenging in that it seeks to find a way to live with the inherent contradictions and seemingly mutual exclusivity of these various approaches. That is, a dialectic approach to accepted that human nature is probably both creative and deterministic; that research goals can be to predict, describe, and change; that the relationship between culture and communication is, most likely, both reciprocal and contested. Specifically, is there a way to address the contextual and power concerns of the critical humanists-structuralists in everyday interpersonal interactions between people from different cultural backgrounds? We propose a dialectic approach that moves us beyond paradigmatic constraints and permits more dynamic thinking about intercultural interaction and research.

Toward a Dialectical Perspective[5]

The notion of dialect is hardly new. Used thousands of years ago by the ancient Greeks and others, its more recent emphases continue to stress the relational, processual, and contradictory nature of knowledge production (Bakhtin, 1981; Baxter, 1990; Cornforth, 1968). Aristotle's famous dictum that "rhetoric is the counterpart of dialectic" emphasizes the significant relationship between modes of expression and modes of knowledge. Dialectic offers intercultural communication researchers a way to think about different ways of knowing in a more comprehensive manner, while retaining the significance of considering how we express this knowledge.

Thus, a dialectical approach to culture and communication offers us the possibility of engaging multiple, but distinct, research paradigms. It offers us the possibility to see the world in multiple ways and to become better prepared to engage in intercultural interaction. This means, of course, that we cannot become enmeshed into any paradigm, to do so flies in the face of dialectic thinking.

We are not advocating any single form of dialectic. The adversarial model utilized in forensic rhetoric may be appropriate in some instances, whereas a more inward, therapeutic model discussed by psychoanalysts may be needed in other situations. Different dialectical forms lead to differing kinds of knowledge. No single dialectical form can satisfy epistemological needs within the complexity of multiple cultures. To reach for a singular dialectical form runs counter to the very notion of dialectical "because dialectical thinking depends so closely on the habitual everyday mode of thought which it is called on to transcend, it can take a number of different and apparently contradictory forms" (Jameson, 1971, p. 308).

Yet, a dialectical approach offers us the possibility of "knowing" about intercultural interaction as a dynamic and changing process. We can begin to see epistemological concerns as an open-ended process, as a process that resists fixed, discrete bits of knowledge, that encompasses the dynamic nature of cultural processes. We draw from the work of critical theorists who initially envisioned their theory as a "theory of contemporary socio-historical reality in which itself was constantly developing and changing" (Kellner, 1989, p. 11). For critical theorists, as well as ourselves, there are many social realities that coexist among the many cultures of the world. Thus, "dialectics for critical theory describe how phenomena are constituted and the interconnections between different phenomena and spheres of social reality" (Best & Kellner, 1991, p. 224).

A dialectical perspective also emphasizes the relational, rather than individual aspects and persons. In intercultural communication research, the dialectical perspective emphasizes the relationship between aspects of intercultural communication, and the importance of viewing these holistically and not in isolation. In intercultural communication practice, the dialectical perspective stresses the importance of relationship. This means that one becomes fully human only in relation to another person and that there is something unique in a relationship that goes beyond the sum of two individuals. This notion is expressed by Yoshikawa (1987) as the "dynamic in-betweenness" of a relationship—what exists beyond the two persons. Research on the notion of third-culture building is one attempt to develop a relational dialectic approach to intercultural interactions (Baley, 1993; Casmir, 1993; Shuter, 1993; Starosta, 1991).

Finally, the most challenging aspect of the dialectical perspective is that it requires holding two contradictory ideals simultaneously, contrary to most formal education in the United States. Most of our assumptions about learning and knowledge assume dichotomy and mutual exclusivity. Dichotomies (e.g., good–evil, subjective–objective) form the core of our philosophical, scientific, and religious traditions.

In contrast, a dialectical perspective recognizes a need to transcend these dichotomies. This notion, well known in Eastern countries as based on the logic of "soku," ("not-one, not-two"), emphasizes that the world is neither monistic nor dualistic (N. Nakayama, 1973, pp. 24–29). Rather, it recognizes and accepts as ordinary, the interdependent and complementary aspects of the seeming opposites (Yoshikawa, 1987, p. 187). In the following sections, we apply the dialectical perspective to intercultural communication theory and research.

A Dialectical Approach to Studying Intercultural Interaction

Interpersonal communication scholars have applied a dialectical approach to relational research (Baxter, 1988, 1990; Baxter & Montgomery, 1996; Montgomery, 1992) and identified basic contradictions or dialectics in relational development (autonomy–connection, novelty–predictability, openness–closedness). Although we do not advocate a simple extension of this interpersonal communication research program, we have identified six similar dialectics that seem to operate interdependently in intercultural interactions: cultural–individual, personal/social–contextual, differences–similarities, static–dynamic, present–future/history–past, and privilege–disadvantage dialectics. These dialectics are neither exhaustive nor mutually exclusive but represent an ongoing exploration of new ways to think about face-to-face intercultural interaction and research.

Cultural–individual dialectic

Scholars and practitioners alike recognize that intercultural communication is both cultural and individual. In any interaction, there are some aspects of communication that are individual and idiosyncratic (e.g., unique nonverbal expressions or language use) as well as aspects that are shared by others in the same cultural groups (e.g., family, gender, ethnicity, etc.). Functionalist research has focused on communication patterns that are shared by particular groups (gender, ethnicity, etc.) and has identified differences between these group patterns. In contrast, critical communication scholars have resisted connecting group membership with any one individual's particular behavior, which leads to essentializing.

A dialectical perspective reminds us that people are both group members and individuals and intercultural interaction is characterized by both. Research could investigate how these two contradictory characteristics work in intercultural interactions. For example, how do people experience the tension between wanting to be seen and treated as individuals, and at the same time have their group identities recognized and affirmed (Collier, 1991)? This tension is often at the heart of the affirmative action debate in the United States—a need to recognize cultural membership and at the same time be treated as an individual and not put in boxes.

Personal/social–contextual dialectic

A dialectical perspective emphasizes the relationship between personal and contextual communication. There are some aspects of communication that remain relatively constant over many contexts. There are also aspects that are contextual. That is, people communicate in particular ways in particular contexts (e.g., professors and students in classrooms), and messages are interpreted in particular ways. Outside the classroom (e.g., at football games or at faculty meetings), professors and students may communicate differently, expressing different aspects of themselves. Intercultural encounters are characterized by both personal and contextual communication. Researchers could investigate how these contradictory characteristics operate in intercultural interactions.

Differences–similarities dialectic

A dialectic approach recognizes the importance of similarities and differences in understanding intercultural communication. The field was founded on the assumption that there are real, important differences that exist between various cultural groups, and functionalist research has established a long tradition of identifying these differences. However, in real life there are a great many similarities in human experience and ways of communicating. Cultural communication researchers in the interpretive tradition have emphasized these similar patterns in specific cultural communities. Critical researchers have emphasized that there may be differences, but these differences are often not benign, but are political and have implications for power relations (Houston, 1992).

There has been a tendency to overemphasize group differences in traditional intercultural communication research—in a way that sets up false dichotomies and rigid expectations. However, a dialectical perspective reminds us that difference and similarity can coexist in intercultural communication interactions. For example, Israelis and Palestinians share a love for their Holy City, Jerusalem. This similarity may be overweighed by the historical differences in meanings of Jerusalem so that the differences work in opposition. Research could examine how differences and similarities work in cooperation or in opposition in intercultural interaction.

For example, how do individuals experience the tension of multiple differences and similarities in their everyday intercultural interactions (class, race, gender, attitudes, beliefs)? Are these aspects or topics that tend to emphasize one or the other? How do individuals deal with this tension? What role does context play in managing this tension?

Static–dynamic dialectic

The static–dynamic dialectic highlights the ever-changing nature of culture and cultural practices, but also underscores our tendency to think about these things as constant. Traditional intercultural research in the functionalist tradition and some interpretive research have emphasized the stability of cultural patterns, for example, values, that remain relatively consistent over periods of time (Hofstede, 1991). Some interpretive research examines varying practices that reflect this value over time (e.g., Carbaugh's study of communication rules on *Donahue* discourse, 1990a). In contrast, critical researchers have emphasized the instability and fleetingness of cultural meanings, for example, Cornyetz's (1994) study of the appropriation of hip-hop in Japan.

So thinking about culture and cultural practices as both static and dynamic helps us navigate through a diverse world and develop new ways of understanding intercultural encounters. Research could investigate how these contradictory forces work in intercultural interactions. How do individuals work with the static and dynamic aspects of intercultural interactions? How is the tension of this dynamic experienced and expressed in intercultural relationships?

Present–future/history–past dialectic

A dialectic in intercultural communication exists between the history–past and the present–future. Much of the functionalist and interpretive scholarship investigating culture and communication has ignored historical forces. Other scholars added history as a variable in understanding contemporary intercultural interaction, for example, Stephan and Stephan's (1996) prior intergroup interaction variable that influences degree of intergroup anxiety. In contrast, critical scholars stress the importance of including history in current analyses of cultural meanings.

A dialectical perspective suggests that we need to balance both an understanding of the past and the present. Also the past is always seen through the lens of the present. For example, Oliver Stone's film, *Nixon*, was criticized because of the interpretation Stone made of (now) historical events and persons. As Stone pointed out, we are always telling our versions of history.

Collier's (1998a) investigations of alliance in ethnic relationships reveal the tensions of the present and past in ethnic relationships. This and other research reveal the importance of balancing an understanding the history, for example, of slavery and the African diaspora, the colonization of indigenous peoples (Morris, 1997), the internment of Japanese Americans (Nakayama, 1997), relationships between Mexico and the U.S., as well as maintaining a focus on the present in interethnic relationships in the United States. How do individuals experience this tension? How do they balance the two in everyday interaction? Many influential factors precede and succeed any intercultural interaction that gives meaning to that interaction.

Privilege–disadvantage dialectic

As individuals, we carry and communicate various types of privilege and disadvantage, the final dialectic. The traditional intercultural communication research mostly ignores issues of privilege and disadvantage (exceptions include Pennington, 1989; Gallois et al., 1995), although these issues are central in critical scholarship. Privilege and disadvantage may be in the form of political, social position, or status. For example, if members of wealthy nations travel to less wealthy countries, the intercultural interactions between these two groups will certainly be influenced by their differential in economic power (Katriel, 1995). Hierarchies and power differentials are not always clear. Individuals may be simultaneously privileged and disadvantaged, or privileged in some contexts, and disadvantaged in others. Research could investigate how the intersections of privilege and disadvantage work in intercultural encounters. Women of color may be simultaneously advantaged (education, economic class) and disadvantaged (gender, race), for example (Houston, 1992). How are these various contradictory privileges and disadvantages felt, expressed, and managed in intercultural interactions? How do context and topic play into the dialectic? Many times, it may not be clear who or how one is privileged or disadvantaged. It may be unstable, fleeting, may depend on the topic, or the context.

Dialectical Intersections

So how do these different dialectics work in everyday interaction? These dialectics are not discrete, but always operate in relation to each other (see Figure 3). We can illustrate these intersections with an example of a relationship between a foreign student from a wealthy family

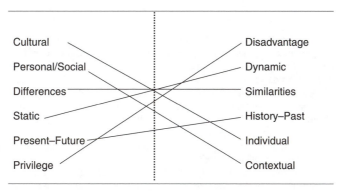

Fig. 3. Intersections of Six Dialectics of Intercultural Interaction

and a U.S. American professor. Using this example we can see how contradictories in several dialectics can occur in interpersonal intercultural interaction. In relation to the personal/social–contextual dialectic, both the student and professor are simultaneously privileged and disadvantaged depending on the context. In talking about class material, for example, the professor is more privileged than the student, but in talking about vacations and travel, the wealthy student may be more privileged.

To focus on another set of dialects, if the topic of international trade barriers comes up, the student may be seen as a cultural representative than an individual and, in this conversation, cultural differences or similarities may be emphasized. When the topic shifts, these relational dialectics also shift—within the same relationship.

These important dialectical relational shifts have not been studied in previous research, and this is what makes the dialectical perspective different from the other three positions identified earlier (liberal pluralism, interparadigmatic borrowing, and multiparadigmatic research). That is, this approach makes explicit the dialectical tension between what previous research topics have been studied (cultural differences, assumed static nature of culture, etc.) and what should be studied (how cultures change, how they are similar, importance of history). The dialectical perspective, then, represents a major epistemological move in our understanding of culture and communication.

Conclusion

In this brief essay we have tried to challenge culture and communication scholars to consider ways that their production of knowledge is related to the epistemological advances made by those in other paradigms. Whereas there cannot be any easy fit among these paradigmatic differences, it is important that we not only recognize these differences, but also seek ways that these epistemological differences can be productive rather than debilitating. Information overload can be daunting, but our dialectical perspective offers intercultural scholars, as well as students and practitioners, a way to grapple with the many different kinds of knowledge we have about cultures and interactions.

In his own thinking about dialectical criticism, Fredric Jameson (1971) observes that there is a breathlessness about this shift from the normal object-oriented activity of the mind to such dialectical self-consciousness—something of the sickening shudder we feel in a elevator's fall or in the sudden dig up in an airliner (p. 308).

This sudden fall in the ways we think about intercultural communication means letting go of the more rigid kinds of knowledge that we have about others and entering into more uncertain ways of knowing about others.

Notes

1. *Cross-cultural communication* denotes studies identifying cultural differences in communication phenomena, both interpersonal and mediated, e.g., Fitch's (1994) study of directives in Boulder, Colorado, and Bogata, Colombia. *Intercultural communication* has focused on the interaction of individuals from various cultural backgrounds in interpersonal contexts, e.g., Houston's (1997) study of Black–White women's interaction, as well as mediated, for example, Pennington's (1989) media study of Jesse Jackson's negotiations with Syria for release of an American POW. *Intracultural/cultural communication* studies identify communication patterns within particular cultural communities, for example, Philipsen's (1976) studies of White, working class male talk in a Chicago neighborhood.
2. These are not necessarily new issues. Scholars had emphasized the need to examine power differentials in intercultural encounters, e.g., Asante, 1987; Folb, 1982; Kramarae, 1981; Smith (aka Asante), 1973, but they were largely ignored (see Moon, 1996; Ribeau, 1997). Concerning relevance, A. Smith (1981), in an indictment of intercultural communication research, stated that the appropriate focus of scholars should be on "relevant" topics—on eliminating poverty, oppression, and not on understanding sojourner communication and other "frivolous" topics.
3. We use the terms *critical humanist* and *critical structuralist* to emphasize the critical theory foundations of these paradigms.
4. One could argue that critical voices have been present in critical ethnography (Conquergood, 1991) and critical rhetoric (McKerrow, 1989), which often address the intersection of culture and communication. This, of course, brings up the question of the boundaries of the study of culture and communication, which is beyond the scope of this essay. What is the appropriate focus for the study of culture and communication? Will cultural studies, critical ethnography, etc., be incorporated along with intercultural communication research to form a larger area of study? Or will intercultural communication researchers simply borrow some of their ideas and retain more narrow boundaries?
5. Some of the material concerning the six dialectics appear in J. N. Martin, T. K. Nakayama, & L. A. Flores (1998). A dialectical approach to intercultural communication. In J. N. Martin, T. K. Nakayama, & L. A. Flores (Eds.), *Readings in cultural contexts* (pp. 5–14). Mountain View, CA: Mayfield.

References

Althusser, L. (1971). *Lenin and philosophy* (B. Brewster, Trans.). New York: Monthly Review Press.

Altman, K. E., & Nakayama, T. K. (1991). Making a critical difference: A difficult dialogue. *Journal of Communication, 41*(4), 116–128.

Asante, M. K. (1987). *The Afrocentric idea*. Philadelphia, PA: Temple University Press.

Asante, M. K., & Gudykunst, W. B. (1989). Preface. In M. K. Asante & W. B. Gudykunst (Eds.), *Handbook of international and intercultural communication* (pp. 7–16). Newbury Park, CA: Sage.

Bakhtin, M. M. (1981). *The dialogic imagination: Four essays by M. M. Bakhtin.* (M. Holquist, Ed., and C. Emerson & M. Holquist, Trans.). Austin, TX: University of Texas Press.

Barnlund, D. C. (1975). *Public and private self in Japan and United States.* Tokyo: Simul Press.

Barnlund, D. C. (1989). *Communicative styles of Japanese and Americans.* Belmont, CA: Wadsworth.

Baxter, L. A. (1988). A dialectical perspective on communication strategies in relationship development. In S. W. Duck (Ed.), *A handbook of personal relationships* (pp. 257–273). New York: Wiley.

Baxter, L. A. (1990). Dialectical contradictions in relationship development. *Journal of Social and Personal Relationships, 7*, 69–88.

Belay, G. (1993). Toward a paradigm shift for intercultural and international communication: New research directions. *Communication Yearbook, 16*, 437–457.

Best, S., & Kellner, D. (1991). *Postmodern theory: Critical interrogations.* New York: Guilford.

Bourdieu, P. (1991). *Language and symbolic power.* Cambridge, MA: Harvard University Press.

Braithwaite, C. A. (1990). Communicative silence: A cross cultural study of Basso's hypothesis. In D. Carbaugh, (Ed.), *Cultural communication and intercultural contact* (pp. 321–328). Hillsdale, NJ: Erlbaum.

Brislin, R. W. (1993). *Understanding culture's influence on behavior.* New York: Harcourt Brace.

Burgoon, J. K. (1995). Cross-cultural and intercultural applications of expectance violations theory. In R. L. Wiseman (Ed.), *Intercultural communication theory* (pp. 194–214). Thousand Oaks, CA: Sage.

Burrell, G., & Morgan, G. (1988). *Sociological paradigms and organizational analysis.* Portsmouth, NH: Heinemann.

Carbaugh, D. (1988a). Comments on "culture" in communication inquiry. *Communication Reports, 1,* 38–41.

Carbaugh, D. (1988b). *Talking American.* Norwood, NJ: Ablex.

Carbaugh, D. (1990a). Communication rules in *Donahue* discourse. In D. Carbaugh (Ed.), *Cultural communication and intercultural contact* (pp. 119–149). Hillsdale, NJ: Erlbaum.

Carbaugh, D. (Ed.). (1990b). *Cultural communication and intercultural contact.* Hillsdale, NJ: Erlbaum.

Casmir, F. L. (1993). Third-culture building: A paradigm shift for international and intercultural communication. *Communication Yearbook, 16,* 407–428.

Collier, M. J. (1991). Conflict competence within African, Mexican and Anglo American friendships. In S. Ting-Toomey & F. Korzenny (Eds.), *Cross-cultural interpersonal communication.* Newbury Park, CA: Sage.

Collier, M. J. (1996). Communication competence problematics in ethic friendships. *Communication Monographs, 63,* 314–337.

Collier, M. J. (1998a). Intercultural friendships as interpersonal alliances. In J. N. Martin, T. K. Nakayama & L. A. Flores (Eds.), *Readings in cultural contexts* (pp. 370–379). Mountain View, CA: Mayfield.

Collier, M. J. (1998b). Researching cultural identity: Reconciling interpretive and postcolonial perspectives. In D. V. Tanno & A. González (Eds.), *Communication and identity across cultures* (pp. 122–147). Thousand Oaks, CA: Sage.

Collier, M. J., & Thomas, M. (1988). Cultural identity in intercultural communication: An interpretive perspective. In Y. Y. Kim & W. B. Gudykunst (Eds.), *Theories in intercultural communication* (pp. 94–120). Newbury Park, CA: Sage.

Conquergood, D. (1991). Rethinking ethnography: Towards a critical cultural politics. *Communication Monographs, 58,* 179–195.

Cornyetz, N. (1994). Feitished Blackness: Hip hop and racial desire in contemporary Japan. *Social Text, 41,* 113–140.

Cornforth, M. (1968). *Materialism and the dialectical method.* New York: International Publishers.

Crawford, L. (1996). Personal ethnography. *Communication Monographs, 63,* 158–170.

Cronen, V. E., Chen, V., & Pearce, W. B. (1988). Coordinated management of meaning: A critical theory. In Y. Y. Kim & W. B. Gudykunst (Eds.), *Theories in intercultural communication* (pp. 66–98). Newbury Park, CA: Sage.

Deetz, S. (1994). The future of the discipline: The challenges, the research, and the social contribution. *Communication Yearbook, 17,* 565–600.

Deetz, S. (1996). Describing differences in approaches to organization sciences: Rethinking Burrell and Morgan and their legacy. *Organization Science, 7,* 119–207.

Derrida, J. (1976). *Of grammatology* (G. Spivak, Trans.). Baltimore, MA: Johns Hopkins University Press.

Dilthey, W. (1976). *Selected writings* (H. P. Rickman, Ed. & Trans.). New York: Cambridge University Press.

Fejes, F. (1986). *Imperialism, media and the good neighbor: New Deal foreign police and United States shortwave broadcasting to Latin America.* Norwood, NJ: Ablex.

Fiske, J. (1987). *Television culture.* New York: Methuen.

Fiske, J. (1989). *Understanding popular culture.* Boston: Unwin Hyman.

Fiske, J. (1993). *Power plays, power works.* New York: Verso.

Fiske, J. (1994). *Media matters: Everyday culture and political change.* Minneapolis, MN: University of Minnesota Press.

Fitch. K. L. (1994). A cross-cultural study of directive sequences and some implications for compliance-gaining research. *Communication Monographs, 61,* 185–209.

Flores, L. (1994). *Shifting visions: Intersections of rhetorical and Chicana feminist theory in the analysis of mass media.* Unpublished dissertation, University of Georgia, Athens, GA.

Folb, E. (1982). Who's got the room at the top? Issues of dominance and nondominance in intracultural communication. In L. A. Samovar & R. E. Porter (Eds.), *Intercultural communication: A reader* (pp. 132–141). Belmont, CA: Wadsworth.

Foucault, M. (1980). *Power/knowledge: Selected interviews and other writings 1972–1977* (C. Gordon, L. Marshall, J. Mepham, & K. Soper, Trans.). New York: Pantheon Books.

Frederic, H. (1986). *Cuban-American radio wars: Ideology in international telecommunications.* Norwood, NJ: Ablex.

Gadamer, H. G. (1976). *Philosophical hermeneutics* (D. E. Linge, Ed. & Trans.). Berkeley, CA: University of California Press.

Gadamer, H. G. (1989). *Truth and method.* New York: Crossroad Publishing.

Gallois, C., Franklyn-Stokes, A., Giles, H., & Coupland, N. (1988). Communication accommodation in intercultural encounters. In Y. Y. Kim & W. B. Gudykunst (Eds.), *Theories in intercultural communication* (pp. 157–185). Beverly Hills, CA: Sage.

Gallois, G., Giles, H., Jones, E., Cargile, A. C., & Ota, H. (1995). Accommodating intercultural encounters: Elaborations and extensions. In R. L. Wiseman (Ed.), *Intercultural communication theory* (pp. 115–147). Thousand Oaks, CA: Sage.

Garner, T. (1994). Oral rhetorical practice in African American culture. In A. González, M. Houston, & V. Chen (Eds.), *Our voices: Essays in culture, ethnicity, and communication* (pp. 81–91). Los Angeles, CA: Roxbury.

Giles, H., Coupland, N., & Coupland, J. (Eds.). (1991). *Contexts of accommodation: Developments in applied sociolinguistics.* Cambridge, UK: Cambridge University Press.

González, A., Houston, M., & Chen, V. (Eds.). (1997). *Our voices: Essays in culture, ethnicity, and communication* (2nd ed). Los Angeles, CA: Roxbury.

González, C., & Krizek, R. (1994, February). *Indigenous ethnography.* Paper presented at the annual meeting of the Western Communication Association, San Jose, CA.

Gramsci, A. (1971). *Selections from the prison notebooks* (Q. Hoare & G. N. Smith, Trans.). New York: International.

Gramsci, A. (1978). *Selections from cultural writings.* Cambridge, MA: Harvard University Press.

Grossberg, L., Nelson, C., & Treichler, P. (Eds.). (1992). *Cultural studies.* New York: Routledge, Chapman, & Hall.

Gudykunst, W. B. (1995). Anxiety/uncertainty management (AUM) theory: Current status. In R. L. Wiseman (Ed.), *Intercultural communication theory* (pp. 8–58). Thousand Oaks, CA: Sage.

Gudykunst, W. B., & Nishida, T. (1989). Theoretical perspectives for studying intercultural communication. In M. K. Asante & W. B. Gudykunst (Eds.), *Handbook of international and intercultural communication* (pp. 17–46). Newbury Park, CA: Sage.

Habermas, J. (1970). On systematically distorted communication. *Inquiry, 13,* 205–218.

Habermas, J. (1981). Modernity versus postmodernity. *New German Critique, 22,* 3–14.

Habermas, J. (1987). *The theory of communicative action: Lifeworld and system* (Vol. 2. T. McCarthy, Trans.). Boston: Beacon Press.

Hall, B. J. (1992). Theories of culture and communication. *Communication Theory, 2,* 50–70.

Hall, S. (1977). Culture, media, and the "ideological effect." In J. Curran, M. Gurevitch, & J. Woollacott (Eds.), *Mass communication and society.* London: Edward Arnold.

Hall, S. (1985). Signification, representation, ideology: Althusser and the post-structuralist debates. *Critical Studies in Mass Communication, 2,* 91–114.

Hamlet, J. D. (1997). Understanding traditional African American preaching. In A. González, M. Houston, & V. Chen (Eds.), *Our voices: Essays in culture, ethnicity, and communication* (2nd ed.; pp. 94–98). Los Angeles, CA: Roxbury.

Hammersly, M. (1992). *What's wrong with ethnography?* New York: Routledge, Chapman, & Hall.

Harman, R. C., & Briggs, N. E. (1991). SIETAR survey: Perceived contributions of the social sciences to intercultural communication. *International Journal of Intercultural Relations, 15*(1), 19–28.

Headland, T., Pike, K., & Harris, M. (Eds.). (1990). *Emics and etics: The insider/outsider debate.* Newbury Park, CA: Sage.

Hebdige, D. (1979). *Subculture: The meaning of style.* London: Methuen.

Hecht, M. L., Larkey, L., & Johnson, J. (1992). African American and European American perceptions of problematic issues in interethnic communication effectiveness. *Human Communication Research, 19,* 209–236.

Hecht, M. L., Collier, M. J., & Ribeau, S. A. (1993). *African American communication: Ethnic identity and cultural interpretation.* Newbury Park, CA: Sage.

Hegde, R. (1998a). Translated enactments: The relational configurations of the Asian Indian immigrant experience. In J. N. Martin, T. K. Nakayama, & L. A. Flores (Eds.), *Readings in cultural contexts* (pp. 315–322). Mountain View, CA: Mayfield.

Hegde, R. (1998b). Swinging the trapeze: The negotiation of identity among Asian Indian immigrant women in the United States. In D. V. Tanno & A. González (Eds.), *Communication and identity across cultures* (pp. 34–55). Thousand Oaks, CA: Sage.

Hofstede, G. (1991). *Cultures and organizations: Software of the mind.* New York: McGraw-Hill.

hooks, b. (1990). *Yearning: Race, gender, and cultural politics.* Boston: South End Press.

Horkheimer, M. & Adorno, T. (1988). *Dialectic of enlightenment* (J. Cumming, Trans.). New York: Continuum.

Houston, M. (1992). The politics of difference: Race, class, and women's communication. In L. F. Rakow (Ed.). *Women making meaning* (pp. 45–59). New York: Routledge, Chapman, & Hall.

Houston, M. (1997). When Black women talk with White women: Why dialogues are difficult. In A. González, M. Houston, & V. Chen (Eds.), *Our voices: Essays in culture, ethnicity, and communication* (pp. 187–194). Los Angeles, CA: Roxbury.

Hymes, D. (1972). Models of the interaction of language and social life. In J. J. Gumperz & D. Hymes (Eds.), *Directions in sociolinguistics: The ethnography of communication* (pp. 35–71). New York: Holt, Rinehart, & Winston.

Jameson, F. (1971). *Marxism and form*. Princeton, NJ: Princeton University Press.

Katriel, T. (1986). *Talking straight: "Dugri" speech in Israeli Sabra culture*. Cambridge, UK: Cambridge University Press.

Katriel, T. (1995). From "context" to "contexts" in intercultural communication research. In R. Wiseman (Ed.), *Intercultural communication theory* (pp. 271–284). Thousand Oaks, CA: Sage.

Kellner, D. (1989). *Critical theory, Marxism and modernity*. Baltimore, MA: Johns Hopkins University Press.

Kim, H. J. (1991). Influence of language and similarity on initial interaction attraction. In S. Ting-Toomey & F. Korzenny (Eds.), *Cross-cultural interpersonal communication* (pp. 213–229). Newbury Park, CA: Sage.

Kim, M.-S. (1994). Cross-cultural comparisons of the perceived importance of interactive constraints. *Human Communication Research, 21*, 128–151.

Kim, M.-S., & Wilson, S. R. (1994). A cross-cultural comparison of implicit theories of requesting. *Communication Monographs, 61*, 210–235.

Kim, M.-S., Hunter, J. E., Miyahara, A., Horvath, A.-M., Bresnahan, M., & Yoon, H.-J. (1996). Individual vs. culture level dimensions of individualism/collectivism: Effects on preferred conversational styles. *Communication Monographs, 63*, 28–49.

Kim, U., Triandis, H. C., Kagitcibasi, I., Choi, S.-C., Yoon, G. (1994). *Individualism and collectivism: Theory, method, and applications*. Thousand Oaks, CA: Sage.

Kim, Y. Y. (1984). Searching for creative integration. In W. B. Gudykunst & Y. Y. Kim (Eds.), *Methods for intercultural communication research* (pp. 15–28). Beverly Hills, CA: Sage.

Kim, Y. Y. (1988). On theories in intercultural communication. In Y. Y. Kim & W. B. Gudykunst (Eds.), *Theories in intercultural communication* (pp. 11–21). Beverly Hills, CA: Sage.

Kim, Y. Y. (1995). Cross-cultural adaptation: An integrative theory. In R. L. Wiseman (Ed.), *Intercultural communication theory* (pp. 170–194). Thousand Oaks, CA: Sage.

Kramarae, C. (1981). *Women and men speaking: Frameworks for analysis*. Rowley, MA: Newbury House.

Kuhn, T. S. (1970). *The structure of scientific revolutions*. Chicago, IL: University of Chicago Press.

Lee, W. S. (1999). One Whiteness veils three uglinesses: From border-crossing to a womanist interrogation of colorism. In T. K. Nakayama & J. N. Martin (Eds.), *Whiteness: The communication of social identity*. Thousand Oaks, CA: Sage.

Lee, W. S., Chung, J., Wang, J. & Hertel, E. (1995). A sociohistorical approach to intercultural communication. *Howard Journal of Communications, 6*, 262–291.

Leeds-Hurwitz, W. (1990). Notes on the history of intercultural communication: The Foreign Service Institute and the mandate for intercultural training. *Quarterly Journal of Speech, 76*, 262–281.

Lukács, G. (1971). *History and class consciousness: Studies in Marxist dialectics* (R. Livingston, Trans.). Cambridge, MA: MIT Press.

Lull, J. (1995). *Media, communication, culture: A global approach*. New York: Columbia University Press.

Marcuse, H. (1964). *One dimensional man*. Boston: Beacon Press.

Martin, J. N., Krizek, R. L., Nakayama, T. K., & Bradford, L. (1996). Exploring Whiteness: A study of self-labels for White Americans. *Communication Quarterly, 44*, 125–144.

Martin, J. N., Hammer, M. R., & Bradford, L. (1994). The influence of cultural and situational contexts on Hispanic and non-Hispanic communication competence behaviors. *Communication Quarterly, 42*, 160–179.

Martin, J. N., Nakayama, T. K. & Flores, L. A. (1998). A dialectical approach to intercultural communication. In J. N. Martin, T. K. Nakayama, & L. A. Flores (Eds.), *Readings in cultural contexts* (pp. 5–14). Mountain View, CA: Mayfield.

McKerrow, R. (1989). Critical rhetoric: Theory and praxis. *Communication Monographs, 56*, 91–111.

McPhail, T. L. (1989). Inquiry in international communication. In M. K. Asante & W. B. Gudykunst (Eds.), *Handbook of international and intercultural communication* (pp. 47–60). Newbury Park, CA: Sage.

Mead, G. H. (1934). *Mind, self, and society*. Chicago: University of Chicago Press.

Meehan, E. R. (1993). Rethinking political economy: Changes and continuity. *Journal of Communication, 43*(4), 105–116.

Merleau-Ponty, M. (1962). *Phenomenology of perception* (C. Smith, Trans.). London: Routledge & Kegan Paul.

Moon, D. G. (1996). Concepts of culture: Implications for intercultural communication research. *Communication Quarterly, 44*, 70–84.

Montgomery, B. M. (1992). Communication as the interface between couples and culture. *Communication Yearbook, 15*, 475–507.

Morris, R. (1997). Living in/between. In A. González, M. Houston, & V. Chen (Eds.), *Our voices: Essays in culture, ethnicity, and communication* (2nd ed.; pp. 163–176). Los Angeles, CA: Roxbury.

Mosco, V. (1996). *The political economy of communication.* Thousand Oaks, CA: Sage.

Mumby, D. (1988). *Communication and power in organizations: Discourse, ideology, and domination.* Norwood, NJ: Ablex.

Mumby, D. K. (1997). Modernism, postmodernism, and communication studies: A rereading of an ongoing debate. *Communication Theory, 7,* 1–28.

Nakayama, N. (1973). *Mujunteki, sosoku no ronri.* Kyoto, Japan: Hyakkaen.

Nakayama, T. K. (1997). Dis/orienting identities: Asian Americans, history, and intercultural communication. In A. González, M. Houston, & V. Chen (Eds.), *Our voices: Essays in culture, ethnicity, and communication* (2nd ed.; pp. 14–20). Los Angeles, CA: Roxbury.

Nakayama, T. K., & Krizek, R. L. (1995). Whiteness: A straight rhetoric. *Quarterly Journal of Speech, 81,* 291–309.

Nakayama, T. K., & Vachon, L. A. (1991). Imperialist victory in peacetimes: State functions and the British cinema industry. *Current Research in Films, 5,* 161–174.

Ono, K. (1998). Problematizing "nation" in intercultural communication research. In D. Tanno & A. González (Eds.), *Communication and identity across cultures* (pp. 34–55). Thousand Oaks, CA: Sage.

Orbe, M. P. (1994). "Remember, it's always Whites' ball": Descriptions of African American male communication. *Communication Quarterly, 42,* 287–300.

Orbe, M. P. (1998). *Constructing co-cultural theory: An explication of culture, power, and communication.* Thousand Oaks, CA: Sage.

Peck, J. (1993/94). Talk about racism: Framing a popular discourse of race on *Oprah Winfrey. Cultural Critique, 5,* 89–126.

Pennington, D. L. (1989). Interpersonal power and influence in intercultural communication. In M. K. Asante & W. B. Gudykunst (Eds.), *Handbook of international and intercultural communication* (pp. 261–274). Newbury Park, CA: Sage.

Philipsen, G. (1976). Speaking "like a man" in Teamsterville: Culture patterns of role enactment in an urban neighborhood. *Quarterly Journal of Speech, 61,* 13–22.

Ribeau, S. A. (1997). How I came to know "in self realization there is truth." In A. González, M. Houston, & V. Chen (Eds.), *Our voices: Essays in culture, ethnicity, and communication* (2nd ed.; pp. 21–27). Los Angeles, CA: Roxbury.

Rogers, E. (1995). *Diffusion of innovations* (4th ed.). New York: Free Press.

Rosaldo, R. (1989). *Culture and truth: The remaking of social analysis.* Boston: Beacon Press.

Schleiermacher, F. D. E. (1977). *Hermeneutics: The handwritten manuscripts* (J. Duke & J. Forstman, Trans.). Missoula, MT: Scholar Press for the American Academy of Religion.

Shuter, R. (1990). The centrality of culture. *Southern Communication Journal, 55,* 237–249.

Shuter, R. (1993). On third-culture building. *Communication Yearbook, 16,* 429–436.

Smith, A. (aka M. K. Asante). (1973). *Transracial communication.* Englewood Cliffs, NJ: Prentice-Hall.

Smith, A. G. (1981). Content decisions in intercultural communication. *Southern Speech Communication Journal, 47,* 252–262.

Starosta, W. J. (1991, May). *Third culture building: Chronological development and the role of third parties.* Paper presented at the annual meeting of the International Communication Association, Chicago, IL.

Stephan, W. G., Stephan, C. W. (1996). *Intergroup relations.* Boulder, CO: Westview Press.

Tanno, D. V. & Jandt, F. E. (1994). Redefining the "other" in multicultural research. *Howard Journal of Communications, 5,* 36–54.

Ting-Toomey, S. (1984). Qualitative research: An overview. In W. B. Gudykunst & Y. Y. Kim (Eds.), *Methods for intercultural communication research* (pp. 169–184). Beverly Hills, CA: Sage.

Ting-Toomey, S. (1986). Conflict communication styles in Black and White subjective cultures. In Y. Y. Kim (Ed.), *Interethic communication: Current research* (pp. 75–88). Newbury Park, CA: Sage.

Ting-Toomey, S. (Ed.). (1994). *The challenge of facework: Cross cultural and interpersonal issues.* Albany: State University of New York Press.

Ting-Toomey, S., & Chung, L. (1996). Cross-cultural interpersonal communication: Theoretical trends and research directions. In W. B. Gudykunst, S. Ting-Toomey, & T. Nishida (Eds.), *Communication in personal relationships across cultures* (pp. 237–262). Thousand Oaks, CA: Sage.

Ting-Toomey, S., Gao, G., Trubisky, P., Yang, Z., Kim, H. S., Lin, S. L., & Nishida, T. (1991). Culture, face maintenance and styles of handling interpersonal conflicts: A study in five cultures. *International Journal of Conflict Management, 2,* 275–296.

Volosinov, V. N. (1973). *Marxism and the philosophy of language* (L. Matejka & I. R. Titunik, Trans.). Cambridge, MA: Harvard University Press.

Wert-Gary, S., Center, C., Brashers, D. E., & Meyers, R. A. (1991). Research topics and methodological orientations in organizational communication: A decade in review. *Communication Studies, 42,* 141–154.

Wiseman, R. L. (Ed.). (1995). *Intercultural communication theory.* Thousand Oaks, CA: Sage.

Yoshikawa, M. J. (1987). The double-swing model of intercultural communication between the East and the West. In D. L. Kincaid (Ed.), *Communication theory: Eastern and Western perspectives* (pp. 319–329). San Diego, CA: Academic Press.

Part III
Contextual Approaches to Culture and Communication

7

Language and Words
Communication in the *Analects* of Confucius

Hui-Ching Chang

> Tradition paints [Confucius] as a strict pedant, laying down precise rules for
> men to follow in their conduct and their thinking. The truth is that he care-
> fully avoided laying down rules, because he believed that no creed formulated
> by another person can excuse any man from the duty of thinking for himself.
> (Herrlee Creel, *Confucius and the Chinese Way*, 1960, p. 1)

Scholars of language and social psychology in Asian nations often invoke Confucianism to
explain Asian communication patterns (Chen, 1993; Chen & Chung, 1994; Cheng, 1987; Oliver,
1971; Yum, 1988). Others have linked Confucianism and language use in social life, showing
how it has influenced Asian cultural concepts important to communication, such as the Chinese
concepts of *kuan-hsi* (relation) (Chang & Holt, 1991), *pao* (reciprocity) (Chang & Holt, 1994),
and *mien-tzu* (face) (Cheng, 1986), as well as the Korean concept of *uye-ri* (righteousness) (Yum,
1987) and the Japanese idea of *ningensei* (human beingness) (Goldman, 1994). This is hardly
surprising, given Confucianism's effect on various Asian societies (Bond & Hwang, 1986; Chan,
1963; Cheng, 1986; Fung, 1983; Goldman, 1994; Hofstede, 1991; Okabe, 1983; Triandis, 1995;
Tu, 1985, 1996; Yum, 1988).

Although Confucian thought is important in shaping attitudes toward language and words
in Asian societies,[1] "Confucianism," as an abstraction used to explain language and social life,
has often been cast in terms of other ideas such as collectivism (Triandis, 1995; Wheeler, Reis, &
Bond, 1989), social orientation (Yang, 1981), and harmony (Oliver, 1971). I will argue that
subsuming Confucianism under these abstractions prevents us from developing appropriate
theories to account for language attitudes in Confucian societies.

Confucian teachings are based on a far more comprehensive and richly textured view of
language and words than is suggested by superordinate sociological and psychological ideas, as
shown by numerous observations about language, society, and cultural practice in the *Analects*
of Confucius, the most important Confucian text.[2] Although the *Analects* extensively treats such
issues, few studies have concentrated on the text of the *Analects* to provide a comprehensive look
at how attitudes toward language are advocated by Confucius;[3] instead, current literature focuses
on the implications of Confucian systems of thought for Asian communication (Cheng, 1987;
Yum, 1988). Even when the *Analects* is discussed, analyses tend to be anecdotal (see Chen &
Chung, 1994). This article redresses this deficiency by looking at how words are treated in
the entire corpus of the *Analects* to formulate more appropriate theoretical perspectives for the
analysis of communication in Confucian societies.

Confucian Philosophy as Key to Asian Communication—Current Interpretations

Most scholars agree that the people in Confucianist cultures emphasize relational hierarchy and social harmony, translating Confucian values into a set of well-defined rules regulating language behaviors for different relationships on different occasions. Bond and Hwang (1986) summarize the key elements of Confucianism:

> In summary, the essential aspects of Confucianism in constructing a Chinese social psychology are the following: (a) man exists through, and is defined by, his relationships to others; (b) these relationships are structured hierarchically; (c) social order is ensured through each party's honouring the requirements in the role relationship.
>
> (p. 216)

Although Bond and Hwang are referring specifically to Chinese, their views are shared by other scholars writing about other Asian societies, influenced by Confucian philosophy. As Yum (1988) puts it, "[The] East Asian preoccupation with social relationships stems from the doctrines of Confucianism, that considers proper relationships to be the basis of society" (p. 374). Yum (1988) further notes that the Confucian ideas of particularism, emphasis on long-term relational development, asymmetrical reciprocity, the drawing of clear distinctions between in-group and out-groups members, use of informal intermediaries, and the overlapping of personal with public relations have led to four characteristics of East Asian communication patterns: (a) process orientation, (b) differentiated linguistic codes, (c) indirect communication emphasis, and (d) receiver centeredness (p. 381).[4]

The logic of these analyses is that relational hierarchical structures compel the individual to emphasize maintaining social harmony and respecting the role of each individual in society, leading, in turn, to language behavior that protects face, avoids conflict, matches behaviors, communicates indirectly, and places greater burdens on the receiver to interpret a given message (Bond & Wang, 1983; Cheng, Bond, & Chan, 1995; Goldman, 1994; Gudykunst & Ting-Toomey, 1992; Kim & Bresnahan, 1994; Kim, Sharkey, & Singelis, 1994; Kim & Wilson, 1994; Ting-Toomey, 1988). In a seminal analysis of Asian communication as observed from classical texts, Oliver (1971) notes, "the primary function of discourse [of Asian rhetoric] is not to enhance the welfare of the individual speaker or listener but to promote harmony" (p. 261).

Due to these emphases, attitudes toward language and words in Confucian societies are said to contrast sharply with those in North America (Gudykunst & Kim, 1992; Oliver, 1971). In addition to Hofstede's (1981) findings that many Asian societies tend to be high on both collectivism and power distance (see also Bond & Wang, 1983; Cheng et al., 1995), Confucian values are seen as virtually interchangeable with collectivist values, as summarized in this description by Gudykunst and Ting-Toomey (1992):

> The value orientation of collectivism, in contrast, constrains members of cultures such as China, Japan, and Korea from speaking boldly through explicit verbal communication style. Collectivist cultures like China, Japan, and Korea emphasize the importance of group harmony and group conformity. Group harmony and group conformity are accomplished through the use of imprecise, ambiguous verbal communication behaviors.
>
> (p. 225)

Although Yum (1988) contends that the individualism–collectivism dichotomy (Triandis, 1988, 1995) "is not identical to the difference between the East Asian's emphasis on social relationships and North American emphasis on individualism" (p. 375), characteristics of Confucian communication described in her article—such as the tendency toward indirectness—are frequently cited as attributes of collectivist cultures (for example, Kim & Bresnahan, 1994). Yum's (1988) examination of Confucianism has been used to explain idiosyncratic features of Asian communication, including high-context communication (Gudykunst & Kim, 1992) and tactics of request (Kim & Bresnahan, 1994; Kim & Wilson, 1994).

These and other lines of research connect Confucianism and collectivism (said to be the principal defining feature of Asian cultures). Confucian philosophy is thus seen as a force inclining Asian cultures toward high-context and collectivist communication that emphasizes role hierarchy and relations rather than the expression of self through direct communication. Inevitably, language behaviors shaped by Confucianism are found to be composed of sets of externally prescribed rules (Goldman, 1994; Oliver, 1971; Yang, 1981), or as Goldman (1994) describes it, "codes of Confucian business and social etiquette requiring adherence to rule-governed interaction" (p. 34). Oliver (1971), in a similar fashion, concludes that Confucian traditions "stressed the value of adhering strictly to patterns of expectations" (p. 262).

Although such studies have contributed to better understanding of Asian communication, they tend to confine their analyses by referring exclusively to the factor of relational hierarchy as espoused by Confucianism. As I look at the *Analects* in detail, it will be clear that the Confucian view of language and words, built on a sophisticated moral and ethical cosmology emphasizing integration between self and others, proves more complex and interesting than the picture resulting from the current focus.

Issues of Words and Speaking in the *Analects*

In the *Analects*, the focus is not on communication as such but on words and speaking. Confucius either explicitly discusses, or refers to, words and speaking throughout the *Analects*. Seventeen of 20 books address these issues in 63 chapters. Examination of these chapters reveals four orientations Confucius takes toward language and words: (a) words define and reflect moral development, (b) beautiful words lacking substance are blameworthy, (c) actions are more important than words, and (d) appropriate speaking relies on rules of propriety. The Confucian analytic framework concentrates not so much on problems associated with people talking to one another and the process of communication but rather on what one chooses to talk about and in what ways.

Words define and reflect moral development

Confucius claimed a direct link between words and virtue, viewing speech as neither simply a tool for mutual understanding nor an instrument for personal gain but an indicator of the speaker's morality. This concern for consistency between internal character and external form points up the most important aspect of Confucian speaking: How moral character is reflected in the individual's words. As a seeker of moral perfection, Confucius avoids plausible words (V, 24) because "plausible words confound virtues" (XV, 26). Because slow speakers are unlikely to pay attention to external appearances, to speak slowly and bluntly may in fact be closer to humanity (*jen*) (XIII, 27).

Confucius elaborates the relation between virtue and words: "Those who are virtuous surely have something good to say, whereas those who have something good to say are not necessarily virtuous" (XIV, 5). If one cultivates oneself inside, character flows out through one's words— words that benefit society (Mao, 1988)—and one will have no problem in speaking. But the opposite is not true: Eloquence is no proof of virtue, and those who merely talk may become eloquent for the sake of eloquence (Soothill, 1968). These are people who can only talk, being unable to put their words into action (Mao, 1988).

Moreover, attitudes toward one's own moral conduct are more important than words.

Responding to Duke Ting's question about the common saying, "a single sentence could make a country prosperous," Confucius explains that such an effect cannot be expected from one sentence. Nevertheless, if Duke Ting were to understand the meaning of some statement, such as "it is difficult to be a prince, nor is it easy to be a minister," then we might say this could almost be considered as an example illustrating the principle that "one sentence can make a country prosperous" (XIII, 15).

Because language is a natural product of moral quality, "From the accuracy or inaccuracy of a man's[5] speech his obliquity or uprightness may be gauged" (Soothill, 1968, p. 932). Being able to detect the moral development of a speaker through careful examination of the words he or she employs is seen as a major task in understanding others. As Confucius put it, "He who does not know the force of words, cannot know men" (XX, 3). Because words are the most accurate index of virtue, to know people is to know their words.

However, this understanding is not simply "knowing who the speaker really is," but an essential task for humanity: Through examining words, one can distinguish good from bad. "Not to speak with one who can be spoken with is to waste a man; to speak with one who cannot be spoken with is to waste one's words. The intelligent man neither wasters his man nor his words" (XV, 7).

Confucius also suggests that people should incorporate moral qualities in their talk, avoiding speech that causes them to stray from virtue. Confucius comments that those who talk incessantly and whose conversation never ascends to what is just and right will have no way to attain virtue (XV, 16). Soothill's (1968) translation of the commentary notes: "When moral obligation does not enter into conversation then talk becomes loose, and a demoralizing spirit is produced" (p. 740). That is not to say that one should lecture others about what is right and wrong; the importance of the lesson lies in the awareness of applying moral obligations as guiding principles for speech. Confucius said that the virtues will necessarily have something good to say. Through enrichment of the mind, one will be able to use moral standards to guide various forms of conduct, among which words are but a single kind. Those who talk continually without regard for what is moral, just, and right do so because they neglect to develop their moral qualities.

Confucius notes that one of the three kinds of beneficial pleasure is to discuss the excellence of others (XVI, 5), exposing discussants to better human qualities, so that such qualities will become a major concern and lead ultimately to gradual change in character toward morality. On the other hand, the virtuous must avoid other kinds of talk: "[The] superior man . . . detests men who proclaim others' misdeeds, men who occupy lower positions [and] slander their superiors, men who are bold and mannerless, and men who are persistently forward and yet obtuse" (XVII, 24). To indulge in such language is to deny oneself the opportunity for spiritual improvement.

To cultivate virtue, one must be cautious about what one says and reflect before speaking. Being quick to speak is incompatible with the cultivation of virtue (Legge, 1985, p. 385). For example, Confucius notes: To proclaim on the road what you hear on the way is to discard virtues" (XVII, 14). If one hears something and repeats it without taking care to consider it sufficiently, one abuses language. Because words can be manipulated (that is, employed in ways that do not reflect a speaker's inner convictions), one who cannot discern the potential defects of language cannot be virtuous.

The virtuous are always careful of their words (I, 14) because (as noted in a quotation from Tzu-Kung in the *Analects*) "The superior man for one word is often deemed wise, and for one word is often deemed foolish" (XIX, 25). Confucius lists nine points with which a superior man must take care, including speaking: "In speaking, his care is to be conscientious" (XV, 10), an attitude equally applicable to learning. In learning, one must broadly study, put aside that which is doubtful, and speak with due caution concerning the rest; in this way, one will seldom incur blame (II, 18). Soothill (1968) notes that "to hear and observe much is the widening of culture; to reserve the doubtful and risky is the essence of selection (discretion); to speak and act warily is the restraining advantage of self-control" (p. 168). Creel (1960) notes that "we must understand what we can, and concerning the rest maintain suspended judgment" (p. 135). Not being demonstrative, the virtuous are often cautious about their words and slow in speaking, and thus, able to discern the good from the bad, qualities that help them to attain virtue.

Along with a cautious attitude toward words, the *Analects* also praised the ability to express oneself with humility. For example, Confucius lauds those who do not boast. The warrior, he says, is the last to flee in the face of defeat, and although this may be considered honorable, the warrior refuses to boast. Instead, he says, "It is not that I dare to be in the rear; my horse would not come [forward]" (VI, 13). This gentle refusal to acknowledge accomplishment is praiseworthy because if one remains humble, one is unsatisfied, and to be unsatisfied with oneself is the best incentive to attain higher levels of virtue.

In discussing the dreams of four students, Confucius relates that one student expressed his ambition in these terms:

> Give me a kingdom of a thousand chariots, hemmed in by two great powers, oppressed by invading troops, with famine suppurated, and let me have its administration—in three years' time I could make it brave and, moreover, make it know the right course to pursue.

At this, Confucius smiled. When another student asked why, Confucius replied, "The administration of a country demands the rule of propriety, but his speech lacked modesty—that is why I smiled at him" (XI, 25). Although Confucius granted his student might have been able to achieve his ambition, the student's lack of modesty showed moral deficiency. Confucius believed that governing a country depends entirely on the ruler's moral qualities (Fung, 1983). Because cultivating moral qualities is the basis for ruling, rulers must be considerate toward subjects and willing to accept advice given by others. Being bold and aggressive in speech shows lack of the most important qualities needed to govern the nation.

From these examples, we observe the importance of humility in speech. To be humble in speech is not merely an external manifestation but the expression of a humble heart seeking life's best experiences to develop moral stature. Virtue is not only the basis for speaking, it is essential to moral development. As King (1985) puts it, "Confucianism is distinctly concerned with the concept of self-cultivation. Indeed, the moral autonomy of the self is unequivocally affirmed by Confucians" (p. 57).

Unfortunately, in scholarly discussion of Confucianism and Confucian philosophy, scant attention is paid to Confucius's dictums about primacy of the self and its moral development. Instead, the Confucian perspective is often rendered as a set of rules guiding specific language behaviors, irrespective of content, precisely the opposite of what Confucius taught. If we do not inquire into the *Analects* to discover the true spirit of the Confucian view of language, we will allow ill-conceived stereotypes about Confucian societies to dictate our analyses of their use of language and words.

Beautiful words lacking substance are blameworthy

The *Analects* shows clearly Confucius's distaste for artifice in speaking. For Confucius, "Beautiful words, insinuating manners, are lacking in human-heartedness [*jen*]" (I, 3). *Jen* is the fundamental perfection of virtue, incorporating all moral qualities that guide human interaction. Beautiful words that do not accord with true feelings but cleverly flatter others are judged hypocritical and, thus, lacking in *jen* (Legge, 1985, p. 126). Commenting on this passage, Mao (1988) notes, "*Jen* emphasizes putting morality into action. In this hypocritical world, if one wants to know the other's morality, one needs to observe another's actual behavior, rather than to evaluate from the other's language and manners alone" (p. 3).

Having lived through the violent Warring States period of Chinese history, Confucius most despised the "sharp tongued" who overthrow the nation (XVII, 18), even while acknowledging that such people can manipulate events: "The keen tongued can make things look the very opposite, the worthy unworthy and vice versa, so that if a Prince believed them, it would not be difficult to overthrow his country" (Soothill, 1968, p. 840). Through artful speech, right and wrong can be confused, and people find themselves unable to attain virtue. Hence, Confucius argues, good people should first distance themselves from the sharp tongued and then avoid contradictory language (XIV, 39).

Unfortunately, glib speakers who confuse moral standards often seem to rule rather than the exception. Observing politics, Confucius grieves: "A decadent age loves flattery and takes pleasure in external charms . . . without these it is hard to get on" (VI, 14; Soothill, 1968, p. 304). One characteristic of the sharp tongued is that their artful speech often does not accord with what they think, but is only uttered verbally (Soothill, 1968). Because of the potential danger inherent in sharp-tongued speech, Confucius said that, to govern, one must "distance [oneself] from specious talkers" (XV, 10).

The wisdom needed to detect falsehood in artful political speech is equally useful in personal life. Much as governors are advised to distance themselves from specious talkers, one should not make friends with such people because they may damage one's virtue. Elaborating the distinction between good and bad qualities of friendship, Confucius described three kinds of harmful friends: "Plausible men, [those with] insinuating manners, and the glib-tongued" (XVI, 4). One must avoid friends who are simply polite without being straightforward, practice insincere flattery, and engage in empty talk without substantial information (Soothill, 1968, p. 788).

This attitude toward words can also be seen in two stories of interactions between Confucius and his students. At one point, Confucius praises a student, noting that although the person seldom speaks, whatever he says hits the right point (XI, 13). Another story concerns making excuses. In an argument over a military action proposed by a student's Prince, but which Confucius thought inappropriate, Confucius criticized the student for not being able to perform his duty as an officer by guiding the Prince to do the right thing. The student replied by telling Confucius the reason why the action was necessary and unavoidable. However, Confucius responded, "A superior man detests those who decline to say plainly that they want a thing and insist on making excuses in regard hereto" (XVI, 1). Such dishonesty, insincerity, and inconsistency between the internal and external stand in opposition to the Confucian view of language.

An important Confucian virtue is "basic stuff" (*chih*, and its accompanying quality, uprightness). To cultivate *chih*, one must project true outward expressions, not deceive others, and reject all empty form and falseness (Fung, 1983). Confucius never hesitated to show his distaste for those who cultivate forms of speaking not consonant with their genuine internal states. As Oliver (1971) puts it, Confucian philosophy "turned attention inward, inviting people to examine themselves, rather than outward, to seek to influence others . . . a man who cannot rectify himself . . . surely cannot improve others" (p. 132).

By attending to internal content and avoiding external manipulation, we let sincerity and truthfulness guide our words. Whether one is sincere in uttering words determines whether one will be accepted by others:

> If you are sincere and truthful in what you say, and trustworthy and circumspect in what you do, even if you are in a barbarian land you will get on with people without any difficulty; if you are not sincere and truthful in what you say, neither are you trustworthy and circumspect in what you do, you will not be able to get on with people in your own home town.
>
> (XV, 5)

The student Tzu-Lu could solve a dispute by "a half sentence" because he never broke a promise (XII, 12). Soothill (1968) notes, Tzu-Lu's "sincerity and acuteness made men submit to his decisions without waiting for him to finish speaking" (p. 582). The power of words, then, rests on such speaker attributes as sincerity and truthfulness. When people trust the speaker's sincerity, words themselves are unimportant, because whatever the speaker says will be accepted.

Because speech comes from within, readiness to speak is also unimportant (V, 4). The *Analects* recounts several instances in which people who do not talk very well are nevertheless virtuous. Observing his student Hui receiving instruction, Confucius notes the importance of conduct as contrasted with the unreliable index of language:

> I have talked with Hui for a whole day and he never raised an objection, as if he were stupid; but when he withdrew and I examined his conduct when not with me, I nevertheless found him fully competent to demonstrate what I had taught him. . . . He was not stupid at all!
>
> (II, 9)

Readiness to speak often leads one to focus on external expression and ignore the internal mind, and hence, one can only engender dislike in others (V, 4). How should one use language for self-expression? As Confucius stated, "in language it is simply required that it convey the meaning" (XV, 40). As long as language is sufficient for clear meaning, whether it is ornate or not is unimportant.

From observations like these, one sees the essence of language and speaking in Confucianism: Language and words must be used according to what is right and appropriate, as determined by the speaker's level of spiritual training. Confucius considered one Chinese classic, the *Book of Odes*, an important teaching resource. Advising students to study the book, Confucius noted: "Odes serve to stimulate the mind, to train observation, to encourage social intercourse, and to modify the vexations of life" (XVII, 9). Thus, the *Book of Odes* serves as a basis for people to engage in social intercourse with others: "If you do not learn the Odes, you will not be fit to converse with" (XVI, 13). Well-cultivated, superior people enrich themselves internally before expressing themselves to others.

These tenets of Confucianism—that external forms are untrustworthy and one should be unwilling to express oneself outwardly until one is cultivated inside—are virtually ignored in scholarly literature. On the contrary, hesitancy in language use is often cast, not as a self-initiated attempt at internal refinement, but the result of society-imposed constraints. Such accounts diminish the essential role played by the speaker in Confucian societies and lead us mistakenly to conclude that language use in Confucian societies is a mechanistic response to structure. This is a considerable distance from the Confucian teaching that beautiful words often are blameworthy because they lack substance.

Actions are more important than words

A third issue regarding the role of speaking is to be deduced from the relation between speaking and actions. According to Confucius, there must be a match between words and actions: "The superior man is ashamed of his speaking exceeding his actions" (XIV, 29). In speaking, the most important thing is to be able to put words into practice; otherwise, words are merely empty form. To Confucius, actions were far more important than speaking. Confucius defined a superior person as one who wishes to be slow in speech but earnest in his actions (IV, 24), or more specifically, as someone who "acts before he speaks, and afterwards speaks according to his actions" (II, 13). Confucius praised the excellence of ancient people in speaking: "People of ancient times did not readily give utterance to their words out of shame lest they should come short in deed" (IV, 22). However, one must also note that making actions correspond with one's words is not the result of blind persistence but rather because such actions accord to what is right (I, 13).

Four important points clarify the Confucian view of word-action correspondence. First, the importance of action in Confucian philosophy is seen in Confucius's emphasis on observing one's words against one's behavior. Confucius cautioned that even if a person's speech and discourse seem solid, one is still not sure that this individual must be a superior person (XI, 20). Legge (1985) notes "we may not hastily judge a man to be good from his discourse" (p. 269). Words create a world that extends beyond one's actions. Therefore, one must not simply trust others' words without checking their deeds: "Observe what the person does. . . . How can a person hide himself!" (II, 10) (see also XII, 20). Although Confucius would like to trust people's words as guarantees of their conduct, unfortunately, such an ideal situation seldom exists in a morally imperfect world. Criticizing one of his students who overslept, Confucius remarked, "Formerly, my attitude toward others was to hear their words and give them credits for their deeds. Now my attitude toward others is to listen to their words and note what they do" (V, 9).

However, checking the conduct of others against their words does not mean that one should make rigid, indiscriminate judgment about others. Confucius taught that "the superior man does not promote a person simply on account of his words, not does he put aside good words because of the man's character" (XV, 22). In other words, when participating in politics, one must be able to discriminate between people and what they say (Soothill, 1968, p. 746). One must be cautious not to be overwhelmed by others' words, but at the same time, one must remain open minded in accepting good words uttered by someone who may be wicked. Even a wicked person may be sincere when uttering good words. Moreover, there are also situations in which one's words are usually good. Master Tseng said, "When a bird is about to die, his notes are mournful; when a man is about to die, his words are good" (VIII, 4).

A second indication of the importance of action in Confucian thought is seen in observations about giving advice. "To words of just admonition can anyone refuse assent?" Confucius asks. "But it is amendment that is of value. With advice gently but persuasively offered can anyone be otherwise than pleased? But it is the application that is of value. Mere interest without application, mere assent without amendment—for such a man I can do nothing whatever" (IX, 23). Even though one may be willing to follow advice, only advice that is applied is important— otherwise, advice has no impact.

Third, because of the worry over being unable to carry out one's words, boasting and exaggerating, together with other forms of extravagant speech, are especially to be avoided because "he who speaks without modesty will perform with difficulty" (XIV, 21).[6] In giving advice to one of his students who had a loose tongue, Confucius said that a virtuous man is one who is hesitant in his speech (XII, 3). Soothill (1968) notes: "The good man is not demonstrative, hence his hesitancy in speech . . . which forms one feature of moral character" (p. 562). Because Confucius emphasized the correspondence between words and actions, if one is unable to perfect linkage, one should simply refuse to say anything. Hence, being hesitant in speech is one way to cultivate virtue (Mao, 1988, p. 185). On the other hand, being sincere in carrying out one's words constitutes only the first step toward humanity. When asked what constitutes a scholar, Confucius replied that the most important factor is a sense of shame, the next being filial and fraternal, and the next being "sincere in what they say and carrying our what they do" (XIII, 20).

Fourth, the relative importance of words and deeds can be seen in the nature of things. Universal principles manifest themselves directly for human beings to contemplate, and for this reason, words may not be important at all. Unfortunately, few people understand the depth of universal principles; rather, they treat language as the only means to acquire truth. This point is exemplified in the following story. "I wish I could do without speaking," Confucius said. "If you do not speak, Sir," asked Tzu-Kung, "what should we disciples pass on to others?" Confucius replied, "What speech does Heaven have? The four seasons run their courses and all things flourish, yet what speech does Heaven have?" (XVII, 19). To this, Soothill (1968, p. 842) translates the commentary as follows: "So every motion of the Sage was a revelation of his profound Truth and essential rectitude, indeed [a manifestation of] Heaven itself, and why wait for speech to see him revealed." The sage wished to model himself after Heaven; for this reason, "it is no wonder that Confucius said very little about the Way of Heaven; he simply preferred to follow Heaven's example and remain speechless on the subject (Liu, 1996, p. 94). Confucius set up examples through his own conduct rather than his words. The discrepancy in recognizing the importance of language in searching for universal principles between Confucius and his students explains why Confucius is considered as the Master (Fung, 1983).

Words are but an imperfect means through which one gets in touch with the world; they are used to compensate for the inability of the human mind to comprehend Heaven's teaching through the manifestation of things. The words of the sage serve to lead people to the fundamental realization of the universe, which then serves as a model for them to emulate. Hence, the superior person stands in awe of the words of sages, whereas the inferior person insults the words of sages (XVI, 8). Here we see the interconnection among moral development, words, and the principles of the universe. When one is able to observe and contemplate the world directly and comes to understand the universal principle, *Tao* (the Way), and to act in accordance with it, words are simply not necessary.[7]

For Confucius, language stands at the nexus between human affairs and the universe. If the universe can manifest itself through the multiplicity of extant things and if actions can speak for themselves, one often need not bother with words. It is unfortunate that such an elevated view of language is almost never encountered in current literature which focuses primarily on the easily observed aspects of language and words in Confucian societies, too frequently concluding that unwillingness to speak results from the overwhelming effects of social structure.

Appropriate speaking relies on rules of propriety

Because speaking has such strong moral connotations, use of language, for Confucius, is not simply an external act following a rigid moral code, but must accord to one's own heart and the cultivation of virtue (Creel, 1960). This attention to the human mind can be refined by attending to *li*, the rules of propriety, which are based on human emotion and the principles of Heaven and Earth (Fung, 1983). Observation of human emotion in turn leads to appropriate speaking according to different situations and relationships.

According to Fung (1983), "All the rules for everything pertaining to human conduct may be included under the terms of *li*" (p. 68). It is only through *li* that one learns to be a superior person, someone able to carry *li* into practice by genuine nature (Fung, 1983). *Li* is the basis of human-heartedness (*jen*). When asked what is *jen*, Confucius contended that to restrain oneself to respond to propriety (*li*) is the essence of *jen*, and that without *li*, one has no way to establish oneself (XVI, 13). Hence, words should be employed to keep away from vulgarity and impropriety (VIII, 4). Confucius further elaborates four aspects of human conduct that must be in accord with *li*: looking, listening, speaking, and moving (XII, 1). Cultivation of virtue must come from one's seemingly insignificant everyday conduct (Mao, 1988), including speaking and behaving.

Li arises from human emotion; hence, one's speech much also correspond to what is appropriate according to human emotion. Propriety implies that the speaker needs to be attuned to emotional concerns relating to the other and flexible in appreciating different contexts.

Because a major focus in Confucianism lies in delineating interpersonal relationships, it is important to see how the content of speech varies according to different types of relationship. For example, although people may consider frankness as expression of sincerity, Confucius contended that frankness without rules of propriety will lead one to rudeness (VIII, 2), and hence be against human emotion. One well-known example is Confucius's contention that a son aggressively criticizing his father for misconduct is not upright because such behavior is against human nature (XIII, 18). Given the emotional tie between the father and son, it is only natural for a father to conceal the misconduct of his son, and the son do the same on behalf of his father. "Mutual screening between father and son is the highest law of Nature, and of humanity" (Soothill, 1968, p. 632). Fung (1983) explains that "the son either wished to get the name of uprightness through sacrificing his father, or lacked feeling toward his father. Hence this could not be true uprightness" (p. 67). Uprightness must be expressed in a refined or cultured way: "Love of straightforwardness without a love to learn finds itself obscured by warped judgment" (XVII, 8).

Talking is a form of politeness as well as an exhibition of "being cultured." In serving superior people, Confucius contends that appropriate speaking depends on the right timing. There are three kinds of errors regarding speaking: speaking before the time to speak, not speaking when it is time to speak, and speaking without observing the superior man's countenance (XVI, 6). One of the virtues discussed in the *Analects* is to speak only at an appropriate time so that people will not be tired of one's talk (XIV, 14). Because the superior man is serious in showing respect toward his own conduct, even in boarding a carriage, he does not talk hastily (X, 17). While eating and while in bed, Confucius did not speak (X, 8). Only by so doing did Confucius feel in accord with etiquette (Fung, 1983).

To speak appropriately, one must have the flexibility to attend to different situations and different types of relationships. For example, in his village, Confucius talked with simplicity and humbleness as if he had not gifts of speech, whereas in the ancestral temple or at the Court, he expressed himself readily and clearly (X, 1). In the village, one interacted with relatives and friends, so that there was no need to speak fluently, whereas in the places such as Court or temple—the source of law—where things must be placed in discrete order, it was necessary that talk be precise, ready, clear, and specific, though spoken with a reserved manner (Legge, 1985, p. 244; Mao, 1988). In talking to people of different ranks, Confucius also conducted himself differently: He was free and straightforward when talking to officers of lower rank, affable and precise when talking to officers of higher rank, and when the Prince was present, he conducted himself respectfully and with self-possession (X, 2). An *Analects* passage by Tzu-Hsia well describes Confucius himself: "The superior man varies from three aspects. Seen from a distance he appears stern, when approached he proves gracious, as you listen to him you find his language firm and serious" (XIX, 9). Here the emphasis is placed on the meaning and spirit of the social forms rather than simply on the outer form and manner of expression. It is imperative that "a man must have a sincere genuineness before he may practice ceremony and etiquette" (Fung, 1983, p. 66).

It should be noted that Confucius himself does not argue against people who are gifted at speech. In one chapter (XI, 2), for example, gifts of speech are considered to be an accomplishment[8] of one of his students. In another chapter (V, 7), Confucius points out that one student—who was famous for his knowledge of rules of ceremony, particularly relating to dress and conversational intercourse (Legge, 1985)—could be employed to converse with guests, even though he did not know whether this student could be said to have perfect virtue. Although Confucius argued against beautiful words because they lack sincerity as their foundation, he viewed speaking appropriately and adjusting to different situations and relationships as a gift. Speaking itself is not against the perfect virtue of *jen*; it is only when words uttered do not accord to humanity that words should be condemned. Appropriate speaking in accordance with moral development is to be highly esteemed.[9]

This flexibility in speaking according to different kinds of situations is especially important when one must deal with a disordered world. "When order prevails in the nation, one may be bold in speech and bold in action, but when the nation is disordered, one may take bold action and should lay restraint on one's speech" (XIV, 4). Soothill's (1968) translation of Chu Hsi's commentary on the *Analects* notes that "the man of honour must hold his convictions unshaken, but there are times when to escape calamity he may not dare to express himself freely" (p. 652). Legge (1985) notes, "What one does must always be right; what one feels need not always be spoken—a lesson of prudence (p. 315). Mao (1988) explains:

> Restraint in one's language is not uttering fake words, nor does it reverse truth and falsehood; it just means that one should be more circumscribed in one's words . . . it is fine if one is restrained in one's words to protect oneself, but it is wrong if it leads the society to calamity.
>
> (p. 214)

When accused of being glib by reclusive Taoists, Confucius replied, "A glib talker I would not dare to be, and I should hate to be obstinately immovable" (XIV, 34). To Confucius, what is more important is to help the nation restore order, a process in which language plays a significant role. So long as one's external expression matches inner genuineness, speaking cannot be faulted. Thus, the Confucian ideal of speaking must be viewed as active and oriented toward the world.[10] The discriminating application of rules for speaking is not what is conventionally considered "playing different games in different situations." One's ability to adjust to different contexts effortlessly is a stage achieved only after a life-long learning process.

Although many investigators have often sought explanations for Asian communication behaviors in the presumed influence of Confucian relational hierarchy, conceptions of relational hierarchy remain very narrowly defined. Instead of a flexible social mechanism attuned to different degrees of emotion and situational factors (as articulated by the *Analects*), scholars tend to construe relational hierarchy as culturally imposed rules clearly spelling out how people of different relations ought to behave toward each other. This not only distorts Confucianism, it also, in general, reinforces mistaken assumptions about how rules are used to guide social actions, whether in language use or otherwise.

Rethinking attitudes toward language and words in Confucian societies

Recapturing the Confucian vision

The Confucian model treats language use as inextricably tied to the speaker's moral reasoning and appreciation of varying relationships and situations based on human emotion, viewing language as merely an imperfect means through which individuals convey ideas. To have force, words must be backed by a highly developed moral character. If one's morality—including one's sincerity, truthfulness, genuine state of mind, and ability to follow propriety—has been appropriately developed, one should be able to formulate messages naturally and spontaneously, and these words will affect others regardless of the form in which they are expressed. Confucius reasoned that words will be effective not because one is able to articulate language to construct images but because listeners will naturally be moved (persuaded) by the virtue of speakers.

Confucius held that one must not be oriented exclusively toward the self but must be cognizant of the presence of others who occupy various social positions. For Confucius, the personal and the social are not two conflicting categories: It is the integration of the two that constitutes the foundation of any individual's morality. More important, the ability to integrate the personal and the social in one's use of language represents not merely constraints imposed by the social rules but also the possibility to achieve understanding of the infinite multitude of possible interpersonal connections and the social fabric they weave. Indeed, the effective communicator is someone who can prioritize actions ahead of words, who appreciates contexts and relationships, and who need not be a particularly fluent speaker. The goal is to refine the language one uses not simply because society formally dictates it but because the formal language itself carries the spirit of social complexity as constituted in the diverse relationships among those who occupy various social roles.

Problems of current interpretation

Although links established in scholarly literature between Asian attitudes towards words and Confucianism (in all of its admittedly considerable complexity) have been valuable, these studies have obviously been limited. As I have shown, among four orientations in the *Analects*, only one—communication according to different relationships—has been extensively discussed, leaving the remaining three essentially ignored, thus resulting in a distorted picture of the Confucian view of language. This should be particularly troubling to scholars of language and social psychology because the key element in constructing theories of language use in Asian cultures (the Confucian view of language) has been misapprehended—if the key element is misunderstood, then the theory as a whole must be called into question.

Especially problematic is the prevailing view that assumes that indirect forms of communication result from role prescriptions that work at the expense of individual self-expression. This assumption, coupled with a narrow rendering of the Confucian idea of different orders of relationships, paints a picture of Asian use of language as a process plagued by restraint and limitation rather than the product of a sophisticated yet flexible moral reasoning that underpins externally manifested communicative activities. This interpretation—laden with Western value judgments—prevents us from developing better theories to account for language attitudes and behaviors in Confucian societies. Specifically, there are five problems with current interpretation.

The first problem may be one of scholarly priorities. By foregrounding the collectivist metaphor (with associated concepts of situational orientation and social harmony), scholars have subordinated the complete Confucian view.[11] Under the powerful influence of the idea of collectivism—particularly as opposed to individualism—scholarly have favored a structural view of Confucian societies that ignores the role of the individual. The harder one tries to differentiate individualism and collectivism, the easier it is to conclude that collectivist (that is, nonindividualist) cultures use language in collectivist ways—that is, according to the dictates of external rules and constraints.

As King says, "[T]he fundamental weakness of the structural conception of Chinese society lies in its failure to recognize that the individuals who comprise the society have selves, which are particularly stressed, as shown above, in Confucian ethics" (King, 1985, p. 60). Countering the widespread view that Confucius emphasized collectivist values, King (1985) offers the notion of "self-centered voluntarism" (p. 57) to show how central Confucian ethics are to Chinese cultures. Triandis (1995) notes that "when reading Confucius . . . one is struck by the extent to which some of his statements urged people to be individualists" (p. 21). By putting individual speakers back into analyses of language in Confucian societies, we will be better able to construct theories not merely about how social structure influences language but also how people use discourse relevant to their moral judgments to create and reconstruct their social identities.

A second problem, closely related to the structural interpretation of Confucian views of language, comes from assuming that social position is incompatible with individual will. Assuming this, scholars conclude that if culture does not emphasize individual free will, it must emphasize control through social position. This dichotomous thinking is a problem not only with cross-cultural research but also with studies of social cognition and language use. Harré (1981) sees this separation of individual and society as problematic: "Not only is much of our social knowledge socially located, but . . . some very important cognitive processes are not inner and private, but public and collective" (p. 212).

Confucius, too, refused to see society as opposed to the individual. As King (1985) says, "Confucians focus on the organic relationship between the individual and society and consider the two inseparable and interdependent . . . the problem is that 'society' is only vaguely defined, as is the idea of 'group' if one is referring to a unit larger than the family" (p. 57). Although the current consensus is that Confucian values emphasize the in-group, the concept of 'in-group"— at least for the Chinese—is not precisely defined (Chang & Holt, 1991; King, 1985; Ward, 1968).[12] Surprisingly, whereas scholars acknowledge that, in the main, individuals are central in producing social discourse, theories of language use in Confucian societies generally ignores the significance of the individual. This leads theorists to disregard the complexity of language behaviors in such cultures and thereby to miss the most noteworthy linguistic achievements of their people.

The connections between individual and society, actualized by dynamic, even-expanding webs of relationships enacted by those in Confucian cultures, engenders an expressive and sophisticated discourse not confined by but integrating social rules. Although current thinking suggests that in using language, speakers should strive to go beyond social rules—to break out of limitations implied by social structure—the Confucian attitude suggests that the ability to integrate social rules with socially enacted language represents a higher level of development that must be seen as less, not more, limited. In accounting for differences between Confucian and non-Confucian societies, we need to look not at differences in how much members' language behaviors are controlled by social rules but how social rules can be actualized differently through language use in Confucian and non-Confucian cultures. We would do well to heed Robinson and Giles (1990), who suggest that research needs to "be open-minded and careful in the application of models derived in one culture when attempting to export them to others" (p. 4). If we can jettison the Western conception that individual will and social positioning are incompatible, we stand a better change of gaining new insight into language behavior in Confucian cultures.

A third problem is the exclusion of moral character from discussions of language use in Confucian societies. As we have seen, Confucius viewed communication according to different orders of relationships as manifesting moral character, a lifelong developmental process through which one learns to let emotion express itself naturally. It is essential, then, to take the moral element into account when constructing theories about language use in Confucian societies. Current accounts limit communicative activity in Confucian cultures only to what society dictates should be said and how, leaving unaddressed questions of how speakers in these cultures, despite relational prescriptions, use sophisticated reasoning that builds on and refines the internal moral foundation.

An example will serve to illustrate. The fact that Chinese, more than Westerners, avoid direct confrontation in conflict situations has less to do with avoidance of conflict to protect social harmony than with the belief that if the conflicting parties are sincere toward each other, the conflict will be resolved in the course of events, without the necessity for conflicting parties to bring up the matter themselves. Moreover, emphasis may be placed on self-examination and self-development before expressing one's own viewpoint, particularly when criticizing the other party. Scholars attempting to theorize about this communicative context (ubiquitous throughout Confucian cultures) are apt to mistakenly conclude that role constraints prevent expression of dissatisfaction toward the other party.

A fourth problem in the current view lies in assuming that personal freedom is the essence of the ability to reason and formulate messages (as implied by the widespread applications of theories about elaborated code and low-context communication). Assuming this, scholars conclude that because it restricts personal freedom, the Confucian dictum that language be used simply to convey ideas without ornamentation is, in either a mental or a social sense, limited.

Confucius said that those who focus too much on linguistic embellishment lose the ability to cultivate themselves internally. Those who utter words lacking in substance are morally deficient. Thus, elaborated code, particularly if unsupported by the speaker's morality or actions, is condemned as merely an expression of meaningless linguistic ornamentation. In theorizing about language use in Confucian societies, scholars should realize that it is possible that restricted speakers may simply be unwilling to use language to create a reality that exceeds what they perceive as their level of internal development.

In other words, theoretical explanations of observed divergence between language use by members of Confucian and non-Confucian cultures may not lie in personal freedom or creativity but rather in another variable, perhaps relating to whether people in Confucian societies consider language use necessary. Scholars should look for causes not solely in the broader social structure but also in the conversants' subjective assessment of the need to speak.

This distinction is particularly important because Confucius saw actions as more important than words—actions speak for themselves. Confucius repeatedly says that words or messages can be done away with if suitable action has occurred. At the very least, there must, in the Confucian ideal, be a match between words and actions. Indeed, one of the ultimate goals of Confucian philosophy is to contemplate the principles of the universe without even using words. It is misguided to assume that Confucianism affects Asian societies either by influencing them to dispense with words as merely as way to avoid disruption of social harmony or else as a helpless bending to the power of omnipotent hierarchical interpersonal structure. In fact, it should now be clear that the emphasis on external formality devoid of substance is the last thing Confucius would advocate.

The final problem with the current view comes from the tendency to explain Confucianism retroactively after analyses about language behaviors in Confucian societies have been made (see Wheeler et al., 1989). The assumption is that what is observed in Confucian societies reflects what was taught by Confucius. Without understanding the complexity of Confucian philosophy, observed communication practices in Confucian societies are likely to be labeled rigid and constraining, compared to the Western ideal of the expressive, free-willed speaker. By tying such practices back to Confucian philosophy, the belief that Confucian values emphasize primarily relational hierarchy and social harmony are reaffirmed.

Although social and political reality in various Asian nations may result in negative interpretations of Confucianism[13] (Liu, 1996), insights about speaking and words in the *Analects* are far more complex, provocative, and interesting than is suggested by current accounts. If we are to construct appropriate theories about language use in Confucian cultures, we must know whether we are making judgments based on hidden Western cultural assumptions or on valid premises that permit us to conduct further analysis.

To appropriately theorize about the Confucian view of language—and perhaps more importantly, how language is used in modern-day Confucianist cultures—one must appreciate the full scope of Confucian perspectives on human emotion, the role of emotion plays in different orders to relationship, the cultivation of virtue and moral character, the coordination of form and substance, the establishment of society, and the overall view of the universe. It is only through such in-depth understanding of the philosophical roots and worldviews of Asian cultures that one can come to understand the meaning of Asian communication.

Epilogue

The semantic dimension of speech (its relation to issues of moral development, need for action, and sense of self) must be explored before venturing into analysis of language behavior in Confucian societies. Because research into the subtle and sophisticated elements of Confucius and Confucianism and their effects on Asian communication have thus far been so narrowly constricted, in the following, I offer a few suggestions concerning theoretical and methodological questions that might be addressed by scholars in the future.

First, how are roles structured and what are their levels of complexity, as understood by speakers of Confucian societies? What precisely are the relations between role hierarchy and these speakers' language behaviors? Although it is true that role relationships in Confucian societies are important in fashioning verbal strategies, the causal connection between the role hierarchy and constrained verbal style cannot be taken for granted.

It is important for scholars to be sensitized to the true referents of the generic term *role* as applied to people of Confucian cultures and how they use this referent to construe their linguistic performances. One could examine the range of manifestations of hierarchical relationships in these societies by examining recorded descriptions in a standard anthropological database such as the Human Relations Area Files. Once the complexity of role hierarchy is understood, scholars will then be in a better position to examine the impact it might have on language behavior. Discourse data on actual conversations of people in Confucian societies should be analyzed to determine how the variable "role hierarchy" relates to the variable "verbal style."

Second, other than structural variables such as role hierarchy, what are some other variables that could account for language behavior in Confucian societies? When analyzing speech behaviors in Confucian societies, account must be taken of other influencing variables. Instead of focusing on role hierarchy as the sole predictor variable for speech behavior, scholars may find it fruitful to introduce individual-level variables such as moral reasoning or emotional consideration either as additional independent variables or as intervening variables to account for language behavior. These variables might be operationalized by asking respondents to generate statements about moral qualities and emotional consideration associated with a specific speech or conversational event and to use these to analyze that event's degree of complexity. It is quite possible that moral reasoning and emotional consideration may prove better predictors for speech behavior than role hierarchy.

Third, apart from commonly used constructs such as collectivism, social harmony, and social orientation, are there alternative ways to describe key features of Confucian societies? Scholars must be dissuaded from giving unjustifiable preference to collectivist metaphors such as social harmony in explaining Confucianism because they fail to adequately account for the subtleties—particularly with respect to the individual's central place—in the Confucian view of communication. One way to do this would be to propose alternative metaphors (in the manner of the "generative metaphors" suggested by Schön, 1979) to account for conversational behavior in Confucian societies (Chang, 1996). As Schön (1979) notes, when metaphors (such as collectivist metaphors) become exhausted from overuse, it is only by introducing fresh, generative metaphors that productive discussion can be reengaged and new insight acquired. For example, if scholars were to describe Confucian societies as emphasizing moral orientation, they would be more likely to acknowledge speakers' active contributions to communicative performance, and not simply as responding to demands of society. This would provide an alternative picture of language behavior in Confucian societies.

Of course, these possibilities only skate the surface of what can be done. The point is that a first step—that of recognizing that what we think we know about Chinese communication and its "Confucian" roots is limited—has now been taken. It is up to scholars of language and social psychology to carry this initial step forward to a new understanding of communication in both Asian and Western cultures.

Notes

1. Several examples from data collected in Taiwan illustrate how Confucian ideas surface in people's speech or conversation. In commenting on why it is not necessary to communicate complaints to one's relational partner, a male respondent said, "Life is like a silent movie," in that much of what is going on is understood without need for verbal explanations. This comment reminds us of *Analects* passage XVII, 19, in which Confucius wonders why Heaven has any need to speak. In another example, a female informant evaluated the Dale Carnegie course in the following terms: "It's better to talk to your parents about these suggestions, because they have sincerity." This echoes the Confucian teaching that words lacking internal foundation are merely external ornamentation. Finally, in interviewing many Taiwanese people regarding whether they should make clear to others what they have done for them, most said it would not be necessary. Almost unanimously, they said, "As long as you try your best, people will know who you are." This statement reflects the Confucian ideal of the person "who wishes to be slow in speech but earnest in actions" (IV, 24).

2. Creel (1960) notes that *Analects* was "not written by [Confucius] but in the main composed near his own time and on the basis of traditions preserved by his disciples" (p. 111).

3. One exception is Oliver (1971), whose approach is rhetorical rather than socio-psychological.

4. Similarly, Chen and Chung (1994) identify the following as indicative of Confucian influence on communication in organizations: (a) explicit communication rules, (b) complementary relationships, (c) in-group/out-group distinction, (d) intermediaries, (e) vague boundaries between personal and public relationships, and (f) similar communication contexts (p. 100).

5. In ancient China, only men were allowed the opportunity to study. The Confucian notion of the "superior man" also refers to women. Moreover, because all of Confucius's students were male, the translation of *Analects* adopts the male pronouns *he* and *him* in light of the sociohistorical circumstances in which the text was composed.

6. Book XIV, chapter 21 of *Analects* has alternative interpretations. Mao (1988), for example, explains this chapter in the following terms: "For a person who is not ashamed of his words, his daily conduct will not be easy" (p. 222). Only if one can face his or her consciousness, can one relate to other people. Such a spiritually elevated state is difficult to attain if the person does not practice virtue in his or her everyday life.

7. This thesis is shared by Confucius with other important figures. Such as Lao-Tzu, in classical Chinese philosophy (see Fung, 1983).

8. The four subject matters mentioned in this chapter—virtue, language, political affairs, and literature—were later called the "four classes" of the Confucian school (Legge, 1985; Mao, 1988). It is interesting to note that language is one of these four classes.

9. Perhaps this is what distinguishes Confucius from the Taoists, who hold that language is more often than not misleading. Taoists exhibit a distaste for language in general, viewing it as an imperfect means of communication. Confucius does not agree with this position.

10. Confucius aimed for balance between internal and external. While maintaining personal virtue, one must also take care of the external world. For Confucius, this meant "looking upon all the worlds as one family, and on China as one person, and he could never for a day forget this" (Soothill, 1968, p. 706).

11. Because Confucian ideals appear to be irreconcilable with Western conceptions, these ideals were subsumed under the umbrella of the collectivist metaphor so that conflicts in cultural values between Confucianism and other perspectives can be resolved (see Xiao, 1995).

12. The Chinese concept of *chia* (home or family), for example, can be extended to include members of a lineage, people who share same interests, and in fact, any person whom another person wants to include. It depends on the individual who serves as the center of a given role relationship (King, 1985).

13. Scholars have pointed to the distinction between Confucian values and Confucianization (as occurred in the case of Chinese) and to the need to take into account historical factors underlying the development of Confucianism (Chang, 1976; King, 1985). King contends that in the Confucian value system, the five cardinal relations were symmetrical. It was through Hsiao Ching that the concept of filial piety became the center of the Chinese ethics system, resulting in asymmetrical relationships that denied recognition of the independent existence of the individual. With further institutional support, Chinese laws underwent a Confucianization that upheld the hierarchical harmony of the family as an unquestioned value. Simply put, problems come from trying to superimpose a governmentally convenient hierarchy onto an essentially unhierarchical philosophical system. Liu (1996) also argues that there are three possible ways to understand Confucianism: as philosophical insights, as a political ideology, and as a storehouse of popular values (p. 111).

References

Bond, M. H., & Hwang, K.-K. (1986). The social psychology of Chinese people. In M. H. Bond (Ed.), *The psychology of the Chinese people* (pp. 213–266). Hong Kong, Oxford University Press.

Bond, M. H., & Wang, S. H. (1983). Aggressive behavior in Chinese society: The problem of maintaining order and social harmony. In A. P. Goldstein & M. Segall (Eds.), *Global perspectives on aggression* (pp. 58–74). New York: Pergamon.

Chan, W.-T. (1963). *A sourcebook in Chinese philosophy.* Princeton, NJ: Princeton University Press.

Chang, H.-C. (1996. November). *"Collectivism" or "competitive bidding": An alternative picture of Chinese communication.* Paper presented at the annual convention of the Speech Communication Association, San Diego, CA.

Chang, H.-C., & Holt, G. R. (1991). More than relationship: Chinese and the principle of *kuan-hsi. Communication Quarterly, 39,* 251–271.

Chang, H.-C., & Holt, G. R. (1994). Debt-repaying mechanism in Chinese relationships: An exploration of the folk concepts of *pao* and human emotional debt. *Research on Language and Social Interaction, 27*(4), 187–351.

Chang, Y. N. (1976). Early Chinese management thought. *California Management Review, 19*(2), 71–76.

Chen, G.-M. (1993). Self-disclosure and Asian students' abilities to cope with social difficulties in the United States. *Journal of Psychology, 127*(6), 603–610.

Chen, G.-M., & Chung, J. (1994). The impact of Confucianism on organizational communication. *Communication Quarterly, 42,* 93–105.

Cheng, C., Bond, M. H., & Chan, S. C. (1995). The perception of ideal best friends by Chinese adolescents. *International Journal of Psychology, 30*(1), 91–108.

Cheng, C.-Y. (1986). The concept of face and its Confucian root. *Journal of Chinese Philosophy, 13,* 329–348.

Cheng, C.-Y. (1987). Chinese philosophy and contemporary human communication theory. In D. L. Kincaid (Ed.), *Communication theory: Eastern and Western perspectives* (pp. 23–43). San Diego, CA: Academic Press.

Creel, H. G. (1960). *Confucius and the Chinese way.* New York: Harper & Row.

Fung, Y.-L. (1983). *A history of Chinese philosophy* (D. Bodde, Trans.). Princeton, NJ: Princeton University Press.

Goldman, A. (1994). The centrality of *ningensei* to Japanese negotiating and interpersonal relationships: Implications for U.S.-Japanese communication. *International Journal of Intercultural Relations, 18*(1), 29–54.

Gudykunst, W. B., & Kim, Y. Y. (1992). *Communicating with strangers: An approach to intercultural communication* (2nd ed.). New York: McGraw-Hill.

Gudykunst, W. B., & Ting-Toomey, S. (1992). Verbal communication styles. In W. B. Gudykunst & Y. Y. Kim (Eds.), *Readings on communicating with strangers* (pp. 223–235). New York: McGraw-Hill.

Harré, R. (1981). Rituals, rhetoric, and social cognition. In J. P. Forgas (Ed.), *Social cognitions* (pp. 211–224). London: Academic Press.

Hofstede, G. (1991). *Cultures and organizations: Software of the mind.* London: McGraw-Hill.

Kim, M.-S., & Bresnahan, M. (1994). A process model of request tactic evaluation. *Discourse Processes, 18,* 317–344.

Kim, M.-S., Sharkey, W. F., & Singelis, T. M. (1994). The relationship between individuals' self-construals and perceived importance of interactive constraints. *International Journal of Intercultural Relations, 18*(1), 117–140.

Kim, M.-S., & Wilson, S. R. (1994). A cross-cultural comparison of implicit theories of requesting. *Communication Monographs, 61,* 210–235.

King, A. Y. C. (1985). The individual and group in Confucianism: A relational perspective. In D. H. Munro (Ed.), *Individualism and holism: Studies in Confucian and Taoist values* (pp. 57–70). Ann Arbor: University of Michigan Press.

Legge, J. (Ed. & Trans.), (1985). *The four books: A Chinese-English version.* Taipei: Culture Book Co.

Liu, S.-H. (1996). Confucian ideals and the real world: A critical review of contemporary neo-Confucian thought. In W.-M. Tu (Ed.), *Confucian traditions in East Asian modernity* (pp. 92–111). Cambridge, MA: Harvard University Press.

Mao, T.-S. (Ed. & Trans). (1988). *Lun-yu-chin-tsu-chin-i* [Analects: Commentary and interpretations of the present day]. Taipei: Taiwan Sun-Wu.

Okabe, R. (1983). Cultural assumptions of East and West: Japan and the United States. In W. B. Gudykunst (Ed.), *Intercultural communication theory* (pp. 21–44). Beverly Hills, CA: Sage.

Oliver, R. T. (1971). *Communication and culture in ancient India and China.* Syracuse, NY: Syracuse University Press.

Robinson, W. P., & Giles, H. (1990). Prologue. In W. P. Robinson & H. Giles (Eds.), *Handbook of language and social psychology* (pp. 1–8). Chichester, UK: Wiley.

Schön, D. A. (1979). A perspective on problem setting in social policy. In A. Ortony (Ed.), *Metaphor and thought* (pp. 251–283). Cambridge: Cambridge University Press.

Soothill, W. E. (Trans.). (1968). *The* Analects *of Confucius*. New York: Paragon Books.

Ting-Toomey, S. (1988). Intercultural conflict styles: A face-negotiation theory. In Y. Kim & W. Gudykunst (Eds.), *Theories in intercultural communication* (pp. 213–256). Newbury Park, CA: Sage.

Triandis, H. (1988). Collectivism vs. Individualism: A reconceptualization of a basic concept in cross-cultural social psychology. In G. K. Verma & C. Bagley (Eds.), *Cross-cultural studies of personality, attitudes, and cognition* (pp. 60–95). New York: Macmilan.

Triandis, H. C. (1995). *Individualism and collectivism*. Boulder, CO: Westview Press.

Tu, W.-M. (1985). Selfhood and otherness in Confucian thought. In A. J. Marsella, G. DeVos, & F. L. K. Hsu (Eds.), *Culture and self: Asian and Western perspectives* (pp. 232–251). New York: Tavistock.

Tu. W.-M. (Ed.). (1996). *Confucian traditions in East Asian modernity*. Cambridge, MA: Harvard University Press.

Ward, B. E. (1968). Sociological self-awareness: Some uses of the conscious model. *Man, 1*, 201–215.

Wheeler, L., Reis, H. T., & Bond, M. H. (1989). Collectivism-individualism in everyday social life: The Middle Kingdom and the melting pot. *Journal of Personality and Social Psychology, 57*(1), 79–86.

Xiao, X. (1995). China encounters Darwinism: A case of intercultural rhetoric. *Quarterly Journal of Speech, 81*, 83–99.

Yang, K. S. (1981). Social orientation and individual modernity among Chinese students in Taiwan. *Journal of Social Psychology, 113*, 159–170.

Yum, J. O. (1987). The practices of *uye-ri* in interpersonal relationships in Korea. In D. L. Kincaid (Ed.), *Communication theory: Eastern and Western perspectives* (pp. 87–100). New York: Academic Press.

Yum, J. O. (1988). The impact of Confucianism on interpersonal relationships and communication patterns in East Asia. *Communication Monographs, 55*, 374–388.

8

Ubuntu in South Africa
A Sociolinguistic Perspective to a Pan-African Concept

Nkonko M. Kamwangamalu

During apartheid, language was used as an instrument of social control and division among the country's various ethnic groups. In the postapartheid era, however, language seems to have become instrumental in the country's efforts to unite its previously divided communities. This is evident in, for instance, TV slogans such as Simunye, which are intended to emphasize the oneness of the new nation; and in concepts such as *ubuntu*, which of late seems to have attracted much attention particularly in the business sector.

My aim is to discuss *ubuntu* from a sociolinguistic perspective. This is not the only perspective from which *ubuntu* could be studied. A socio-historical study would equally make an important contribution to understanding this pan-African concept. Such a study would have a wider scope to include an analysis of *ubuntu* not only in the African context but also in the Western context. It would, for instance, focus on the roots of notions such as *humanitas* (humanity), *humanismus* (humanism) and *caritas* (dearness, affection, caring), for they are related in many ways to the concept of *ubuntu*.

The paper is divided into three main sections. The first part considers some of the tenets of *ubuntu*, with a focus on "interdependence" and "communalism". To underline the sociolinguistic nature of *ubuntu*, these tenets will be illustrated with a selection of Bantu proverbs, for proverbs constitute one of the media through which the virtues of *ubuntu* were transferred from one generation to another. This paper stresses, as does Tshimpaka Yanga (1996, p. 12), that "the relevance of *ubuntu* as a universal African conception of life should not be blurred in unstated attempts to sacrifice a continental ideal for some form of ethnic philosophy".

The second section critically examines the uses to which *ubuntu* has been put in South Africa, especially in the business sector. I argue that for a society where *ubuntu* has been eroded as a result of apartheid, what is needed, is revival rather than commercialization of the virtues of *ubuntu*. Suggestions are made for a bottom-up revival, so that the country can bring first its communities, not its business sector, together and build a new nation, based on the virtues of *ubuntu*.

Then I consider briefly whether *ubuntu* is uniquely African, or whether its virtues can be found in other societies and cultures. Using historical facts such as slavery, colonialism and apartheid in Africa, and holocaust and Naziism in the West, I challenge the *unqualified* claim in some studies that the virtues of *ubuntu*, such as "respect for human dignity", "figures very strongly in Western thinking" (Prinsloo, 1996, p. 120).

Ubuntu: A Pan-African Concept

Morphologically, *ubuntu*, a Nguni term which translates as "personhood", "humanness", consists of the augment prefix u-, the abstract noun prefix bu-, and the noun stem -ntu, meaning "person" in Bantu languages. The concept of *ubuntu* is also found in many African languages, though not necessarily under the same name. Quoting Kagame (1976), Yanga (1997, p. 13) remarks that this concept has phonological variants in a number of African languages: *umundu* in Kikuyu and *umuntu* in Kimeru, both languages spoken in Kenya; *bumuntu* in kiSukuma and kiHaya, both spoken in Tanzania; *vumuntu* in shiTsonga and shiTswa of Mozambique; *bomoto* in Bobangi, spoken in the Democratic Republic of Congo; *gimuntu* in kiKongo and giKwese, spoken in the Democratic Republic of Congo and Angola, respectively.

Sociolinguistically, *ubuntu* is a multidimensional concept which represents the core values of African ontologies: respect for any human being, for human dignity and for human life, collective sharedness, obedience, humility, solidarity, caring, hospitality, interdependence, communalism, to list but a few. What this means, to paraphrase Kwame Gyekye (1987), is that despite Africa's cultural diversity, threads of underlying affinity do run through the beliefs, customs, value systems, and sociopolitical institutions and practices of the various African societies. Of the value systems, one that is found in most of these societies is the *ubuntu* system, of which recent literature offers the following definitions:

- *Ubuntu* means humanness. It is the humanistic experience of treating all people with respect, granting them their human dignity. Being human encompasses values like universal brotherhood for Africans, sharing, treating and respecting other people as human beings (Bhengu, 1996, p. 5).
- *Ubuntu* is a process and philosophy which reflects the African heritage, traditions, culture, customs, beliefs, value systems and the extended family structures (Makhudu, 1993, p. 40).
- *Ubuntu* is the key to all African values and involves humanness, a good disposition towards others, and a moral nature. It describes the significance of group solidarity and interdependence in African culture. It places great value on dignity, respect, conformity and reconciliation in the midst of conflict and hardship (Mthembu, 1996, p. 216).
- *Ubuntu* is the "collective consciousness" of the people of Africa. It involves alms-giving, being sympathetic, caring, sensitive to the needs of others, being respectful, considerate, patient and kind (Prinsloo, 1996, pp. 113–114).
- The concept of *ubuntu* is understood as a collective solidarity whereby the self is perceived primarily in relation to the perception of others, that is, persons are perceived less as independent of one another, and more as interdependent of one another (Laden, 1997, p. 134).
- *Ubuntu* is a statement about being human, about fundamental things that qualify a person to be a person. . . . Being human is achieved as a person shows characteristics that qualify him or her to be so regarded . . . *Ubuntu* is about how you relate to people and is . . . a fountain from which actions and attitudes flow (Dandala, 1996, pp. 70, 72).

These definitions, and others, have one theme in common: *ubuntu* is a value system which governs societies across the African continent. It is a system against whose values the members of a community measure their "humanness". These values, like the *ubuntu* system from which they flow, are not innate but are rather acquired in society and are transmitted from one generation to another by means of oral genres such as fables, proverbs, myths, riddles, and story-telling. Below I discuss two of these values, communalism and interdependence, and illustrate them with proverbs from Ciluba, a Bantu language spoken in the Democratic Republic of Congo (formerly Zaire).

Some Core Values of *Ubuntu*

Ubuntu *as communalism*

Communalism is one of the core values of *ubuntu*. It is a value according to which the interest of the individual is subordinate to that of the group. In other words, the group constitutes the focus of the activities of the individual members of the society at large. Communalism insists that the good of all determines the good of each or, put differently, the welfare of each is dependent on the welfare of all. As Adonisi (1994, p. 311) observes, "traditional African values foster a communalistic world-view towards life". Nobody in an African context lives for himself. We live for the community. Africa, wrote Sekou Toure, is fundamentally communocratic. The collective life and social solidarity give it a basis of humanism which many peoples might envy (see Sekou Toure, quoted in Gyekye, 1987, p. 209). These human qualities, argues Sekou Toure, also mean that an individual cannot imagine organizing his life outside that of his family, village or clan.

The view that Africa is communalistic is also expressed in Jomo Kenyatta's comments about the traditional life of the Kiguyu people in Kenya. He points out that according to Gikuyu ways of thinking,

> nobody is an isolated individual. Or rather, his uniqueness is a secondary fact about him; first and foremost he is several people's relative and several people's contemporary . . . this fact is the basis of his sense of moral responsibility and social obligation.
>
> (Kenyatta, 1965, p. 297, quoted in Gyekye, 1987, p. 209)

What Jomo Kenyatta says about the Gikuyu people is equally true of any ethnic group in Africa whose ways of life are governed by *ubuntu*. From Dakar in Senegal to Addis-Ababa in Ethiopia, and from Cairo in Egypt to Pretoria in South Africa, one finds evidence of *ubuntu* and of one of its cardinal virtues, communalism, in particular. One must admit, though, that as a result of contacts with Western cultures, communalism is perhaps not as much practised in urban Africa as it is in rural Africa. Comparative studies of *ubuntu* might shed light on the extent to which communalism is practised in these areas. It suffices to note, however, that "in Africa, communalism is a strong and binding network of relationships" (Mthembu, 1996, p. 220). Children, for example, belong not only to their biological parents, but are also under the authority and control of any adult in the community. Kinship terms attest to the nature of the relationships that bind the members of a community together. In South Africa and elsewhere in the continent, a member of a community can use the term *sister*, for instance, to refer to any female and not necessarily to one's sibling. Similarly, children are taught from young age that they must refer to anyone who is the same age as their father/mother as *father/mother*, and never to call such people by their names as this would be considered disrespectful.

In what remains of traditional Africa, communalism as core value of the *ubuntu* system is taught not at school but rather through oral genres such as proverbs, fables, riddles, etc. The following Ciluba proverbs are illustrative. They clearly underscore the rationale behind communalism and support the point that Gyekye (1987, p. 156) makes in relation to Akan proverbs in Ghana, "that extreme individualism could not thrive in traditional African culture; and that in spite of individual talents and capacities, the individual ought to be aware of his or her insufficiency to achieve his or her welfare through solitary effort".

(a) **Ngonga umwe katu udila pa mukaba** [Lit: "One bell cannot ring on the belt."] (One finger cannot lift up a thing.)
(b) **Tshiadima umwe tshiadia bangi** [Lit: "Harvested by one, eaten by many."]
(c) **Nkunda ya bangi itu iboba ne mata** [Lit: "Beans cooked by many can cook with saliva."] (Unity is strength.)

(d) **Babidi** kabakukumi batu bakushiya diulu nsoso [Lit: "If two people fight against one person they will win the fight."]

These proverbs teach communalism, and unity in particular. One notes that each of the proverbs makes reference to numbers: In (a) umwe "one" is followed by the negative particle katu "not" to stress the fact that one only finds strength in working in and with the community; in (b) umwe is used to stress the fact that in Africa we live for the community, and that what one achieves through individual effort, one must share with the members of the community; in (c) bangi "many" is the plural form of umwe "one" and serves also to underline the importance of collectiveness or unity, much as does babidi "two" in (d). The fact that these proverbs extol communalism does not necessarily imply negation of individualism. Rather, and to quote Gyekye (1987, p. 156), "communalism is the recognition of the limited character of the possibilities of the individual, which limited possibilities whittle away the individual's self-sufficiency". The Ciluba proverb *Bayaya waya biashala washadilamu* [Lit: "Go when everyone is going, if you stay behind, you stay for good."], for instance, extols individual competitiveness but it does not necessarily undermine communalism.

Ubuntu *as interdependence*

The essence of *ubuntu* is that an individual owes his or her existence to the existence of others. "I am" because "you are" and you are because "I am". Mbigi and Maree (1995, p. 2) put it this way, "the cardinal belief of Ubuntu is that a man can only be a man through others"; while Bhengu (1996, p. 2) says that "the person . . . cannot exist of himself, by himself, for himself; he comes from a social cluster, [and] exists in a social cluster . . .". This interpersonal character of *ubuntu* is the source of many of its distinctive virtues that have been highlighted in the literature, such as patience, hospitality, loyalty, respect, conviviality, sociability, vitality, endurance, sympathy, obedience, sharing, to list but a few (Shutte, 1996; Prinsloo, 1996; Mbigi and Maree, 1995).

Interdependence corresponds to the concept of *organic solidarity*, which Emile Durkheim, uses in his theory of social production of culture. Organic solidarity, which Durkheim (1915) contrasts with *mechanic solidarity*, is intended as an explanation for how modern societies, with people specializing in so many different areas, hold together. What it entails, is that these societies hold together because their members exchange services with one another, e.g. a farmer exchanges his produce with the teacher who, in return, educates his children. On the other hand, mechanic solidarity, which corresponds to communalism in the *ubuntu* system, "is a practice according to which traditional societies held together because the shared beliefs and understandings of a people constituted their collective consciousness, and this collective consciousness governed their thoughts, attitudes, and practices" (Griswold, 1994, p. 46).

Interdependence is valued highly in Africa, much as it is in Asia. However, in the West, independence rather than interdependence is the norm. Consequently, these two values, independence and interdependence, tend to clash when those who hold them come into contact. Consider, for instance, the concept of the nursing home, which is an integral part of the Western medicine but is rejected outright in Africa and Asia. In intercultural communication, concepts such as these can cause a clash of cultures. For instance, Yousef (1978, pp. 56–58), reports the clash between the Thompsons, a middle-class American family and their African friend, Grace, a Zambian student, who found it strange if not downright unfeeling and irresponsible that the Thompsons were planning to put Mr. Thompson's elderly mother in a nursing home. Yousef explains that Grace's reaction is based on her having grown up in a high-context culture, while the Thompsons' behaviour is based on their having grown up in a low-context culture. High context-cultures are marked by behavioural patterns of interdependence and they reflect patterns and value systems of people intensely involved in each other's lives; patterns according to which members of a household are bound for life in cycles of expectations and obligations to each other and to their extended families, friends, tribes, and clans. In cultures such as these the group, as Hinkel (1995, p. 331) points out, defines and controls the individual, that is the individual owes his/her existence to the existence of the group. Unlike high-context cultures, low-context cultures emphasize independence. Therefore, relationships among the members of these cultures are looser and less binding than is the case in high-context cultures. Like other virtues of *ubuntu* (e.g. communalism, conviviality, etc.), in traditional Africa interdependence is taught through oral genres, as illustrated in the following Ciluba proverbs.

(a) **Muntu apa muntu apa ki mbowa** [Lit: "A man here a man there means no fear."] (We can achieve anything if we support one another.)

(b) **Mwena mutumba mmwanenu** [Lit: "A neighbour is a sibling."] (Care for your neighbours in the same was as you do for your siblings.)

(c) **Bukwata nyanebe mbukukwata** [Lit: "Your friend's problem is your problem."]

(d) **Bubedi bwa disu mbubedi bwa diulu** [Lit: "The sickness of the eye is the sickness of the nose."] (Your neighbour's problem is your problem.)

These proverbs indicate the value of mutual aid and interdependence as necessary conditions not only for an individual's welfare, but also for the welfare of the community as a whole. Interdependence has implications for South African society, and particularly for the walls that apartheid erected among the country's communities. For instance, if neighbours treat one another as siblings in the *ubuntu* sense, as Bhengu (1996, p. 3) puts it, "regard my neighbours' mind as an open book of discovered knowledge, recognize my neighbours as the reverse side of an entity to which I am the obverse", the walls that apartheid erected among the communities will not take long to come down. Bringing these walls down is, in my view, one of the most serious challenges that post-apartheid South Africa faces at the moment.

The values of *ubuntu* are, of course, too numerous to discuss them all here. However, I assume that those illustrated above, interdependence and communalism, provide a glimpse into what *ubuntu* is about and how it is transmitted from one generation to another in the African context.

Ubuntu, Culture and the Business Sector in South Africa

I shall argue that *ubuntu* is first and foremost a social rather than a business concept. Therefore, if post-apartheid South Africa is to build a society based on *ubuntu*, one must first raise awareness about and revive the apartheid-eroded virtues of *ubuntu* at the grassroots level before one embarks on disseminating these virtues in the business sector. Doing the opposite, as seems to be the case, is tantamount to building a house without first laying a foundation.

Ubuntu *and culture*

Culture is the socially learned, shared assemblage of practices, perceptions, attitudes, world view, value system and beliefs that determine the texture of our lives as members of a given community (e.g. Sapir, 1963; Bowers, 1992). Quoting Peterson (1979), Griswold (1994, p. 3) remarks that when sociologists, for instance, talk about culture they usually mean one of four things: norms, values, beliefs, or expressive symbols. Roughly, Griswold notes, norms are the way people behave in a given society, values are what they hold dear, beliefs are how they think the universe operates, and expressive symbols are representations, often representations of social norms, values, and beliefs themselves. We express these values, beliefs, perceptions, etc. in a number of ways, one of which is language. As Hyde (1994, p. 300) observes, "though people are not necessarily prisoners of their language, it is undoubtedly true that the way a culture sees the world is reflected in its language". This is because "as people come to value certain things and do them in a certain way, they come to use their language in ways that reflect what they value and what they do" (Wardhaugh, 1992, p. 218). The concept of the nursing home referred to earlier, which according to Yousef (1978) caused the clash of cultures between an American family and their African guest, illustrates how what is considered a value in one community or culture may not be so regarded in another. What people value, culturally or otherwise, is context-bound. Accordingly, "while management principles are universal, the context in which they are implemented is critical to the form and shape they should take in any particular environment" (Lessem and Nussbaum, 1996, p. 11). It is against this background that *ubuntu* seems to have found its way into the business sector in South Africa.

Ubuntu *and the business sector*

In present-day South Africa, *ubuntu* has become the hallmark of the business sector. Its use in this sector is, among other things, primarily intended to enable business leaders to understand the cultural and behavioural context in which they are developing their approach to business; to develop management principles which incorporate African values; to give cultures that were previously kept apart by apartheid an opportunity to celebrate their diversity and build on the strengths of that diversity; and to enable business leaders to shift paradigms in the conduct of business (Mbigi, 1995; Lessem, 1996). Shifting paradigms entails, in the words of Lessem (1996, p. 7), "changing management style from dictatorship to relationship, shifting orientation from manager to mentor, engaging in affirmative action, and thereby reversing discrimination and, finally, following the indigenous African management practice of *ubuntu*", practice which builds on virtues such as those discussed in previous sections, namely interdependence and communalism. The popularity of *ubuntu* in the business stems both from these and several other ingredients regarded as critical to Western psychological therapies—warmth, forgiveness, compassion, respect, dignity, empathy, supportiveness, co-operation, mutual understanding and a shared world view, ingredients which can be used profitably in the business sector. These ingredients contrast, as Adonisi (1994, p. 311) observes, with clinical approaches. The latter, to a large extent, reflect positivistic assumptions about people, tend to elevate the individual above his social group, encourage the individual to strive for personal goals, and in the process compete against the very social entity that has brought individuals into being. Because *ubuntu* insists on the spirit of togetherness, "it is inconceivable that individual careers can be formed and actualised outside of the communal context that provides meaning and anchors in life for people" (Adonisi, 1994, p. 311). In this regard, Lessem (1996, p. 187) remarks pointedly that "unless business leaders in southern Africa can tap such a spirit of 'ubuntu', align it with eastern and western management techniques and turn it into a material force for reconstruction and development, they will have no collective or individual future." Accordingly, *ubuntu* is expected "to transform our economic practices and make us as competitive as any other economy that has transformed itself by discovering the fundamental values of its social context" (Dandala, 1996, p. 71).

The next section looks at how the business sector disseminates *ubuntu* to transform economic practices and increase production.

Disseminating ubuntu *in the business sector*

Since *ubuntu* is now seen as Godsend to help business prosper, management has developed strategies to disseminate the values of *ubuntu* in the business sector. Some of these strategies include, for instance, conferences, seminars, workshops as well as training courses on *ubuntu*. The focus of all these activities has been on the teamwork and sense of group responsibility flowing from *ubuntu*—in contrast to the sometimes destructive individualism and over-competitiveness in Western systems. Besides, books have been written to advise companies on how best they can use *ubuntu* to manage their business, ensure good human relationships among their personnel and, above all, have a competitive edge. Among the books, one notes the following, *African Management: Philosophies, Concepts, and Applications* (Chrissie, Lessem, & Mbigi, 1994); *Sawubona Africa: Embracing Four Worlds in South African Management* (Lessem & Nussbaum, 1996); *Ubuntu: The Spirit of African Transformation Management* (Mbigi & Maree, 1995).

All the above is good news indeed, but only in so far as no profit is lost or no company goes bankrupt. However, one must pause and ask: Is *ubuntu* really about profit-making? Isn't the basic point of departure for *ubuntu* the view of man as social being? How much *ubuntu* do business leaders, as social beings, practice themselves at the grassroot level? Do they, for instance, treat their neighbours as siblings as required in the *ubuntu* culture? To what extent does business encourage free flow of information within its ranks? From the *ubuntu* perspective, members of a group or company are dependent on one another for their own welfare as well as for the welfare of the group or company as a whole. Therefore, Khoza (1994) cautions that one cannot cultivate a community spirit, which companies claim to pursue in their business, by withholding information from one another. In short, slogans such as "information is power" (Adonisi, 1994), whose goal is to guard knowledge, defy the virtues of the very *ubuntu* system the business sector claims to promote.

It seems to me that the efforts to extol *ubuntu* via published literature, training courses, workshops, and conferences risk remaining a pie in the sky if those involved in these efforts do not perceive the contrast between the virtues of *ubuntu* and the profit-based *modus operandi* of the business sector. On this particular point, South Africa is perhaps the only country in Africa where *ubuntu* is so much talked about. This is understandable especially as *ubuntu* has been eroded by apartheid and the walls it has erected among communities. In other African countries, however, *ubuntu* is the norm, it is felt, it is practised and reflected in the daily behaviours of the members of a community. With the walls that divide South Africa still standing tall, one wonders whether efforts to revive *ubuntu* shouldn't focus on bringing these walls down first rather than on teaching companies how to use *ubuntu* to remain competitive.

I now shall turn to the last part of this paper and examine briefly whether *ubuntu* is uniquely African or whether its virtues can be found in other cultures. I shall argue that some of the virtues of *ubuntu*, such as interdependence, may be unique to African and Asian cultures, for these are high-context cultures, as described earlier. Other virtues, such as hospitality, compassion, empathy, tolerance, respect, etc. could be found in other cultures.

Ubuntu in Other Cultures

One issue that Western philosophers have raised in regard to *ubuntu* is whether it is unique to Africa or whether its virtues can be found in other societies around the world (Broodryk, 1996; Prinsloo, 1996; Shutte, 1994). Broodryk (1996) notes that for something to be unique, it needs to be extra-ordinary and incomparable. Consequently, when one considers the uniqueness of *ubuntuism*, one has to ask whether there are characteristics (e.g. compassion, respect, hospitality, solidarity, togetherness, etc.) which cannot be identified in any other *-isms*, of which he lists the following: Communism, Marxism, Communalism, Capitalism, Liberalism and Conservatism. After describing the characteristics of each of these ideologies, Broodryk (1996, pp. 31–35) argues that "if 'unique' means unusual, incomparable or extra-ordinary, then *ubuntuism* is not unique to one culture, for all people have this magic gift or sadly lack it. In some of us, these qualities exist". Makhudu (1993) supports this view by saying that the qualities of *ubuntu* or humanness exist in every person, though I must emphasize, once again, that these qualities are not innate but are rather acquired through socialization. Along these lines, Edgard Sienaert (1984, p. 226), quoting Paul Renucci (1953, p. 9), views *humanism* as

> the will to seize the whole history of art and thought and to mobilize it to serve man, the most perfectible of all beings and the only one able to understand and master the universe. The main task of a humanistic enterprise is to destroy dark zones and barriers of the past, to discover and put back in use the treasures of science, wisdom and beauty that have become obtuse or have been forgotten or despised. It (humanism) is not to reject anything of the past without prior serious and patient investigation; it is to look into the errors and crimes of the past and to ensure that, by studying them, they are never committed again.
>
> (my translation)

Ubuntu is indeed unique to Africa, where the Bantu languages from which it derives are spoken. However, the values it evokes seem to be universal since they are apparently shared by societies world over, as the above and the following quotations suggest. For instance, Prinsloo (1996, p. 120) points out that "human dignity figures very strongly in Western thinking, especially in legal and religious contexts and forms a strong basis for (Western) humanism". He goes on to say that "sharing" is also regarded as part and parcel of socialism and even of capitalism where participatory management is or was applied. Thus, argues Prinsloo, "*ubuntu* shares a world spirit and serves, perhaps, to emphasize this world spirit and remind Western and other thinkers of its importance" (1996, p. 120). This discovery, Prinsloo concludes, can lead to a joint application of principles of human dignity to all spheres of life in order to create relatively harmonious communities. Unlike Prinsloo, and in what appears to be an afterthought, Broodryk (1996, p. 36) notes that some aspects of *ubuntu* may be unique to Africa.

> *Ubuntu* may be different from other ideologies on the aspect of humanism. This humanism appears to be more intense than humanistic approaches in other ideologies. What the motivation of this is, is unclear. Could it be that this is a result of former colonial situations where the humanity of people was shattered?

There is, as an anonymous reviewer has remarked, the need to engage, at least briefly, in the semantics of humanism to avoid blurring the meaning of this concept. If the first sentence in the above quotation is anything to go by, it seems that Broodryk distinguishes between *ubuntu* and *humanism*. To him, *ubuntu* is an ideology of which humanism is but an aspect. It seems to me, however, that *ubuntu* can be encoded in English as *humanism*. Put differently, *ubuntu* means humanism, the art of being human. Therefore, trying to separate the two, as Broodryk does, is misleading and can create confusion.

If one assumes with Broodryk and others that *ubuntuism* is neither unique nor "purely African", and that "human dignity figures very strongly in Western thinking" (Prinsloo, 1996, p. 120), then a number of historical facts, among them holocaust, Naziism, slavery, colonialism and apartheid, require an explanation. How could these facts originate in the West where, if Prinsloo and others are right, there is a strong belief in human dignity and in the values of humanism. This is an important question, but one which is beyond the scope of this paper.

Similar questions can be raised in regard to pre-colonial, equally dehumanizing practices, such as *muti* and *witchcraft*-related killings in the South African context. Are these practices *ubuntuistically* acceptable? With regard to witchcraft for instance, Nekhudzhiga of the Institute for Multi-Party Democracy (Braamfontein), cited in Yanga (1996, p. 17) from *The Citizen*, 5 May 1996 remarks that:

it is not a question of whether witchcraft is a reality or myth. Many men, women and children are dead through witchcraft, suspicion and related activities . . . Can we in South Africa at this point continue with that type of belief, that to improve the status of an individual, we sacrifice another? Is that our culture? Is this what *Ubuntu* is all about?

Besides, how can Africa, a continent which has produced innumerable political human monsters and dictators, have humanistic pretensions. It seems to me that *ubuntu* (i.e. *humanism*) is an ideal whose virtues are perhaps too numerous and of too high a standard for any human being or community, whether in Africa or in the West, to conform to them all. Black South African communities, for instance, though well aware of the virtues of *ubuntu*, have not been able to live up to them, for they continue to engage in dehumanizing practices such as *muti*, a practice which involves killing a human being for the purpose of using his body's parts to advance one's own cause or status in the community. Similarly, apartheid was designed in South Africa despite the fact that its architects were well aware of the virtue of humanism (Broodryk, 1996; Prinsloo, 1996).

Conclusion

This paper has critically examined the concept of *ubuntu* and its use in African societies, with a focus on South Africa. I have argued that *ubuntu* is first and foremost a social rather than a business-related ideal. Therefore, there is a need to understand, revive, and promote the virtues of *ubuntu* first at the social, grassroot level, to practice *ubuntu* in our own communities and with own neighbours if one is to build a better society, a society where neighbours treat one another not just as neighbours but as siblings in the *ubuntu* sense; a society where people acknowledge and value interdependence and develop mutual respect for their diverse cultures. Only after we have made progress in these areas can we claim to be good agents for societal change and for the spread of *ubuntu* in other sectors including the business and management sector.

The need for developing *ubuntu* culture is expressed in the following letter, quoted in Sonja Laden (1997, p. 135) from *Drum Magazine* (1995). This letter, incidently, calls for "reviving the spirit of neighbourliness (Ubuntu) in our communities":

Looking back over the years, some of us can remember how important it was to have the companionship of neighbours. Calling each other *Makhi* or *buur*, we helped each other in all areas of life. Alas, those happy days of borrowing and lending anything from *letswai* (salt) to money without fear of getting cheated, are gone . . . If we let *ubuntu* live, our souls, minds, hearts, and bodies will benefit. Let there be that neighbourly spirit of love, warmth, friendliness, kindness, joy and security. And of course Neighbourhood Watch must be every person's job.

References

Adonisi, M. (1994). The career in community. In P. Christie, R. Lessem & L. Mbigi. (Eds.) *African management: Philosophies, concepts, and applications* (pp. 309–314). Randburg: Knowledge Resources (Pty) Ltd.

Bhengu, M. J. (1996). *Ubuntu: The essence of democracy.* Cape Town: Novalis Press.

Bowers, R. (1992). Memories, metaphors, maxims, and myths: language learning and cultural awareness. *ELT Journal, 46*(1), 29–38.

Broodryk, J. (1996). Is Ubuntuism unique? In J. Malherbe (Ed.), *Decolonizing the mind: Proceedings of the 2nd Colloquium on African Philosophy* (pp. 31–37). Pretoria: UNISA Research Unit for African Philosophy.

Christie, P., Lessem, R. & Mbigi, L. (Eds.). (1994). *African management: Philosophies, concepts, and applications.* Randburg: Knowledge Resources (Pty) Ltd.

Dandala, H. M. (1996). Cows never die: Embracing African cosmology in the process of economic growth. In R. Lessem & B. Nussbaum (Eds.), *Sawubona Africa: Embracing four worlds in South African management* (pp. 69–85). Sandton: Zebra Press.

Durkheim, E. (1915,1965). *The elementary forms of the religious life* (J. W. Swain, Trans.). New York: Free Press.

Griswold, W. (1994). *Cultures and societies in a changing world.* London: Pine Forge Press.

Gyekye, K. (1987). *An essay on African philosophical thought: The Akan conceptual scheme.* Cambridge: Cambridge University Press.

Hinkel, E. (1995). The use of modal verbs as a reflection of cultural values. *TESOL Quarterly, 29*(2), 325–344.

Hyde, M. (1994). The teaching of English in Morocco: the place of culture. *ELT Journal, 48*(4), 295–305.

Kagame, A. (1976). *La philosophie bantu comparee.* Paris: Presence Africaine.

Kenyatta, J. (1965). *Facing Mount Kenya.* New York: Vintage.

Khoza, R. (1994). The need for an Afrocentric approach to management. In P. Christie, R. Lessem, & L. Mbigi (Eds.), *African management: Philosophies, concepts, and applications* (pp. 117–124). Randburg: Knowledge Resources (Pty) Ltd.

Laden, S. (1997). Middle-class matters, or How to keep Whites whiter, Colours Brighter, and Blacks Beautiful. *Critical Arts, 11*(1–2), 120–141.

Lessem, R. (1996). South Africa's business-sphere. In R. Lesse & B. Nussbaum (Eds.), *Sawubona Africa: Embracing four worlds in South African management* (pp. 35–46). Sandton: Zebra Press.

Lessem, R. (1996). *From hunter to rainmaker: The Southern African businessphere.* Johannesburg: Knowledge Resources.

Lessem, R. and Nussbaum, B. (Eds.). (1996). *Sawubona Africa: Embracing four worlds in South African management.* Sandton: Zebra Press.

Makhudu, N. (1993, August). Cultivating a climate of co-operation through Ubuntu. *Enterprise Magazine, 48,* 40–42.

Mbigi, L. and Maree, J. (1995). *Ubuntu: The spirit of African transformation management.* Randburg: Knowledge Resources.

Mthembu, D. (1996). African values: Discovering the indegenous roots of management. In R. Lessem & B. Nussbaum (Eds.), *Sawubona Africa: Embracing four worlds in South African management* (pp. 215–226). Sandton: Zebra Press.

Peterson, R. A. (1979). Revitalizing the culture concept. *Annual Review of Sociology, 5,* 137–166.

Prinsloo, E. (1996). The Ubuntu style of participatory management. In J. G. Malherbe (Ed.), *Decolonizing the mind: Proceedings of the Second Colloquim on African Philosophy* (pp. 112–127). Pretoria: UNISA Research Unit for African Philosophy.

Sapir, E. (1963). *Language.* London: Hart-Davis.

Shutte, A. (1994, July). *The Ubuntu project.* Paper presented at the 22nd Congress of Philosophical Society of Southern Africa, University Natal, Durban.

Sienart, E. (1984) *Les lais de marie de France. Du conte merveilleux a la nouvelle psychologique.* Paris: Editions Champions.

Wardhaugh, R. (1992). *An introduction to sociolinguistics* (2nd ed.). Cambridge: Blackwell.

Yanga, T. (1996, May). *African studies and the concept of Ubuntu.* Paper presented at the Southern African Folklore Society Regional Conference. Hebron College of Education, Johannesburg.

Yanga, T. (1997, September). *African languages and the discourse of African Renaissance.* Paper presented at the Transformation Forum of South Africa Conference on African Renaissance: Setting the Agenda for the 21st Century. Johannesburg.

Yousef, F.S. (1978). Communication patterns: some aspects of non-verbal behaviour in intercultural communication. In E. L. Ross (Ed.), *Interethnic communication: Southern Anthropological Society Proceedings 12,* 49–62. Athens, GA: University of Georgia Press.

9

Constructing the Other
A Critical Reading of *The Joy Luck Club*

Jing Yin

In 1993, Amy Tan's (1989) best-seller novel *The Joy Luck Club* was made into a movie with the same title by Disney. With the two-million-copy book sale, Tan became an overnight celebrity in the early 1990s. Tan's enormous success symbolized the acceptance of Asian Americans to the mainstream American culture. The movie production further added to this fervor. The movie, *The Joy Luck Club* (directed by Wayne Wang), soon proved a box-office hit. It was ranked 48 in terms of box-office income in the fiscal year of 1993. It generated approximately $32,901,136 in the U.S. domestic market alone. *The New York Times*' Century Box Office ranked this movie as one of the Top Three Movies of that year.

The movie, just like the book, was hailed by many for two reasons: (a) the universal female theme and (b) Asian actors moving into mainstream. For example, Linda Lopez McAlister (1993) applauded the movie for the universal mother–daughter bonding:

And though these mothers and daughters are specifically Chinese, the theme is universal and speaks to every woman who ever had a mother and/or a daughter, across ethnic and racial differences.

Film critic Roger Ebert (1993) credited the movie as a breakthrough for Asian actors moving from margin to center:

The movie is a celebration, too, of the richness of Asian-American acting talent . . . But often they were marginalized, or used in "exotic" roles, or placed in stories that were based on what made them different from the dominant culture, instead of what makes them human and universal. "The Joy Luck Club" is like a flowering of talent that has been waiting so long to be celebrated.

The Washington Post praised this film as "nourishing for its avoidance of Asian stereotypes" (Howe, 1993). In fact, another review in *The Washington Post* blamed the movie for its eagerness to present Asian American women in a positive light to fit its "feminist ideology" (Hinson, 1993).

All these reviews shared the same theme—Asians or Asian Americans are not "human and universal" until they become acceptable to the mainstream (dominant culture). The claim of universality is essentially problematic in that rather than representing a full range of human beings, it in fact projects or naturalizes particular groups—for example, White, middle class, heterosexual, able-bodied, male, etc.—as "human and universal," while it designates others as less human. Thus, the claim of universality works as a mechanism of exclusion that perpetuates existing social hierarchies and power structures.

The claim of universality works in all social domains involving power. This particular film, however, concentrates this claim on the issue of race. Asians or Asian Americans can be upgraded to the "human and universal" category only if they can produce elements shared by the White audience. This assumption requires Asians or Asian Americans, or all racial or ethnic minorities for that matter, to give up their own cultural values in order to be assimilated into the mainstream U.S. culture (M. McAlister, 1992; Yep, 2002).

Despite the universality that critics credited it with, the movie *The Joy Luck Club* reinforced stereotypical images of Chinese and Chinese Americans. In her website titled "Why *The Joy Luck Club* Sucks," Al Wong (1997), a Chinese-American, wrote that the movie is full of stereotypes of Chinese Americans or Asian Americans. For example, the movie actually perpetuated the stereotype of Chinese women as sexual objects, the "China Doll" (e.g., see Sun, 2003, for a review of stereotypical media portrayals of Asian American women).

Moreover, rather than breaking stereotypes, this movie further reaffirmed the notion of Asia as the monolithic Other.[1] Indeed this Hollywood presentation confounded the negotiations and struggles over identities engaged in by Asian Americans or Asians. Kathleen Wong(Lau) (2002) documented one incident in which a well-meaning White woman claimed to have learned a lot about her Korean American colleague's culture from this movie. Thus, although Asian Americans are permitted to join the elite class financially as the "model minority," they still could not escape cultural and political marginalization. They are seen as forever foreign although they have been living in the United States for several generations, longer than many European descents (Nakayama, 1988). This double bind is what M. McAlister (1992) called the *new Orientalist/Assimilationist paradigm*, which "simultaneously insists on the exotic 'otherness' of Asian culture *and* on the necessity—for Asian Americans—of putting aside all but the most superficial elements of that culture in order to be assimilated into America" (p. 104).

The popularity and the ostensible progressiveness of *The Joy Luck Club* made it the representative voice of Asian Americans. A couple of years ago, several White female colleagues of mine, after viewing this movie, showed tremendous sympathy toward me, the "poor" (oppressed) Chinese girl. Shohat (1991, p. 51) argued that Western films assume "the ethnographic and quasi-archaeological power" in presenting Others and in turn defining the "Western" self. It constructs Chineseness, Asianness, and Asian Americanness for its audiences, Asian or non-Asian alike. Unlike Tan's novel, which has been both praised and criticized (e.g., V. Chen, 1995; M. McAlister, 1992), with the exception of Al Wong's (1997) critique of stereotypes, the film has not been critically analyzed as a politically charged cultural text. The movie deserves scholarly attention especially in the context that the U.S. cultural politics reduces the experience of racial minorities into mere ornamentation to sustain the myth of a diverse society without fundamentally challenging the racial hierarchy (M. McAlister, 1992). A critical examination of the movie *The Joy Luck Club* can help us disentangle how such cultural politics and media representations contribute to the struggle of meanings over cultural or racial identities.

Articulating the Movie Text

Many communication researchers agree that the mass media are the most powerful storytellers in modern society (Severin & Tankard, 1997). Indeed the original motivation for communication study in the United States was the fear of mischievous effects of the media (McQuail, 1987). The media have become an important source of information and interpretation, especially for what could not be obtained through first-hand experiences (Nimmo & Comb, 1990). Western films, as a form of popular culture, function as "Philosophy, Egyptology, Anthropology,

Historiography and Geography" in constructing other (non-Western) cultures (Shohat, 1991). A very useful way to tackle the discursive power of a movie is to examine it as socially, politically, culturally, and historically situated text.

My treatment of the text draws from critical and cultural studies. This tradition of research focuses on two central issues: (a) the politics of textuality (the nature of signification) and (b) the relationship between the cultural and the social (Grossberg, 1984). These two central issues lead to dual tasks for the researcher: a hermeneutics of faith and a hermeneutics of suspicion. A hermeneutics of faith deals with interpreting the meaning of the text; whereas a hermeneutics of suspicion requires examining the connection between the text and the context in which the text is produced, distributed, and consumed. The intersection of these two hermeneutics defines the "ideological function" of the text (Grossberg, 1984, p. 393).

Examining textual power from this perspective, Althusser (1971) argued that rather than merely reflecting the social order, or producing a system of meaning supporting the existing social order, the media text works as practices that present its own meaning system as real or natural. Thus, the power of the text is not reflecting or confirming, but normalizing or naturalizing certain practices. Building on Althusser's argument and Ernesto Laclau's (1977) book *Politics and Ideology in Marxist Theory*, Stuart Hall (1986) contended that the mechanism of the media text to reinforce normalcy as well as marginality is "articulation." That is, the media text does not simply distort or misrepresent the reality (consciously or unconsciously). Rather, it works through the process that forms "the connection that can make a unity of two different elements, under certain conditions" (p. 53). This connection is "a linkage which is not necessary, determined, absolute, and essential for all time" (p. 53). In other words, articulation is the connection between two distinct discursive elements that would not ordinarily or naturally be connected. It is through articulation that a linkage is established. The discursive unity created by articulation is arbitrary and contingent. Thus, articulation is also a process of intervention of ideology into language. The dominant group that has institutional, material, and discursive resources naturalizes its own practices through the control of articulation. The struggle over meaning is essentially the struggle over articulation.

The theory of articulation is not confined to the domain of discourse. It also has implications for social forces. Unlike orthodox Marxists, Hall (1986) rejected the necessary correlation between ideology and social class (or social forces). He maintained that ideological elements do not have necessary belongingness. A particular form of ideology does not intrinsically belong to a particular social-economic class. Rather, such connection is contingent and non-necessary. One's social identity (class, gender, race, sexuality, etc.) does not necessarily determine one's consciousness. It is through articulation that an ideology discovers and speaks to its political subjects. An ideology that enables people to make sense of the world and their own positions can also function to unify those people, political subjects, as a social force or class. For example, being a female does not necessarily make a woman a feminist. She can be a feminist only if she accepts the articulation of feminist ideology and uses it to interpret social affairs. By the same token, a man can also subscribe to feminist ideology even if he does not have a female identity.

It is precisely because articulation is not necessary, inherent, or determined that any articulation can be broken down and rearticulated in different ways (Hall, 1986). This is where the role of human agency comes into play. Rather than merely the products of dominant discourse, human beings, as social actors, can intervene in the articulation process. Thus, they can resist the dominant discourse through a process of deconstruction-reconstruction.

Therefore, the investigation of the process of how certain meanings and practices are "articulated" or made a coherent unity not only is important to understand the function of media texts in naturalizing dominant experiences and identities while marginalizing those of the dominated, but also is critical for challenging the dominant discourse and producing the possibility of hope. Giroux (2000) argued that "texts are now not only as objects of struggle in challenging dominant modes of racial and colonial authority but also as pedagogical resources to rewrite the possibilities for new narratives, identities, and cultural spaces" (p. 494). His contention that media texts should be treated as forms of public pedagogical resource involves more than deconstruction, it further includes a process of re-construction or re-articulation.

A critique of the movie *The Joy Luck Club* is an excellent way to engage in public pedagogy. This film was accepted by many in the United States as a "classic," "the representative voice of Asian-Americans." Indeed, intercultural communication researchers and educators even use this movie (as well as Tan's book) to teach Chinese cultural values and communication styles (e.g., Athanases, 1993; Hamilton, 1999; Sueda, 1993). Feminist critics either challenge this movie as an example of female oppression in China, or celebrate it as alternative female narratives or Asian American feminist literature (e.g., V. Chen, 1995; X. Chen, 1994; Lu, 1998). Many viewers (including Asian Americans) believe that this movie represented authentic Chineseness or even Asianness. A Caucasian woman claimed this movie taught her a lot about her Korean American colleague's culture (Wong(Lau), 2002). Many of my American students argue that this movie is very accurate, authentic, and non-stereotypical because Amy Tan and Wayne Wang (the director of the film) are Asian Americans. When hearing my project on *The Joy Luck Club*, colleagues, friends, and students always would question me "How on earth could you bash such a nice (positive) movie about Chinese culture?" The "ethnographic" power that this movie assumed in the mainstream U.S. culture makes it problematic and dangerous in the increasingly diverse society in which we dwell.[2] Thus, we need to critically read this Hollywood movie to explore how the articulation process contributes to the struggle over meanings of cultural or racial identities.

My reading of *The Joy Luck Club* is grounded in sociolinguistics and critical discourse analysis. Sociolinguistics studies the use of language with regard to the interlocutors' social/cultural identities, relations, and contexts (e.g., Fowler, 1996; Gee, 1999; Halliday, 1971; Hatch, 1992). For example, Fowler's (1996) theory of "point of view" of a narrative tackles the relationships among characters and with the larger context. Critical discourse analysis deals with "the role of discourse in the (re)production and challenge of dominance" (van Dijk, 1998, p. 367). Van Dijk (1988a, 1988b, 1997) and Fairclough (1992, 1995) examined how the dominant ideology is perpetuated by the structure and content of news. The integration of these two approaches enables the researcher to not only interpret the meanings of the film, but also discern the ideologies articulated in the movie text.

My treatment of this film is not a typical "textual analysis." Textual analysts seldom delineate their methods in their research, they, nevertheless, primarily rely on Freudian, Foucaultian, or Lacanian psychoanalysis of "desire," which is manifested is the gendered "gaze" (Olesen, 1998). The theory of "gaze" deals with how the power relations between the origin of the gaze (e.g., Western males) and the object of the gaze (e.g., women, non-Western cultures, nature, etc.) are communicated in visual terms (Chow, 1995). Critics of the psychoanalytical film approach contend that the preoccupation on sexual desires ignores other factors such as race and class, as well as the importance of the context (e.g., Pribram, 1988). De Lauretis (1984) proposed to explore alternative film analysis methods, for example, semiotic theories of iconicity and narrativity. Therefore, rather than focusing on the subconscious psyche, my approach emphasizes the actual use of language in the movie text. Inspired by sociolinguistics and critical discourse analysis, I examine the film *The Joy Luck Club* as a socially, politically, culturally, and historically situated text.

Clashes of Cultures[3]

Hall's theory of articulation directs our attention to the connections between certain meanings and practices established by the text. My analysis of the movie *The Joy Luck Club* focuses on the articulation process by which the movie text associated specific meanings with Chinese and American cultures.[4]

This movie presents a series of stories about four Chinese mothers and their American-born daughters. The development of the mother/daughter relationships centered on conflicts, with the mothers' attempts to maintain control on the one hand and the daughters' wishes to run free. Contrary to what film critics claimed to be universal women bonding, the movie articulated the mother/daughter conflicts as clashes between the American and Chinese cultures.

An example of such construction is June's piano lessons. June had no interest in the piano; however, her mother forced her to play it in order to compete with Auntie Lindo, whose daughter was a gifted chess champion. Lacking genuine interest and internal motivation, June resented the piano lessons. As a result, her debut ended in disaster. After that, June saw no reason to continue this torture, but her mother would not give up the idea. Then a conflict took place (see Example 1).

Example 1:

1 Mother: Four o'clock. Turn off TV. Practice piano time. What I say? Four o'clock.
2 June: I am not gonna play anymore. Why should I?
3 Mother: What did you say?
4 June: I am not your slave. This isn't China. You can't make me!
5 Mother: Get up!
6 June: No! No, I won't! No!
7 Mother: (grabs June and forces her to sit in front of the piano).
8 June: You want me to be someone I am not. I'll never be the kind of daughter you
9 want me to be.
10 Mother: There two kind of daughters, obedient or follow own mind. Only one kind of
11 daughter could live in this house, obedient kind.
12 June: Then I wish I wasn't your daughter! I wish you weren't my Mom!

This story was narrated from June's point of view. June, as the narrator, was the center of the sympathetic portrayal. She was a child who had her own will and opinion. She resisted her mother's imposing things on her against her own will. In Lines 2 and 6, she verbally declared that she would not continue practicing the piano, which she perceived as an imposition. For her, she could only be what she is rather than "someone I am not" (Line 8). In addition to this declaration, she resorted to her right of freedom by saying "I am not your slave!" (Line 4). In the same line she backed her utterance up by insisting that such imposition was not the norm in the United States, "This is not China. You can't make me!"

A story can be constructed in different ways from different perspectives. The point of view of a narrative determines the relationships among characters and with the outside world. It reflects the ideology of the author (or the film makers) (Fowler, 1996). In this case, the character June was given the power to define her relationship with her mother and to make sense of the world. Her insistence on individual freedom echoes the myth of the American culture, which makes her the "normal."

The construction of her mother was through June's eyes. The mother was portrayed as a bit abusive, verbally and physically. She tried to shape her daughter's future according to her own ideal without considering her daughter's feelings. Faced with June's resistance, the mother resorted to verbal demands "get up" (Line 5), physical force (Line 7), and her authority by virtue of her status as mother. She put emphasis on the obligations of the daughter and used it as a threat, "There two kinds of daughters, obedient or follow own mind. Only one kind of daughter could live in this house, obedient kind" (Lines 10–11).

From June's point of view, her mother's action was defined as imposition and her intention was defined as unjustified, using June to compete with Auntie Lindo. The mother's perspective was ignored, as a result, she was deprived of the power to voice her interpretation of the issue. Furthermore, the mother's reasoning—asking the daughter to be obedient—does not resonate with the norms and values of the mainstream U.S. American culture, which makes her abnormal or less humane. The mother, thus, contrary to June, was presented as the oppressive Other.

Cross-generation conflict may not be particular to any culture, but what needs to be noted here is that the conflicts in this movie were constructed as cultural rather than idiosyncratic or universal. Throughout the movie, the mother–daughter conflicts were constructed in one pattern, that is, all the daughters were trying to assert their well-deserved individuality, where the mothers tried to prevent that for reasons that were bizarre or ridiculous. For example, Lindo, Waverly's mother, used her daughter's chess championship to show off in Chinatown, which was seen as an embarrassment by Waverly. In a quarrel with her mother, Waverly also perceived her mother as a force of repression: "I'm never gonna play chess again! You can't make me! You can torture me all you want. I still won't!"

Thus, by representing the conflicts as patterned, this movie suggests that those conflicts were in fact clashes between the American and Chinese cultures. With the absence of a White center, the American-born daughters, who were eager to be assimilated into the White middle-class American culture, were promoted to the center, while the Chinese mothers represented the Other, Chinese culture. In addition, this movie further associated specific values with each culture. The American culture was linked to freedom and humanism, whereas Chinese culture was connected to abuse (e.g., "You can torture me all you want"), coercion, and irrationality. Through this type of articulation, the movie constructed the dichotomy between the humane Self and the sexist, oppressive, mysterious, inscrutable, exotic, and savage cultural/racial Other (Bhabha, 1994; Said, 1978). The reinforcement of the Other in turn sustains the myth of the positive and normal Western Self (Jandt & Tanno, 2001).

In this movie, the construction of the two cultures was accomplished through dichotomized articulation. The American culture was presented as normal and competent, while Chinese culture was depicted as deficient. This manifested in the languages that the mothers and daughters speak. Although both mothers and daughters speak English on most occasions, the mothers' English is broken or fractured with a Chinese accent, (e.g., "What I say" in Line 1 and "There two kind of daughters, obedient or follow own mind" in Line 10 in Example 1). This kind of pidgin English was viewed as deficient or stupid by their daughters. In sharp contrast to their mothers, the daughters speak perfect White middle-class American English. This both reflects and reinforces the linguistic prejudice that is prevalent in the American society. The so-called "standard English" (i.e., that of White middle class), is considered as intelligent and uplifting. Any deviation from this norm is seen as stupid, uneducated, or deficient. In this movie, the mothers' less perfect English was a source of embarrassment for the daughters. At times, they assumed that their mothers were too incompetent to communicate with others so they volunteered to serve as translators. By so doing, they helped silence the mothers.

However, contrary to the contempt of the mothers' failure in acquiring a second language, English, the daughters' inability to understand their mothers' Chinese was represented as unproblematic. The Chinese language, which was impenetrable to the daughters, was linked to conspiracy or corruption. The two different types of speech codes—systems of symbols, which can be more than one language (Philipsen, 1992)—thus, were articulated in association with different values: one stupid, impenetrable, and cunning; the other competent, promising, and uplifting. Indeed, White middle-class American English was treated as the norm against which the mothers' language was evaluated and judged. The Chinese language was constructed as a barrier to assimilation into the mainstream American culture.

This dichotomized articulation is also manifested in the construction of the rational Self versus the irrational Other. American cultural values, represented by the daughters, were presented as rational and reasonable, whereas Chinese cultural values associated with the mothers were made to appear irrational or ridiculous. The mother–daughter bonding stories were indeed a cluster of value collisions. For example, Lindo and Waverley's conflicts were often around cultural/relational assumptions. They had an argument before Waverley's wedding (see Example 2). Waverly had offered to accompany her mother to the beauty parlor before the wedding, but later she called Lindo to excuse herself.

Example 2:

14 Mother: So you see I still kept my promise to my mother. But years later, things were
15 somewhat different with my daughter Waverly's wedding.
16 (Phone rings)
17 Mother: Wei.
18 Waverly: Ma, It's me.
19 Mother: Oh, Waverly-ya, you already at the beauty parlor?
20 Waverly: No.
21 Mother: No?
22 Waverly: No. I'm . . . I have a headache.
23 Mother: Headache? You have a headache so you cannot keep your promise to your
24   mother?
25 Waverly: Ma!
26 Mother: No, don't come. Why should I want you to come? Why not you telling me
27   you don't want to come?
28 Waverly: Ma, that's not what I said!
29 Mother: What's wrong with the way I look now. I just go to wedding with my old
30   hair. (hangs up the phone)
31 Waverly: Shit! She always does that!

In this story, two different assumptions were underlying their communication. For the mother, a daughter should not consider herself as the center of everything, and she should give higher priority to her mother. Once a promise is made to the mother, it should be kept (e.g., Lines 14–15, 23–24). However, for Waverly, breaking an arrangement is no big deal, and it can hardly be seen as breaking a serious promise. Her individual interests should be given highest priority in any consideration. It is not necessary for her to sacrifice herself for her mother. She could cancel a previous arrangement with her mother for a good reason, "I'm . . . I have a headache" (Line 22).

The different assumptions resulted in frustration on both sides. Lindo and Waverly both assumed that the other party was insincere and manipulative. The mother perceived that her daughter was not willing to be there for her (Lines 26–27) and was telling her excuses, that is, a "headache" (Line 23). The daughter interpreted that her mother was ignoring her personal will and need. For Waverly, her mother was very authoritarian and tried to coerce her to do things against her own wish.

Unlike the story of June's piano lesson, this story was narrated from the mother's point of view. However, like the previous story, this story did not shed positive light on the mother. Walter Fisher (1984, 1985, 1987) argued that persuasion can take place only if audiences accept the truthfulness of the text. By truthfulness, Fisher does not mean the authenticity of the text or some notion of absolute truth. It is whether the text resonates with the values shared by audiences. In this case, to most of the middle-class audience members in the United States, who share individualistic beliefs and values, Waverly's reason for not going to the beauty parlor is more acceptable than her mother's request to keep her promise. Lindo's requests were based on collectivistic assumptions. They do not ring true to American audiences. As a result, she sounded demanding and needy. By merely presenting the mother's behavior without necessary contextalization (i.e., to put those behaviors in their historical, cultural backgrounds within which those behaviors were generated and shared), the movie constructed Chinese cultural values as strange, oppressive, and less humane. Once more, Chinese culture was articulated as the strange, exotic, mysterious, and inscrutable cultural/racial Other, as opposed to the normal positive American Self.

Representation of Cultures

The movie *The Joy Luck Club* as part of the new Orientalist/Assimilationist discourse simultaneously insists on "universality" and "otherness" (M. McAlister, 1992). In other words, it directs Asians or Asian Americans to be assimilated into the mainstream American culture, at the same time it denies them the opportunity for full participation (Yep, 2002). On the one hand, cultural heritages of ethnic or racial minorities were always associated with negative meanings, such as uncivilized, backward, poverty, etc.[5] This results in self-hatred and hatred of the Other. Shedding those cultural identities was made an imperative for liberation, freedom, and prosperity (Morris, 2004). However, on the other hand, ethnic or racial minorities are forever seen as foreign. Certain cultural symbols such as Chinatown, sushi, and karate were insisted upon to maintain the exotic "otherness" (M. McAlister, 1992). In this section, I will use this film as a case study to delineate the articulation strategies of new orientalist/assimilationist discourses.

The media text works through conditioning audience members' interpretations (Hall, 1980). Audience members from marginalized groups might be able to read the text oppositionally, but to do so requires extra work and the access to counter-rhetorics (Condit, 1991). That is, members of marginalized groups need to realize the dominant meaning of the text before they can engage in oppositional readings. Although recognizing the potential resistance of audience members, this study focuses on the process through which the text exercises its ideological power through different articulations (S. Hall, 1986).

In this section, I will focus on three types of articulation through which the movie text established certain discursive connections to construct the positive Self and the negative Other. These three types of articulation include: selective presentation, attribution, and subsumption.

Selective presentation

The primary power of media text is selective presentation (S. Hall, 1980). In the process of selection and representation, certain discursive elements were allowed to appear in the text, while others were excluded. This selectionre-presentation process defines the range of potential interpretations (Corner, 1983). Wolfe (1992) argued that, rather than idiosyncratic, interpretation of the text is "a culturally determined practice rooted in codes shared by message-makers and -consumers belonging to the same culture" (p. 272). The text constitutes meanings for the audience by highlighting certain meanings while excluding others (Carragee, 1990). Even when the audience engages in critical or oppositional reading, he or she still first realizes the preferred reading of the text (Condit, 1991; Corner, 1983). Thus, what is included in and what is excluded from a text are crucial to understand the ideological nature of the text.

The film *The Joy Luck Club*, like any other forms of cultural texts, is the product of selective representation. The producers of the film, consciously or unconsciously, chose to include only the negative aspects of Chinese culture, while excluding the positives. All the mothers' stories, which took place in China, were tragedies.

Lindo's mother arranged for her to marry a 10-year-or-so-old boy whom she had never met before the wedding. Her cruel mother-in-law treated her as a reproduction machine and constantly blamed her for not having a baby with the boy, who was too young to be a husband. Yingying was married to a womanizer husband. She killed her own baby because of the rage she felt due to her husband's infidelity and abuse. Suyan left her twin baby girls in the street while taking refuge during the war. An Mei lived in the misery of her mother. An Mei's mother was thrown out of the family by her own mother because she had been raped on a trip. Homeless and pregnant, An Mei's mother was forced to marry the rapist. Eventually, she committed suicide to end her suffering.

All these Chinese stories were presented as examples of irrationality or madness. The movie discourse invites the audience to believe that it is Chinese culture, which is cruel, oppressive, and irrational, that predetermined and caused the mothers' agony. Leaving Chinese culture is a literal and figurative escape from misery and suffering. The representation of the mothers' stories thus articulated Chinese culture as the negative, sexist, repressive, and inhumane cultural Other.

Contrary to the negative Other, Chinese culture, the representation of the American culture showed the positives only. The United States was constructed as a haven for the oppressed mothers. Only in the United States could they leave that suffering behind. And only in the new country were they able to provide their daughters with material comfort. The only thing that prevented them from further prospering is the baggage that they carried from China. This baggage was not only the barrier that prevented them from being assimilated into the mainstream American culture, but also the cause of the mother–daughter conflicts. Indeed, the movie constructed the mothers as the carriers of the negative Other, Chinese culture, who would pollute the positive Self.

Although American culture was not constructed as homogeneous as in the case of Chinese culture, it included only the middle-class culture. The middle class was projected as the universal class in the United States. The movie implies that anyone who comes to the United States will automatically become a member of the middle class. All the Chinese mothers, who had been miserable in China, got married, had children, and bought big houses after they came to the United States. Any deviation from the "American dream" can be attributed to laziness or stupidity of the individual. And none of them had a place in this movie.

The daughters' stories further conformed to this theme. Unlike their mothers' experiences in China, the daughters' encounters in the United States were constructed as generally positive. Waverly's White middle-class fiancée had genuine interests in Waverly as an individual and her cultural baggage, her family. He made efforts to adapt to exotic Chinese customs. Rose's husband rescued her from his mother's blatant racism. It was Rose's subservient Chinese character and lack of spirit that made her unlovable. Once she got rid of them, her husband fell in love with her all over again. The only incident that was completely negative was Lena's marriage to a Chinese American man, who was not fully American. This Chinese American man was Lena's employer and made seven times more than she did. However, this calculating man insisted on Lena paying 50 percent for all their expenses.

This movie thus associated Chinese culture with the negative—war and chaos, lack of freedom, gender inequality, brutality, and savageness—while it connected the American culture to the positive—freedom, prosperity, and civilization. Selective presentation is critical to the construction of the dichotomous relationship of the positive Self and the negative Other, because the positive Self image is possible only when it is placed against the negative Other that represents the lack of values (Jandt & Tanno, 2001). This film *The Joy Luck Club* presented a direct contrast of the Self and the Other in the opening narration:

On her journey she [the Chinese woman] cooed to the swan: "In America I will have a daughter, just like me. But over there, nobody will say her worth is measured by the loudness of her husband's belch. Over there, nobody will look down on her, because I will make her speak only perfect American English. And over there, she will always be too full to swallow any sorrow."

This narration juxtaposed the negative China and the promises of the new land, the United States. Compared with China, the patriarchal and hierarchical society, the United States was presented as a place that promised gender equality and free competition based on individual ability and achievement—being able to "speak only perfect American English." Above all, the United States was associated with happiness or pleasure, as opposed to China, which was connected to "sorrow." In this movie, the abstract concept of happiness or pleasure was further substantiated with consumerism in June's narration:

Now the woman was old. And she had a daughter growing up speaking only English, and swallowing more Coca-Cola than sorrow.

The selective representation was achieved not only through the principle of inclusion/ exclusion, but also through de-contextualization. In addition to representing the negatives only, this film abstracted Chinese communicative acts out of the socio-cultural contexts in which they are socially constructed, shared, and intelligible.

Philipsen (1992) argued that any type of talk (or other communicative acts) is culturally and historically constituted. It reflects a distinct way of thinking or distinct system of meanings. It can be understood properly only in that local context. Once the communicative act is removed from its local context, misinterpretation or misunderstanding might occur. *The Joy Luck Club* abstracted some Chinese communicative acts, which are based on Chinese frame of reference, and re-signified them into the White middle-class American system of meanings. This process of appropriation robs off the original meanings—bound by the historical and cultural forces yet multiaccentuate (Fowler, 1996)—and enciphers them into the system that fits American middle-class ideology (Ono & Buescher, 2001). The issue here is not that re-signification or appropriation distorts some authentic meaning. Rather, it contributes to establish, maintain, and reinforce certain ideology—White middle-class American ideology in this case—while challenging, contesting, and undermining others (i.e., Chinese cultural values).

For example, one theme throughout the movie is the notion of "hope." In her introduction to the Joy Luck Club, a casual association of the Chinese mothers, June narrated:

For so many years these women feasted, forgot past wrongs, laughed and played, lost and won, and told the best stories. Each week they hoped to be lucky. And that hope was their only joy. Their connections with each other had more to do with hope than joy or luck.

This notion of "hope" was originated in Chinese culture and was bounded by its historical and cultural contexts. In Chinese culture, people are understood in regards to their relations to the collective rather than as individuals (Chen & Starosta, 1998). A person is not a complete entity without considering his or her origins (ancestors) and decedents. The ancestor–self–offspring circle constitutes the past–present–future entity of the individual. The notion of hope needs to be interpreted in relation to the Chinese notion of personhood. It is more than the wish that one has for oneself. It is something that people wish, expect, plan, and attempt for themselves and their offspring. Oftentimes a hope for a particular family member would also mean sacrifice on the part of other members. The family, as a whole, would work toward that hope. Thus, hope involves more than wishes. It is associated with interdependence, sacrifice, and hard work. Hopes for children are considered as a responsibility of parents. Not being able to fulfill this responsibility is viewed as the failure of being a person.

However, the term hope was deprived of its historical–cultural contexts in the film and was re-contextualized and given the frame of reference of the White middle-class American culture. As a result, the Chinese notion of hope, with the presence of its form only, was interpreted as restraints and burdens on the free will of the individual. The daughters, who identify themselves with middle-class Americans, resented this Chinese version of hope and perceived it as a barrier to being "normal" and "free."

In the film *The Joy Luck Club*, selective representation is the primary form of articulation that constructed Chinese culture as the negative Other, and the middle-class American culture as the positive Self. Through strategic exclusion, it represented Chinese culture as the composite of the lack of values, the racial Other, which in turn confirmed the positive Self image of the United States. Moreover, the articulation process is more than establishing connections. It is achieved also through obscuring or disengaging connections that would not serve the interest of the dominant group. This film disconnected Chinese communicative acts of their culture-specific interpretive framework in which they are constituted and socially shared. By so doing, it denied the potential for positive interpretations of Chinese cultural values and communicative acts.

Culture vs. personality

Another type of articulation in this film is attribution. Attribution is the process of making sense of certain behaviors or events. Attribution is an attempt for people to explain human experiences by locating some sort of cause. It provides a sense of closure for people. Attribution, however, is also a means of articulation because it makes connections of human actions to specific reasons, thus assigning specific meanings to those actions.

The movie *The Joy Luck Club* used different attribution mechanisms in representing Chinese and American cultures. The mothers' miserable experiences were attributed to Chinese culture. However, the daughters' encounters with mean people in the American society were attributed to individual personalities.

In this movie, Chinese culture was constructed as a monolithic collective. Each member was a representative or a part of the whole entity. Any individual negative incident or wrongdoing was rooted in the collective. Culture, in this case, is treated as a script, which determines the behaviors of its members (B. "J." Hall, 1992). It is the cruel, sexist, irrational nature of the culture that predetermined the fates of all the four women (the mothers). Compared to the negative force of the culture, individual efforts and struggles for change were futile or negligible.

All the four mothers' stories, as argued earlier, were tragedies. Although different women have different experiences, all those experiences were represented in similar ways. They all happened in an irrational manner, in madness. The audience was told that there was no rationality in Chinese culture and that Chinese people were different. In fact, Mark R. Leeper (1993) remarked on the movie:

> Yet by the time the full story is revealed we have seen how *different* mainland Chinese culture is from our own and we will come to understand Suyuan's actions.
>
> (emphasis added)

The attribution of the mothers' dreadful experiences to Chinese culture rather than particular situations accented the notion of Chinese culture as the cruel, sexist, inscrutable, irrational Other. This reaffirmed that all the Chinese cultural values were opposite to enlightenment, freedom, or humanity. Thus it reinforced the notion that members of minority groups need to cast off their cultural values in order to be liberated or emancipated (Morris, 2004).

Contrary to the representation of Chinese culture, the American culture was constructed as an aggregation of individuals. Each individual is responsible for his or her own rational choices rather than for the group as a whole. Negative experiences in American culture can be interpreted as encountering particular kinds of individuals, some jerks, who are different from the "decent" middle class. In this case, culture is viewed as a loosely structured community, in which all the rational members reside. Culture, thus, is not directly connected to individual incidents. Nor is it deterministic force on personal actions. Individuals (i.e., their personalities, psyches, or pathology) are responsible for their behaviors and the subsequent consequences. As a result, members of this community can change their lives by alternating their behaviors.

Ignoring inequalities caused by the social political system in the United States, the movie constructed a free world, the positive Self, which promises everyone equal opportunity. It connected the U.S. American culture to "true humanity," or universal humanity. This humanity is also that standard against which all other cultures should be evaluated and judged.

Specifically, in this movie, the unpleasant experiences in the daughters' stories were attributed to the individuals rather than culture. For example, in her marriage to a Chinese American man, Lena had to pay for 50 percent of their expenses, despite the fact that Lena worked for that man and only made one-seventh of his salary. This Chinese-American man, unlike Chinese men in China who were blatantly brutal, was portrayed as a jerk as opposed to the model immigrants that the daughters represented.[6] Thus, the movie implied that what kind of person one turns out to be in American culture is completely a personal matter. Any link between the devious behavior of a particular person and the American culture or the whole system was denied. Furthermore, the jerk image of the Chinese-American man also reaffirmed the notion that Asian-Americans, by their association with the negative Other, were not fully American. They remain as outsider or foreigner no matter what.

Unlike Lena's Chinese American husband, the White males in Waverly and Rose's lives were represented as positive. Waverly's fiancé was a lovely White middle-class man, who was interested in exploring the exotic Chinese American culture. In order to be accepted by his future in-laws, he even tried to acquire some exotic Chinese customs, for example, using chopsticks to eat. However, this "well-meaning" White person was still rejected by the mean, picky, authoritative, and inscrutable Chinese mother, Lindo. This story invites audiences to view Chinese culture through the voyeurist lens. Chinese culture, like any racial Others, is treated as a primitive land, which invites the White man to venture and to conquer.

Rose's White upper-class husband, Ted, had a more heroic image in this movie. When she first met Ted's parents, Rose was faced with Ted's mother's blatant racism (see Example 3). Mrs. Jordan, Ted's mother, like many White people who are blind to their own discriminative attitude and behavior, claimed that her family was a "liberal family" (Line 32). However, despite that claim, she felt no hesitation to express her objection to Rose because of her cultural or racial background (Lines 35–37). She further justified her discrimination by saying that is "the way the world is" (Line 41) and "how unpopular Vietnam is" (Lines 41–42).

Example 3:

32 Mrs. Jordan: I want you to know, Rose, that we're a very liberal family.
33 Rose narrating: I couldn't believe what she was telling me. It came straight out of
34   some awful racist movie, like *The World of Susie Wang.*
35 Mrs. Jordan: Ted is going to be working with his father's company, and he's
36   going to be judged by people of a different standard,
     publishers,
37   authors, critics and their wives. And they wouldn't be as
38   understanding as we are.
39 Rose: Mrs. Jordan, you sound as if Ted and I are getting married. That is
40   hardly the case.

41 Mrs. Jordan: Oh, I know dear, It's just, that well the way the world is, how
42   unpopular Vietnam is.
43 Rose: I am not a Vietnamese. I am an American.
44 Mrs. Jordan: Of course you are. It's just, I understand you. That's all I am
45   trying to say. Do you understand?
46 Ted: Mom.
47 Mrs. Jordan: Hello, darling. We're having a wonderful conversation.
48 Ted: You know I always knew you were a . . . jerk. But shit, this is the
49   first time in my life I am ashamed of you.
50 Mrs. Jordan: How dare you use that language? I think you better apologize right
51   now!
52 Ted: I'm sorry Mom, you made a fucking asshole of yourself in front of
53   the woman I love. We're out of here Rose.

Although the movie exposed and criticizes the racist elements in American culture, it still constructed racism as an individual matter. Mrs. Jordan was depicted as a super-conservative and hypocritical woman, who was not to be seen as a representative of the whole culture. Rose's narration in Lines 33–34 implied that this was an atypical encounter for a Chinese American like herself. By presenting racism as aberrant incidents, the movie further projected the United States as a free land with no systematic inequalities. That is, although some terrible incidents might happen, the system in the United States is generally good. Rose's response further confirmed this projection. Instead of claiming her Chinese heritage, Rose defended herself by avowing her identity as "an American" (Line 43). This assertion was a double bind. It was of course Rose's attempt to fight back against Mrs. Jordan's discrimination and to gain an equal standing. At the same time, however, it assumed that the identity of "an American" was superior to any other. It also reflected the illusion that model minorities such as the daughters were permitted to become full members of the mainstream U.S. American culture.

As the story developed, Ted came to Rose's rescue. He confronted his mother by declaring "I always know you were a . . . jerk" (Lines 48–49). This again convinced the audience that the presence of racism depends on the particular individual. Therefore, racism has nothing to do with the social structure or larger ideology. Furthermore, the conflict pertaining to the racial issue was revolved in a sexist fashion in which the female was weak and needed to be rescued by her hero.

In a nutshell, attribution is another means of articulation in the constructing of cultures in this movie. The mothers' sufferings were attributed to the collective, Chinese culture, which was portrayed as homogenous. Chinese culture predetermined the fates of its people, which could not be changed by human efforts. The attribution to the collective deprived Chinese people of human agency and made Chinese culture into the negative Other, which is opposite to the positive or normal Self. On the other hand, negative incidents in United States were explained as a result of individuals (jerks) who should be accountable for their own actions. This attribution transformed societal or system issues into the personal. It thus denied the need for collective actions to challenge the existing social and political relationships.

Class, gender vs. culture

Still another type of articulation in the movie *The Joy Luck Club* is the subsumption of class and gender to culture. Ono and Buescher (2001) noted that in Disney's appropriation of other cultures, the boundaries of class, gender, and race collapse, that is, racism and sexism are intertwined in the process of commodification. The media text evokes racial and gender inequality simultaneously. Therefore it should not be read through a single lens. However, in any text, not all the three elements have equal weight. One may be more prominent. It subordinates the other two. In *The Joy Luck Club*, the issues of class and gender are subsumed to the issue of culture (race). Class and gender are denied or translated into the cultural or racial terms.

For instance, in this movie, class was never a real issue. In Chinese culture, where human suffering was pervasive, class was somehow not the cause of grief. Chinese people lived dreadful lives regardless of their socio-economic standings. A rich girl (Yingying) was married to a womanizer husband; a wealthy widow (An Mei's mother) was raped by a brutal rich guy and was deserted by her own family; a wife of a military officer (Suyuan) lost her babies during the war. Even in the case of Lindo, who came from a poor family and was married into a rich one through a family arrangement, class was not accented as the cause of Lindo's misery. She was not sold because of the situation of her family. It was the bizarre "arranged marriage" custom in Chinese culture that resulted in her unhappy life. By rendering socio-economic classes irrelevant or negligible, *The Joy Luck Club* laid the blame on Chinese culture, the negative Other.

In American culture, class was further diminished. All the Chinese immigrants and their descendants were model immigrants, who join the middle class through working hard in the free land. All the Americans that those Chinese immigrants encountered were middle or upper-middle class. Class struggles did not exist in the movie. The concept of class itself becomes an invisible category beyond commonsense.

The subsumption of class into culture helped construct a hierarchy of cultures, with Chinese culture at the bottom, American culture at the top, and Chinese American culture in the middle. In this movie the American White middle class was the center of true humanity, to which Chinese culture, the negative Other, was the complete opposite. Unlike their mothers, who were the real exotic Other, the Chinese American daughters were becoming closer to the mainstream American culture through assimilation. When the White center was absent, the American-born daughters were promoted to the center as model minorities to confirm that the system in the United States is working (Nakayama, 1988). Such subsumption reinforces the idea that shedding one's cultural identity is the only means of liberation and prosperity (Morris, 2004).

Although the movie temporarily promoted the daughters to the center with the absence of the White center, it still managed to construct the Chinese-American culture as a collective. When the White center did appear, the American-born daughters were demoted to the margin again. Thus, despite their economic success, Asian Americans are never real members of the Self no matter how hard they have been trying (Takaki, 1998; Yep, 2002). They are required to keep certain cultural elements as ornaments to sustain their Otherness. Contrary to mainstream film critics' arguments, *The Joy Luck Club* reinforced stereotypical images of Chinese or Chinese American women as "the lotus baby" or "China doll," the sexual object (Sun, 2003) and Chinese men as sexist and brutal. Those stereotypes perpetuate the foreignness or otherness of Chinese Americans who have lived in the United States for generations.

Unlike class, gender did play a major role in this movie. However, instead of patriarchy, the movie attributed female issues to Chinese culture, the cultural/racial Other. Rather than men, this movie depicted those Chinese women who endorsed cruel cultural customs as the real cause of female sufferings. Lindo's unhappy marriage was arranged by her own mother, although her father was also present in the movie. It was not the cruel and insensitive boy-husband, but her ridiculous mother-in-law who expected her to have a baby with the 10-year-old husband. Instead of the man who raped her, the grief endured by An Mei's mother was caused by her own mother and that man's second wife. Her own mother's intolerance forced her to marry the rapist. And that man's second wife had trapped An Mei's mother for the rape and later took her baby away. It was women themselves, rather than men, who caused pain for other women. Unlike feminist scholars who argue that in the process of hegemony women are inscribed in dominant patriarchal ideology (e.g., hooks, 1994), this movie ascribed it to Chinese culture. Gender thus collapses into the cultural in the film *The Joy Luck Club*.

What needs to be noted is that although this movie challenged women's problems in the context of Chinese culture, it turned blind to gender issues in the United States. The movie defined the gender issue as a unique Chinese problem, which did not exist in the United States. It projected that in the United States, women would enjoy equal rights as men do, a myth ascribed by people both in and outside the United States. For example, June's mother believed: "In America I will have a daughter, just like me. But over there, nobody will say her worth is measured by the loudness of her husband's belch."

Even in cases when the gender issue did arise, such as in Rose's marriage, the movie managed to categorize it as a Chinese problem. Rose gave up her chance to study abroad in order to support her husband's career. However, after a while her husband found her boring and had an extramarital affair. Instead of addressing it as a gender issue, the movie constructed that it was the Chinese cultural baggage that prevented Rose from speaking up for herself. An Mei, Rose's mother, explained the situation in the following words:

> I tell you the story because I was raised the Chinese way. I was taught to desire nothing, to swallow other people's misery, and to eat my own bitterness. And even though I taught my daughter the opposite, but still she came out the same way. Maybe it is because she was born to me and she was born a girl, I was born to my mother and I was born a girl. All of us like stairs, one after another, going up, going down, but always the same way.

The different articulation of gender issues in this movie subsumed gender to culture. It in fact reaffirmed the racist "saving brown women from brown men" ideology (Shohat, 1991). Ironically, while constantly lamenting the cruel treatments of women in China, and presuming that women have the rights they deserve in the United States, this movie actually helped to legitimize and perpetuate the vulnerable images of females by presenting them as objects of being protected, rescued, and loved by males. Rose was rescued by her boyfriend from the insult of his "jerk" mother and thus fell in love with her hero.

Concluding Thoughts

This study used Stuart Hall's theory of articulation to analyze the film *The Joy Luck Club*. Through articulation, this movie constructed Chinese culture as the sexist, oppressive, mysterious, inscrutable, exotic, and savage cultural Other (Bhabha, 1994; Said, 1978). The representation of the negative Other in turn sustains the myth of the White middle-class American culture as the positive Self. This construction reflects the new Orientalist/Assimilationist paradigm, which simultaneously requires Asian Americans to be assimilated into mainstream American culture and maintains the exotic "otherness" of Asian cultures (M. McAlister, 1992). On the one hand, it insists that members of minority groups need to cast off their cultural identities and to obey and follow the rules of the dominant group. On the other hand, however, it would not permit those people to fully participate in creating those rules (Yep, 2002).

My reading of the film *The Joy Luck Club* in this study may not represent the interpretations of average audience members. Radway (1984) reminded us that the audiences or readers may use interpretive strategies different from literary critics. Textual analysis is elitist for it privileges the readings of scholars rather than those of the average audience (Turner, 1990). The arguments made in this article may be different from the interpretations of ordinary audience members. However, a critical examination of popular culture texts is a political project that aims at empowerment and emancipation. It is an attempt to understand the power of the film as a politically charged cultural text and as part of public pedagogy (Giroux, 2002).

Scholars such as Tanno (1997), Tanno and Jandt (1993/1994) and Jandt and Tanno (2001) have raised our awareness about the knowledge production process that perpetuates the monolithic cultural Other as the object of research. They argue that we need to encode self-determination through "appreciation of differences" and "label appropriation" (the practice of labeling through conscious choices) in multicultural research and education. Popular culture is equally, if not more, powerful in the creation and perpetuation of the negative cultural/racial Other. It has ethnographical power in constructing non-Western cultures (Shohat, 1991). Treating popular culture as resources for public pedagogy involves more than a critical analysis (deconstruction) of a particular cultural text. Rather it should be seen as an opportunity for empowerment, that is, it should include the possibility for alternative narratives or reconstruction. Tanno and Jandt's suggestions would certainly be very helpful in teaching popular culture as public pedagogy. However, the real appreciation of differences can only be realized when conscious choices have been made to reverse the negative representation of non-Western cultures. Asante (1998) reminded us that what members of minority groups desperately need is positive interpretations of their cultural values. A productive reconstruction of popular texts should strive to go beyond challenging the myths associated with the negative cultural Other to provide positive and contextualized interpretations of those cultural values.

Acknowledgments

I wish to thank Dr. Carolyn A. Stroman, Dr. Fred E. Jandt, and the other anonymous reviewer for their insightful comments and helpful suggestions. I also thank Dr. Henry A. Giroux at McMaster University, Canada, Dr. Bradford "J" Hall at the University of New Mexico, and Dr. William Kelly at the University of California, Los Angeles for their consistent support and encouragement. An earlier version of this paper was presented at the National Communication Association Meeting, New Orleans, LA, November 2002.

Notes

1. For mainstream film critics and the White middle class American audience, Asian or Asian-Americans all look alike. They seem to see no need to differentiate Asians from Asian-Americans, or Chinese/Chinese Americans from other groups of Asians/Asian Americans.
2. Certainly audience members could read this movie in multiple ways. V. N. Volosinov's (Mikhail Bakhtin's) (1986) theories of polyphony and multiaccentuality and John Fiskes' (1987) notion of polysemy suggest that the media text provides semantic potentials for multiple interpretations. Reception researchers demonstrate such multiple interpretations in their audience research (e.g., Liebes, 1988, 1990; Lull, 1980a, 1980b, 1982; Morley, 1980, 1986; Radway, 1983, 1984). The text, nevertheless, conditions audience members' interpretations (S. Hall, 1980). The use of words in the text tends to reduce the polyphonic, multiaccentual, or polysemic nature of signs and symbols to one direction by suppressing other meanings (Fowler, 1996). Audience members could restore the polyphony or multiaccentuality in critical reading, however they often need to realize the "primary" meaning before they could apply a different frame of reference to the text (Corner, 1983; Hay, 1989; Wolfe, 1992).
3. Raymond Williams (1976, p. 87) noted "culture is one of the two or three most complicated words in the English language." He outlined the three most widely accepted uses of this term: (a) "a general process of intellectual, spiritual, and aesthetic development," (b) "a particular way of life, whether of a people, a period, a group, or humanity in general," and (c) "the works and practices of intellectual and especially artistic activity" (p. 90). In this particular case, I adopted the second definition of culture, which is based on ethnicity or race, and sometimes class.
4. The movie is not a simple translation of Tan's book. It is a reproduction—a new process of articulation. Compared to Tan's book, this movie is more complicit to the dominant ideology and leaves less room for different interpretations.
5. Such ideology in fact confounds class with ethnicity, race, or culture. It also disguises the system structure that work against all marginalized groups (Wong(Lau), 2004).
6. Sun (2003) argued that Asian American males are more silenced, marginalized and stereotyped in media representation than their female counterparts. When Asian American females were getting a certain amount of recognition, Asian American males were virtually non-existent in the media.

References

Althusser, L. (1971). Ideology and ideological state apparatuses. In B. Brewster (Ed.), *Lenin and philosophy and other essay* (pp. 127–186). New York: Monthly Review Press.

Asante, M. K. (1998). *The Afrocentric idea* (rev. ed.). Philadelphia, PA: Temple University Press.

Athanases, S. Z. (1993). Cross-cultural swapping of mother and grandmother tales in a tenth grade discussion of *The Joy Luck Club*. *Communication Education, 42*, 281–287.

Bhabha, H. K. (1994). *The location of culture*. London: Routledge.

Carragee, K. M. (1990). Interpretive media study and interpretive social science. *Critical Studies in Mass Communication, 7*, 81–96.

Chen, G.-M. & Starosta, J. W. (1998). *Foundations of intercultural communication*. Boston: Allyn and Bacon.

Chen, V. (1995). Chinese American women, language and moving subjectivity. *Women and Language, 18*(1), 3–8.

Chen, X. (1994). Reading mother's tale reconstructing women's space in Amy Tan and Zhang Jie. *Chinese Literature: Essays, Articles, Reviews (CLEAR), 16*, 111–132.

Chow, R. (1995). *Primitive passions: Visuality, sexuality, ethnography, and contemporary Chinese cinema*. New York: Columbia University Press.

Condit, C. M. (1991). The rhetorical limits of polysemy. In R. K. Avery & D. Eason (Eds.), *Critical perspectives on media and society* (pp. 365–386). New York: Guilford.

Corner, J. (1983). Textuality, communication and media power. In H. Davis & P. Walton (Eds.), *Language, image, and media* (pp. 266–281). Oxford: Basil Blackwell.

De Lauretis, T. (1984). *Alice doesn't: Feminism, semiotics, cinema*. London: Macmillan.

Ebert, Roger. (1993, September 17). Memories of Chinese-American women unfold at *Joy Luck Club*. *Chicago Sun-Times*, p. 48.

Fairclough, N. (1992). *Discourse and social change*. Cambridge: Polity Press.

Fairclough, N. (1995). *Media discourse*. New York: E. Arnold.

Fisher, W. R. (1984). Narration as a human communication paradigm: The case of public moral argument. *Communication Monographs, 51*, 1–22.

Fisher, W. R. (1985). The narrative paradigm: An elaboration. *Communication Monographs, 52*, 347–367.

Fisher, W. R. (1987). Judging the quality of audience and narrative rationality. In J. L. Golden & J. J. Pilotta (Eds.), *Studies in honor of Chaïm Perelman*. Boston: D. Reidel.

Fiske, J. (1986). Television: Polysemy and popularity. *Critical Studies in Mass Communication, 3*, 391–408.

Fowler, R. (1996). *Linguistic criticism* (2nd ed.). New York: Oxford University Press.

Gee, J. P. (1999). *An introduction to discourse analysis: Theory and method*. London: Routledge.

Giroux, H. A. (2000). Racial politics, pedagogy, and the crisis of representation in academic multiculturalism. *Social Identities, 6*, 493–510.

Grossberg, L. (1984). Strategies of Marxist cultural interpretation. *Critical Studies in Mass Communication, 1*, 392–421.

Hall, B. "J." (1992). Theories of culture and communication. *Communication Theory, 2*, 50–70.

Hall, S. (1980). Encoding/Decoding. In S. Hall, D. Hobson, A. Lowe, & P. Willis (Eds.), *Culture, media, language: Working papers in cultural studies* 1972–1979 (pp. 128–138). London: Hutchinson.

Hall, S. (1986). On postmodernism and articulation: An interview with Stuart Hall (Edited by L. Grossberg). *Journal of Communication Inquiry, 10*, 45–60.

Halliday, M. A. K. (1971). Linguistic function and literary style: An inquiry into the language of William Golding's *The Inheritors*. In S. Chatman (Ed.), *Literary style: A symposium* (pp. 330–368). London: Oxford University Press.

Hamilton, P. (1999). Feng shui, astrology, and the five elements: Traditional Chinese belief in Amy Tan's *The Joy Luck Club*. *MELUS, 24*, 125–145.

Hatch, E. (1992). *Discourse and language education*. Cambridge, England: Cambridge University Press.

Hay, J. (1989). Advertising as cultural text. In B. Dervin et al. (Eds.), *Rethinking Communication* (Vol. 2, pp. 129–152). Newbury Park, CA: Sage.

Hinson, H. (1993, September 24). *Joy Luck Club*: Misfortune smiles. *The Washington Post*, p.C1. com/wp-srv/style/longterm/movies/videos/thejoyluckclubrhinsona0a844.htm

hook, b. (1994). *Outlaw culture: Resisting representations*. New York: Routledge.

Howe, D. (1993, September 24). My mother: Mah-Jong. *The Washington Post*, p. N42.

Jandt, F. E. & Tanno, D. V. (2001). Decoding domination, encoding self-determination: Intercultural communication research processes. *Howard Journal of Communications, 12*, 119–135.

Laclau, E. (1977). *Politics and ideology in Marxist theory: Capitalism, fascism, and populism*. London: NLB.

Leeper, M. L. (1993). *The Joy Luck Club.* http://us.imdb.com/Reviews/21/2152.

Liebes, T. (1988). Cultural differences in the retelling of television fiction. *Critical Studies in Mass Communication, 5,* 277–292.

Liebes, T. (1990). Cultural difference in the retelling of television fiction. In B. L. Brook, R. L. Scott, & J. W. Chesebro (Eds.), *Methods of rhetorical criticism* (pp. 461–476). Detroit, IL: Wayne State University Press.

Lu, J. (1998). Enacting Asian American transformations: An interethnic perspective. *MELUS, 23,* 85–99.

Lull, J. (1980a). The social uses of television. *Human Communication Research, 6*(3), 197–209.

Lull, J. (1980b). Family communication patterns and the social uses of television. *Communication Research, 7,* 319–334.

Lull, J. (1982). How families select television programs: A mass-observational study. *Journal of Broadcasting and Electronic Media, 26,* 801–811.

McAlister, L. L. (1993). *The Joy Luck Club:* A review. http://www.inform.umd.edu/EdRes/Topic/WomensStudies/FilmReviews/joy-luck-club-mcalister

McAlister, M. (1992). (Mis)Reading *The Joy Luck Club. Asian America: Journal of Culture and the Arts, 1,* 102–118.

McQuail, D. (1987). *Mass communication theory* (2nd ed.). London: Sage.

Morley, D. (1980). *The "nationwide" audience: Structuring and decoding.* London: British Film Institute.

Morley, D. (1986). *Family television.* London: Comedia.

Morris, R. (2004). Living in/between. In A. Gonzalez, M. Houston, & V. Chen (Eds.), *Our voices: Essays in culture, ethnicity, and communication* (4th ed., pp. 217–227). Los Angeles, CA: Roxbury.

Nakayama, T. K. (1988). "Model minority" and the media: Discourse on Asian America. *Journal of Communication Inquiry, 12,* 65–73.

Nakayama, T. K. (1994). Show/down time: "Race," gender, sexuality, and popular culture. *Critical Studies in Mass Communication, 11,* 162–179.

Nimmo, D. & Comb, J. E. (1990). *Mediated political realities.* New York: Longman.

Olesen, V. (1998). Feminisms and models of qualitative research. In N. K. Denzin & Y. S. Lincoln (Eds.), *The landscape of qualitative research* (pp. 300–332). Thousand Oaks, CA: Sage.

Ono, K. A. & Buescher, D. T. (2001). Deciphering *Pocahontas:* Unpacking the commodification of a Native American woman. *Critical Studies in Media Communication, 18,* 23–43.

Philipsen, G. (1992). *Speaking culturally: Explorations in social communication.* Albany, NY: State University of New York Press.

Pribram, E. D. (1988). Introduction. In E. D. Pribram (Ed.), *Female spectators: Looking at film and television* (pp. 1–11). London: Verso.

Radway, J. (1983). Women read the romance: The interaction of text and context. *Feminist Studies, 9*(1), 53–78.

Said, E. W. (1978). *Orientalism.* New York: Vintage.

Severin, W. T. & Tankard, J. W. (1997). *Communication theories: Origins, methods, and uses in mass media* (3rd ed.). London: Longman.

Shohat, E. (1991). Gender and culture of empire: Toward a feminism ethnography of the cinema. *Quarterly Review of Film & Video, 13,* 45–84.

Sueda, K. (1993). An analysis of *The Joy Luck Club* from the perspective of intercultural communication. *Hokusei Review, 30,* 79–105.

Sun, C. F. (2003). Ling Woo in historical context: The new face of Asian American Stereotypes on television. In G. Dines & J. M. Humez (Eds.), *Race, gender, and class in media: A text-reader* (pp. 656–664). Thousand Oaks, CA: Sage.

Takaki, R. (1998). *A larger memory: A history of our diversity, with voice.* Boston: Little, Brown & Co.

Tan, A. (1989). *The Joy Luck Club.* New York: G. P. Putman's Sons.

Tanno, D. V. (1997). Ethical implications of the ethnic "text" in multicultural communication studies. In J. M. Makau & R. C. Arnett (Eds.), *Communication ethic in an age of diversity* (pp. 73–88). Chicago: University of Illinois Press.

Tanno, D. V. & Jandt, F. E. (1993/1994). Redefining the "other" in multicultural research. *Howard Journal of Communications, 5,* 36–45.

Turner, G. (1990). *British cultural studies: An introduction.* Boston: Unwin Hyman.

van Dijk, T. A. (1988a). *News as discourse.* Hillsdale, NJ: Lawrence Erlbaum Associates.

van Dijk, T. A. (1988b). *News analysis: Case studies of international and national news in the press.* Hillsdale, NJ: Lawrence Erlbaum Associates.

van Dijk, T. A. (1997). Discourse as interaction in society. In T. A. van Dijk (Ed.), *Discourse as social interaction* (pp. 1–37). London: Sage.

van Dijk, T. A. (1998). Principles of discourse analysis. In J. Cheshire & P. Trudgill (Eds.), *The sociolinguistics reader: Gender and discourse* (Vol. 2, pp. 367–393). London: Arnold.

Volosinov, V. N. (1986). *Marxism and the philosophy of language* (L. Matejka & I. R. Titunik, Trans.). Cambridge, MA: Harvard University Press.

Williams, R. (1976). *Keywords: A vocabulary of culture and society.* London: Fontana.

Wong, A. (1997). *Why The Joy Luck Club sucks.* http://www.olagrande.net/~webguy/writings/joysucks.html#Stereotypes

Wong(Lau), K. (2002). Migration across generations: Whose identity is authentic? In J. N. Martin, T. K., Nakayama, & L. A. Flores (Eds.), Readings *in intercultural communication: Experiences and contexts* (2nd ed., pp. 95–101). Boston: McGraw-Hill.

Wong(Lau), K. (2004). Working through identity: Understanding class in the context of race, ethnicity, and gender. In A. Gonzalez, M. Houston, & V. Chen (Eds.), *Our voices: Essays in culture, ethnicity, and communication* (4th ed., pp. 256–263). Los Angeles, CA: Roxbury.

Wolfe, A. S. (1992). Who's gotta have it? The ownership of meaning and mass media texts. *Critical Studies in Mass Communication, 9,* 261–276.

Yep, G. (2002). My three cultures: Navigating the multicultural identity landscape. In J. N. Martin, T. K. Nakayama, & L. A. Flores (Eds.), *Readings in intercultural communication: Experiences and contexts* (2nd ed., pp. 60–66). Boston: McGraw-Hill.

10

The Four Seasons of Ethnography
A Creation-Centered Ontology for Ethnography

*Sarah Amira De la Garza**

1. Background

My first professional encounters with the study of culture came under the tutelage of Asante (1987, 1988, 1990) to whom I was assigned as research assistant at the State University of New York at Buffalo in 1980. He taught me much about the interaction between ontology and notions of race and ethnic identity by exposing me to his work on Afrocentricity and sensitizing me to the ways ethnicity and race manifested in organizational and academic politics. I was then a student of organizational and interpersonal communication. Dr Asante has remained my friend and mentor over the last two decades, and his influence has been tremendous. During that time, I was encouraged to study ethnography from anthropologist Fred Gearing, known for his work among Native Americans. I was also taught statistics, methods of network analysis, conversation analysis, organizational auditing, and interactive computerized surveys. This multi-methodological approach would continue to characterize my experience as a doctoral student at the University of Texas at Austin, where I studied sociolinguistics with the British linguist Bickerton (1992, 1996), conversation analysis with the late Hopper (1992), variable analytic research with Ed Hayes and with John Daly (see Daly et al., 1997, 1998), rhetorical analysis with Hart (1987, 1996) and grounded theory and ethnography with Browning (see Browning & Shetler, 2000) and the sociologist Snow (1993).

While a Fulbright professor in the city of Chihuahua, Mexico during 1988–1989, I was sent to the faculty of psychology at the Universidad Autónoma de Chihuahua to teach qualitative research methods. This was the first year of the administration of President Salinas de Gortari, and a massive effort to 'modernize' Mexico was underway, with government expectations of unquestioned solidarity. During that year, I conducted a study of the identity of Chihuahuans during this process of modernization. Based on my daily observations that many Mexicans seemed to pride themselves on both their modernity and their traditionalism, I wanted to see what they would choose if faced with questions designed to identify their preference. The study was multi-methodological and conducted in various phases, including interviews, focus groups, and factor analysis of survey items generated to reflect an array of views held to be either modern or traditional according to the work of Inkeles and Smith (1971). What I found was that Mexicans in Chihuahua could not be identified as 'either/or,' but *both* modern *and* traditional. The resulting paper which I presented at a 1991 border studies conference in Mexico (González & Cole, 1991) questioned the cultural assumptions of factor analytic methodologies and their appropriateness for use in cultures that do not value exclusive binary categorization of experience.

If contradiction is not culturally problematic, then consistency in response can not be taken to be an indication of validity.

Reliability becomes practically moot as an issue.

It was largely in this sort of intellectual environment that I was led to question how it is that persons come to believe they understand a culture in the first place. I could see what I believed to be a tremendous interplay between the methodologies accepted for the study of culture and the cultures themselves that produced those methodologies.

Upon my return from Mexico, I spent the time from December of 1989 to July 1992, preparing for, engaging in, and writing an ethnographic exploration of the sharing of Native American (chiefly Lakota) spirituality between 'Indians and non-Indians' (see González, 1997). During that time, I watched the constant construction and deconstruction of individuals' ethnic identities as such related to the rights of access, ownership, practice, and dissemination of spiritual traditions and practices. Additionally, I witnessed debates on the rights of individuals to define themselves ethnically. The individuals I confronted and grew to know well during this study were marginal in many ways. The 'white' non-Indians identifying with Native American cultural traditions, changing their names, abandoning their families and disassociating from their own cultural histories, were 'choosing' this identity as a voice against the 'meanings' of being non-Indian. It was a way to disassociate one's self from the history of one's cultural group and to identify with an idealized other. In a fascinating way, the re-identification that took place allowed for high levels of self-deprecation and rejection of one's family and history as a perceived way to increase the 'correctness' or 'worth' of the self. The Native Americans sharing and teaching spiritual practices also were creating and maintaining an identity that had privileges of sovereignty and ownership of their traditional ways. This manipulation of ethnicities drew my attention because of the implicit awareness of the significance of identification, in many instances seemingly related to a desire to disassociate from cultural, familial, national, or personal histories of oppression, abuse, failure, waste, and other manifestations of domination. I realized that in many ways, this dynamic seemed present in the methodological trends in our field.

The Four Seasons of Ethnography are introduced as a methodology for ethnography that stemmed from my awareness that the dynamics we find in often problematic intercultural contexts are often pervasive in studies of culture. I considered the reality that the taken-for-granted approaches to reasoning and rhetoric which we put forth as academic discourse were themselves exemplars of a greater cultural ontology that assumes hierarchical relations of domination. How could I proceed to seek insight into the questions that motivated me without further reifying those structures? In 1987, Molefi Asante suggested a different, Afrocentric, ontology for rhetoric, and demonstrated its implications. Asante's approach to reconceptualizing taken-for-granted ontologically rooted structures motivated me. I asked myself, what would the ethnographic study of others look like if it were done from a perspective that at this point in our history is not taken-for-granted?

This is the question that motivated me in 1991 to begin formulating a methodological approach to ethnography that grew out of a cultural ontology of organic, circular order, one that I call 'creation-centered' (Fox, 1991, 1994, 1996), significantly different from a received western, linear, mechanical and positivistic worldview. I was frustrated by the outcomes of works inspired by Lincoln and Guba's (1985) hallmark work on the 'naturalistic' paradigm. The enthusiastic 'new' research which graduate students and others developed often seemed to me to simply 'dress up' otherwise still western, linear understanding. I struggled with the growing awareness that my own indigenous[1] cultural ontological position was informing a different reading of Lincoln and Guba. The Four Seasons of Ethnography evolved from my gradual realization that the same methods can be used within different methodologies, reflecting the source ontologies which themselves reflect cultural location and taken-for-granted assumptions. I was inspired by the joint works of scientists and theologians Capra and Steindl-Rast (1992) and

Swimme and Berry (1992). They were able to critique the mechanistic worldview without rejecting its contributions. The objective and subjective were part of the same experience, not in different boxes. I wanted to do the same. The problems I saw with our received view were not because it was 'evil', but because when treated as if it is a separate view, its implications are problematic. I searched non-traditional sources for insight, including my own cultural positioning as a woman scholar of Mexican mestizo ancestry.

2. Birth of the Four Seasons as Ontology for Ethnography

Capra and Steindl-Rast (1992) discuss paradigmatic conflicts in the natural sciences. In their dialogue, Capra claims that the traditional scientific paradigm does not allow for any work conducted from other paradigmatic perspectives *to even be called* 'science'. However, they assert, this does not mean that science is not possible from other perspectives. Systematic observation and development of theory are the necessary components for the development of a science. The oral traditions of the creation-centered non-materialist and organic cultures of the world are replete with assertions of 'learning by watching'. The cycles of nature become the experiential source of a circular cultural ontology. The scientific knowledge of people not governed exclusively by positivist rules for knowing is oftentimes disregarded due to the implicit and tacit forms of their accustomed methodologies. In order for science conducted within these paradigms distinct to the traditional western academic 'received' view to be understood, the ways of those alternatives must be articulated.

Capra and Steindl-Rast explain that social communities, and indeed cultures, are themselves paradigmatic and therefore offer alternatives to the traditional ways to do science. However, the European/American models for science, based on domination and control, they say, have become so prevalent, that even in nations whose everyday cultures are quite distinct, scientific work tends to reflect the traditional 'western' paradigm. When the methodology is driven by the paradigmatic source, the work will always reflect that paradigm, regardless of the culture or personal/political leanings and preferences of the researchers.

The Four Seasons is my attempt to reformulate the task of ethnography, as it might be viewed through the methodology of a circular ontology as experienced and often expressed by Native American 'Indian'[2] cultures. My own experience as a child was heavily influenced by the lessons taught to me by my Mexican Indian-Spanish grandparents. The 'folk' theories of my grandfather Manuel (of Comanche and Rarámuri Mexican ancestry) were all based on his systematic observation of human behavior and nature. His life as a social and political activist was rooted in these tacit theories and aided by his spiritual practice of praying to the Mother at sunrise, noon, and sunset each day. My grandmother Fina (of Lipán Apache Mexican ancestry) was a champion unobtrusive observer, sitting dutifully by her window each day watching the community come and go in the Mexican barrio where I lived as a child. We called her *juzgona*,[3] teasingly referring to her opinions freely given based on those observations. She had a daily spiritual practice and was a weather-watcher, often walking many miles in a day to gather and deliver the herbs that were needed by someone in the community.

My grandfather Cosme of Basque and Sephardic Spanish ancestry, was a silent, meditative man who read rigorously and compared the newspaper reports daily, able to provide situated opinions on the circumstances that surrounded him. Orphaned after his father was murdered by a conspiratorial group of Texans seeking to gain access to lands owned by Mexicans, he spent time during his childhood as a servant to an Anglo-Texan family and watched his last name changed from the Basque *Urueta* to *Ureta*, which was easier for Anglos to pronounce. Developing alcoholism in his adult years, he taught me of the pain existing in the spaces 'between', not too different from the pain of having to present our cultural realities through only one set of lenses (see González, 1995).

Mama Carmelita, my paternal grandmother, kept daily journals for over 50 years, and she wrote in them faithfully each night, recording the events of the day and her observations of those events. She shared her reflections on the present by comparing it to her experience growing into womanhood—the daughter of a soldier in the Mexican Revolution, and fleeing to the USA from the religious oppression of post-revolutionary Mexico. From her I learned of the pain of hegemony and of the complexity of a life story, as well as the strength that can be maintained through dutiful practice of recording one's accounts.

These were my models for my ethnographic practice and research identity, long before I used such terms. They provided the cultural ontology that served as the backdrop for my practice of ethnographic methods I would one day learn. From them all, I learned a methodology that was rooted in a spirituality of the seasons of life, action gauged in response to one's environment. It is from this ontology, garnered through the lived experience of indigenous culture and years of commited study and practice of the metaphysical spiritual traditions of my Native American ancestors, that the Four Seasons were born.

3. Ontology and Methodology

If rooted firmly in the taken-for-granted assumptions of an ontological position, the methodology for the application of particular methods will reflect the ontology in the ways the methods are developed, utilized and interpreted. The results of one's research can not be assumed to reflect a particular ontological position, simply because of the prototypic appearance of the methods. Research by many in the social sciences has moved increasingly toward a validation of a relativist ontology, often in the guise of postmodernism, at other times simply reflecting the politics of positionality. This has been reflected in the utilization of qualitative, narrative, situational, and autobiographical methodologies for data collection, analysis, and writing (Denzin, 1996; Ellis & Bochner, 1996; Goodall, 1989, 1991, 1996, 2000; Banks & Banks, 1998).

It has been my experience in the pedagogy of qualitative research methods that recent converts and zealous students new to the freedom of applied relativism will often be drawn by the aesthetics and/or emotional appeal of the subjective methodologies, not fully understanding the ontological approach that supports them. An ontology involves far more than a difference of opinion; it is the basic structuring set of assumptions of what can be taken as real. It follows that then an absence of ontological awareness, comprehension, or commitment can appear in taken-for-granted claims of ontological validity which are assumed simply on the evidence of the subjective methodologies used. The resultant problems in definition and accountability can result in seriously naïve claims about the significance of methods on face value alone. Altheide and Johnson (1994) warn ethnographers of the central importance of accountability in ethnographic work. Without an honest accounting of one's methods and decisions along the path of an emergent design (Lincoln & Guba, 1985), it is difficult to learn the nature of one's craft, or one's assumptions. The most positivistic, linear, and deterministic of assumptions can be cloaked in the sheep's clothing of qualitative methods assumed to be on face value ontologically distinct in their application due to a nontraditional textual form.

This argument is particularly relevant to the presentation of the Four Seasons of Ethnography methodology. The methods that are utilized will be familiar to students and advocates of ethnography. The Four Seasons methodology does not assume to introduce new methods, per se, but rather to demonstrate the application of a variety of already familiar ethnographic methods, along with other familiar methods from introspective and analytic traditions, *when rooted in a holistic ontology of circular order*. What results is a research process and outcome that is intentionally and necessarily both personally and academically tentative and dynamic. Like the circular progress of a spiral, the researcher and theories develop cumulatively and rhythmically, with no claims of absolute knowledge. Rather, the results are reported with *tentative certainty* (González, 1994, 1999), a paradoxical term which is characteristic of a respect for the power of nature to determine the circumstances or 'facts' of our human experience. Conceptual dynamism, or 'new ideas,' are only 'new' in that they revisit where we have already been, as fundamental to the ideas' present and equally dynamic state. History and tradition are fundamental to our current understanding. Theory is not to be refuted or disproven, but contextualized and amplified. Things get bigger, not smaller and tighter, as we understand them.

4. Guiding Ideals of the 'Received View' of Ethnography

When I refer to the 'ethnographic method', I am assuming the array of methods which in consort become both process and outcome of a study of the creation and maintenance of meanings which can serve to identify social groups and their individual members. This creation and maintenance of meanings can happen through (among innumerable others) conversation, nonverbal behavior, routines and rituals (both formal and informal), and even through personal introspection. The methods for its study, however, are fairly straightforward, and the Four Seasons methodology incorporates them: pre-ethnography, ethnography proper (immersion, observation, and interviews utilizing field notes and transcriptions), synthesis and analysis of transcriptions and notes, and the decisions and actions of writing an account of the cultural aspects explored. A classic explication of this sort of methodology can be found in Glaser and Strauss (1967), and Buraway et al. (1991) present a strong collection of the sorts of ethnographic essays that result from solid participant observation ethnography. The following comparison of guiding ideals of traditional ontologically framed work is not a rejection of such exemplary ethnographic works, but is rather a comparative explication, for the purposes of demonstrating how significant decision points in research might end in different ontologically based research strategies and actions.

I borrow the term 'guiding ideals' from Guba's *The Paradigm Dialog* (1990), in which Guba describes the 'ideals' which guide the work within positivistic, naturalistic (constructivist), and critical theory research. The guiding ideal, in effect, serves as an implicit ideological marker by which the researcher can gauge his or her 'success' within the given paradigm of research. I have expanded the use of the term to include multiple ideals which exist on a taken-for-granted level due to the cultural situatedness of 'western' research. Guba's use, I believe, accounts for ideals which characterize the conscious intent of researchers who ascribe to a given 'paradigm'. My extension of the use takes into account the very powerful ideals which are driven by cultural assumptions, in such a fashion that they are not recognized as driving ideals, but rather as taken-for-granted reality or nature. The force of these ideals persists, I believe, in the same fashion that one's primary cultural frames persist and resurface during intense experience.

It is important to mention that the separation presented in these two sets of ideals is itself part of our received view. Although the Four Seasons is presented in this text as separate, care should be taken to note that it incorporates the other as part of the many, many ways in which we experience our realities during the seasons of our experience. As Swimme and Berry (1992) point out:

> No experience can be simplistically divided up into inner and outer aspects where the outer aspects . . . refer simply to the objectively existing universe, and the inner refers simply to the subjectivity . . . the elements of experience cannot be assigned a simple, univocal origin.
>
> (1992, p. 40)

Similarly, it is hoped that the following dualist presentation can be recognized as a heuristic and not as the definition of a battleground of separate opposites. Following are four 'guiding ideals' of the received view and also of the Four Seasons ontology.

Received guiding ideal #1: Opportunism. This ideal is often discussed under the mantel of linear and material orientations to time and process. I have called it opportunism in that underlying beliefs about the passing of time, including the concepts of 'losing' and 'wasting' of time manifest themselves in activity for the sake of activity before an opportunity 'is lost' or 'passes by'. Interviews might be conducted because a member of the culture is present 'today' and might not be there 'tomorrow', even if the researcher is not really aware of a purposive need for the interview.

The linear and material orientation to process manifests itself in beliefs that research methods and outcomes should reflect predictable forms. Therefore, if data and observations do not lend themselves to the planned form or design, the form takes precedence over the integrity of the data. Linear and material orientations to time allow for the existence of the myth of 'one time' opportunities. Because time can be 'lost', it is important to plan and schedule one's research. These beliefs, rooted in the same basic cultural assumption, create a guiding ideal that values and rewards 'seizing the opportunity' and encourages the perception of 'windows of opportunity'. An action orientation to field work develops, in which 'doing' something is necessary for it to be regarded as an appropriate 'use' of time.

Received guiding ideal #2: Independence of researcher. The idea that the researcher is somehow separate from that being studied, a key epistemological issue, is at the root of this ideal. Culturally, the ability to conceive of such a separation must exist within a belief system that unitizes the world and believes that somehow the separation of entities allows for manipulation of one by another. In many ways, this guiding ideal is actually a necessary condition for the existence of the third guiding ideal, entitlement. The independent researcher can engage in any multitude of activities and relationships while in the field and by implicit definition not consider the effects and implications of the activity on his or her understanding of the culture. The belief in independence allows for immersion research to be understood as 'researcher in contact with culture' and not more radically, 'researcher *as part* of cultural context'.

Although much traditional literature on ethnography discusses at great length the reality of involvements and relationships 'in the field', and encourages methods to deal with this, it should be noted that the assumption is that methods are intended to correct and remedy the 'problems' which arise when the independence of the researcher is violated. (See Stringer, 1996 for an excellent explication of these sorts of dynamics.) Such 'violating' influence is not regarded as an integral part of the research process itself.

Similarly, a reaction formation response is possible by those who inherently remain western in their primary cultural orientation (Hall, 1983), as unpalatable as it might be to some on political or personal grounds. In this case, a hypersubjectivity and epistemology of involvement is adopted, not as a taken-for-granted position, but as a hypervigilant reaction to the independence position. I have seen this often in graduate students who adopt an ideological opposition to 'tradition', only to reify the validity of the traditional stances through their vehement adoption of 'non-traditional' methods. Their reason for the adoption is anti-traditional, rather than organically rooted in a differing ontology. This distinction is precarious, but vital to the understanding of ontology in research.

Guiding ideal #3: Entitlement. Entitlement is similarly linked to a set of cultural assumptions, in this case, regarding one's relationship to experience and the world. Social hierarchy is a taken-for-granted, and the human being, translated as self, is seen as in a dominant relationship to that which is external to him or her, including nature and the unusual. Therefore, frustrations exist when this dominance can not be exercised, as in being able to determine the form and nature of data or experience a priori.

It is manifested most intriguingly on the relation-concept level, a level that exists when one's access to information is dependent on the cooperative provision of that information by an external party. Since the taken-for-granted natural relationship is one of dominance to anything external to the familiar self, simply having a question is seen as grounds for being able to obtain one's 'answer' upon demand. Curiosity becomes sufficient grounds for entry into a culture and/ or community for study. Tanno and Jandt (1994) provide an insightful discussion of these sorts of entitlement dynamics.

Information gathered throughout one's ethnography is in the control of the owner, as ownership is a manifestation of dominance. Ownership implies ability to control activities, form, or presentation. Therefore, this guiding ideal of entitlement demonstrates itself in any number of issues of assumed access, rights to information, representation, and respect and/or understanding of interpersonal and social boundaries.

It is of interest as well that aspects of the self not known or understood could be seen as unwelcome intrusions, therefore making honest reflection difficult, too.

Guiding ideal #4: Primacy of rationality. Spiritual, physical-material, and psycho-emotional experience are made valid subjects of the rational interpretive voice. Historically rooted, the 'splits' between the dimensions of human experience are often simplified in discussions as 'mind–body' dualisms, etc. The framing of human experience as either mind or body itself implies the primacy of the *rational thought* as mind, by positioning all other experience within the realm of the body (the physical, emotional and spiritual), with the extreme forms found in physiological explanations provided for spiritual and emotional experience. Given that the paradigm assumes the duality, it is logical that the resulting science would provide explanations which would support the collapsing of categories of human experience (Asante, 1987).

While 'in the field', this can be seen by the insatiable need to explain all things within already accepted categories. It can become extremely problematic when the particular meaning of a cultural phenomenon is so primary to a culture that its members take its definition for granted through its simple or implicit reality to them. The instant that the ethnographer begins, on his or her own, to speculate explanations for these implicit meanings, the rationality of the ethnographer is privileged above the authentic embodied experience of the participants in the culture.[4]

The primacy of the rational is particularly of issue in the creation of texts that describe cultural experience. Because the written word and many academic forms are rooted in the same cultural assumptions, an authentic rendering of the understanding that might have been attained is made difficult if not impossible. What occurs in the privileging of the rational voice is essentially a veiled repetition of the cultural theme of dominance of the self which operates through the preceding ideals. Ultimately, it will be the interpretation of the rational writer that is assumed as the voice of the 'other'.

5. Guiding Ideals of the Four Seasons

The guiding ideals for a creation-centered circular ontology, as assumed by the Four Seasons methodology are presented below.

Four Seasons guiding ideal #1: Natural cycles (appropriateness). The most central guiding ideal is rooted in the belief that all natural experience is ordered in cycles, which are then reflected in the processes and experiences of all living beings. With the Four Seasons, one such cycle is used to demonstrate the circular process of preparation, growth, harvest, and rest with 'rest' moving naturally into 'preparation' without a fixed point of experiential demarcation.

These cycles are inevitable and multiple, layered upon each other due to the multiplicity of experiential domains, yet all continuing in their natural rotation. For instance, a sudden frost in spring may impede the preparation for growth of crops in summer, thereby affecting the fall harvest, and the nature of winter experience. These natural realities are used allegorically in their application to methodology.

The awareness of this cycle carries with it the interdependent notions of appropriateness and necessity, which can be confused with opportunity if the spiraling nature of circular order is not experienced ontologically. Opportunity is never 'lost', simply delayed for the reoccurrence of a season. This perspective requires that predetermined designs and outcomes be abandoned as dictators of activity. A sensitivity to seasonal cues must develop to appropriately respond throughout one's research, requiring much of the researcher as a human instrument. If the seeds are not planted at the appropriate time, in other words, allowing for the development of deep analytic skills and awareness-in-practice of the value of all forms of research-related experience, researchers not accustomed to such necessary heightened awareness can find it fatiguing. In the worst cases, researchers might lend themselves to a fatalistic approach in which they avoid the interaction of the human instrument with experience. A balanced system involves a human being who makes wise choices on the basis of awareness of the cycles and their influence on one's environs.

Four Seasons guiding ideal #2: Interdependence of all things (awareness). The interdependence of all things deals with the arbitrary nature of boundaries that we construct for ourselves in our social experience. However, it does not imply by arbitrary that they are unnecessary or without value. Rather, the awareness of the nature of boundaries calls for a further awareness of the obfuscation that occurs if we reify boundaries and perceive separateness where we have constructed it for functionalist reasons.

This guiding ideal will manifest itself most obviously in the seeming disregard for rigid disciplinary and academic dictates of what 'counts' as a source of knowledge or information. This is particularly apparent in the formal establishment of one's expertise, or theoretical sensitivity,[5] during which sources of information and insight might come from any academic discipline, from fiction, popular culture and the media, or other non-traditional fonts of knowledge and insight.

In the field, it manifests in the awareness of the inability to compartmentalize experience as 'data collection' or 'just being there'. Similarly, interviews begin with the first contacts and efforts to schedule an interview and continue with everyday encounters, rather than simply in the asking of formal guided questions. All that exists and occurs within a culture is data and related to the awareness of meanings for the persons for whom it provides primary human grounds for interpretation and execution of experience.

Personal relationships in the field, including those of the researcher with 'outsiders', become related to the study. What develops in one who operates within this ontology is an extension of the heightened awareness referred to in guiding ideal #3. One realizes that all experience is part of the whole process. Therefore, a discipline for one's life as an ethnographer must develop which respects the process and eventual report as a demonstration not just of the *focus* of the study, but also of the nature of the researcher, as part of that study.

Four Seasons guiding ideal #3: Preparedness. The spiritual traditions of those people whose practices are rooted in the observation and notion of interdependence with nature always have an element present that incorporates the awareness of the nature of cyclic processes. This element is the notion of preparedness, that one simply can not enter into that for which he or she is not prepared appropriately. A seed will not grow without being planted! This manifests itself in the appearance of personal reflexivity in the reports of one's ethnographic research, and the value given to rich descriptions of personal and experiential context for one's 'findings'. The coexisting ideal of appropriateness governs implicitly the awareness that an honest and authentic report of context will demonstrate the meaning of those findings, including the interpretations and assumed meanings reported by the researcher. In many ways this guiding ideal incorporates the notion of letting go of control, giving the upper hand to 'nature' (see Gonzaález, 1997). An example of this can be identified when I was studying the sharing of spirituality between non-Indian and Indian (Native American) persons. While preparing, the many layers of my own mixed Native American/Mexican/Spanish ancestry and my corresponding attitudes and feelings about 'culture sharing' had to be the object of my own deep reflection and honesty. I relied heavily on members of the groups I got to know throughout the ethnography for their observations on my observations. I could not have done this at a time in my life when I was tightly attached to my identity or opinions as somehow factual. I find graduate students, who want to study major life events while learning methods, are often hampered when they face the reality of their (un)readiness. There is no crime in this—no defect—it is perhaps simply not the season for that topic. The importance of heightened personal awareness can not be stressed too much.

Four Seasons guiding ideal #4: Harmony/balance (discipline). The preceding ideals, with their necessary responsiveness to the awareness of nature and relationships within it, will manifest themselves in the ultimate awareness that all forms of experience must be respected and given attention, due to their interdependent nature. As such, the rational is no more valuable than the spiritual, the material no more significant than the emotional. The awareness that builds due to the belief that all things are interdependent will ultimately lead to the growth of one's personal discipline and rigor as a human instrument and ethnographic scholar. This discipline will be rooted, not in the expectations of one's academic field or career, but in the awareness that what is not taken care of now will inevitably be dealt with again in a future cycle of seasons.

One's methodology in the field will begin to reflect a cyclical awareness of experience within individual events and situations. Field notes and forms of recording experience will respect the natural cycles that the researcher is living. The ultimate report will reflect an insightful selection of what can be reported, and in what form, so as not to upset the balance of meaning.

Ethics are incorporated into this highly intuitive form of discipline. The taken-for-granted requirements for competent and 'rigorous' methodology are authenticity and honesty with one's self as the research is conducted and texts written and shared. The skill of introspection and the ability to accept and process feedback regarding very personal aspects of one's work are probably the most important attributes of a researcher who functions within this ontology. The instrument in ethnographic qualitative research is, as so well stated by Lincoln and Guba (1985), a *human instrument.* We, the ethnographers, hold the information, insights, and conceptual turns of our research. We gather the data and process it. Nothing is produced that has not been part of us, as researchers. The research is intimate, organic and interdependent.

This sort of 'naturalist' paradigm is best described for me in the writings of Lincoln and Guba (1985). I have adopted and adapted insights from naturalism in my exposition of the Four Seasons. This naturalist paradigm which they presented in their 1985 work could also be called a 'constructivist' paradigm (Guba, 1990), or even the 'holographic' paradigm (Lincoln & Guba, 1985; Talbot, 1991). Sometimes it is simply referred to as qualitative research. Some might call it 'postmodern'. In juxtaposing the paradigm of positivism with these views as I apply them in this work, I have preferred to call the ontology of the Four Seasons a paradigm of *paradoxical tentativeness.* It is the tentative and paradoxical nature of knowing which characterizes the Four Seasons, due to the cyclical nature of experience and discovery. All 'new' knowledge is also paradoxically old, necessarily reflecting all preceding knowledge that led to its discovery. And as the cycles continue, any findings are necessarily tentative. A good example, related to nature, is a weather report.

Lincoln and Guba (1985) do an admirable job arguing that a worldview or paradigm is more than just an *alternative* perspective. It is not just 'standing in a different place'. It is seeing with *different eyes.* Based on this, all experience, not just the research process, would differ for someone operating from a paradigm of paradoxical tentativeness. One of the most significant differences is found in the subjectivity–objectivity dialectic. The paradoxical tentativeness paradigm places emphasis on the subjective experience, while the positivist places emphasis on the objective. However, within paradoxical tentativeness, objectivity is paradoxically incorporated as a form of subjective experience of equal value to (not privileged above) all others. This is accomplished through the conscious acknowledgement of the functional, yet arbitrary, boundaries, which result in a variety of standpoints. In a sense, boundaries and bracketing of those boundaries (Becker, 1992), are a manifestation of the illusion of objectivity which is necessary to operate within constructed realities. Objectivity in this sense, however, does not imply the lack of influence by external factors, rather it highlights the awareness of the researcher regarding the influence of individual factors. Since all such factors can never be accounted for, boundaries are simply an illusory heuristic for the purposes of cooperative human behavior.

The scholar who operates from the circular paradigm of paradoxical tentativeness acknowledges the *human instrument*, the researcher as a whole person, as the means of collecting, synthesizing, and analyzing data. In ethnography, the field worker in the midst of a culture being studied, is *through* his or her experience—physically, socioemotionally, rationally, and spiritually—'collecting data'. Because of this, a profound awareness and understanding of the nature of the constructed boundaries of one's own identity and personal experience is critical to being an effective 'human instrument'. In positivist research, much time is spent in the preparation and 'perfection' of a good research instrument. There is a constant awareness that the nature and quality of one's data and findings is dependent on the nature and quality of one's instrument. Unfortunately, while there is much romanticism about the human instrument, and much lip service about the need to prepare for one's ethnographic experience, there has been little yet existing that approaches what might be adequate forms of preparation of the human instrument, as required by the circular ontology of paradoxical tentativeness (for an exception to this, one might look at the work of Goodall, 2000).

Viewing the ethnographic process from a creation-centered cyclical perspective provides a means for framing one's preparation for fieldwork. By using this approach, I have also found a means for framing the entire ethnographic process—it is a spiritual enterprise, situated in a human context (González, in press). As creation-centered, I have chosen to view the ethnographic process through the cycles of the Four Seasons of nature. Creation-centered cultures share a close relationship with nature, and with the yearly cycles that govern life. Spiritual and social rituals reflect those cycles, respecting the interdependence between all things. Depending on geography, the seasons may have different characteristics, but cycles still exist, and at all levels of experience. This holographic reality is today being recognized by scholars and technologists (Talbot, 1991). When someone is culturally predisposed to view things ontologically and paradigmatically as circular and paradoxically tentative, the assumptions behind the Four Seasons will not be problematic; they are in sync with reality. For others, culturally 'western', linear and objectivist in their assumptions about reality, the Four Seasons will be a serious challenge to learn. But as many persons not culturally 'western' seem to succeed at mastering methodologies foreign to their ontologies and implicit paradigms, I believe the methodology of the Four Seasons can be learned—but hope that it might be a less traumatic experience.

I personally believe that the experience reported by many underrepresented groups in the academy, who have been forced into conducting and reporting their ethnographic work through lenses of an ontology and paradigm that is in discord with their own, is an example of the trauma which can occur if forced to repeatedly prove one's value as a scholar through an alien ontological position (see Padilla & Chávez Chávez, 1995, for graphic narrative accounts of Latina/os in US higher education). For this reason, I personally do not believe it ethical (or sound) to expect persons to totally 'deconstruct' and eliminate the present ontology or paradigm as requisite for acceptance as a member of the academy or one of its subgroups.

This much said, I believe that because the ideals of the positivist paradigm and its resultant ontology predispose persons to believe in the existence of truth vs. non-truth, any other way of looking at the world will tend to be viewed as inferior through those lenses crafted to perceive dichotomies of value. As such, I can understand why some would move to 'eliminate' the positivist paradigm. This desire is a residue of positivistic thinking. Paradigmatic change should be voluntary, based on the gradual awakening and changing of individuals and society. Imposition would simply be a replication of the hierarchical domination already present. With paradoxical tentativeness, even forces experienced as oppositional and destructive or dominating reflect something of the interdependent cyclical world in which we live. To deny the reality of variance is foolish, nor can we control it any more than we can control tornadoes or earthquakes.

It is the *application* of the methods within a paradigm that often demonstrates the ontological positioning of the researcher. I believe that the Four Seasons methodology is very compatible with what I have read concerning the naturalist/constructivist paradigm. Paradoxical tentativeness and holographic interdependent realities are difficult to handle, but especially so if one does not implicitly operate in his or her world according to these ideals. Just rationally or intellectually 'agreeing' with a concept, or 'seeing its point' is not the same as taking it for granted in the application of one's research methods.

In order to present the Four Seasons in a language that will trigger fewer predisposing constructs, I will largely abandon social science style in writing in favor of the language of ceremony from creation-based cultures that do indeed have a circular ontology. I gather much from my direct experience in ritual. What follows in an attempt to describe the essence of a Four Seasons approach to methodology.

6. The Nature of the Four Seasons

In creation-centered traditions, ceremony is much more than the ritual proper. Ceremony involves phases, which like seasons, reflect the natural process of the ceremony, itself reflecting the cycles in creation. There is a preparation, or 'spring', as I will call it, which is the foundation for all that will come. It is followed by the 'summer', or actual recognizable ritual acts. The 'fall', or harvesting portion of a ceremony is the time when the fruits of the ceremony are shared and celebrated communally. The 'winter' is the time of rest and waiting, and it is often the time when the meaning of the ceremony is received and understood. The phases of nature can be observed to provide wisdom about the phases of all human experience. What follows is a description of the ethnographic process using the four seasons to highlight the methodology and significance of the season to the overall ethnographic project.

6.1. Spring

Like the fast of the firstborn before the first Passover seder, or the fasting and ritual purification before the traditional Lakota *hanbleceya*,[6] the spring of ethnography is that time during which the ethnographer must prepare for what is ahead (Fig. 1). It is the foundation of all the work that will come. During this time, there is much speculation and dreaming about what the ethnographic project will be like. The future is uncertain, and there is excitement, anticipation, and often some reservation. In the traditional ways, one is a fool not to have some measure of fear. It demonstrates a lack of respect for what is about to be experienced. Likewise, not having some measure of fear about one's ethnographic experience demonstrates immaturity and serious naiveté concerning the entrance into the lifeworld of others.

In some ceremonial traditions, it is necessary to ask permission to be allowed to participate in the ceremony. Preparation can not begin until that is granted. Often, in the western social scientific traditions, there is an assumed 'right' to study what one is curious about. From the perspective of the Four Seasons, this is always presumptuous and disrespectful, demonstrating clearly the inappropriateness of timing for the research. In creation-centered traditions, a demonstration of sincere respect is of utmost importance. This respect might be demonstrated

Fig. 1. Synthesis of Integral Concepts for the Four Seasons of Ethnography

Spring
Related Metaphors:
- preparation, purification, tilling the soil, vision/vigil, childhood

Basic Nature:
- foundation for all the work that will come
- dreams of what might be
- establishment of patterns of interaction and behavior
- playful/experimental, not compulsively rule-bound
- planting of "seeds," the ideas and relationships that will later blossom
- "fasting"—the gradual removal from the habituated and familiar
- meditation, focusing, introspection

Methods/Tasks:
- getting permission, allowing "insiders" to tell you honestly if they perceive you as ready or able to understand them
- assessment of tacit knowledge, theoretical sensitivity, personal biases, expectations, triggers, shadow issues
- learning how to bracket through practice at spontaneous reaction and positioned analyses of self
- reading, media viewing, passive observation of relevant contexts and cultural sites
- identification of boundaries, foci, and targets for inquiry/investigation
- personal journaling

Cautions:
- dependent on the researcher's indigenous time orientation and/or ontology, could be tempted to "skip" spring
- assuming understanding of issues and topics prior to exposure or introspection/reflection
- "spring fever"—laziness due to zealous enthusiasm, no attention to detail
- being pragmatically blinded—having personal or professional motives that make you reluctant to admit your limitations or possible ethical problems—not willing to adjust when the blind spots are pointed out

Summer
Related Metaphors:
- growth, labor, community-building, work, youth

Basic Nature:
- intensity
- requires nourishment, "rain"
- attention to details and nurturing
- testing of limits on all dimensions
- rebellion, conflict, "heat"
- rules are semi-learned, form is emerging

Methods/Tasks:
- gathering data in field notes
- participant observation
- coding
- interviewing
- personal journaling & daily "checks"
- theoretical memos and constant comparison
- member-checking

Cautions:
- culture shock—need to be aware of one's reactions and perceptions and how these affect experience
- establishment of personal relationships in the field can complicate the process—especially if deep emotions are experienced, such as intimacy, conflict, jealousy, competition
- tendency to resist the need to practice bracketing, and need to consider having a confidant
- temptation to believe that participation and observation are clearly separate activities
- exhaustion—being sure to respect the needs of the self to regenerate and recuperate

Autumn
Related Metaphors:
- harvesting, release, celebration, adulthood

Basic Nature:
- "reaping what was sowed"
- community celebration
- "gestalt" of experience begins to form
- winding down, breaking away
- self knowledge
- feasting and celebration of accomplishments

Methods/Tasks:
- compiling all gathered forms of data
- theoretical saturation is reached, memos have been developed and tried in the field
- celebration of completion of field work
- leave-taking behaviors which respect the relationships formed
- leaving the field
- organization of materials
- decisions about focus begin to be made
- personal journaling

Cautions:
- overwhelming feeling may consume you as you realize the breadth of data
- temptation to believe it's "over" in order to avoid the equivocality of memos and perspectives
- going native as they realize they are not indigenously "in-group" but are feeling the natural emotional pains of separation and accommodation
- for indigenous ethnographers, the relief of being able to relax and refrain from frequent bracketing of their everyday experience can tempt them to forget that writing will require much of the same
- ethics regarding commitments to people and communities must be remembered
- preparation for re-entry culture shock should be done
- personal journaling should not be stopped

Winter

Related Metaphors:
- incubation, hibernation, retreat, waiting, solitude, elder

Basic Nature:
- slower pace
- conservation of energy
- wisdom
- incubation period of creativity
- success is determined by previous "year"
- confronation of "mortality", cold

Methods/Tasks:
- writing the ethnography
- submissions, revisions, performances
- decisions regarding extent to which your knowledge will be shared
- journaling about new tacit knowledge, theoretical sensitivity, and personal development
- speculation on future directions, both personally and professionally
- decision regarding how relationships from the field will be maintained
- rest

Cautions:
- freezing: writer's block
- believing there is nothing more to be known
- abandoning tentativeness when asked to report
- not resting or taking time to reflect on the process
- being driven by constraints rather than allowing the work to be grounded and naturally evolving
- freezing: discovery of issues that make reporting difficult on ethical grounds

through patient waiting to receive word that one can participate. Some people wait years to know that the time is right to participate in a ceremony. Similarly, just knowing that you want to study something does not mean it is the right time to do so. Respect is about 'looking at something again', getting to really know it. It is not about rushing.

During the spring, the human instrument is being prepared for fieldwork. This is a time for much introspection and honest observation of the self. What are your strengths and flaws? This will tell you much about your methodological preferences and choices once you are out in the field. The blatant extrovert, for example, will often want to rely mostly on interviews and conversation, while the more introvert researcher will want to be an unobtrusive observer. By honestly accepting these bits of information about the self, you can prepare for your study, knowing what other types of data you will need to strengthen your work, knowing what methods will best triangulate with what you personally prefer. Personal 'flaws' are not problems. They are what characterize you. What you think is a flaw simply tells you what is culturally valued, not what is 'wrong with you'. They are guides that lead you in the direction of what you might need. Because of this, the ethnographer who refuses to see his or her own characteristics, both positive and negative, is limited. Denial guarantees that you will not see the weaknesses in your method, because you do not see the weaknesses in your instrument—you.

During the spring of ethnography, you should honestly assess your biases. Unlike positivist research, biases are not problematic. They are part of your subjectivity, and they provide insight into the unique perspective that you will provide in your ethnography. Without an awareness of them, however, you will not *know* what your perspective is, and neither will your eventual reader. It will weaken your finished work. Some examples of work that have been done utilizing this ontology are those of Krizek (1994), Stage (1997), Broadfoot (1995) and Mendoza (1999).

Further introspection should guide you to look for your limitations and boundaries in terms of what you are personally capable of stomaching and tolerating. This will tell you what the scope of your study can be. Because as tentativists we do not pretend to represent whole populations with our work, it is not necessary that we have a scope that specifically accounts for all aspects of a culture. The holographic nature of reality will interestingly enough provide you with information about the breadth of the culture if you are watching carefully, with an eye of wholeness rather than separateness.

Respect others. Boundaries, because they are socially constructed, are there for a reason. Crossing them has implications—a price—and you will pay it, one way or another. In traditional ways of creation-centered practices, violating order in a ceremony is a grave transgression that carries a spiritual, if not physical, price. There are things that can and can not be done. During the spring of ethnography, we listen to others who have gone before us and know of the culture. They can help us to identify the rules. We are not all-privileged in all situations. Research does not entitle us to be able to enter, ask or do as we wish. Like in a ceremony, there are limits and boundaries of appropriateness. Spend time identifying them. Listen when they are identified to you by others, and respect them. One of my students learned this very powerfully when in her curiosity while in a sweat lodge in Porcupine, SD, taking an ethnography class in field methods which I was teaching, she attempted to approach the man who was running the ceremony. He very curtly informed her that it was not to be allowed—ceremony time was not the time for doing anything but ceremony.

Search your heart. This is very important, and is perhaps the most important aspect of preparation. *Why* are you doing this? A traditional medicine person will turn you away if you do not at some level know why you want to participate in a ceremony. If you don't know why you want to study something in this highly intimate way, then maybe you aren't ready. Spend more time reading, studying other things, learning about yourself. If you are impatient or rebellious, take time to figure out *why*. You are about to enter into other people's life worlds. Be honest about your motives, even if they are embarrassing. Don't do it disrespectfully. And this goes for looking at your own life as the subject of ethnography as well! It is a grave disrespect to participate in a ceremony 'just to see what it's like', or to talk about it publicly just for the attention. There has to be a conscious spiritual reason, not just an assumption of spirituality. Likewise, in ethnography, what is your reason? And be honest. If you don't know what your reasons are, you aren't ready. Learn to wait. Sometimes, the ethnographic process will startle you if you can not answer this. One student, while coding her field notes, was stunned when her biases against men became glaringly apparent in that she had not included any codes of negative experiences of women in a matriarchal society. She was forced to see that she had an underlying agenda for the study, which, had it not been recognized when she submitted her codes for grading, would have led her to write a report that systematically distorted what she experienced.

6.2. Summer

Just as with seasons, one wakes to the summer of ethnography gradually. It is an emergent progression from one fluid state to another. Suddenly one day you realize that you are in the midst of field work proper; you are no longer preparing. This emergent realization is only possible if preparation has been adequately conducted, for spring is actually a gradual entry into the field, a sort of 'pre-ethnography'. If this pre-ethnography has not taken place, then one feels a jolt with what can be a violently rejected culture shock. What is considered a normal part of field work from a traditional academic perspective (culture shock) is a sign of not being able to be present where you are. Preparation in the spring should teach you how to handle this more appropriately, so you can handle the culture shock better. You can not force seasons to change, and from this perspective you can not begin your work until it's time.

During the summer, it is the time to maintain steady involvement with the culture. It is the time for discipline, but not as in traditional conceptions of rigor. Discipline here implies that you have become a disciple of the culture. You are learning it not as an outsider, but in order to be part of it, *as yourself.* It is never the same to merely watch a ceremony as it is to participate in it. The level of depth of understanding you can attain through this type of participation is true understanding rooted in experience. And you need not change yourself. Change occurs naturally—when it doesn't, it is a form of violence. Summer is a time of intense realizations.

It is this intensity, this 'heat', which will determine how the rest of the year will proceed. Like an all-consuming summer heat, it can not be escaped, even at night when alone in bed. This is what true immersion fieldwork is like. That is what is so frightening and threatening about it. It is during the summer that one is most apt to want to cry, 'I wanna go home!' but not out of culture shock. Rather, like in a ceremony, because heat makes one quickly realize what is really involved. Making it through the summer of ethnography means working even when fatigued, heat-exhausted, and weary. This fatigue will be mental, emotional, and spiritual as well as physical.

The skilled ethnographer in the field learns to believe in the circle of time, in the inevitability of changes. If there is too much focus on one's specific experience, the product of the eth-nography will be narrow and non-holistic. It will not capture the essence of the culture. Rather, each and every experience within the culture is an example of the *whole* culture. And the essence, therefore, is tentative and paradoxical. Wisdom begins to grow from this aspect of summer, as fruit that reaches its full size and begins to ripen. The Sun Dancer in Lakota tradition learns the meaning of his or her people through the dance. The dancer who focuses on his or her thirst *rather than the dance,* can not understand its essence anymore than an ethnographer who focuses on specific behaviors and the recording of those specific behaviors can understand that which gives them meaning—the context, the culture.

Summer is a time of paradox. The heat makes the body naturally lazy, but work at the same time must pick up if one is to be ready for fall. Because of this, work during the summer of ethnography must always be tempered by efforts to conserve energy. The amplitude of experi-ence that offers itself in the summer provides the ground for learning one's limits as a human instrument. As relationships build and fatigue grows, the potential for conflict and confronta-tion of personal biases increases. It is in the summer that the idealized 'subjects' in the field lose their romance. They become people—ordinary people with human frailties and faults. It is in this aspect of the summer that the value of honesty during the spring can best be appreciated. Having 'sold' one's self to get access by making the human instrument seem 'too good to be true', or denying the reality of one's limitations, will become apparent as the immersed human instrument shows his or her humanity along with that of the native members of the culture. The irony is that it is the conflict that begins to arise here which is integral to obtaining a true understanding of another culture.

Until one learns to engage in conflict and *stay*, one does not know what members of a culture are like. The does not mean *watching* conflict between others, it means accepting one's own involvement in conflict as a member of the social dynamics of the field. It means perceiving this conflict not as a 'methodological *issue*', but as lived cultural experience. Not only the enjoyable or entrancing is worthy of our attention. I remember the problems I had with my landlady during the early stages of ethnographic work in Mexico in the fall of 1998. She lectured me daily on religion and morality, and when she found me buying a gift bottle of tequila in a grocery store, she snatched the money out of my hand and attempted to influence my behavior. I spent much time interviewing other women informally about this encounter, and in the process, learned much about the roles of women in conflict in Mexico. Rather than try to explain my position ad nauseum, I tried to find out why they found the situation to be permissible, although aggressive. This was not an enjoyable phase of my ethnography, but vital.

Having planted one's crops and leaving them when they begin to be choked by weeds is not the way to prepare for a good harvest. It is similarly the undesirability of one's work that tests the human instrument's ability to obtain the 'data' which will allow an ethnography that demonstrates true understanding to be written. It is always possible to alter one's tasks by focusing on journals and note-taking, on categorizing and interviewing, during this phase. The seasonal approach to ethnography sees those enterprises as important, but *not central* to one's work. What is central is the involvement with the culture, and although we have called it 'immersion' into a culture, it is more like *infusion*. The human instrument must be steeped in the culture, allowing him or herself to be transformed through the research. Only through this transformation will he or she ever understand the culture implicitly. This is what will enable him or her to write the essence of a culture rather than describe it.

What is needed in the summer is the ability to let the indigenous participants in the culture teach the human instrument how to function as a human being in their world. This is *not* in order to understand them as 'subjects', but to fully participate as one's self in their world. This means that aspects of his or her personality and preferred ways of doing things will need to be put aside for the duration of the research. One learns to make choices within the cultural frame—sacrifice and laboring are needed. This is not in order to demonstrate skill or endurance, but because the human instrument is gathering data in the way he or she best does it—through experience. It becomes part of him or her. I once heard the head dancer of a Lakota Sun Dance joking with a group of non-Indian dancers after a particularly grueling day of dancing, 'Put *that* one in your book, Jim!' At another time, he added, 'Some things aren't able to be known 'out there' with pictures and words; some things can only be known inside.' When the human instrument begins to know this intuitively rather than intellectually, fall is approaching.

6.3. *Fall*

The intuitive sense of knowing in an implicit unexplainable way is as comforting as the first cool breeze of autumn after a long hot summer. Autumn is the cool down; it is exhilarating and intoxicating to reach a sense of completion that is dangerously misleading. The year is not over, but it feels as if the work is. This is the stage when the ethnographer needs to concentrate on his or her task, because it is at this point that winter is anticipated. And winter is the deadliest of seasons if one is not prepared. Winter will be the time of writing and publishing, of sharing one's work publicly. Without a good harvest, one's efforts will be for naught.

In the autumn of fieldwork, the human instrument begins to reframe the experiences of the summer. Instead of saying, 'I wanna go home', he or she is more apt to say, '*I don't know* if I wanna go home'. Having made it through conflict with members of the culture, there is apt to be a sense of bonding and comfort with the 'host' culture. This is when it is tempting to believe that one has actually become a member of the culture. While decisions to continue relationships with members or aspects of the cultures studied may indeed be part of the life experience of many ethnographers, caution needs to be taken as a researcher during the fall. The ethnographic task from a circular, holistic perspective is to understand the culture as a whole. By being lured into purely subjective personal experience with no 'eye' for the whole picture, the ethnographic task is endangered. This is when one's journals and notebooks again become important. Summer's tasks are misleading in that they could lead one to believe that that is when note-taking is most important. From this perspective, it is actually autumn when most notes should be recorded. It is during autumn that theoretical memos should be written and necessary interviews conducted. It is the time to harvest. And this is a harvest from within the human instrument.

During autumn, the researcher should know enough about the culture to know what is being analyzed. Earlier, in the spring, the focus was on preparation of the instrument. In the summer, it was on learning the culture. Once both seasons have passed, memos can be written. From a holographic perspective, there is no problem in recording events at this time, and not only when in their midst. It does not mean that no notes can or should be taken during the summer, but merely that it is not the sole time, nor always the most appropriate. With repeated experience in the field over years, one's memory will begin to develop in ways that will facilitate harvesting in the fall. The fruit gathered in the summer is far from ready for harvesting. One must wait until fall. Clarity of one's experience is a characteristic of a well-prepared fall, like crisp clear autumn nights. Now, decisions on the perspectives for analysis must be made.

From a creation-centered perspective, all knowledge is valuable, but wisdom is only attained from completion of cycles. The insight of wisdom into a culture requires tenacity and willingness to wait until one is *ready* to 'know'. And even then, 'knowing' is tentative. It is during the fall that the temptation will grow to believe that one has certainty about the culture. That is why I have formulated the concept of 'tentative certainty' to characterize the knowledge acquired through creation-centered ethnography stemming from a circular ontology. Rooted in relativity, tentative certainty respects the boundaries of subjective context as determinants of what is known. During the fall, the ethnographer begins to create categories for what he or she has experienced, and to chronicle experiences within those categories. Categories are related to each other in explanatory expositions called theoretical memos (Glaser & Strauss, 1967). But at all times, these relationships and category assignments are subject to redefinition; they are tentative. Practicing this frame of mind during the autumn prepares one for writing in the winter. One's writing can not reflect tentativeness if the writer does not intrinsically experience it. It is not being 'wishy-washy' or noncommittal; it is the ability to believe something wholeheartedly without being attached to it. Learning how to detach one's self from things held dear, including one's ideas, was at first practiced in the spring by bracketing one's biases and limitations. Later it was practiced in the summer by learning to continue in endeavors when one does not rationally want to continue. In the fall, it is practiced through expressions of tentative certainty. All three seasons ultimately prepare for winter.

6.4. *Winter*

In the winter, the researcher 'leaves the field'. In classic fieldwork, this is meant literally. The researcher breaks away physically from personal contact and presence. This may or may not be the case with indigenous ethnography, but the human instrument must still somehow break away from dynamic lived experience to write about it. The very act of recording in writing the essence of culture changes it to something it is not. It freezes it. And the possible deathly consequences of winter's deep freezes are excellent metaphors for the costs of careless writing.

Writing about a culture, even when one is or has become a member of it, always involves leaving the culture in one's mind. This is why during the winter of ethnography, I believe it is necessary for the human instrument to physically retreat. This is not in order to leave one's subjects and setting, but rather to contemplate the separations one will create with writing. Some might call this 'considering ethics'. But the issue is not whether one is right or wrong ethically—it is considering what will be given back to the people with one's work. It is time to consider what the human instrument has experienced subjectively. It is a time to anticipate one's future life, having been through the ethnographic experience. It is a time to journal honestly while simultaneously explicating one's theories and ideas about the culture.

In the winter, the human instrument can not become so absorbed in his or her work that the self is neglected. Winter is a cold time. It is often lonely. Writing about a culture removes you from it, so that even if you are part of it, you no longer are in the same way. This is the winter of ethnography. Even if relationships established in the field are maintained, writing about it in a way that will become public transforms the writer. The human instrument has done something which will reflect back on him or her, *and* the culture about which is written. In traditional creation-centered societies, this is at the core of justice without need for elaborate legal systems. If what you do will reflect back, or come back, to you, then actions must logically be careful. What one writes about the people will inevitably come back to the writer in his or her life. It is not a light enterprise. In fact, it is quite serious.

Words are sacred in creation-centered traditions. They create realities with which we must live. Discussing open systems in human communication, we sometimes talk about irreversibility. In traditional creation-centered views, it is not just that something cannot be reversed; it is that whatever we say will keep moving along the circle of life and *come back* to us. Words are spiritual—they carry with them power and energy which lives through them. It is this spiritual force of words which enables them to create reality. It is also the reason behind the unwillingness of traditional native people to speak when they have nothing to say. Similarly, the human instrument should write to *say something*. One should not express out of obedience or strict obligation; one should express only when there is something to say. Accordingly, what is expressed by someone who truly believes it, is serious. It is not taken back. It has been *ex-* pressed, sent *out*, with an understanding that its spiritual force will come back to the sender.

This is what winter is all about. It is the culmination of all that the other seasons have involved. And it, like the other three seasons, can last for a very long time. One should not be tempted to think that the annual aspect of the seasonal metaphor implies that the Four Seasons of Ethnography reflects a calendar year. The Four Seasons highlight many real aspects of a creation-centered approach to ethnography, but the seasons of a year are fairly fixed in terms of their duration. In ethnography, the duration of seasons is determined by the subjective, spiritual experience of readiness on the part of the human instrument during a cycle that has its own rhythms.

This intuitive sense of knowing when to 'go on' to the next season means that one's work may not correspond to formal organizational requirements. But if we are honest with ourselves, formal organizational requirements rarely are natural. The Four Seasons propose an approach to understanding other cultures that is creation-based, organic, and not imposed. It requires new definitions of academic performance. For example, I believe that the well-developed and supported theoretical memo must begin to be recognized as a viable contribution to scholarship. Similarly, entries from 'spring journals' must begin to be accepted methodological reports. By allowing work that reflects the progress at all seasons to be recognized as the viable scholarship it is, ethnographers who use the Four Seasons approach to 'govern' their research would find they can be productive even before the ethnography is 'done'. All seasons are beautiful and sacred in their own way. To stress the works of one season above another is to work in an unbalanced way. When there is a lack of balance, something will fall or break eventually. By choosing to do ethnography as a reflection of the natural, organic, order in the universe, I am choosing to do my research in a way that allows me to maintain balance and harmony.

Maintaining balance in this sense does not mean eliminating conflict. Harmony does not mean carefully orchestrated synchrony. Balance is the precarious experience of dynamic tension, with the constant awareness that 'things could tip' at any point in time, if a move is made too abruptly or too dramatically with too much force. From a state of balance, all actions are 'weighed' with regard to their effect on the balance. It is not a position of comfort. It is the position of dialectic tension, of the constant awareness of opposites. Balance is the union of those opposites, and rather than eliminate the tension, it is the *experience* of it. Similarly, harmony is like the morning song of birds waking to the new day. They all sing different songs at the same time, at different paces, but with respect to each other's song. All come through. To do ethnography from a place of harmony does not mean it is without conflict or challenges or displeasure. It means that the goal of one's voice is authenticity and mutual participation. In order to do this, all the seasons must be lived fully. From this position, one would eventually come to the place of not having to ask oneself, 'Why do I do what I do?' When balance and harmony become a way of life, then one's work is merely an extension of it, and its purpose is not compartmentalized as distinct from other aspects of life (Fox, 1994). Harmony and balance exist when individuals are themselves, and when they act from a confident awareness of that knowledge. Our ethnographic work begins to answer, not the demands of structured organizations or careers, but the question of a source far greater—a question that asks, 'What is the reason for which I am called to do this work?' (Kamenetz, 1998). Imagine if birds, if trees and four-legged animals, waited for their career plans to tell them what they should do next!

Native, creation-centered people living traditional earth-based lives, have always learned how to act organically—by watching nature. Many of the traditional tales and stories of animals are reflections of the awareness developed of archetypal organic ordering (Taylor, 1998) that is developed from observing and living an experience of creation, of nature. As such, animals and plants are seen to have the same potential as humans and vice versa. This approach to looking at members of 'other' cultures has much to offer those who have been overly affected by the notions of scientific objectivity and the myth of possible separation of parts. Everything is related, and therefore what we do in our work with others will inevitably be done to us.

7. Afterward

There is an old Hopi story about Coyote and her efforts to get food for her pups. On one of her ventures, she encounters a sacred kiva, and she is overcome by curiosity. Her curiosity is so great that she violates norms in order to look into the hole on top. What she sees is lots of people— four-leggeds, birds, humans—all learning how to transform themselves into other creatures. Twice, their magic is interrupted because they realize that someone is watching, and they search for her outside the kiva, taking time from their normal activities to stop the interference. On the second search, they find her and take her in. They might as well—she has already seen them at work. Coyote is asked if she would like to learn their secret. She decides she will become a rabbit, because then she could run much faster and catch her prey. Like the others, she jumps through a hoop and is transformed into the animal she desired to be. They then tell her to go on her way and to come back another time, when they will tell her how to return to her previous form. When she leaves, the others laugh at her naivete and ignorance. Imagine, they think, she actually thought they would tell her all their secrets! Meanwhile, Coyote runs home in the form of a rabbit, and upon arriving home to her hungry pups, they eat her.

Ultimately, her own were the ones who suffered from her venture. Had she only tried to live her own life, rather than attempting to know what was not meant to be her knowledge—by attempting to do her work in the form of another.

There are many lessons here for us as ethnographers if we will only pay attention to the creation around us.

Notes

* This article was originally published under the author's former name of María Cristina González.
1. I use the term 'indigenous' to refer to a cultural conceptual 'place' of origin, as opposed to specific physical location or nation-state identification.
2. Native American peoples, as I use the term, includes those cultures that populated the lands from what is now Arctic Canada and Alaska to the southern tip of South America, prior to the arrival of European refugees, conquerors and settlers.
3. One who observes in order to judge or give an opinion.
4. This would seem somewhat less likely in an indigenous ethnography, if the ethnographer were particularly reflexive and possessing a high awareness of his or her own culture. The strength of the received view is demonstrated in that academic socialization can function to distance a cultural member from his or her own culture.
5. This formal academic preparation which utilizes theories and literature to serve as a backdrop for awareness I refer to as theoretical sensitivity, broadening the use of the term coined by Glaser and Strauss in their 1967 work, *The Discovery of Grounded Theory*.
6. Literally, 'crying for a vision', the Lakota ceremony popularly called a 'vision quest', which entails being placed in a pit or up on a hill to await one's vision.

References

Altheide, D. L., & Johnson, J. M. (1994). Criteria for assessing interpretive validity in qualitative research. In Y. Lincoln & N. Denzin (Eds.), *Handbook of qualitative research*. Thousand Oaks, CA: Sage.
Asante, M. K. (1987). *The Afrocentric idea*. Philadelphia, PA: Temple University Press.
Asante, M. K. (1988). *Afrocentricity*. Trenton, NJ: Africa World Press.
Asante, M. K. (1990). *Kemet, Afrocentricity and knowledge*. Trenton, NJ: Africa World Press.
Banks, S., & Banks, A. (1998). *Fiction and social research: by ice or fire*. Thousand Oaks, CA: AltaMira Press.
Becker, C. (1992). *Living and relating: an introduction to phenomenology*. Newbury Park, CA: Sage.
Bickerton, D. (1992). *Language and species*. Chicago: University of Chicago Press.
Bickerton, D. (1996). *Language and human behavior*. Seattle: University of Washington Press.
Broadfoot, K. (1995). *Theory of a faceted cultural self: the role of communication*. Unpublished Master's Thesis, Arizona State University, Tempe, AZ, USA.
Browning, L. D., & Shetler, J. C. (2000). *Sematech: saving the US semiconductor industry*. College Station: Texas A&M University Press.
Buraway, M., Burton, A., Ferguson, A. A., Fox, K. J., Gamson, J., Gartrell, N., Hurst, L., Hurzman, C., Salzinger, L., Schiffman, J., & Ui, S. (1991). *Ethnography unbound: power and resistance in the modern metropolis*. Berkeley: University of California Press.
Capra, F., & Steindl-Rast, D. (1992). *Belonging to the universe: explorations on the frontiers of science and spirituality*. San Francisco, CA: Harper.
Daly, J. A., McCroskey, J. C., & Ayres, J. (1997). *Avoiding communication: shyness, reticence and communication apprehension*. Cresskill, NJ: Hampton Press.
Daly, J. A., McCroskey, J. C., & Martin, M. (1998). *Communication and personality: trait perspectives*. Cresskill, NJ: Hampton Press.
Denzin, N. (1996). *Interpretive ethnography: ethnographic practices in the 21st century*. Newbury Park, CA: Sage.
Ellis, C., & Bochner, A. (1996). *Composing ethnography: alternative forms of qualitative writing*. Newbury Park, CA: Sage.
Fox, M. (1991). *Creation spirituality: liberating gifts for the peoples of the Earth*. San Francisco, CA: Harper.

Fox, M. (1994). *The reinvention of work.* San Francisco, CA: Harper.

Fox, M. (1996). *Original blessing: a primer in creation spirituality.* Santa Fe, NM: Bear and Company.

Glaser, B., & Strauss, A. (1967). *Discovery of grounded theory.* Chicago, IL: Aldine.

González, M. C. (1994). An invitation to leap from a trinitarian ontology in health communication research to a spiritually inclusive quatrain. In S. Deetz (Ed.), *Communication Yearbook XVII.* Newbury Park, CA: Sage.

González, M. C. (1995). In search of the voice I always had. In R. Padilla & R. Chávez Chavéz (Eds.), *The leaning ivory tower: Latino professors in American universities.* Albany, NY: SUNY Press.

González, M. C. (1997). Painting the white face red: intercultural contact presented through poetic ethnography. In J. Martin, T. Nakayama & L. Flores (Eds.), *Readings in cultural context.* Mountain View, CA: Mayfield.

González, M. C. (2003) Ethnography as spiritual practice: a change in the taken for granted (or an epistemological break with science). In J. Mandelbaum & P. Glenn (Eds.), *Festschrift for Robert Hopper.* Hillsdale, NJ: Erlbaum.

González, M. C., & Cole, M. (1991). The development of a culture based scale of modernity in Chihuahua: a meaning-centered approach. In Conference on Border Issues of the Instituto Norteamericno de Cultura, Chihuahua, Mexico.

Goodall, H. L. (1989). *Casing a promised land: the autobiography of an organizational detective as cultural ethnographer.* Carbondale: Southern Illinois Press.

Goodall, H. L. (1991). *Living in the rock 'n' roll mystery: reading context, self and others as clues.* Carbondale: Southern Illinois Press.

Goodall, H. L. (1996). *Divine signs: connecting spirit to community.* Carbondale: Southern Illinois Press.

Goodall, H. L. (2000). *Doing ethnographic research.* Thousand Oaks, CA: AltaMira Press.

Guba, E. (1990). *Paradigm dialog.* Newbury Park, CA: Sage.

Hall, E. (1983). *The dance of life: the other dimension of time.* New York: Anchor.

Hart, R. (1987). *The sound of leadership: presidential communication in the modern age.* Chicago: University of Chicago Press.

Hart, R. (1996). *Modern rhetorical criticism.* Needham Heights, MA: Allyn & Bacon.

Hopper, R. (1992). *Telephone conversations.* Bloomington, IN: Indiana University Press.

Inkeles, A., & Smith, D. H. (1971). *Becoming modern: individual change in six developing nations.* Cambridge, MA: Harvard University Press.

Kamenetz, R. (1998). In *Stalking Elijah: adventures with today's Jewish mystical masters.* San Francisco, CA: Harper.

Lincoln, Y., & Guba, E. (1985). *Naturalistic inquiry.* Newbury Park, CA: Sage.

Mendoza, L. (1999). In Annual meeting of the National Communication Association, Chicago.

Padilla, R., & Chávez Chávez, R. (Eds.) (1995). *The leaning ivory tower: Latino professors in American universities.* Albany, NY: SUNY Press.

Snow, D. A. (1993). *Down on their luck: a study of homeless street people.* Berkeley: University of California Press.

Stage, C. (1997). *An examination of organizational communication cultures in American subsidiaries doing business in Thailand.* Unpublished doctoral dissertation, Arizona State University, Tempe, AZ, USA.

Stringer, E. T. (1996). *Action research: a handbook for practitioners.* Newbury Park, CA: Sage.

Swimme, B., & Berry, T. (1992). *The universe story.* San Francisco, CA: Harper Collins.

Talbot, M. (1991). *Holographic universe.* New York: Harper Collins.

Tanno, D. V., & Jandt, F. E. (1994). Redefining the 'other' in multicultural research. *Howard Journal of Communications, 5,* 36–45.

Taylor, J. (1998). *The living labyrinth: exploring universal themes in myths, dreams and the symbolism of waking life.* Mahwah, NJ: Paulist Press.

Part IV
Impact of Globalization on Intercultural Communication

11

The Hegemony of English and Strategies for Linguistic Pluralism
Proposing the Ecology of Language Paradigm

Yukio Tsuda

One of the most important tasks that scholars ought to perform is to discover questions out of the taken-for-granted knowledge of existing reality. The question I want to raise in this essay concerns the use of English, which is very much taken for granted in international communication today. Speaking from a non-English-speaking perspective, I believe the use of English should not be taken for granted but should be examined as a problem of linguistic hegemony. It is evident that English is the de facto language of international communication today. It is also evident, however, that the dominance of English causes not only linguistic and communicative inequality but also feelings of anxiety and insecurity, especially on the part of non-English-speaking people in a rapidly globalizing world. Thus, there is a need to propose a paradigm to counterattack the hegemony of English so that linguistic and cultural pluralism will be secured.

Here I want to achieve two goals. One is to raise the problem of the hegemony of English by discussing the two aspects: neocolonialism and globalism. The other goal is to discuss what I call the "Ecology of Language Paradigm" as a counterstrategy to the hegemony of English and its implications for international communication and linguistic pluralism. Addressing the problem of linguistic hegemony is crucial to developing human and cultural security.

Dominance of English as Neocolonialism

It is often said that English is the most widely used language for international and intercultural communication. A number of linguists have tracked the global spread of English and have shown that it is the most prevalent language today. Ammon, for example, points out several statistical indicators of the dominance of English. The number of English speakers has grown to 1.5 billion people. English is designated as an official language in as many as 62 nations. English is the most dominant language in scientific communication, being the language of 70–80 percent of academic publications. English is the de facto official and working language in most international organizations. English is the most-taught foreign language around the world (Ammon, 1992, pp. 78–81).

English is indeed the most dominant language and operates as a common medium for international communication. Because it is dominant, however, English is also the "hegemonic" and "neocolonialist" language. It creates both a structure of linguistic and communicative inequality and discrimination between speakers of English and speakers of other languages and a form of indirect rule over many aspects of life.

The use of English has been taken for granted in most international interactions, and it has almost never been called into question. In the English-dominated Western academic community, the use of English has never been perceived as the problematic, as far as I know. Strangely enough, international and intercultural communication studies are quite indifferent to the dominance of English, while sociolinguistics centers on the objective description of the spread of English and thus legitimates the function of English as an international language.

I have been attempting to critically examine the dominance of English as the problematic in international communication (Tsuda, 1986, 1990, 1992, 1993a, 1993b, 1994, 1996). I have found that the dominance of English causes serious consequences, which include: (1) linguistic and communicative inequality to the great disadvantage of the speakers of languages other than English; (2) discrimination against non-English-speaking people and those who are not proficient in English; and (3) colonization of the consciousness of non-English-speakers, causing them to develop linguistic, cultural, and psychological dependency upon, and identification with, English, its culture and people.

Linguistic and communicative inequality

In a situation where English dominates communication, the non-English-speaking people are inevitably disadvantaged. They become mute and deaf and are therefore prevented from fully participating in communication. Let us look at an example from international conferences.

Takahashi, a Japanese anthropologist, having observed the proceedings of an international conference where English was the only official language, argues that English-dominated international conferences are bound to serve as an arena for linguistic and communicative discrimination (Takahashi, 1991). In his view, native speakers of English take full advantage of the linguistic and communicative inequality to their own benefit. Takahashi reports on his observation as follows:

> There is a great gap in the working knowledge of English between native speakers and non-native speakers, especially those speakers whose mother tongues are linguistically distant from English. Thus, native speakers of English intentionally try to push non-native speakers out of discussions by making a full use of tactics that stem from phonetic, idiomatic, syntactic, and pragmatic characteristics unique only in English . . . . For example, they step up the speed of speech, use a large number of jargons and idioms, or make utterances that are grammatically complex . . . . These communicative tactics are used to take advantage of lower proficiency of non-native speakers in English.
>
> (Takahashi, 1991, pp. 188–189)

As Takahashi observed, it seems that native speakers of English in the English-dominated conferences, use their linguistic advantage to magnify their power so that they can establish an unequal and asymmetrical relationship with the non-English-speakers and thus push them out of the mainstream of communication.

There are a great many other examples of linguistic and communicative inequality arising from the dominance of English, but it is sufficient to report one more.

W. J. Coughlin, an American journalist, wrote about the *mokusatsu* mistake that lead to the atomic bombing of Hiroshima and Nagasaki (Coughlin, 1953). He reported that the Japanese prime minister's response of *Mokusatsu* to the Allies' demand for complete surrender was misinterpreted to mean "reject" the demand, driving American President Harry Truman to decide on the atomic bombing. *Mokusatsu* actually means both "ignore" and "no comment."

The point in this historic misunderstanding of a word is that in the English-dominated Japan–U.S. communication, the Americans always have semantic control and the subtle nuances of Japanese semantics are "ignored" or "overlooked." In other words, in English-dominated communication, English speakers are in a position to control communication to their own advantage.

Linguistic discrimination and social inequality

The dominance of English also creates prejudices and stereotypes that, in turn, create discrimination against those who do not or cannot speak English. For example, those who cannot speak English fluently are labeled incompetent and thus insulted and perceived to be inferior.

Let me present two examples of discrimination as a result of the dominance of English. The first example comes from a *Time* magazine article that reports on a Chinese immigrant to the United States. He was confined in a mental institution for 31 years because of "the incomprehensible English" he spoke. The article reports that when the Chinese visited a doctor, he was diagnosed as "abnormal" because of the English he spoke (*Time*, January 9, 1984).

The second example illustrates discrimination among non-native speakers of English. Kazuo Kojima, a Japanese journalist, wrote an essay about the role of English as a basis of discrimination in Southeast Asia (Kojima, 1996). Being able to speak English is such a source of pride for the people in these countries that some proficient speakers of English are inclined to insult and discriminate against those who cannot speak English. Kojima himself heard an Indian say, "Iraqis are beasts, because they can't speak English."

I believe this is a rather extreme case, and most Indians do not hold such a discriminatory attitude. These two examples suggest, however, that the dominance of English is such that the stereotypes and prejudice are easily created and lead to discriminatory perceptions and attitudes toward those who do not and cannot speak English. In other words, English, because of its dominant prestigious status, functions as a basis of discrimination and therefore legitimates and reproduces the perceptions of linguistic prejudice and discrimination.

Discriminatory perceptions and attitudes toward non-English-speakers justify the social hierarchy, which places native speakers of English at the top of the order with non-native speakers of English placed in the middle and the people who do not speak English placed at the bottom. The dominance of English is such that proficiency in the language serves as a criterion by which to classify people.

Thus, native speakers of English reign as a prestigious ruling class of international communication: they can easily express their ideas any time, while non-native speakers and people who do not speaker English constitute the "muted" working class of international communication: they are compelled to learn English and have difficulty expressing their ideas. This is what I call the "Class Structure of International Communication" on the basis of proficiency of English.

Colonization of the consciousness

The third and ultimate consequence of the dominance of English is what is usually called "colonization of the consciousness," which refers to the mental control of the colonized by the colonizer. Colonization of the mind occurs as a result of the domination of the colonizer's language over the language of the colonized. Ngugi wa Thiong'o, an African writer famous for his book, *Decolonizing the Mind*, describes how colonialism takes control of the mind of the colonized.

> [Colonialism's] most important area of domination was the mental universe of the colonized, the control, through culture, of how people perceived themselves and their relationship to the world. . . .

For colonialism this involved two aspects of the same process: the destruction or the deliberate undervaluing of a people's culture, their art, dances, religions, history, geography, education, orature and literature, and the conscious elevation of the language of the colonizer. The domination of a people's language by the languages of the colonizing nations was crucial to the domination of the mental universe of the colonized (Ngugi, 1981, p. 160).

As Ngugi clearly points out, linguistic domination leads to mental control. This implies that the global dominance of English today is leading to the control of the mind of the global population by speakers of English and their nations and governments.

Ngugi also points out that mental control is made possible by a combination of "the destruction or the deliberate undervaluing of a people's culture" and "the conscious elevation of the language of the colonizer."

In the face of this mental controlling, the colonized/dominated are usually coerced into complying with the force of mental controlling, which facilitates the execution of the colonization of the mind. In short, the dominated are led to identify with the dominator and glorify the dominator's language while devaluing their own language and culture. This psychological identification with the dominators and their language is the ultimate result of the colonization of the mind. The process of colonization of the mind, which involves identification, glorification, and devaluing, is clearly reflected in an African sociolinguist's comment on linguistic imperialism:

> The phenomenon in which the minds and lives of the speakers of a language are dominated by another language to the point where they believe that they can and should use only that foreign language when it comes to transactions dealing with the more advanced aspects of life such as education, philosophy, literature, government, the administration of justice, etc. . . . . Linguistic imperialism has a subtle way of warping the minds, attitudes, and aspirations of even the most noble in a society and of preventing him from appreciating and realizing the full potentialities of the indigenous languages.
>
> (Quoted in Phillipson, 1992, p. 56)

The sociolinguist is aware of the mental control that dominated suffers, but most of the dominated unknowingly comply with the force of mental colonization.

Learners of English, as they try to master the language, unknowingly fall prey to the colonization of the mind. The following passage by a Japanese student well exemplifies the mental control of learners of English by English:

> The primary goal of this journey was to learn the American way of life, not to mention learning how to speak English a lot better. To learn how English really works, it would be best to take out all the Japanese words from my brain and fill it up with English instead. I must use English all the time, even when I speak to myself, write my diary, and speak to a dog!
>
> (Quoted in Tsuda, 1990, p. 145)

What we witness here is not mere linguistic and cultural learning but the transformation of a person's mind, from a Japanese mind to an English-centered one—the colonization of a person's mind and the conscious devaluating her own language.

Dominance of English as Globalism

While the dominance of English as neocolonialism occurs at the level of international interpersonal communication, the dominance of English as globalism operates at the level of international mass communication, which involves issues such as cultural and media imperialism,

Americanization of global culture, McDonaldization and Dallasization of society, unequal flow of international news and information, dominance of English on the Internet, and so on. In short, the dominance of English operates as a means of promoting globalization. The dominance of English no doubt facilitates globalization. Globalization, in turn, assumes and encourages the use and dominance of English. In other words, the dominance of English is a reflection of the structure of global relations.

Australian applied linguist A. Pennycook, for example, points out the interrelationship between the dominance of English and the structure of global relations:

> [I]ts widespread use threatens other languages; it has become the language of power and prestige in many countries, thus acting as a crucial gatekeeper to social and economic progress; its use in particular domains, especially professional, may exacerbate different power relationships and may render these domains more inaccessible to many people; its position in the world gives it a role also as an international gatekeeper, regulating the international flow of people; it is closely linked to national and increasingly non-national forms of culture and knowledge that are dominant in the world; and it is also bound up with aspects of global relations, such as spread of capitalism, development aid and the dominance particularly of North American Media.
>
> (Pennycook, 1994, p. 13)

Thus addressing the dominance of English is crucial to understanding the structure of global relations.

According to sociolinguist Roland Robertson, one of the most prominent scholars on globalization, globalization as a concept refers to "the crystallization of the entire world as a single place" (quoted in Arnason, 1990, p. 220) or "the compression of the world and the intensification of consciousness of the world as a whole" (Robertson, 1992, p. 8).

Globalization in a more concrete sense is taking place primarily in economic domains in which transnational corporations act as agents to conduct business and trade beyond national borders. As a result, we live in a global culture in which our lives are filled with products and information imported from overseas.

Globalism, therefore, is a belief or a form of knowledge that globalization should happen. Globalism accepts globalization as natural, inevitable, and beneficial for all (Pennycook, 1994).

As I mentioned, however, globalization, in fact, causes the Americanization of world culture and McDonaldization of society: it is not a process carefully planned but a mere affirmation of the structure of the unequal global relations in which a few center nations dominate over the periphery nations.

Thus globalism justifies globalization as it is occurring today. Globalism prevents us from recognizing the three consequences of globalization: Anglo-Americanization, transnationalization, and commercialization of contemporary life.

Globalization as Anglo-Americanization

The most serious problem caused by globalization is the Anglo-Americanization of the world culture, based on the Anglo-American monopoly of the global information and entertainment market.

Take movies, for example. Of 87 countries surveyed in 1992, as many as 63 countries imported the largest number of movies shown from the United States, and 20 out of 25 European countries showed 60–70 percent American movies. Also in Japan, more than half of the movies shown are imported from the United States (Tsuda, 1996).

It seems that the dominance of American products is evident in the entire international mass communication market: American videos, music, news, magazines, TV programs, and so on, are exported throughout the world. This inevitably results in "ideological control" of the world population, especially by the United States. American ways of feeling and thinking have become very visible and therefore influential as American cultural and information products have been received and welcomed by the whole population of the world.

Thus, Anglo-Americanization and globalization go hand in hand, putting the United States in a position to be able to control, influence, and dominate other countries in terms of values, beliefs, and thought. The dominance of American media products provides the United States with a power to promote and facilitate globalization as well as to spread their values across the world. It also facilitates the global spread of English. The rest of the world is simply bombarded with images, ideas, and values that are not their own. Americanization and globalization thus cause ideological invasions of countries throughout the world and interfere with cultural and political self-determination of most of the countries.

Globalization as Transnationalization

The most striking characteristic of globalization is its transnationalizing force. Due to rapid developments in telecommunication technologies and networks such as communication satellites, personal computers, and the Internet, most messages and information are disseminated on a global scale, easily going beyond national borders. These transnational messages are so powerful that the image from the West is believed to have influenced the people of East Germany and caused the collapse of the Berlin Wall. This leads us to believe that whoever controls the channels and media of transnational telecommunication can control global relations. Rather, I would say the present system of transnational telecommunication, which is heavily dominated by the advanced Western capitalist countries, is merely a reflection of the unequal power structure between the center countries and the periphery countries.

Although there was an urgent demand for a more nearly equal flow of international information, as demonstrated in the UNESCO attempt to establish a "New World Information and Communication Order" started in the 1970s, such a call from the non-Western nations has been mostly ignored by the United States and the United Kingdom as they withdrew from UNESCO in the middle of the 1980s.

The introduction of the "Information Superhighway" by the United States and the global spread of the Internet in the 1990s resulted in loss of interest in the issues of imbalance and inequality in the flow of international information. Above all, the dominance of English on the Internet and in international information is not merely creating inequality in communication and homogenization of culture but is also affirming and reinforcing the structure of inequality between English and other languages.

Thus the transnationalizing aspect of globalization does not contribute to the establishment of a more nearly equal international communication. Rather, globalization consolidates the power structure of global relations in which the advanced capitalist countries such as the United States dominate all the rest.

Globalization as Commercialization

Today for the English-speaking countries English is the best commodity that can be exported throughout the world. English is the best-selling product every year. This means that the English-speaking countries have more linguistic capital than countries of other languages. Because English is the most widely used and taught language, it is accepted easily in almost any place in the world. Because of this great communicability and acceptability, English-language related products ranging from movies, videos, and compact discs to jeans, T-shirts, discos, and so on are exported and consumed all over the world. One of the problems with this globalization of English products is that it creates "cultural domination" by the United States as well as by transnational corporations over the non-Western countries and the Third World. Herbert Schiller, an American critical scholar, characterizes the global spread of cultural domination as "transnational corporate cultural domination" (Schiller, 1991) which causes the commercialization of our life:

> Excluding the public's voice, denying the right to political expression, extolling shopping as the primary activity of human existence, owned privately, the mall is the foremost expression of contemporary capitalism, providing the daily social experience of millions of people. If the transnational corporate order has a vision, possibly an absurd notion, surely it must be that of a global shopping mall.
>
> (Shiller, 1989, p. 43)

Schiller thus points out that American and transnational corporations' cultural domination spreads in all the spheres of our daily lives, commercializing all our physical and mental spaces.

American cultural products such as Disneyland, rock and roll, McDonald's, and so forth appeal to and satisfy the libido of the people, thus transforming them into mere consumers of these products who willingly continue to purchase them without really knowing that they are trapped in a cycle of consumption. Once trapped in the cycle, people accept it as inevitable and thus become happily enslaved to consuming English products.

Globalization of English products thus not only gives rise to "cultural domination" of the United States and transnational corporations but also causes commercialization of all spheres of life. We become consumers willing to purchase English products, unknowingly helping to reproduce the structure of cultural domination and commercialization of life.

The Ecology of Language as Counterstrategy to the Hegemony of English

We have seen in the above discussions that the hegemony of English creates and reproduces inequality, discrimination, and colonization of the mind as well as Americanization, transnationalization, and commercialization of contemporary life. In order to solve these problems and realize equal and emancipatory communication, the Ecology of Language Paradigm is very much needed as a theory of resisting the hegemony of English. The Ecology of Language Paradigm serves as a theory or perspective for promoting a more nearly equal language and communication policy of world.

I first talked about the Ecology of Language Paradigm in 1993 in Honolulu at the East-West Center's Internationalization Forum. The two paradigms are as follows:

> The Diffusion of English Paradigm, which is a dominant position not only in the Anglo-American world but also in the former British colonies in Asia and Africa, is characterized by theoretical orientations such as capitalism, science and technology, modernization, monolingualism, ideological globalization and internationalization, transnationalization, Americanization, homogenization of world culture, and linguistic, cultural, and media imperialism.
>
> In contrast, an alternative theoretical orientation critical of the Diffusion of English Paradigm is what I call the Ecology of Language Paradigm. This paradigm is based on the theoretical positions such as the human rights perspective, equality in communication, multilingualism, maintenance of languages and cultures, protection of national sovereignties, and promotion of foreign language education.
>
> (Tsuda, 1994, pp. 58–59)

Thus the Diffusion of English Paradigm, or what I call the Hegemony of English Paradigm, evidently serves Western capitalism and civilization, while the Ecology of Language Paradigm is critical to the underlying philosophy of Western civilization, which advances modernization.

For example, the philosophy of language in the Hegemony of English Paradigm is basically functionalism in that it sees language as a mere tool or instrument for communication and fails to understand that it is an essential component of culture and identity. Thus the Hegemony of English Paradigm disconnects language from culture and the people using it.

On the other hand, the Ecology of Language Paradigm assumes that language is culture and is a source of personal identity. Moreover, in the Ecology of Language Paradigm language is a precious environment that creates us and our culture. Language is not a mere instrument but is an environment that influences and shapes us.

Also, the Ecology of Language Paradigm holds that language is people and people are language. Therefore, inequality among languages means inequality among people. The death pf one language is the death of its speakers.

Based on these views of language, the Ecology of Language Paradigm advocates: (1) the right to language; (2) equality in communication; and (3) multilingualism and multiculturalism. By advocating these goals, the Ecology of Language Paradigm attempts to promote linguistic and cultural security for the non-English-speaking people. Let us look at each of them.

The right to language

The Ecology of Language Paradigm regards "the right to language" as an essential right for every person. The "right to language" primarily refers to an individual's right and freedom to use a language of his or her choice in any circumstances. It therefore assumes an individual's right and freedom not to use a language that is not his or her choice but is imposed.

The central concept of "the right to language" resides in the use and recognition of an individual's "mother tongues." Tove Skutnabb-Kangas and Robert Phillipson, authors of *Linguistic Human Rights,* define "linguistic human rights' and "mother tongues" as follows:

> We will provisionally regard linguistic human rights in relation to the mother tongue(s) as consisting of the right to identify with it/them, and to education and public services through the medium of it/them. Mother tongues are here defined as "the language(s) one has learned first and identifies with." In relation to other languages we will regard linguistic human rights as consisting of the right to learn an official language in the country of residence, in its standard form.
>
> (Skutnabb-Kangas & Phillipson, 1995, p. 71)

Skutnabb-Kangas and Phillipson emphasize two factors in their definition. One is "identification with an individual's mother tongues." They believe that emotional attachment to one's mother tongues should be recognized as a part of "the right to language." Second, they emphasize social participation and integration. They recognize language as a channel that enables people to participate and integrate into society. They recognize access to an official language as a part of linguistic human rights.

Therefore, we can provisionally say that "the right to language" involves an individual's right to use, learn, and identify with a language of his or her choice including his or her mother tongues and official languages of the country in which he or she lives.

Equality in communication

The prerequisite for equality in international communication is equality among languages. If a speaker of language A and a speaker of language B communicate by speaking either one of the two languages, inequality in communication occurs.

One of the most influential factors justifying the use of English in international communication is the taken-for-granted assumption that English should be used. English-speaking people unconsciously believe English to be used by all people; that is, they unconsciously have a linguistic imperialist consciousness. Meanwhile, non-English speaking people assume that the use of English is inevitable, indicating the colonization of the mind on their part.

A consciousness revolution is thus needed to alleviate imperialistic consciousness as well as colonization of the mind.

One practical approach to establishing equality in international communication is "linguistic localism," or the use of local languages by all participants in communication. For example, when an international conference meets in France, every participant speaks French; if a conference is held in Japan, Japanese should be used. By practicing linguistic localism we can develop an intercultural awareness of sharing the burden of using and learning foreign languages.

Effective use of translators and interpreters is also encouraged to promote equal use of languages.

Use of a third language, or what I call "neutralingual communication," is another approach. When an American and a Chinese communicate in a third language, such as French, Russian, or Malay, they engage in linguistically equal communication in comparison with communication in English, which favors the American one-sidedly.

Another strategy for promoting equality in communication is equalizing the linguistic handicaps of the participants in communication. For example, if each one of us speaks a foreign language or a planned, constructed language such as Esperanto, we will be able to establish equality in our linguistic handicaps, which will lead to equality in communication.

The primary reason for emphasizing equality in communication is that it will establish "symmetry" among people, enabling them to exchange ideas without much constraint, as German social theorist Jürgen Habermas points out when he talks about "the ideal speech situation":

> pure intersubjectivity exists only when there is complete symmetry in the distribution of assertion and dispute, revelation and concealment, prescription and conformity, among the partners of communication.
>
> (Habermas, 1970, p. 371)

Of all the symmetries, linguistic symmetry is the most important for realizing equality in communication and "the ideal speech situation."

Multilingualism and multiculturalism

Multilingualism and multiculturalism can also be called "linguistic and cultural pluralism," suggesting a critical theoretical position against monolingualism and monoculturalism, which aim at one language and one culture in a society.

The history of modernization was a process of building monolingual and monocultural societies, as the standard languages were developed for efficient communication at the expense of innumerable local languages and dialects. As a result, linguistic hierarchization emerged, and it caused social stratification and inequality as well as discrimination. Globalization as it is occurring today is bringing about a new "global class society" in which English and Anglo-American culture dominate as a "global ruling class."

Linguistic and cultural pluralism is counterstrategy against the force of monolingualism and monoculturalism. It opposes monolithic singularism because diversity is the most important index of a truly democratic society. Pluralism is a philosophy of tolerance and conviviality that pursues a harmonious coexistence of different cultures, languages, and people. Pluralism also pays most attention to minorities, the dominated, and the disadvantaged, as it believes that these people should be given equal opportunities.

Thus, linguistic and cultural pluralism not only criticizes monolingualism and monoculturalism but also serves an important indicator of whether a certain society is truly democratic or not. The philosophy of pluralism is very necessary if we really wish to realize the democratization of international communication.

Implication of the ecology of language paradigm

The ideas and goals advocated by the Ecology of Language Paradigm should be incorporated into the theories and practices of international communication, especially for the purpose of democratizing it. Let me summarize some of the implications of the Ecology of Language Paradigm for the betterment of international communication today.

1. The Ecology of Language provides a critical perspective for the present English-dominated international communication and raises consciousness about issues such as the right to language and equality in communication.
2. The Ecology of Language serves non-English-speaking people by providing a theoretical base for building strategies to fight the hegemony of English and promote their cultural security and empowerment. In other words, it serves as a strategy for creating a balance of cultural and linguistic power between English and other languages.
3. The Ecology of Language provides a theoretical foundation for the development of a global language policy, especially from the position of promoting multilingualism and multiculturalism.
4. The Ecology of Language serves English-speaking people by providing them with a critical awareness and knowledge with regard to the dominance of English, raising the consciousness about equality in communication, the right to language, and linguistic and cultural pluralism.

The Ecology of Language Paradigm is not without faults and weaknesses. Perhaps linguistic and cultural isolationism is one likely pitfall. If multilingualism, for example, is pursued to the extreme at the expense of everything else, the speakers of minority languages might be confined in their languages and thus unable to communicate with the world outside of their linguistic and cultural boundaries. In order to prevent linguistic and cultural isolation, we should recognize "ecology-conscious" ideas such as "communication globalism" and "liberal localism" developed by Majid Tehranian (1993) and integrate them into the Ecology of Language Paradigm.

Conclusion

Whenever I criticize the hegemony of English, I am asked the same question: "I understand what you are talking about. But look, English is the lingua franca today. How can we communicate without it?"

I am not denying the use and learning of English. Rather, what I am challenging is the very knowledge or consciousness that makes it possible for people to ask such a question: the knowledge that takes for granted the existing reality, accepts it as natural, inevitable, and even beneficial; the knowledge that refuses to envision the alternative.

We need to examine the existing reality and then try to fill the gap between the status quo and the ideal by exploring the problems and providing solutions to them.

In conclusion, I would like to make three suggestions.

The first one is directed to scholars of international and intercultural communication. That is, I suggest that the hegemony of English should become the subject of academic inquiry in the area of international and intercultural communication, especially in the English-speaking countries.

The second suggestion is directed to English-language teaching professionals. I suggest that the English-language education should incorporate the Ecology of Language Paradigm into the contents and methods of teaching as well as teacher education.

The last suggestion goes to all speakers of English. I suggest that both native speakers and non-native speakers of English learn the philosophy of the Ecology of Language so that they will become more sensitive to the ethical aspects of international communication.

References

Ammon, U. (1992). *Gengo-to sono chii* (Y. Hieda & H. Yamashita, Trans.). Tokyo: Sangensha.

Arnason, J. P. (1990). Nationalism, globalization and modernity. In M. Featherstone (Ed.), *Global culture* (pp. 207–236). London: Sage.

Coughlin, W. J. (1953). The great *mokusatsu* mistake: Was this the deadliest error of our time? *Harper's Magazine, 206*(1234), 31–40.

Habermas, J. (1970). Towards a theory of communicative competence. *Inquiry, 13,* 360–375.

Kojima, K. (1996, January 9). Eigoken-no kuni-ga harau daishou. *Mainichi Shimbun.*

Ngugi wa Thiong'o. (1981). *Decolonizing the mind: The politics of language in African literature.* London: J. Currey.

Pennycook, A. (1994). *The cultural politics of English as an international language.* London: Longman.

Phillipson, R. (1992). *Linguistic imperialism.* London: Oxford University Press.

Robertson, R. (1992). *Globalization: Social theory and global culture.* London: Sage.

Schiller, H. (1989). Disney, Dallas and electronic date flows: The transnationalization of culture. In C. W. Thomsen (Ed.), *Cultural transfer or electronic imperialism?* (pp. 33–43). Heidelberg: Carl Winter Universitatverlag.

Schiller, H. (1991). Not yet the Post-Imperialism Era? *Critical Studies in Mass Communication, 8,* 13–28.

Skutnabb-Kangas, T., & Phillipson, R. (Eds.). (1995). *Linguistic human rights: Overcoming linguistic discrimination.* Berlin: Mouton de Gruyter.

Takahashi, J. (1991). Kokusai kaigi-ni miru Nihonjin-no ibunka koushou. In J. Takahashi et al. (Eds.), *Ibunka-eno sutoratejii* (pp. 181–201). Tokyo: Kawashima Shoten.

Tehranian, M. (1993). Ethics discourse and the new world dysorder: A communitarian perspective. In C. Roach (Ed.), *Communication and culture in war and peace* (pp. 192–215). Newbury Park, CA: Sage.

Tsuda, Y. (1986). *Language inequality and distortion in intercultural communication: A critical theory approach.* Amsterdam: John Benjamins.

Tsuda, Y. (1990). *Eigo shihai-no kouzou* [*The structure of the dominance of English*]. Tokyo: Daisan Shokan.

Tsuda, Y. (1992). The dominance of English and linguistic discrimination. *Media Development, 39*(1), 32–34.

Tsuda, Y. (Ed.) (1993a). *Eigo shihai-eno iron* [*Objections to the dominance of English*]. Tokyo: Daisan Shokan.

Tsuda, Y. (1993b). Communication in English: Is it anti-cultural? *Journal of Development Communication, 4*(1), 68–78.

Tsuda, Y. (1994). The diffusion of English: Its impact on culture and communication. *Keio Communication Review, 16,* 48–61.

Tsuda, Y. (1996). *Shinryaku-suru Eigo, hangeki-suru Nihongo* [*The invading English, the counterattacking Japanese*]. Tokyo: PHP.

12

The Intersecting Hegemonic Discourses of an Asian Mail-Order Bride Catalog

Pilipina "Oriental Butterfly" Dolls for Sale

Rona Tamiko Halualani

Western societies typically associate romance with magic, altruism, love affairs, and heterosexual marriage (Adelman & Ahuvia, 1991; Radway, 1984, 1986). But the ideology grounding this perspective on romance—at least reflected in popular texts—also tends to reinforce patriarchal power structures, male domination, and female subordination in social relations (Modleski, 1982; Mussel, 1984; Snitow, 1979). While Radway (1986) demonstrates how individuals might find pleasure from such seemingly oppressive texts, most scholars identify the ways texts laden with patriarchal signification exert authority and create self-promoting images. This knowledge, in turn, can be used as a potential source of resistance for female readers (Radway, 1984, 1986; Rakow, 1986).

The ideology of "romance" is conceived as an extension of hegemony, or "the various means through which those who support the dominant ideology in a culture are able to continually to reproduce that ideology in cultural institutions and products while gaining the tactic approval of those whom the ideology oppresses" (Dow, 1990, p. 262; Fiske, 1987; Fitlin, 1982; Gramsci, 1971; Hall, 1980). A hegemonic tool for supporting Anglo patriarchal ideology, romance in popular culture texts like novels and soap operas celebrates the male and simultaneously punishes a masochistic female (Modleski, 1982). This seductive, illusory romance also underscores Asian mail-order bride catalogues and the firms that produce them. These discourses manufacture a sexually and racially differentiated power relationship between Anglo male consumers and Pilipina female products.[1]

Asian Romance is one such mail-order bride firm. It uses a hegemonic construction of romance to sustain dominant Anglo patriarchal ideology at the expense of a subordinated Asian Pilipina female image through various intersecting discursive strategies: commodification, opposition and inoculation, euphemization, and racist ideology embedded in a specialized "Oriental Butterfly" grammar. These strategies, which intermingle economic, sexual, and racial hegemony, create an ideal product—the Pilipina "Oriental Butterfly" doll—that functions as a self-reflexive mirror of the face of Anglo patriarchal power. Just as Marchetti (1993, p. 6) discovered in Hollywood film discourses, the *Asian Romance* mail-order bride firm employs a set of discursive codes which "create a mythic image of Asia that empowers the West and rationalizes Euro-American authority over the Asian [female] other."

While some scholars describe the mail-order bride phenomenon (Chow, 1991; Joseph, 1984), others critique Asian mail-order bride services in terms of the subjugation of different Asian women (Lai, 1988; Villapando, 1989). None, however, uses cultural feminism as a framework for uncovering the intricate and intersecting discourses in such services for how Anglo patriarchal capitalist hegemony is affirmed under the guise of romance. This essay analyzes the interrelated hegemonic operations manifest in *Asian Romance*, an Asian mail-order bride catalog that functions rhetorically to celebrate dominant Anglo patriarchal ideology and perpetuate the colonization of the Asian Pacific "other."

The Lens of Feminist Cultural Studies

Drawing from cultural studies and feminist criticism, feminist cultural studies investigates socio-political constructions of women, women's subordination on the basis of gender, race, and class, especially in media representations, and women's resistance to such definitions (Baehr & Dyer, 1987; Hobson, 1982; Lont, 1993; McRobbie & Wartella, 1986). Textual analyses uncover the "ideological underpinnings of social structures . . . and their effects on the humans who create and inhabit those forms" (Bowen & Watt, 1993, p. 4). Feminist cultural studies scholars also recognize that many media images "reflect not only sexism but . . . other forms of oppression based on class, race, and nationality" (Lont, 1993, p. 241; Baehr, 1981); in addition, they hold economics, politics, and socio-cultural factors responsible for creating ideology in texts. Consequently, feminist cultural studies show strains of Marxism because it embraces the view that capitalist social structures exploit and oppress individuals, especially women (Lont, 1993; Steeves, 1987). Thus, because it highlights the "critical intersection of race, class, ethnic background, and gender" in capitalistic systems (Treichler & Wartella, 1986, p. 2), feminist cultural studies is an appropriate approach from which to examine *Asian Romance*.

Ideology and hegemony are two principle constructs of feminist cultural studies. Schwichtenberg (1989) used both to investigate representations of "femininity" and women, and drew from the work of other scholars to develop these critical instruments and the "diffusion of consent" (Hall, 1982). They are also associated with power relations and, specifically, with the ways in which symbolic forms "establish and sustain relations of domination" (Thompson, 1990, p. 58).

Hegemony refers to the continuous and intricate reworking of dominant interests to win and re-win the willing consent of subordinate groups (Althusser, 1971; Fiske, 1987; Gramsci, 1971). The difference between hegemony and ideology is that the former seeks to win consent and reproduce dominant ideas largely through coopting oppositional elements that protest prevalent ideologies. Symbolic forms, then, become sites of struggle between dominant and subordinate interests; these tensions embody various shades of domination, opposition, resistance, and recuperation (Fishe, 1987; Schwichtenberg, 1989). In addition, discourses reflecting hegemonic practices often incorporate oppositional, negotiated, and decoratively designed ideas especially when capitalist economics are at issue (Almquist, 1984; Chow, 1991; Gitlin, 1986; Lai, 1988). Ideology and hegemony, then, provide the critical foundation for exploring forms of domination and their operations within symbols, language, and discourses.

When applied specifically to Pilipina women, however, this feminist cultural studies approach runs the risk of oppressing women at another level—a meta-critical level if you will. Pilipina women comprise a group symbolizing the convergence of gender, race, and sexuality (hooks, 1984). For these reasons, Asian feminist scholars argue that Asian Pacific women and their experiences have been articulated only under the broader concerns of "women" and "feminism," concerns which reflect mostly "white middle class women's interests" (Chia, 1983; Chow, 1989, 1991; Dill, 1983; Loo & Ong, 1982; Yamada, 1981), and further push Asian Pacific women to the margins of academic discourse (Chia, 1983; Chow, 1989). Chow (1991) and Yamada (1981) ground their analyses of Asian Pacific women within the political intersection of gender, race, class, and culture, and within the more traditional social contexts of an Asian patriarchal hierarchy. Only by viewing Asian Pacific women within a cultural milieu of male domination, role constraint, and subordinate placement in their own Asian communities can their experiences be adequately uncovered and chronicled (Chia, 1983; Chow, 1989, 1991; Yamada, 1981). This analysis of *Asian Romance* commences via a feminist cultural studies framework but with sensitivity toward Pilipina women so as to avoid marginalizing their identity under the generic labels "feminist" and "women."

Hegemony and the Ideology of Patriarchal Romance

The Asian mail-order bride trade, begun in the early 1940's, continues to be a booming enterprise today throughout Europe, Australia, and parts of the United States (JCAL, 1985; Joseph, 1984; Lai, 1988; Serita, 1984; Villapando, 1989). The contemporary version differs only in that what once were family arranged unions are now more impersonal financial transactions based on gender and racial imbalances (JACL, 1985; Villapando, 1989). Approximately fifty of these bride services operate in America. Sporting names like "Love Overseas" and "Lotus Blossom," they advertise brides from Thailand, Malaysia, Singapore, and the Philippines in mainstream newspapers and magazine publications (JACL, 1985; Joseph, 1984; Villapando, 1989).

Several articles discussing this phenomenon attempt to characterize both women and men who procure the services of mail-order bride firms. Brides, for example, are likely to be vulnerable and dependent on their new husbands (JACL, 1985; Joseph, 1984; Lai, 1988; Serita, 1984; Villapando, 1989). Because money is exchanged for them, they also may feel emotional and financial obligations to meet their husbands' needs and demands (JACL, 1985; Lai, 1985; Serita, 1984; Villapando, 1989). Also, Asian brides who are unfamiliar with the United States' immigration procedures and the American legal system are significantly disadvantaged for this lack of knowledge can potentially be used by male spouses as a mechanism of control and guarantee of dominance in the marriage (JACL, 1985; Lai, 1988; Serita, 1984; Villapando, 1989).

In contrast, male clients tend to be active initiators of the "marriage" transaction (JACL, 1985; Joseph, 1984; Lai, 1988; Serita, 1984; Villapando, 1989). The customer profile features older, divorced European and Anglo American men interested in traditional family oriented Asian women (JACL, 1985, Joseph, 1984; Lai, 1988; Serita, 1984; Villapando, 1989). One man's explanation is illustrative: "I wanted a wife who isn't career-oriented, who participates very little in the world outside, who does not have high aspirations, who is useful, and whose life revolves around me" (Joseph, 1984, p. 1).

These "marriage agencies" package Asian women as goods for sale. Catalogs and videos come complete with pictures and answers to such questions as "How would you described your breasts?" and "Do you believe in women's liberation?" (Serita, 1984, p. 39; Villapando, 1989). Other catalog descriptions read: "They love to do things to make their husbands happy", and "Most, if not all, are very feminine, loyal, loving, and virgins" (Lai, 1988, p. 168). Asian brides are depicted as obedient and erotic, the keys to fulfilling males' demands (JACL, 1985; Serita, 1984; Villapando, 1989). Thus, these Asian women are marketed as "exotic, subservient wife imports" for sale and as alternatives for men sick of independent "liberal" Western women (JACL, 1985; Joseph, 1984; Lai, 1988; Serita, 1984; Villapando, 1989).

In resurfacing, however, firms trading in marriage define themselves not as the archaic "mail-order bride services" of yesterday, but as contemporary "romance manufacturers" or "introduction agencies" (Lai, 1988; Serrati, 1984; Villapando, 1989). One of these companies is *Asian Romance*, a Davis, California business run by husband and wife, Michael and Chantal Donahue. Relocated to Davis from the San Francisco Bay Area in 1991, the firm publishes a bi-monthly magazine/catalog targeted for Anglo males. The catalog features pictures and biographical information (age, height, weight, education) of Pilipina women, a description of the company's services, an order form, and cartons depicting Anglo male and Pilipina bride romance. *Asian Romance* provides a complex set of discourses sexually and racially reproducing the mythic image of "Oriental femininity."

The hegemonic force of romance which constructs dominant and subordinate relations based on gender and race appears in four major forms throughout the Asian Romance catalog: commodification, opposition and inoculation, euphemization, and racist ideology. These devises promote Anglo patriarchal superiority in economic, social, and sexual spheres.

Commodification

Commodification is product of capitalism and mass media. As Fiske (1987, p. 259) notes. "the circulation of commodities in the marketplace is . . . the circulation of meaning and identities." Goldman and Wilson (1983) explain the ideological role of this hegemonic device both practically and symbolically. Practically, the meaning of a commodity is determined by its use or exchange value; its symbolic value depends upon the degree to which it functions as a "commodity-sign." A commodity-sign consists of two parts: a "signifying unit" or signifier is an object, picture, or individual, while "signified meaning" is the image associated with the signifier. Thus, when individuals purchase a product, they also acquire its associated image. As Goldman and Wilson (1983) illustrate, a Mercedes Benz automobile may be useful as a car but it is more symbolically valued for the social status it allegedly offers to purchasers. Thus, it functions as a commodity-sign because what it signifies is equated with what it is. The power of the commodity form lies in its ability to lead purchasers to see the sign only in terms of what it signifies, or to be what one buys (Goldman & Wilson, 1983).

Commodification in Asian mail-order bride catalogues legitimizes the American capitalist system and its dominant social relation of gendered and racialized domination–subordination (Almoquist, 1984; Chow, 1991; Gitlin, 1986; Goldman & Wilson, 1983; Lai, 1989). An instrument of hegemony, commodification strips Pilipina women of their uniqueness as humans and transforms them into signifying products of Anglo male power that can be purchased, attained, and therefore socially legitimated (Goldman & Wilson, 1983). Sexual and racial oppressions emerge as socially accessible products. Thus, through commodification, ethnic gender is rendered inferior and objectified, and Anglo male ideology is affirmed. *Asian Romance* texts use three recurrent tactics—abstraction, equivalence, and reification—to complete the commodification of the Pilipina female and facilitate the ideology of patriarchal romance.

Abstraction. Abstraction detaches a commodity from its unique properties and separates consumers from real contexts (Goldman & Wilson, 1983). The effect is to connect consumers and products exclusively through consumption. Through abstraction, human characteristics become "exchangeable"; as a result, consumers acquire certain qualities by purchasing a product. As Fiske (1987) observes, glamorous models on game shows represent sexuality and are objectified along with the commodities they display; sexuality, then, can be purchased by consumers. Ideally, abstraction creates a new context which suppresses uniqueness and individuality.

In the *Asian Romance* text, abstraction occurs through replacing the individuality of the male consumer and the female commodity with generalized identities. For instance, male consumers are referred to as "American gentlemen," "gentlemen," and "serious marriage-minded gentlemen," thus depicting them by virtue of social standing. The ambiguity of this label valorizes the white male customer, adding prestige and respectability to his persona.

Similarly, Pilipina women find their identities muted. For example, they are visually presented in identical pictures which are also numbered and equal in shape. Such a portrait is, in Kuhn's (1985, p. 9) terms, "highly coded discourse which, among other things, constructs whatever is in the image as objects of consumption—consumption by looking, as well as often quite literally by purchase." Pilipina women are products sold on a shelf. Moreover, all are shown from the neck up. The photograph highlights lips, eyes, hair, and cheekbones. These fragments are "zones of consumption" that signify femininity (Goldman, Heath, & Smith, 1991, p. 337), and convey the message that "femaleness and femininity are constructed as a set of bodily attributes reducible to a sexuality which puts itself on display for a masculine spectator" (Kuhn, 1985, p. 43).

Biographical accounts of the women accompany the pictures. They feature other physical characteristics or "zones of consumption," as the following example indicates:

101. (Name) _____
DOB: 1/4/63, HT: 5'4, WT: 107 lbs. Education: B.S. in Accounting. **Occupation:** Accountant. Describes herself as caring, devoted simple lady with no vices. Seeks correspondence with honest loving marriage-minded gentlemen age 28 to 45.

Bold print attends a woman's height, weight, and assigned number. These elements depersonalize bride-to-be because they abstract generic "feminine" features only. Pilipina women are also positioned as numbered entries in three columns with date of birth, height, and weight dominating their descriptions. Compared to these features, their names are almost invisible. In arrangement, Pilipina brides are assigned by consecutive number, a characteristic intimating the irrelevance of their personal identities. They are also typically labeled as "select attractive Pilipina ladies," "beautiful ladies," and "most attractive, young ladies." These women are not just any commodities, but beautiful, youthful products. Furthermore, the term "lady" is associated with Pilipina brides, but not as a counterpart to their "gentlemenly" purchasers; rather, the label is derogatory for it is connected to images of fragility and helplessness. Female subordination through this term reflects the view that language "maintains the secondary status of women by defining them and their place" (Henley, 1987, p. 3; Eitzen & Zinn, 1989). Pilipina women are attractive generic feminine commodities, not surprisingly, references to individual personalities, interests, and thoughts are virtually nonexistent.

The texts' abstraction of persons into roles of consumer and commodity hierarchically position the Anglo male as a superior gentleman in relation to the Pilipina woman as a sexualized, racialized, and objectified commodity for sale. Visually and verbally, the consumption process enables the abstracted consumer to purchase and possess the abstracted product.

Equivalence. Because commodification elevates exchange value over use value, any commodity can become equivalent to any other commodity as long as an overarching or universal form of equivalence—like money—exists. Equivalence functions in such a way that the commodity form's particularities are suppressed and replaced with a standardized value designating its worth (Goldman & Wilson, 1983).

Economic and economical equivalence is evident throughout *Asian Romance,* but particularly through order forms, discount details, and product guarantees. The catalogues' exchange value—in American dollars—ranges from $57 to $285 depending upon the type and number of orders made. The worth of the Pilipina women is defined in economic terms as well for inclusion of one picture costs approximately 50 cents. Pilipina women equal commodities because they are advertised in catalogs. Subscribers check a "box" to purchase a yearly subscription or specialty issues advertising living, "generic" sexual products.

Asian Romance features "Supersaver" deals which offer bargains and discounts; that is, more pictures of women for less money. One such bargains is a "Supersaver 1000 Packet" which includes black and white photographs of over 1000 Pilipina women, one issue of the magazine, pictures and addresses of 95 women, three issues of *Asian Romance Bi-Monthly* with 300+ women featured, the "Ladies Ages 30 to 50" issue with 350 women featured, and the "Black and White Bonus Issue" featuring 300 women. In addition, a purchaser might choose the "*Asian Romance* Guide to Marriage By Correspondence" and several immigration forms for the prospective bride's entry into the United States. Other "Supersaver" deals offer the "Supersaver 1000 Packet" plus one of the specialty issues mentioned above in either the black-white or color format.

Some special interest issues showcase women according to their age and occupation. For example, a "Teenage Issue" features Pilipina women around the age of 17; another is the "Ladies Ages 30 to 50 Issue." Those related to occupations include a "Nurse and Health Professionals Issue," and "Teachers and Accountants Issue." All issues portray Pilipina women similarly as zones of consumption. Special issues simply frame Pilipina objects more specifically according to the preferred interests of Anglo male customers. The "Supersaver" discounts reflect the equivalence of women as commodities through demographic preferences of male customers and through the bargain principle of chalking them as "cheap" products.

Commodification is augmented by *Asian Romance*'s commitment to quality: it provides its male customers with a "Marriage Guarantee Card." This product guarantee states that if the client is not married within a year, he is entitled to a free subscription of the catalog. Pilipina women are again equated with product commodities through a "Satisfaction Guaranteed or Your Money Back" certification.

Reification. Reification refers to the process by which a commodity comes to mean something else. In this case, the Pilipina woman reifies Anglo patriarchal power and superiority, and has value only as a mirror for that image. Subject becomes object through a process in which the "tendency for social relations to be transformed into things" results in endowing commodified products with desirable human traits and attributes (Goldman & Wilson, 1983, p. 128). Buying a product enables a consumer associatively to gain a certain quality of social relation because that product represents an "active" ready-made package of attractive qualities.

In the context of the *Asian Romance* catalog, reification occurs by way of a textual sequence that positions the male client to purchase the Pilipina commodity and then to conceptualize himself as part of a group of prestigious male customers. Initially, through ordering and purchasing Pilipina women, customers demonstrate their purchasing power and affirm their economic status in a competitive capitalistic society. Similarly, this purchase affirms a sense of masculinity as it reinforces males as "breadwinners" who foot the bill for the catalogues, marriage guides, visa forms, and other publications required to secure a spouse.

The *Asian Romance* texts' identification of customers as an elite, select group of "serious, marriage-minded American gentlemen" furthers the principle of reification. For example, the statement, "We expect that . . . the serious marriage-minded gentleman is already convinced of the many advantages to having a loving Asian lady for a wife," demonstrates the positioning of the male client as a superior gentleman in pursuit of a good investment. Social prestige underlies this statement: "We maintain a high standard in the solicitation of new subscribers." This enables the male to envision himself as an exclusive member of a social club. Similar to Adelman and Ahuvia's (1991, p. 285) conclusion about dating and introducing services, *Asian Romance* projects an image of elite clientele for "increased social legitimacy" and popularity.

Visual elements accompany the language of reification. Comic strips scattered throughout the publication construct the male client in elitist ways. For example, one cartoon frames a conservatively dressed "nerdy" Anglo male client, replete with bow tie and glasses, displaying an exotic, long-tressed, petite Pilipina wife. Other men around him admire his acquisition with such statements as "How'd Hank even find such a gorgeous wife?" and "Maybe she has a sister!" Because the cartoon focuses principally on the relationship between the male client and the male spectators, the Pilipina bride emerges as a trophy reinforcing the client's masculinity to other men. The male consumer, then, gains social status by owning a product that other men would like to possess. In this comic strip, men engage in a "spectator sport," a competition whose purpose is to gain respect from one another (Friedman, 1985). This male customer also generates sexual power because he has purchased a body to use for sexual pleasure; the bride occupying this body, of course, is presumed willing to accommodate his sexual needs.

Through his economic purchasing power, the male consumer gains social standing and ownership of a physical, sexual product; he also, however, enjoys control or dominance in terms of gaze and later possession. The spectator of the *Asian Romance* magazine "can choose to gaze at length, to retune again and again, to a favorite photography and like voyeurism, there is a pleasure in looking, a pleasure of power and the look a controlling one" (Kuhn, 1985, p. 28). But, this male spectator is allowed to go one step further: he can purchase these objects of visual pleasure.

Further, Kuhn (1985, p. 26) observes that "photographs stand as evidence that whatever is inside the frame of the image really happened, was really there: it is authentic, convincing, true." In other words, photographs are not mere images but, according to Sontag (1986, p. 392), "interpretations of the real." Whereas a painting refers to a central subject, a photograph appears to be the actual subject or "an extension of the subject and a potent means of acquiring it, of gaining control over it." Thus, photographs redefine, "enlarge," and "imprison" reality (Sontag, 1986, pp. 393, 397). Viewers of photos in *Asian Romance* are likely to associate Pilipina women with qualities implied by the photographic images—commodified products for sale. Acting on those images, the male consumer can also possess the reality of them, thus materializing and consummating the commodification of Pilipina females. Subscribing to the catalogues provides the customer with economic, social, and sexual power and reifies masculine control over Pilipina femininity as well as a social relationship grounded in domination–subordination. To the degree that this hegemonic discourse of commodification circulates in *Asian Romance* through abstraction, equivalence, and reification, so too does its end product, commodified and fetishized Pilipina oppression (Goldman & Smith, 1983).

Opposition and inoculation

As mentioned earlier, hegemony embodies various means through which a dominant ideology is continually reproduced in cultural institutions and products (Dow, 1990; Fiske, 1987; Gitlin, 1986). One marker of hegemony in a capitalist system is its ability to "domesticate oppositions, absorbing it into forms compatible with the core ideological structures" (Gitlin, 1986, p. 526). Barthes (1972) refers to this practice as "inoculation," arguing that inoculation protects the dominant ideology from radical change by incorporating small amounts of oppositional ideology. Thus, a hegemonic social text leaks alternative viewpoints in order to achieve popularity and power over thought simultaneously (Dow, 1990; Fiske, 1987; Gitlin, 1986). Gitlin's (1986, p. 526) observation that "consent is managed by absorption as well as by exclusion" is supported by Dow (1990) who notes that those embracing an oppositional ideology may be satisfied that their demands are being addressed even if the creators of a text make only cosmetic changes. Such appropriated ideologies, then, are small "patches" scattered across a larger pervasive ideological structure and connected by dominant ideological seams. Hence, inoculation relies on the premise that "major social conflicts are transported into the cultural system where the hegemonic process frames them, form and content both, into compatibility with dominant systems of meaning (Gitlin, 1986, p. 527).

The commodified dialogue of *Asian Romance* presents contradictory images juxtaposing a dominant patriarchal discourse with that of a feminist Pilipina discourse. What emerges are divergent images of the Pilipina woman as sexy, submissive object and independent, modern woman, and marriage as male ownership and equal partnership.

Pilipina Women as Sex Objects and Independent Subjects. Asian Romance shapes the Pilipina woman as a sexualized and racialized object through recurring visual and verbal images promoting exotica and obedience. For example, photographs of women accompanied by a biographical section listing their height, weight, and age emphasize the values of physical appearance and attractiveness. Women's marketability stems from pictures and measurements. Much of the same occurs with the visual construction of the Pilipina woman in comic strips. She appears in these frames as sensuous, as "exotic" with long black tresses and skimpy tank tops and skirts. Her erotic physical appearance—long flowing hair, curvaceous body, and form-fitting clothing—constructs pleasurable images visually and sexually.

The texts also portray the Pilipina women as obedient and submissive. For instance, the *Asian Romance* text reads, "Finding your lifetime partner—an attractive unspoiled Asian lady who is enthusiastically devoted to pleasing you—may be easier than you ever dreamed." Here the Asian woman is described as willingly subservient to her potential mate. Moreover, the statement "old fashioned, wholesome family values never went out of style in the Philippines" links tradition and family to female ethnic subservience. The owner of *Asian Romance* captures this patriarchal ideology in the catalog's introduction as he speaks of his wife, a former Asian mail-order bride: "Her gentle smile, soft touch, and sweet love songs have turned my heart into butter." Complacency and demureness, then, are also characteristic of the Pilipina bride.

An oppositional discourse presenting the Pilipina woman as an independent, educated worker coexists with the portrait of the sexy, submissive wife. As the biological entry illustrates, "education" is a key quality for Pilipina women are depicted as articulate and intelligent. Specialized "working women" issues also paint teachers, nurses, and accountants as "sign objects meant to stand for feminist goals of independence and professional success" (Goldman, Heath, & Wilson, 1991, p. 336). In one sample letter, for example, a Pilipina woman describes her civil engineering and problem-solving background as acquired skills enabling her to accomplish her goal of becoming a "pathfinder of civilization." *Asian Romance* appears to endorse feminist ideology through specters of educational and occupational achievements, individual freedoms, and ambition. Collectively, these discourses portray Pilipina women as passive objects of desire and active, empowered subjects of substance simultaneously. Yet, the contradictory images recuperate dominant patriarchal ideology by intimating that even independent, educated, working Pilipina women are motivated to find happiness and satisfaction through serving their Anglo male mates.

Marriage as Male Ownership and Equal Partnership. *Asian Romance* also incorporates contradictory discourses on marriage. Marriage as male ownership dominates the discourses, but the texts also emphasize marriage as an equal partnership and an intimate relationship grounded in common values.

The order form is a telling example of the dominant patriarchal discourse for it defines marriage as "Pilipina product ownership." The male customer controls the institution of marriage by purchasing a wife; included in this transaction are his instructions regarding all of the details of marriage. Because only male buyers have access to information enabling them to make decisions about who their "brides" will be affirms the legitimacy of the power of male clients over Pilipina women. Michael Donahue, the magazine's owner, reinforces this discourse of subjugation by including his own comments, but not those of his wife, Chantal, in promotional publications for *Asian Romance*. However, an oppositional discourse emphasizing marriage as an equal partnership underlines *Asian Romance* texts. For example, terms like "common values," "sharing," and "relationship" frequently appear in the magazine. In addition, the catalog's cover sports a picture of Michael and Chantal Donahue together (both of whom allegedly jointly own the business), and their signatures appear on the backcover, thus offering the illusion of equality in marriage.

The contrary images of marriage as male ownership and equal partnership work together to produce an ideology of marriage centered in white male control and power. Apparently, marriage is an equal partnership as long as he wills it. This paradoxical form of "inoculation" simply maintains dominant Anglo patriarchal ideology. While oppositional images are "domesticated into hegemonic forms," as Gitlin (1987, p. 510) explains, "commercial culture does not manufacture ideology; it relays and reproduces and processes and packages and focuses ideology that is constantly arising."

The inclusion of alternative feminist principles fostering images of modern women and marriage as equal partnership further legitimize the commodification of Pilipina women. While the *Asian Romance* catalog fuses the images of the smart, independent, ambitious working woman and the beautiful, sexy, exotic, and pleasing object, these women's apparent willingness to conform to such images justifies their commodification and warrants Anglo male power. Thus, instead of displaying "feminism," the ideological function of these oppositional discourses signifies the notion of subordination of Pilipina femininity (Golden, Heath, & Smith, 1991).

Euphemization

The catalog's inoculation of oppositional discourses and their attendant feminist principles merges with an ideological model Thompson (1990, p. 62) calls "euphemization," or a process by which "actions, institutions, or social relations are described or redescribed in terms of which elicit a positive valuation." *Asian Romance* attempts to distance itself from the "degrading, archaic mail-order bride services" by redefining itself euphemistically as a "romance manufacturer" and "a business to find lifetime partners." Relabeling hegemonically obscures the activity of advertising women of sale, and at the same time, substitutes mystical images of love, romance, and intrigue in order to continue the patriarchal signification of women and extend Anglo male superiority.

Racist ideology

While *Asian Romance* highlights gendered and capitalist codes, a related aspect of the commodification of Pilipina women is a racist ideology which propagates an unequal power relationship between Pilipina women and white American men that generalizes to relations between Pacific Asia and America. Serita (1984) argues that since the 19th century the United States' domination of the Philippines entails an arrogance and self-acclaimed superiority over people considered to be "forever foreign" and "unassimilable"; who represent the "Yellow Peril" (Lai, 1985). More specifically, Matsui (1987) and Villapando (1989) indict American imperialism for oppression both racially and sexually. *Asian Romance* continues the tradition by reinforcing images of Suzie Wong and exotic, obedient Asian women.

The racist discourse evident in *Asian Romance* is articulated in "images, concepts, and premises which provide the frameworks through which we represent, interpret, understand, and 'make sense' of some aspects of social existence" (Hall, 1981, p. 8). These discursive structures operate unconsciously to help racist ideologies and ethnocentric ideas become "naturalized" as social constructions. Three themes of what Hall (1985, p. 15) terms "a grammar of race" advance this ideology of racism: themes of domination and subordination, stereotypes, and the language of nature. Through them, *Asian Romance* functions to establish a social relation of Anglo male domination and Pilipina female subordination.

Themes of Domination and Subordination. One "naturalized" media construction of the "white eye" position privileges perceptions of the Anglo race. This gaze is "always outside the frame" but it sees and positions "everything within it" (Hall, 1981, p. 14). Michael Donahue's "white eye" position shapes the *Asian Romance* text by recreating the age-old image of Asian Pacific women as "Oriental Butterflies." She is a woman with "extraordinary sexual power" but also is a "quiet, unassuming, and non-threatening doll" (Lai, 1988, p. 167; Serrati, 1984; Villapando, 1989). Clearly misconceptions, nevertheless Asian women's "exotic and erotic but . . . passive and submissive" persona constitutes the marketing image of today's mail-order bride services (JACL, 1985; Joseph, 1984; Lai, 1988; Serrati, 1984; Villapando, 1989). The "Oriental Butterfly" image emerges from the larger imperialist discourse of Orientalism, or the "Western style for dominating, restricting, and having authority over the Orient." Borne of the 19th century involvement in the East, the discourse of Orientalism invented an ideal vision of the

West as superior ruler and the East as submissive servant (Said, 1978, p. 3). In the context of the *Asian Romance* catalog, this Orientalist vision transforms the Pilipina woman into an Oriental "other."

The *Asian Romance* grammar positions the Pilipina women as the "Oriental Butterfly" with its description of "devoted, faithful, beautiful women," and numbered photo entries with matching order forms. As shelf products, Pilipina women exist solely for the white male consumer's use. By contrast, the white male surfaces as an elite social member with the power to exert economic, social, and sexual control over these Pilipina products. For instance, the text addresses customers as "Dear Sir" or "suitable American gentlemen," and portrays white males showing off their Pilipina products to other white men. Moreover, relations of "white male consumer" domination and "Pilipina product" subordination become fixed with order forms and lists of prices.

The Oriental Butterfly image constitutes a form of inferential racism, or a set of ethnocentric beliefs that reflect no overt evidence of racism (Hall, 1981). The catalog naturalizes Pilipina women through depicting them as obedient passive wives and uninhibited sex goddesses "enthusiastically devoted to pleasing." These "faithful" wives are attractive and curvaceous, ready and willing to be sold. The unequal power relationship of the white male over the Pilipina woman, then, is constructed so as to make Pilipina slavery appear characteristic of the social world.

Stereotypes. Ideological discourse also operates through stereotypes and erroneous yet carefully constructed images privileging Anglo superiority. Once again, the texts embrace one positive stereotype for white men: the socially elite, financially secure white customer in control. His confidence soars as he scans hundreds of photos of prospective brides and orders the best value. The Asian woman stereotype, however, is markedly more negative. She is a sexually available girl who is also exotic and eager to please. Attractive, educated, and virginal, she is simultaneously erotic and submissive. Thus, Pilipina women are generalized into a subordinate Oriental Other through which Western men can colonize and control.

Language of Nature. Reproducing racism occurs in physical signs and racial characteristics comprising the language of nature. *Asian Romance* portrays the Pilipina bride as a curvy yet petite woman with long black hair and almond shaped eyes. In contrast, the white customer is a blond, older male whose conservative attire includes a bow tie. Such caricatures are symbols of difference, markers of subordination and domination respectively.

Asian Romance's discourse grammar is also overtly racist because it includes the open and mass publication of racist thoughts and images (Hall, 1981). Because the *Asian Romance* catalog and its services are accessible by phone or mail request, this public catalog pushes acceptance of the "sexploitation" of Pilipina women and the stereotypes attending Pacific Asian females. *Asian Romance* constructs a seemingly "natural order of rank" which is actually an ethnocentric hold over the Pilipina women (Hall, 1981, p. 14). The catalog's ideological underpinnings portray Asian women in "servant-like" images.

Conclusions

The Pilipina "Oriental Butterfly" doll symbolizes the economic, sexual, and racial convergence of *Asian Romance*'s varied forms of hegemony. This "doll" represents the commodified form of a capitalistic social system as well as the sexualized signification of "woman" as objective product. The Pilipina doll's shading symbolizes the racial otherness attached to the product while the "Oriental Butterfly" mystique reflects the intersection of the colonization of gender and race in the shadow of the Western male dominator (Said, 1978). The Pilipina mail-order bride image, then, functions hegemonically to celebrate superior Anglo-American male ideology. Visually and textually transformed into the Pilipina "Oriental Butterfly" doll, the Pilipina woman ceases to exist.

The *Asian Romance* catalog therefore can be read as reinforcing a central Anglo patriarchal voice. But while this analysis concludes that *Asian Romance* sustains "white, bourgeois, western values" in a variety of hegemonic ways, the study does not stop here (Serrati, 1984, p, 41). In the name of feminist cultural studies, another discourse must be examined: The voice of Pilipina brides. Numerous possible sources of resistance may exist in discourses if viewed from Pilipina women's perspectives. For instance, many Pilipina mail-order brides are motivated to escape their country's poverty and to send money back to their families at home (JACL, 1985; Serrati, 1984; Villapando, 1989). In addition to this, marrying an American citizen affords many Pilipinas an expedient way to enter the United States and become naturalized citizens (JACL, 1985; Villapando, 1989). Consequently, Pilipina brides may well participate in an active process of "bargaining with [Anglo] patriarchy" to "negotiate and adapt to the set of rules that guide and constrain gender relations . . . in order to maximize power and options within a patriarchal structure" (Kibria, 1990, p. 9; Kadiyoti, 1988). If brides use *Asian Romance* and other such firms for their own purposes, and therefore participate willingly in their own commodification, then their choices ultimately prevent Anglo patriarchal hegemonic ideology from taking hold of Pilipina subjective identity. Only through examination of bride services from the perspective of both groom *and* bride can the complexities and implications of hegemony and patriarchal signification be understood.

Note

1. "Pilipina" identities women from the Philippines. The term "Filipino" is not used for it is an anglicized form. According to Lai (1988), in Tagalog, the national language of the Philippines, the word is pronounced with a "p" sound.

References

Adelman, M. B., & Ahuvia, A. C. (1991). Mediated channels for mate seeking: A solution to involuntary singlehood? *Critical Studies in Mass Communication, 8*, 273–289.

Almquist, E. M. (1984). Race and ethnicity in the lives of minority women. In J. Freeman (Ed.), *Women: A feminist perspective* (pp. 23–45). Palo Alto, CA: Mayfield.

Althusser, L. (1971). Ideology and ideological state apparatuses. In *Lenin and philosophy and other essays* (pp. 127–186). New York: Monthly Review Press.

Aquino, B. A. (1979). The history of Philipino women in Hawaii. *Ridge, 7*, 17–21.

Baehr, H. (1981). The impact of feminism on media studies—just another commercial break? In D. Spender (Ed.), *Men's studies modified: The impact of feminism in the academic discipline.* Oxford: Pergamon.

Baechr, H., & Dyer, G. (1987). *Boxed in: Women in television.* New York: Pandora.

Barthes, R. (1973). *Mythologies.* New York: Hill & Wang.

Bowen, S. Perlmutter, & Wyatt, N. (1993). Visions of synthesis, vision of critique. In S. Bowen & N. Wyatt (eds.), *Transforming visions: Feminist critiques in communication studies.* Cresskill, NJ: Hampton.

Chia, A. Y. (1983). *Toward a holistic paradigm for Asian American women's studies: A synthesis of feminist scholarship and women of color's feminist politics.* Paper presented at the Fifth Annual Conference of the National Women's Studies Association, Columbus, OH.

Chow, E. N. (1989). The feminist movement: Where are all the Asian American women? In Asian Women United of California (Eds.), *Making waves: An anthology of writings by and about Asian American women* (pp. 362–377). Boston: Beacon.

Chow, E. N. (1991). The development of feminist consciousness among Asian-American women. In J. Lorber & S. A. Farrell (Eds.), *The social construction of gender* (pp. 255–268). Newbury Park, CA: Sage.

Dill, B. T. (1983). Race, class, and gender: Prospects for an all-inclusive sisterhood. *Feminist Studies, 9*, 131–150.

Dow, B. J. (1990). Hegemony, feminist criticism and the *Mary Tyler Moore Show. Critical Studies in Mass Communication, 7*, 261–274.

Eitzen, D. S., & Zinn, M. B. (1989). The de-athleticization of women: The naming and gender making of collegiate sport teams. *Sociology of Sport Journal, 6*, 362–370.

Fiske, J. (1987). British cultural studies and television. In R. C. Allen (Ed.), *Channels of discourse, reassembled* (pp. 284–326). Chapel Hill, NC: University of North Carolina Press.

Fiske, J. (1987). *Television culture.* New York: Routledge.

Friedman, M. (1985, July). To wild guys at a party, rape isn't a crime. It's a spectator sport. *Mademoiselle,* pp. 104–105.

Gitlin, T. (1987). Prime time television: The hegemonic process in TV entertainment. In H. Newcomb (Ed.), *Television, the critical review* (pp. 507–529). New York: Oxford University Press.

Goldman, R., Heath, D., & Smith, S. L. (1991). Commodity feminism. *Critical Studies in Mass Communication, 8,* 333–351.

Goldman, R., & Wilson, J. (1983). Appearance and essence: The commodity form revealed in perfume advertisement. In McNall (Ed.), *Current perspective in social theory* (Vol. 4, pp. 119–142). Greenwich, CT: JAL Press.

Gramsci, A. (1971). *Selections from the prison notebooks* (Q. Hoare & G. Nowell-Smith, Eds. & Trans.). New York: International Publishers.

Hall, S. (1980a). Cultural Studies and the centre: Some problematics and problems. In S. Hall, D. Hobson, A. Lowe, & P. Willis (Eds.), *Culture, media, language: Working papers in cultural studies, 1972–1979* (pp. 15–47). London: Hutchinson.

Hall, S. (1980b). Encoding/Decoding. In S. Hall, D. Hobson, A. Lowe, & P. Willis (Eds.), *Culture, media, language: Working papers in cultural studies, 1972–1979* (pp. 128–139). London: Hutchinson.

Hall, S. (1981). The whites of their eyes: Racist ideologies and the media. In G. Bridges & R. Brunt (Eds.), *Silver linings: Some strategies of the eighties* (pp. 7–23). London: Lawrence and Wishart.

Hall, S. (1982). The rediscovery of "ideology": Return of the repressed in media studies. In M. Gurevitch, T. Bennett, J. Curran, & J. Woollacott (Eds.), *Culture, society, and the media* (pp. 56–90). London: Methuen.

Henley, N. M. (1987). This new species that seeks a new language: On sexism in language and language change. In J. Penfield (Ed.), *Women and language in transition* (pp. 3–27). Albany, NY: State University of New York Press.

Hobson, D. (1982). *Crossroads: The drama of a soap opera.* London: Methuen.

hooks, b. (1984). *Feminist theory: From margin to center.* Boston: Southend.

Japanese American Citizens League (JACL). (1985, February 22). JACL report on Asian bride catalogs. *Pacific Citizen,* pp. 10–11.

Johnson, R. (1986). What is cultural studies anyway? *Social Text, 16,* 38–80.

Joseph, R. A. (1984, January 25). American men find Asian brides fill the unliberated bill. *Wall Street Journal,* pp. 1, 22.

Kandiyoti, D. (1988). Bargaining with patriarchy. *Gender & Society, 2,* 274–291.

Kibria, N. (1990). Power, patriarchy, and gender conflict in the Vietnamese immigrant community. *Gender & Society, 4*(1), 9–24.

Kuhn, A. (1985). *The power of the image: Essays on representation and sexuality.* New York: Routledge and Kegan Paul.

Lai, T. (1985, June). Asian women: Resisting the violence. *Working Together,* pp. 1–3.

Lai, T. (1988). Asian American women: Not for sale. In J. Cochran, D. Langston, & C. Woodward (Eds.), *Changing our power: An introduction to women's studies* (pp. 163–171). Dubuque, IA: Kendall-Hunt.

Lont, C. M. (1993). Feminist critique of mass communication research. In S. Bowen & N. Wyatt (Eds.), *Transforming visions: Feminist critiques in communication studies.* Cresskill, NJ : Hampton.

Loo, C., & Ong, P. (1983). Slaying demons with a sewing needle: Feminist issues for Chinatown women. *Berkeley Journal of Sociology, 27,* 77–88.

McRobbie, A., & Garber, J. (1975). Girls and subcultures: An exploration. *Working Papers in Cultural Studies, 7–8,* 209–222.

Marchetti, G. (1993). *Romance and the "yellow peril": Race, sex, and discursive strategies in Hollywood fiction.* Berkeley, CA: University of California Press.

Matsui, J. (1987). Women forging a future: Emerging Asian feminist movements. In Y. Matsui (Ed.), *Women's Asia* (pp. 143–157). London: Red Books.

Modleski, T. (1982). *Loving with a vengeance: Mass produced fantasies for women.* Hampden, CT: Archon Books.

Mulvey, L. (1975). Visual pleasure and narrative cinema. *Screen, 16,* 6–18.

Mussell, K. (1984). *Fantasy and reconciliation: Contemporary formulas of women's romance fiction.* Westport, CT: Greenwood.

Radway, J. A. (1984). *Reading the romance: Women, patriarchy, and popular literature.* Chapel Hill, NC: University of North Carolina Press.

Radway, J. A. (1986). Identifying ideological seams: Mass culture, analytical method, and political practice. *Communication, 9*, 93–123.

Rakow, L. F. (1986). Feminist approaches to popular culture: Giving patriarchy its due. *Communication, 9*, 19–41.

Richardson, L. W. (1981). *The dynamics of sex and gender* (2nd ed). Boston: Houghton Mifflin.

Said, E. (1978). *Orientalism*. New York: Vintage Books.

Schwichtenberg, C. (1989). Feminist cultural studies. *Critical Studies in Mass Communication, 6*, 202–208.

Serita, T. (1984). Mail order sexploitation. *Bridge*, pp. 39–41.

Snitow, A. B. (1979). Mass market romance: Pornography for women is different. *Radical History Review, 20*, 141–161.

Sontag, S. (1986). The imprisoning of reality. In G. Gumpert & R. Cathcart (Eds.), *Intermedia: Interpersonal communication in a media world* (pp. 391–400). New York: Oxford University Press.

Steeves, H. L. (1987). Feminist theories and media studies. *Critical Studies in Mass Communication, 4*, 95–135.

Thompson, J. (1990). *Ideology and modern culture*. Palo Alto, CA: Stanford University Press.

Treichler, P. A., & Wartella, E. (1986). Interventions: Feminist theory and communication studies. *Communication, 9*, 1–18.

Villapando, V. (1989). The business of selling mail-order brides. In Asian Women United of California (Eds.), *Making waves: An anthology of writings by and about Asian American women* (pp. 318–326). Boston: Beacon.

Yamada, M. (1981). Asian Pacific American women and feminism. In C. Moraga & G. Anzaldua (Eds.), *This bride called me back: Writings by radical women of color* (pp. 71–75). Watertown, MA: Persephone.

13

Currents in History, Cultural Domination, and Mass Communication in the Caribbean

Humphrey A. Regis

One of the major turns in "international" mass communication took place in the enunciation of the relationship between mass communication and "development." Earlier in the history of theory, policy, and practice in that area, the predominant framework essentially saw the communication as playing missionary roles of sorts—helping the transfer of a certain character (Lerner, 1958), certain technologies (Rogers, 1969), and certain techniques (Rogers, 1969) from the more powerful and "developed" societies to the less powerful and "undeveloped" societies. The first role seemed to be captured in the idea that mass communication may serve as a transmitter and "magic multiplier" of a certain "modernization ethic," and the second and third seemed to be captured in the attention that many experts gave to the role of mass communication in the adoption of certain "innovations." At the root of these roles was the assumption that with the help of the mass media the advances that Europeans made in the Industrial Revolution and after World War II would be replicated in other parts of the world (see Melkote, 2002, and Cambridge, 2002 for elaborations of these issues).

Later in the history of the enunciation of that relationship, many experts from the less powerful societies, together with colleagues from the more powerful societies, proposed other frameworks that saw the communication as playing responsive roles of sorts—helping people realize their aspirations and surmount difficulties they perceive or encounter in their lives (Rogers, 1976). The first specific role recognized that the beneficiaries of development indeed had aspirations and saw mass communication as helping them realize these aspirations. The second saw resource or situational or contextual difficulties as retarding achievement and saw a combination that includes mass communication and the alleviation of the difficulties (or the creation of new opportunities through the introduction of facilitating resources or situations or contexts) as helping this achievement (also see Melkote, 2002, and Cambridge, 2002 for more substantial elaborations of these issues).

It seems that at the foundation of the second framework was the consideration of the history of the less powerful societies. That history indicates, for example, that in such locations as the Congo, Niger, Nile, Tigris/Euphrates, and Indus river valleys, and the Limpopo/Zambezi and meso-America regions, many of these societies have centuries- or millennia-old records of aspiration and achievement. It also indicates that in the lives of individual members of these societies today, aspiration may not translate into achievement in part because of frustrating personal cirsumstances, local situations, national conditions, and/or global contexts. The framework seems to propose, as the uses and gratifications (McGuire, 1974) and third-variable (Comstock et al., 1978) theories seem to propose, that a combination that includes the design of appropriate mass media messages and the creation of personal and local and national and global enablers is one key to the type of beneficiary-defined achievement or realization that it calls "development."

It seems that just as the study of the history of the world from the perspectives of several of the currently more powerful societies propelled the development of the earlier framework for the elaboration of the relationship between mass communication and development, the study of the history from these perspectives propelled the development of the early framework for the elaboration of the relationship between mass communication and cultural domination. It also seems that just as the study of the history from the perspectives of the currently less powerful societies spawned the later framework for understanding the relationship between mass communication and development, the study of the history from these perspectives spawns another framework that on the one hand challenges and on the other hand complements the established one in the elaboration of the relationship between mass communication and cultural domination.

This chapter elaborates these issues and articulates the implications of them in the study of Caribbean People of African Descent, but the implications are applicable in the lives of People of the African Continent, members of the World African Community, and ultimately the peoples of the less powerful societies in general. The chapter defines culture and cultural domination. It describes representative observations from recent history that may have inspired the conceptualization of the earlier framework the writer calls cultural domination by importation or exportation, as well as three perspectives for the elaboration of the relationship between mass communication and this domination. It describes observations from the ancient, recent, and current history of members of the Community in the Caribbean and the Continent that point to the need for the consideration of a second framework the writer calls cultural domination by re-importation or re-exportation, and proposes that the three perspectives apply in the elaboration of the relationship between mass communication and this domination. Then it brings this application to life as it proposes research programs, agendas, questions, and hypotheses that arise from the conceptualization of the relationship and are applicable in the lives of Caribbean People of African Descent, People of the African Continent, members of the World African Community, and peoples of the less powerful societies. The chapter argues that just as the responsiveness framework liberated the development of theory, policy, and practice in mass communication and development, the re-importation or re-exportation framework liberates the development of theory, policy, and practice with regard to the relationship between mass communication and cultural definition and continuance and change in the lives of these peoples. It also argues that the proposed relationship between mass communication and cultural domination by re-importation or re-exportation reveals the need for the study of mass communication to be inspired by other disciplines, especially the study of the millennia-long history of the World African Community.

Culture

Some views of culture define it in cognitive terms, some define it in affective terms, and some define it in behavioral terms. Tan (1985) integrated these emphases by defining culture as the interrelated cognitions, affects, and behaviors that members of a society share. McDonald (1986) emphasized the normative implications of these cognitions, affects, and behaviors by noting that they provide the reference points by which members of a society give meaning and validation to their beliefs, attitudes, and behaviors. And Benedict (1934) summarized the essence of these definitions by proposing that culture may be seen as personality writ large—the culture of a society may be seen as the collective personality of its members.

The culture is expressed in domains. These are areas of existence in which individual members of the society express themselves or the society as a whole expresses itself. From observations of members or the society in these domains, one may identify patterns that point to the characteristics of the culture. The domains are infinite in number and include agriculture, politics, religion, government, clothing, housing, recreation, grooming, trading, music, sanitation, and reasoning.

In each domain, the culture may be described through continuums called dimensions, with each dimension having at one end the extreme of one characteristic and at the other end the extreme of a contrasting characteristic. As McGuire (1974) proposed, in the case of individuals, they include the cognitive vs. affective, preservation-oriented vs. growth-oriented, internally oriented vs. externally oriented, and active vs. passive dimensions. As Diop (1978) proposed, in the case of societies, they include the matriarchal vs. patriarchal, individualistic vs. collectivistic, and oriented-toward-xenophobia vs. oriented-toward-xenophilia dimensions. Of course, the ends of a dimension are not always diametrically opposed characteristics. One end may be the near absence and the other the extremely strong presence of a certain characteristic, such as the belief in original sin (Diop, 1978).

Within any dimension, a society may be located at an extreme end, more toward this end than toward a second, balanced between the two ends, more toward the second end than toward the first, or extremely at the second. Diop (1978) applied this idea in his attempt to describe the traditional culture complexes of African and European peoples. He concluded that the former have tended to be more collectivistic than individualistic and the latter more individualistic than collectivistic, the former more matriarchal than patriarchal and the latter more patriarchal than matriarchal, and the former more inclined toward xenophilia than toward xenophobia and the latter more toward xenophobia than toward xenophilia. Thus along each dimension Diop was describing the location of each culture complex, its attribute. And as Tan (1985) and McDonald (1986) most probably would argue, each of these attributes will have cognitive, affective, and behavioral aspects.

The totality here called the culture of a society may be seen as the sum of the attributes (or locations on dimensions) the society displays in the sum of the domains of its existence. If each society were seen as an island, the domains of its existence may be seen as regions that constitute it, the dimensions of its domains may be seen as land masses that make up its regions, and its attribute along a dimension may be seen as the elevation of a land mass. The location of a society at an extreme end of one dimension may be seen as equivalent to the low elevation of the corresponding land mass, and the location of the society at the other extreme end as equivalent to the high elevation of that land mass. Thus the territory of an island may be seen as the aggregate of the elevations (of the aggregate of land masses) in the aggregate of regions that constitute it. And the culture of a society may be defined as the aggregate of the attributes (along the aggregate of dimensions) in the aggregate of the domains that make up its expressions of its existence.

Cultural change in a society may be seen as change in an attribute, or in its location along any dimension or dimensions in any domain or domains. It also may be seen as cognitive, affective, or behavioral, but it probably will be in all of these aspects of an attribute, as Tan (1985) and others report these aspects are interrelated. And it may be the result of experiences members of the society have among themselves, with other societies, or in their natural environment (Diop, 1978).

The change due to experience with other societies may be placed in three categories. The first is change by symmetry or balanced interaction, in which there is a balance between the flow of influence in one direction and the flow in the other. The change also may be by asymmetry or imbalanced interaction, in which there is a greater flow of influence in one direction than in the other. The second category is change by incidental domination, in which the imbalance is not the result of the intention and/or deliberate action of either of the interacting societies or third parties. The third is cultivated domination (often called imperialism), in which the imbalance is the result of this intention and/or deliberate action. The literature of mass communication and cultural domination, as represented in certain treatises (Chinweizu, 1975; Hamelink, 1983; Schiller, 1969, 1976) and reviews (Hur, 1982; Salwen, 1991; Schiller, 1991; Sreberny-Mohammadi, 1997; Tamborini and Choi, 1990), seems to focus to a great degree on the relationship between mass communication and incidental domination and/or between mass communication and cultivated domination, but there seem to be some noteworthy exceptions to this pattern (Galtung, 1980; Mazrui, 1976).

The Established Framework

One instance of cultural change that seems to capture the essence of the established framework for the elaboration of cultural domination seems to be as follows:

> A few years ago, Ethiopian radio imported dramatic programs from the United States. Around the time of the Christmas season, these programs promoted the European and American tradition of Christmas trees and gift giving. Ethiopia is a Coptic Christian country, where Christmas was strictly a religious holiday. However, the American programming led to a demand for Christmas trees and gift giving. . . . The trees had to be shipped in from the [United States]!
>
> (Dennis, 1984, p. 183)

Another instance is the subject of a more recent report (Becker & Burwell, 1999) on conceptions of ideal weight, related attitudes, and related behavior held by secondary school girls in Fiji.

> The researchers compared the views of a sample taken in 1995, one month after Fiji began receiving Western television programs via satellite, with one taken in 1998. In a culture [in which] slimness was deemed unattractive, there was a marked increase in the percentage of girls who desired to lose weight and therefore dieted or engaged in bulimic behavior to slim down. And the increased tendencies were more pronounced among those who watched television the most. Whereas just 3% of the girls in the 1995 survey reported inducing vomiting to lose weight, 15% of the 1998 sample did so. And the girls who watched television the most were 50% more likely to describe themselves as too fat and 30% more likely to diet than the others. Moreover, the study found an increased incidence of depression related to self image. The girls told the researchers they admired women characters on Melrose Place and Beverly Hills 90210, two of their favorite programs, and they wanted to be like those hourglass-shaped characters.
>
> (reported in Ibelema, 2001, p. 28)

These reports capture a process that has these stages: the more powerful society develops a cultural characteristic or attribute; the originating more powerful society exports the attribute or characteristic (or, the less powerful society imports it); then the less powerful society adopts it. This represents the framework one may call cultural domination by exportation from the point of view of the more powerful or by importation from that of the less powerful (see examples and discussions in Salwen, 1991; Schiller, 1969, 1976, 1991; Sreberny-Mohammadi, 1997).

The instances also seem to suggest three perspectives of the role and significance of mass communication within the framework. One is the correlation perspective that holds that the mass communication in which the members of a society engage will have elements that reflect the cultural attributes of the society: thus the stress on material trappings in the observance of

Christmas and the emphasis on slimness of the female figure were attributes of the sending society that were embedded in the mass media content its members prepared for their consumption. One is the transmission perspective that holds that the mass media serve as conduits for the movement of representations of cultural attributes from one culture to another: the radio programs served such a function in the United States/Ethiopia scenario and the satellite broadcasts did so in the United States/Fiji scenario. (The perspective also holds that the characteristics of the message originators, mass media, or message receivers all have an effect on the degree of fidelity between the "real" attributes of the depicted society and the "impression" the receivers develop of the attributes.) And one is the persuasion perspective that holds that the mass media promote in the receiver not only the understanding but also the adoption of the attributes of the originator; so the radio and satellite programs may have contributed to the adoption of the American attributes by their respective audiences.

The Proposed Framework

A review of a number of developments in the histories of members of the World African Community—People of the African Continent (PACs) and People of African Descent (PADs, including those in the Caribbean)—point to the need for another framework for the study of cultural definition, continuance, or change under the influence of external groups. This framework captured in the histories of cultural attributes and related expressions that the two populations have exchanged with each other and with other groups is called cultural influence by re-importation or re-exportation, and has an aspect that is called cultural domination by re-importation or re-exportation. The correlation, transmission, and persuasion perspectives of the relationship between mass communication and cultural domination by importation/exportation also find application in the elaboration of the relationship between mass communication and this proposed cultural domination.

One of the developments actually is a progression that spans millennia. According to Jackson (1985), a people of Central Africa (that he says we call the Pygmies today) have had a belief system that centers on "a Father-God . . . a Virgin Mother . . . (and) a Savior-God Son" (p. 175). The belief system holds that the Father-God impregnated the Virgin Mother, who gave birth to the Savior-God, who "died for the salvation of his people, arose from the dead, and finally ascended into Heaven" (p. 175). Finch (1991) reports that Massey (1883, 1970, 1992), in "36 years of mind-bending labor" (p. 129), has among other things traced similar ideas to Africa, and writes that "The Christ myth, instead of being a spontaneous upsurge of a new divine dispensation (started in Palestine about 2,000 years ago), was traced back by Massey some 10,000 years [to] Central Africa" (p. 180). This leads to the proposition that the drama of the Son of God as an instrument for the redemption of humanity that is the cornerstone of Christianity has an antecedent that goes to Central Africa 10,000 years ago (Finch, 1991; Jackson, 1985). It was interpreted and localized in the lives of the Kemetu (the so-called Ancient Egyptians of the Nile Valley) as far back as 6,000 years ago (Finch, 1991). It has since appeared in the religions of other ancient societies (see Jackson, 1972) and was appropriated by the ancient Roman empire under its emperor Constantine (ben Jochannan, 1991). And it has been re-exported in recent and present times—the era of colonialism and imperialism and "globalization"—by the recent and present western component or extension of this empire to the descendants, and cousins of the descendants, of these ancient African peoples.

One other aspect of this progression that also spans millennia seems to be captured by ben Jochannan thus:

> The co-option of the "sacred scriptures" (and the tenets in them) by various religious groups was common among the ancients. This [co-option] came down through the

adaptation of basic tenets from indigenous Nile Valley Africans' "Mystery System" into Judaism. Christendom extended [this co-option] when it made Judaism its foundation. From this historical background [these tenets have] re-entered the various indigenous African traditional religions through colonialism and imperialism.

(ben Jochannan, 1991, p. 167)

and, of course, "globalization."

Indeed, perhaps on the basis of the similarities and identities between the essential idea, many major myths, many major symbols, and many major practices in Christianity and others in Africa, the comparison of the ages of the Christian idea and myths and symbols and practices and those in Africa, and the relationships between early Christian peoples and ancient Africans that seem to explain the similarities and identities between the Christian and the African, Diop (1991, p. 3) asserts:

Insofar as [Kemet] is the distant mother of Western culture and sciences, as will emerge from the reading of [*Civilization or Barbarism*], most of the ideas that we (Africans) call foreign are oftentimes nothing but mixed up, reversed, modified, elaborated images of the creations of our African ancestors, such as Judaism, Christianity, Islam. . . . One can see how fundamentally improper is the notion, so often repeated, of the importation of foreign ideologies into Africa. It stems from a perfect ignorance of the African past.

Liverpool (2001) appears to trace a comparable progression in the evolution of highlife music in West Africa. He reports that People of the African Continent taken by Europeans to enslavement in the Americas (including the Caribbean) brought with them a multitude of ideational, lyrical, structural, expressional, and contextual music traditions, and People of African Descent in the Caribbean (especially Trinidad) maintained or modified these traditions. He proposes that a certain inclination toward continuity in symbolism or artifact or performance explains the maintenance, that a certain inventiveness employing local materials and cultivated by local conditions explains the modifications, and that one of the results of these processes is the contemporary calypso. Then he explains how in recent years this calypso has been re-exported by PACs and PADs to West Africa, contributing there to the development of the contemporary music genre called highlife.

Orlean (2002) describes a perhaps similar recent process and centuries-old progression that appear to have contributed to the development of contemporary soukous music in Central Africa. The recent process takes off from the fact that many Central Africans have taken their music to performances in Europe. She indicates that the Africans also have taken their music to European recording studios and the resulting recordings have gone back Africa. Indeed, she wrote, "Even though there was nowhere to buy African music in France in the [mid-1970s], much of it was actually being recorded in studios in Paris and in Brussels and shipped back to Africa" (p. 114). She also seems to trace a comparable but centuries-old progression with regard to the development of soukous: the carrying of music from Africa by PACs brought to enslavement to the western hemisphere by Europeans, the combining of the African music with Spanish elements in Cuba to form the rumba, the receiving and acceptance of the rumba in Central Africa since the 1930s, and then the weaving of the rumba and "indigenous village music" (p. 115) into the melange that is called the contemporary soukous. Then taking some liberty she concludes, "Soukous had left home, absorbed a new culture, returned home, and was being absorbed and reinterpreted once again" (p. 115).

Parris (2001) also traces a comparable progression in the valuation of Caribbean literary giants by Caribbean people. Of these giants, he makes a special case of the poet Claude McKay, who had received little praise for his talents in his native Jamaica or the wider Caribbean. He became one of the most articulate voices of the Harlem Renaissance, became very successful and respected among PADs in the United States, and garnered additional success among other populations in the United States and in other parts of the world. Only after that did he receive so much recognition and even adulation in the Caribbean that he inspired a major theme in the works of Caribbean writers—"the return to peasant roots and the rejection of middle class society" (p. 100).

From the *Trinidad Guardian* of March 8, 1970 (as reported by Lowenthal, 1972) we find indications of a more recent but in some ways similar progression in the following observation: "Remember how we (Trinidadians) used to turn up (our) noses at roti? The Yankees come and say it too nice (it is very nice). So now roti (is to be found) in every social fete (party). Is that kind of people we are, yes." To the writer of this observation, Trinidadians developed a culinary culture in which the roti had a certain presence or valuation, they introduced Americans stationed in the island during and after World War II to the roti, the Americans seemed to elevate it more than the Trinidadians had elevated it before, reports of this elevation reached the Trinidadians, and finally in their culinary culture they went on to elevate the roti very much more than they had done so before and to a degree that was consistent with the implicit or explicit American elevation.

In each progression described above, one may identify a five-stage process that seems to start and end at an originating society that includes members of the World African Community: the society develops and expresses a cultural attribute (most of these reports highlight a cognitive or affective or behavioral aspect of the attribute, but each attribute would have cognitive and affective and behavioral aspects); the society exports the attribute to another society, or the other society imports the attribute; the receiving society modifies the attribute in ways that are consistent with the characteristics of its culture; the originating society re-imports, or the receiving society re-exports, these modifications; and finally the receiving society may adopt the modifications (to varying degrees, of course). Thus these progressions seem to illustrate a process one may call cultural influence by re-importation (from the perspective of the originator) or re-exportation (from that of the modifier).

Cases in Caribbean Music

Since popular music may be one of the most trafficked of human expressions, it would seem reasonable to look for re-importation or re-exportation scenarios within this domain. And indeed, over the last several decades, the music of Caribbean members of the World African Community has seen modifications that appear to be the results of influence by re-importation or re-exportation, with such influence flowing from external and more powerful societies or their extensions or surrogates to the region more than it flows from the region to these entities.

Several of these changes, as reported by Lashley (2001), seem to have taken place in the world of calypso in the first half of the 1900s. He reports that early in the history of the music its pioneers and performers and aficionados were viewed by many in the island of Trinidad as "the scum of the earth;" in the 1930s calypsonians went to the United States and received a warm welcome, recording contracts, and performance engagements (including one before President F. D. Roosevelt); and after this the earlier and rather widespread contempt turned into "justifiable pride" (p. 85) in Trinidad (p. 87):

> The apparent acceptance given to the calypso by musicians and audiences overseas had created a cultural resurgence in the art form. The calypsonians and their work found more acceptance in their homeland. . . . Ignorance had been replaced by awareness, prejudice by pride; the scoffers had become devotees. There was none too aloof, vain, or arrogant as not to honor the calypso and calypsonian alike. Trinidadians were seeing themselves anew.

Lashley (2001) also reports that the anticipation by Trinidadian calypsonians of what the United States market wanted in the calypso songs it patronized led to several changes in their performance of the music. Some calypsonians started to incorporate these changes so much that one leader said that to him these calypsonians became less genuine representatives than they had been before of the local calypso milieu. It seems that the use of the music in social communication among members of the originating less powerful society changed in part in compliance with modifications desired in the music by the external more powerful society. Indeed, Lashley (2001) notes that the trend continues, with calypsonians not just imitating American music but electronically fusing segments from American songs into what are supposed to be their original compositions.

One other area of change noted by Lashley (2001) was in the length of time during the year in which Trinidadians played the calypso over the airwaves. He reports that because of the sentiments of Christians in the land, at first the calypso mainly was publicly performed in the period just before Lent. He also reports that the Americans stationed in Trinidad during and after World War II patronized the music and played it on their radio station throughout the year. Then he reports that two researchers have observed that after this American practice there was an increase in the period each year during which the population played the music in public places and on the airwaves.

In the reggae music culture, the writer has observed three changes that took place in the 1970s and followed the exportation of the music to the United States and other more powerful countries. In each of these changes, there seems to have been the repetition of the progression Lashley reports to have taken place in the world of calypso.

Like other musical social commentaries, those whose writers use the reggae form describe the world and espouse ways of correcting its problems, improving its conditions, and achieving its ideals. In these commentaries, the writers have the option of stressing as a key to these activities a certain symmetry perspective that sees human beings as collaborators or a certain asymmetry perspective that sees them as adversaries. During the 1960s and early 1970s, each perspective had its presence in the Jamaican and Caribbean reggae culture, but after the mid-1970s the asymmetry perspective seemed to have had a greater presence than before. The songs with this latter perspective divide the world into opposing camps, such as Rastafari vs. Baldhead or Babylon, as well as the righteous vs. the heathen, the system vs. the suffering, the good vs. the bad, or us vs. them. They locate the writers, interpreters, or performers of works in one camp and certain others in another. They proclaim members of the first camp to be victims of problems and members of the second to be causes of the problems. They even imply or declare that the solution to the problems essentially lay in the triumph of the first camp and the demise of the second.

African Caribbean music always has included songs with social critical content. Thus up to the mid-1970s, music aficionados of the region did not distinguish reggae from the other music genres on the basis of the presence of this content in them. In addition, they did not describe reggae on the basis of the presence of this content in it. They described it on the basis of the feature that indeed distinguished it from other Jamaican or Caribbean music: its rhythm, accents, structure, or form. This aspect of the culture is captured in the definition of reggae provided by two of its keenest observers (Weber & Skinner, 2001, p. 151) thirty years after the beginning of the 1970s: "It is characterized by the foregrounding of syncopated bass and drum rhythms, an emphasis on the down beat (beats 1 and 3) rather than the backbeat (beats 2 and 4, which are emphasized in rock and blues), a prominent afterbeat or 'skank' voiced on guitars and/or keyboards, a call-and-response vocal style, and a strong orientation toward audience participation." Indeed, to this definition they add the following distinction (p. 161): "An important difference between reggae and Euro-American pop music is the significance in reggae of drum-and-bass patterns or 'riddims.' In reggae, the riddim rather than the lyric is considered to be the essence of the song."

After the mid-1970s, among many aficionados there was a noticeable shift in the elements emphasized in the definition of reggae. First, they changed from stressing form more than content to stressing content (especially the intention or the writer or interpreter or performer understood from an analysis of the content) more than form as the key criterion to be considered. Second, of all the content in reggae songs, they stressed Rastafari and the dichotomization of humanity into opposing camps more than before and more than other content. The resulting definitions include the following: reggae is the music of Rastafari; reggae is the music of Jah (the name for the Rastafari concept of God); reggae is the music that speaks against oppression; and reggae is the music of revolution.

One noteworthy feature of reggae, calypso, cadence, compas direct and other African Caribbean music cultures is that they traditionally have accorded the acclaimed musician the status of member rather than that of idol. This is found in the status accorded the most acclaimed calypsonian, on whom Caribbean people have been heaping accolades for many decades because they have regarded his work as superlative, but who for almost half a century has remained, to almost all of the Caribbean people, "one of the boys" or "one of the fellas" or "one of us."

Since the mid-1970s, in Jamaican and Caribbean reggae, there has been a noticeable shift in the range of status labels aficionados have accorded acclaimed musicians. That change is illustrated by the degree to which they have elevated the person and works of Robert "Bob" Marley. Before the mid-1970s, many disregarded much of his work, called much of it typical or ordinary, and used labels such as singer, musician, or music player to refer to him. Since the mid-1970s, they have paid far more attention to the work, have rated it (including those works they had ignored or dismissed) as superlatively or uniquely authentic, and even have tended to refer to Marley as leader, visionary, prophet, and yes, indeed, messiah.

There are many reasons why these changes took place in the Jamaican and Caribbean reggae culture, but while many explanations may clarify specific changes, one seems to clarify all of them. During much of the 1970s—and especially from the mid-1970s—the music was the subject of a major exportation and promotion campaign that took it to the United States and other more powerful countries. Audiences in these destinations—especially those in the United States—developed their reggae culture by interpreting the original reggae culture within the context of their historical and cultural milieu. In this reconceptualization, they changed the presence or importance of certain elements to levels that were different from the presence or importance accorded the elements in the original culture. In keeping with their greater tendency toward individualism and the idolization of individual musicians, their reggae culture accorded the elevation of single individuals to the status of idol a greater presence than it had in the original culture, and they accorded the status of idol to the only systematically, continually, and heavily promoted musician, Bob Marley. In keeping with the counterculture element in their current milieu, their reggae culture embraced the way of life of Rastafari that represented an alternative to the main stream far more than the original culture had done so, and claimed that reggae was an embodiment of Rastafari (see Zaid, 2001). In addition, in keeping with their greater emphasis on asymmetry than symmetry in relations, their reggae culture conceived of the world in dichotomous or oppositional terms (see Bangs, 1978; Frost, 1990) far more than the original culture had done so. Furthermore, their culture defined reggae to a greater degree on the basis of content and a lesser degree on the basis of rhythm, in contrast to the tendency in the originating culture to define it on the basis of form more than on the basis of content. The culture celebrated many songs that reflected this definition, with the best known of these songs being "The Harder They Come," "I Shot the Sheriff," and "Get Up, Stand Up." To the writer of this exposition, after these modifications, the adulation of Marley, the presence of Rastafari, the definition of reggae more on the basis of content than on the basis of rhythm, and the definition of reggae on the basis of the presence in reggae songs of the idea of a fundamental dichotomization and opposition in humanity, became much more pronounced than before in the Jamaican and Caribbean reggae culture.

As was the case with the progressions described earlier, those having to do with the calypso in the early part and reggae in the later years of the 1900s seem to include five stages: first, an African Caribbean music culture developed a genre that was characterized by certain attributes (origination); second, the culture exported the expressions of the attributes to the more powerful societies (exportation); fourth, these societies carried out modifications of the expressions and hence the attributes (modification); third, the societies re-exported or the African Caribbean music culture re-imported the modifications (re-importation, or re-exportation); and fifth, the Caribbean music culture appears to have changed in ways that seem consistent with the modifications (adoption).

Mass Communication Perspectives

As is the case with the importation/exportation framework, the re-importation or re-exportation framework allows for consideration of the correlation, transmission, and persuasion perspectives in the elaboration of the role and significance of mass communication in the process it describes. Indeed, the perspectives yield a number of programs, agendas, questions, or hypotheses for the study of this role and significance. Each of these areas of research will be described below, and as much as possible illustrated in both the world of calypso and the world of reggae.

The correlation perspective

The correlation perspective comes to life in the description of changes in the length of the time in the year during which Trinidadians engaged widely in the public displaying of the calypso. It is likely that the earlier local limitation of the period corresponded with an earlier local limitation of airplay on local radio stations, the later American extension of the period corresponded with a later greater airplay by radio stations controlled by the Americans, and the even later local extension of the period corresponded with an even later extension of the airplay natives accorded the music.

This perspective also comes to life in research possibilities in the study of reggae. Three observations of the writer are that the dichotomization of humanity in lyrics of reggae songs, the definition of reggae on the basis of content, and the idolization of acclaimed musicians by reggae aficionados had a certain low presence in the Jamaican and Caribbean music culture in the early 1970s, a greater presence in the United States reggae culture in the middle-to-late 1970s, and then a greater presence than before in the Jamaican and Caribbean reggae culture after the mid-1970s. These may be tested through the hypothesis that text that proposed or endorsed the dichotomization of humanity, the definition on the basis of content, and the idolization of acclaimed musicians had a relatively low presence in Jamaican and other Caribbean mass media in the early 1970s, a greater presence in United States mass media in the middle-to-late 1970s, and a greater presence than before in Jamaican and other Caribbean mass media after the mid-1970s.

The transmission perspective

The transmission perspective has to do with the movement of cultural attributes from the originator of these attributes to the external group and the movement of modifications in these attributes from the external group to the originator, and so presents opportunities for the study of players and means and methods in the exportation and re-importation or re-exportation stages. It seems easy to focus on such obvious and superficial issues as the types of media used by these players and in these processes, but perhaps a more fruitful and revealing investigation would focus on the objectives of the players in the processes and on their use of the media to achieve these objectives.

The need for this primary focus arises from an important report from Zaid (2001). He says that in the early phases of the exportation of reggae from Jamaica to the more powerful societies its exporters presented it as an embodiment of "the aesthetic form that effectively 'directed and organized' the perceptions of Rastafarians" (p. 143). This leads one to ponder the possibility that this characterization may have been cultivated by these exporters as they sought to maximize the popularity of the music among audiences in which such characterizations would have resonated, since these audiences mainly included critical university students and counterculture proponents seeking alternatives to the "establishment," and the lifestyle proposed by Rastafari represented one such alternative. Thus one issue is what are the motivations of exporters (that may be media services), what influences their representations of the culture of the African originators in the destinations of their exports, and as a result, how rooted in the originators are their representations of the culture.

The need for this primary focus also arises from another report from Zaid (2001). He says that early in its history, reggae had a singles-based format, but one of its major promoters had the need to market it in ways that optimized its success in the more powerful societies and thus convinced its originators to produce it in an album format for these societies. One possibility is that this promoter communicated to the originators an interpretation of the modifications desired by the more powerful societies that would lead to the maximization of returns to the promoter. Thus another major issue is what are the motivations of re-importers or re-exporters (that may be media services), how do the motivations influence their representations of the modifications carried out or desired by the more powerful societies, and given these influences, how authentic are their representations of the responses of the more powerful societies to the culture of the African originators.

The report on the importation of United States television programs into Fiji gives the impression that the programs provided a certain representation of the American conception of the ideal female figure but did not deal with the issue of how much that ideal appeared on other media importations (for example, newspapers, magazines, radio programs, and other television programs) from the United States to Fiji. In the exportation stage of the process of cultural domination by re-importation or re-exportation, one related issue is the pervasiveness of representations of an attribute of the culture of the originating society of African peoples that members of the society exchange with each other in the aggregate of media content that flows from that originating society to the more powerful society. And in the re-importation or re-exportation stage, the comparable issue is the pervasiveness of representations of the modifications that are made by the more powerful society and that members of that society exchange with each other within the aggregate of media content that flows from the more powerful society to the originating society of African peoples.

The report on the importation of United States television programs into Fiji also did not cover the issue of the presence of United States media representations of the American conception of the ideal female figure in the television programming, and hence the television audience, in Fiji. In the exportation stage, one related issue is the penetration of media content from the originating society of African peoples in the mass media system of the more powerful society, and in the re-importation or re-exportation stage, a comparable issue is the penetration of media content from the more powerful society in the media system of the originating society of African peoples.

The assumption here is that the greater the pervasiveness or penetration of media content that comes from and describes one society within the media system and audience of a receiving society, the greater the probability that truly accurate representations of the cultural attributes of the sender will be developed by the receiver. This pervasiveness or penetration could be considered in the elaboration of the transmission of representations of cultural attributes from originating societies of African peoples to more powerful societies, as well as the transmission of the modifications of these attributes from the more powerful societies to the African peoples. These issues seem important in the study of situations in which the societies may be interlocked in the relationship this exposition calls cultural domination by re-importation or re-exportation.

One inclination would be to assume the originating society of African peoples to be the exporter of the representations of its culture that flow to the more powerful societies. But the historical and contemporary reality is that the external, more powerful society may be the one playing this role. This was the case in recent times, because as Martin (1983) reports, the media that many colonizers established in their colonies served mainly to connect these colonies to the homes of the colonizers. Thus information about a colony often flowed from that colony to the more powerful dominator and then to another colony, even though that second colony may be close to the first one. Indeed, Ibelema (2001) indicates that such a state of affairs obtains today in linkages between neighboring peoples in Africa. This means that information that flows among members of a society of African peoples (or between societies of African peoples that constitute a culture complex) about elements of their culture may be in the hands of the media of an external and more powerful society, and so the understanding that the African peoples develop of their supposedly common cultural attributes and related expressions may be shaped by the media of that external and more powerful society.

The degree to which this is the case in the Caribbean cultural arena is very important, since it is a fact that much of the definition, description, and illustration of what many in the region viewed as "authentic" or "roots" in reggae in the 1970s seemed to flow from Jamaica through the media of the more powerful societies and then to such other parts of the Greater Caribbean as the Bahamas and the Eastern Caribbean. Indeed, one observer of and expert on Caribbean mass communications (Walrond, 1991) recalled that during and after the mid-1970s Caribbean newspapers carried many definitions, descriptions, illustrations, critiques, and evaluations of reggae performers, reggae works, and/or the reggae genre. But, she noted, many of these articles were reproductions of media content that was written by observers from, primarily intended for audiences in, and even first published by, the print media of the United States and other more powerful countries.

The issue here is the centrality of the media of an external and perhaps more powerful society in the conversation that takes place among members of a society of African peoples, or among societies of African peoples that constitute a culture complex, in the elaboration of, the evaluation of, and the response to, what they see as natural, normal, representative, or authentic in their culture. The extremely great importance of this centrality among People of African Descent in the Caribbean lies in the observation by Alleyne (1994) that Caribbean people tend to display "an undue reliance on Western arbiters regarding the value and representation of [Caribbean] creativity" (p. 76).

The persuasion perspective

At the foundation of the persuasion perspective is the proposition that the mass media promote the adoption by members of the originating society of African peoples of modifications that have been made of their culture in the more powerful societies. One model for the elaboration of the role and significance of mass communication in the achievement of this outcome appears to be captured in the bullet or hypodermic theses on mass media effects, and argues that the messages in the mass media are powerful causes of effects. It seems to propose that mass media reports on the modifications carried out in the more powerful society on elements in the culture of the society of African peoples may instantly and even powerfully move the African peoples to adopt these modifications. Another model for this elaboration seems to be captured in the cultivation and social learning theses on mass media effects, and argues that the messages are moderately powerful promoters of effects over long periods. It seems to propose that the exposure to and the consumption of reports on the modifications would lead over an extended period to the adoption of them.

But a review of the histories of societies of African peoples and the more powerful societies leads to the recognition of the need to consider as the explanation for this adoption a combination that includes mass communication, inclinations of individuals in both groups of societies that seem to be consequences of the histories, and conditions in the contexts that affect both groups and also appear to be consequences of the histories. The consideration of the inclinations of the individuals is justified by the uses and gratifications perspective of mass communication effects (see McGuire, 1974) that proposes that human beings, in response to their psychological makeup or internal stimuli or external stimuli, develop needs they may try to satisfy through the consumption or application of mass media messages, and the "effects" of the messages indeed may be the satisfaction of these needs. The consideration of the conditions is also justified by the third-variable perspective of mass communication effects (Comstock et al., 1978), which proposes that the conditions may impel human beings in certain directions, mass media messages also may impel them in these directions, and the "effect" of the messages may be the outcome of the synergy in the combination that includes the conditions and the mass communication.

The history in question spans not only 400 years but almost 4,000 years. It includes the development of the southern cradle of civilization (that includes Africa) with its greater orientation toward feminine attributes, collectivism, cooperation, interpenetration, equilibrium, symbiosis, and complementarity than toward their opposites. It also includes the development of the northern cradle of civilization (that includes Europe) with its greater orientation toward masculine attributes, individualism, competition, penetration of others, overwhelming of others, subjugation of others, and the use of others for self interest, than toward their opposites (for an elaboration of these observations, see Diop, 1978, 1974; Finch, 1991). One of the implications from two of the major works of Diop (1974, 1978) is that in the study of global relations it is extremely important to consider not only the characteristics of the southern peoples but also those of the northern ones. Indeed, one of the major ideas of Diop, as summarized by Finch (1991), seems to suggest that the interplay between the psychologies, related priorities, and related activities of the two major cradles of civilization over more than 3,500 years seems to explain the contemporary global condition (p. 60):

> Summarizing Diop's viewpoint, we can say that the (more symmetry-oriented) matriarchy of the southern cradle and the (more asymmetry-oriented) patriarchy of the northern cradle sprang up more or less independently, but became ineluctable antagonists. The (more symmetry-oriented) matriarchal south, which first attained civilization, (has) *succumbed* (emphasis added by this writer) to the politico-military onslaughts of the (more asymmetry-oriented) patriarchal north occurring in waves for more than 3,500 years after 1,700 B.C. The outcome of this repeated *onslaught* (emphasis added by this writer) over thousands of years is seen in the contemporary military, political, and economic pre-eminence of the western world.

Thus the elaboration of the domination of the cultures of the mostly "southern" less powerful societies of African peoples by the mostly "northern" more powerful societies by re-importation or re-exportation must include the consideration of the relationship between mass communication and the characteristics of both groups of societies that may explain the adoption by the African peoples of modifications made in their culture by the more powerful. The elaboration recognizes that the result of the millennia-old drama between the two "cradles" includes not only the overwhelming, domination, and exploitation of the southern peoples by the northern ones, but also the cultivation in the southerners by the northerners of a profound and powerful orientation to the northerners as a reference group, and the cultivation by the northerners of an international order that is marked by the centrality of the northerners and their extensions, outposts, or surrogates in global affairs. In this orientation and centrality we may find keys to the roles of the mass media in the adoption in the societies of African peoples— indeed, the southern and less powerful peoples of today in general—of modifications of their culture that are carried out in the more powerful societies.

A reference group (see Kelley, 1968; Kemper, 1969) is one that subjects bear in mind as they respond to stimuli, conceptualize conditions, or realize terminating conditions. This may be a normative reference group that defines these responses, conceptualizations, or realizations for subjects, or a comparison reference group whose example guides the subjects. The inclination of subjects to consider cognitions, affects, and behaviors of the reference group is their orientation toward the group (Regis, 2001d) and would seem to have three aspects. Attention valuation is the degree to which subjects would like their cognitions, affects, and behaviors to receive the attention of the reference group (this attention is important, since it would be followed by the reaction of the reference group and perhaps the adjustment of the cognition, affect, or behavior by the subject). Validation valuation is the degree to which subjects would like their cognitions, affects, or behaviors to be endorsed by the reference group (this validation is important because, as Festinger, 1968, notes, without it the cognitions, affects, or behaviors in question may be unstable). Imitation inclination is the degree to which subjects develop, maintain, or change their cognitions, affects, or behaviors by imitating those they perceive to be held or endorsed or pronounced by the reference group.

In the Caribbean, one major outcome of the domination of the peoples of the "south" by those of the "north" has been the cultivation in the descendants of the former of a very strong orientation toward the descendants of the latter. It is a recurring subject in reports of experts who have studied the region carefully (for example, see Brown, 2001; Ibelema, 2001; Lashley, 2001; Liverpool, 2001; Lowenthal, 1972; Parris, 2001; Regis, 2001a, 2001b, 2001c; Skinner, 2001; Weber and Skinner, 2001). It also is captured in the important observation by Alleyne (1994) that Caribbean people display "an undue reliance on Western arbiters regarding the value and representation of [Caribbean] creativity" (p. 76). Given this orientation, one project could involve the study of the degree to which there may be a certain contest or synergy between mass communication and each type of orientation (attention valuation, validation valuation, imitation inclination) toward each type of reference group (normative, comparison) in the more powerful societies in the adoption by Caribbean People of African Descent of those modifications that may be made by the more powerful societies in their culture and after that re-imported by or re-exported to the Caribbean.

This project could have at least two components. The first springs from the inclination of Caribbean People of African Descent, as members of the World African Community (WAC), toward the collectivism that Diop (1978) sees as historically characteristic of African peoples. It proposes that this inclination is expressed in their emphasis on collective participation in (or the popularity that symbolizes collective participation in) expressions of culture, and further proposes that there will be an emphasis on such participation (or the popularity that symbolizes it) in the more powerful societies, and studies the relationship between mass communication and the perception of this participation (or popularity) in their adoption of the modifications. The second springs from the recognition of the fact Caribbean PADs and other members of the WAC have been subjected by the more powerful societies to a colonialistic socialization that cultivates in the Caribbean PADs the idea that they are inferior and the more powerful peoples are superior. It proposes that among Caribbean PADs there has been as a result a heightened valuation of validation from the more powerful societies, and studies the relationship between mass communication and this valuation of validation in their adoption of the modifications. The third compares the mass communication, the inclination among Caribbean PADs toward collectivism, the orientation of Caribbean PADs toward the more powerful societies, the synergy between these factors, and the contests among these factors, in their adoption of the modifications. The foundation of the project and its components could be the uses and gratifications perspective (see McGuire, 1974) and/or the third-variable perspective (see Comstock et al., 1978) of mass communication effects.

In the Caribbean, the orientation toward the more powerful societies seems to be complemented by the structural and operational order that is the corollary of the centrality of these societies in the recent and present global order. The centrality was in the communication domain in the colonial era of decades or centuries ago (Martin, 1983) and continues in this domain today (Ibelema, 2001). It comes to life in a system in which messages flow from a Caribbean island (or less powerful society) through a colonial dominator (or its extensions, outposts, or surrogates) and to another Caribbean island (or less powerful society), and focuses on the centrality of the more powerful societies and their agents as enablers. It was in the sugar industry decades and centuries ago (see Augier et al., 1974) and continues in the recording industry today (see Orlean, 2002) as part of a global order that includes the presence of "resources" in the Caribbean (or less powerful societies), the exportation of these resources to the more powerful societies (or their extensions, outposts, or surrogates), the processing of them in the more powerful or their agents, the re-importation or re-exportation of the results of the processing to the Caribbean (or less powerful), and the adoption of these results in the Caribbean (or less powerful), and focuses on the roles of the more powerful societies or their agents as economic patronizers, product reformulators, and marketers.

In recent years, this order has existed in the process that includes the development of proposals for the addressing of local needs by technocrats in the Caribbean (and, in general, the less powerful societies), the presentation of these proposals to international agencies under the influence of the more powerful societies or their agents, the modification of the proposals before funding by the agencies, and the adoption of the modifications by the Caribbean (or less powerful societies), and focuses on the role of the more powerful societies and their agents as financers and validators of the proposals. It also has taken the form of this common occurrence in the education systems of the smaller islands of the English-speaking Eastern Caribbean: island governments seek foreign aid in the improvement of the systems; technocrats from the more powerful societies serve as providers of the expertise that drives the development of ideas for the utilization of the "aid"; local teachers provide ideas for the improvement of the systems, but the technocrats validate, modify, and augment the ideas, and present the results as recommendations to the island governments and the providers of the aid. The technocrats operate as agents of the more powerful societies and as intermediaries between the local teachers and their governments, and in this role they incorporate those modifications that represent the ideas of their more powerful societies into ideas the local teachers could have shared directly with local technocrats and governments. Thus ideas for the operation and improvement of the education systems flow from local teachers, through validating and/or reformulating technocrats representing the more powerful societies, to local technocrats and governments.

These agents of the more powerful societies—the patronizers, reformulators, marketers, financers, and validators—may act as reference groups whose policies, actions, or reactions may amount to the modification of the features of individual attributes and related expressions, or the presence of individual attributes and related expressions, in the culture of the Caribbean (and the less powerful societies). This leads to another subject for study: the degree to which there is a certain synergy or contest between mass communication, the Caribbean orientation toward these reference groups, and the centrality of these reference groups in the global order, in the adoption by Caribbean People of African Descent of modifications that are made by the groups specifically and the more powerful societies in general in African Caribbean culture, and re-imported by or re-exported to the region. The project could study the mass communication, each orientation, combinations of these factors, or the synergy or contestation among these factors or combinations, in this adoption. The conceptual foundation of this project also could be the uses and gratifications perspective (see McGuire, 1974) and the third-variable perspective (see Comstock et al., 1978) of mass communication effects.

Conclusion

The assumption that guides this exposition is not new. It has guided the elaboration of the relationship between mass communication and other phenomena. For example, it has guided the elaboration of the relationship between mass communication and development and between mass communication and cultural domination by importation or exportation. It is that mass communication can play the part of a correlate, a transmitter, or a persuader in human conditions and processes.

But there is one approach to the elaboration of mass communication that these expositions have not employed very extensively but that calls for attention. This is the elaboration and investigation of the nature of mass communication variables, and the relationships that involve mass communication variables, under the inspiration of other disciplines. Regis (2001b), proposes that among members of the World African Community the orientation toward collectivism in life in general (an aspect of group psychology) has a parallel in the presence of call-and-response in the composition and performance of music (an aspect of cultural expression). Bromley and Bowles (1995), propose that the idea of relative constancy that argues that "consumer spending on mass media was relative to the gross national product and was constant over time" (p. 14) and lies in the domain of financial management has a parallel in the idea that "the amount of time consumers spend with mass media may be constant and finite over time" (p. 15) that is in the domain of time management. And Frith and Wesson (1991) propose that the greater orientation of American life than British life toward individualism (an element in group psychology) has a parallel in the more frequent use of individuals than groups in advertisements in American magazines (an element in mass communication) and in contrast the more frequent use of groups than individuals in advertisements in British magazines (another element in mass communication). In each case, the study of phenomena in one discipline seems to be inspired by the study of those in another discipline. Thus one project among Caribbean People of African Descent, members of the World African Community in general, and perhaps other peoples with "southern" historical roots, could be the study of the nature and significance of the role of mass communication in cultural domination by re-importation or re-exportation under the inspiration of ideas from theoretical historical analysis, such as the two-cradle theory of Diop.

In such works as *The African Origin of Civilization* (1974) and *The Cultural Unity of Black Africa* (1978), Diop dwells to some degree on the historical fact of the overwhelming and subjugation of the southern peoples of the world (represented to some degree by the less powerful societies of today) by the northern peoples (represented to some degree by the more powerful societies). In Africa and the Caribbean, some argue that the major outcome of this overwhelming and subjugation has been the exploitation of the human and other resources of the southern lands for the benefit of the northern peoples. But one also may argue that a major outcome is the cultivation, internalization, and perpetuation in the southern peoples of a mindset that sees them as inferior and the northern peoples as superior and has as its corollary the cultivation, internalization, and perpetuation in them of a substantial orientation toward the northern peoples as reference groups. That mindset and orientation see the northern peoples as keys to the attainment of development and civilization and salvation but serves the continuation of the millennia-old overwhelming, subjugation, and exploitation. It appears to be captured in the sentiment, expressed repeatedly in an election season in what many may call a "post-colonial, independent, sovereign" island in the Eastern Caribbean, that "Bon Dieu voye un nom blanc pou sovay nous" ("God has sent a white man to save us").

In the elaboration and investigation of cultural domination, on the one hand the importation/exportation framework perpetuates this state of affairs by conceptualizing the domination as a process or condition that begins with the assumption of the more powerful societies as originators of cultural attributes or expressions and ends with the assumption of the less powerful societies as recipients and adopters of these attributes and expressions. But the re-importation or re-exportation framework begins to make breaches in this state of affairs by conceptualizing the domination as a process or condition that starts with the assumption that the less powerful societies are originators of cultural attributes and expressions in a process or condition that ultimately ends within them. It could be seen as a liberating framework, but at its foundation is the study of the millennia-old history of Caribbean People of African Descent, People of the African Continent, other members of the World African Community, and the other peoples with deep roots in the "southern" cradle of civilization.

References

Alleyne, M. (1994). Positive vibration? Capitalist textual hegemony and Bob Marley. *Bulletin of Eastern Caribbean Affairs, 19*(3), 76–84.

Augier, F., Gordon, S., Hall, D., & Reckord, M. (1974). *The making of the West Indies.* Port of Spain, Trinidad, and Kingston, Jamaica: Longman Caribbean.

Bangs, L. (1978, June 1). Bob Marley aims high, misses big: Tepid cliches and tourist bait. *Rolling Stone,* p. 56.

Becker, A., & Burwell, R. (1999). Acculturation and disordered eating in Fiji. Paper presented at the annual meeting of the American Psychiatric Association, Washington, DC.

Benedict, R. (1934). *Patterns of culture.* Boston, MA: Houghton Mifflin.

ben Jochannan, J. (1991). *African origins of the major Western religions.* Baltimore, MD: Black Classic Press.

Bromley, R., & Bowles, D. (1995). Impact of Internet on use of traditional news media. *Newspaper Research Journal, 16*(2), 14–27.

Brown, A. (2001). Caribbean cultures, global mass communication, technology, and opportunity in the twenty-first century. In H. Regis (Ed.), *Culture and mass communication in the Caribbean: Domination, dialogue, dispersion* (pp. 169–184). Gainesville, FL: University Press of Florida.

Cambridge, V. (2002). Milestones in communication and national development. In Y. Kamalipour (Ed.), *Global communication* (pp. 141–160). Belmont, CA: Wadsworth/Thomson Learning.

Chinweizu. (1975). *The West and the rest of us: White predators, black slavers, and the African elite.* New York: Vintage Books.

Comstock, G., Chaffee, S., Katzman, N., McCombs, M., & Roberts, D. (1978). *Television and human behavior.* New York: Columbia University Press.

Dennis, E. (1984). The U.S. is guilty of communications imperialism. In E. Dennis & J. Merrill (Eds.), *Basic issues in mass communication* (pp. 183–190). New York: Macmillan.

Diop, C. (1974). *The African origin of civilization: Myth or reality.* Westport, CT: Lawrence Hill.

Diop, C. (1978). *The cultural unity of Black Africa.* Chicago, IL: Third World Press.

Diop, C. (1991). *Civilization or barbarism.* New York: Lawrence Hill Books.

Festinger, L. (1968). A theory of social comparison processes. In H. Hyman & E. Singer (Eds.), *Readings in reference group theory and research* (pp. 123–146). New York: The Free Press.

Finch, C. (1991). *Echoes of the Old Darkland: Themes from the African Eden.* Decatur, GA: Khenti, Inc.

Frith, K., & Wesson, D. (1991). A comparison of cultural values in British and American print advertising: A study of magazines. *Journalism Quarterly, 68*(1–2), 216–221.

Frost, L. (1990). DJ Reggae: Slackness becomes standard. *Caribbean Review, 16*(3/4), 6, 74.

Galtung, J. (1980). *The true worlds: A transnational perspective.* New York: Free Press.

Hamelink, C. (1983). *Cultural autonomy in global communications: Planning national information policy.* New York: Longman.

Hur, K. (1982). International mass communication research: A critical review of theory and methods. In M. Burgoon (Ed.), *Communication yearbook, 6,* (pp. 531–554). Beverly Hills, CA: Sage.

Ibelema, M. (2001). Perspectives on mass communication and cultural domination. In H. Regis (Ed.), *Culture and mass communication in the Caribbean: Domination, dialogue, dispersion* (pp. 15–36). Gainesville, FL: University Press of Florida.

Jackson, J. (1972). *Man, God, and civilization.* New York: Citadel Press.

Jackson, J. (1985). *Christianity before Christ.* Austin, TX: American Atheist Press.

Kelley, H. (1968). Two functions of reference groups. In H. Hyman & E. Singer (Eds.), *Readings in reference group theory and research* (pp. 77–83). New York: The Free Press.

Kemper. T. (1969). Reference groups, socialization, and achievement. In E. Borgatta (Ed.), *Social psychology: Readings and perspectives* (pp. 297–312). Chicago, IL: Rand McNally.

Lashley, L. (2001). Decades of change in Calypso culture. In H. Regis (Ed.), *Culture and mass communication in the Caribbean: Domination, dialogue, dispersion* (pp. 83–93). Gainesville, FL: University Press of Florida.

Lerner, D. (1958). *The passing of traditional society: Modernizing the Middle East.* New York: The Free Press.

Liverpool, H. (2001). Re-exportation and musical traditions surrounding the African Masquerade. In H. Regis (Ed.), *Culture and mass communication in the Caribbean: Domination, dialogue, dispersion* (pp. 63–82). Gainesville, FL: University Press of Florida.

Lowenthal, D. (1972). *West Indian societies.* New York: Oxford University Press.

McDonald, H. (1986). *The normative basis of culture.* Baton Rouge, LA: Louisiana State University Press.

McGuire, W. (1974). Psychological motives and communication gratification. In J. Blumler & E. Katz (Eds.), *The uses of mass communications: Current perspectives on gratifications research* (pp. 167–196). Beverly Hills, CA: Sage.

Martin, L. (1983). Africa. In J. C. Merrill (Ed.), *Global journalism: A survey of the world's mass media* (pp. 190–248). New York: Longman.

Massey, G. (1883). *Natural Genesis,* Vol. 2. London: Williams & Norgate.

Massey, G. (1970). *Ancient Egypt,* Vol. 2. New York: Weiser.

Massey, G. (1992). The historical (Jewish) Jesus and the mythical (Egyptian) Christ. In G. Massey (Ed.), *Gerald Massey's lectures* (pp. 1–25). Brooklyn, NY: A&S Books.

Mazrui, A. (1976). *A world federation of cultures: An African perspective.* New York: Free Press.

Melkote, S. (2002). Theories of development communication. In W. Gudykunst & B. Mody (Eds.), *Handbook of international and intercultural communication* (pp. 419–436). Thousand Oaks, CA: Sage.

Orlean, S. (2002, October 14 & 21). The Congo sound: How a record store in Paris became a center of African music. *The New Yorker,* pp. 114–120.

Parris, E. (2001). The re-exportation of the Caribbean literary artist. In H. Regis (Ed.), *Culture and mass communication in the Caribbean: Domination, dialogue, dispersion* (pp. 95–119). Gainesville, FL: University Press of Florida.

Regis, H. (2001a). Introduction. In H. Regis (Ed.), *Culture and mass communication in the Caribbean: Domination, dialogue, dispersion* (pp. 3–14). Gainesville, FL: University Press of Florida.

Regis, H. (2001b). Caribbean desire for popularity for the works of Caribbean musicians. In H. Regis (Ed.), *Culture and mass communication in the Caribbean: Domination, dialogue, dispersion* (pp. 185–197). Gainesville, FL: University Press of Florida.

Regis, H. (2001c). Mass communication, orientation, and connection of Eastern Caribbean people to reference groups. In H. Regis (Ed.), *Culture and mass communication in the Caribbean: Domination, dialogue, dispersion* (pp. 199–212). Gainesville, FL: University Press of Florida.

Regis, H. (2001d). An integrative framework for study and elaboration of culture and mass communication in the Caribbean. In H. Regis (Ed.), *Culture and mass communication in the Caribbean: Domination, dialogue, dispersion* (pp. 215–239). Gainesville, FL: University Press of Florida.

Rogers, E. (1969). *Modernization among peasants.* New York: Holt, Rinehart, & Winston.

Rogers, E. (1976). Communication and development: The passing of the dominant paradigm. In E. Rogers (Ed.), *Communication and development: Critical perspectives* (pp. 121–148). Beverly Hills, CA: Sage.

Salwen, M. (1991). Cultural imperialism: A media effects approach. *Critical Studies in Mass Communication, 8,* 29–38.

Schiller, H. (1969). *Mass communication and American Empire.* New York: Augustus M. Kelly.

Schiller, H. (1976). *Communications and cultural domination.* White Plains, NY: International Arts and Sciences Press.

Schiller, H. (1991). Not yet the post-imperialist era. *Critical Studies in Mass Communication, 8,* 13–28.

Skinner, E. (2001). Empirical research on mass communication and cultural domination in the Caribbean. In H. Regis (Ed.), *Culture and mass communication in the Caribbean: Domination, dialogue, dispersion* (pp. 37–62). Gainesville, FL: University Press of Florida.

Sreberny-Mohammadi, A. (1997). The many cultural faces of imperialism. In P. Golding & P. Harris (Eds.), *Beyond cultural imperialism: Globalization, communication, and the New International Order* (pp. 49–68). Thousand Oaks, CA: Sage.

Tamborini, R., & Choi, J. (1990). The role of cultural diversity in cultivation research. In N. Signorielli and M. Morgan (Eds.), *Cultivation analysis: New directions in media effects research* (pp. 157–180). Newbury Park, CA: Sage.

Tan, A. (1985). *Mass communication theories and research.* New York: John Wiley and Sons.

Walrond, L. (1991). Personal interview with writer, Ideas Management, St. Michael, Barbados.

Weber, T., & Skinner, E. (2001). Theorizing Reggae and small media: Social movements in globalization. In H. Regis (Ed.), *Culture and mass communication in the Caribbean: Domination, dialogue, dispersion* (pp. 149–163). Gainesville, FL: University Press of Florida.

Zaid, B. (2001). Bakhtin's dialogic model and popular music: Bob Marley and the Wailers as a case study. In H. Regis (Ed.), *Culture and mass communication in the Caribbean: Domination, dialogue, dispersion* (pp. 139–148). Gainesville, FL: University Press of Florida.

Part V
Identity and Intercultural Communication Competence

14

Intercultural Communication Competence
A Synthesis

Guo-Ming Chen & William J. Starosta

As we grow increasingly aware of the global interdependence of people and cultures, we confront ever shifting cultural, ecological, economic, and technological realities that define the shrinking world of the twenty-first century. The development of new ways of living in the world together is pivotal to further human progress; we must learn how to see things through the eyes of others and add their knowledge to our personal repertories. Such a global mind-set can result only from competent communication among peoples from diverse cultures.

Intercultural Communication Competence: Why?

The citizens of the twenty-first century must learn to see through the eyes, hearts, and minds of people from cultures other than their own. Several important trends of the late twentieth century have transformed the world into a global village: technology development, globalization of the economy, widespread population migrations, the development of multiculturalism, and the demise of the nation-state in favor of sub- and supranational identifications. In order to live meaningfully and productively in this world, individuals must develop their intercultural communication competence.

Technology development

The development of communication and transportation technology linking every part of the world has served to interconnect almost every aspect of life at the onset of the twenty-first century (Frederick, 1003; Porter & Samovar, 1994). Today the flow of ideas and information increasingly transcends national boundaries. People can also travel to anywhere in the world much more quickly than ever before. The faster travel speeds wrought by transportation technology have introduced increasing face-to-face communication among people from different cultures.

Globalization and economy

The progress of communication and transportation technology has rendered global markets more accessible and the business world more interrelated and international than in the past. Regional trade alliances have become the "new world order." The trend toward a global economy is bringing people from different cultures together. It requires representatives from multinational corporations to communicate with those in other parts of the world to retain a competitive space in the global economic arena. The interdependence among international economies reflects the important role that intercultural communication plays now and will play increasingly in the next century. The development of greater intercultural understanding has become an essential element of global business (Adler, 1991; Mead, 1990).

Widespread population migrations

As cultural interconnectedness has increased as a result of technology advancement, we have also witnessed remarkable population migrations across national borders. The United States especially has felt the impacts of this trend. In 1990, the U.S. Census revealed that the first generation foreign-born population in the United Sates had reached almost 20 million. About 8.7 million immigrants entered the United States between 1980 and 1990. At least 32 million persons residing in the United State speak a first language other than English, and 14 million of these do not speak English fluently. These figures indicate that the increasing numbers of immigrants have restructured the fabric of American society. The United States has become much more culturally diverse than it has been in the past.

This multiethnic structure makes intercultural contact among co-cultures inevitable. Members of the various co-cultures and ethic groups residing in the United States must learn to adjust to one another's identities. This trend demands that individuals learn to communicate in ways that are effective in such a diversifying society (Nieto, 1992).

The development of multiculturalism

The changing demographics described above stand to affect every aspect of life in the United States. Johnston and Packer (1987), for example, predict that the increasing diversity of workplace and social life in the United States will dramatically affect organizational life in the twenty-first century. The new workforce will comprise persons who are diverse in race, culture, age, gender, and language. Cultural diversity, or multiculturalism, will become the norm rather the exception in American life. Thus, intercultural communication scholars need to address those issues that will help people learn to work and live together without being deterred by the differences they may bring to their encounters. The development of greater intercultural understanding and intercultural communication competence is an essential part of human life in the contemporary age.

De-Emphasis on the nation-state

As new immigrants arrive and co-cultures make headway in achieving fuller participation in U.S. society, the very idea of national identity will surely change. Increasingly, the United States is pulled into regional alliances, such as NATO or NAFTA, that are larger than the nation. In addition, we see the reassertion of ethnic and gender differences within the nation; for instance, women have begun to talk as women, African Americans as African Americans, and Native Americans as Native Americans. The ability to negotiate the meanings and priorities of diverse identities has become a prerequisite of attaining interpersonal competence in modern society (Collier & Thomas, 1988).

The five trends described above combine to provide a foundation for the indispensability of intercultural communication competence in our increasingly global society. The world has become more interdependent and interconnected, and the nation-state has become more culturally heterogeneous. These developments foster within individuals multiple, simultaneous identities in terms of culture, ethnicity, race, religion, nationality, and gender (Belay, 1993). Intercultural communication competence therefore functions to nourish a human personality in which people are aware of their multiple identities and are able to maintain a multicultural coexistence in order to develop a "global civic culture" (Boulding, 1988). In other words, intercultural communication competence transforms a monocultural person into a multicultural person. This transformation is achieved through symmetrical interdependence that enables persons to demonstrate "tolerance for differences and mutual respect among cultures as a mark of enlightened national and global citizenship" in individual, social, business, and political institutions levels (Belay, 1993).

Based on this theoretical foundation, the following discussion of intercultural communication competence is divided into five sections. These address, in turn, the nature of communication competence, approaches to the study of intercultural communication competence, a model of intercultural communication competence, a critique and directions for future research, and a summary and conclusion.

The Nature of Communication Competence

Although 50 years of conceptualizing have provided a theoretical and practical foundation for intercultural communication, it remains a fresh field. The study of intercultural communication dates back to the works of political scientists and anthropologists in the 1940s and 1950s. Whereas linguist Edward Sapir wrote about this topic in the 1920s, it took Benjamin Whorf to frame his work more fully as a communication question. As sociologists, linguists, and communication scholars have developed an interest in intercultural communication, two separate schools of thought—cultural dialogue and cultural criticism—now inform research in intercultural communication (Asante, Newmark, & Blake, 1979). Both schools have spawned significant research in intercultural communication. One of the main topics studied by the two groups is intercultural communication competence, or the effective means whereby individuals can understand cultural commonalities and move beyond cultural differences in order to reach the ideal goals advocated by cultural dialogists and cultural critics. But, we ask, What is communication competence?

Definition of communication competence

Two concepts have long been applied in discussions of communication competence: effectiveness and appropriateness. *Effectiveness* refers to an individual's ability to produce intended effects through interaction with the environment. This ability is treated either as a basic human skill that is obtained through learning and socializing processes (Weinstein, 1969; White, 1959) or as an acquired ability that is related neither to personal intellect nor to education (Foote & Cottrell, 1955; Holland & Baird, 1968). In either case, the ability is understood to increase as the individual's awareness of relevant factors increases (Argyris, 1965a, 1965b). In addition, ideally, competent communicators should be able to control and manipulate their environments to attain personal goals. In order to maximize such goals, individuals must be able to identify them, get relevant information about them, accurately predict others' responses, select communication strategies, implement those communication strategies, and accurately access the interaction results (Parks, 1985, 1994).

A more systematic view of effectiveness in communication relates the concept to both interactants. To be competent in communication, a person must not only feel competent, but his or her ability should be observed and confirmed by the people with whom he or she interacts. Thus, communication competence should be judged based on individuals' abilities to formulate and achieve objectives, to collaborate effectively with others, and to adapt to situational variations (Bochner & Kelly, 1974). Rubin (1983) has further considered communication competence to be a kind of impression based on the individual's perception, an impression the individual forms of both his and her own and others' behaviors. Through this impression, a person makes guesses about the internal states of those with whom he or she is interacting.

Finally, Wiemann (1977) synthesizes the concept of communication competence from the perspective of effectiveness. He conceptualizes communication competence as "the ability of an interactant to choose among available communicative behaviors in order that he may successfully accomplish his own interpersonal goals during an encounter while maintaining the face and line of his fellow interactants within the constraints of the situation" (p. 198). This definition argues simultaneously that competent communication is other oriented and that communicators have to accomplish their own goals.

Whereas some scholars conceive of communication competence as a function of perceived effectiveness, others look at it from the viewpoint of *appropriateness*. Wiemann and Backlund (1980) explain appropriateness in the communication process as follows:

> Appropriateness generally refers to the ability of an interactant to meet the basic contextual requirements of the situation—to be effective in general sense.... These contextual requirements include: (1) The verbal context, that is, making sense in terms of wording, of statement, and of topic; (2) the relationship context, that is, the structuring, type and style of messages so that they are consonant with the particular relationship at hand; and (3) the environmental context, that is, the consideration of constraints imposed on message making by the symbolic and physical environments.
>
> (p. 191)

The "appropriateness of behavior" thus implicates three kinds of ability. First is the ability to recognize how context constrains communication, so that one acts and speaks appropriately by combining capabilities and social knowledge to recognize that different situations give rise to different sets of rules (Lee, 1979; Trenholm & Rose, 1981). Second is the ability to avoid inappropriate responses. An inappropriate response is defined as "one which unnecessarily abrasive, intense, or bizarre. It is also likely to result in negative consequences that could have been averted, without sacrifice of the goal, by the more appropriate actions" (Getter & Nowinski, 1981, p. 303). Third is the ability to fulfill appropriately such communication functions as controlling, sharing feelings, informing, ritualizing, and imagining (Allen & Wood, 1978). We extend Grice's (1975) recommendations concerning appropriateness in interaction to include the following:

1. Say just enough—not too little or too much.
2. Do not say something that is false—or speak about something for which you lack evidence.
3. Relate your contribution to the topic and situation.
4. Be clear about what you are saying, and say it with dispatch.

These guidelines specify the four elements of appropriate communication: quantity, quality, relevance, and manner of message sending.

To summarize, communication competences requires appropriateness, and "the fundamental criteria of appropriateness are that the interactants perceive that they understand the content of the encounter and have not had their norms and rules violated too extensively" (Spitzberg & Cupach, 1984, p. 101).

Definition of intercultural communication competence

The literature treats intercultural communication competence in much the same way as it does communication competence in general (Hammer, 1988; Lustig & Koester, 1993; Martin, 1989;

Ruben, 1989; Spitzberg, 1988, 1989; Wiseman & Koester, 1993). The only difference is, in addition to looking at communication competence as effective and appropriate interaction, intercultural communication scholars place more emphasis on contextual factors. They conceive of communication competence not only as effective and appropriate interaction between people, but as effective and appropriate interaction between people who identify with particular physical and symbolic environments. This orientation resembles that of communication scholars who emphasize competence as a context-specific behavior (Spitzberg & Cupach, 1984).

Although researchers conceive of communication competence as the ability to interact effectively and appropriately with others, their definitions betray greater or lesser degrees of ambiguity, confusion, and imprecision. For example, from Wiemann's (1977) synthesized definition, the question arises, What constitute "available communicative behaviors" and "constraints of the situation"? These concepts are not clear, and require definition. To alleviate the problem in defining communication competence and to apply the concept to intercultural settings, intercultural communication competence can be conceived of as the ability to negotiate cultural meanings and to execute appropriately effective communication behaviors that recognize the interactants' multiple identities in a specific environment. This definition emphasizes that competent persons must know not only how to interact effectively and appropriately with people and environment, but also how to fulfill their own communication goals by respecting and affirming the multilevel cultural identities of those with whom they interact.

Types of competence

How do individuals interact across multiple cultural identities? Spitzberg and Cupach (1984) propose seven generic types of competence: fundamental competence, social competence, social skills, interpersonal competence, linguistic competence, communicative competence, and relational competence. *Fundamental competence* involves the general ability to adapt effectively to a new environment in order to achieve goals. In this sense, fundamental competence comprises the cognitive capacities that individual communicators need to be effective cross-situationally. *Social competence* involves specific, rather than general, abilities. Spitzberg and Cupach include within social competence the skills of empathy, role taking, cognitive complexity, and interaction management. *Interpersonal competence* is the ability to accomplish tasks and achieve goals through successful communication. Even though interpersonal competence is part of both fundamental competence and social competence, it is especially related to how individuals execute certain skills to control their environments in order to achieve goals in particular communication situations. Linguistic competence and communicative competence both relate to language and messages in the interaction process. *Linguistic competence* (a concept that stems from the work of Chomsky, 1965) is specifically the ability to use language properly. *Communicative competence* entails not only the knowledge of how to use language, but also knowledge about how to execute one's language knowledge appropriately. To be communicatively competent, a person must be able to convey messages appropriately in a given context of interaction. Finally, *relational competence* comprises many of the other six kinds of competence, but independent and reciprocal processes of interactions are among its most important aspects. An individual must establish certain degrees of relationships with others before he or she can interact effectively with them and achieve his or her goals. Such relationships cross multiple dimensions of language, profession, ethnicity, and nation.

Spitzberg and Cupach's view of competence suggests that individuals have unitary and unchanging cultural identities. By contrast, we view cultures as a set of preferences and possibilities that inform, rather than determine, given interactions. Communicators both shape and are shaped by these familiar meanings. Especially as individuals draw from multiple identities, interactions may not perfectly resemble any one cultural expectation.

Approaches to the Study of Intercultural Communication Competence

To understand the mutual negotiation of cultural meanings in intercultural communication, Dinges (1983) and Collier (1989) have classified the study of intercultural communication competence into different approaches. Dinges (1983) identifies six approaches to the study of intercultural communication competence: "overseasmanship," subjective culture, multicultural person, social behaviorism, topology, and intercultural communicator. The overseasmanship approach, first presented by Cleveland, Mangone, and Adams (1960), identifies common factors in effective performances among sojourners, or individuals on extended, nonpermanent stays in cultures other than their own. To be considered competent according to this approach, a sojourner must show the ability to convert lessons from a variety of foreign experiences into effective job-related skills.

The subjective culture (isomorphic attribution) approach requires individuals to have the ability to understand the causes of interactants' behaviors and reward them appropriately, and to modify their own behaviors suitably according to the demands of the setting (Triandis, 1976, 1977). This ability to understand the reasons that members of other cultures give for their behaviors must be based on accurate cognition of the differences in cognitive structure between cultures.

The multicultural person approach emphasizes that a competence person must be able to adapt to exceedingly difficult circumstances by transcending his or her usual adaptive limits (Alder, 1975, 1982). The individual must learn to move in and out of different contexts, to maintain coherence in different situations, and to be dynamic.

The social behaviorism (culture learning) approach emphasizes that successful intercultural coping strategies depend more on the individual's predeparture experiences, such as training and sojourning in another country, than on inherent characteristics or personality (Guthrie, 1975). That is, to be competent in intercultural interaction, a person must learn discriminative stimuli to obtain social rewards and to avoid punishments that will create hardship (David, 1972).

The typology approach develops different models of intercultural communication competence. Most of the models place sojourners' behavioral styles on a continuum from most to least effective. For example, Brislin (1981) proposes that a successful intercultural interaction must be based on the sojourner's attitudes, traits, and social skills. He asserts that nonethnocentrism and nonprejudicial judgments are the most valuable attitudes for effective intercultural interaction. Ethnocentrism is the judgment of an unfamiliar practice by the standards and norms familiar to one's own group or culture. The major adaptive personal traits Brislin mentions include personality strength, intelligence, tolerance, social relations skills, recognition of the potential for benefit, and task orientation. Important social skills are knowledge of subject and language, positive orientation to opportunities, effective communication skills, and the ability to use personal traits to complete tasks.

Finally, the intercultural communicator approach emphasizes that successful intercultural interaction centers on communication processes among people from different cultures. In other words, to be interculturally competent, an individual must be able to establish interpersonal relationships by understanding others through the effective exchange of verbal and nonverbal behaviors (Hall, 1959, 1966, 1976).

Collier (1989) identifies four categories of approaches to intercultural communication competence: ethnography of speaking, cross-cultural attitude, behavioral skills, and cultural identity. The ethnography of speaking approach assumes that meaning, conduct, and cultural membership are interdependent, thus, competence must be contextually defined (Geertz, 1973; Hymes, 1971, 1972). In order to achieve communication goals, an individual must correctly perceive, select, and interpret the specific features of the code in interaction and integrate these with other cultural knowledge and communication skills (Saville-Troike, 1982). The cross-cultural attitude approach assumes that understanding the culture of those with whom one is communicating and developing a positive attitude toward that culture are the keys to attaining communication competence across cultures. Studies by Chen (1989), Abe and Wiseman (1983), Gudykunst, Wiseman, and Hammer (1977), and Wiseman and Abe (1984) have examined the concept from this perspective. The behavioral skills approach assumes that "humans are goal directed and choice making beings, and that humans can distinguish between skills which will be effective and skills which will not be effective" in interaction (Collier, 1989, p. 294). Thus, competent persons are able to identify and adopt those effective skills in intercultural interaction (Chen, 1992; Hammer, 1989; Ruben, 1976, 1977; Ruben & Kealey, 1979). Finally, the cultural identity approach assumes that communication competence is a dynamic and emergent process in which interactants are able to improve the quality of their experience by recognizing the existence of each other's cultural identities (Collier, 1989, 1994; Cupach & Imahori, 1993). Thus, interculturally competent persons must know how to negotiate and respect meanings of cultural symbols and norms that are changing during their interactions (Collier & Thomas, 1988; Y. Y. Kim, 1994a). In addition, Ward and Searle (1991) have found that cultural identity significantly affects adaptation to a new culture.

Although the approaches described above provide useful perspectives from which to study intercultural communication competence, they fail to give a holistic picture that can reflect the global civic culture in which people can mutually negotiate their multiple identities. In the following section we attempt to synthesize these approaches into a model of intercultural communication competence.

A Model of Intercultural Communication Competence

After scrutinizing the existing approaches to the study of intercultural communication competence, we can synthesize them into a model of "interactive-multiculture building" (Belay, 1993). The model aims at promoting interactants' ability to acknowledge, respect, tolerate, and integrate cultural differences, so that they can qualify for enlightened global citizenship. The model represents a transformational process of symmetrical interdependence that can be explained from three perspectives: (a) affective, or intercultural sensitivity; (b) cognitive, or intercultural awareness, and (c) behavioral, or intercultural adroitness.

The affective process: intercultural sensitivity

The affective perspective of intercultural communication competence focuses on personal emotions or the changes in feelings that are caused by particular situations, people, and environments (Triandis, 1977). The affective process especially carries a notion that interculturally competent persons are able to project and receive positive responses before, during, and after intercultural interactions. These positive emotional responses will in turn lead to acknowledgement of and respect for cultural differences. This process is the development of intercultural sensitivity (Bennett, 1986; Bhawuk & Brislin, 1992; Chen & Tan, 1995; Gudykunst, Ting-Toomey, & Wiseman, 1991).

Four personal attitudes form the foundation of the affective perspective on intercultural communication competence: self-concept, open-mindedness, nonjudgmental attitudes, and social relaxation. *Self-concept* refers to the way in which a person sees him- or herself. An individual's self-concept not only serves as his or her key to communication, but it mediates how the person relates to the world. One of the most important elements of the self-concept is self-esteem. Adler and Towne (1993) have summarized research in this area, and they note that the communication behaviors of high self-esteem individuals and low self-esteem individuals differ significantly. Persons with high self-esteem, compared with persons with low self-esteem, are more likely to think well of others, are more accepted by others, perform well when being watched, feel more comfortable when working with superiors, and can defend themselves against the negative comments of others. Persons with high self-esteem also tend to feel more positively toward out-group members. In intercultural encounters, which often involve psychological stresses associated with the need to complete a task and establish relationships with others, self-esteem helps individuals to calculate whether or not they can fulfill particular needs (Brislin, 1981; Ehrlich, 1973; Ting-Toomey, 1993).

Other aspects of self-concept can also affect intercultural communication. For instance, an interculturally competent person must have a good, optimistic outlook that inspires confidence in his or her interactions with others (Foote & Cottrell, 1995; Hawes & Kealey, 1979, 1981); must show a stable and extroverted personality (Gardner, 1962); and must show self-reliance, perseverance, and reliability (Harris, 1973; Smith, 1966). All these personality traits combine to cultivate a positive self-concept that can lead to intercultural communication competence (Chen, 1995b; Scollon & Scollon, 1995).

Open-mindedness refers to individuals' willingness to express themselves openly when it is appropriate and to accept others' explanations. This positive trait is parallel to one of the characteristics of a multicultural person, who is willing to accept different patterns of life and to accept, psychologically and socially, a multipilicity of realities (Alder, 1977). In other words, open-minded persons possess an internalized broadened concept of the world that enables them to understand that an idea can be rendered in many different ways (Bennett, 1986; Hart & Burks, 1972). Open-mindedness entails a willingness to recognize, appreciate, and accept different views and ideas in intercultural interaction. It allows people to understand and acknowledge other people's needs and, further, can transform such understanding to actions (Smith, 1966; Yum, 1989). It is a process of mutual validation and confirmation of cultural identities that fosters a favorable impression in intercultural communication (Ting-Toomey, 1989).

Being *nonjudgmental* means holding no prejudices that will prevent one from listening sincerely to others during intercultural communication. At the same time, being nonjudgmental allows others to be psychologically satisfied and happy that they have been listened to actively. Mutual satisfaction of interactants is a measure of intercultural communication competence (Hammer, 1989; Ruben, 1988).

Nonjudgmental and open-minded attitudes nurture a feeling of enjoyment of cultural differences in intercultural interactions. Interculturally competent persons not only need to acknowledge and accept cultural differences, but should establish a sentiment of enjoyment, which usually leads to a satisfactory feeling toward intercultural encounters (Chen & Tan, 1995). Researchers have identified three kinds of enjoyment in intercultural interactions that are necessary for intercultural communication competence: (a) the enjoyment of interacting with people from different cultures (Randolph, Landis, & Tzeng, 1977), (b) the enjoyment of improving working relations with others from different cultures (Fiedler, Mitchell, & Triandis, 1971), and (c) the enjoyment of carrying out one's own duties in another culture (Gudykunst, Hammer, & Wiseman, 1977).

Finally, *social relaxation* refers to the ability to reveal little anxious emotion in intercultural communication. It is assumed that a series of crises usually occur in the initial experiences of sojourners, and feelings of anxiety usually originate from the psychological lack of security that individuals feel when entering new situations (Gudykunst & Hammer, 1988; Herman & Schield, 1961; Sanders & Wiseman, 1993; Stephan & Stephan, 1992). The symptoms of social anxiety include excessive perspiration, rocking movements, rigidity of posture, speech disturbances, hesitations, and lowered response tendencies (Spitzberg & Cupach, 1984; Wiemann, 1977). To be competent in intercultural communication, an individual must overcome such stumbling blocks, which can include feelings of anxiety when communication with those from different cultures (Barna, 1994).

The four personal attributes described above form the affective basis of intercultural communication competence. They enable an individual to be sensitive enough during intercultural interactions to acknowledge and respect cultural differences. They increase the level of a person's compatibility with a new cultural environment, and thus help alleviate the impact of cultural shock (Kim, 1988, 1991; Kim & Gudykunst, 1988; Oberg, 1960; Smalley, 1963). In other words, they expedite the process of psychological adaptation by increasing a person's general psychological well-being, self-satisfaction, and contentment within a new environment.

In general, psychological adaptation in intercultural interaction is associated with the ability to cope in situations where social difficulties cause frustrations, stress, and alienation due to cultural differences (Furnham & Bochner, 1982; Rogers & Ward, 1993). A great deal of research based on the affective perspective of intercultural communication competence has addressed individuals' abilities to handle psychological stress in new environments (Hammer, 1987; Hammer, Gudykunst, & Wiseman, 1978; Searle & Ward, 1990; Ward & Searle, 1991; Wiseman & Abe, 1984). However, this line of research needs to be extended to examine how people can identify their own multiple identities in the process of psychological adaptation during intercultural encounters.

To summarize, affectively, intercultural communication competence demands positive emotion that enables individuals to be sensitive enough to acknowledge and respect cultural differences. The affective process of intercultural communication is built on four personal attributes: self-concept, open-mindedness, nonjudgmental attitudes, and social relaxation.

The cognitive process: intercultural awareness

The cognitive perspective of intercultural communication competence emphasizes the changing of personal thinking about the environment through the understanding of the distinct characteristics of one's own and others' cultures (Triandis, 1977). It is the process of reducing the level of situational ambiguity and uncertainty in intercultural interactions. With little visible discomfort, confusion, or nervousness, an individual can adapt to situational demands in a new environment with no noticeable personal, interpersonal, or group consequences, and can cope with the changing environment rapidly and comfortably (Ruben, 1976; Ruben & Kealey, 1979).

The cognitive process of intercultural communication competence, then, provides an opportunity for the individual to develop an awareness of cultural dynamics and to discern multiple identities in order to maintain a state of multicultural coexistence. This is the ability of intercultural awareness, which comprises two aspects of understanding: self-awareness and cultural awareness (Brislin, Landis, & Brandt, 1983; Gudykunst et al., 1991; Pruegger & Rogers, 1993).

The implementation of conversationally competent behaviors in interaction requires self-awareness, the individual's ability to monitor or be aware of him- or herself (Spitzberg & Cupach, 1984). Self-awareness facilitates competent intercultural communication and helps a person to adjust to cultures other than his or her own (Brislin, 1981; Gudykunst, 1993; Triandis, 1977). A person who is high in self-awareness or self-monitoring is likely to be sensitive to the expressions and self-presentation of his or her counterparts in intercultural communication, and knows how to use these behavioral cues to guide his or her own self-presentation (Berger & Douglas, 1982; Chen, 1995b; Gudykunst, Yang, & Nishida, 1987; Hammer, 1989).

The factors that account for self-awareness or self-monitoring include (a) concern with the social appropriateness of one's self-presentation, (b) attention to social comparison information as cues to situationally appropriate expressive self-presentation, (c) the ability to control and modify one's self-presentation, (d) the use of this ability in particular situations, and (e) the modification of one's expressive behavior to meet the requirements of particular situations

(Snyder, 1974, 1979, 1987). These factors play important roles in the process of intercultural communication (Gudykunst & Ting-Toomey, 1988; Trubisky, Ting-Toomey, & Lin, 1991).

Cultural awareness refers to an understanding of the conventions of one's own and others' cultures that affect how people think and behave. This includes understanding the commonalities of human behavior and differences in cultural patterns. Based on some of the universal commonalities of human behavior, such as eye contact, turn talking, gesturing, and the use of politeness norms, an individual can begin to understand how people from diverse cultures adapt such universal behaviors to the unique expectations of intercultural communication settings (Bond, 1988; Brown, 1991; Fiske, 1992; John, 1990; Kiesler, 1983; Schwartz, 1990; Schwartz & Bilsky, 1987; Schwartz & Sagiv, 1995; Strack & Lorr, 1990; White, 1980). The process of becoming culturally aware promotes not only the understanding of cultural variability but also positive feelings toward the search for a common ground of multicultural coexistence. Cross-cultural understanding alerts individuals as to those points where differences come into play.

Thus, understanding the dimensions of cultural variability provides ways of identifying how communication differs across cultures. In important studies on the dimensions of cultural variability, Parsons (1951) has identified five pattern variables, Kluckhohn and Strodtbeck (1960) have identified five cultural value orientations, Hall (1976) has labeled culture as high-context or low-context, and Hofstede (1980) has named four dimensions of cultural variability.

Because all cultures tend to favor particular ways of processing the data around us, misunderstandings concerning these differing thought patterns often lead to problems in intercultural communication. Therefore, to be effective in intercultural interaction, an individual must first learn how arguments are supported and knowledge is determined in the culture in which he or she will be interacting (Glenn & Glenn, 1981; Harris & Moran, 1987; Oliver, 1962). In other words, before a person can modify his or her communication patterns to be congruent with the cues given by unfamiliar interactants, he or she must understand any cultural differences that exist (Hall, 1959; Hall & Whyte, 1963). If interactants change their behaviors to be congruent with those of their culturally different counterparts, they may improve their chances of reaching mutual understanding and of maintaining a fruitful multicultural coexistence. Many studies have tried to identify the myriad ways in which cultures differ (Althen, 1992; Barnlund & Yoshioka, 1990; Chang & Holt, 1991; Chen & Chung, 1994; L. Chen, 1993; Cocroft & Ting-Toomey, 1994; Fitch, 1994; Goldman, 1994; Hecht, Sedano, & Ribeau, 1993; Ishii, 1992; Ishii & Bruneau, 1994; Kim & Wilson, 1994; Klopf, 1992; H. Ma, 1990; R. Ma, 1992; Marriott, 1993; Martin, Hecht, & Larkey, 1994; Stewart & Bennett, 1991; Suzuki & Rancer, 1994; Ting-Toomey, 1991; White & Barnet, 1995).

The development of cultural awareness resembles the idea of making a "cultural map" or "cultural theme"; the emphasis is on the importance of cultural knowledge for competent intercultural communication. Kluckhohn (1948) asserts that cultural awareness requires an understanding of a "cultural map": "If a map is accurate, and you can read it, you won't get lost; if you know a culture, you will know your way around in the life of a society" (p. 28). Turner (1968) indicates that to be aware of a culture means that one understands the "cultural theme"—the thread that goes through a culture and organizes it as a recognizable system. The theme acts as a guide for people's thinking and behavior, and appears repeatedly in daily life.

The key components of a cultural map or theme that affect intercultural communication competence include social values, social customs, social norms, and social systems. Studies by Abe and Wiseman (1983), Chen (1989), Hammer et al. (1978), Jain and Kussman (1994), Lustig and Koester (1993), Martin (1987, 1989), and Yum (1988) have shown that intercultural communication competence requires an understanding of these cultural components. As more than one cultural identity comes into play, maps are overlaid on other maps, and themes upon themes.

To summarize, individuals tend to be more competent in intercultural communication as they acquire greater degrees of cultural awareness and self-awareness. Self-awareness involves knowledge of one's own personal identity; cultural awareness involves understanding how cultures vary. Both combine to provide a framework for communication competence in a global society (Barnlund, 1994).

The behavioral process: intercultural adroitness

The behavioral perspective of intercultural communication competence stresses how to act effectively in intercultural interactions. Intercultural adroitness, the ability to get the job done and attain communication goals in intercultural interactions, comes into play. Intercultural adroitness corresponds to communication skills. It consists of those verbal and nonverbal behaviors that enable us to be effective in interactions. Such behaviors in intercultural communication include message skills, appropriate self-disclosure, behavioral flexibility, interaction management, and social skills.

Message skills, in the context of intercultural communication, refers to the ability to use the language of a culture other than one's own. Intercultural communication competence begins with message skills, which include the following: linguistic competence, or the knowledge of the rules underlying the use of language (Chomsky, 1965); the ability to code skillfully and to create recognizable messages in the process of communication (M. Kim, 1994; Y. Y. Kim, 1994b; Milhouse, 1993; Parks, 1976; Weber, 1994); the ability to understand one's counterpart's language; and the ability to recognize the meanings of nonverbal behaviors (Anderson, 1994; Barna, 1994; Dolphin, 1994). Many studies have shown that fluency in the other culture's language is the key element in effective intercultural interaction (Deutsch & Won, 1963; Giles, 1977; Martin & Hammer, 1989; Morris, 1960; Selltiz, Christ, Havel, & Cook, 1963; Sewell & Davidsen, 1956; Ting-Toomey & Korzenny, 1989).

Besides language itself, message skills include the ability to use descriptive and supportive messages in the process of interaction. The use of descriptive messages entails the use of concrete and specific feedback as opposed to judgment of anther's behaviors. Nonjudgmental attitudes help interactants to avoid defensive reactions from their counterparts (Bochner & Kelly, 1974; Gibb, 1961; Hammer, 1989). Supportiveness is the sine qua non for effective communication. It is important for communicators to know how to support others effectively and to reward them in communication with cues such as head nods, eye contact, facial expressions, and physical proximity (Olebe & Koester, 1989; Parks, 1985; 1994; Ruben, 1976, 1977, 1988; Spitzberg, 1991; Wiemann, 1977).

Message skills are tempered by self-disclosure, or the willingness to reveal information about oneself openly and appropriately to one's counterparts during intercultural interactions. What is considered appropriate self-disclosure varies among cultures, as do appropriate topics of conversation and appropriate forms of address for persons at varying levels of intimacy and at given levels of social hierarchy (Chen, 1995a; Nakanishi, 1987; Nakanishi & Johnson, 1993). In addition, to be classified as self-discourse, messages must be intentional and the information revealed to others must be significant and previously unknown to them (Adler & Towne, 1993). Appropriate self-disclosure is one of the main elements of individual competence in communication, and can lead to achievement of personal communication goals (Bochner & Kelly, 1974; Spitzberg, 1991).

The contextual ambiguity common in interactions between people from different cultures produces a predictably high level of uncertainty (Gudykunst, 1985). Reduction of this uncertainty level can often be achieved through mutual self-disclosure. Studies have demonstrated appropriate self-disclosure to be one of the components of intercultural communication competence, especially regarding depth and breadth of self-disclosure (Chen, 1989, 1990, 1993b). This finding helps to illustrate the social penetration model, wherein relationships develop from superficial to more personal levels through the depth and breadth of information individuals disclose (Altman & Taylor, 1973; Gudykunst & Nishida, 1983, 1986; Knapp, 1978).

Behavioral flexibility is the ability to select appropriate behaviors in different contexts and situations (Bochner & Kelly, 1974). This concept makes up the creativity or flexibility dimension of intercultural communication competence. Behaviorally flexible persons are accurate and adaptable when attending to information, and are able to perform different behavioral strategies in order to achieve communication goals (Parks, 1985). Behavioral flexibility is considered a dimension of intercultural communication competence (Chen, 1992; Imahori & Lanigan, 1989; Martin, 1987; Martin & Hammer, 1989; Ruben, 1977; Spitzberg, 1994; Wiemann, 1977). It is expressed through verbal immediacy cues; behaviorally flexible individuals know how to use different kinds of intimate verbal behaviors to establish interpersonal relationships. Moreover, behaviorally flexible persons must be good at "the alternation and co-occurrence of specific speech choices which mark the status and affiliative relationships of interactants (Wiemann, 1977, p. 199).

Interaction management is the ability to speak in turn in conversation and to initiate and terminate conversation appropriately. This encompasses also the ability to structure and maintain the procedure of a conversation (Spitzberg & Cupach, 1984), or the ability to develop a topic smoothly in interaction. Individuals with good interaction management skills allow all participants in a discussion the chance to contribute. Interaction management is one of the major dimensions of intercultural communication competence (Chen, 1989; Olebe & Koester, 1989; Ruben & Kealey, 1979; Spitzberg, 1994). Guidelines for effective management of interactions in U.S. culture include the following, summarized by Wiemann (1977): (a) Interruptions are not permitted, (b) only one person may talk at a time, (c) speakers' turns should be appropriately interchanged, and (d) speakers should pay full attention to their counterparts. These standards do not apply to all cultures, clearly; for instance, African and African American interaction rules allow two speakers to talk at one time, at least briefly, during shifts between speakers (Sanders, 1995). Moreover, the African American tradition of "call and response" may be falsely interpreted by European Americans as "interruption"; rather, it represents the cocreation of messages.

Communication skills also include such social skills as empathy and identity maintenance. Empathy, or the ability to feel the same emotions as another person (Alder & Towne, 1993), has been long recognized as a central element of effective interpersonal communication. This ability has also been called "affective sensitivity" (Campbell, Kagan, & Krathwohl, 1971), "telepathic or intuition sensitivity" (Gardner, 1962), and "perspective taking" (Parks, 1976). Empathic persons are able to judge accurately their communication counterparts' behavior or internal states (Parks, 1994). Empathic individuals are usually able to respond accurately to the feelings and thoughts of those with whom they are interacting, and so this trait is highly valuable in intercultural communication (Chen, 1992; Chen & Tan, 1995; Ruben, 1976, 1977). In interaction, empathic persons generally demonstrate reciprocity of affect displays, verbal responses that show understanding, and active listening. Empathy is viewed as one of the elements of intercultural communication competence (Bennett, 1979, 1986; Gudykunst, 1993; Hwang, Chase, & Kelly, 1980; Yum, 1988).

Identity maintenance refers to the ability to maintain one's counterpart's identity in interaction. Because the need to learn who we are is one of the reasons we communicate with others, communicatively competent persons not only understand themselves in interaction but also inform their counterparts about who they are. Thus, in order to achieve smooth interaction, a communicatively competent person maintains his or her counterpart's identity. The skill of identity maintenance is learned through experience, and the use of identity maintenance skills varies with different situations and different personal goals (Collier, 1989; Parks, 1976; Ting-Toomey, 1989, 1993) and with movement from one salient identity to another.

To summarize, individuals become more competent in intercultural communication as they improve their degree of intercultural adroitness, which involves message skills, knowledge regarding appropriate self-disclosure, behavioral flexibility, interaction management, and social skills. The behavioral perspective of intercultural communication competence emphasizes the ability to act effectively to achieve the goal of multicultural interdependence and interconnectedness in the global village.

The three perspectives of the intercultural communication competence model described above form the three sides of an equilateral triangle. All are equally important, and all are inseparable, forming a holistic picture of intercultural communication competence. The model integrates different approaches to the study of intercultural communication competence specified by scholars (Collier, 1989; Dinges, 1983). It provides a guideline for future research in this area.

Critique and Directions for Future Research

Since the germination of the field of intercultural communication in the early 1950s, communication scholars have continued to search for better models to explain the concept of intercultural communication competence. After more than four decades, communication scholars have produced an abundance of literature in this line of research. Unfortunately, however, this literature is fragmentary and lacks a holistic view. Consequently, scholars in the area of intercultural communication competence have been unable to provide a consistent framework for an understanding of the notion of interdependence and interconnectedness of the complex multicultural dynamics in the contemporary age. Operationally, they have failed to provide a clear direction for the development of a valid and reliable intercultural communication competence instrument that is appropriate to our current global society.

The problem originates in the lack of a proper interpretation of global interaction processes. The trends of technology development, globalization of the economy, widespread population migration, development of multiculturalism, and the demise of the nation-state in favor of sub- and supranational identifications have shrunk and multiculturalized the world, and traditional perceptions of *self* and *other* must be redefined. The global context of human communication and the need to pursue a state of multicultural coexistence require that we abolish the boundaries separating *me* and *you*, *us* and *them*, and develop a theory of communication competence that takes into account individuals' multiple identities. Although a few researchers have shown interest in this line of research (Casmir, 1993; Collier, 1989; Collier & Thomas, 1988; Hecht & Ribeau, 1991; Starosta & Olorunnisola, 1995), the study of intercultural communication must take it one step further.

In addition to this philosophical issue, the study of intercultural communication competence has other problems. We describe below some of the specific areas scholars should address in future research.

At the conceptual level, intercultural communication competence scholars face five challenges. First, as the concept of intercultural communication competence grows more sophisticated, it becomes confused with the definition of the term *competence*. Argument continues as to whether competence is an inherent ability (trait) or a learned ability (state). Although we understand *competence* to refer to personal attributes and to communication skills, future research needs to figure out whether trait competence and state competence can be treated separately or must be considered together.

The second challenge for the study of communication competence centers on whether *competence* refers to knowledge or performance. Chomsky (1965) considers competence to be simply the knowledge of the speaker-hearer's language, and Phillips (1983) considers Chomsky's competence to be merely the first step toward communication competence. He conceives of competence as the understanding of a new situation and its requirements. Chomsky and

Phillips treat competence as an individual's knowledge. Although McCroskey (1982) and Spitzberg (1983) further identify distinctions among motivation, knowledge, and skills for the conceptualization of communication competence, the existing definitions suffer from a degree of incompleteness, especially when we apply the concept to intercultural settings, in which we have to consider that the process of communication demands not only situational knowledge but behavioral skills as well. Future research ought to include both knowledge and performance as elements of intercultural communication competence.

Third, the confusion between the term *effectiveness* and *competence* must be resolved if we are to arrive at a clear conception of communication competence. Many scholars use the word *effectiveness* instead of *competence* (e.g., Hammer et al., 1978; Ruben, 1988). Others use *effectiveness* and *competence* interchangeably (e.g., Ruben, 1976, 1977; Ruben & Kealey, 1979). Usage of these terms should be standardized in future studies. We believe that *competence* is the preferable word, especially in intercultural communication settings. As we have indicated, effectiveness is only one of two elements in a conceptualization of competence. The second, appropriateness, plays a role of equal significance. In other words, to be competent in intercultural interaction, individuals must communicate both effectively and appropriately.

Fourth, culture-general versus culture-specific approaches to the study of intercultural communication competence continue to be a problem. Most of the existing research on intercultural communication competence has taken a culture-general approach. The current trend in this line of research strongly demands balance between the two approaches. Recent studies, for instance, have begun to examine communication competence from Chinese, Indian, Japanese, and Korean perspectives (Chen, 1993a; Hedge, 1993; Miyahara, 1993; Yum, 1993). A coherent theme around which these researchers conceptualize communication competence is "harmony," which appears to be an element of most Asian cultures. Studying intercultural communication competence from a culture-specific perspective in order to find common themes within cultures may shed new light on the field.

Finally, the application of studies in intercultural communication competence has been confined mainly to the intercultural adaptation process of sojourning in a new culture. We suggest that the scope of intercultural communication cannot be divorced from the full scope of the communication environment of the global civic culture, which can be conceptualized as having interpersonal, group, organizational, national, and supranational levels.

On the operational level, we face three challenges. First, we have to clarify where intercultural communication competence resides. Ruben (1989) proposes three alternatives:

1. The message sender alternative claims that competence is what an individual displays or possesses.
2. The message receiver alternative claims that competence is based on the evaluation of the message receiver, no matter what the sender possesses.
3. The dyadic, or systemic, or culture-based alternative claims that competence is based on relational, social, or cultural rules instead of on an individual such as the sender and the receiver.

The Western cultural orientation to the study of intercultural communication competence tends to focus on the first two of these alternatives. Other cultures, such as Asian cultures, seem to focus more on the third alternative. For instance, the measurement of communication competence from the Japanese cultural perspective seems to focus on the concept of "group" as a unit of analysis (Miyahara, 1994); from the Korean cultural perspective, communication competence tends to be observed from an interpersonal rather than an individual point of view (Yum, 1994).

Second, we must decide how intercultural communication competence should be assessed. Use of self-report scales, other-report scales, or the two together remains possible. If intercultural communication competence is a product of personal attributes and behavioral skills, then both self- and other-report methods should be used. Yet, although the use of both methods in combination assures the external validity of the data, it becomes difficult to bridge any discrepancy between the self- and other-report measures unless a more acceptable scale is created. This problem becomes critical in an intercultural communication setting. For example, people from different cultures may have different perceptions of or attitudes toward the processes and instruments used in the study, including scale items and how to use particular scales (Campbell, 1969; Klopf & Cambra, 1983; Martin, 1993).

Third, and finally, how should we measure intercultural communication competence? Although we have proposed three perspectives from which to view the measurement of intercultural communication competence, we can clearly see that the existing literature in this area strongly reflects a Eurocentric point of view. This Western bias has caused a reliance on the positivism tradition, which in turn identifies a set of Western-oriented elements as the components of intercultural communication competence. We urge future researchers to try to discover more and different elements to account for intercultural communication competence from non-Western cultural perspectives. For instance, instead of following the above components of intercultural communication competence, Chen (1994) notes that the four elements of communication competence from the Chinese cultural perspective are the ability to control emotion, the ability to express feelings indirectly, the ability to save another's face, and the ability to recognize distinctions in relations with in-group members versus relations with out-group members. Similarly, Yum (1994) identifies five elements that can be used to measure communication competence from the Korean cultural perspective: empathy, sensitivity, indirectness, being reserved, and transcendentality. Thus, an instrument that is sufficient for the measurement of intercultural communication competence may have to account for multiple voices, multiple competencies, and multiple identities.

Summary and Conclusion

As we encounter ever greater cultural and co-cultural diversity, the careful study of intercultural communication competence becomes increasing important. Only through competent intercultural communication can persons from different cultures understand each other. Sitaram and Cogdell (1976) proclaim, "All people of the world should study intercultural communication." This broad dictum emphasizes the necessity for all of us to learn more about ourselves and members of cultures other than our own.

Communication competence has been studied for many years, but its application to intercultural interaction continues to evolve. In this chapter we have extracted three perspectives on intercultural communication competence from the existing literature. We have considered how the *competence* relates to the intercultural setting. The six types of competence discussed in this chapter—fundamental, social, interpersonal, linguistic, communicative, and relational—can be treated as interdependent dimensions of communication competence. We have also argued that culture and communication competence are inseparable.

The approaches to the study of intercultural communication competence discussed above lead to a three-perspective model: (a) The *affective* perspective represents intercultural sensitivity, promoted through positive self-concept, open-mindedness, nonjudgmental attitudes, and social relaxation; (b) the *cognitive* perspective represents cultural awareness, which includes self-awareness and the understanding of one's own and others' cultures; and (c) the *behavioral* perspective represents intercultural adroitness based on message skills, appropriate self-disclosure, behavioral flexibility, interaction management, and social skills. We have proposed directions for future research along these lines, focusing on the conceptual and operational problems that scholars face.

The indispensability of intercultural communication competence in our increasingly global society demands that communication scholars enhance the functions of the concept and expand the scope of research in this area. The study of intercultural communication competence should be extended to include research concerning the multiple identities that individuals maintain in our interdependent and interconnected global society. The scope of intercultural communication competence should penetrate different levels of intercultural communication to ensure the integration of various communication demands in terms of culture, ethnicity, race, gender, and religion. These processes will require a functional and theoretical reorientation for the study of intercultural communication competence (Taylor, 1994).

References

Abe, H., & Wiseman, R. L. (1983). A cross-cultural confirmation of the dimensions of intercultural effectiveness. *International Journal of Intercultural Relations, 7*, 53–67.

Adler, N. J. (1991). *International dimensions of organizational behavior.* Belmont, CA: Wadsworth.

Adler, P. (1975). The transnational experience: An alternative view of culture shock. *Journal of Humanistic Psychology, 15*, 13–23.

Adler, P. (1977). Beyond cultural identity: Reflections upon cultural and multicultural man. In R. Brislin (Ed.), *Cultural learning: Concepts, applications, and research.* Honolulu: University of Hawaii Press.

Adler, P. (1982). Beyond cultural identity: Reflections upon cultural and multicultural man. In L. A. Samovar & R. E. Porter (Eds.), *Intercultural communication: A reader* (pp. 389–405). Belmont, CA: Wadsworth.

Adler, R. B., & Towne, N. (1993). *Looking out/looking in.* New York: Harcourt Brace Jovanovich.

Allen, R. R., & Wood, B. S. (1978). Beyond reading and writing to communication competence. *Communication Education, 27*, 286–292.

Althen, G. (1992). The Americans have to say everything. *Communication Quarterly, 40*, 413–421.

Altman, I., & Taylor, D. (1973). *Social penetration: The development of interpersonal relationships.* New York: Holt, Rinehart & Wilson.

Anderson, J. W. (1994). A comparison of Arab and American conceptions of "effective" persuasion. In L. A. Samovar & R. E. Porter (Eds.), *Intercultural communication: A reader* (pp. 104–113). Belmont, CA: Wadsworth.

Argyris, C. (1956a). Explorations in interpersonal competence, I. *Journal of Applied Behavioral Science, 1*, 58–83.

Argyris, C. (1956b). Explorations in interpersonal competence, II. *Journal of Applied Behavioral Science, 1*, 255–269.

Asante, M. K., Newmark, E., & Blake, C. A. (1979). *Handbook of intercultural communication.* Beverly Hills, CA: Sage.

Barna, L. M. (1994). Intercultural communication stumbling blocks. In L. A. Samovar & R. E. Porter (Eds.), *Intercultural communication: A reader* (pp. 337–346). Belmont, CA: Wadsworth.

Barnlund, D. C. (1994). Communication in a global village. In L. A. Samovar & R. E. Porter (Eds.), *Intercultural communication: A reader* (pp. 95–103). Belmont, CA: Wadsworth.

Barnlund, D. C., & Yoshioka, M. (1990). Apologies: Japanese and American styles. *International Journal of Intercultural Relations, 14*, 193–206.

Belay, G. (1993). Toward a paradigm shift for intercultural and international communication: New research directions. In S. A. Deetz (Ed.), *Communication yearbook 16* (pp. 437–457). Newbury Park, CA: Sage.

Bennett, M. J. (1979). Overcoming the golden rule: Sympathy and empathy. In D. Nimmo (Ed.), *Communication yearbook 3* (pp. 407–433). New Brunswick, NJ: Transaction.

Berger, C. R., & Douglas, W. (1982). Thought and talk: Excuse me, "but have I been talking to myself?" In F. E. X. Dance (Ed.), *Human communication theory: Comparative essays* (pp. 42–60). New York: Harper & Row.

Bhawuk, D. P. S., & Brislin, R. (1992). The measurement of intercultural sensitivity using the concepts of individualism and collectivism. *International Journal of Intercultural Relations, 16*, 413–436.

Bochner, A. P., & Kelly, C. W. (1974). Interpersonal competence: Rationale, philosophy, and implementation of a conceptual framework. *Speech Teacher, 23*, 279–301.

Bond, M. H. (1988). Finding universal dimensions of individual variation in multicultural studies of values: The Rokeach and Chinese value surveys. *Journal of Personality and Social Psychology, 55*, 1009–1015.

Boulding, E. (1988). *Building a global civic culture: Education for an interdependent world.* New York: Columbia University Press.

Brislin, R. W. (1981). *Cross-cultural encounters: Face-to-face interaction.* Elmsford, NY: Pergamon.

Brislin, R. W., Landis, D., & Brandt, M. E. (1983). Conceptualizations of intercultural behavior and training. In D. Landis & R. W. Brislin (Eds.), *Handbook of intercultural training; Vol. 1. Issues in theory and design* (pp. 1–35). Elmsford, NY: Pergamon.

Brown, D. E. (1991). *Human universals.* Philadelphia, PA: Temple University Press.

Campbell, D. T. (1969). Reforms as experiment. *American Psychology, 24,* 409–429.

Campbell, R. J., Kagan, N., & Krathwohl, D. R. (1971). The development and validation of a scale to measure affective sensitivity (empathy). *Journal of Counseling Psychology, 18,* 407–412.

Casmir, F. L. (1993). Third-culture building: A paradigm shift for international and intercultural communication. In S. A. Deetz (Ed.), *Communication yearbook 16* (pp. 407–428). Newbury Park, CA: Sage.

Chang, H. C., & Holt, G. R. (1991). More than relationship: Chinese interaction and the principle of *kuan-hsi. Communication Quarterly, 39,* 251–271.

Chen. G.-M. (1989). Relationships of the dimensions of intercultural communication competence. *Communication Quarterly, 37,* 118–133.

Chen, G.-M. (1990). Intercultural communication competence: Some perspectives of research. *Howard Journal of Communications, 2,* 243–261.

Chen, G.-M. (1992). A test of intercultural communication competence. *Intercultural Communication Studies, 2,* 63–82.

Chen, G.-M. (1993a, November). *Communication competence: A Chinese perspective.* Paper presented at the annual meeting of the Speech Communication Association, Miami Beach, FL.

Chen, G.-M. (1993b). Self-disclosure and Asian students' abilities to cope with social difficulties in the United States. *Journal of Psychology, 127,* 603–610.

Chen, G.-M. (1994, November). *A conceptualization and measurement of communication competence: A Chinese perspective.* Paper presented at the annual meeting of the Speech Communication Association, New Orleans, LA.

Chen, G.-M. (1995a). Differences in self-disclosure patterns among Americans versus Chinese: A comparative study. *Journal of Cross-Cultural Psychology, 26,* 84–91.

Chen, G.-M. (1995b). A model of intercultural communication competence: *Mass Communication Research, 50,* 81–95.

Chen, G.-M., & Chung, J. (1994). The impact of Confucianism on organizational communication. *Communication Quarterly, 42,* 93–105.

Chen, G.-M., & Tan, L. (1995, April). *A theory of intercultural sensitivity.* Paper presented at the annual meeting of the Eastern Communication Association, Pittsburgh, PA.

Chen, L. (1993). Chinese and North Americans: An epistemological exploration of intercultural communication. *Howard Journal of Communications, 4,* 342–357.

Chomsky, N. (1965). *Aspects of the theory of syntax.* Cambridge: MIT Press.

Cleveland, H., Mangone, G. J., & Adams, J. C. (1960). *The overseas Americans.* New York: McGraw-Hill.

Cocroft, B. K., & Ting-Toomey, S. (1994). Facework in Japan and the United States. *International Journal of Intercultural Relations, 18,* 469–506.

Collier, M. J. (1989). Cultural and intercultural communication competence: Current approaches and directions for future research. *International Journal of Intercultural Relations, 13,* 287–302.

Collier, M. J. (1994). Cultural identity and intercultural communication. In L. A. Samovar & R. E. Porter (Eds.), *Intercultural communication: A reader* (pp. 36–44). Belmont, CA: Wadsworth.

Collier, M. J., & Thomas, M. (1988). Cultural identity: An interpretive perspectives. In Y. Y. Kim & W. B. Gudykunst (Eds.), *Theories in intercultural communication* (pp. 99–120). Newbury Park, CA: Sage.

Cupach, W. R., & Imahori, T. T. (1993). Identity management theory: Communication competence in intercultural episodes and relationships. In R. L. Wiseman & J. Koester (Eds.), *Intercultural communication competence* (pp. 112–131). Newbury Park, CA: Sage.

David, K. (1972). Intercultural adjustment and applications of reinforcement theory to problems of culture shock. *Trends, 4,* 1–64.

Deutsch, S. E., & Won, G. Y. M. (1963). Some factors in the adjustment of foreign nationals in the United States. *Journal of Social Issues, 19,* 115–122.

Dinges, N. (1983). Intercultural competence. In D. Landis & R. W. Brislin (Eds.), *Handbook of intercultural training: Vol. I. Issues in theory and design* (pp. 176–202). Elmsford, NY: Pergamon.

Dolphin, C. Z. (1994). Variables in the use of personal space in intercultural transactions. In L. A. Samovar & R. E. Porter (Eds.), *Intercultural communication: A reader* (pp. 252–263). Belmont, CA: Wadsworth.

Ehrlich, H. (1973). *The social psychology of prejudice.* New York: John Wiley.

Fiedler, F., Mitchell, T., & Triandis, H. (1971). The culture assimilator: An approach to cross-cultural training. *Journal of Applied Psychology, 55,* 95–102.

Fiske, A. P. (1992). The four elementary forms of sociality: Framework for a unified theory of social relations. *Psychological Review, 99,* 689–723.

Fitch, K. L. (1994). A cross-cultural study of directive sequences and some implications for compliance-gaining research. *Communication Monographs, 61,* 185–210.

Foote, N. N., & Cottrell, L. S. (1955). *Identity and interpersonal competence.* Chicago: University of Chicago Press.

Frederick, H. H. (1993). *Global communication and international relations.* Belmont, CA: Wadsworth.

Furnham, A., & Bochner, S. (1982). Social difficulty in foreign cultures: An empirical analysis of culture shock. In S. Bochner (Ed.), *Cultures in contact: Studies in cross-cultural interaction.* Elmsford, NY: Pergamon.

Gardner, G. H. (1962). Cross-cultural communication. *Journal of Social Psychology, 58,* 241–256.

Geertz, C. (1973). *The interpretation of cultures: Selected essays.* New York: Basic Books.

Getter, H., & Nowinski, J. K. (1981). A free response test of interpersonal effectiveness. *Journal of Personality Assessment, 45,* 301–308.

Gibb, J. (1961). Defensive communication. *Journal of Communication, 11,* 141–148.

Giles, H. (Ed.). (1977). *Language, ethnicity, and intergroup.* London: Academic Press.

Glenn, E. S., & Glenn, C. G. (1981). *Man and mankind: Conflict and communication between cultures.* Norwood, NJ: Ablex.

Goldman, A. (1994). The centrality of "ningensei" to Japanese negotiation and interpersonal relationships: Implications for U.S.–Japanese communication. *International Journal of Intercultural Relations, 18,* 29–54.

Grice, H. P. (1975). Logic and conversation. In P. Cole & J. Morgan (Eds.), *Syntax and semantics 3: Speech acts* (pp. 107–142). New York: Academic Press.

Gudykunst, W. B. (1985). A model of uncertainty reduction in intercultural encounters. *Journal of Language and Social Psychology, 4,* 79–98.

Gudykunst, W. B. (1993). Toward a theory of effective interpersonal and intergroup communication: An anxiety/uncertainty management (AUM) perspective. In R. L. Wiseman & J. Koester (Eds.), *Intercultural communication competence* (pp. 33–71). Newbury Park, CA: Sage.

Gudykunst. W. B., & Hammer, M. R. (1988). Strangers and hosts: An uncertainty reduction based theory of intercultural adaptation. In Y. Y. Kim & W. B. Gudykunst (Eds.), *Cross-cultural adaptation: Current approaches* (pp. 106–139). Newbury Park, CA: Sage.

Gudykunst. W. B., Hammer, M. R., & Wiseman, R. (1977). An analysis of an integrated approach to cross-cultural training. *International Journal of Intercultural Relations, 2,* 99–110.

Gudykunst. W. B., & Nishida, T. (1983). Social penetration in Japanese and American close friendships. In R. Bostrom (Ed.), *Communication yearbook 7* (pp. 592–610). Beverly Hills, CA: Sage.

Gudykunst. W. B., & Nishida, T. (1986). The influence of cultural variability on perceptions of communication behavior associated with relationship terms. *Human Communication Research, 13,* 147–166.

Gudykunst. W. B., & Ting-Toomey, S. (1988). Affective communication across cultures. *American Behavioral Scientist, 31,* 384–400.

Gudykunst. W. B., Ting-Toomey, S., & Wiseman, R. (1991). Taming the beast: Designing a course in intercultural communication. *Communication Education, 40,* 272–286.

Gudykunst. W. B., Wiseman, R., & Hammer, M. R. (1977). Determinants of a sojourner's attitudinal satisfaction: A path model. In B. D. Ruben (Ed.), *Communication yearbook 1* (pp. 415–425). New Brunswick, NJ: Transaction.

Gudykunst. W. B., Yang, S. M., & Nishida, T. (1987). Cultural differences in self-consciousness and unself-consciousness. *Communication Research, 14,* 7–36.

Guthrie, G. (1975). A behavioral analysis of culture learning. In R. W. Brislin, S. Bochner, & W. J. Lonner (Eds.), *Cross-cultural perspectives on learning.* New York: John Wiley.

Hall, E. T. (1959). *The silent language.* Garden City, NY: Doubleday.

Hall, E. T. (1966). *The hidden dimension.* Garden City, NY: Anchor.

Hall, E. T. (1976). *Beyond Cultures.* Garden City, NY: Anchor.

Hall. E. T., & Whyte, W. F. (1963). Intercultural communication; A guide to men of action. *Practical Anthropology, 9,* 83–108.

Hammer, M. R. (1987). Behavioral dimensions of intercultural effectiveness: A replication and extension. *International Journal of Intercultural Relations, 11,* 65–88.

Hammer, M. R. (1988, November). *Communication skills and intercultural communication competence: A review and research agenda.* Paper presented at the annual meeting of the Speech Communication Association, New Orleans, LA.

Hammer, M. R. (1989). Intercultural communication competence. In M. K. Asante & W. B. Gudykunst (Eds.), *Handbook of international and intercultural communication* (pp. 247–260). Newbury Park, CA: Sage.

Hammer, M. R., Gudykunst, W. B., & Wiseman, R. (1978). Dimensions of intercultural effectiveness. *International Journal of Intercultural Relations, 2,* 382–393.

Harris, J. G. (1973). A science of the South Pacific: An analysis of the character structure of the Peace Corp volunteer. *American Psychologist, 28,* 232–247.

Harris, P. R., & Moran, R. T. (1987). *Managing cultural differences.* Houston, TX: Gulf.

Hart, R. P., & Burks, D. M. (1972). Rhetorical sensitivity and social interaction. *Speech Monographs, 39,* 75–91.

Hawes, F., & Kealey, D. J. (1979). *Canadians in development: An empirical study of adaptation and effectiveness on overseas assignment* (Technical report). Ottawa: Canadian International Development Agency.

Hawes, F., & Kealey, D. J. (1981). An empirical study of Canadian technical assistance. *International Journal of Intercultural Relations, 5,* 239–258.

Hecht, M. L., & Ribeau, S. (1991). Sociocultural roots of ethnic identity: A look at black America. *Journal of Black Studies, 21,* 501–513.

Hecht, M. L., Sedano, M. V., & Ribeau, S. R. (1993). Understanding culture, communication, and research: Applications to Chicanos and Mexican American. *International Journal of Intercultural Relations, 17,* 157–166.

Hedge, R. (1993, November). *Communication competence: An Indian perspective.* Paper presented at the annual meeting of the Speech Communication Association, Miami Beach, FL.

Herman, S., & Schield, E. (1961). The stranger group in cross-cultural situations. *Sociometry, 24,* 165–176.

Hofstede, G. (1980). *Culture's consequences: International differences in work-related values.* Beverly Hills, CA: Sage.

Holland, J. L., & Baird, L. L. (1968). An interpersonal competence scale. *Educational and Psychological Measurement, 28,* 503–510.

Hwang, J. C., Chase, L. J., & Kelly, C. W. (1980). An intercultural examination of communication competence. *Communication, 9,* 70–79.

Hymes, D. (1971). Competence and performance in linguistic theory. In R. Huxley & E. Ingram (Eds.), *Language acquisition: Models and methods* (pp. 3–26). New York: Academic Press.

Hymes, D. (1972). Models of the interaction of language and social life. In J. Gumperz & D. Hymes (Eds.), *Directions in sociolinguistics: The ethnography of communication* (pp. 1–71). New York: Holt, Rinehart & Winston.

Imahori, T. T., & Lanigan, M. L. (1989). Relational models of intercultural communication competence. *International Journal of Intercultural Relations, 13,* 269–286.

Ishii, S. (1992). Buddhist preaching: The persistent main undercurrent of Japanese traditional rhetorical communication. *Communication Quarterly, 40,* 391–397.

Ishii, S., & Bruneau, T. (1994). Silence and silences in cross-cultural perspective: Japan and the United States. In L. A. Samovar & R. E. Porter (Eds.), *Intercultural communication: A reader* (pp. 246–251). Belmont, CA: Wadsworth.

Jain, N. C., & Kussman, E. D. (1994). Dominant cultural patterns of Hindus in India. In L. A. Samovar & R. E. Porter (Eds.), *Intercultural communication: A reader* (pp. 95–103). Belmont, CA: Wadsworth.

John, O. P. (1990). The "big five" factor taxonomy: Dimensions of personality in the natural language and in questionnaires. In L. A. Pervin (Ed.), *Handbook of personality: Theory and research* (pp. 66–100). New York: Guilford.

Johnston, W. B., & Packer, A. H. (1987). *Workforce 2000: Work and workers for the 21st century.* Indianapolis: Hudson Institute.

Kiesler, D. J. (1983). The 1982 interpersonal circle: A taxonomy for complementary in human transactions. *Psychological Review, 90,* 185–214.

Kim, M. (1994). Cross-cultural comparisons of the perceived importance of conversational constraints. *Human Communication Research, 21,* 128–151.

Kim, M., & Wilson, S. R. (1994). A cross-cultural comparison of implicit theories of requesting. *Communication Monographs, 61,* 210–235.

Kim, Y. Y. (1988). *Communication and cross-cultural adaptation.* Clevedon, England: Multilingual Matters.

Kim, Y. Y. (1991). Communication and cross-cultural adaptation. In L. A. Samovar & R. E. Porter (Eds.), *Intercultural communication: A reader* (pp. 383–391). Belmont, CA: Wadsworth.

Kim, Y. Y. (1994a). Beyond cultural identity. *Intercultural Communication Studies, 4,* 1–24.

Kim, Y. Y. (1994b). Interethnic communication: The context and the behavior. In S. A. Deetz (Ed.), *Communication yearbook 17* (pp. 511–538). Thousand Oaks, CA: Sage.

Kim, Y. Y., & Gudykunst, W. B. (Eds.). (1988). *Cross-cultural adaptation: Current approaches*. Newbury Park, CA: Sage.

Klopf, D. W. (Ed.). (1992). Communication practices in the Pacific basin [Special section]. *Communication Quarterly, 40*, 368–428.

Klopf, D. W., & Cambra, R. E. (1983). Communication apprehension in foreign settings: The results of exploratory research. *Communication, 12*, 37–51.

Kluckhohn, C. (1948). *Mirror of man*. New York: McGraw-Hill.

Kluckhohn, C., & Strodtbeck. F. (1960). *Variations in value orientations*. New York: Row, Peterson.

Knapp, M. (1978). *Social intercourse: From greetings to goodbye*. Boston: Allyn & Bacon.

Lee, L. (1979). Is social competence independent of cultural context? *American Psychologist, 34*, 795–796.

Lustig, M. W., & Koester, J. (1993). *Intercultural competence: Interpersonal communication across cultures*. New York: HarperCollins.

Ma, H. K. (1990). The Chinese Taoist perspective on human development. *International Journal of Intercultural Relations, 14*, 235–250.

Ma, R. (1992). The role of unofficial intermediaries in interpersonal conflicts in the Chinese culture. *Communication Quarterly, 40*, 269–278.

Marriott, H. (1993). Politeness phenomena in Japanese intercultural business communication. *Intercultural Communication Studies, 3*, 15–38.

Martin, J. N. (1987). The relationships between student sojourner perceptions of intercultural competence and previous sojourn experience. *International Journal of Intercultural Relations, 11*, 337–355.

Martin, J. N. (Ed.). (1989). Intercultural communication competence [Special issue]. *International Journal of Intercultural Relations, 13*(3).

Martin, J. N. (1993). Intercultural communication competence: A review. In R. L. Wiseman & J. Koester (Eds.), *Intercultural communication competence* (pp. 16–32). Newbury Park, CA: Sage.

Martin, J. N., & Hammer, M. R. (1989). Behavioral categories of intercultural communication competence: Everyday communicators' perceptions. *International Journal of Intercultural Relations, 13*, 303–332.

Martin, J. N, Hecht, M. L., & Larkey, L. K. (1994). Conversational improvement strategies for interethnic communication: African American and European American perspectives. *Communication Monographs, 61*, 236–255.

McCroskey, J. C. (1982). Communication competence and performance: A research and pedagogical perspective. *Communication Education, 31*, 1–7.

Mead, R. (1990). *Cross-cultural management of communication*. New York: John Wiley.

Mihouse, V. H. (1993). The applicability of interpersonal communication competence to the intercultural communication context. In R. L. Wiseman & J. Koester (Eds.), *Intercultural communication competence* (pp. 184–203). Newbury Park, CA: Sage.

Miyahara, A. (1993, November). *Communication competence: A Japanese perspective*. Paper presented at the annual meeting of the Speech Communication Association, Miami Beach, FL.

Miyahara, A. (1994, November). *A conceptualization and measurement of communication competence: A Japanese perspective*. Paper presented at the annual meeting of the Speech Communication Association, New Orleans, LA.

Morris, R. T. (1960). *The two-way mirror: National status of foreign students' adjustment*. Minneapolis: University of Minnesota Press.

Nakanishi, M. (1987). Perceptions of self-disclosure in initial interaction: A Japanese sample. *Human Communication Research, 13*, 167–190.

Nakanishi, M., & Johnson, K. M. (1993). Implications of self-disclosure on conversational logics, perceived communication competence, and social attraction. In R. L. Wiseman & J. Koester (Eds.), *Intercultural communication competence* (pp. 168–183). Newbury Park, CA: Sage.

Nieto, S. (1992). *Affirming diversity*. New York: Longman.

Oberg, K. (1960). Culture shock: Adjustment to new cultural environments. *Practical Anthropology, 7*, 177–182.

Olebe, M., & Koester, J. (1989). Exploring the cross-cultural equivalence of the Behavioral Assessment Scale for intercultural communication. *International Journal of Intercultural Relations, 13*, 333–347.

Oliver, R. T. (1962). *Culture and communication: The problem of penetrating national and cultural boundaries*. Springfield, IL: Charles C. Thomas.

Parks, M. R. (1976, December). *Communication competence*. Paper presented at the annual meeting of the Speech Communication Association, San Francisco, CA.

Parks, M. R. (1985). Interpersonal communication and the quest for personal competence. In M. L. Knapp & G. R. Miller (Eds.), *Handbook of interpersonal communication* (pp. 171–201). Beverly Hills, CA: Sage.

Parks, M. R. (1994). Communication competence and interpersonal control. In M. L. Knapp & G. R. Miller

(Eds.), *Handbook of interpersonal communication* (2nd ed., pp. 589–618). Thousand Oaks, CA: Sage.

Parsons, T. (1951). *The social system.* Glencoe, IL: Free Press.

Phillips, G. M. (1983). A competent view of "competence." *Communication Education, 33,* 25–36.

Porter, R. E., & Samovar, L. A. (1994). An introduction to intercultural communication. In L. A. Samovar & R. E. Porter (Eds.), *Intercultural communication: A reader* (pp. 4–25). Belmont, CA: Wadsworth.

Pruegger, V. J., & Rogers, T. B. (1993). Development of a scale to measure cross-cultural sensitivity in the Canadian context. *Canadian Journal of Behavioural Science, 25,* 615–621.

Randolph, G., Landis, D., & Tzeng, O. (1977). The effects of time and practice upon culture assimilator training. *International Journal of Intercultural Relations, 1,* 105–119.

Rogers, J., & Ward, C. (1993). Expectation-experience discrepancies and psychological adjustment during cross-cultural reentry. *International Journal of Intercultural Relations, 17,* 185–196.

Ruben, B. D. (1976). Assessing communication competency for intercultural adaptation. *Group and Organization Studies, 1,* 334–354.

Ruben, B. D. (1977) Guidelines for cross-cultural communication effectiveness. *Group and Organization Studies, 2,* 470–479.

Ruben, B. D. (1988). Human communication and cross-cultural effectiveness. In L. A. Samovar & R. E. Porter (Eds.), *Intercultural communication: A reader* (pp. 331–338). Belmont, CA: Wadsworth.

Ruben, B. D. (1989). The study of cross-cultural competence: Traditions and contemporary issues. *International Journal of Intercultural Relations, 13,* 229–240.

Ruben, B. D., & Kealey, D. J. (1979). Behavioral assessment of communication competency and the prediction of cross-cultural adaptation. *International Journal of Intercultural Relations, 3,* 15–47.

Rubin, R. B. (1983, November). *Conceptualizing communication competence: Directions for research and instruction.* Paper presented at the annual meeting of the Speech Communication Association, Washington, DC.

Sanders, J. A., & Wiseman, R. L. (1993). Uncertainty reduction among ethnicities in the United States. *Intercultural Communication Studies, 3,* 1–14.

Sanders, O. (1995). *A multi-phase analysis of African American women's communication at a public transit setting.* Unpublished doctoral dissertation, Howard University, Washington, DC.

Saville-Troike, M. (1982). *The ethnography of communication: An introduction.* Baltimore, MD: University Park Press.

Schwartz, S. (1990). Individualism-collectivism. *Journal of Cross-Cultural Psychology, 21,* 139–157.

Schwartz, S., & Bilsky, W. (1987). Toward a psychological structure of human values. *Journal of Personality and Social Psychology, 58,* 878–891.

Schwartz, S., & Sagiv, L. (1995). Identifying culture-specifics in the content and structure of values. *Journal of Cross-Cultural Psychology, 26,* 92–116.

Scollon, R., & Scollon, S. (1995). *Intercultural communication: A discursive approach.* Oxford: Basil Blackwell.

Searle, W., & Ward, C. (1990). The prediction of psychological and sociocultural adjustment during cross-cultural transitions. *International Journal of Intercultural Relations, 14,* 449–464.

Selltiz, C., Christ, J. R., Havel, J., & Cook, S. (1963). *Attitudes and social relations of foreign students in the United States.* Minneapolis: University of Minnesota Press.

Sewell, W. H., & Davidsen, O. M. (1956). The adjustment of Scandinavian students. *Journal of Social Issues, 12,* 9–19.

Sitaram, K. S., & Cogdell, R. T. (1976). *Foundations of intercultural communication.* Columbus, OH: Merrill.

Smalley, W. A. (1963). Culture shock, language shock, and the shock of self-discovery. *Practical Anthropology, 10,* 49–56.

Smith, M. B. (1966). Explorations in competence: A study of Peace Corps teachers in Ghana. *American Psychologist, 21,* 555–556.

Snyder, M. (1974). Self-monitoring of expressive behavior. *Journal of Personality and Social Psychology, 30,* 526–537.

Snyder, M. (1979). Cognitive, behavioral, and interpersonal consequences of self-monitoring. In P. Pliner, K. R. Blankenstein, I. M. Spigel, T. Alloway, & L. Krames (Eds.), *Advances in the study of communication and affect: Perception of emotion in self and others* (pp. 181–201). New York: Plenum.

Snyder, M. (1987). *Public appearances, private realities.* New York: Friedman.

Spitzberg, B. H. (1983). Communication competence as knowledge, skill, and impression. *Communication Education, 32,* 323–329.

Spitzberg, B. H. (1988, November). *Progress and pitfalls in conceptualizing and researching intercultural communication competence.* Paper presented at the annual meeting of the Speech Communication Association, New Orleans, LA.

Spitzberg, B. H. (1989). Issues in the development of a theory of interpersonal competence in the intercultural context. *International Journal of Intercultural Relations, 13,* 241–268.

Spitzberg, B. H. (1991). Intercultural communication competence. In L. A. Samovar & R. E. Porter (Eds.), *Intercultural communication: A reader* (pp. 353–365). Belmont, CA: Wadsworth.

Spitzberg, B. H. (1994). A model of intercultural communication competence. In L. A. Samovar & R. E. Porter (Eds.), *Intercultural communication: A reader* (pp. 347–359). Belmont, CA: Wadsworth.

Spitzberg, B. H., & Cupach, W. R. (1984). *Interpersonal communication competence.* Beverly Hill, CA: Sage.

Starosta, W. J., & Olorunnisola, A. A. (1995, April). *A meta-model for third culture development.* Paper presented at the annual meeting of the Eastern Communication Association, Pittsburgh, PA.

Stephan, C. W., & Stephan, W. G. (1992). Reducing intercultural anxiety through intercultural contact. *International Journal of Intercultural Relations, 16,* 89–106.

Stewart, E. C., & Bennett, M. J. (1991). *American cultural patterns: A cross-cultural perspective.* Yarmouth, ME: Intercultural Press.

Strack, S., & Lorr, M. (1990). Three approaches to interpersonal behavior and their common factors. *Journal of Personality Assessment, 54,* 782–790.

Suzuki, S., & Rancer, A. S. (1994). Argumentativeness and verbal aggressiveness: Testing for conceptual and measurement equivalence across cultures. *Communication Monographs, 61,* 256–279.

Taylor, E. W. (1994). A learning model for becoming interculturally competent. *International Journal of Intercultural Relations, 18,* 389–408.

Ting-Toomey, S. (1989). Identity and interpersonal bond. In M. K. Asante & W. B. Gudykunst (Eds.), *Handbook of international and intercultural communication* (pp. 351–373). Newbury Park, CA: Sage.

Ting-Toomey, S. (1991). Intimacy expressions in three cultures: France, Japan, and the United States. *International Journal of Intercultural Relations, 15,* 29–46.

Ting-Toomey, S. (1993). Communication resourcefulness: An identity negotiation perspective. In R. L. Wiseman & J. Koester (Eds.), *Intercultural communication competence* (pp. 72–111). Newbury Park, CA: Sage.

Ting-Toomey, S., & Korzenny, F. (Eds.). (1989). *Language, communication, and culture: Current directions.* Newbury Park, CA: Sage.

Trenholm, S., & Ross, T. (1981). The compliant communicator: Teacher perceptions of classroom behavior. *Western Journal of Speech Communication, 45,* 13–26.

Triandis, H. C. (1976). *Interpersonal behavior.* Monterey, CA: Brooks/Cole.

Triandis, H. C. (1977). Subjective culture and interpersonal relations across cultures. In L. Loeb-Adler (Ed.), Issues in cross-cultural research [Special issue]. *Annual of the New York Academy of Sciences, 285,* 418–434.

Trubisky, P., Ting-Toomey, S., & Lin, S. (1991). The influence of individualism-collectivism and self-monitoring on conflict styles. *International Journal of Intercultural Relations, 15,* 65–84.

Turner, C. V. (1968). The Sinasina "big man" complex: A central culture theme. *Practical Anthropology, 15,* 16–23.

Ward, C., & Searle, W. (1991). The impact of value discrepancy and cultural identity on psychological and sociocultural adjustment of sojourners. *International Journal of Intercultural Relations, 15,* 209–226.

Weber, S. N. (1994). The need to be: The socio-cultural significance of black language. In L. A. Samovar & R. E. Porter (Eds.), *Intercultural communication: A reader* (pp. 221–226). Belmont, CA: Wadsworth.

Weinstein, E. A. (1969). The development of interpersonal competence. In D. A. Goslin (Ed.), *Handbook of socialization theory and research* (pp. 753–775). Chicago: Rand McNally.

White, G. M. (1980). Conceptual universals in interpersonal language. *American Anthropologist, 82,* 759–781.

White, M. I., & Barnet, S. (Eds.). (1995). *Comparing cultures: Readings on contemporary Japan for American writers.* Boston: Bedford.

White, R. W. (1959). Motivation reconsidered: The concept of competence. *Psychological Review, 66,* 297–333.

Wiemann, J. M. (1977). Explication and test of a model of communicative competence. *Human Communication Research, 3,* 195–213.

Wiemann, J. M., & Backlund, P. (1980). Current theory and research in communicative competence. *Review of Educational Research, 50,* 185–199.

Wiseman, R. L., & Abe, H. (1984). Finding and explaining differences: A reply to Gudykunst and Hammer. *International Journal of Intercultural Relations, 8,* 11–16.

Wiseman, R. L., & Koester, J. (Eds.). (1993). *Intercultural communication competence.* Newbury Park, CA: Sage.

Yum, J. O. (1988). The impact of Confucianism on interpersonal relationships and communication patterns in East Asia. *Communication Monographs, 55,* 374–388.

Yum, J. O. (1989, November). *Communication sensitivity and empathy in culturally diverse organizations.* Paper presented at the annual meeting of the Speech Communication Association, San Francisco, CA.

Yum, J. O. (1993, November). *Communication competence: A Korean perspective.* Paper presented at the annual meeting of the Speech Communication Association, Miami Beach, FL.

Yum, J. O. (1994, November). *A conceptualization and measurement of communication competence: A Korean perspective.* Paper presented at the annual meeting of the Speech Communication Association, New Orleans, LA.

15

Beyond Multicultural Man
Complexities of Identity

Lise M. Sparrow

In 1976, Peter Adler characterized the experience of what he called "multicultural man". His article was an important think-piece for the field of intercultural communication. His articulate description of a "new kind of man", who might "embody the attributes and characteristics that prepare him to serve as a facilitator and catalyst for contacts between cultures" (Adler, 1977, p. 38), provided for the basis for considerable discussion about the types of persons best suited for working across cultures and was included in a primary text used in intercultural communication courses (Samovar and Porter, 1985) and in many compilations of intercultural training materials.

In his article "Beyond Cultural Identity: Reflections on Cultural and Multicultural Man" (1977), Adler suggested that the conditions of contemporary history may be creating "a new kind of man" whose identity is based: not on a "belongingness" which implies either owning or being owned by culture, but on a style of self-consciousness that is capable of negotiating ever new formations of reality. This person, he said, "lives on the boundary", is "fluid and mobile", and committed to people's essential similarities as well as their differences. "What is new about this type of person and unique to our time is a fundamental change in the structure and process of identity" (Adler, 1977, p. 26).

More recently, Janet Bennett's work (1993a) on "cultural marginality" cites the story of Barack Obama, the first black elected president of the *Harvard Law Review*. She says he seems to claim for himself "an identity that is beyond any single cultural perspective" and posits that he and other "constructive marginals . . . are coming to terms with the reality that all knowledge is constructed and that what they will ultimately value and believe is what they choose . . ." (Bennett, 1993a, p. 128).

Milton Bennett (1993b) similarly argues that these marginals, who have reached the final stage of development with respect to his model of intercultural sensitivity, are "outside all cultural frames of reference by virtue of their ability to consciously raise any assumption to a meta level (level of self-reference)". Adler and the Bennetts represent important current thinking about what it is to be multicultural and of the constructivist view of identity development.

As an instructor of intercultural communication, I initially found these articles to be exceptionally useful with the students in our master's degree programs at the School for International Training, most of whom had lived overseas extensively and spoke many languages other than English. More than 20% of the student body comes each year from outside the United States, and of the Americans, the ethnic and racial diversity has increased markedly over the past decade. Differences in gender, age, sexual orientation, and religious affiliation have also become a much more explicit part of informal conversation as well as of the curriculum. Managing these personal and cultural differences has become a central challenge for participants in our programs and has inevitably forced students to become more self-aware and to make conscious choices about their interactions with others.

As such, in the context of our courses, Adler's view of what it means to be a multicultural person faced considerable scrutiny. Students in our programs questioned the article both because it was based solely on the experiences of men and because many of Adler's assumptions about what it takes to work effectively in intercultural settings did not match their own experiences overseas. Though the Bennetts' more recent work on marginality explicitly addresses the inherent challenges to identity of extended multicultural experience, students often questioned whether one could really choose to act on one's values if those values were not recognized in the contexts in which they lived as professionals.

One Taiwanese woman, for example, in a final paper for a course entitled Culture, Identity and Ethnic Diversity, reflected on her dependence on men for her identity:

> It was necessary in the high-context Chinese culture . . . for a man to designate my status identity.

Students of color similarly claim that the opportunity to construct an individual identity is a luxury available only to those in dominant social categories. A Somali woman interviewed as part of the study described in the latter part of this paper, talked about cultures in a similar way, as limiting her interactions:

> In order for me to function I have to be able to do what these people do while I still feel comfortable . . . I always have to check and when I check I think, did I say or do that right?

International students add that the very concept of an individual identity is Euro-centric. A woman from Hong Kong wrote in her final paper:

> Unlike American culture which recognizes individual identity as rooted in personal accomplishment . . . (in my) society one's identity is rooted in groups . . . my identity was not my own to establish and/or earn.

As those with unclear membership in any one culture have talked about the importance of connection, rather than marginality. One man wrote:

> I have found that even as I seem to free myself from the particulars of my life, the particulars always remain in my life and nurture it much like a plowing of weeds nurture a garden. My particulars are always part of my life . . . the ultimate protection from the insufferable hubris of "terminal uniqueness".

The fact that Anglo-American men in our program have tended to identify strongly with Adler's description of a multicultural person has also been of great interest to me, especially given that women, people of color and international students generally state that individuality and self-constructed identity are neither possible nor desirable from their points of view.

In response to these diverse critiques, I eventually stopped including the Adler article in the students' core curriculum. Nonetheless, students in our program have continued to express a compelling desire to define what it means to be a multicultural person and to discuss to what extent the solutions posed by the Bennetts' "constructive marginality" are valid for women and ethnic minorities. It is the purpose of this paper to consider these differences in the experiences of multicultural identity, both through a review of literature related to the definition of self and the development of identity, and through the results of a small research project. Inasmuch as Adler states that his multicultural man's disembodied mind may very well represent "an affirmation of individual identity at a higher level of social, psychological and cultural integration" (Adler, 1977, p. 38), it would seem important to continue to explore his as well as alternative views of identity and to explore the intrapsychic dilemmas of such people. Questions which I hope to address in this paper are first, whether the ideal of a free-acting individual is in itself a western or male viewpoint and second, whether it is an optimal view at all. In his paper Adler enjoins others to further research and exploration. That was the essential purpose of the study which is the subject of this paper.

1. Review of Literature

As stated above, Adler's description of the multicultural person has been paralleled in the recent description by Janet Bennett of "cultural marginality" (1993a), and in the final "integration stage" (Bennett, 1993a, p. 59) of the "Developmental Model of Intercultural Sensitivity" (1993b) described by Milton Bennett. In discussing the last stage of his model, Bennett states that "people can function in relationship to cultures while staying outside the constraints of any particular one" (Bennett, 1993b, p. 60). Tillich (1966) also suggested that the future will demand that one live with tension and movement:

> It is in truth not standing still, but rather a crossing and return, a repetition of return and crossing, back and forth—the aim of which is to create a third area beyond the bounded territories, an area where one can stand for a time without being enclosed in something tightly bounded.
>
> (Tillich, 1966, p. 111)

Yoshikawa (1987), similarly posits an integration of eastern and western perspectives in which the communicator "is not limited by given social and cultural realities" but operates in "the sphere of 'between' where the limitation and possibility of man and culture unfold . . . (and) one has a transcending experience" (Yoshikawa, 1987, p. 328).

These theories are based in the "radical constructivist" view (von Glaserfeld, 1984) of communication which suggests that it is, in fact, possible to escape the influence of one's own reality. Bennett (1993a) describes the optimal stage of identity as that in which people:

> are outside all frames of reference by virtue of their ability to consciously raise assumption to a meta-level level of self-reference. In other words, there is no natural cultural identity for a marginal person.
>
> (Bennett, 1993a, p. 63)

The assumption of these theories is that marginality and the experience of transcendence are not only possible but that they are "the most powerful position from which to exercise intercultural sensitivity" (Bennett, 1993a, p. 65).

This Cartesian concept of a mind, detached from experience, capable of determining an objective reality, while still the ideal model of many intellectual and ethical theories based on work with white western male respondents (Kohlberg, 1976; Levinson, 1978; Murray, 1938; Perry, 1970; Rogers, 1956; Spence, 1985), has, however, been brought into question recently by feminists (Benack, 1982; Belenky, Clinchy, Goldberger & Tarule, 1986; Gilligan, 1982; Josselson, 1987; Loevinger, 1962; Marcia, 1980). The importance of a sense of belonging and relationship, both to one's own background and ultimately to that of others, is highlighted as optimal in many current racial and ethnic identity development theories (Myers et al., 1991; Hecht, Collier & Ribeau, 1993). Cross-cultural research (Geertz 1984; Kakar, 1989, 1991; Sampson, 1985; Schweder, 1991; Schweder & Bourne, 1982), and post-modern educators also suggest that cultural and sociopolitical factors influence identity development (Freire, 1985; Giroux, 1983; Katz, 1985; Leung, 1990; Nieto, 1992). Similarly, within the field of communication as well, the "social constructionist" view (Gergen & Davis, 1985; Hoffman, 1993; Schweder, 1991) suggests that the very frames of reference we use to construct our identities are rooted in our social experiences. Research in bilingual and feminist education, psychology and intercultural competence have, in fact, consistently shown that it is in "connection" (Belenky et al., 1986), interaction (Bateson, 1972; Hoffman, 1993) and "sharing meaning" (Collier & Thomas, 1988) that growth, mediation and communication occur.

1.1. Cross-cultural differences in the concept of self

The idea that a mind can isolate itself from its experience has also been problematized frequently by those outside western cultural paradigms. Balagangadara (1991) suggests, in stark contrast to this concept, that while:

> the Western man feels the presence of "something deep inside himself" even if he is unable to say what it is [and] builds an identity for such a self [which] is what makes such an endowed organism unique . . . By contrast, the Easterner would experience nothing, or some kind of hollowness, the psychological identity of such a self is a construction of the "other", an agent is constituted by the actions which an organism performs, or . . . is the actions performed and nothing more.
>
> (Balagangadara, 1991, p. 103)

Further, he states, those actions are without meaning unless construed or "ascribed" in some way by another.

Similarly, in his paper contrasting concepts of self in China and the United States, Pratt (1991, p. 302) states:

> The Chinese construction of the self and location of personality appears to be derived primarily from the cultural, social, and political spheres of influence with an emphasis on continuity of family, societal roles, the supremacy of hierarchical relationships, compliance with authority, and the maintenance of stability. The resulting self finds an identity that is externally ascribed, subordinated to the collective, seeks fulfillment through the performance of duty, and would have little meaningful existence apart from ordained roles and patterns of affiliation. If this is true, the Chinese self is, largely, an externally ascribed, highly malleable, and socially constructed entity—part of an intricate composite that, like a hologram, is representative of the whole, even when removed from it.

In contrast, he says the individual in the United States:

> is recognized as the starting point for construing the social order, and the self is considered a psychological construct as much as an artifact of cultural, social and political influences.

The intricate holographic conception of self within China poses a stark contrast to the psychologically constructed conception within the United States.

Rosaldo (1982, p. 228) also contrasts the Ilongot concept of the self to the traditional western model:

What Ilongots lack from a perspective such as ours is something like our notion of an inner self continuous through time, a self whose actions can be judged in terms of sincerity, integrity, and commitment . . . Ilongots do not see their inmost hearts as constant causes, independent of their acts . . . what matters is the act itself and not the personal statement it purportedly involves.

Finally, Geertz (1976, p. 225) makes a similar contrast with the Javanese, Balinese and Moroccan concepts of self:

The Western conception of the person as a bounded, unique, more or less integrated motivational and cognitive universe, a dynamic center of awareness, emotion, judgment and action organized into a distinctive whole and set contrastively both against other such wholes and against its social and natural background, is, however incorrigible it may seem to us, a rather peculiar idea within the context of the world's cultures.

These examples provide the basis for questioning whether the concept of an individuated self, capable of free choice and action is not a construct of western languages and cultures.

1.2. African American views of the self

Looking at this same issue within the American context, one finds that African-Americans, as one example, also cite contrasts with the dominant western view of the self. Hecht et al. (1993) posit that African-Americans by and large identify themselves not so much as individuals, but as linked across time and space, and as altering self-concept in relation to the situation and in "relationship to other members of the group and to members of other groups" (Hecht et al., 1993, p. 40). Asante (1987) extends this by emphasizing the contextually determined interrelationship of feeling, knowing and acting and posits that, in contrast to Bennett's (1993b) position that we are best served by a meta-stance outside our experience, "in Afrology [sic] the study of an object is best performed when all three components are interrelated". Asante further states: "One becomes human only in the midst of others" (p. 79). bell hooks similarly contrasts Adler's emphasis on marginality with her African-American community growing up, and with her need as she grew up to understand both the dominant white culture and her own African-American culture, and to see both as part of a whole:

We looked both from the outside in and the inside out. We focused our attention on the center as well as on the margin. We understood both. This mode of seeing reminded us of the existence of a whole universe, a main body made up of both margin and center.

(hooks, 1990, p. 149)

1.3. Gender differences in the concept of self

Current research into western female identity also contrasts that of western men. Relating directly to the issue of marginality, Chodorow (1976) asserts that boys have the early challenge of disconnecting themselves from an identification with their mothers while girls are encouraged to "maintain more connected, fluid relationships" (Enns, 1991, p. 212). Miller (1986) extends this to say that, in contrast to men, women are:

trained to be involved with emotions, to sense physical, emotional and mental growth and ultimately have a greater recognition of the essential cooperative nature of human existence

(Miller, 1986, p. 38)

Belenky et al. (1986) put forth a view of female identity, much like that of hooks, that is situated in and develops through relationship: "You let the inside out and the outside in". In women they say, "there is an impetus to try to deal with life, internal and external, in all its complexity" (Belenky et al., 1986, p. 128). In emphasizing the differences between men and women's moral development, Gilligan (1982) has been perhaps most successful in pointing out both the impetus for men to develop a sense of individual self-identity and for women to emphasize contextual and relational aspects of experience and ultimately, of choice:

> For Stephen leaving childhood means renouncing relationships in order to protect his freedom of self-expression. For Mary, "farewell to childhood" means renouncing freedom of self-expression in order to protect others and preserve relationships.
>
> (Gilligan, 1982, p. 157)

She notes that for women:

> The standard of judgment that informs their assessment of self is a standard of relation-ship, an ethic of nurturance, responsibility, and care.
>
> (Gilligan, 1982, p. 159)

Recent research in intercultural adjustment (Mendenhall & Oddou, 1985; Parker & McEvoy, 1993) also supports the view that marginality is a trait more typical of men and that, in fact, the relational and communication skills associated more often with women are the most appropriate precursors to adjustment and interaction with host country nationals. Parallel to gender-related research in psychology (Gilligan, 1982; Miller, 1986), Kealey's (1990) study in cross-cultural effectiveness reported that:

> women are more highly rated than men on many of the skills and attitudes associated with women than men overseas; relation-building, flexibility and appreciation for contextual variation were attributes cited both as present to a greater extent in women than in men and as contributing significantly to overseas effectiveness.
>
> (Kealey, 1990, p. 29)

1.4. Postmodern views of identity

Parallel to these gender-related distinctions one finds that models of psychological development (Erikson, 1964; Kegan, 1982) based on research with white men, have consistently emphasized the development of an individuated self, one optimally capable of making increasingly abstract moral decisions (Kohlberg, 1976). Similarly, radical constructivists (von Glasersfeld, 1984; Watzlawick, 1984) describe a self which constructs its own unique meaning from experience and then is responsible for the implications of that meaning. However, for social constructionists (Gergen, 1982; Hoffman, 1993), who claim to offer a post-modern view of identity:

> the line between individual and social becomes tenuous . . . an idea is constructed together with others; then is internalized in the private mind; then rejoins the common mind; and so forth.
>
> (Hoffman, 1993a, p. 204)

Social psychologists (Hecht et al., 1993) have also proposed an "interpenetration" model of development and say that "the self and society cannot be defined apart from each other". These latter theorists focus on ethnic and racial identities and highlight the distinction between identities that are "internally defined (subjective, perceived, or private identity) and those that are externally imposed (objective, actual, or public identity)". These views:

> allow[s] for both the individual and the social perspectives, the dialectic between the levels and the interpenetration of each level as well as structural properties of interactional and societal systems.
>
> (Hecht et al., 1993, pp. 42–43)

Similarly, critical theory (Poster, 1989), which is concerned with the sociopolitical dimensions of identity, suggests that human beings "participate willingly at the level of everyday life in the reproduction of their own dehumanization and exploitation" (Giroux, 1983, p. 157) and that society defines and limits self-definition as a means of maintaining dominant cultural paradigms. What they term post-modern "subjectivity":

> relates to issues of identity, intentionality and desire (and) is a deeply political issue that is inextricably related to social and cultural forces that extend far beyond the self-consciousness of the so-called humanist.
>
> (Giroux, 1991, p. 30)

Through the lens of these theories one might say that only members of dominant paradigms can have the luxurious illusion of objectivity or of a self which is free of social realities.

1.5. Complexities of identity

As a final contrast, Myers et al. (1991) examine the "complexity" of the impact of race, gender and ethnicity on identity and suggest that "the optimal conceptual system" is seen as multi-dimensional: "encompassing ancestors, those yet unborn, nature, and community" (Myers et al., 1991, p. 55) and that it is in connection with the spiritual, rather than individual awareness, that one transcends culture. Social identity theories (Brown & Levinson, 1978; Hardiman & Jackson, 1992; Hecht et al., 1993; Hoare, 1991; Kim, 1981; Phinney, 1990) however, point to the impact of these physiological and social realities on one's capacity to self-define and negotiate identity, and that even spiritual beliefs are socially constructed.

Perhaps appropriately, Gergen (1982) states:

> it is becoming increasingly apparent to investigators in this domain that developmental trajectories over the lifespan are highly variable; neither with respect to psychological functioning nor overt conduct does there appear to be transhistorical generality in lifespan trajectory . . . A virtual infinity of developmental forms seems possible, and which form emerges may depend on confluence of particulars, the existence of which is fundamentally unsystematic.
>
> (Gergen, 1982, p. 161)

Identity development theory, for example, suggests, that White and Black identity development differ (Hardiman, 1982; Hardiman & Jackson, 1992; Tatum, 1992), as do male and female identity development (Chodorow, 1976; Enns, 1991; Gilligan, 1982), and further that ethnic identity and multiple minority identities create complex variations and alternatives to standard developmental models (Martinez, 1994; Reynolds & Pope, 1991; Root, 1992). Ivey, Ivey and Simek-Morgan (1993) have, in fact, developed a "multicultural cube" in which some 19 factors: five contextual variables, nine multicultural issues and four developmental stages interact in determining the identity of one individual. Ultimate stages in these various trajectories tend to point to the capacity to integrate cultural identities within oneself, rather than to transcend them as constructivists suggest is possible.

In summary, it appears that to speak of multicultural identity apart from social realities is increasingly difficult once one focuses on non-western, non-dominant experiences of identity. "Interpenetration" (Asante, 1987) and "interaction" (Hecht et al., 1993, p. 46) tend to bespeak these identity processes.

2. Interviews with Multicultural People

2.1. Research methodology

The small study discussed here was a further investigation and documentation of the experiences of women and people of color with respect to the experience of multicultural identity. Initial data which contributed to this investigation were approximately 300 essays written for a course mentioned previously entitled "Culture, Identity, and Ethnic Diversity", taught by the author. In these essays students were to define culture, its influence in their lives and to describe ways culture affected choices they could see themselves making in the future. Having compiled and examined these essays, all written by students with at least 2 years of intercultural experience and having determined that women and people of color articulated experiences at greatest variance from the Adler article, and from the experiences of Anglo-American men, a series of interviews was carried out. While Adler had focused on the experiences of four men, 20 in-depth interviews totalling up to 6 h for each person were the final source of data for this study.

In addition to interviews with four men who were of western backgrounds similar to those described by Adler, six other men from more varied ethnic and cultural backgrounds, and 10 women were interviewed. Some were from biracial families, and some were bicultural. All had lived extensively (defined as 2 years minimum) in at least three cultures and were at least bilingual, the criteria used in the initial identification of multicultural people for the study. Respondents came originally from Australia, Canada, China, Colombia, India, Iran, Italy, Jamaica, Japan, Malaysia, Russia, Saudi Arabia, Somalia, Uganda, the United States, Viet Nam, Zaire, Saudi Arabia, and South Africa. Adler speaks of his individuals having "embraced only to let go [of] one frame of reference in favor of yet another". The premise of this study was that the challenges posed by life in three cultures, complemented by those of operating effectively in at least two languages assured the same kind of shift and the development of a multicultural identity.

Rather than pre-dispose the interviewees to a particular way of describing their experiences, a methodology called "in-depth interviewing", developed by Irving Seidman (1991) was selected. He notes:

> At the root of in-depth interviewing is an interest in understanding the experience of other people and the meaning they make of that experience.
>
> (Seidman, 1991, p. 8)

The three-part interviews, each part up to 2 h in length, were intended specifically to help portray a social constructionist view of reality. The interviewer encouraged narrative description to highlight how respondents remember and make meaning of their experiences. In this study, for example, the interviewer began with the query "what is it like to be a multicultural person", and followed in later interviews with questions relating to their sense of "self". Seidman insists that only by engaging deeply with a person and by recording and studying the way they construct and explain their experiences can we come to a deeper understanding of human experience and of how meaning is made of human dilemmas.

While he suggests an open-ended form of questioning which "reflectively" (Rogers, 1980) follows the thoughts of the interviewee in exploring a particular issue, the technique of "circular questioning" (Tomm, 1985) was also used. This form of questioning is based on the idea that selves are created in interaction and is intended to highlight contextual and relational aspects of human experience. Rather than suppose that there is one answer to any question the interviewer follows the themes of the interviewee while seeking constantly to contextualize answers. Sample questions in response to the recounting of a particular event might be: did you respond the same way to members of your family when you were in Africa, when you were a student, etc.? The interviewer consistently clarifies the contexts and asks for descriptions of interlocutors, and for the degree of which an interviewee would make choices or behave according to consistent values or in relation to contextual variation. While the methodology allowed for the social construc- tionist view of identity to be expressed, the range of possible answers allowed for the construc- tivist model of identity to emerge as well, which it did in some instances. In fact, those with views similar to Adler were still able to describe their experiences in ways which denied the impact of context or relationship, while others for who these factors played important roles were allowed to flesh out intricacies of their experiences in ways which more quantitative interview methodologies may not have allowed.

It needs to be noted, however, that there are significant limitations to the study. It was a small, though in-depth study into the lives of only 20 people. More often than not interviewees were not being interviewed in their native languages, and in the majority of the interviews, the interviewer was not of the same race or ethnic background of the interviewee. These factors can be seen to have limited the comfort of the interviewees in describing their life experiences and the reliability of the results. While involvement in some form of intercultural work was a criteria for identifying skilled interculturalists in the selection of the interviewees and they varied widely in terms of their backgrounds, all are or were students, teachers, trainers or managers in one of three contrasting (one urban, one suburban and one rural) college communities. This was significant in that it may also have limited the types of responses received.

There are also limitations to this paper inasmuch as it is difficult in other than thematic and anecdotal ways to describe the human experience described in a qualitative study of this kind. While differences in age, gender, race and class of the respondents in this study provide a contrast to Adler's work, this paper cannot adequately address the complexity of multicultural experience nor can the conclusions be seen as anything more than suggestions of what it means to be, as were Adler's men, multicultural within the United States context, or of directions for further study.

2.2. Four women

In his article, Adler described four men, two of whom he had interviewed, and two of con- temporary significance, Norman O. Brown and Carlos Castaneda. In further describing the results of this study, representative case studies of four women will be provided. This will be followed by a summary of themes which were highlighted in both the students' essays and in the interviews conducted.

2.2.1. Case study 1

Marhaba is a Somali woman in her early twenties. She was born in the United States when her parents were students and was taken with her younger sister, at the age of three, to live with her father's parents in Tanzania. Her parents finished their studies in the US and later divorced. Five years later she moved with her grandparents to Somalia. Her mother then returned to Somalia and lived both with her own parents and in the house of her ex-husband's parents with her two daughters. At that point, Marhaba spent time in the homes of both her grandparents. She finished high school at a French lisee, fluent in French, the Swahili of her paternal grandparents, and Somali, and was somewhat familiar with English. As her father had remained in the United States she was able, at the age of sixteen to join him and his new family, to attend a well-known US university and to pursue a Master's Degree and teaching credential.

At the time she was interviewed she was working supervising teachers and student-teaching. She was proud of her background and yet clearly sensitive to ethnic and cultural differences in the classroom she taught. She expressed anger at her college advisor who seemed racially biased and judgmental towards international students. She was articulate about the experience of change. She spoke of life as "a lottery, like gambling", because people went from positions of power to jail, from riches to poverty "like a roller coaster" in Somalia. As such she talks about always learning: "there's always something to learn from here and there's always something to learn from home . . . I am always here learning".

2.2.2. Case study 2

To Duc Hanh is a Vietnamese woman, 63 years old at the time of the interview. She was schooled in a French Catholic boarding school in Viet Nam and later attended university at the Sorbonne. In France she married a Vietnamese man and returned to Viet Nam to raise a family. She later divorced and in 1975 escaped Viet Nam and has lived for the past 18 years in California. She has received a doctoral degree in education from the University of California at Berkeley and currently teaches multicultural education to teachers of LEP (Limited English Proficiency) students. Holding herself graciously and speaking in an educated English, she refers often in conversation to French philosophers and American psychologists, and speaks enthusiastically of Vietnamese poetry and music

> there is no such thing as "I" in Vietnamese . . . we define ourselves in relationship . . . if I talk to my mother, the "I" for me is "daughter", the you is for mother, it's in a relationship always. If I talk to my children the mother would be me and the daughter or son would be them.

As she speaks of her present life in the United States, however, she notes a change:

> Since the elements and the needs of my family are changing then my responsibilities and duties are changing and so I change: I perceive myself as creating my own identity . . . and a person who is choosing and creating my own self.

2.2.3. Case study 3

Ayse is an ethnic East Indian woman who was raised in Uganda and was forced, as a teenager, to leave in 1972. As a refugee, she worked initially in a chicken factory in England and later attended secondary school there. In 1975, she was able to join her family in Canada where she attended University. Having received her Master's Degree in the US, she is in her early forties and teaches English as a Second Language in Canada. She speaks articulately about the place of language in her identity. At home, she says she spoke Kachi, bastardized with Swahili. Though she rarely uses them now, she grew up speaking Hindi and Gujarati as well. At her father's garage in Uganda she spoke Swahili and in school and all during her studies she has used English.

Though her accent in recognizably East Indian she notes that, never having been to India, she feels far closer to Africa, though it is her Muslim faith which she refers to as home. She has married a man of her same faith who similarly escaped from Uganda to England and finally, Canada. In their shared faith and relationship she notes, she is most herself. She grants her faith credit for the strength needed to endure her painful life as refugee, and for the opportunity to earn a Master's Degree now to be a teacher of Afghani refugees.

2.2.4. Case study 4

Susanna Harrington was born in South America and lived and travelled with her family throughout the continent as the child of a diplomat. As a teenager she travelled frequently between counties after her parents' divorce. More recently, she has married an American man, received her Master's Degree in the US and works as a teacher of English as a Second Language in an American high school. Many of her students are Hispanic, mainly Puerto Ricans. She speaks compellingly of her shock at the ignorance of her first American students who assumed all Hispanics were servants or laborers and with sadness at the effects of her parents' divorce. Now in her thirties, she is enthusiastic about her young daughter, takes great solace in her relationship to her husband and his family, and is inspired by the commitment to humanity she shares with them:

> I have learned to deal better with issues of power. I am aware that I have been the oppressor and the oppressed in different instances in my life. It is my intention to strive for equality in the classroom and to avoid imposing my agenda or power on students.

3. Analysis of Interviews and Essays

These women reflect the numerous factors and complexities involved in multicultural experience. Education, divorce, political turmoil and diplomacy along with economic fluctuations, intermarriage, business and tourism combine in infinite ways to provide the impetus for individuals to take on multicultural lives. The very fact that this study included the experiences of women and people of color meant also that the sociopolitical dimensions of identity came to light in most interviews. A woman of nobility and prestige in her home country had to struggle with visa problems and racism as an instructor at a Southern university. Another woman from a comfortable middle class family suffered the degradation of a grueling factory job as a refugee. Similarly, women in intercultural partnerships found themselves without the familiar support of customs to support their expectations of their partners.

Nonetheless, it was obvious, both from the students' essays and from the interviews with men that Adler's portrait of multicultural men was in many ways accurate. All the western men expressly articulated an aspect of the experience of marginality, especially as a sense of detachment. While women spoke of reconnecting with the religions, languages and ethnic traditions they had grown up with, the men interviewed tended, like Adler's men, to find connection and integration through the kinds of mental exercises described by Bennett (1979) and George Kelly (1955):

> the creative capacity of the living thing to represent the environment, not merely to *respond* [author's italics] to it . . . [to] do something about it if it doesn't suit him.
>
> (Kelly, 1955, p. 15)

One man, of Caribbean origin found his belonging in an Eastern religious practice, a Saudi man in Hindu poetry, a Japanese man in western philosophy. Similar to Adler's four men, the four western men interviewed had each chosen lives apart from their native cultures yet linked to some form of intercultural communication. In reviewing both the essays and the other experiences described for this study, however, significant differences began to emerge and transcripts were culled for themes common to all or most of the respondents.

There were differences in the ways marginality was described as well as in the ways individuals managed entry into new situations. The "marginality" mentioned by non-dominant respondents came more often in relation to lack of privilege within particular social contexts than to an abiding sense of "marginal" identity, per se. Similarly, while they articulately spoke of their learned abilities to shift in relation to their surroundings, most all defined themselves in terms of their genders, families, their languages and religions and, often, in relation to the expectations of different contexts. While able to transcend cultural viewpoints and adjust to cultural differences, they viewed themselves as significantly rooted in the customs and values of certain communities and as committed using their global contacts to improve those same communities. Ayse, for example, maintained her commitment to the Muslim community even while living in Canada, Hanh to Vietnamese refugees while living in California.

3.1. *Experiences with sexism, racism, prejudice and stereotyping*

> Some people patronize you, some want to protect you, some want to ignore you or ignore part of you . . . and I am aware of their attitude and say that's the way they are and that is where they are at this moment in their life.
>
> (Hahn, see Section 2.2.2.)

Bennett's work (Bennett, M. J., 1993, p. 65) suggests that this experience of not being accepted is a type of marginality which can be transcended by the development of intercultural sensitivity which, in turn, helps them "construe the experience of personal 'differentness' as a natural outgrowth of highly developed sensitivity to cultural relativity" and that:

> if there is to be a "meta-ethic" (Barnlund, 1979) that can restrain . . . cultural-value conflict and guide respectful dialogue, it must come from those whose allegiance is only to life itself.

Women, in particular, however, in spite of their commitments to intercultural communication spoke consistently of their identities in relation to contexts of being excluded or included on the basis of their race, religion, ethnicity and gender. A biracial woman wrote in her essay:

> I ponder if others see me first as a black woman and then as a person who eats, drinks, breathes, etc.

Regardless of their self-perceptions both men and women of color inevitably mentioned having had to struggle in the United States with the focus on race and ethnicity. Often having originated in cultures where they were members of the majority, and in some cases of the elite, this shift to minority status had often been unanticipated. For Susanna, for example, whose life within a diplomatic family had taught and allowed her the vantage point of the type of intermediary described by Adler and Bennett, it was a painful realization that her role as a teacher was limited by her students' assumptions that she was a Hispanic immigrant and by their prejudices associated with this stereotype.

Another example of this forced awareness came to light in interviews with three black Africans. For all three, coming to the United States was disturbing as they were unaccustomed to a culture adapted so much to whiteness. Not only did they struggle in mundane ways, e.g. finding cosmetics and hair products to fit their needs but they described the stereotyping of African-Americans in our society as more exaggerated than in their countries. Having come from post-colonial countries where blacks are dominant, two were able to keep perspective on their experiences and maintain a sense of self-esteem. For one Zairean woman who comes from nobility in her native culture and who lives and teaches in a large urban setting, the issue of maintaining self-esteem in the face of constant oppression is an abiding issue. She sees her and her husband's struggles with lawyers and employment as at least partially caused by racism. Similarly, a Kenyan woman consciously made choices to choose relationships with Africans and European-Americans before struggling with the dilemmas raised as they confronted the experiences of African-Americans in the US. A third, a South African man, who had grown up under apartheid, who had developed a sense of self-esteem in the anti-apartheid movement, had the capacity to maintain a very strong commitment to South African nationalism and still work with European Americans doing anti-oppression and literacy work in the US.

Similarly, three others of international backgrounds, who had grown up with privilege, were initially shocked by the prejudice and racism they encountered because of their lack of linguistic competence and ethnic backgrounds. Hanh still reports frustration at the attitudes of people she meets:

> I have been here 18 years and if somebody had been to Viet Nam and spoke the language they would think they knew that country very well. Americans are still WHITE AMER-ICA. Anglo-America. Americans still think of me as a foreigner. You see even though I'm a citizen and I've been here some are still very surprised that I know English, use funny words and joke in English. They say how did you do it. Eighteen years and they can't believe I know all of that?

Many of the women also spoke of having been abused, others of having been denied privileges both in their native cultures and in North America because of their gender. Their multicultural perspectives did not exempt them from the perceptions of women and people of color held by their various host cultures. Hanh reported:

> I was married to a man who was extremely traditional. Coming back from France, he was for the first 3 years the perfect French gentleman, then he became again the master of the house and wanted me to obey him.

The woman from Zaire commented on her experience as a professional in a way that was reflective of some of the other women's experiences as well:

> I had a job at the university teaching men. Women would see me as smart and send me to sit with the men and superior. So I needed to sit with the men and discuss with them. So I would discuss with them and they would tell me I'm still a woman. So I didn't have any place where I could identify myself.

Struggles with prejudice were reported again and again as women accustomed to privilege and status confronted oppressive sociopolitical realities. These realities and the experiences of marginality they caused posed a harsh contrast to the privileged men in the Adler article, whose multicultural experiences were a result of choice and education, and whose marginality was a "style of self- consciousness" (Adler, 1977, p. 26).

Ayse, having lived through many difficult experiences, stated firmly:

> I may behave differently, I may try to fit into the mold but . . . over the years I have come to know that I will not be pushed down, I will not be trampled . . . you respect who I am and I will respect you.

While this firmness of stance reflects the type of self-reflectiveness encouraged by M. J. Bennett it also reflects the constant social pressures on those with non-dominant status. It also suggests that while "mediation . . . [is] accomplished best by someone not enmeshed in any reference group" (Bennett, 1993, p. 65) we must also consider the extent to which social realities limit the choice and options of mediators and examine critically the fact that most successful international mediators are currently male.

3.2. Shifting identities according to context

> The multicultural style of identity is premised on a fluid, dynamic movement of the self, an ability to move in and out of contexts, and an ability to maintain some inner coherence through varieties of situations.
>
> > (Adler, 1976, p. 37)

Respondents, both in essays and interviews within this study, also spoke of their experiences of constructing new identities, but always within existing cultural definitions. While many spoke specifically of the influence of language proficiency on their adjustment and comfort in new cultures, there was also frequent mention of the concept of an almost chameleon-like capacity to blend in and become harmonious with different settings. Susanna describes this well:

> I think of myself not as a unified cultural being but as a communion of different cultural beings. Due to the fact that I have spent time in different cultural environments I have developed several cultural identities that diverge and converge according to the need of the moment.

Shifts in identity seemed to happen intuitively and many seemed to take this capacity for granted. Another woman, for example, involved in a bicultural marriage entitled her essay: "The phone is ringing, who will I be?", indicating the extent to which the person with whom she was about to communicate determined a temporary identity. Other women asked such questions to help them respond, as "in what setting", "give me an example of a situation". For the women in this study their concepts of identity were statements of relationship. In contrast to Adler's men who saw themselves as somewhat empowered to choose which milieus would affect them, these women saw themselves as choosing who and how to be in whatever relationship and often considered others as holding or wielding power from which they might be excluded. This adjustment was sometimes described as painful. One Anglo-American student gave her essay the title "Where can I really be me?", as she felt her marriage to a man from another culture asked to give up aspects of self which had had importance. Marhaba states fatalistically:

> I don't think people change who they are. You can try to change but I think I am still the same person . . . but I'm aware. I can never change who I am but I can change my awareness. I'm with this person now and I'm going to be careful how I handle this because I don't know how I'm going to handle it but I am aware.

A question the interviewer asked of all the interviewees was whether or where there was a place where they felt they were completely themselves. One woman flipped the response in a way that was reflective of many others, responding that she would more accurately respond to a question phrased: "With whom or where do you like best, the person who you find yourself being?" For most respondents, in fact, responses affirmed a recognition that who they were was a reflection of the situation in which they found themselves. For many, for example, it was "at home", for others it was a place where there were other interculturalists, for others it was a place or relationship which allowed them to express more fully all the parts of themselves. In some accounts there was a sense of satisfaction that they had "become a better person" in new contexts but, concomitantly, that that identity could exist only in the new context. An example of this was clear in the accounts of a Malaysian woman who had been increasingly abused by her husband and abandoned by her parents as she achieved success as a professor in Malaysia and yet was dismayed by the extent to which these same achievements were taken for granted in an American university setting.

For the multicultural women in this study, context, at least as much, if not more than any cognitive capacity for self reflection, affected their social identity, self-esteem, and experiences of marginality as well. Overall these responses reflect views of identity which are interactive with and responsive to context, in which the construction of identity is less conscious than it is intuitive, and wherein self-awareness comes after the fact as reflection, rather than as a "choice" in immediate response to a new context.

3.3. Having deep roots

Adler ends his article with a quote from Harold Taylor (1969) which states that:

> There is a new kind of man in the world, conscious of the age that is past and aware of the one now in being, aware of the radical differences between the two . . .
>
> (Taylor, 1969, p. 39)

Implicit in this statement is the "willingness to accept the lack of precedent" or as von Glasersfeld proposes, the existence of "cognitive organisms that are capable of constructing for themselves, on the basis of their own experience, a more or less reliable world" (von Glasersfeld, 1984, p. 38). Similar to Adler and Bennett these authors propose the existence of a mental, imaginative capacity to transcend reality and construct new possibilities.

While every woman interviewed was committed to some form of global transformation, they also spoke of the importance of family, relationships, and community. Mostly women of color, they saw themselves as socially marginal to dominant cultures in many instances but rather than valuing that marginality as a form of freedom or opportunity for detachment, they worked to redefine their lives, relationships, and communities to create and foster a sense of belonging. Marhaba speaks of her race:

> For a person who's black . . . it's very important for someone not to disregard it. [it's ridiculous to] say we are human beings and the other things [just] come with it.

and a Latin American woman of her gender, "I guess, at core, I am a mother, a daughter and ultimately, a woman".

All female respondents, in fact, used concepts such as "rootedness" or "belonging" to describe themselves and talked, without exception of the challenges of connecting with others and of not judging others who failed to treat them with respect. The respondents had all demonstrated competence through their professions and had worked effectively in intercultural settings. Many spoke of grounding their lives in meaningful relationships. One woman spoke at length of her ethnicity and religion as central to her life, as a focus from which she could embrace others. Another spoke of the importance of settling down, having a family and living in community as essential for her as she continued her work in intercultural settings. Ayse notes:

> As a result of all these differences and having been forced to adapt to this new culture, I have developed another cultural identity which is capable of surviving in this new environment but that has its roots in the past. This identity functions like a second personality that appears when it is necessary to adopt a culturally appropriate behavior in the new culture.

Two women who had been refugees spoke of parts of themselves which were developed in their native cultures and which they had found ways of nurturing in their new environments, largely through associating with members of their native cultures. The Zairean woman said clearly:

That's my roots, that's where I come from, that speaks to me, that is home, although I feel very much a citizen of the world.

When asked if she ever feels marginal or disconnected, Ayse notes that she doesn't think of connection abstractly as much as in terms of groups or individuals:

I can always connect with some people. I start with one or two rather than with groups.

Adler described multicultural man as "a person who is always in the process of becoming a part of and apart from a given cultural context" (Adler, 1977, p. 31). The women in this study, on the other hand, clearly strive to root themselves in aspects of their identity which give them a sense of power and possibility. For some women it was their relationships to their families that provided a "sense of home"; for many women of color it was a commitment and bond with others of their race or ethnic background; for others, it was their religion; for others, their work. Ayse remarks:

While I am aware that I am visibly different from others I have found many things in others which are the same.

3.4. Commitment to others

A strength of multicultural women is their capacity to reflect on and work with sociopolitical realities. By virtue of their life experiences the women in the study had become aware of themselves and their capacities as well as of the extent to which sociopolitical realities affect their lives. The receptivity and support of their host communities, or, alternatively, the prejudice or hostility found in different contexts and relationships shaped aspects of their identities and served to either foster or prevent growth in certain areas. To some extent each one had found an identity through teaching which allowed them to relate to others and serve as guides in the multicultural realities of their students. Having successfully negotiated the storms of cultural adjustment and language acquisition, these women had discovered a variety of ways to help others with the same challenges. While some were motivated by a certain degree of anger, others by a need for self-sufficiency, all spoke of a compelling desire and commitment to make their experiences of use to others.

3.5. An alternative image

While a clear-cut graphic design was chosen by Adler to portray the solitary concept of identity described by Adler, definitions of self of the women interviewed suggest a more organic image, perhaps a plant or tree rooted and grounded in aspects of self which connect them to others and to community. The image in Fig. 1 was created life-size by a female student depicting her identity for an intercultural communications course. Just as Adler's men claim multifaceted and evolving identities, women tend to move from their grounding in gender, ethnicity, religion and race into the multiple and dynamic circumstances which serve to further affect and shape their identities. The women interviewed in this small study spoke repeatedly in metaphors reminiscent of roots which grow deeper and deeper as allowed by the receptiveness, or "soil" of a situation. One older woman found she worked more and more to develop connections to her native culture as she grew older, realizing that the strength she gained allowed her to grow and to reach more deeply into and appreciate aspects of American culture as well.

The image of a tree to depict multicultural women's identity, whose commitments are strengthened as they deepen their connections and roots in community also suggests a contrast

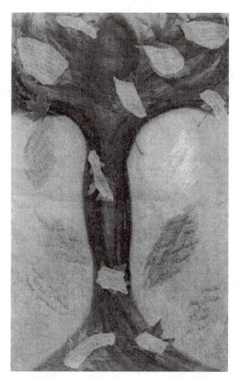

Fig. 1. An alternative view of multicultural identity.

to the marginal men of Adler's article who stand outside relationship to maintain their senses of self. Much like biological trees, the length of whose roots into the earth and height above the earth are often equivalent in, these multicultural women reflect uniquely adapted identities and commitments to global interaction. Just as trees adjust their growth to climate and season, women's ways of expressing themselves grow in relation to their experiences of relationship and community. Similarly, the intricate root and branch systems which grow in relationship to the soil and elements, reflect the dynamic complexity and individuality of organisms whose development happens in relationship to context, a concept essential to biological models of development (Maturana & Varela, 1987) as well and suggestive of the more chaotic view of communication. According to Barnlund's ecological approach to communication (1981) "the environmental dimension deserves far more attention than it receives". This is echoed in the interviews which embody identities profoundly affected by their relations to interpersonal experiences and sociopolitical realities.

4. Further Considerations

For interculturalists, maintaining a positive self concept is an essential challenge. While this small study offers some insights into the relation of sociopolitical realities to the self-definitions of multicultural persons, four issues present themselves for further consideration. "Marginality", "in-betweenness", and "uniqueness" are terms used by Adler, Bennett, and radical constructivists to highlight a definition of a highly individuated and optimal human capable of mediating effectively between cultures. "Commitment" is similarly used in reference to human unity, rather than to specific communities. These terms take on new meaning in the lives of women and people of color and are deserving of further research, as will be briefly discussed below.

4.1. Marginality

Marginality, the concept that "in each human being there obtains a core which is separable and different from everything else" and its concomitant "reflexivity; the self is aware of itself as a self" (Balagangadara, 1991) is central to the work of interculturalists (Adler, 1977; Bennett, 1993a, 1993b) and is fundamental to constructivism (Watzlawick, 1984), upon which so much of intercultural communication theory is based. This small study would suggest that men are more likely to have that sense of separateness and that that is in part a result of their dominant status in western societies.

As such, definitions of self are inextricably linked to the cultures and languages as they describe the self, and within those cultures and languages, the freedom to define oneself is dependent on relationships of power:

> Our beliefs and values are inextricably caught up in networks of power and desire, and resistance to power and desire.
>
> (Gee, 1990, p. iii)

For the women in this study, context, these "networks of power and desire", affect their social identity, self-esteem and experiences of marginality at least as much, if not more than, any cognitive capacity for self-reflection.

4.2. In-betweenness

This brief study also suggests that most multicultural people will inevitably experience minority status in the course of their lives, and will be affected, as were the women in this study, by the rocky soils of human interaction. While the work of Adler states that the experience of multiculturalism as such results in "in-between attitudes" (Dawson, 1969) or "dynamic in-betweenness" (Yoshikawa, 1987), the experiences of the respondents in this study suggest otherwise. Social identity theories (Banks, 1988; Hardiman & Jackson, 1992; Myers et al., 1991) also suggest that the final stages of identity development are instead integrative, and that the "in-betweenness" is a stage preceding the optimal, similar to that of Janet Bennett's "encapsulated marginality" (Bennett, 1993a). This suggests that the re-connection to one's social identities from a vantage point of appreciation and belonging is necessary both for self-esteem and for professional work with and beyond issues of prejudice and exclusion.

Furthermore, "empathy" (Bennett, 1979; Fantini, 1991; Kealey 1990) is often on the list of characteristics of effective interculturalists. While Bennett (1979) has suggested this "empathy" can be learned as an intuitive imaginative skill, respondents in this study suggest that women with multicultural backgrounds are most effective in communities of belonging to which they have personal connection and experience. Similarly Parker and McEvoy (1993) found that "prior international experience and the amount of time spent with host country nationals" (Parker & McEvoy, 1993, p. 374) facilitate both cultural adjustment and work effectiveness. This research highlights that true empathy and interpersonal skills rise naturally and organically from healthy relationships with one's own family and communities of origin and from a commitment to significant interaction with others.

4.3. Uniqueness

The results of this study suggest that multicultural identity as a "sense of uniqueness" can have as much to do with the contextual variations in which humans find themselves, and with the linguistic competency and strategies for appropriate interaction which they have learned, as with an unusual capacity for cognitive or emotional detachment.

An interesting variation on the experience of uniqueness was articulated in the interview with a Russian woman, who was later in life identified as "gifted", as she described her struggles as an adolescent within a restrictive educational system. As two of Adler's men might be classified as "geniuses" within our culture's definitions, and gifted in the "psychophilosophical" domain described by Adler (1977, p. 29), other research (Csikszentmihaly, Rathunde & Whalen, 1993) might consider giftedness in relationship to experience of uniqueness. The "very gifted" often interact in rarefied margins of society and typically struggle with issues of belonging. Whether this capacity for complex cognitive creativity is the same as a multicultural perspective deserves further investigation.

Furthermore, it became clear in this study that individuals develop in a variety of ways, depending on almost infinite variables, and that their ways of understanding and describing their development can vary significantly. Gender, religion, racial and ethnic backgrounds, socio-economic status and language competence all interact within specific contextual realities to configure personal and social identities. We might then expect that the definitions of self will be as varied as the cultures and subcultures whose languages describe them, and that there will be increasing variations on the experience of multiculturalism and perhaps a need for a "chaos theory" of identity. Jenkins suggested, in fact, that there is no one analysis, no final set of units, no one set of relations, no claim to reducibility, in short no unified account of anything (Jenkins, 1974, p. 787), and Barnlund proposed that:

> The study of human communication concerns the process by which meanings are formed within and among people and the conditions that determine their character and consequences.

He further urges:

> Two caveats are in order: One is that figure and ground are essential to each other: without figure there is no ground and without ground no figure is discernible.

Similarly the experiences of the people in this study would suggest that uniqueness exists only in relation to something recognized as familiar. For most people in this study their capacity to work effectively depended on their relationship to their context and host culture, and in turn that the more clearly they could define who they were in terms of social variables and context, the more clearly they were able to define and articulate universal values which they hoped to embody and promote.

4.4. Commitment to community action

Although Bennett's statement that "cultural mediation . . . be accomplished best by someone . . . not enmeshed in any reference group" (Bennett, M. J., 1993, p. 65) and Adler's (1977, p. 38) that "these 'mediating' individuals incorporate the essential characteristics of multicultural man" may be seen as an ideal; members of non-dominant groups may, nonetheless, be unable to fulfill them because of the identities ascribed to them in specific contexts. Janet Bennett's portrayal of Barack Obama effectively portrays the former characteristics, yet he is beset by conflict within his circumstances:

> European-American students complain that too much attention is paid to his race: African American students are angered that he failed to select more African-Americans for positions at the Review. Some question his motives . . . some point to his record of social responsibility and apparent commitment to community work and political affairs.

Nonetheless, respondents in this study portray another form of effective intercultural endeavor, one highly referenced to community yet holding the vision of enhanced possibilities gained from broader social experience. Nancy Adler's work (1997) researching global women leaders also suggests that women leaders often, in fact, symbolize unity and connection within their own countries while also demonstrating the capacity to work effectively internationally:

> Chamorro's ability to bring all the members of her family together for Sunday dinner each week achieved near legendary status in Nicaragua (Saint-Germain, 1993, p. 80) . . . [and] Aquino, and widow of the slain opposition leader was seen as the only person who could credibly unify the people of the Phillipines following Benigno Aquino's death.
>
> (Adler, 1997, p. 23–24)

The lives of Waangari Maatai in Kenya and Vezna Terselic in Croatia provide a similar contrast. Having started the "Green Belt Movement" in Africa, a widespread movement of women planting trees to re-engender the wildlife and lifestyle of Kenyans, Maatai has now gone on to become a global leader in environmental circles and thus, a prominent Kenyan political figure. Similarly, Terselic, who is coordinator of the Anti-War Campaign in Croatia, an organization whose purpose is the mediating of grievances incurred during the recent war, has been nominated for the Nobel Peace Prize and has gained global stature for her commitment to the peaceful resolution of global conflict. The people in this study point also to the importance of balancing "dynamic in-betweenness" (Yoshikawa, 1987) with the motivation and commitment to work with one's local communities for positive social change.

The second purpose of this study was the identification of characteristics essential to working effectively within international and multicultural communities and a deeply rooted understanding of the uniqueness and potentials of individual communities becomes immediately evident in the successful commitments of the respondents in this study. Community development theory also points inevitably to issues of appropriateness and sustainability, both logical extensions of these attributes. In concert with an appreciation for other realities, and an experienced view of the global condition, this sense of belonging and commitment might ultimately provide the type of integrative action and commitment needed in the current complex global environment.

5. Conclusion

This paper began with the articulation of the concerns voiced by students in a course on cultural identity, who claimed that the 1977 article by Peter Adler on multicultural identity did not adequately address the complexities of this experience. Similarly, the review of related literature called for deeper exploration into the factors that influence multicultural identity development. Analysis of the contents of student essays and interviews with multicultural people highlighted gender differences and the ways in which multicultural people define marginality, shift their identities, define their roots and ultimately commit to lives of service to others. Ultimately, the terms marginality, in-betweenness and uniqueness as they relate to multicultural identity are in need of further consideration. There must also be a broader investigation of the nature and value of multicultural experience and identity than that described in Adler's 1977 article, one more in line with post-modern views of chaos, relativity and social constructionism. While the Cartesian capacities for objectivity, detachment, and cognitive sophistication which he described are valuable attributes in an interculturalist, the results of this study and its brief investigation of research into non-western and multicultural identity development theories suggest that the capacity for subjectivity, connection and commitment to specific communities provide an important complement to Adler's ideas. It is hoped that this study will suggest the importance of ongoing exploration of multiculturalism and its relationship to positive social change.

References

Adler, P. (1977). Beyond cultural identity: reflections on cultural and multicultural man. In R. W. Brislin (Ed.), *Culture learning: Concepts, application and research* (pp. 24–41). Honolulu, HI: University of Hawaii Press.

Asante, M. (1987). *The Afrocentric idea.* Philadelphia, PA: Temple Press.

Balagangadara, S. N. (1991). Comparative anthropology and moral domains: an essay on selfless morality and the moral self. *Cultural Dynamics, 1,* 1.

Banks, J. (1988). *Multiethnic education.* Boston, MA: Allyn and Bacon Inc.

Barnlund, D. C. (1981). Toward an ecology of communication. In C. Wilder-Mott & J. H. Weakland (Eds.), *Rigor and imagination.* New York: Praeger.

Bateson, G. (1972). *Steps to an ecology of mind.* New York: Ballantine.

Benack, S. (1982). The coding of dimensions of epistemological thought in young men and women. *Moral Education Forum, 7,* 3–24.

Belenky, M. J., Clinchy, B. M., Goldberger, N. R., & Tarule, J. M. (1986). *Women's ways of knowing.* New York: Basic Books.

Bennett, J. (1993). Cultural marginality: identity issues in intercultural training. In R. M. Paige (Ed.), *Education for the intercultural experience.* Yarmouth, ME: Intercultural Press.

Bennett, M. J. (1979). Overcoming the golden rule: sympathy and empathy. In D. Nimmo (Ed.), *Communication yearbook 3.* Washington DC: International Communication Association.

Bennett, M. J. (1993). Towards ethnorelativism: a developmental model of intercultural sensitivity. In R. M. Paige (Ed.), *Education for the intercultural experience.* Yarmouth, ME: Intercultural Press.

Brown, P., & Levinson, S. (1978). Universals in language usage: politeness phenomena. In E. Goody (Ed.), *Questions and politeness* (pp. 56–289). London: Cambridge University Press.

Chodorow, N. (1976). *The reproduction of mothering.* Berkeley: University of California Press.

Collier, M. J., & Thomas, M. (1988). Cultural identity: an interpretive perspective. In Y. Y. Kim & W. B. Gudykunst (Eds.), *Theories in intercultural communication.* Newbury Park, CA: Sage.

Csikszentmihaly, M., Rathunde, K., & Whalen, S. (1993). *Talented teenagers: Roots of success and failure.* New York: Cambridge University Press.

Dawson, J. L. M. (1969). Attitude change and conflict. *Australian Journal of Psychology, 21,* 101–116.

Enns, C. Z. (1991). The "new" relationship models of women's identity: a review and critique for counselors. *Journal of Counseling and Development, 69* January/February.

Erikson, E. H. (1964). *Insight and responsibility.* New York: WW Norton and Co.

Fantini, A. (1991). Becoming better global citizens: the promise of intercultural competence. In *Intercultural education.*

Freire, P. (1985). *The politics of education.* New York: Bergin and Garvey.

Gee, J. (1990). *Social linguistics and literacies: Ideology in discourses.* Bristol, PA: Falmer Press.

Geertz, C. (1984). From the native's point of view. In R. Schweder & R. Levine (Eds.), *Culture theory* (pp. 123–136). Cambridge, England: Cambridge University Press.

Gergen, K. (1982). *Towards transformation in social knowledge.* New York: Springer-Verlag.

Gergen, K., & Davis, K. (1985). *The social construction of the person.* New York: Springer-Verlag.

Gilligan, C. (1982). *A different voice.* Cambridge, MA: Harvard University Press.

Giroux, H. (1983). *Theory and resistance in education: A pedagogy for the opposition.* New York: Bergin and Garvey.

Giroux, H. (1991). *Postmodernism, feminism, and cultural politics: Redrawing educational boundaries.* Albany, NY: State University of New York Press.

Hardiman, R. (1982). White identity development: a process oriented model for describing the racial consciousness of white Americans. Unpublished dissertation, University of Massachusetts, Amherst, MA.

Hardiman, R., & Jackson, B. W. (1992). Racial identity development: understanding racial dynamics in college classrooms and on campus. In M. Adams (Ed.), *Promoting diversity in college classrooms: Innovative responses for the curriculum, faculty, and institutions* New Directions for Teaching and learning, no. 52. San Francisco: Jossey Bass.

Hecht, M., Collier, M., & Ribeau, S. (1993). *African American communication: Ethnic identity and cultural interpretation.* Newbury Park, CA: Sage Publications.

Hoare, C. (1991). Psychological identity development and cultural others. *Journal of Counseling and Development, 70,* 45–53.

Hoffman, L. (1993). Exchanging voices: a collaborative approach to family therapy. London: Karnac Books.

hooks, b. (1990). *Yearning: race, gender, and cultural politics.* Boston: South End Press.

Ivey, A., Ivey, M. B., & Simek-Morgan, L. (1993). *Counseling and psychotherapy: A multicultural perspective.* Needham Heights, MA: Simon and Schuster.

Jenkins, J. (1974). Remember that old theory of memory, well, forget it? *American Psychologist*, 785–795.

Josselson, R. (1987). *Finding herself: Pathways to identity development in women*. San Francisco: Jossey-Bass.

Kakar, S. (1989). *Intimate relations*. Chicago: The University of Chicago Press.

Kakar, S. (1991). Western science, eastern minds. *The Wilson Quarterly*, 15(1), 109–116.

Katz, J. H. (1985). The sociopolitical nature of counseling. *The Counseling Psychologist*, 13(4), 615–624.

Kealey, D. J. (1990). *Cross-cultural effectiveness: A study of Canadian technical advisors overseas*. Quebec: Canadian International Development Agency.

Kegan, R. (1982). *Problem and process in human development*. Cambridge, MA: Harvard University Press.

Kim, J. (1981). *Process of Asian American identity development: A study of Japanese American women's perception of their struggle to achieve positive identities as Americans of Asian Ancestry*. Cambridge, MA: University of Massachusetts Graduate School.

Kohlberg, L. (1976). Moral stages and moralization: the cognitive-developmental approach. In T. Lickona (Ed.), *Moral development and behavior: Theory, research and social issues*. New York: Rinehart and Winston.

Leung, E. K. (1990). Early risks: transition from culturally/linguistically diverse homes to formal schooling. *Journal of Educational Issues of Language Minority Students*, Volume 7 Special issue, Summer. Boise, ID: Boise State University.

Levinson, D. (1978). *The seasons of a man's life*. New York: Knopf.

Loevinger, J. (1962). *Ego development*. San Francisco: Jossey-Bass.

Marcia, J. F. (1980). Development and validation of ego identity status. *Journal of Personality and Social Psychology, 3*.

Martinez, I. (1994). Quien soy? Who am I? Identity issues for Puerto Rican adolescents. In P. E. Salett & D. R. Koslow (Eds.), *Race, ethnicity and self*. Washington, DC: NMCI Publications.

Maturana, H. R., & Varela, F. J. (1987). *The tree of knowledge*. Boston: Shambala.

Mendenhall, M., & Oddou, G. (1985). The dimensions of expatriate acculturation: a review. *Academy of Management Review, 10*, 39–47.

Miller, J. B. (1986). *Toward a new psychology of women* (2nd ed.). Boston: Beacon.

Murray, H. A. (1938). *Explorations in personality*. New York: Oxford University Press.

Myers, L., Speight, S., Highlen, P., Cox, C., Reynolds, A., Adams, E., & Hanley, C. (1991). Identity development and worldview: toward an optimal conceptualization Special issue: Multiculturalism as a fourth force in counseling No. 1. *Journal of Counseling and Development, 70*, September/October, pp. 53–55.

Nieto, S. (1992). *Affirming diversity*. White Plains, NY: Longman.

Parker, B., & McEvoy, G. (1993). Model of intercultural adjustment. *International Journal of Intercultural Relations, 17*(3), 355–380.

Perry, W. G. (1970). *Forms of intellectual and ethical development in the college years*. New York: Holt, Rinehart and Winston.

Phinney, J. (1990). Ethnic identity in adolescents and adults: review of research. *Psychological Bulletin, 108*(3), 499–514.

Poster, M. (1989). *Critical theory and poststructuralism*. Ithaca, NY: Cornell University Press.

Pratt, D. D. (1991). Conceptions of self within China and the United States: contrasting foundations for adult education. *International Journal of Intercultural Relations, 15, 3*.

Reynolds, A., & Pope, R. (1991). The complexities of diversity: exploring multiple oppressions. *Journal of Counseling and Development, 70*.

Rogers, C. R. (1956). What it means to become a person. In C. E. Moustakas (Ed.), *The self* (pp. 195–211). New York: Harper Colophon.

Rogers, C. R. (1980). *A way of being*. Boston: Houghton Mifflin.

Root, M. (1992). *Racially mixed people in America*. Newbury Park, CA: Sage Publications Inc.

Rosaldo, M. (1982). The things we do with words: Ilongot speech acts and speech act theory in philosophy. *Language in Society, 11*.

Samovar, L., & Porter, R. (1985). *Intercultural communication: A reader* (4th ed.). Belmont, CA: Wadsworth Publishers.

Sampson, E. E. (1985). The decentralization of identity. *American Psychologist, 40*(11), 1203–1211.

Spence, J. T. (1985). Achievement American style: the rewards and costs of individualism. *American Psychologist, 40*, 1285–1295.

Schweder, R. (1991). The social construction of the person. In R. Schweder (Ed.), *Thinking through cultures*. Cambridge, MA: Harvard University Press.

Schweder, R., & Bourne, E. (1982). Does the concept of the person vary cross-culturally? In A. J. Marsella & G. White (Eds.), *Cultural concepts of mental health and therapy*. Boston: Reidel and Company.

Seidman, I. E. (1991). *Interviewing as qualitative research: a guide for research in education and social sciences*. New York: Teacher's College Press.

Tatum, B. (1992). Talking about race, learning about racism: the application of racial identity development theory in the classroom. *Harvard Educational Review, 62*(1), 1–24.

Taylor, H. (1969). Toward a world university. *Saturday Review, 24,* 52.

Tillich, P. (1966). *The future of religions.* New York: Harper & Row.

Tomm, K. (1985). Circular questioning: a multifaceted clinical tool. In *Applications of systemic family therapy.* New York: Grune and Stratton.

von Glasersfeld, E. (1984). An introduction to radical constructivism. In P. Watzlawick (Ed.), *The invented reality.* New York: WW Norton & Co.

Watzlawick, P. (1984). *The invented reality.* New York: WW Norton & Co.

Yoshikawa, M. J. (1987). The double swing model of intercultural communication between the East and the West. In D. L. Kincaid (Ed.), *Communication theory: Eastern and Western perspectives.* San Diego: Academic Press.

16

Applying a Critical Metatheoretical Approach to Intercultural Relations
The Case of U.S.–Japanese Communication

William Kelly

U.S. Americans scholars initially researched U.S.–Japanese communication in the 1970s (Condon & Saito, 1974, 1976; Barnlund, 1975). They emphasized differences in patterns of self-disclosure and in values between members of the two cultures. Since that time, the research approach to U.S.–Japanese communication has hardly changed. Intercultural scholars still focus on cultural differences between the two nations along dimensions such as individualism/collectivism (Yamaguchi, 1994).

What is striking is that intercultural researchers have largely ignored the larger political and economic context and the ways in which this context influences interpersonal communication between U.S. Americans and Japanese. They also have failed to systematically address issues of history and power. It is as if Perry's forcible opening of Japan in 1853, World War II, the U.S. Occupation of Japan, and the long-standing trade disputes had never occurred.

A new research direction is needed based on a critical metatheoretical perspective. A critical approach brings to light the ways in which both U.S. Americans and Japanese have been influenced by power dynamics related to Japan's defeat in the Second World War, its political subordination the United States, and its rise to economic superpower status. A critical approach emphasizes that relations between U.S. Americans and Japanese have never been equal due to structural factors within the world political economy. Until the influence of structural forces on U.S.–Japan communication is recognized, the applicability of intercultural communication concepts to actual communication between members of these two cultures will remain partial and limited.

Critical approaches have emphasized the importance of structural factors, power relations, and historical context, but they have tended to focus only on mass media discourse, thereby neglecting interpersonal communication across cultures (Martin & Nakayama, 1999). The value of the present article is that it attempts to compensate for such neglect by focusing on interpersonal communication between U.S. Americans and Japanese. By utilizing a critical approach, I connect communication at the interpersonal level with the larger international context.

I will first compare difference-based and critical metatheoretical approaches to intercultural communication. Second, I will present my personal experience as a case study of U.S.–Japanese communication. Third, I will analyze this personal experience to demonstrate the ability of a critical metatheoretical approach to deal with interpersonal communication across cultures. Finally, I will summarize the advantages of a critical metatheoretical approach to intercultural communication and suggest some new directions for future theorizing concerning U.S.–Japanese relations.

Comparing CD and Critical Approaches to Intercultural Communication

I will use the abbreviation "CD" to refer to the traditional social scientific approaches based on the analysis of cultural differences that have made up the mainstream of the intercultural communication field since the early 1980s. A classic statement of the difference-based approach to intercultural communication was made by Barnlund (1998). He stated the requirements for human survival in the global village with its diverse cultures in the following terms. "What seems most critical is to find ways of gaining entrance into the assumptive worlds of another culture, to identify the norms that govern face-to-face relations, and to equip people to function within a social system that is foreign but no longer incomprehensible" (p. 37). Thus the task of the interculturalist is to discover the ways in which cultures can be distinguished by studying differences in cultural meaning. There have been many studies of U.S.–Japanese communication that have almost exclusively focused on the study of cultural differences (e.g., Condon & Saito, 1974, 1976; Barnlund, 1975, 1989; Okabe, 1983; Ishii, 1985; Hall & Hall, 1987; Gudykunst, 1993).

The CD approach will be contrasted with a critical metatheoretical approach. I define a critical approach as similar to what Martin and Nakayama (1999) call a critical humanist perspective, incorporating critical theory deriving from the Frankfurt school, cultural studies, and postcolonial perspectives. The central tenet of such a critical approach is an emphasis on relations of power between different cultural groups. There is also a concomitant rejection of the fundamental premise of the CD approach that the study of cultural difference provides the key to intercultural understanding.

Critical metatheoretical approaches have only recently begun to have an impact within the field of intercultural communication, and this newer trend within the intercultural communication field has recently blossomed (Martin & Nakayama, 2000; Martin, Nakayama, & Flores, 1998; Nakayama & Martin, 1999; Gonzalez, Houston, & Chen, 2000; Orbe, 1998; Gonzalez & Tanno 1997; Tanno & Gonzalez 1998; Gonzalez & Tanno 2000). Outside the intercultural communication field, Young (1996), an Australian social theorist, has written an impressive philosophical critique of theoretical perspectives on intercultural relations from a Habermasian perspective. Another noteworthy effort has been made by Dahlen (1997), a Swedish anthropologist, who has critiqued the training aspect of the intercultural communication field for its dependence on outdated anthropological models. Nevertheless, with regard to the specific area of U.S.–Japanese interpersonal communication, few critical studies have been carried out.

I will now present CD and critical perspectives formulated in highly general terms. By presenting them in such generic terms, the ways in which CD and critical approaches deal with the various dimensions of intercultural communication can come more clearly into focus, thereby highlighting their differences. I will distinguish between a difference-based and a critical approach to intercultural communication in five areas: (1) notion of culture, (2) similarity/difference, (3) relations of power, (4) importance of history, and (5) communication competence.

Notion of culture

Two well-known theorists who have studied the influence of culture on communication are E. Hall (1959) and Hofstede (1991). E. Hall (1959) posits a cultural unconscious that influences people to communicate in certain fashions beneath their conscious awareness. For Hofstede (1991), culture is the programming of the mind that operates like computer software. These theorists share a belief that the understanding of social structural and economic influences upon culture does not make a major contribution to the theory and practice of intercultural communication.

In S. Hall's (1986) reinterpretation of Marxism, however, culture is the realm in which a contest of ideas takes place. These ideas are themselves influenced by the positioning of their proponents within the social structure. Therefore, culture cannot be understood without reference to the social context within which ideas are formulated. Such material factors such as people's class, race, and gender do not determine the content of ideas, but they do have a considerable influence upon people's thinking.

As a contested site, culture cannot simply be viewed as an arena of shared meanings and values in the manner of CD theorists (Moon, 1996; Ono, 1998). Hegemonic concepts of culture are subject to challenge by those whose voices have not been represented in the present construction of that culture. The culture that reflects the interests of more powerful groups may be resisted directly or indirectly by members of subordinated groups.

Similarity/difference

Bennett (1998) writes that "the topic of difference—understanding it, appreciating it, respecting it—is central to all practical treatments of intercultural communication" (p. 2). From his CD stance, all universalist perspectives are ways of minimizing difference. Bennett believes that those who claim that recognition of human similarity is a positive factor in promoting effective intercultural communication are guilty of trying to impose their cultural beliefs on the other. They are denying difference in order to preserve an attachment to their own cultural beliefs and values while avoiding the need to accept and appreciate other ways of life.

Young's (1996) work illustrates a critical metatheoretical perspective on similarity/difference. His aim is to provide a theoretical approach that is capable of dealing with the remnants of imperialism and colonialism. Such an approach must be capable of allowing us to celebrate differences but not at the expense of denying our common humanity. His plea is for a middle path between the universalism that was used to justify European conquest and rule over weaker nations and the relativism that often leads to separatism and ethnic conflict.

Critical anthropologists and postcolonial theorists have also argued against the tendency to emphasize cultural differences in research. They have seen the emphasis on difference as a way of "making other." In their view, this celebration of difference stems from an absolute division that has been constructed between West and non-West. As Said (1987) points, out, such a division, historically, has been used to justify the power exercised by the West over others. By viewing cultures as separate and bounded entities existing in isolation, the Orient appears as radically other. The West is constructed as masculine, democratic, progressive, dynamic, rational, and moral; the Orient as feminine, sensual, backward, and duplicitous.

Relations of power

The main premises of the CD standpoint on power and the reasons for rejecting a critical approach to power have been expressed by Bennett (1998). Bennett does not deny the existence of power differentials that have an impact on communication. Yet he believes that the examination of power relations leads into politically charged discussion that is beyond the province of the intercultural communication field. Discussions of ideological discourse should be avoided since they create much heat and little light. "When communication behavior is labeled as 'Marxist,' or 'imperialist,' or 'racist,' or 'sexist,' the human aspects of that behavior are overshadowed by the reifications of principle. Polarization usually supplants any hope of inclusivity, and further exploration of communication differences is drowned out by the political commotion" (pp. 10–11).

From the CD perspective, the research focus should be on communication difficulties between members of different cultures that are "well-meaning clashes" (Ting-Toomey, 1999). A well-meaning clash occurs when all parties in an intercultural encounter follow their own cultural script and behave in accordance with their own cultural norms, rules and values.

A critical approach to the role of power relations in communication recognizes the negative role of ideology whereby meaning is constructed and conveyed in the service of power (Thompson, 1990). Systematically asymmetrical relations of power are structures of domination within which members of less powerful groups are expected to act in accordance with particular scripts and social roles. As Young notes (1996), such a pattern of behavior is inimical to the dignity and self-respect of subordinated groups, prevents them from pursuing their own interests and needs in an unhindered fashion, and maintains social inequality and their own subordination. Under such conditions, members of dominant groups will tend to enforce social expectations that reinforce their own dominant position and power, whereas members of subordinate groups may resist them.

Critical interculturalists, therefore, do not focus only on miscommunication due to cultural differences. There are also important occasions when the structure of people's roles, tasks, and situation does not allow the basic needs of subordinated group members to be realized. In addition, the meanings that may be employed are often limited by distorted communicative frameworks and by ideological practices. When there are relationships of domination and subordination, members of dominant groups will tend to impose their reality on members of subordinated groups. As a result, members of oppressed groups who question or reject the existential claims of members of the dominant group violate the socially and politically constructed interaction norms of that speech context (Young, 1996).

Historical context

Among CD theorists, Bennett (1998) has explicitly rejected the notion that historical understanding should play a major part in intercultural communication. History should be downplayed, he believes, because it usually has little connection with current behavior. He does recognize that an understanding of history may help us to interpret present behavior that is a response to past mistreatment by another group. Nevertheless, his overall view is that a focus on historical context is a distraction from analyzing the influence of culture on face-to-face interaction in the present.

Postcolonial theorists as far back as Fanon and Memmi have pointed to the need for historical reconstruction of the colonial period in order to uncover the ambivalent and symbiotic relationship between colonizer and colonized whose effects have continued to the present time. The colonized may have identified with the colonizer, and the colonizer may have applied great violence against the colonized (Gandhi, 1998). Bhabha (1994) sees the task of the theorist as bringing back to consciousness the memories of events that the colonized person's mind could not accept. In this way, the blocked memories can be released and their influence upon present behavior can be neutralized.

There tend to be two phases of identity construction that occur once the colonized has thrown off identification with the colonizer (S. Hall, 1996). The first is when colonized peoples try to decolonize their minds by making efforts to recover a pure culture that existed before the colonial intrusion. The second phase may follow after cultural integrity has been regained. In this phase, the influence of the colonizer is admitted, and a new hybrid culture is created that faces toward the future rather than the past.

Communication competence

The CD view of communication competence is that it has three major dimensions: affective, cognitive, and behavioral (Chen & Starosta, 1996). The affective domain centers on intercultural sensitivity; the cognitive dimension includes self-awareness, cultural self-awareness, and knowledge of other cultures; and the focus of the behavioral realm is on skill development. Intercultural sensitivity is defined as acceptance of another culture, but the issue of whether members of the dominant culture have sufficient motivation to give up their power and privilege is not addressed. The CD theorist views the cognitive dimension in terms of thought patterns and social values, norms, customs, and systems, but no mention is made of the historical relations between nations and their present relations of power.

From a critical metatheoretical perspective, Young (1996) claims that traditional interculturalists fail to provide an adequate theory of context and circumstances because their treatments do not address the realities of political economy and human emotions such as pride. The communication ideal that Young proposes is based on Habermas's notion of open speech and unconstrained communication. He maintains that all communicators regardless of cultural background have some notion of communication that is free from external intervention and oriented toward what is true, what is right, and what is sincere. In the process of communicating, people can choose whether or not to follow this ideal, and he views such choices as a continuum with rationality at one pole and power/knowledge or ideology at the other. From this standpoint, communicative competence means speaking authentically, accurately, and appropriately with regard to the social relationship, as well as a willingness on the part of those in positions of power to cooperate with those who resist domination.

Personal Experience as Evidence

In this article, I will share my own personal experience as evidence to support the usefulness of a critical approach to intercultural communication. This experience involves living in Japan for nineteen years and considerable familiarity with Japanese life, including marriage to a Japanese woman and the raising of two children. I have used published accounts to add credibility to my reports, but my own experience provides the primary evidence for the value of a critical approach in understanding U.S.–Japanese intercultural communication.

Was my experience representative? Countercultural and mainstream U.S. Americans were living in Japan as well as those who were sent by their company or by the U.S. government. Despite the different backgrounds and circumstances, I found that we all tended to share certain attitudes and behavior toward Japanese people. We generally felt superior to Japanese people and played the role of a teacher, since we consciously or unconsciously understood ourselves to be members of the leading nation in the world and expected others to communicate on our terms. I am not claiming that all U.S. Americans had this type of attitude, but in my observation, a large majority of the Americans that I encountered in Japan did have such an attitude.

There are several advantages of relying on personal experience. One is that there is an active personal involvement that provides the flavor of what it felt like for a white American male to be interacting with Japanese people in Japan. Another advantage is that we have a chance to listen to a distinctive voce, that of a white American male trying to unlearn privilege. In addition, there is the close connection between experience and theorizing that Kondo (1990) addresses. It is our participation and immersion in events that enables us to create order and meaning. Living in Japan led me to perceive power as an issue for intercultural communication and to take an interest in critical approaches.

Using personal experience as data, I will argue that a critical metatheroetical perspective can be applied to the understanding of interpersonal communication across cultures. I will examine my personal experience and show how these experiences can be interpreted on the basis of a critical approach with regard to notions of culture, similarity/difference, relations of power, historical context, and communication competence. My argument is that the application of critical concepts enables us to understand my communication as a white American male with Japanese people in Japan in useful and valuable ways that a CD approach cannot match. The personal experience that I will analyze in terms of critical concepts includes the ways in which

I first benefited from privilege as a white American in Japan, the changes in outlook that I underwent while living in Japan, and the reasons for my letting go of my colonial attitude towards Japanese people.

Taking up the White Man's Burden

As an English teacher and sympathizer with Western countercultural trends, I entered a milieu of like-minded people who seemed interested in making sufficient money either to resume traveling, to accumulate savings, or to enable them to go out and enjoy themselves. Not unlike the adventurers and misfits who partially made up European colonial society, many of us did not experience comfort or success in our own country. Consequently, it was pleasant to have status, money, and popularity merely on the basis of being white. As Iyer (1991) points out, there was a comfortable groove for U.S. Americans in Japan: "being taken as an exotic, or a demigod, was one of the hardest states to abandon" (p. 190).

For Western men, the availability of Japanese women has been a big attraction. Especially when I first lived in Japan, the romantic image of the Western male was very strong. There was never a shortage of Japanese women in Tokyo who could be met at discos, parties, English classes, or through friends. Some Japanese women accepted the image that Western men were more kind and less sexist as well as more romantic than Japanese men. Western men, including myself, often took Japanese women lightly and enjoyed the psychologically secure relationship that we had with them. For example, I felt more confident and secure being with Japanese women inasmuch as their standards seemed lower. At a time of rapid gender role changes in the United States, Japanese women tended to follow traditional gender roles and were pleased to have a white partner. The ability to enjoy such status and privilege was rooted in a colonial-type relationship between the United States and Japan. In Ma's (1996) words, "If America's position as Japan's conqueror and savior helped to reinforce a general sense of awe and respect toward Westerners, then it also produced a colonial attitude among Western men . . . who believe they can easily 'lord it over' the Japanese" (pp. 107–108).

Not long after I arrived in Tokyo, I went on a television program with a large international audience and made up stories about my unusual sexual experiences in Japan and then came back the next week and did a commentary on a film about streaking in California. For that first show, I dressed in five-color Balinese pants, wore a batik shirt, and was somewhat drunk. During my first year in Tokyo, I was a movie extra, a secretary at an international health conference, lectured and taught at well-known Japanese companies on American thinking and values, and made much money teaching English at prestigious Japanese companies.

My way of life with its freedom and excitement seemed much better than that of the typical Japanese salaried workers I taught. I looked down on them and frequently told them that I did not want to settle down and live a regular life. In a condescending way, I implied that they were stuck in their routine lives, while I was not. I preferred not to recognize that it was my white privilege that allowed me to be accepted and to get jobs in foreign countries. Japanese people, for example, did not have the same opportunities to get well-paying jobs teaching the Japanese language or doing Japanese-language rewriting and editing in other countries.

As part of my exciting life, I hitchhiked all over Japan during the 1970s and early 1980s. White people could easily get rides from Japanese drivers, although Japanese people themselves generally could not, and sometimes we were brought to where we wanted to go, even if it was far from the driver's actual destination. Kerr (1996) talked about hitchhiking in the Japanese countryside in the early 1970s as a wonderful experience during which he was treated "extremely well." Japanese people showed tremendous curiosity and kindness to him, and it was an easy time for foreigners.

Discussions with other European Americans about Japan usually led to sharing of complaints about Japan or, at best, predictions that Japan was in for deep trouble due to its stubborn unwillingness to internationalize. One U.S. friend who had studied philosophy at Columbia University said that Japanese people have no morality, power always prevails in Japan, and weaker groups are mercilessly exploited. He refused to believe that the income inequality was far greater in the United States than in Japan during the 1980s.

There was a certain predictability in the interactions between white Americans and Japanese throughout the 1970s and early 1980s. Japanese were almost always expected to speak English, show interest in the United States, compliment and flatter white Americans, and do what was possible to make white Americans feel good. When white Americans said something, Japanese were not supposed to contradict it. At the same time, though, we would criticize Japanese for being so reserved and unable to express themselves.

White American arrogance was greatly in evidence at that time, a phenomenon that CD approaches cannot account for. When I taught at Mitsui & Co., one of the leading trading companies in Japan, in 1974, a student asked me to go with him to Kamakura. I replied that I had already been to Kamakura and wanted to go somewhere new. My casual dismissal of this invitation could be interpreted as unawareness of the importance of face saving in Japan, that is, in terms of cultural ignorance. But my behavior could also be interpreted as the kind of arrogance often displayed by those occupying dominant positions within a colonial-type relationship. It could be interpreted in terms of my enjoying power and privilege rather than as a failure to acknowledge cultural differences. Since I felt that I was a kind of minor star in Japan as a white American and that Japanese were interchangeable as acquaintances, I think that arrogance of power is a more accurate explanation for my behavior.

White Americans had reality-defining power in most circumstances where they came together with Japanese people. As critical theorists have noted, the form of domination that tends to prevail in today's world is the power to define reality. In the case of white Americans in Japan, we often took advantage of U.S. cultural hegemony in our attempts to impose our ways of thinking on Japanese people. It was not until the early 1980s and the sudden popularity of Japanese-style management in the West, that the idea of learning from Japan first surfaced. Before that time, it was always tacitly understood that when Japanese and Americans came together in Japan, the Americans taught and the Japanese learned. Until intercultural scholars recognize these contextual factors, they will not be able to account for the distorted patterns of communication that have had such a strong impact upon U.S.–Japanese intercultural relations.

The issue of communication competence is related to that of power. In the CD account of communication competence, neither recognition of power differences between the communicators nor a willingness to give up one's privileges is a precondition for communication competence. The idea that the politics of communication can prevent effective communication is not entertained. Since the CD approach ignores the political dimension, it creates the impression that knowledge, affect, and skills are sufficient conditions for the presence of communication competence.

My experience shows that until I admitted that I was taking advantage of my skin color, nationality, and culture, I did not seriously consider developing the knowledge of Japanese culture and language, the feeling toward Japanese people, and the communication skills that would enable me to relate to Japanese people beyond a very superficial level. Much personal development and reflection had to take place before I was willing to leave the world of English conversation and segregated foreign ghettos. A critical metatheoretical approach emphasizes the importance of the politics of communication, and in my case the political choice was whether to continue accepting the U.S–Japanese communication hierarchy. This political decision determined the very possibility of my achieving communication competence.

The Well-Worn Paths of "English Conversation"

As an English teacher in the world of "English conversation," I experienced the situation that Lummis (1977) described in his critique of that world. Over the years, the situation became less extreme, but I believe Lummis's description is accurate for the period covered before Japan's rise to economic eminence. In those days, in order to teach English in Japan, it was not necessary to be qualified as a language teacher or to speak Japanese or know anything about Japanese culture and society. It was enough to give Japanese people a chance to meet a foreigner and to be entertained. Consequently, a teacher could talk about anything during the class and preparation was hardly necessary. Our salaries were also higher than those of Japanese teachers of English who were qualified and experienced.

When teaching at Mitsubishi Corporation, the leading trading company in Japan in 1974, I remember doing some teaching for one hour and entertaining and exchanging ideas with students for the other hour of the class. Once I even arm-wrestled the ten male students in the class. It was also generally understood that English teachers would be white, even if not native speakers, and that native speakers of other colors would usually not be hired under "normal" circumstances.

In those days when I walked around Tokyo, I had experiences of being stopped by young Japanese who asked me in a fawning manner if they could practice their English. Lummis (1977) describes how Japanese learn English conversation from whites in an extremely alienating manner and then speak to white people in the same depersonalized way. "Typically 'English conversation' is characterized by an attitude of obsequiousness, banality, a peculiar flatness or monotone, and practically no hint as to the identity or personality of the speaker" (p. 21). I looked down on these speakers of English conversation as having a slave mentality and tried to avoid them.

At the first meeting of the Society for Intercultural Education, Training and Research (SIETAR) Japan that I attended in the late 1980s, I noticed that U.S. Americans who had recently arrived in Japan would discuss Japanese culture and communication while Japanese remained silent. All meetings were held in English at that time, and native speakers had a tremendous linguistic advantage that enabled them to dominate discussions at these meetings. The purpose of the organization was to promote intercultural communication, but it seemed that U.S. ethnocentrism was being promoted instead.

The English language also played a part in the way Japanese were often treated at public meetings by U.S. native speakers of English. Tsuda (1999) notes that native speakers often take advantage of their English proficiency and push non-native speakers aside during discussions by stepping up their speaking speed, using much jargon and idiomatic expressions, or making grammatically complex statements. Thus some Japanese and other non-native speakers feel inhibited when speaking English. "I have constantly observed that non-native speakers of English apologize for their inability to speak English correctly, make excuses for their poor English, and ask for the native English speaker's indulgence and forgiveness" (Trifonovitch, 1981, p. 213).

My experience of communication between U.S. Americans and Japanese points to some well-worn tracks along which conversations have tended to travel. There is already a deep groove in the world of "English conversation" that is difficult to avoid for both European American teachers and Japanese students. It is a groove that was formed as a result of unequal power relations between the two groups in which white Americans in Japan play the role of teacher, whether working as an English teacher or not, and Japanese are the students, despite the fact that the setting is Japan. A personal example of this phenomenon was telling one of my students about the advantages of living a free and adventurous life beyond social obligations and ties. My efforts went as far as trying to convince him that my way of life was better than his cramped and restrained existence as a salaried worker at a Japanese company.

In this artificial world, not only are the conversations often boring, trivial, and shallow, but white Americans never learn much about Japan or expand their identity. They do not have to go through a difficult struggle of adaptation to the various aspects of Japanese culture because the Japanese people are expected to do all the adapting. European Americans just have to "be themselves" and let Japanese help them whenever they have to deal with anything new or unusual that they are not used to.

As part of the norms of English conversation, I expected Japanese to assimilate to my culture. I also felt superior to them. Due to their culture, I believed that Japanese would never reach the goals of individual freedom, rational thinking in daily life, and speaking English like a U.S. American. Therefore, they would always remain aspiring U.S. Americans, not capable of achieving equality. During my first stay in Japan, I gave up any attempt to study Japanese and concentrated mostly on making and saving money.

Like many other Western English teachers in Japan, I scathingly criticized the Japanese educational system for the inability of Japanese people to speak English. By emphasizing only reading and writing, by forcing students to pass difficult school entrance exams in English grammar, and by allowing Japanese English teachers who could not speak English themselves to teach, the Japanese Ministry of Education ensured that Japanese people would not learn how to speak English in school. Reischauer (1988) intimated that an important reason for this deliberate policy was that the Japanese government was afraid Japanese people would lose their Japaneseness through exposure to Western people. What I failed to recognize until much later was that this fear of the Japanese government was not unfounded.

When I came to Japan, the easiest path for me to take was to enter the domain of English conversation. Consciously, I was not a cultural imperialist but it felt comfortable and reassuring to enter a world where I could make money, be looked up to, and not have to adapt to a new language and culture. This world was built upon structurally distorted communication in which the English language, U.S. culture, and white Americans were assumed to be superior within a colonial relationship. This example reveals the importance of the material as well as the symbolic realm for the understanding of culture. It was the material conditions of white U.S. power and privilege that led me to assume a stance of superiority in relation to the Japanese people I encountered. The communication grooves that I unthinkingly entered when I began living in Japan were the outcome of a colonial relationship between the United States and Japan.

Role Models and Catalysts

A U.S. American I met, whose behavior contrasted in many ways with those of the other whites that I knew, really opened my eyes. He did not teach English and had little money, his friends were mostly Japanese intellectuals and artists, and he spoke almost perfect Japanese while acting in a manner that was nearly indistinguishable from that of most Japanese people.

I learned about another side of Japanese life from him as I heard about Japanese people who had self-respect and communicated with foreign people on their own terms in Japanese about things that mattered. These Japanese had no desire to imitate white Americans and to learn English because it was fashionable. His knowledge and understanding of Japanese society and culture seemed enviable, and through him I came to know what more equal and meaningful communication with Japanese was like, what it would require of me, and what the rewards might be.

A critical metatheoretical analysis of the behavior of the Japanese people with whom my American friend associated, would emphasize that they were resisting the unequal world of English conversation by refusing to enter it. They were also contesting the third culture that had been created by U.S. Americans and Japanese during and after the U.S. Occupation of Japan. By using the Japanese language and style of communication, these Japanese people were rejecting the role of student and setting up new norms for relations between white Americans and Japanese.

This example also illustrates the contested nature of the relationship between U.S. and Japanese. In creating a third culture, U.S. Americans and Japanese can choose to relate largely on U.S. terms, on Japanese terms in opposition to the prevailing norms, or create their own hybridized third culture. Japanese people who resist U.S. cultural hegemony may contest English-language dominance and Western communication norms. Their desire is to overcome the legacy of a Japanese colonial mentality. On the other hand, Western people who are anti-colonial may also contest these same norms when interacting with Japanese.

When I left Japan for the first time, I exited through Okinawa. There I met a man from western Japan with whom I went around the island for a few days. Even though I could only speak a little Japanese, and he could speak no English, we somehow communicated in a very natural and warm way. I appreciated so much that I was not treated as an English speaker and felt free of all stereotyped roles. His humanity deeply impressed me in a way that I could not easily explain. Although I did not keep in contact with him, I knew that if I returned to Japan, I would learn the Japanese language and would try to meet more people like him. Through meeting this person, I began to understand at a deep level that Japanese also had a desire for self-expression, for personal integrity, for equal relations with others. Eventually, I was able to reach a level of understanding that accepted both the common humanity of U.S. Americans and Japanese and our differences in cultural background.

I came to realize that my attempt to teach Japanese people and carry the white man's burden enmeshed me in contradictions. I looked down on Japanese because they imitated the United States, yet I taught them to become more like white Americans and received gratification through their acknowledgement of my cultural superiority in the world of English conversation. I felt negatively about Japanese people because I maintained a belief in their difference, yet I was holding out to them the promise of erasing that difference by teaching them English.

As long as I believed in a racial/cultural hierarchy, I could not accept Japanese people's humanity. And it was by accepting their humanity that I also accepted their uniqueness and allowed them to choose their own way of life. Thus both similarity and difference need to be recognized (Hirai, 1987), and as critical theorists have pointed out, an emphasis on difference alone can lead to greater objectification of the Other (Dahlen, 1997).

On Being a Racial Minority in Japan: Lessons from History

The other area of experience which greatly affected my perception of Japan and Japanese people was that of racial discrimination. In the early 1970s, I lived in a block of apartments in Tokyo where only foreigners lived. After I married a Japanese woman, I thought I would be able to live anywhere, but that was not always the case. There was a house my wife really wanted to rent, but the landlady said that no foreigners were allowed. My wife got the real estate person to intercede and finally the landlady relented on condition that I prove that I was not black by showing my face at the real estate office.

Later, in the early 1990s, I tried to help U.S. friends who could not speak Japanese to rent an apartment in Tokyo. One agent of a small real estate went into a panic when I entered. She said that no Japanese would rent to a foreigner in that area. The larger real estate agents were helpful, but they had to mention that a foreigner wanted to rent whenever they called the owner by phone. The refusal rate for whites was about 50% in the areas of Tokyo that I visited, and landlords and landladies asked no questions about where the person worked, whether the person could speak Japanese, had a guarantor, or had been in Japan long enough to understand Japanese customs.

For whites, not to mention people of darker skin, marrying a Japanese could cause huge family problems. Moreover, foreigners could not get loans, enter certain establishments, or have the same jobs as Japanese. In these cases, appeals could not be made since there were few laws that could deter racial discrimination, and it was customary for such discrimination to exist.

For many white Americans, racial discrimination is a new and very unwelcome experience that leads them to complain bitterly about Japan and the Japanese. But such conditions are not like racial discrimination in the United States where the darker "races" are treated as inferior in most respects. In Japan, whites are treated better than Japanese as long as they stay in their circumscribed area and remain honored guests. The consequence of this type of treatment is that a white cannot forget his or her difference. I had many experiences where I would speak fluent Japanese and the person I was speaking to would reply in broken English. The message I received in those situations was that it did not matter how long I lived in Japan—I would always be treated as a foreigner.

How can this situation be explained? Does my experience show that Japanese are typically racist like most people in the world, including U.S. Americans? Ivan Hall (1998), who has lived in Japan over thirty years, views the Japanese concept of internationalization as openness to foreign things but not to foreign people. "Japan's concept of 'internationalization' as a controlled ingestion of foreign civilization while keeping foreigners themselves at bay, rests on a perception of racial and cultural homogeneity as something that is both dynamically creative and easily destroyed" (p. 175). He goes on to say that "the Japanese simply do not want non-Japanese physically present among them for any length of time, embedded as individuals in the working institutions of their society. As short-term feted guests or curiosities, yes; but not as fixed human furniture" (p. 178).

My own explanation of Japanese discrimination was similar to Hall's during my early years in Japan. I felt the same outrage at Japanese insularity and the same frustration about being kept at arms length by many Japanese. But reading about Japanese history really helped me to see racial discrimination against white people with new eyes. No longer could I simply agree with the statement that Japanese are the world's most racist people put forward by Crichton (1992) in *Rising Sun*.

The history of postwar U.S.–Japanese relations made it apparent to me that Japanese racial discrimination against whites has often been a defensive measure to keep members of a powerful nation within well-defined spheres. The goal has been to maintain a private area for Japanese people where the overbearing Western presence and gaze were absent and where Japanese could be "themselves." Dealing with Western people on Western terms within relations of unequal power has been a tiring and strenuous experience for many Japanese people, and there has been a desire to make certain areas of Japanese life off-limits to Westerners. Although racism is also involved, it is hardly of a simple and unambiguous type. It is far too simple to dismiss people who have experienced a series of wrenching identity crises lasting through nearly a century and a half of contact with the West as mere racists.

My reading of hooks (1995) on black separatist thought confirmed my early recognition that an oppressed group needs to have a space of its own. The Japanese experience in communicating with white Americans resembles what blacks experience when communicating with whites in the United States. African Americans are expected to communicate like European Americans and have to endure a lack of respect and sensitivity on the part of whites. Similarly, Japanese are often stereotyped by Westerners as little men who are ineffective and inconsequential or else as samurais in suits who are bent on economic conquest of the world (Littlewood, 1996). Thus Japanese who have to frequently deal with Western people need the same kind of respite and space of their own as black Americans, and that is one reason why white people are sometimes excluded.

The ways in which the United States has treated Japan since Japan first became its economic competitor at the end of the nineteenth century also made a deep impression on me. I read about the Yellow Peril threat that was spread after the Japanese victory over Russia in 1904, the segregation of East Asian pupils in San Francisco in 1906, the refusal of the Allied powers to enact the racial equality clause at the Versailles Peace Conference after World War I, and the exclusion of Japanese and Chinese immigrants from entering the United States in 1924 which Nitobe, Japan's most famous internationalist, described as a slap on the cheek from a best friend that occurred suddenly and without provocation (Iriye, 1972; Schodt, 1994).

My study of Japanese history helped me to fathom why Japanese had a pronounced complex toward whites and behaved in such a stilted manner toward them. The Western intrusion into Japan and the other areas of Asia, in Van der Post's (1977) view, had produced intolerable frustration due to Western people's arrogant belief in their own superiority and their forcible transformation of Asian ways of life. The frustration that Asian peoples experienced was the result of not being able to remain "their own special selves." In communicating with Western people, the various Asian peoples were required to step out of themselves and become someone other to themselves. Van der Post (1977) wrote that "it was almost as if the peoples of Asia had only to come into the presence of a European to be hypnotized out of being themselves, and forced to live a kind of tranced life in his presence that was not their own" (p. 36).

Later I realized that the U.S. anger toward Japan at the time of Japan's economic rise and the ensuing Japanese resentment against the United States was a partial reenactment of a tragic drama that had already been staged during World War II. I concluded that many U.S. Americans were being high-handed and arrogant in their criticisms of Japan in the late 1980s, just as they had been since the time of Perry's intrusion into Japan in 1853. When the United States heavily criticized Japan for its unfair trade and refusal to adopt laissez-faire capitalism, I thought that a strange reversal was taking place. Japanese people who had suffered a severe identity crisis due to Western intrusion were now being blamed for trying to preserve their present way of life and their agency.

Instead of complaining about Japanese racism, I began to focus on the long history of white racism against Japanese people and the various ways that such racism was resurfacing in a particularly severe manner due to Japan's increasing economic strength in the 1980s. I also needed to recognize the colonial context of U.S.–Japanese relations since the middle of the nineteenth century. The result of the "opening" of Japan through Perry's gunboat diplomacy was that "Japanese experienced feelings of helplessness, and it left a psychologically critical and traumatic wound upon the Japanese psyche" (Tsuda, 1993, p. 73). Through this understanding of Japan's predicament, I was able to resist the often intense pressure from U.S. American people and media to view Japan negatively in the late 1980s and early 1990s.

The value of a critical understanding of history was that I recognized that Japanese reluctance to allow Western people a firm footing in Japan has been largely a defensive measure for protecting Japanese cultural space. It can be traced to the historical experience of Western attempts to impose their values on Japan in the name of the white man's burden, Christianity, and civilization. Viewed in this manner, the Japanese tendency to adopt an exclusive identity is part of the historical process of moving from a colonized identity to one based on the recovery of a cultural heritage that had existed before the Western intrusion. Therefore, I cannot agree with CD theorists who believe that historical concerns distance one from present issues. Rather, historical consciousness can make the present comprehensible in all its complexity for the first time.

A Power Shift in U.S.–Japanese Relations

My efforts to communicate with Japanese people in a truly respectful manner were assisted by the diminishing of the unequal power relations between the United States and Japan. I noticed that by the 1990s, there were more Japanese with experience of the West that were no longer so positive about Westerners, and especially Americans. They expected white people to learn the Japanese language and communicate in a more Japanese way. In the intercultural communication field, too, during the 1990s, one Japanese pioneer said that there was no connection between English-language teaching and the teaching of intercultural communication. Another well-known interculturalist made a video for studying intercultural communication in the Japanese language, implying that Japanese, not English, should be the bridge language in Japan.

At this time, it seemed that U.S. whites, at least in Tokyo, did not stand out as much as before and they could blend in more easily with Japanese people. There had been a large increase in the number of whites living in Tokyo over the years, many Japanese had gone overseas to work or study, and there was less of an inferiority complex among Japanese towards white Americans. The result is that European Americans have been very gradually losing their place of privilege. And as a beneficial side-effect of this process, they find it a little easier to enter the inside world of Japanese people.

A critical approach is valuable for understanding this gradual process of change in Japanese communication behavior toward white Americans, because it points to the effect of power on hierarchical relations of communication. Power does not determine communication patterns in any simple causal sense, but it does have a major impact on the direction that communication takes within intercultural relations. Although U.S.–Japanese communication is still affected in numerous ways by the legacy of the U.S. Occupation of Japan, Japan's economic power has given Japanese people a new pride that has lessened their inferiority feelings toward white Americans. They are less willing to automatically defer to white Americans.

Former Prime Minister Hosokawa's open disagreement with President Clinton on trade issues and his refusal to accede to U.S. wishes in 1994 was a highly symbolic event in the bilateral relationship. It signaled the growth of Japanese pride, a large step toward an independent Japanese foreign policy, and an important move toward equal relations between Japanese and U.S. Americans. It was also an act of resistance, in the same manner as the refusals of Japanese interculturalists to automatically give the English language priority over Japanese in intercultural relations taking place in Japan.

Conclusion: Intercultural Communication in a Postcolonial World

My analysis of my personal experience in Japan indicates the many ways in which a critical approach illuminates important dimensions of interpersonal relations across cultures. Through a critical metatheoretical perspective, we come to understand that U.S.–Japanese communication has been affected by material factors and that its third-culture communication has been contested. This third culture or in-between space cannot be viewed in an abstract manner, as if the larger context of preponderant U.S. military power and cultural hegemony has had no impact on U.S.–Japanese communication.

There is also a need to emphasize both the similarities and differences between U.S. Americans and Japanese, since a single-minded focus on difference may obscure the humanity of members of the other cultural group. In my case, I had to recognize the humanity of Japanese people before I was able to progress toward accepting them as equals. The CD approach may lead to an overemphasis on difference that reinforces the tendency of members of dominant cultures to view members of less powerful cultures as opposite and inferior to themselves.

A critical metatheoretical approach sheds light on the world of English conversation by focusing on power relations and structural factors that lead to patterns of distorted communication. Teachers of English define reality for their Japanese students in an institutional setting according to whose norms white people are superior. The result is that Japanese are taught to acknowledge the superiority of U.S. culture and its communication patterns in comparison to their own cultural and communication norms.

Another value of such a critical approach is that it enables us to understand the ways in which the past has influenced the present and how identity has developed over time. My study of the history of relations between Japan and the West played a large role in my letting go of colonial attitudes toward Japanese people.

In addition, I have described the advantages of a critical metatheoretical approach for communication competence. For me, communication competence defined in CD terms was not even conceivable until I decided to give up my white privilege and to make the initial efforts to study the Japanese language, learn about Japanese culture and communication, and begin to communicate on Japanese terms as well as those of my own culture.

There are many connections that can be made between my analysis of U.S.–Japanese communication based on a critical metatheoretical approach and the concerns of specific critical approaches such as those of postcolonial theory and feminism. Since my personal experience is taken from white American–Japanese encounters, it may seem that this setting is not connected with colonial politics. In the examination of my experience, however, I have shown that the context was, and to a lesser degree still is, a colonial-type setting. Although Japan lost its political self-determination for only seven years from 1945 to 1951, it has nevertheless experienced U.S. cultural hegemony and a considerable degree of political subordination throughout the entire postwar period, only moving toward a more independent foreign policy in recent years. This asymmetry of power in the international sphere has been carried over into interpersonal communication between European Americans and Japanese.

The U.S.–Japanese relationship has been a postcolonial one of a special type. Japan's economic strength makes this relationship more equal than any other relationship between the United States and nonwhite nations. A more equal relationship between nations makes it easier for less distorted communication between members of the two nations to occur. Yet this is also an unstable situation because white Americans whose dominance is endangered may react with outrage at the prospect of more equal communication and take steps to defend their privilege. Such a state of affairs existed in the late 1980s and early 1990s.

Equal relations between white Americans and Japanese is an ideal case that the CD approach is better equipped to deal with, since present power relations would not play a role in communication. However, existing relations between the United States and Japan are still unequal, and the shortcomings of the CD approach become apparent under these circumstances. Unlike the CD approach, a critical metatheoretical perspective directs our attention to the stance of the members of the dominant culture within the unequal relationship. A focus on the standpoint of dominant white Americans enables us to focus on the main reason for communication problems within the U.S.–Japanese relationship: the asymmetrical distribution of power and the communication behavior of white Americans that reproduces the present structure. Japanese complicity may also contribute to the reproduction of the unequal relationship, but the onus is on the members of the dominant group to make the first step toward dissolving unequal relations at both structural and individual levels.

In shifting our focus from cultural differences to the attitudes and behavior of white Americans, we move into the terrain of research on whiteness. So far, this research has mostly examined the power and privilege of members of the dominant white group in the United States (Nakayama & Krizek, 1995; Fine et al., 1997; Lipsitz, 1998). An exception to this research trend is Shome (1999) who has written on the power and privilege of whiteness within India. I believe that similar examinations of white power and privilege in Japan are warranted. Such research would complement intercultural research on cultural differences and provide a sense of the larger context that has tended to be lacking until now in the intercultural communication field.

The experiences that I have presented can also be analyzed from a feminist point of view, and feminist postcolonial theoretical analysis has already appeared within the communication discipline (Hedge, 1998). In the case of U.S.–Japanese relations, the "Madame Butterfly" image analyzed by Ma (1996) is a fruitful place to pursue such a feminist inquiry, and Kondo (1997) has exposed the connection between gender, Orientalism, and essentialism in the construction and maintenance of this image. The critical metatheoretical approach that I have outlined also can be supplemented by postmodernist approaches (Mumby, 1997; Chen, 1996; Spivak, 1999) that retain a critical dimension and focus on issues of power and the larger historical and political context.

In the early 21st century, non-Western peoples are proceeding with their efforts to mentally decolonize. With the increasing power of non-Western nations, particularly those in East Asia, the key issue is whether U.S. Americans and other Western people are willing to communicate in a way that facilitates relations of equality. For intercultural communication scholars, it is necessary to craft an approach that will aid in our understanding of the present world context. When dealing with U.S.–Japan communication, the prevailing emphasis on cultural differences limits the ability of practitioners to cope with issues of history, power, and privilege. My presentation of a critical metatheoretical approach to U.S.–Japanese communication based on personal experience is a contribution toward overcoming such limits. It also provides an example of how context affects interpersonal communication that can be of value when studying relations between members of any nations whose power is asymmetrical.

References

Barnlund, D. C. (1975). *The public and private self in Japan and the United States.* Tokyo: Simul Press.

Barnlund, D. C. (1989). *Communication styles of Japanese and Americans: Images and realities.* Belmont, CA: Wadsworth.

Barnlund, D. C. (1998). Communication in a global village. In M. J. Bennett (Ed.), *Basic concepts of intercultural communication: Selected readings* (pp. 35–51). Yarmouth, ME: Intercultural Press.

Bennett, M. J. (1998). Intercultural communication: A current perspective. In M. J. Bennett (Ed.), *Basic concepts of intercultural communication: Selected readings* (pp. 1–34). Yarmouth, ME: Intercultural Press.

Bhabha, H. (1994). *The location of culture.* London: Routledge.

Chen, G. M., & Starosta, W. J. (1996). Intercultural communication competence: A synthesis. *Communication Yearbook, 19,* 353–384.

Chen, K. H. (1996). Post-marxism: Between/beyond critical postmodernism and cultural studies. In D. Morley & K. H. Chen (Eds.), *Stuart Hall: Critical dialogues in cultural studies* (pp. 309–325). London: Routledge.

Condon, J. C., & Saito, M. (Eds.). (1974). *Intercultural encounters with Japan.* Tokyo: Simul Press.

Condon, J. C., & Saito, M. (Eds.). (1976). *Communication across cultures for what?* Tokyo: Simul Press.

Crichton, M. (1992). *Rising sun.* New York: Knopf.

Dahlen, T. (1997). *Among the interculturalists: An emergent profession and its packaging of knowledge.* Stockholm, Sweden: Stockholm University, Department of Social Anthropology.

Fine, M., Weis, L., Powell, L. C., & Wong, L. M. (Eds.). (1997). *Off white: Readings on race, power, and society.* New York: Routledge.

Gandhi, L. (1998). *Postcolonial theory: A critical introduction.* New York: Columbia University Press.

Gonzalez, A., Houston, M., & Chen, V. (Eds.). (2000). *Our voices: Essays in culture, ethnicity, and communication* (3rd ed.). Los Angeles, CA: Roxbury.

Gonzalez, A., & Tanno, D. V. (Eds.). (1997). *Politics, communication, and culture.* Thousand Oaks, CA: Sage.

Gonzalez, A., & Tanno, D. V. (Eds.). (2000). *Rhetoric in intercultural contexts.* Thousand Oaks, CA: Sage.

Gudykunst, W. (Ed.). (1993). *Communication in Japan and the United States.* Albany, NY: State University of New York Press.

Hall, E. T. (1959). *The silent language.* New York: Doubleday.

Hall, E. T., & Hall, M. R. (1987). *Hidden differences: Doing business with the Japanese.* New York: Doubleday.

Hall, I. (1998). *Cartels of the mind: Japan's intellectual closed shop.* New York: Norton.

Hall, S. (1986). The problem of ideology: Marxism without guarantees. In D. Morley & K. H. Chen (Eds.), *Stuart Hall: Critical dialogues in cultural studies* (pp. 25–46). London: Routledge.

Hedge, R. (1998). A view from elsewhere: Locating difference and the politics of representation from a transnational feminist perspective. *Communication Theory, 8,* 271–297.

Hirai, K. (1987). Conceptualizing a similarity-oriented framework for intercultural communication study. *Journal of the College of Arts and Sciences, Showa University, 18*, 1–19.

Hofstede, G. (1991). *Cultures and organizations.* London: McGraw-Hill.

hooks, b. (1995). *Killing rage: Ending racism.* New York: Henry Holt.

Iriye, A. (1972). *Pacific estrangement: Japanese and American expansion, 1897–1911.* Cambridge, MA: Harvard University Press.

Ishii, S. (1985). Thought patterns as modes of rhetoric: The United States and Japan. In L. A. Samovar & R. E. Porter (Eds.), *Intercultural communication: A reader* (4th ed., pp. 97–102). Belmont, CA: Wadsworth.

Iyer, P. (1991). *The lady and the monk.* New York: Knopf.

Kerr, A. (1996). *Lost Japan.* Oakland, CA: Lonely Planet.

Kondo, D. (1990). *Crafting selves: Power, gender, and discourses in a Japanese workplace.* Chicago, IL: University of Chicago Press.

Kondo, D. (1997). *About face: Performing race in fashion and theater.* New York: Routledge.

Lipsitz, G. (1998). *The possessive investment in whiteness: How white people profit from identity politics.* Philadelphia, PA: Temple University Press.

Littlewood, I. (1996). *The idea of Japan: Western images, Western myths.* London: Secker & Warburg.

Lummis, C. D. (1977). English conversation as ideology. In Y. Kurokawa (Ed.), *Essays on language* (pp. 1–26). Tokyo: Kirihara Shoten.

Ma, K. (1996). *The modern Madame Butterfly: Fantasy and reality in Japanese cross-cultural relationships.* Tokyo: Tuttle.

Martin, J. N., & Nakayama, T. K. (1999). Thinking dialectically about culture and communication. *Communication Theory, 9*, 1–25.

Martin, J. N., & Nakayama, T. K. (Eds.). (2000). *Intercultural communication in contexts* (2nd ed.). Mountain View, CA: Mayfield.

Martin, J. N., Nakayama, T. K., & Flores, L. A. (Eds.). (1998). *Readings in cultural contexts.* Mountain View, CA: Mayfield.

Moon, D. (1997). Concepts of "culture": Implications for intercultural communication research. *Communication Quarterly, 44*, 70–84.

Mumby, D. (1997). Modernism, postmodernism, and communication studies. *Communication Theory, 7*, 1–28.

Nakayama, T. K., & Martin, J. N. (Eds.). (1999). *Whiteness: The communication of social identity.* Thousand Oaks, CA: Sage.

Nakayama, T. K., & Krizek, R. L. (1995). Whiteness: A strategic rhetoric. *Quarterly Journal of Speech, 81*, 291–309.

Ono, K. (1998). Problematizing "nation" in intercultural communication research. In D. V. Tanno & A. Gonzalez (Eds.), *Communication and identity across cultures* (pp. 193–202). Thousand Oaks, CA: Sage.

Okabe, R. (1983). Cultural assumptions of East and West: Japan and the United States. In W. B. Gudykunst (Ed.), *Intercultural communication theory: Current perspectives* (pp. 21–44). Thousand Oaks, CA: Sage.

Orbe, M. (1998). *Constructing co-cultural theory: An explication of culture, power, and communication.* Thousand Oaks, CA: Sage.

Reischauer, E. O. (1988). *The Japanese today: Change and continuity.* Cambridge, MA: Harvard University Press.

Said, E. (1978). *Orientalism.* New York: Pantheon.

Schodt, F. (1994). *American and the four Japans.* Berkeley, CA: Stone Bridge Press.

Shome, R. (1999). Whiteness and the politics of location: Postcolonial reflections. In T. K. Nakayama & J. N. Martin (Eds.), *Whiteness: The communication of social identity* (pp. 107–128). Thousand Oaks, CA: Sage.

Spivak, G. (1990). *The post-colonial critic: Interviews, strategies, dialogues.* New York: Routledge.

Spivak, G. (1999). *The critique of postcolonial reason.* Cambridge, MA: Harvard University Press.

Tanno, D. V., & Gonzalez, A. (Eds.). (1998). *Communication and identity across cultures.* Thousand Oaks, CA: Sage.

Thompson, J. (1990). *Ideology and modern culture.* Stanford, CA: Stanford University Press.

Ting-Toomey, S. (1999). *Communicating across cultures.* New York: Guilford Press.

Trifonovitch, G. (1981). English as an international language: An attitudinal approach. In L. E. Smith (Ed.), *English for cross-cultural communication* (pp. 211–215). London: Macmillan.

Tsuda, Y. (1993). Communication in English: Is it anti-cultural? *Journal of Development Communication, 4*, 69–78.

Tsuda, Y. (1999). The hegemony of English and strategies for linguistic pluralism: Proposing the Ecology of Language Paradigm. In M. Tehranian (Ed.), *Worlds apart: Human security and global governance* (pp. 153–167). London: I. B. Tauris.

Van der Post, L. (1977). *The night of the new moon.* Harmondsworth, UK: Penguin.

Yamaguchi, S. (1994). Collectivism among the Japanese: A perspective from the self. In U. Kim et al. (Eds.), *Individualism and collectivism: Theory, method, and applications* (pp. 175–188). Thousand Oaks, CA: Sage.

Young, R. E. (1996). *Intercultural communication: Pragmatics, genealogy, deconstruction.* Clevedon, UK: Multilingual Matters.

Part VI
Ethical Considerations in Intercultural Communication

17

Theoretical Perspectives on Islam and Communication

Hamid Mowlana

Introduction

A number of studies on international communication over the last several decades reveal two essential characteristics. One is the ethnocentric orientation of mass communication systems of the highly developed and industrialized nations, and the second is the "asymmetric" circulation of information in the world. These two characteristics dominate the world mass media system and indeed are responsible for uneven treatment of events, imbalances in news and information, and also the unequal distribution of power in the world system.

It is precisely here that a need for professional code of ethics among Muslim journalists around the world seems imperative and their creation of a network of professional world associations both timely and inevitable. The fact that until now there have been almost no such associations at the international level illustrates the low priority given to information and news among and between the Islamic countries. It also indicates a century-long inattention to the lack of growth in media organizations which is, in part, a consequence of decades of repression, colonialism, and government control.

From the Islamic Revolution in Iran to the occupation of Afghanistan by the former Soviet Union, from the Persian Gulf War to the American invasion of Iraq, the last two decades have witnessed profound and worldwide revolutionary movements of an Islamic nature as well as systematic and continuous conflicts which have embraced Muslim lands. The developments in the Islamic world not only have been reported during this period with a good deal of bias, distortion, and ethnocentricism by non-Muslim media but also the great portion of what has been reported has been provided mainly by the Western media and journalists.

Research shows that 99 percent of world events do not come to the attention of readers simply because they are eliminated and considered as unimportant or irrelevant by the media. The Islamic world, in particular, has been on the receiving end of a good share of this modus operandi. For example, consider six levels of the so called common selections of news in mass communication: (1) sources of production of information and news; (2) journalists and correspondents; (3) central offices of news agencies; (4) local newspapers and editorial offices; (5) mass media editors, and finally (6) recipients, meaning readers or viewers. It has been reported empirically that 98 percent of news and information is eliminated in the second through the sixth levels with 92 percent elimination from the second through the fifth, not to mention the elimination resulting from the process of selectivity on the part of readers and viewers. This Darwinian law of selectivity, once translated and applied to events and developments in the Islamic world (which constitutes one-fourth of the world's population) can indeed have enormous impact on individual and collective perceptions about Islam and its followers. The crucial question is not how strongly the control is exercised but instead by whom, under what conditions, and for what purpose.

A Call for a World Organization of Muslim Journalists

A cursory look at the list of existing media and journalist associations around the world quickly shows how the media are organized and mobilized on the basis of nationality, regionalism, ethnicity, and even religious premises and are among the most active nongovernmental organizations around the world. Yet, remarkably, today, there are no professional associations of Islamic journalists which can set professional and ethical criteria for news reporting, protect the rights of individual Muslim journalists, and promote education and training of young men and women who represent a major source of human resources for Islamic culture and civilization.

Why is it important for Islamic journalists to have a network of associations binding their professional mission? The answer lies in the very core of Islamic political culture for Islam is not only a religion but also a total way of life for millions of people around the world. Unlike other major cultural systems, Islam transcends geographical as well as racial and ethnic boundaries and strives for universality of human kind. In short, the socio-cultural elements inherent in and among the Islamic community, *ummah*, provide a common ground and outline a necessity for the type of news reporting that is vital to understanding events in the world community. Such a network of Muslim journalist and media associations and professional organizations also can play an important role as vanguards and promoters of professional aims within the existing systems of international organizations. A network of professional associations, thus, not only can enhance the exchange of information among and between various geographical areas known as the Islamic world but also can stimulate the ongoing mobilization of journalists and their common interests.

What should be the tenets underlying the formation and the mobilization of such networks of associations? It must be recalled that news values in the Islamic world differ considerably from the general news values in the non-Islamic world and, more specifically, the West. For example, take the concept of so called "hard news" common in the Western media with its "five Ws" syndrome of "what, when, where, why, and who" which is promoted as universal. The real problem is that the recipient of such five Ws news never is allowed to conceive of news as a whole but only in fragments because the structure of the whole is at odds with what is considered "hard facts." The priorities given to news values in the West, such as human interests, proximity, novelty, consequence, and prominence, are totally different from those valued in Islamic contexts.

For example, the notion of proximity in the Western media primarily is a geographical as well as spatial concept. To apply this concept, in its orthodox sense, to the Islamic world would eliminate news coming from distant places such as Indonesia, China, Africa, or Latin America when the media and its audiences are located somewhere in the United States or the Middle East. Proximity in an Islamic context is neither geographical nor spatial but rather cultural—that is to say, events of the Islamic community of *ummah* are and must be relevant to the entire Muslim world regardless of nationalities and countries. The factors of human interest or prominence are by themselves not adequate justification for reporting of news in the Islamic context. News and information for the *ummah* are social commodities and not cultural industries.

One of the disadvantages arising from Western reporting of the contemporary Islamic world is that news of both cooperative and conflict-filled natures are treated not in an Islamic context but in the generic journalistic culture over decades in Europe and the United States. Thus, a major result is incomplete presentation, if not actual and chronic misrepresentation, of events in the Islamic world as they occur. This reductive refinement of the concept of information and news has been a gradual process extending over several decades and, indeed, has been responsible for a good deal of misperceptions and even bias. This, in itself, has provided a kind of journalistic "fundamentalism," which claims universalism, under which such issues as "Islamic fundamentalism" are unfairly lumped.

In a changing and volatile world—where values and ideas are constantly in transition and where internal and external events of nations are becoming more unpredictable leading to profound political, economic, and cultural transformation—Muslim journalists around the globe must define their own informational and cultural territories as well as their own professional and ethical standards. One of the weaknesses in the world of Islamic media is the fact that there is a low level of participation of either individuals or associations in regional and international gatherings and conferences. Correspondingly, the power of the West—that is to say, the European and American journalists and media—resides in the fact that they are systematic and constant participants in a variety of international conferences, symposia, seminars, as well as international and regional organizations. It is through this process of participation as well as professional acculturation that individuals can hope to contribute to the process of decision making as well as learn how to influence the agenda of international organizations.

This is well illustrated by an example from the Persian Gulf War of 1990–91. During this international political crises, journalists and correspondents from the major Islamic countries opposing the intervention of the United States and the coalition forces not only were not allowed to be part of the news pool or to cover the countries involved in the war but also the stream of information coming from the war front was controlled and manipulated either by the governments involved or the Western news sources. The existence of a strong professional association of Muslim journalists would have made a definite difference in that it could have exerted pressure collectively to obtain at least part of the privileges extended to other groups and have voiced their grievances on professional and institutional levels for all the world to hear. Additionally, on the "home front," the existence of such Islamic professional journalistic associations could give proper recognition to the coverage of such events as the annual *hajj* (pilgrimage) as a major religio-political and socio-cultural occurrence to counteract its trivialization through non-Muslim media channels.

An underlying premise of such a network of professional associations is the Islamic world view which considers news and information as a process of distribution of knowledge. In short, from the Islamic perspective, mass media organizations as well as their personnel are engaged in a delicate stage centering around both the production and distribution of knowledge. This is because facts by themselves do not have meaning in Islam but, once placed in a proper Islamic social structure, constitute information leading to knowledge.

A number of concepts comprising the world view of Islam could be the information and social basis of such a network of journalists. They include among others the concept of *tawhid* (unity of God), the concept of *ilm* (knowledge), the meaning of *taqwa* (fear of God), the process of *adl* (justice), the notion of *ijma* (consensus), *shura* (consultation), the doctrine of *amanat* (public interest), and last but not least the *ummah* (the larger Islamic community).

Definition of Terms

A social system is a process of interaction of individuals within a larger unit called society, which exhibits the property that Ibn Khaldun, an Islamic thinker, called solidarity (*assabieh*), a term also employed later by Durkheim in his works. A social system is not the value itself, but a system of values and actions of individuals which are associated in terms of symbolic meaning. On the other hand, values are instruments of maintaining the cultural integrity and cohesion of society, serving to legitimize the modes of more concrete actions (Kroeber & Parsons, 1958). Here, we are concerned with the question of cultural systems and how they interact with problems of conceptualization, theorization, and practices of information and communication. What impact do cultural settings have on the studies of communication? What communication theories and practices do they foster?

The Islamic world consists of a vast and diverse geo-political area stretching from Indonesia and the Pacific Ocean in the east to Morocco and the Atlantic coast in the west, from central Asia and the Himalayas in the north to the southern African nations and the Indian Ocean. As one of the major religions of the world, Islam encompasses one quarter of the world's population—over a billion people. From the death of the Prophet (SAAS) (572–632 A.D.) and the period of the first four Caliphs (632–661 A.D.), to the end of World War I and the demise of the Ottoman Empire, the Islamic community has been a major world power. In the context of decolonization and increasing numbers of sovereign nation-states, the Islamic world politically, economically, and often culturally began to integrate into the existing sphere of the Western-dominated modern world system. The contacts between the Islamic world and the West in the 19th and 20th centuries increased the absorption of many Islamic countries into quasi-secular political entities ranging from hereditary monarchies to modern Western and/or military style republics. This also resulted in pronounced conflicts between modern secularism and the Islamic tradition of *al shari'a*, the canonical law of Islam.

In order to understand the current journalism practices in the Islamic world and to assess its future directions, it is necessary to examine a number of the fundamental principles upon which the Islamic communication framework has been built, and how the Islamic societies have come under constraints as a result of global political, economic, and cultural developments over the last century. The central foci of analysis will be on the fundamental principles of Islamic ethical methods in communication and on the objectives and aims of social communication. I use the term social communication here in its broader sense to include all kinds of communication, including journalism and mass communication, in an Islamic context. This understanding should help clarify the function of some of the modern institutions of communication in contemporary Islamic societies.

A distinction should be made between the Islamic term of social communication or *tabligh* (propagation) and the general concepts of communication, journalism, propaganda, and agitation commonly used in contemporary literature. The word "communication" comes from the Latin *communico*, meaning "share," and it is essentially a social process referring to the act of imparting, conveying, or exchanging ideas, knowledge, or information. It is a process of access or means of access between two or more persons or places. Also implicit and explicit in this definition is a notion of some degree of trust without which communication cannot take place. In its reductive approach (mathematical, technical, and some scientific analysis) communication is associated with the concept of information linking the process with chance events and various possible outcomes. This "atomic" view gives emphasis to quantitative and linear aspects of the process and not to its cultural and cognitive meanings (e.g., Cherry, 1961; Kirschenmann, 1970; Shannon & Weaver, 1961; Wiener, 1961, 1967). Journalism, as defined in the West, is the collection, writing, editing, and publishing of news or news articles, opinions, and commentaries through newspapers, magazines, broadcasting, and other modern media.

The term "propaganda" is a Western concept and was used for the first time by a committee of Cardinals (founded in 1622 by Pope Gregory) of the Roman Catholic Church having the care and oversight of foreign missions. Propaganda comes from the Latin word *propagare* and originally meant propagating the gospel and establishing the Church in non-Christian countries. The contemporary usage of the term propaganda in its political, sociological, and commercial contexts, however, dates back to the beginning of the 20th century. Since World War I, its definition has evolved to connote an instrument of persuasion and manipulation of individuals and collective behavior in national and international scenes (e.g., Lasswell, Lerner & Speier, 1980).[1]

Thus, according to French sociologist Jacques Ellul (1965), "propaganda is a set of methods employed by an organized group that wants to bring about the active or passive participation in its action of a mass of individuals psychologically unified through psychological manipulations and incorporated in an organization" (p. 61). In a somewhat similar fashion, Harold D. Lasswell (1942) has defined propaganda as "the manipulation of symbols as a means of influencing attitudes on controversial matters" (p. 106). This follows the common definition of propaganda as spreading ideology, doctrine, or ideas, and of agitation as an instrument for arousing people to spontaneous action. The Communist position on propaganda and agitation differs method-ologically from that of Lasswell. As defined by Vladimir I. Lenin (1935–1939), "A propagandist presents many ideas to one or a few persons; an agitator presents only one or a few ideas, but he presents them to a mass of people" (p. 85).

Note that contemporary propagandists, therefore, do not need to be believers in an ideology or a doctrine. Here propagandists are people in the service of the State, the party, the political or commercial campaign, or any other organization that is ready to use their expertise. Propagandists are technicians, bureaucrats, and specialists who may eventually come to despise the ideology itself.

Propagation, on the other hand, is dissemination and diffusion of some principle, belief, or practice. The Islamic word for propagation, *tabligh*, means the increase or spread of a belief by natural reproduction; it is an extension in space and time. It is the action of branching out. Social communication, journalism, and *tabligh* in an Islamic context have an ethical boundary and a set of guiding principles. In a broader sense, *tabligh* is a theory of communication and ethics. This theory of communication and global community integration is well stated by Ibn Khaldun (1967) in *The Muqaddimah* (*An Introduction to History*). Here he cites "truthful propagation" (*tabligh*) and group cohesion (*assabieh*) as two fundamental factors in the rise of world powers as States and large communities (Ibn Khaldun, 1336/1957, pp. 301–316, 1967, pp. 123–127). Thus journalism as a production, gathering, and dissemination of information, news, and opinion is an extension of *tabligh* in its broadest sense.

Communication and Ethics: Their Boundaries and Frontiers

A study of social communication in Islamic society in the early days and certainly before the rise of the modern nation-state system has a unique element to it (Mutahhari, 1361/1982, 1977). This was because it was rooted in oral and social traditions and the notion of *ummah* or greater Islamic community. Also the geographical entities now called Islamic countries were not heavily influenced by Western methods, conducts, and regimes in conflict with the major tenets of Islam. With the exception of the Islamic Republic of Iran, which is founded on the Islamic notion of the state, the remaining Islamic countries have state systems which are a mixture of the modern and traditional monarchial or republican systems. Thus their legal and ethical codes are heavily influenced by non-Islamic frames of reference. In many current analyses, great confusion arises from the failure to make a distinction between a nation-state and an Islamic state. It should be emphasized that while the nation-state is a *political* state, the Islamic state is a *muttagi* or religio-political and "God fearing" community or state. The ecological terrain of social com-munication in an Islamic community emphasizes intra personal/interpersonal communication over impersonal types, social communication over atomistic communication, and intercultural communication over nationalism.

Moving from the process of social communication to the definition of ethics, it must be emphasized that the boundaries of the study called "ethics" vary from culture to culture. For the purpose of the present study a method of ethics is defined to mean any rational procedure by which we determine what an individual human being as a person and as a member of a community ought to do as a "right" action by voluntary means. By using the word "individual" as a member of community this definition does not make a distinction between ethics and politics. From an Islamic perspective, the study and conduct of politics cannot be separated from the methods of ethics; the need is to determine what ought to be and not to analyze what merely is. Consequently, the conception of ethics here essentially deals with the Islamic perceptions of conduct as an inquiry into the nature the unity of God, humankind, and nature, and the method of attaining it (Mutahhari, 1985).

Since the Enlightenment, the West gradually divorced religion from secular life. Ethical conduct of the everyday life was left to an individual's conscience as long as such actions did not conflict with the perceived public morality. In Islam, this separation of the religious from the secular sphere did not materialize, and if attempts were made by the late modernizers to do this the process was never completed. Thus, throughout the Islamic societies not only did religion encompass a person wholly but also it shaped the conduct of the individuals in general through application of Islamic socio-religious ethics. In short, whereas modern ethics in the West became predominately social in nature, in Islamic societies that power remained social as well as religious. As the Quran says: "The noblest of you in the sight of Allah is the best of you in conduct" (49:13). In the Islamic tradition, the word *adab* means discipline of the mind or every praiseworthy conduct by which a person is excelled.

Until the 19th century Islamic canonical law, *al shari'a*, provided the main if not the complete legal underpinnings of social and economic conduct in Muslim societies. The intimate contact between Islam and modern Western industrial countries, coupled with the process of colonization of substantial parts of Asia and Africa, introduced a number of Western standards and values to these societies. Thus at the beginning of the 20th century and with the introduction of modern means of communication, transportation, and technologies, the fields of civil and commercial transactions proved particularly prominent for change and new methods of conduct.

The first foothold of European law, criminal and commercial, in the Islamic countries (particularly in the Ottoman empire) was advanced as a result of the systems of Capitulations, which ensured that the European citizens residing in the Middle East and a large part of Africa would not be governed by the Islamic laws and conduct of ethics but by their own laws and traditions. Furthermore, the reform movements such as the Tanzimat in the Ottoman (1839–1876) and the Constitutional reform in Iran (1906–1911) were indeed direct translations of French and other European codes which tended to establish secularism and injected the kinds of rules of conduct that were particularly European. In Egypt that process, from 1875 onward, went even further in the adaptation of European laws in such fields as commerce and maritime and included the enactment of civil codes which were basically modeled on French laws and contained only a few provisions drawn from *shari'a*.

For example, in the fields of journalism and media practices many Islamic countries adopted the concepts, norms, and legal codes of the West without considering the broader notion of laws and ethics in Islam. It should be remembered that the body of Islamic laws and ethics are classified according to a scale of values: obligatory (*vajeb*), recommended (*mostahab*), permitted (*mobah*), disapproved (*makroh*), and prohibited (*haram*). There is unanimity among the various schools of Islamic jurisprudence in such matters as prohibited and obligatory categories and the differences are usually regarding the disapproved or undesirable and recommended categories. This is the difference of degree which is called *ikhtlaf* and not the difference of categories or extremes which are referred to as *iftragh*. The existence of a unanimous standard is unique to Islamic jurisprudence. The Western study of law and ethics does not fulfill these conditions.

Communication and Ethical Thinking and Practices in Islamic Societies

The current ethical thinking and practices in Islamic societies, especially as they might relate to community, communication, and social interactions, are usually based on two different but important dimensions:

1. Normative religious ethics as explained in the primary source of Islam, the Quran and the traditions (*al-sunna*) of the Prophet and the *Imams*.
2. Normative secular ethics ranging from Greek tradition of popular Platoism, to the Persian tradition of giving advice to sultans and wazirs about government and politics, to the more contemporary ethical frameworks introduced by the West through "modernization," "development," "industrialization," and "secular humanism."

In the first category, the study of ethical principles in the religious tradition dates back to the eighth and ninth centuries during which two lines of argument were developed: the rationalist, those who subscribed to rational opinion, *ra'y*, argued that where there is no clear guidance from the Quran or tradition, the Islamic judges and lawyers might make their own rational judgments on moral and ethical questions. The traditionalist insisted that ethical and moral judgments can be based only on the Quran and tradition. This led to major debates among the various groups which are well-known in the study of the Mu'tazilites, the Asharis, the Shafi'is, and the Hanbalis, who took different positions on the questions of ethics in classical Islam.

In addition to these varied schools of thought, there is also a strong tradition in the mainstream of Islamic philosophy. This is seen mainly as the contribution of Islamic philosophers on *akhlag* (character) in the works of such philosophers as Farabi (870–950), Ibn Sina or Avicenna (980–1037), and Ibn Rushd or Averroes (1126–98), all of whom have contributed significantly to our knowledge about the sources of mystical as well as Sufi and Hellenic traditions in the classical Islamic system of ethics.

It was Ibn Khaldun, the father of sociology, however, who theorized about communication as a social institution which grew according to the need of the community. Social communication in terms of *tabligh* provided for a vast number of people from diverse races, languages, and histories a common forum for participation in a shared culture which was Islam. According to Ibn Khaldun, the states, governments and political systems of wide power and large authority have their origin in religious principles based either on prophethood and propagation or on a truthful *tabligh* carried out by *khatibis* (orators/communicators) (Ibn Khaldun, 1336/1957, pp. 310–316, 1967, pp. 125–127). Ibn Khaldun was one of the first thinkers to point out that communication based on ethics is the web of human society and that the flow of such communication determines the direction and the pace of dynamic social development. To him, combinations of the *assabieh* feelings and social communication approach provided a more dynamic view of organizational behavior than can be readily derived from the more conventional concepts of states, of hierarchical position, and of role which usually had been used in the discussion of politics, government, and large social organization. He thus concluded that propagation cannot materialize without group feeling. The relationship of social communication and Islam, therefore, emerges from the very nature of these two institutions. One is the source of society's values; the other propagates, disseminates, and maintains the value system of society, the *ummah* or community.

In the Islamic tradition of epistemology, the sustained discussion on ethics in Islam has been discussed in the *kalam* literature, the theologian's discussion and debate on the sources of right. Following is an outline of a number of fundamental Islamic concepts that have been the basis of Islamic communication ethics, and sense of community and should be at the heart of any journalistic ethics and duties of Muslim journalists. These concepts are the sources of much of the contemporary social, political, and economic debates in the Muslim world, especially in regard to normative secular ethics and in relation to the influences and values coming from the West and the non-Islamic traditions.

The Theory of *Tawhid*

The first and most fundamental outlook regarding man and universe in Islam is the theory of *tawhid*, which implies the unity, coherence, and harmony between all parts of the universe. Thus one of the most basic ethical pillars of the Islamic world is born: the existence of purpose in the creation and the liberation and freedom of humankind from bondage and servitude to multiple varieties of non-Gods. It stands for the necessity of exclusive servitude to God, and it negates any communication and messages, intellectual, cultural, economic, or political, that subjugates humankind to creatures. The principle of *tawhid* also negates any right of sovereignty and guardianship of anyone over human society except God. Society can be expected to be free from all deviations and excesses only when the affairs of society are delegated by a Power Transcendental to an individual or a council of rulers, with a power commensurate with responsibilities within the Islamic legal framework.

Thus, all man-made laws and ethical codes that arrogate judgment to themselves, or to any authority or institution other than in obedience or enforcement of "Allah's Own Judgment," are void. Therefore, all man-made laws, communication contents, mass media, and public forums that attempt to put restraints upon Allah's sovereignty must be void. The concept of *tawhid*, if exercised, provides the principal guide in drawing the boundaries of political, social, and cultural legitimation by a given communication system. The content of *tabligh* must not be in the direction to create and perpetuate political, social, economic, and cultural idols; nor are they allowed under this principle to promote the cult of personality.

Under the principle of *tawhid* another fundamental ethical consideration in *tabligh* becomes clear: the destruction of thought structures based on dualism, racialism, tribalism, and familial superiority. The function of communication order in Islamic society, according to the principle, is to break idols, to break the dependence on the outsiders, and to set the *ummah* or community in motion toward the future. Thus, one of the important functions of *tabligh* is to destroy myths. In our contemporary world these myths may include "power," "progress," and "modernization." Personalities as they represent these must not be superhumanized and superdefined. One of these dualism, according to this principle, is the secular notion of the separation of religion and politics.

The principle of *tawhid* also requires the absence of any economic, political, intellectual, or other centers, including the media, in which power can be amassed. The freedom of expression, assembly, and that of the media of communication do not have meaning when there is no social accountability on the part of the individual and institutions. The fight against the cult of personality and that of any social institutions associated with it is the fight against the communication system which attempts to propagate it.

Additional consideration under the ethical framework of *tawhid* is to campaign against the material foundations of dualism. Since among the characteristics of dualism is a desire for superiority through wealth, the content of journalism and social communication must not stress the value of wealth over spiritual growth and elimination of dividing lines and forms.

The doctrine of Responsibility, Guidance, and Action

A second principle guiding the ethical boundaries of *tabligh* in Islam is the doctrine of *amr bi al-ma'ruf wa nahy'an al munkar* or "commanding to the right and prohibiting from the wrong." Implicit and explicit in this principle is the notion of individual and group responsibility for preparing the succeeding generation to accept the Islamic precepts and make use of them. Muslims have the responsibility of guiding one another, and each generation has the responsibility of guiding the next. The Quranic verse explains this: "Call people to the path of your Lord with wisdom and mild exhortation. Reason with them in the most courteous manner. Your

Lord best knows those who stray from His path and best knows those who are rightly guided" (16:125). This points out the responsibilities of Muslims in guiding each other, especially those individuals and institutions who are charged with the responsibilities of leadership and propagation of Islamic ideals. This includes all the institutions of social communication such as the press, radio, television, and cinema, as well as the individual citizens of each community.

Thus, a special concept of social responsibility theory is designed around the ethical doctrine of "commanding to the right and prohibiting from the wrong." This concept has taken on an extra dimension of its own in the Islamic communities and societies through history since Islam as an all-inclusive systematic religion is an interrelated set of ideas and realities covering the entire area of human notion and action, beliefs and practices, thought, word, and deed. This is particularly important in light of the fact that Islam is not only a set of theological propositions, as are many other religions, but is also a set of comprehensive legal frameworks that govern every action of the individual in society and in the world at large.

For example, on the social and collective level the doctrine has been practiced systematically in the mosque in the Islamic societies. The mosque as a major channel of social and public communication has always been a pivot of spiritual and cultural movements since the days of the Prophet. It has fulfilled not only the role of purification of the soul, but also the acquisition of knowledge and public affairs information. Mosques and major universities existed side by side or within one another for many years in Egypt, Iran, Spain, and many parts of central Asia and other Islamic areas. In fact, many mosques were the centers of higher education in the Islamic tradition. Today in a number of Islamic societies the systems of "mass communication" have been well integrated within the classical and traditional systems of social communication of the mosque, especially the Friday prayers (Mowlana, 1979, 1985).[2] The result has been a high level of organization and mobilization, making the process of political, cultural, economic, and military participation extremely effective.

It is here that the concept of martyrdom (*shahadat*) in Islam and the concept of Holy Struggle (*jihad*) may only be understood if the doctrine of enjoying good and forbidding evil outlined here is properly appreciated. The term Islam is derived from the Arabic root *salama*, meaning surrender and peace or peaceful submission to the Will of Allah. Thus the concept of martyrdom, like all other Islamic concepts, is fully related to the concept of *tawhid*, or the absolute unity of God, humankind, and universe. In this sense, under the social responsibility theory of "commanding to the right and prohibiting from the wrong," the concept of *jihad* is no exception. Thus, from an Islamic perspective and ethical framework, martyrdom and struggle cannot be explained purely in terms of intercession and mediation; they should be understood within the framework of the principle of causality and not solely as spiritual mediation. In short, according to Islam, there is no martyrdom without struggle and *tabligh* in the course of Allah.

The Concept of Community

A third fundamental concept in determining the nature and boundaries of *tabligh* and that of social ethics, particularly as it might relate to the political life of the individual and Islamic society, is *ummah* or community. The concept of *ummah* transcends national borders and political boundaries. Islamic community transcends the notion of the modern nation-state system: an Islamic community is a religio-economic concept and is only present when it is nourished and governed by Islam. The notion of community in Islam makes no sharp distinction between public and private; therefore, what is required of the community at large is likewise required of every individual member. Accordingly, the *ummah* must be exemplary, setting the highest standards of performance and the reference point for others. It must avoid excesses and extravagances, be steadfast and consistent, know what to accept and what to reject, have principles and at the same time remain adaptable to the changing aspect of human life.

Under the concept of *ummah*, race is not accepted as a foundation of the state. Values follow piety and the social system of Islam is based on equity, justice, and ownership of the people. There is no individual or class of individuals to dominate, exploit, or corrupt the state. Intercultural and international communication (the emphasis here is on nationality and not the nation-state) are the necessary ingredients of Islamic *ummah*. The Quran says: ". . . We created you from a single (pair) of a male and a female, and made you into nations and tribes, that you may know each other (not that you may despise each other). Verily the most honored of you in the sight of God is (he who is) the most righteous of you" (Sura 49, 13).

In the Islamic *ummah* the sovereignty of the "state" belongs to God, and not to the ruler nor even to the people themselves. The ruler or leaders are only acting executives chosen by the people to serve them according to the Law of Islam and the concept of *tawhid*. Every citizen in the Islamic "state" is required to offer his best advice on common matters and must be entitled to do so. Thus consultative methods in politics are not only recognized but are a moral and ethical duty of the people and the ruler. Furthermore, man, according to Islam, possesses liberty and free will, so that by intervening in the operation of the norms of society, and by manipulating them creatively in accordance with the Quran and tradition, he may plan and lay foundations for a better future for both the individual and society.

Under the *ummah*, Islam has a new concept of community. One of the most important aspects of *ummah* is that Islam does not differentiate between the individuals as members of its community. Race, ethnicity, tribalism, nationalism, have no place to distinguish one member of the community from the rest. Nationalities, cultural differences, geographical factors are recognized but domination based on nationality is rejected. It is the individual and its relations to the community that is valued; however, this relationship alone is not the sole purpose in itself, both the individual and society must make their relationship clear to God: Are the individuals in society against God or under God? *Ummah*, as a social organization, emphasizes communality and collectivity based on Islamic tenets and not inter-individualism. The social contract which becomes the basis of *ummah* is not based on free will of undefined choice but subject to higher norms: the will of Allah. Communal cohesion is based on divine rights and not on natural rights. The term theocracy, often cited in the West, thus, cannot apply to the Islamic community since the notion of church as an institution is foreign to Islam, which as a religion combines both spiritual and temporal powers. It is an ideology possessing no centralized body yet its monotheism implies a single global order advocating the universality of moral principles. The *ummah* is beyond the nation-state in that the notion of community in Islam cannot be compared to the stage series of societal development found in Western community histories—principally that of an independent and an incorporated "political community" or "military community" (19).

Modernization movements in Islamic societies over the last 100 years failed in part because they were unable to elaborate a coherent doctrine based on the unity of spiritual and temporal powers, the interconnection of what is known as civil society and the state. Islamic "reformism," despite its idealistic unity, failed to take into account the multidimensional aspects of the society which was the *ummah*. Instead, its political culture, its mode of mobilization, and its administrative framework became ingrained in the concept of the modern nation-state system and its bureaucracy. Attempts were made to shift the models but not the dominant paradigm which stood in contrast to the meaning of the *ummah* (Chay, 1990; Mattelart, 1990; Mowlana & Wilson, 1990; Said, 1978; Schiller, 1990; Shari-ati, 1980; Smythe, 1981; Tran, 1987; Walker, 1984).

It is in this political, spiritual, and ethical framework that journalism must play a pervasive role in preservation and maintenance of the unity of the Islamic community. Thus, communication on both interpersonal and social levels becomes both basic and vital to the functioning of the *ummah*, for it sustains and encourages the integral and harmonious relationship between God, the individual, and society.

The Principle of *Taqwa*

A fourth principle outlined here to explain the ethical framework of journalism in Islamic societies is the concept of *taqwa* or, roughly translated, piety. In Islamic societies *taqwa* is commonly used in reference to individual "fear of God" and the ability to guard oneself against the unethical forces which might surrender the environment; however, the concept of *taqwa* goes beyond this common notion of piety. It is the individual, spiritual, moral, ethical, and psychological capacity to raise oneself to that higher level which makes a person almost immune from the excessive material desires of the world, elevating the individual to a higher level of prophetic self-consciousness.

The assumption is that human beings possess in their nature a set of divine elements which are other than the material constituents that exist in animals, plants, and inanimate objects. Human beings are endowed with innate greatness and dignity. Recognizing that freedom of choice is a condition for the fulfillment of obligation, the person is held responsible to perform his or her obligations within the Islamic framework of ethics. In short, it is recognized that human beings perform some of their actions only under the influence of a series of ethical emotions rather than with an intention of gaining a benefit or of repelling a harm. Thus, as a virtue and as an important element in the ethical framework of Islamic communication both on the individual and community levels, *taqwa* should be the underpinning ingredient in almost every action of a Muslim.

For example, fasting is an institution which has been practiced by different peoples in different times and places. In modern times, fasting has taken the two extreme forms of either ritualism and hunger strikes or dieting. Islamic fasting, however, is different in the sense that if it does not emanate from and lead to *taqwa*, it cannot be regarded as fasting. The Quran says: "O, you believers and faithful, fasting is prescribed for you as it was prescribed for those before you in order that you may develop *taqwa* (piety)" (2:183). On the leadership level of the *ummah* and community, it is the high level of *taqwa* that must be valued and counted the most. Technical knowledge, managerial ability, scientific know-how, communication skills, etc., if not associated with *taqwa*, cannot and should not be the sole criteria for promotion in an Islamic context. In the Islamic tradition, the conduct of politics and journalism is associated with *taqwa* and those who do not possess a degree of *taqwa* have faced the crisis of legitimacy.

The Meaning of *Amanat*

The fifth and final principle outlined in this paper is the concept of *Amanat*. The term *Amanat* signifies great responsibility which the Almighty God has imposed on the human being for his or her deeds in this world. The most relevant view of this concept as it may apply to the conduct of the press and the media is that *Amanat* refers to Divine Vicegerency for which human beings alone are fit and none else can share this honor with him. The Holy Quran says: Surely, we offered the *Amanat* into the heavens and the earth and the hills, but they refused to hear it and were afraid of it, and man took it up. Verily, he (human beings) was unjust, and ignorant (xxxiii: 72).

Thus, human beings fitness for Divine Vicegerange is lower, conditioned by the fact that he or she must practice the lofty code morality which brings him or her to the supreme being. Off all the created beings human beings are certainly the best and noblest (Ashraf-ul-makhlughat). Here it may be noted that rights and obligations are interdependent. Serving the public interest, therefore, becomes one of the principal ethical duties of the media.

Amanat means obligatory duties (faraiz). One aspect of *amanat* is that is can only be given to one who has the capability and power to shoulder the burden of its responsibilities and fulfill the commandments of Allah. Thus in Islam real progress of moral and not just material, for the latter refers to the transitory things of life. The liberty in Islam has quite a different meaning from that understood in the West. It is neither a prerogative nor an absolute right of the individual.

Conclusion

An attempt to evaluate the Islamic implications of our knowledge of the dynamics of communication ecology has been made here. A number of concepts have been introduced and examined in order to understand the phenomenon of communication and ethics in an Islamic context. It was shown that Muslim thinkers and philosophers throughout history not only recognized the importance of communication and ethics in determining the cultural profile of the Islamic civilization but also regarded the propitious equilibrium of spatial and temporal biases in Islam as an established fact. Over the last century, however, and especially during the last four decades, a dualism and contradiction have been created within the Islamic countries as a result of the introduction of the secular nationalist framework and the accompanying new concepts and methods of communication and ethics. A crisis of legitimacy has been created as a result of a conflict between the "official culture" of the ruling elites, which in many cases now represents and promotes Western influence, and the "traditional Islamic culture" of the masses rooted in centuries of religio-political and socio-ethical experience.

Nowhere is this communication and ethical conflict better illustrated than in the structure and use of the means of communication at the disposal of both cultures. The overwhelming evidence suggests that Muslim societies have, by and large, not responded positively to modern communication ethics coming from outside their own culture; nor in the post-colonial Muslim world has the political and communication system acquired from the West gained a broad popular base. On the contrary, such political and communication systems have become increasingly authoritarian, dictatorial, and military. Thus, as stated earlier, in Muslim societies today there exist two competing and mutually exclusive ethical methods and frameworks: the imported political culture of the ruling classes, and the indigenous political culture of the Muslim masses.

A look at the pre-modernist reform movements of the 18th and 19th centuries which swept over a large part of the Muslim world might offer some lessons. These movements were generated from the heart of the Islamic world itself and were directed toward correcting social evils and raising the moral standards of the community. Such movements appealed to the Muslims to awaken and liberate themselves from Western economic, political, military, and cultural domination, and to carry out the necessary internal reforms that would make for ethical and moral regeneration and strength. It would be a mistake to consider these movements as being primarily the result of Western influence on the Muslim world. All of these movements, without exception, emphasized a return to the tradition and ethics of Islam.[3] The current movements in the Islamic world are simply a continuation of the pre-modernist movements which tried to resolve contradictions created by exogenous forces.

Here, the central question is not one of economics but of culture, ethics, and *tabligh*. It is in this context that contemporary movements in the Islamic lands must be studied and understood. The question which Muslims have to answer, therefore, is how best to devise structural changes and institutional setups that would help to maintain the precious communication and ethical balance which has been traditionally part of the Islamic civilization.

As I have outlined elsewhere, the crucial question for the Islamic societies is whether the emerging global information communication community is a moral and ethical community or just another stage in the unfolding pictures of the transformation in which the West is the center and the Islamic world the periphery. Throughout Islamic history, especially in the early centuries, information was not a commodity but a moral and ethical imperative. Thus, through an

Islamic perspective, it seems that linguistic and political vocabularies and concepts, now at the center of global politics, both celebrate the arrival of a new communication age and hold the key to ultimate information control.

Notes

1. See Harold D. Lasswell, Daniel Lerner, and Hans Speier (1980) edited *Propaganda and Communication in World History*, Three volumes published by University of Hawaii Press. The first volume deals with "The Symbolic Instrument in Early Times," while the second volume concerns the "Emergence of Public Opinion in the West." The third volume deals with the contemporary world situation.
2. For a review of global information and international communication, see Mowlana (1986, 1988).
3. See *Sahifeh Noor: Majmoe Rahnemood ha'i Imam Khomeini, 18 Volumes* (1361–1365). For a comparative view of journalism and media ethics see Cooper, with Christians, Plude, & White (1989); Philip Schlesinger & Hamid Mowlana (1993), Mowlana (1994, 1996); Christians, Ferre, & Fackler (1993); Merrill (1997).

References

Cherry, C. (1961). *On human communication.* Cambridge, MA: MIT Press.

Chay, J. (Ed.). (1990). *Culture and international relations.* New York: Praeger.

Christians, C., Ferre, J., & Fackler, M. (1993). *Good news: Social ethics and the press.* New York: Oxford University Press.

Cooper, T. W., Christians, C. G., Plude, F. F., & White, R. A. (Eds.). (1989). *Communication ethics and global change.* White Plains, NY: Longman.

Ellul, J. (1965). *Propaganda: The formation of men's attitudes.* New York: Vintage.

Ibn Khaldun, (1336/1957). *Muqaddimah* (Vol. 1) (M. P. Gonabadi, Trans into Persian). Tehran: Bongahe Tarjumeh va Nashreh Ketab.

Ibn Khaldun, (1967). *The Introduction to History: The Mugaddimah* (F. Rosenthal, Trans from Arabic, N.J. Dowood, Abridged and Eds). London: Routledge and Kegan, Paul.

Kirschenmann, P. P. (1970). *Information and reflection: On some problems of cybernetics and how contemporary dialectical materialism copes with them.* Dordrecht, Holland: D. Reidel.

Kroeber, A. L., & Parsons, T. (1958). The concepts of culture and of social systems. *American Sociological Review, 23,* 582–583.

Lasswell, H. D. (1942). Communication research and politics. In D. Waples (Ed.), *Print, radio, and film in a democracy.* Chicago, IL: University of Chicago Press.

Lasswell, H. D., Lerner, D. & Speier, H. (Eds). (1980). *Propaganda and communication in world history.* Honolulu, HI: University of Hawaii Press.

Lenin, V. I. (1935–1939). *Selected works II* (J. Fineberg, Ed.). New York: Macmillan.

Mattelart, A. (1990). *Communication and class struggle: Vol. 3 New historical subjects.* New York: International General.

Merrill, J. C. (1997). *Philosophical foundations for news media.* New York: St. Martin.

Mowlana, H. (1979). Technology versus tradition: Communication in the Iranian revolution. *Journal of Communication, 29*(3), 107–112.

Mowlana, H. (1985). Communication for political change: The Iranian revolution. In G. Gerbner & M. Siefert (Eds.), *World communication: A handbook.* New York: Longman.

Mowlana, H. (1986). *Global information and world communication: New frontiers in international relations.* White Plains, NY: Longman.

Mowlana, H. (1988). Mass media systems and communication. In M. Adams (Ed.), *The Middle East: A handbook.* London: Muller, Blond and White.

Mowlana, H. (1994). Civil society, information society, and Islamic society. In S. Splichal, A. Calabrese, C. Sparks, W. Lafayette (Eds.), *Information society and civil society: Contemporary perspectives on the changing world order* (pp. 208–232). West Lafayette, IN: Purdue University Press.

Mowlana, H. (1996). *Global communication in transition: The end of diversity.* Thousand Oaks, CA: Sage.

Mowlana, H., & Wilson, L. J. (1990). *The passing of modernity: Communication and the transformation of society.* White Plains, NY: Longman.

Mutahhari, M. (1977). *Nahjul balagha: Sermons, letters and sayings of Hazrat Ali* (S. M. Ashari Jafery, Trans.). Elmhurst, New York: Tahrike Tarsile Quran.

Mutahhari, M. (1361/1982). *Majmoe Ghoftarha* (Collection of speeches). Teheran: Sadra.

Mutahhari, M. (1985). *Fundamentals of Islamic thought: God, man, and universe.* Berkeley, CA: Mizan.

Nahjul, B. (1977). *Sermons, letters, and saying of Hazrat Ali.* (S. M. Ashari Jafery, Trans.). Elmhurst, NY: Tahrike Tarsile Quran.

Sahifeh Noor: Majmoe Rahnemood ha'i Imam Khomeini, 18 Volumes (1361–1365). Tehran: Vezarate Ershad Islami.

Said, E. W. (1978). *Orientalism.* New York: Vintage.

Schiller, H. I. (1990). *Culture, Inc.* New York: Oxford University Press.

Schlesinger, P., & Mowlana, H. (Eds.). (1993). *Islam and communication* [Special Issue]. *Media Culture and Society, 15*(1).

Shannon, C. E., & Weaver, W. (1961). *The mathematical theory of communication.* Urbana, IL: University of Illinois Press.

Shari-ati, A. (1980). *Marxism and other Western fallacies* (R. Campbell, Trans from Persian). Berkeley, CA: Mizan.

Smythe, D. W. (1981). *Dependency road: Communications, capitalism, consciousness, and Canada.* NJ: Ablex.

Tran, V. D. (1987). *Independence, liberation, revolution: An approach to the understanding of the Third World.* Norwood, NJ: Ablex.

Walker, R. B. J. (Ed). (1984). *Culture, ideology, and world order.* Boulder, CO: Westview.

Wiener, N. (1961). *Cybernetics, or control and communication in animal and the machine* (new ed.). Cambridge, MA: MIT Press.

Wiener, N. (1967). *The human use of human beings: Cybernetics and society.* New York: Avon.

18

Ethics and the Discourse on Ethics in Post-Colonial India

Anantha Sudhaker Babbili

> My language is aphoristic; it lacks precision. It is, therefore, open to several interpretations.
>
> (Lord Krishna's conversation with Dharmadev, *The Collected Works of Mahatma Gandhi*, Government of India, 1958, p. 485)

> If we define ethics as involving intention, will, freedom, the relation of one individual to another, we are imposing a western concept on India. Admittedly, Hinduism has little or no ethics in this sense. But if ethics involves a set of standard behavior based on duty, social custom, religious faith in *karma*, then Hinduism puts a high premium on moral conduct. Hinduism has no concern for others as others, as individuals deserving separate treatment, but it does have concern for others as members of the group or as part of Universal Reality.
>
> (Father Raymond Panikkar as quoted in Lacy, 1965, p. 27)

The chapter deals with Indian ethics in its cultural context and with the intellectual challenge that the discourse on ethics in a post-colonial situation offers. It begins with the latter to arrive at the former. In doing so, the chapter explores the perplexing morass of ethical reasoning that dictates Indian daily life. The discursive analysis hopes to sketch a normative vision and describe an encompassing theory of discourse on ethics.

The intent here is to introduce the student of ethics to the ethical schemata of India. And this task is not easy. The journey into Indian ethics is essentially an excursion into the contestable terrain of conflicting cultural narratives—native and those imposed from the outside. Thus, any narrative on Indian ethics must first wrestle with the difficulty of dealing with ethics in its post-colonial condition.[1] It must provide a descriptive in the context of contemporary India's geography, society, culture, and politics. Also, to imagine the particular location of ethics, one must understand the history of the culture and society. The philosophical basis for the specific principles governing Indian life can then be discussed meaningfully from an indigenous "ethical systems" perspective.

The study of Indian ethics calls for eschewing the traditional dualisms that exist in Western thought. The typical dichotomies of subject–object, fact–value, individual–society, material–spiritual, good–evil, and so forth are inconsequential for understanding Indian society and ethics. The Western need to *understand* is basically puzzling to Indians. One seeks the experience of the Self [*Atman*] to find one's *dharma* [duty and righteousness]—not to explain away but to accept, not to articulate but to experience. Telling a story is as important as speaking the truth, but most often, it is telling the story that indicates profound insight not preaching truth as one sees it.

In India, everything important is told in paradoxes. Oliver (1971) writes that subtlety is the hallmark of the Indian mind. The rhetorical milieu includes the manner of talk, how people address each other on what topics, styles of conversation, non-verbal cues, and intended effects between senders and receivers. Nothing is as it first appears. What is said must be understood in terms of what has been left unsaid. "Opposites are coordinates; contradictions are illusionary. The world is a dramatic portrayal of God playing hide and seek with Himself—trying to reassemble all the divergent parts into their original unity" (Oliver, 1971, pp. 15–16). Death is life; continuity is change.

The potent force of such Indian ethical paradoxes and conduct can be seen in Mahatma Gandhi's twin battle (Gandhi, 1948; Misra & Gangal, 1981) against British colonial rule in India based on *dharma* and *ahimsa* [nonviolence]—destined to permanently change the colonizer as well as the colonized (Nandy, 1983). Gandhi's ability to translate social ethics and ethical ideals into political action laid the foundations for achieving social justice for millions for the first time in world history through nonviolence. With a clever use of nonverbal methods evoking the cultural ethics laden in the texts and epics of nationhood, he struck a chord of unity among its diverse people and effectively disarmed a colonial military machine.

Geography and the Cultural Ethos

Understanding the land—the geography of modern India and its geographical formulations—is critical to comprehending Indian ethics.[2] Major battles between good and evil have been fought in mythology that carry insight into ethics. The *Mahabharata* and *Ramayana* point into wars and warriors, virtuous and treacherous gods, benevolent and punishing gods, and to goddesses and androgynous gods. They describe gods who provoked warfare, gods who switched sides, gods that are human, partly human, partly non-human, partly from the rest of the animal kingdom, half-god, half-human, half-animal, perfect, and imperfect gods. Three million of them—each reflecting virtues and antivirtues—reside in one of the oldest civilizations that extends from the Indus River to the Himalaya mountains, from the genesis of the sacred rivers Brahmaputra and Ganga to the Vindhya mountains, and from central plains to the lush greenery of Kanyakumari at the tip of south India. The sage then shows, following different ways of enumerating them, how each of these views could make sense (Davis as cited in Lopez, 1995, p. 3). The narratives that have sprung from this land domiciled between the Indus and Ganges rivers are indeed peculiar to India and Indians, though their imprint can be seen in the Greek and Roman, Chinese and European civilizations (Halbfass, 1988).

Contemporary studies of Indian ethics cannot be understood without coming to terms with its post-independent (after 1947) political, cultural, social, and religious fragments. Located in southern Asia between the Arabian Sea, Bay of Bengal, and Indian Ocean, between Bangladesh and Pakistan (both creations from the former "India" of the colonial era), India experienced Islamic colonialism for nearly three centuries until the arrival of the British in the 1600s. Ethnically, 72% of the nearly 950 million Indians are Indo-Aryans and 25% are Dravidians of the south. Indians, however, never really identify themselves along ethnic lines as Aryan or Dravidian. India harbors many religions, including the Hindu majority (80%), Muslim (14%), Christian (2.4%), Sikh (2%), Buddhist (0.7%), Jains (0.5%), and other faiths. Religious plurality—including Zoroastrianism with origins in Persia and in Judaism—is a historical reality, although the fundamentalist backlash from the Hindu Right against two colonialisms—Christian and Islamic—is presently a feature of Indian politics. Linguistically, India has had a burst of creative languages over the past 5,000 years. There are 18 major languages with their own unique alphabet and script, which formed the basis of statehoods; yet there are 25 languages spoken by 1 million or more Indians and more than 1,100 dialects—some with written scripts and others strictly oral. Literacy rates in 1991 were estimated as 63.86% for males and 39.42% for females. Agriculture and village-cottage industries take the lion's share of the labor force. Politically, the colonial imprint can be seen on India's political structure (federal republic) and on its legal system (based on English common law), although compromises with Islamic law to appease the Muslim minority are often allowed.

India is the world's largest and most populous democracy, with 950 million people. Governance of India is virtually unimaginable with such a multitude of classes, castes, subcastes, religions, regionalisms, linguistic divisions, and a population nearing 1 billion. Yet suffrage is extended universally to citizens 18 years and older, and they have exhibited in India's post-independent history a vibrant propensity for democratic institutions and a disdain for dictatorships. The Indian constitution embraces a social activism that encourages equality for caste and religion. Reservations in employment and in higher education akin to affirmative action in the United States have been in place since 1947, and accommodations to the lower castes have gradually increased—much to the chagrin of the upper castes. However, as governmental measures to eradicate caste discrimination take root, discrimination based on economic status has begun to emerge as even more important than the traditional caste distinctions. The gap between the rich and poor is wide and gets wider every year.

Communication in culturally diverse environment is a given in India. The India model of communication can be called at best a "mixed system," with a blend of written and oral traditions. Print media include 30,000 newspapers with a combined circulation of 60 million. Government ownership of newspapers is disallowed. Daily newspapers 3,000 strong—although relying heavily on government-approved newsprint—provide the most vocal criticism of political and social institutions. The broadcasting system, however, is under the government's control, ensuring public interest with a balance of regional, linguistic, and religious representations on radio and television. Radio, with its appeal for nonliterate audiences reaches about 94% of India, and television has a nearly 84% reach, the latter confined to India's middle class. India boasts the world's largest film industry with about 900 full-length feature films produced every year. Bombay, India's Hollywood, produces the largest number of films in the Hindi language, spoken by about 30% of Indians. Films are seen by 100 million people every week in 13,000 cinema halls. Often, the largest buildings in small villages are the temple and the cinema hall. Although most films ape Western story-telling, violence, and escapism, many do construct narratives of caste injustice, marriages based on love (as opposed to forced or arranged marriages), the triumph of the lower and poorer castes of people over the upper caste and the arrogant elite, the triumph of the gentler and the androgynous over the powerful and hypermasculine (Nandy, 1995). Films and government-sponsored television productions aim to propagate religious tolerance, national unity, and environmental protection. Radio shows promote development programs and cultural cohesion. The broadcast media deal with subject matter that relates to tradition and the family as a unit. Films, in particular, critically examine the cultural consequences of Westernization even as they follow the cinematic logic established by the West. Cable TV and imported programming are on the rise.

When partitioned from British Indian, Pakistan chose to become an Islamic Republic, whereas India made secularism as inherent part of its plurality (Sen, 1993) by choosing a secular constitution for its Hindus and Muslims. Although diversity and tolerance within Hinduism did not come with Western secularism, they have become a political necessity. It was a moral and ethical choice that neutralized temporarily sectarian nationalism, ultra-right Hindu fundamentalism, and militant obscurantism until India gained the strength to stand on its own feet in the wake of independence from the British.

Ethics and Religion in India

India's social ethics cannot be understood without locating them in a broad definition of religion. The caution here is that Hinduism must be understood in pre-colonial terms to extract the nation's ethical underpinnings. Hinduism is a collection of a broad group of south Asian religions. It has been challenged by other religions that came to exist in the region—Buddhism, Islam, and Christianity—but it remains the most prevalent. Hinduism is one of the world's oldest continuously recorded religions dating from 4500 to 1200 B.C.E. A text was already edited and put into final shape by about 1200 B.C.E. (Davis, cited in Lopez, 1995, p. 3). Both terms, Hinduism and India, were framed by outsiders—the former an invention of the last century by the British and the latter the coinage by the Greeks and Persians referring to a geographical location rather than a collection of beliefs and peoples (Lopez, 1995; Sen, 1993). The word "Hindu" was coined by the Arab colonizers referring to people who lived near the Sindhu river. It was later incorporated into the Indian lexicon by Indians eager to construct for themselves a counterpart to the seemingly monolithic Christianity of the colonizers (Lopez, 1995, p. 6).

Because ethics is derived from Hinduism as a whole, it is pertinent to discuss the term *Hinduism*. It remains useful for describing and categorizing the various schools of thought and practice that have sprung up within a shared Indian society and have employed a common religious vocabulary. However, applying this single term to a wide array of Indian religious phenomena across a historical continuity raises some obvious questions (Lopez, 1995, p. 6).

What is the center of Hinduism? And who determines this center, if any? Scholars and Indians have largely adopted two contrasting views on this matter that have a bearing on ethics—one centralist and the other pluralist. Centralists identify a pan-Indian hegemonic, orthodox tradition transmitted primarily through the Sanskrit language, chiefly by the Brahmanic upper caste. Davis contends that the tradition centers around a Vedic lineage of texts that includes the Vedas themselves but also the *Mimamsa, Dharmasastra*, and *Vedanta* corpuses (Lopez, 1995).[3] Vernacular challenges to Sanskrit questioning the caste order and rejecting the authority of the Vedas may periodically show up as a rebellion against the center, but the orthodox, through the adept use of inclusion and repressive tolerance, have managed to prevail in authority. The pluralists envision a decentered profusion of ideas and practices all tolerated and incorporated under Hinduism (Lopez, 1995).

The textual history of Hinduism and of Indian religions begins in 4000 B.C.E. and since then has encouraged its own versions of dissent, lively religious interaction, and criticism through satire and polemic. Various contending religious narratives have vied to each present a view of divinity, human society, human purposes, and social ethics as more compelling than the others. As quoted in Lopez (1995), Davis writes,

> One finds such all-encompassing visions presented in many Hindu texts or group of texts at different periods of history: the Vedas, the Epics, the puranic theologies of Vishnu and Siva, the medieval texts of the bhakti movements, and the formulations of synthetic Hinduism by modern reformers.
>
> (p. 7)

The theoretical exegesis of Indian ethics flows from such a synthesis of Indian thought. To speak of Hinduism as a "religion" in India is not to say much of anything at all theoretically or analytically. Hinduism defies a Western category of religions, encompassing actually "a diversity of gods, texts, and social practice, and a variety of ontologies and epistemologies. Without an organized church, it is innocent of orthodoxy, heterodoxy and heresy" (quoted by Larson, 1995, p. 279). Religion—a fundamental anthropological notion on analogy with culture, language, and society—goes beyond the theoretical categories of European history of religions, theology, and

Western social science (Larson, 1995, pp. 280–281). Uniquely, "India has been instructive in exhibiting forms of religion in which determinate cognitive formulation regarding ultimate truth is neither essential nor possible" (Larson, 1995, p. 281).

The anthologies that hold the treasures of Indian thought, Indian morality, and human virtue are the *Rg Veda* (the Vedic period of Indian history stretches roughly from 2500 to 500 B.C.E.), the collection of hymns that form the bedrock of the Hindu tradition; the *Upanishads* (700 to 300 B.C.E.), the story of creation and classic discourses that form the foundation for Hindu religious and philosophical speculation; the *Bhagavad Gita* (400 B.C.E. to 400 A.D.), the basic text of religious and philosophical synthesis and basic scripture of Hindu devotionalism; the *Mahabharata* (400 B.C.E. to 400 A.D.), the political history of humankind with contending moralities and nondualistic thought; and the *Ramayana* (200 B.C.E.), the second of the great epics that exemplifies the fundamental values and tensions in the classical tradition.

No one text represents a complete statement of Buddhism, but the *Dhammapada* comes closest to the basic discourse, which teaches that the greatest sin is ignorance or thoughtlessness and that the holy life begins with, and is founded upon, moral earnestness and the spirit of inquiry and self-examination. India ethical extrapolations can also be found in the fables of *Panchatantra*, which uses classic Indian humor to spell out five doctrines of conduct or modes of action, namely, confidence or firmness of mind, creation of prosperity or affluence, earnest endeavor, friendship, and knowledge. *Panchatantra* reveals the ancient Indian affinity towards non-human beings and the sanctity of nature by evoking the imagery of animals when discussing the doctrines of conduct—especially for children. The basic authority for India's legal and moral philosophy today seems to be the *Code of Manu*, a text written between 600 B.C.E. and 300 A.D. that contains a mythological rationalization for the caste system and family ethics (Doniger & Smith, 1991). Thus, ethics in India stems from those basic Hindu religious texts that are often considered cultural and philosophical texts.

Hindu philosophy teaches that the metaphysical ideal is higher than the ethical ideal (Brown, 1970; Crawford, 1974, p. 229); nevertheless, both are synthetically related. Those who have achieved the mystical state of *moksa* [liberation] does not consciously follow the ethical path but neither can they deviate from it. The path of an enlightened person is paved with virtue (Crawford, 1974, p. 230). Love and compassion to all creatures are the spontaneous products of wisdom. This thought, for example, is relevant to an ecologically conscious world. Ecology presupposes ethics. To attain a right relationship with nature, modern human beings must assume vital obligations for the web of life in which their own life is wonderfully woven. Material investments do not recover and preserve nature. The obligation to life forms is a matter of conscience—an individual's ecological conscience. The ecological conscience views the human being as a spectator and participant in nature.

> This means, if we are going to be scientific in our approach, we cannot speak of man and nature, but of man in nature. The first view is anthropocentric; the second is biocentric. The first view has characterized Western man's approach to nature; the second has been more characteristic of the Hindu perspective.
>
> (Crawford, 1995, p. 177)

The outlook on life underlying the *summum bonum* of Hindu ethics is fundamentally cosmic. The essential self is not only identified with the group or society or nation or even with the whole human race, but it is inclusive of these and much more. The nature of the self in Hinduism includes all lesser forms of existence, and therefore, it also has an ecological conscience. Crawford (1974) cites this passage from the *Upanishads*: "The essential self or the vital essence of man is the same as that in a gnat, the same as that in an elephant, the same as that in these three worlds, indeed the same as that in the whole universe" (p. 232).

The Nature of Ethics and Continuity in India

Hindus call their religion *Sanatana Dharma*, which literally means "Eternal Law." The term does not imply that the ethical ideals connected with religion are eternal in the sense of being fixed, static, and unchanging. To the contrary, Hindu ethics

> like the river Ganges, has been in a state of ceaseless flow during the ages, constantly changing its course and currents relative to the hard, intervening realities of Indian history. Under the rubric of eternal law and universal law, Hindu ethics combines continuity with dynamic diversity.
>
> (Crawford, 1974, p. i)

Hinduism does not have a science of morals fashioned after some Aristotelian or Thomistic model (Crawford, 1974, p. xiv). However, it does have a moral philosophy that postulates a *summun bonum* and specifies the proper means to achieve it. This highest ideal is the state of *moksa* or liberation where one finds self-fulfillment and deepest bliss. *Moksa* serves as the ultimate standard of right conduct; it measures the value of an act by the extent to which it either helps or hinders the attainment of freedom. Actions most distinctly oriented to *moksa* are those characterized by truth, non-violence, sacrifice, and renunciation (Crawford, 1974, p. xiv).

In the ancient texts, the earliest India scribe, Sage Narada, was charged with the responsibility of mediating messages between the mighty deities and their earthly subjects. Narada was given the basic objective of establishing *lokakalyan* [universal peace and prosperity]. In his role, he depicts himself as the master oral communicator who sought liaison between the rulers and the ruled and as one who kept an empathetic discourse between the people and the various kingdoms of the gods. It is essential to notice the fact that sages, when narrating each other's intentions and motives in the interest of maintaining peace and tranquility, would deliberately slant the truth. Even when the clever role of Narada was to be found out, he would still be revered for his intent to keep peace between people over truth-telling. Similarly, the two great epics *Mahabharata* and *Ramayana* are wrought with such paradoxes in human action. The former text includes *Bhagavad Gita*—the conversation between Lord Krishna the chariot driver and Arjuna the ultimate warrior on one's *dharma* and ethics of being. *Bhagavad Gita* is the famous philosophical dialogue that lays foundation for Indian ethical conduct in the present life. Nondualisms and contradictions prevail in which the choice between good and evil is never clear-cut.

Indian ethics appear most often as subtle manifestations of human conduct in the narratives of prominent cultural and religious texts, traditions, and customs. These narratives carry diverse interpretations (Richman, 1991), multiple and authoritative translations into other Indian languages, dialects, and semantics within oral traditions, vernacular expression and ahistorical arrangements. In addition, Buddhist doctrines espoused in *Dhammapada* shed light on problems of human existence, goals of Buddhism (King, 1946), Buddhist ethics, the problem of evil, and ethics for laypersons. The dominant Hindu ethics revolve around the issues of moral obligation. Indian texts point to minute details of Indian life that expound on the ethics of environmental protection, universal morality, and the ideal of human perfection, knowledge as virtue, the parallelism of thought and action, and intersections of theory and practice.

The original texts of Hinduism reflect throughout a continuity of ethical discourse in the midst of paradoxes and contradictions (Govinda Das, 1947; Herman, 1991). The Vedic period produced the oldest known book in human civilization, the *Rg Veda*, which contains no evidence of caste, child marriage, prohibition of widow remarriage, or other such antisocial practices. "Women wore the sacred thread of Brahminism, participated in metaphysical discourse, and enjoyed a moral and intellectual status never achieved since then" (Lacy, 1965, p. 14). Ethics during the Vedic period espoused obedience to divine law. "*Rta*, the law or order of the world . . . provides the standard of morality. . . . Virtue was conformity to the cosmic law" (Gandhi, 1948; quoted by Lacy, 1965). *Rta* contains discourses on love and fear, kindness and benevolence, order and duty. Out of *rta* comes the central ethical concept of *dharma* in subsequent moral philosophy. During the Vedic age, life was viewed in an affirmative sense rather than according to the later ideal of renunciation. Only after did the ideal of high ethnicity become withdrawal rather than service, spiritual achievement not abasement (Lacy, 1965, p. 15).

Upanishads essentially nullifies ethics as commonly defined. Under the *Upanishads*, a person's highest spiritual aim is to blend the individual soul (*Atman*) with the Universal-Ultimate Reality, the *Brahman* (not to be confused with the upper caste Hindu Brahmin) creating *Brahman-Atman*, a supramoral Soul. Because the spiritual goal processes no moral characteristics, the process of salvation includes no moral challenge. The *Upanishads* contain various instructions: to speak the truth, respect gods and ancestors, honor parents and guests, and control desires. Another reason for the nullification of ethics in the *Upanishads* is the denial of the material world because the only reality is represented in the *Brahman-Atman's* impersonal and supramoral Soul. The physical universe and human existence are *maya* [illusion], and *lila* [play]. In such a society, one may have prescribed duties, but any free, spontaneous, creative relationship to other beings becomes imaginary and meaningless. The attainment of *nirvana*, a Hindu-Buddhist term for the extinction of desire and attachment, is a transcendence of all relativity and relationships. A devout Hindu or Buddhist would find supreme union with the *Brahman* as the ultimate, positive, and ecstatic experience (Lacy, 1965, p. 16). But, clearly, in the arena of human ethics and in a traditional epistemological view, this concept of salvation offers neither guidance nor incentive.

Another reason for the de-emphasis of ethics in the *Upanishads* is the emphasis on two doctrines crucial to all subsequent Hinduism: *karma* and *samsara*. Ethically speaking, the law of *karma* simply recognizes that a person reaps what a person sows—if not in this life, then in a life to come. According to *samsara*, all those who die without achieving *nirvana* will reappear in another and yet another birth, either higher or lower in the orders of creation and social scale (Herman, 1991). Many Indians and some Westerners today, without justifying caste discriminations in any sense, uphold the doctrine of *karma* on various grounds. Metaphorically speaking, it provides a consistent theory of evil and suffering.

> No theistic system, including Christianity, has been able to reconcile the goodness and omnipotence of God with a world of pain and sin. . . . The Hindu advocate of *karma* may be quite right that such a belief provides a powerful incentive for personal ethics . . . At best, therefore, these basic Hindu beliefs inspire a self-centered morality (and social ethics), whose sole criterion for ethical behavior is the merit being stored up by *karma*.
>
> (Lacy, 1965, p. 17)

By the time the *Code of Manu* (Doniger & Smith, 1991) makes an appearance in the continuum of Indian philosophical thought, it is obvious that neither lawmakers nor philosophers of ancient India sought to construct a systematic ethical theory. Morality consisted of obedience to the divine law, expressed less in legal commandments than in social custom and religious sanction. Not unlike *Rg Veda*, the *Code of Manu* offers a mythological rationalization of ethical behavior through the caste system: that the Brahmins must be priests wielding verbal authority, the Kshatriyas must be the warriors to defend the *raj*, the Vaisyas craftsmen, traders and farmers are to be used for manual skills, the Shudras servants for performing menial tasks, and India's outcasts (the *harijans*) are the untouchables. Many enlightened Hindus have discarded all justifications of the caste system, and the brutal exploitation of caste stands universally condemned.

Although many Indians, including Mahatma Gandhi and Rabindranath Tagore, believed in the *varna-dharma* (caste obligations) for different reasons, Gandhi, particularly became an active crusader against caste with the profound belief that caste was alien to Hinduism having found no support in the *Vedas* (Crawford, 1974, p. 220).

Every social, economic, and cultural justification of the caste system was purchased at a great price—the loss of freedom and the sacrifice of social progress. Freedom was lost because the individual was required to submit totally to the system; social progress was sacrificed because the principle of heredity was the sole determinant of a person's role in life (Crawford, 1974, p. 219). The doctrine of *karma* could explain one's present position in relation to the past and even provide incentive to perform good deeds with a view to meriting a higher caste in the future existence, but too often this doctrine was only a moral rationalization of social inequalities (Crawford, 1974, p. 219).

However, the inherent quality of Hinduism—the many voices of dissent against the hierarchical order of caste—had always been vibrant. It should not be assumed that the Hindu embarrassment over the caste system developed only from the contact with Western ideals of liberty, equality, and fraternity. "Actually there has always been a counter movement, questioning and controverting the rigidity and inviolability of the principle of heredity" (Crawford, 1974, p. 219). Regardless of the assigned caste, one reaches the state of the *Brahman* if one observes "truth, charity, fortitude, good conduct, gentleness, austerity, and compassion," says Yudhisthira in *Mahabharata*. The actual attainment of the Ultimate Soul—the *Atman*, the *Brahman*—is contingent on one's ability to denounce the social status and caste affiliation and embrace nothingness. Unlike earlier texts, the *Code of Manu* codified family ethics and a lower status for women. Pre-puberty marriage, polygamy, divorce, voluntary *sati* [widow cremation] and bans against widow remarriage—all found acceptance in this book of Hindu law.

The epic *Mahabharata* anchored the major problem of Hindu social ethics. This text represents the sublime pinnacle of morality even as it describes an impersonal superdeity who deprives his followers of the involvement essential to genuine ethical choice. Compassion, forgiveness, devotion, life without love or desire or goodness are cast in genuinely problematical terms. Because Hinduism encompasses a wide variety of beliefs and interpretations with no official orthodoxy or hierarchy, the philosophy of India that is captured in this epic demands no logical consistency or precision. Completely contradictory conclusions may be drawn by equally competent scholars and devotees; any objective appraisal leads to the generalization of ethical theory and to observations of moral practice (Lacy, 1965, p. 14).

The centripetal ethical arguments of *Mahabharata* find their home in the *Bhagavad Gita*, the song of the celestial Lord. Millions of Hindus turn to it for daily inspiration and guidance; many can recite the entire text. The central theme of *Gita* is this: Perform your duty with detachment. The most dominant school of Hindu philosophy has emphasized detachment—the freedom from emotional involvement and from concern for consequences. The other school gaining influence in modern India today puts stress on action and on courageously making decisions. The result is the classic collision between "world-and-life negation" and "world-and-life-affirmation" in Indian ethics (Lacy, 1965, p. 20). Consequently, Hinduism does not deny dilemmas. The epics and other cultural texts are not just works of antiquity but embody the social sinews that connect past with present and make the epics timeless treasuries of true dilemmas.

Dharma, Ahimsa, and Ethical Values

Although the earlier texts based morality on law and ritual, *Gita* gives new weight to the personal conscience. Though the union with the Supreme Soul is based on spiritual terms, it calls for benevolence toward others. "Morality, which is eternal . . . consists of universal friendliness (and) is fraught with beneficence to all creatures" (*Santiparva* 262: 5; quoted by Lacy, 1965, p. 20). True detachment is problematic when one considers this passage from *Gita*:

> Neither with eye, nor with mind, nor with voice should one injure another. . . . He indeed is exalted in heaven who looks on all other beings with an eye of affection, who comforts them in affliction, gives them (food) and speaks kindly to them becoming one (with them) in their grief and joy.
>
> (Lacy, 1965, p. 20)

It is in the *Bhagavad Gita* that the inner tension of Hindu ethics pulls at one's soul. What is unmistakably clear is the final message of the *Gita*: "Perform thou right action (regulated, prescribed duty) for action is superior to inaction. . . . Therefore, without attachment, constantly perform action which is duty, for and by performing action without attachment, (a person) verily reacheth the supreme" (III: 8, 19; quoted by Lacy, 1965, p. 21). Both action and escape may lead to salvation, but the former is the nobler choice. One of the lessons of *Gita* is that all persons should do their own duty, fulfill their own *karma*, and accept their lot in life. "Better one's own duty, though destitute of merit, than the duty [*dharma*] of another, well discharged" (III: 35, cf. XVII: 47; quoted by Lacy, 1965, p. 22). It is better to be a good slave than an immoral master. Here a moral standard is implied, though it is no more than a fulfillment of duty.

Equality is also emphasized in the *Gita*. Some scholars contend that if the basic element of Hindu ethics can be examined apart from the caste system, or even within the framework of a single caste or community, it would have many advantages (Creel, 1977; Lacy, 1965, pp. 22–23). Lord Krishna insists in his discourse with Arjuna that detachment leads to the virtues of impartiality, fairness, and justice—at least within the group. The equality of *dharma* (meaning here that each has his or her ordained duty) to many Hindus represents an excuse for non-involvement and a lack of concern for others. One of the Hindu arguments in defense of *karma* is that it puts ethical responsibility where it belongs, on persons themselves leaving them dependent neither on other people nor on the whim of God. Such a view, admittedly and without apology, leaves no room for vicarious suffering by the innocent nor for atonement by an incarnate deity (Lacy, 1965, pp. 20–25).

The major element of Hindu ethics developed in the *Gita* is the concept of *dharma*. Whereas in ancient Vedic times, *dharma* meant the whole body of truth, the cosmic law, Buddhism narrowed it to a particular set of teachings, to the creed and the doctrines. Hinduism, on the other hand, gradually expanded the idea until *dharma* came to mean the all-inclusive focus of ethics. *Dharma*, in the text of the *Gita*, can be translated as duty, righteousness, customs, traditions, law, nature, justice, virtue, merit, and morality (Khan, 1965; Noble, 1915).

The unattached individual lives the life of virtue. *Dharma* or virtue has three forms: virtues of the body—charity, helping the needy, social service; virtues of speech—truthfulness, benevolence, gentleness; and virtues of the mind—kindness, unworldliness, and piety. *Gita*, India's sermon on the mount several centuries before Christ, makes *dharma* the pillar of all virtues.

> *Dharma* is the cosmic process, the Kantian moral law, the Quaker Inner Light, the Communist dialectic. It is the Decalogue, the Mosaic Covenant, and the "righteousness" of prophecy. For the Hindu it is what he does and why he does it.
>
> (Lacy, 1965, p. 23)

Lord Krishna, towards the end of *Gita*, spells out the attributes of the righteous person:

> Fearlessness, cleanness of life, steadfastness in the Yoga of wisdom, alms-giving, self-restraint and sacrifice and study of the Scriptures, austerity and straightforwardness,

harmlessness, truth, absence of wrath, renunciation, peacefulness, absence of crookedness, compassion to living beings, uncovetousness, mildness, absence of fickleness, vigor, forgiveness, fortitude, purity, absence of envy and pride—these are his who is born with the divine properties.

(XVI: 1–3)

The final phrase tosses responsibility to one's *karma*, denying the freedom essential for moral action. However, the significance of *Gita* for Hindu ethics lies in the dialogue Indians have with Lord Krishna, finding him a god concerned with human problems, human temptations, and human values. Lacy (1965, p. 24) maintains that the faith Krishna offers and rewards is more tolerant and more universalistic. Therein lies Hinduism's chief claim to superiority. Whatever the weakness of nonattachment, duty, and eclecticism in formulating ethics, the freedom and open-mindedness of Hinduism provide a strong appeal.

The true nature of moral character espoused by the *Gita* depends on the faithful performance of duty without regard to consequences: "Thy business is with action only, never with its fruits; so let not the fruit of action be thy motive, not be thou to inaction attached" (II: 47; Lacy, 1965, p. 25). One follows without question the universal law of *dharma* and the particular law of *karma*.[4] Whereas Hinduism draws a sharp distinction between the spiritual and material, the eternal and temporal, these dimensions of existence are polarized but correlated within the concept of *dharma*. *Dharma*, writes R. N. Dandekar, is a "unique joint product of the speculative and practical wisdom of the Hindus" (quoted by Crawford, 1974, p. 202). *Dharma* describes many modes of conduct, including speak the truth, do not be negligent of truth; do not be negligent of virtue; do not be negligent of welfare, of prosperity, of study and teaching, of duties to the gods and to the fathers; live as one to whom a mother is a god and to whom a father is a god and to whom a teacher is a god; those things that are irreproachable should be practiced and no others; only good deeds should be revered, not others; one should give with faith, one should give plenty, with modesty, with fear, and with sympathy (Crawford, 1974, pp. 211–212)

What are the universal duties of human beings? One sacrifices because of debt to the community, because one is culturally and experientially indebted to humanity and must, therefore, serve the universal good. The 10 laws of Manu also operate on those premises of virtuous conduct in *dharma*: steadfastness, forgiveness, application, nonappropriation, cleanliness, repression of the sensuous appetites, wisdom, learning, veracity, and restraint of anger. Also, although speaking truth is customarily good, if telling the truth will result in the death of an innocent, it is prudentially expedient to tell lies. In such cases, the end justifies the means. Here, one can see that Hindu ethics is not absolutist and unbending, but is reflective and contextual in its approach to ethical problems. However, to safeguard this situationalism from degenerating into privatism, the *dharma sastras* make it clear that exceptions are only to be made for the sake of others, not for one's own private advantage (Crawford, 1974, p. 223).

Dharma must be understood in relation to other values in society (Radhakrishnan, 1989). The traditional categories of *kama, artha, moksa,* and *dharma* are used to express an inclusive recognition of temporal values of which *moksa* is on the highest of the hierarchy. *Kama* refers to artistic or emotional or sensual experience or a combination of them; *artha* refers to economic and material interests; *dharma* comprises duties in the world or the requirements of the social order; and *moksa* is supreme freedom or realization or highest intuitive knowledge of reality.[5] When *dharma* is interpreted as the capstone of earthly value, the major contrast is between the transcendental realm of *moksa* and the empirical, limited, and relative realm of *dharma, kama,* and *artha*. The great Indian philosopher Sri Aurobindo spoke of the Indian social system as an attempt to achieve the harmony of the complex factors of these values, in which *dharma* is the guiding principle of the social order founded on an innate law of individuals and of societies. *Dharma* stands as a contrast to *moksa*'s spiritual freedom (Creel, 1977, pp. 45–57).[6]

Dharma represents the moral order of the universe that ensures the victory of righteousness over evil, so that a weak person can hope to defeat the strong through righteousness (Jhingran, 1989, p. 167). The naïve belief that *dharma* [righteousness] or *satya* [truth] always wins in the end so characterizes the Indian ethos that the Indian government has accepted the phrase, *satyameva jayate* [truth alone triumphs], as the motif on the national emblem. *Dharma*, in all of its ethical tentacles, embraces both virtue and duty. Certain moral terms like nonviolence, truthfulness, and forgiveness denote both virtues and duties.

A human being of *dharma* demonstrates the ethical behavior in several ways: kindness towards all, forbearance, nonhostility, cleanliness, quietude, doing good acts, freedom from avarice, and freedom from convetedness. Unless accompanied by the practice of these universal virtues, fulfillment of religious duties is considered useless. Throughout Sanskrit literature, there are many more listings of moral virtues, including purity, charity, mercy, self-restraint, control of the senses, patience, absence of pride and anger, intelligence, modesty, spiritual knowledge, helping the distressed, serving the elderly, speaking the truth [*satya*], agreeableness of speech, indifference to material well-being, and piety.

Gita teaches fearlessness, purity of heart, nonviolence, truth, serenity, absence of enmity, compassion for creatures, absence of hatred, whereas *Mahabharata* enumerates forgiveness, patience, nonviolence, equality towards all creatures, truthfulness, simplicity, magnanimity, non-greed, compassion, and speaking gently and pleasantly. According to the scriptures, if *dharma* is conceived in terms of nonviolence and compassion, it presents a universal morality in that, "those who follow the principle of universal love and are adorned with mercy towards all living creatures are called Godly" (Jhingran, 1989, pp. 173–179).

Paradoxically, truth is perhaps the most important cardinal virtue of Hindu *dharma*. It is unanimously recognized and cherished in all the traditions of Hinduism. Truth is the highest *dharma* and the source of all other virtues. Manu's law says being guided by truth in one's action is the greatest virtue, whereas acting in disregard to it is the greatest sin (Jhingran, 1989, p. 170). To be truthful means never to indulge in any kind of lies or slanderous and malicious talk and to adhere to the highest measure of rectitude in one's conduct. It also means knowing the metaphysical nature of reality [*satya*] and acting in harmony with it. However, as noted earlier, Hindu texts also make allowances for untruthful representations to protect the innocent. As Krishna argues, a promise-keeping and truth-telling cannot be unconditional obligations when they conflict with the avoidance of grossly unjust and criminal acts such as patricide or fratricide (Jhingran, 1989).

The cardinal virtue of Hinduism that equals *dharma* in importance is *ahimsa* (nonviolence). Nonviolence along with truth in *dharma* forms the basis of the entire superstructure of Hindu religio-culture. The ethical principle of nonviolence introduced into Hinduism through the direct influence of Buddhism and Jainism, eventually came to be accepted as the guiding principle of life. *Ahimsa* is the all-encompassing ideal both in its concept and scope. The contemporary example in Indian history is Mahatma Gandhi, who used *ahimsa* as a potent weapon in India's independence movement against the British Empire. Gandhi literally interpreted the term as never hurting another in any way and harboring positive feelings of friendship and goodwill towards all—including one's own enemies. The ideal of *ahimsa* means that a human being must never hurt others physically or mentally or cause fear in them or in any creature. Absolute harmlessness and friendliness towards all beings are expected in *ahimsa*. The *Mahabharata* contends that a human being who causes no harm to others through body, mind, and speech, and who never thinks ill of others, reaches the stage of supreme *Brahman* (Jhingran, 1989, p. 191).

The real worth of *ahimsa* lies in its exceptionally broad application—expanding from individuals, their group, community, nation, world, nature and all the living things therein, and eventually to the cosmos. All living beings from gods and humans to smallest creatures are *jivas*.

(The term *jiva* is used for the individual soul basically referring to one who has life breath.) *Ahimsa* is applicable to all and in all circumstances of life. Nowhere in the history of human thought have the animal kingdom and the plant kingdom been treated as deserving equal consideration and kindness as human beings as in the concept of nonviolence. Millions of Indians reject meat eating on the sole consideration that animals are killed for meat have the same *jiva* as humans. Animals cannot be killed, beaten, or treated cruelly.

Closely associated with *ahimsa*, then, is the virtue of compassion or universal kindness to all beings. The puritan Jain concept of *ahimsa* allows taking the life of a plant if and only it helps in the survival of another living being. Vegetarians who rely on plants do so with extreme apology and for frugal subsistence. Kindness, compassion, and nonviolence are to be nurtured and practiced by all in day-to-day life. Other branches of Hinduism affirm that kindness toward others or magnanimity toward other living creatures motivates great souls to work for the good of suffering human beings. Jhingran admits that it is always difficult to say what exactly Hinduism means by doing good to others (*paropakara*). "It definitely includes magnanimity and philanthropic works, as digging wells, planting trees, etc., though perhaps active physical service is not included" (Jhingran, 1989, pp. 190–191). Prominent Hindu philosophers come down squarely on each end of the spectrum of compassion. Some contend that a human being must not merely provide physical service but ought to help follow humans obtain freedom from transmigratory existence. Others emphasize the need to provide for the physical needs of the masses before offering them spiritual guidance. Universal love and compassion are integral to the concept of *ahimsa*. Truth is an end to which *ahimsa* is the means.

Ethics in Contemporary India

India's hybrid discourse of modernity and of progress involves a search for a new beginning. All the ethical ideals discussed here—*dharma* and *ahimsa*, in particular—have to be recast in terms of a modern and post-colonial India. This task is essentially an urban phenomenon, though the outcome will have a drastic impact on India's rural life.

Modern India now confronts the compelling challenges paramount to the survival of her civilization: the secular as religion, the community as a citizen, caste politics and economic inequality, Hindu–Muslim discord, regionalism, linguistic divisions and the burden of English, social harmony and welfare, status of women, unity and plurality, individuals and the social order, cultural integration, protection of environment and wildlife, population control and family planning, abortion and the dilemmas of life and death, and the challenges brought forth by Western dominance in culture, education, urban values, and ways of thinking. India's success in confronting these challenges depends on her ability to harness the resources of her philosophy and ethical ideals to bring them to bear on her native solutions.

The public rhetoric of the government and the constitution of India is built on the concept of a secular state in a country that is overwhelmingly Hindu. India is indeed a secular state, but it is also much more than that (Larson, 1995, p. 284). It combines a Gandhian–Nehruvian model of a Neo-Hindu civilization-state. Its Gandhian nationalist ideology has a Nehruvian variant in terms of socialism, with nonalignment existing alongside the liberal democratic traditions of the Indian National Congress. The reformist impulses of Hindu religious movements have a quasi-protestant veneer of individualism and the privatization of religious belief. India's multilayered cultural heritage of the Indic, the Indo-Brahmanical, and Indo-Anglian, however, reflects the conventional mind-set of India's high-caste ruling elite. It is a breathtaking exercise in the "solution of synthesis" (Larson, 1995, p. 285) and what John F. Kennedy called an "experiment in democracy." Gerald Larson (1995) writes,

It is also useful to see the Neo-Hindu "secular state" . . . as a Gandhian-Nehruvian Indic civil religion that exists alongside the many other religious traditions in modern India, a civil religion mainly of high caste, English-educated and English-speaking elites in government, the modern industrialized economy, the professions, communications and the academy.

(p. 285)

India's hybrid discourse of modernity includes the pervasive use of the terms "secular" and "secular state" whereas some Indian leaders refer to India as a "nation of Hindu chauvinism," "upper caste Hindu *raj*," and so forth. The Kashmiri Muslims see it as a repressive, totalitarian Hindu regime that rules by the barrel of the gun (Larson, 1995, p. 285).

Given the contentious environment between dominant religions ranging from Hinduism to Islam, from Jainism to Sikhism, and all faiths that lie in between, the secularist ideology borrowed from the West and later codified in the constitution of India raises a nebulous specter of Hinduism's ability to embrace tolerance. However, post-colonial critics such as Nandy (as quoted by Larson, 1995) are skeptical about secularism:

To build a more tolerant society we shall have to defy the imperialism of categories of our times which allows the concept of secularism . . . to hegemonize the idea of tolerance, so that any one who is not secular becomes definitionally intolerant.

(Larson, 1995, p. 290)

The notion that tolerance came to India through Western secularism is what Nandy appropriately resists. The prevailing models of dissent, diversity, and tolerance in early and modern Hinduism continue to elude the post-colonial, urban, English-educated Indian. To build a tolerant India, one has to retrieve the modern-day *dharma* from the cultural narrative of authentic and tolerant India rather than depend on the disarming and yet alien ideologies associated with Western secularism.

It would be a mistake to trace the . . . religious formulation of the "secular state" solely to the Western and largely Protestant notions of secularization, individualism and the privatization of religious belief, although it certainly is the case that these Protestant notions appear to be dominant in modern Indian discourse.

(Larson, 1995, p. 291)

As Larson notes, India's communities within communities within communities represent fundamental and major features of social reality in terms of the traditional or premodern caste system with its religio-hierarchical ranking based on ritual purity. These multiple layers of communities are the fundamental structure of modern, secular India with its caste, tribes, backward classes, caste associations, sectarian movements, extended families with carefully arranged marriages, and any number of other minority communities based on language, religion, or regional culture. For India, it has become the ultimate challenge to make relevant the concept of *dharma* to retrieve unity and harmony within India's 4,599 or more distinct communities in the midst of hundreds of languages and dialects. In this cultural milieu, the notion of community becomes central to the understanding of what India has been and continues to be. Political scientists have coined the term "community-ship" to parallel the notion of "citizenship" as one way of capturing this dimension of India's hybrid discourse of modernity. In modern India, the claims of community-ship are at least as strong and maybe much stronger than the claims of citizenship. This notion of community-ship takes the place of communalism, nationalism, secularism, sectarianism, and other inaccurate and divisive notions in Indian society (Larson, 1995).

Two major social explosions in the early 1990s occurred in the area of caste politics and Hindu–Muslim relations. The first was associated with the government-initiated Mandal Commission, which studied the status of lower caste Indians and proposed higher quotas for their employment and educational access and privileges. When the commission released its report late in 1990, members of different castes pitted against each other in a manner that was never before seen in India's history. The backlash in the guise of student protests and upper-caste reaction resulted in urban violence and self-immolations. The government's quest to balance tradition with equality and fairness in the face of injustice exemplifies how India is confronting the challenges posed by caste politics and modernity. Questions of entitlement, the search for alternative political and cultural traditions, human rights and economic rights for lower caste and untouchable populations, the classification and politics of community in today's India are all best seen in the contemporary formation of narratives on caste. The fact remains, however, that the lower-caste people—particularly in the villages—live under a hegemony of the Brahmanic and other upper castes and subcastes that is oppressive and often cruelly inhumane.

The second incident was associated with the holy city of Ayodhya that pitted Hindus and Muslims against each other over the control of a sacred site (cf. Breckenridge & Van Der Veer, 1994, pp. 314–315).[7] In a dramatic entry into the arena of conflict, Hindus wanted to demolish a mosque supposedly built on the site of the birthplace of Lord Rama. Fundamentalist religious groups and political parties turned this confrontation into a national settling-of-scores between Hindus and Muslims. India witnessed perhaps its most serious Hindu–Muslim rioting since the partition of 1947. The number of dead ran into thousands across the country and the mosque was demolished by Hindu militants to "recapture injured Hindu pride" (Hardgrave & Kochanek, 1993, p. 182). The Muslims in India, although a minority of less than 15%, number more than 100 million—making India the fourth most populous Muslim nation in the world, after Indonesia, Bangladesh, and Pakistan. India's Muslims, however, are heterogeneous.

> They are not only culturally varied (distinguished, for example, by language and custom among the Urdu-speaking Muslims of North India and Andhra Pradesh, the Malayalee-speaking Mappillas of Kerala, and the Tamil-speaking Labbais of Tamil Nadu), they are also divided on religion and politics. They range from Islamic fundamentalists to secular Communists.
>
> (Hardgrave & Kochanek, 1993, p. 183)

Many Indian Muslims today feel threatened and look to the government as their protector. They have traditionally supported the Indian Congress Party for its commitment to secular ideology. Although the vast majority of Muslims remain depressed in rural areas, there is a rising urban middle class, many of whom have ties to the economic pipeline in the Middle East. India's ethical balance has consistently strived to accommodate Islam's Shariat law and India's uniform civil code—a dual legal system that accommodates Muslim injunctions of faith. This does not always come without acrimony. Urban communal riots are regular and constant because most rural Muslims are too weak to offer resistance or pose a threat. Hindu chauvinism and the militant Islamic factions are fortunately considered as extremes politically moderate India as a whole, but the continued Hindu hegemony will pose problems for Indian morality in the coming decades (Hardgrave & Kochanek, 1993, pp. 175–205). Even though the constitution of India has abolished untouchablity and discrimination on the grounds of religion, race, caste, sex, or birthplace, tension between religions will remain a challenge to the formation of a permanent reconciliatory ethics in Indian society.

Regional cultures and linguistic groups have also asserted their right to dominance in post-independent India. The divisions between the North and the South, between the Hindi-speaking northerners and the southerners who speak Tamil, Kannada, Malayalum, and Telugu have become pronounced. The South with its longer traditions in art, music, dance, drama, and literature perceives the North as politically dominant and culturally bullish. Similar situations exist between Northeast and West. Regional conflicts and politics based on language are common and pose a constant threat to India's unity and harmony.

English that forms the "link language" extends its hegemony and control over other languages, and yet it is the *lingua franca* that has continued to serve the nation in the post-independent era. Critics have argued that colonialism manifests its power and entangles the colonized people "in webs of cohesion and domination; the most insidious—because not often perceived as a tool of conquest—is the superimposition of the colonial language over the languages of the subject people" (Niranjana, Sudhir, & Dhareshwar, 1993, p. 334). Conquest of the language was a necessary adjunct of economic and political conquest (Suleri, 1992). Nonetheless, the demands for regional autonomy are tied to questions of dominance among Indian languages.

The concept of *dharma* and *ahimsa*, which provides the rationale for Indian ethics, specifically promotes unity of existence, the oneness of all, social harmony, social welfare, and plurality. The struggle for social harmony, the growth of the women's movement for equal status in India, and cultural-social integration have gathered increased momentum during the last two decades. *Dharma* with its established kinship among fellow human beings runs into its toughest contemporary test in these areas of social upheaval. Noted Indian philosopher Radhakrishnan, as quoted by Creel (1977), says that it is *dharma* that must be evoked to keep society together and nurture "national solidarity, cultural and social integration, equality of women" (p. 86). Women's struggle[8] involves increased political participation, access to higher education, liberation from social practices that have historically been oppressive—that is, the dowry system, nonmarriage of the widow, the rare but alarming practice of *sati* (self-immolation of the widow),[9] and a revolt against the oppressive ideology of the masculine at the societal level (Niranjana et al., 1993).

It is interesting and instructive to juxtapose the advocacy of social integration with that of individual ethics. The individual and the social order remain suspended in an enigmatic relationship in India. Individuals determine *dharma* in the process of reaching *moksa* [liberation]. Gandhi stressed discipline, self-control, and individual purity as necessary foundations of social righteousness. Social justice is deemed a spontaneous reflection of justice in individual life, and the moral discipline of individuals is considered the key to social reconstruction. If individual perfection is emphasized, social welfare will follow automatically (as cited by Creel, 1986, p. 101). The closest Hindu ethical tenet associated with individual discipline is the idea of *sva-dharma* [service to humanity], which is reflected in Gandhi's view of *swadeshi* [respect for the indigenous]. Gandhi wished to preserve the ancient village structure with its reciprocal patterns of duty and inward-looking solutions to native problems. Gandhi defended this position with the argument that only traditional villages will resist Western materialism and permit a modest social development that leaves people time to pursue spiritual growth. The other reason for his position was that there is an innate law that arranges people in the social order determining their stations and roles in society. *Swaraj* [home rule] and *swadeshi* [preference for things native] became hallmarks in Gandhi's struggle for independence; modern India strives to anchor these terms in *dharma* and *ahimsa* as the country comes to terms with her hybrid discourse of modernity.

Typical of *Gita*'s moral dilemmas tugging at the heart and mind is the modern Indian's quest for tranquility in the midst of chaos. As Crawford (1974) notes,

Hindu ethics is a moral system which acknowledges genuine moral dilemmas. We encounter a dilemma when values to which we are equally committed are brought into conflict, so that the honoring of one value necessitates the violation of the other. The Hindu position is to be distinguished both from the religious fundamentalist, who views dilemmas in the light of revelation, and the secular rationalist, who views them as problems to be solved by the use of reason. For the one, the problem is the need for better faith; for the other, it is the need for superior knowledge. In either case, there are no genuine dilemmas.

(p. 6)

What, then, is the applicability of *ahimsa* to India and to the Indians? Perhaps the question ought to be: What is the relevance of *ahimsa* to the world at large (Tahtinen, 1976; Walli, 1974)? The dilemmas of life and death are continuous. The view that life in the womb is not tissue of the mother's body but a separate life bearing the essential marks of humanity before the time of conception is *ahimsa*. "In the Indian view, perhaps the greatest hiatus in Western religions is the failure to explain birth" (Oliver, 1971). *Ahimsa* is also present in the rules of hospitality; gentleness; care for the young and aged; kindness to the land, birds, insects, animals, and the child in the womb. One can locate the concept of *ahimsa* (and *dharma*) in India's politics of population control and family planning. How India will reconcile a burgeoning population with voluntary family planning strategies remains to be seen. India will reach the 1 billion mark in population by the year 2000. Hindu philosophy equates death with life and life with death. Life exists before one is conceived and life exists even after cremation. *Samsara*, the eternal cycle of life, is a metaphysical reality until one reaches *moksa* through one's doing of *dharma* to perfection. The contemporary Indian struggles to find a compromise in the paradoxes that are offered in today's world.

One of the most pertinent principles of early Hindu ethics concerns the sanctity of the natural environment. Hindu philosophy is a rich repository of ideas, attitudes, ethics, and values that can furnish the necessary principles for a proper management of the physical environment (Crawford, 1995, p. 169). Indian environmental thinking dates back to the earliest of the pre-Aryan religions and cultures around 4500 to 3000 B.C.E. Rituals that emphasized the figurines of mother goddesses and representations of other gods were accompanied by animals and plants. A great deal of the imagery of poetry and religion reveal to the human imagination a nature that seemed living and animate. Lord Krishna rides on a cow, Lord Brahma's main transportation is the gentle bull, Goddess Lakshmi sits on a lotus flower, Lord Ganesha is half god and half elephant. Lord Vishnu is protected by a cobra that is coiled around his neck. The universe itself at the time of creation was supported by a serpent that eventually became the pillar on which life itself rested. Hindus have reflected long and hard on the relationship God has with humans and physical nature of the world. The principles of unity, of interconnectedness, of interdependence and of restraint are reflected not only in the evolving governmental policies in India but more so in the village life.

The struggle to bring economic development into rural India is the largest battle between the Western model of technology-driven social progress and Gandhi's *swadeshi* principle empowering villagers to attain self-sufficiency through cottage industries. The next two decades will determine what direction India will pursue. The speculative wisdom of India is essentially intuitive and cosmic. It purports the view of a deep ecology that places people *in* nature, as opposed to a shallow ecology that is anthropocentric and that ascribes to Homo sapiens a position of dominance and superiority *over* nature (Crawford, 1995, p. 177). Issues in biodiversity are related to Hinduism's nondiscriminatory embrace of all life forms, including the lowliest plants and insects. It is interesting that Hindu ethics is sensitive to the moral and practical difficulties of its post-colonial condition. The destruction caused by poverty and population, the struggle to feed their burgeoning members have not diminished the people's worship of nature—more so in the nonurban Indian milieu. The flexibility of Indian ethics makes accommodation and relevance possible to contemporary situations. For example, the concept of *dharma*, is essentially a dynamic notion open to processes of change as different situations arise. The general idea behind Hinduism's environmental ethics is that the individual *Atman* is one with the universal *Brahman*. This *Brahman* force is manifest uniformly in the divinity of human, animal, and plant life on earth. All these entities live an apparently independent existence, but they all emanate from *Brahman*—oneness in all, which transcends the natural divisions between people and people and between humankind and nature. "Its ecumenism is existential and environmental. It sees humanity in nature and nature in humanity" (Crawford, 1995, p. 200).

India's opposition to the signing of the Comprehensive Test Ban Treaty (CTBT) to ban nuclear testing is based on India's global consciousness in which all humans are viewed as members of a single family; that solidarity is seen as extending beyond human welfare to include all creation. India's sole condition to signing of the CTBT is that every nuclear weapon must be destroyed before the CTBT must go into effect. India's view on this treaty is a rare display of a developing country standing up to the global powers. The conquest of nature is unreal and people's sense of separateness is the product of ignorance. Referring to Hinduism's environmental ethics, Crawford (1995) writes,

> This calls for self-knowledge. Humans cannot act ethically toward nature as long as they are ignorant of themselves. Lacking a sense of universal identity, people cannot identify with the trees and the mountains, nor can we feel empathy for the beasts of the fields. Nature is perceived as mechanical because people have become mechanical. Nature is perceived as empty because we have become empty. We manipulate nature because we manipulate ourselves. The loss of our relation to nature is the corollary of the loss of our own lives.
>
> (pp. 168–202)

Conclusion

This chapter has attempted to glean a vast array of cultural sources and interpretations in India to highlight her ethical orientation in the context of her post-colonial condition. Ethics in India is beset by the challenges of continuity and change both in its ethical ideals and normative orientation.

On this journey, readers may discover for themselves what traits of the ancient philosophical and religious traditions of India can invigorate an ethics of communication and contribute to the universal ethical project so badly needed for the 21st century. Perhaps the most practical insight from this tradition is its emphasis of virtue ethics. The moral person is indispensable. People who are truthful, forthright, gentle, and compassionate are able to perform their duties—also as communicators—without analytical recourse to ethics codes or so called standards. This point can be of great significance for media professionals having to make complicated decisions against immediate deadlines. There are no shortcuts in ethics: being is prior to acting, and nothing can substitute the ongoing struggle of becoming moral persons.

Morality, however, is not acquired in isolation. Moral practice usually, if not always, relates to others. The curious meshing of individual and social ethics derives from the notion of relatedness. If individuals are truthful to others, acting justly toward them, charitable and helpful to them, they will be able to attain (as it were) self-fulfillment and freedom (*moksa*). The principle of relatedness is even more evident in the radical demand of universal kindness to all beings, better known as nonviolence.

The basis of this relatedness is a cosmic order, embracing both the local and global. Only its awareness and contemplation can ultimately make humans genuinely human and, thus, moral beings. As Crawford (1995, p. 202) points out, the basic message of Hindu ethics in the ancient idea of *Rta* is that harmony is already here. We do not have to create it, only discover it.

Notes

1. Any normative discourse on Indian ethics must necessarily take into consideration the hermeneutic situation of the 20th century, the Orientalist constructions (Said, 1978, 1993) in Western epistemologies, and the problem of authenticity (Halfbass, 1988, 1991). For three centuries, the construction of non-Western ethics, particularly those of India, was mainly the project of the Anglo-Saxon curiosity. With its bias rooted in the Euro-Enlightenment, the Anglo-Saxon project initiated and appropriated the discourse on philosophy and ethics. Halfbass (1988) and Nandy (1983) contend that a degree of intellectual honesty in the East–West conversation and the balance between the colonized and the colonizer must be restored for an authentic understanding of the ethics of "the Other." Most discourses were founded on the European understanding of Indian ethics, which later became the staple of higher education and pedagogy of the Indian elite. The latter, although claiming their Indianness with authority, legitimated European thought as more authentic and "objective." Consequently, any discourse on non-Western ethos begins as a response to that which has been already erected. However, it is beyond the scope of this chapter to demonstrate the difficulties in scholarship relating to ethics when one attempts to look for native sources of ethics, its rhetorical composition, its terms, its categories, its meanings and its dogma—in the midst of the 20th-century hermeneutics of suspicion.

   This dilemma gives the reader a sense of the challenge facing colonial scholarship. It must at the same time not romanticize one's civilization and attempt to restore a native hermeneutics in the quest for authenticity. Rhetorical continuity, evaluation of communicative acts, the undecidability of truth, the nonfoundational aspects of ethics, the multiplicity of meanings, the multitude of discourses within one tradition, such competing narratives as strong versus the meek and dominant versus the subservient, the lack of acceptable grounds for ethical values, the categories of ethics, and the understanding of Self—all present the self-aware Indian a genuine problematic in conversing with a non-Indian about ethics. Colonial societies were not simply colonized politically and economically; more importantly, they were colonized culturally and intellectually. One needs to be mindful of the intellectual colonialism (Oommen, 1995) in which the present-day discourses between societies take place. This is particularly critical for the understanding of the ethics of India.

2. In this chapter, I have used Hindu–India interchangeably. I have chosen to use the word Hindu *faute de mieux* for India. Hindu is any native-born inhabitant of India, whatever his or her ancestry or faith. But in the article, such "Hindus" as Mohammedans and Parsis have been excluded (see Hopkins, 1924).

3. I have avoided the diacritical signs, the *visargas*, thus minimizing the use of Sanskrit words.

4. This type of determinism explains not only the lack of missionary outreach in Hinduism (because a faith is bestowed on us at birth) but also the resistance to religious conversion or cultural change (Lacy, 1965, p. 25). It also explains why even the *Gita* has not inspired many Hindus to creative social and ethical reforms.

5. Because these values are prevalent in all of the epics and *sastras*, any attempt to simply or venture into deductivist analysis will prove to be difficult due to the sheer ambiguity of the concepts.

6. Questions of *dharma* and the regulations of social life were not the province of the Indian philosopher. As Rangaswami Aiyangar (as quoted by Creel, 1977) says, "Writers on philosophy . . . take for granted a life lived according to the dictates of *dharma*, and do not, therefore, expatiate on them. Ethics do not accordingly form a separate branch of Indian philosophy" (p. 21).

7. The Hindu–Muslim communal strife in the city of Ayodhya is a classic study of political rhetoric and public action in post-colonial India. Soon after India gained freedom from Britain in 1947, the ultra-right Hindus rekindled an old controversy over the site of the Islamic mosque, Babri Masjid. They contested the same site as the Ramajanmabhoomi—the birthplace of Lord Rama. The secular interventions from the government and courts temporarily restrained the attempt of Hindu fundamentalist political parties' to take over the sacred site. Neither the Muslims nor the Hindus could legitimately claim the site as their own for four decades. In February 1986, the district court decision to unlock the doors of the Babri Masjid assuring unhindered access for Hindu worship ignited the communal tension once again. It was destined to explode 6 years later. In 1992, the climax came in the wake of the call by the Hindu-revivalist organization, Vishwa Hindu Parishad, "to liberate Lord Rama from the Muslim jail." On December 6, the Hindu mob demolished and razed the mosque to the ground stunning predominantly moderate Hindu India. The national news media agonized over the onslaught of secularism in India.

8. For Indian feminism and women's movement for social and economic equality, see Niranjana et al. (1993); Kishwa and Ruth (1984); and Jeffrey (1979).

9. *Sati*, the idea of compulsory suicide on the funeral pyre of one's husband, has been an ancient rite, though not widespread, in northern India. Strangely, the texts of earlier Hinduism do not carry references to this practice. In modern India over the last 50 years, sporadic cases of sati have been confined mainly to one state in northern India and, within that state, to one region (Nandy, 1995, p. 34). The British construction of Indian history emphasized such generalizations of *sati* as a widespread practice to justify its own oppression of the heathens. The *Rg Veda*, *Ramayana*, *Mahabharata* and other Hindu scriptures, on the contrary, carry directives to honor and respect widows, who were allowed to marry anyone without restrictions.

References

Breckenridge, C. A., & Van Der Veer, P. (1994). *Orientalism and the postcolonial predicament.* Delphi, India: Oxford University Press.

Brown, N. W. (1970). *Man in universe: Some continuities in Indian thought.* Berkeley, CA: University of California Press.

Coward, H. G., Lipner, J. J., & Young, K. K. (1989). *Hindu ethics.* Albany, NY: State University of New York Press.

Crawford, C. S. (1974). *The evolution of Hindu ethical ideals.* Calcutta, India: Firma K. L. Mukhopadhyay.

Crawford, C. S. (1995). *Dilemmas of life and death: Hindu ethics in a North American context.* Albany, NY: State University of New York Press.

Creel, A. B. (1977). *Dharma in Hindu ethics.* Columbia, MO: South Asia books.

Doniger, W., & Smith, B. K. (Eds.). (1991). *Laws of Manu.* New Delhi, India: Penguin.

Gandhi, M. C. (1948). *The story of my experiments with truth.* New York: Public Affairs Press.

Government of India (1958). *The collected works of Mahatma Gandhi* (Vol. 53, Appendix III). Delhi, India: Ministry of Information and Broadcasting, Publications Division.

Govinda Das, B. (1947). *Hindu ethics: Principles of Hindu religio-social regeneration.* Madras: G. A. Natesan.

Halfbass, W. (1988). *India and Europe: An essay in understanding.* Albany, NY: State University of New York Press.

Halfbass, W. (1991). *Tradition and reflection: Explorations in Indian thought.* Albany, NY: State University of New York Press.

Hardgrave, R. Jr., & Kochanek, S. A. (1993). *India government and politics in a developing nation.* Orlando, FL: Harcourt Brace Jovanovich.

Herman, A. L. (1991). *A brief introduction to Hinduism: Religion, philosophy, and ways of liberation.* Boulder, CO: Westview.

Hopkins, W. E. (1924). *Ethics in India.* New Haven, CT: Yale University Press.

Jeffrey, P. (1979). *Indian women in Purdah.* London: Zed.

Jhingran, S. (1989). *Aspects of Hindu morality.* Delhi: Motilal Banarsidass.

Khan, B. (1965). *The concept of dharma in Valmiki Ramayana.* New Delhi, India: Munshi Ram Manohar Lal.

King, W. L. (1946). *Buddhism and Christianity: Some bridges of understanding.* Philadelphia, PA: Westminster.

Krishna, D. (1991). *India philosophy: A counter perspective.* New York: Oxford University Press.

Kishwar, M., & Ruth, V. (1984). *In search of answers: Indian women's voices form Manushi.* London: Zed.

Lacy, C. (1965). *The conscience of India.* San Francisco, CA: Holt, Rinehart & Winston.

Larson. G. J. (1995). *India's agony over religion.* Albany, NY: State University of New York Press.

Larson, G., & Deutsch, E. (Eds.) (1988). *Interpreting across boundaries: New essays in comparative philosophy.* Princeton, NJ: Princeton University Press.

Lopez, D. S. (Ed.). (1995). *Religions of India in practice.* Princeton, NJ: Princeton University Press.

Misra, K. P., & Gangal, S. C. (1981). *Gandhi and the contemporary world.* Delhi, India: Chanakya.

Nandy, A. (1983). *The intimate enemy: loss and recovery of self under colonialism.* New York: Oxford University Press.

Nandy, A. (1995). *The savage Freud and other essays.* New York: Oxford University Press.

Niranjana, T., Sudhir, P., & Dhareshwar, V. (1993). *Interrogating modernity: Culture and colonialism in India.* Calcutta: Seagull.

Noble, M. E. (1915). *Religion and dharma.* London: Longmans, Green and Co.

Oliver, R. T. (1971). *Communication and culture in ancient India and China.* Syracuse, NY: Syracuse University Press.

Oommen, T. K. (1995). *Alien concepts and South Asian reality.* New Delhi, India: Sage.

Radhakrishnan, S. (1989). *Indian philosophy*. New York: Oxford University Press.

Richman, P. (1991). *Many Ramayanas: The diversity of a narrative tradition in South Asia*. Oxford, UK: Oxford University Press.

Said, E. W. (1978). *Orientalism*. New York: Vintage.

Said, E. W. (1993). *Culture and imperialism*. New York: Knopf.

Sen, A. (1993, April 8). The threats to secular India. *New York Times Review*, pp. 26–32.

Suleri, S. (1982). *The rhetoric of English India*. Chicago, IL: University of Chicago Press.

Tahtinen, U. (1976). *Ahimsa: Non-violence in Indian tradition*. London: Rider.

Walli, K. (1974). *The conception of ahimsa in Indian thought*. Varanasi, India: Bharata Manisha.

19
Peace and the Middle East

Edward W. Said

I'm going to talk about peace in the Middle East, in the context of the continuing Persian Gulf War, since it isn't really over as you know, but also in the context of the question of Palestine that is most important to me and to I suppose many people in this room and elsewhere in the country. The immediate situation at present is rather dramatic. There is a persisting conflict between the United States and Iraq. There is also, rather dramatically, not only the peace process which was begun in 1991 by the Secretary of State acting on the instructions of the President, but also, for the first time, a rather dramatic conflict between the United States and Israel over the question of $10 billion loan guarantees to Israel.

But both of these questions need to be looked at in their historical and above all in their moral context. The first point is one that has to do with the war the United States fought against Iraq in January through March of 1991. My own position on the war is a simple one. I was against and remain against the invasion and annexation of Kuwait by Iraq. The arguments given were spurious. The notion of invading, in a Bismarckian fashion, a neighboring Arab country and claiming to unify it on the basis of principles of Arab unity, is an outrageous breach of international law and is intolerable and unacceptable. But I also was against and remain against the United States-inspired war against Iraq because although principles were solicited and mentioned many times by the President, in actuality principles were not at stake. There was a rather showy recourse to the United Nations. The President persists to this say in talking about the United Nations as if it was acting on its own and not, in fact, spurred on by the United States to take the positions that it did. The falseness of the position taken by the United States, which claimed to be acting on principles against aggression and so on, was made more manifest when at the same time massive abuses of human rights, massive abuses of international law, massive abuses of the rights of an entire people, namely the Palestinian people, were being committed barely a thousand miles away in Palestine by the Israelis with the support and subsidy of the United States.

So it really wasn't a war fought on principles, or if they were principles they were very lackadaisically applied. Since 1974, Turkey has been in occupation of half of Cyprus, and there have been numerous U.N. resolutions suggesting that Turkey should withdraw. The United States didn't go to war against Turkey. Similarly, there have been numerous U.N. resolutions against the Israeli occupation of the West Bank and Gaza, against the occupation of South Lebanon, against the occupation and annexation of the Golan Heights and Jerusalem. But the United States has not gone to war against Israel. Far from that, it has continued to supply Israel with military and economic support.

No, the issue in the case of the invasion of Iraq by Kuwait was oil and remains oil and the strategic importance of the Gulf region to the United States for its own purposes. The war has now been fought, and there were a lot of parades in June. But it's important and sobering to survey the results of the war, not from the point of view of rhetoric and high sounding principles, but rather from what in fact is taking place on the ground in the region in which the war was fought.

One of the first results of the war was a huge number of Iraqi deaths. The United States and its allies only lost a few hundred men. Iraq by conservative estimates lost 100,000 people, probably more. This amounts to about one-half of one percent of the total 1990 Iraqi population of 18.8 million people. We're talking about an equivalent loss of life in U.S. terms of 1,257,000 people. This is approximately equal to the combined total of U.S. deaths in the Civil War, World War I, World War II, the Korean War and The Vietnam War. [Figures based on 1991 Almanac.] The war also accomplished the massive destruction of Baghdad, which to most Americans is just a spot on the map. But in the eyes of the Arab world, Baghdad is one of the greatest cities in the Islamic and Arab world. Baghdad was the capital of the Abbasid Empire for hundreds of years. It was destroyed by the Mongols in the thirteenth century, and then by the United States in the twentieth century. But more important than that, Baghdad is the city which in the twentieth century was and is the most renowned for the richness of its culture. Most of the great poets, writers, painters and architects of the contemporary Arab world come from Baghdad. So I think it's important to understand the horrendous meaning to Arabs and Muslims of the destruction of Baghdad by a Western power acting in an imperialist way. The bombing of Baghdad was roughly equivalent, in Western European terms, to the destruction of both Rome and Athens, and has instilled in the inhabitants of the region fear and hatred of the United States. Saddam Hussein is a tyrant, he is an unattractive, horrendously bloody human being whose regime is a repressive one. There's no use lying about that. That's a fact. But despite that, the massive destruction of a city like Baghdad has meant in the Arab and Islamic world a great deal of resentment against the United States and an even deeper resentment of so many of the rulers of the Arab world who, like those of Egypt, Syria and Saudi Arabia, were allied with the United States in this war.

The economic, social and political problems of the Arab world after the war remain grave and in fact are aggravated. There is still a tremendous disparity between the wealth of the Gulf states, which produce a vast amount of oil with a very tiny population and invest most of the money abroad, and the rest of the Arab world—countries, for example, like Egypt or the Sudan. It is estimated that eight million people will die of famine in the Sudan, where the average per capita income is about $200, compared with $15,000 in the Gulf, where most of the oil is found. The war contributed absolutely nothing to the problem of the distribution of wealth and resources in the Arab world. As another result of the war, there has been an increase in hostility toward the United States. Paradoxically, one of the aims of the war, to unseat Saddam Hussein—not only to get him out of Kuwait but to destroy his power—has been a total failure. Saddam Hussein remains in power, and ironically enough, just as he was supported by many of the rulers of the area and by the United States before the war, he is similarly supported now, after the war, by many of the rulers in the area. He remains in power and is able to continue to repress his population. Except for the starvation, various forms of disease due to malnutrition, and unsanitary conditions that the war has brought its people, there has been no change in Iraq.

Most celebrations of the war tended to focus on the amazing technological superiority of the United States, on the fact that George Bush now feels good that he's won a war, that Collin Powell is an exceptional general, General Schwarzkopf has gotten $5 million contract to write his memoirs, and so on. All of these results of the war, that everybody felt that the United States was opposing aggression, that we have to police the world, all of that stuff I don't want to go into. It's been brooded about but not sufficiently analyzed. The most important negative result of the war is not the destruction, not the horrendous toll wreaked upon the Iraqi people nor upon the many hundreds of thousands, probably millions of refugees created by the war, nor the tremendous ecological and environmental damage done by the war. That was done jointly. I think you'd be wrong if you were to say it was just Saddam Hussein. The United States contributed its fair share to the pollution of the atmosphere, the blowing up of wells, burying people alive and all kinds of other things.

Although we in the U.S. are not often prone to think in these ways, the most grievous negative result of the war was that even though the United States is the most significant outside force, the battle for democracy in the Middle East has not been helped by the U.S. at all. People in the Middle East, whether they are Arabs or Jews or others are also interested in democracy, and improving their lot. Through arm sales, support to governments, and economic, social, political and cultural missions in the Arab world, the United States has been the most significant outside power in the Middle East, much more so than Britain, France or the Soviet Union. Given this exorbitant influence, it is shameful that the U.S. has remained committed to the support of various unpopular dictatorships, whether they happen to be Arab or, in the case of Israel for the Palestinians, the Israeli government. It is very difficult to find one struggle for human rights, for women's rights, for minority rights in the Arab or the Islamic world or generally speaking the Middle East that the U.S. has supported or enhanced.

We really need to re-examine the pieties, exuberance and triumphalism of the war and try to remember that although we sit many thousands of miles away, the ongoing struggle against misery, oppression, persecution, which we have opposed, still continues. People still want a change in their status. They still want an enhanced and empowered life for themselves. But in all of this I'm very sorry to say that the United States has not helped that struggle at all.

The most important question for most Arabs and certainly for Palestinians is "linkage." Remember in the months leading up to the war how the Secretary of State and the President would say, "There is no linkage." As a professor of literature and somebody who spends a lot of his time dealing with language, linkage is a very ugly word. It's aesthetically unpleasant. "Connection" is a much better word. "Linkage" sounds like a technological neologism of some sort. But the idea is that, "No, we are entitled by an act of Olympian indifference and Archimedean withdrawal to pick whatever struggle we want to focus on for our own purposes. There is no connection between this question and any other question." Whereas "linkage" most accurately descried U.S. policy itself. It was the United States that not only originally supported Saddam Hussein but during the Iran–Iraq war was to support both sides, the Iranians and the Iraqis so that in the words of one policy maker they would "bleed each other to death." The U.S. has been involved. That is the connection. The United States has been involved not only in the emergence of Saddam and the war against him but also in other big question, the question of Palestine.

Whether policy makers like it or not, there is a connection, and the connection is—in both instances—dispossession, invasion, annexation and the massive abuse of human rights, for which the word Palestine has become the symbol. It's important to remember that the President and others in the international community of "white men," including France, Britain, and Germany and so forth, constitute all the people who had colonized the Third World and now stand in judgment over all of these little "colored people" who are running around. There's a great deal of racism involved here. It would be difficult to imagine that the kinds of epithets hurled at Arabs and non-Europeans generally could be, with equal impunity, hurled against other white people. We have listened to everyone who had an opinion about international law including the President, the Secretary of State, the British Foreign Minister, Douglas Hurd, and the French President. But is was very difficult not to remember that since 1967, when Israel occupied the West Bank and Gaza and the Golan Heights and Sinai, there have been 64—not 12, as in the case of Iraq—U.N. resolutions condemning the illegal Israeli occupation of territories. Israel had annexed territories against the will of the international community, and there were 29 more resolutions that would have been passed had the U.S. not vetoed them. It's horrific to think that the United States would mobilize an army, navy and air force over 600,000 men and women to fight to liberate Kuwait, and, yet, would do nothing when a scant eight years before the Israeli army had occupied Lebanon and laid siege to the city of Beirut. I speak with some passion on the subject because my family was besieged by the Israelis at the time. They were all in West Beirut. The Israelis had not only laid siege to the city; they had cut off water and electricity, and had forbidden the flow of medicines and food across the siege lines. A city that numbered about 750,000 people. And this in full view of the world! The proclaimed purpose of this was to destroy the PLO which, General Sharon said at the time, was threatening Israel. At the time the PLO fighters barely numbered 10 or 12 thousand men and women, armed with rifles and a few artillery pieces. No air force, no navy. The Israeli army, navy and air force conducted continuous bombardments of the city, on some days over 150 sorties. At that point I was at the United Nations, anxiously following the debate in the Security Council. A resolution was put forward, in which the Security Council urged Israel to open the siege lines to permit, for humanitarian purposes, the passage of medicines and other essential things for the besieged inhabitants of Beirut.

What was the fate of that resolution? It was vetoed by the United States. On what grounds, you might well ask? Why would anybody want to veto a resolution that spoke of medicines going across a line? The argument presented then was that the resolution was not "even-handed." It requires the imagination and the anger of a Jonathan Swift. It's like *Gulliver's Travels*. But of course there was no Palestinian army besieging Tel Aviv at the time. So the phrase "even-handedness" had the same kind of cruel irony to it as the U.S. bombing of Baghdad and claiming that it was doing so because of U.N. resolutions, principles and international law. What about the 64 U.N. resolutions that have gone unheeded against the Israeli occupation of the West Bank?

This brings us finally to the major question: As the United States was conducting a war that was destructive, wasteful, and mostly negative in its consequences for the people who have to live their lives in the Middle East, what was happening about a thousand miles to the west? As you know, in 1967 Israel occupied the West Bank and Gaza, the last remaining parts of Palestine. In 1948 when Israel was created, approximately 800,000 Palestinians were driven out. They have become the exiled population to which I belong, this is to say, a population today of about 3.5 million people who are scattered throughout the Arab world in places like Lebanon, in Jordan, Syria, partly in the Gulf, in Egypt, in parts of North Africa, Europe and North and South America. There were two Palestinian populations left behind. One accounted for about 120,000 people who did not leave and became Palestinian citizens of Israel in 1948. They number today about 800,000. Many of them live in their original places of residence, as second-class citizens of Israel. The second Palestinian population remains on the West Bank and Gaza, and their number today is approximately 2 million. They live under a military occupation in modern history. Here is where a little attention to facts and realities needs our scrupulous and fair scrutiny.

I think it's important first of all to understand that since 1967 those people on the West Bank and Gaza have had no political rights whatsoever. This means quite literally that they are entitled *to no representation at all*. They're not allowed to vote. They're not allowed to send representatives, whether to their own or Israeli institutions. They are taxed well beyond and above what most Israeli citizens are taxed. They are forbidden a huge number of things that in most other parts of the world are taken for granted, and certainly taken for granted by Israeli Jews. It's very important to understand who is doing the persecuting, the oppressing, and who is the oppressed. Much of the rhetoric of the Middle East in this country is so skewed as to cause the "average American"—the person who watches Peter Jennings, the MacNeil-Lehrer report, or *Nightline*, or reads the newspapers—to forget that it isn't Palestinians versus Israelis, two equals locked in what is sometimes referred to as an "ancient contest." The fact is that first of all this is not an ancient contest. It is a very modern contest that has to do with the appearance on the land in which I and many hundreds of thousands of Palestinians grew up, and of a wave of immigrants, largely from Europe and the United States, who displaced many of us in the process of establishing a Jewish national home in Palestine. In the past the Jews were the classical victims of persecution. They were the people who suffered the Holocaust. They were the people who suffered the ravages for centuries, for millennia, of anti-Semitism and persecution, largely in Europe at Christian hands. The Jews came to Palestine and one of the slogans they used at the time was "this is a land without people for a people without land." These people who came to Palestine and established Israel in 1948 did two things. One is they shattered and destroyed the largely Arab existing society that was there in 1948. Second, they became the oppressors of the Palestinians. This is the important point. We're not talking about a pre-historic or ancient conflict, nor are we talking about a perfectly symmetrical one. We're talking about a conflict in which one community, which was the community of victims in Europe and other parts of the world, came to Palestine and created another community of victims, who are the Palestinians. So it is important to understand the Palestinians today are the victims of the victims, which is a very difficult position for Palestinians to occupy, because the Israeli Jews who oppress them today are no ordinary people. They're not white settlers in South Africa. They're not French settlers in Algeria. They are a people who have a history of suffering behind them which gives them a moral stature that is quite unique in modern history. And it is a suffering that has been imposed upon them that has made them a very remarkable and unusual people. But so far as Palestinians are concerned, we have never seen that side. What we saw was the side of the people who came and took our land from us, dispossessed us, took our homes from us and threw us out and supplanted our state and our society with theirs.

But, you might say, this is ancient history. It happened in 1948. Israel is a state, recognized. What about the present? This is what I'm talking about now. I'm simply talking about the history as a background to the present, because history never ends very simply. There isn't a clear line that cuts histories off. History continues. In 1967 Israel occupied the west of Palestine, so that all of historical Palestine is now controlled by Israel. And I return now to the question of Palestine under military occupation since 1967. We're not talking about a matter of two weeks, which is as long as the Iraqi occupation of Kuwait lasted before the United States marshalled the United Nations and started sending troops and six months later conducted a war against Iraq. We're talking about 24 years of military occupation, during which time there have been numerous U.N. resolutions saying that Israel has to give up the land. But it's much more important to understand what is happening on the land for the almost two million Palestinians who live in Gaza and the West Bank. First of all, they have no political rights. What does this mean? It means that they have to pay taxes at a higher rate than paid by average Israeli citizens. More to the point: for those taxes Israel has never published a budget of what it spends on the West Bank and Gaza. So they pay taxes and don't know where the money goes because they are not entitled to ask. Taxes simply go in a sense to maintain the occupation, perhaps paying for the Israeli army to occupy the West Bank and Gaza. But the citizens of the West Bank and Gaza continue to pay taxes at astronomical levels, sometimes three times higher than those paid for by Israeli citizens, who by the way get free schools and health care and so on.

Israel has forbidden these Palestinians—and this is a crucial point not often recognized and known—to conduct themselves as if they belonged to a national community. All of us Palestinians consider ourselves to be Palestinians. But on the West Bank and Gaza the word "Palestine" is forbidden by military law. It's against the law to pronounce the word "Palestine." It is even against the law to use the colors of the Palestinian flag or to show the Palestinian flag. You've seen pictures during the intifada of young kids waving the flag around. That is a capital offense in Israel. The colors of the Palestinian flag, for example, once used on a birthday cake in Gaza, earned the users of those colors a term in jail. An artist, also in Gaza, using the colors of the Palestinian flag—black, white, red and green—in painting was sent to jail for six months. So there is, in addition to the taxation and the absence of political rights, also a programmatic war against the very concept of Palestine, as if what Israel has in mind is the extermination of Palestinian national identity.

A third connected measure is that Palestinians in the West Bank and Gaza under Israeli military occupation are subject to the closure of schools and universities. I speak now of the period in particular after the beginning of the intifada, from December 1987 until the present. What is astonishing to me is that beginning in February 1988 Israel closed all seven universities on the West Bank and Gaza, and for many, many months at a time closed the schools and high schools and vocational schools there, all as punitive measures, using the excuse that they were doing this to prevent terrorism. We're not talking about one school. We're not talking about one university. We're talking about *all* the schools and universities, with the result that Israel had in fact denied an entire generation of Palestinian children their education. So that today seven, eight and nine year-old children are illiterate because they haven't been able to attend school. And Israel has made alternative education illegal, so that if you try to educate your children in little groups, you find out that too is against the law. There is a code against these attempts by Palestinians to lead their own lives, a code of military law now numbering over a thousand. They're done by edict, and there's no appeal against them. So schools and universities, including Bir Zeit, the leading university on the West Bank and Gaza, are still closed. It is a scandal. A scandal, ladies and gentlemen, that Israel, which is the state of the Jewish people, the people of The Book, the people who are above all others committed to learning, to humane values, to moral values inscribed in the Old Testament, should be in the position of persecuting another people not only in general but in specific on matters to do with education. There are over a thousand books banned on the West Bank and Gaza today. I supported the movement to prevent Salman Rushdie from being censored by the Iranian government or possibly being killed. I believe absolutely in the right to freedom of speech and opinion. The moral hypocrisy is that at the same time that we were demonstrating for Salman Rushdie's rights, *The Merchant of Venice*, Plato's *Republic*, and *Hamlet* were forbidden on the West Bank by the Israeli government. To this day the leading university is closed. In all of the expressions about the need for freedom of opinion and democracy that we hear from the President and every elected official in this country, where is the discussion about opening the universities in Palestine? That entire institutions of learning should be closed by the Israeli government on the grounds that they are incitements to terrorism, these are colossal, outrageous breaches of moral law.

But that's not all. Since after the first year of the occupation, the Israeli government has been programmatically confiscating land, so that today we are talking about 55 percent of the West Bank and Gaza that has been stolen from the native inhabitants. Because the President has decided that the settlements are an obstacle to peace you are finally beginning to hear about it. During the period of the Carter presidency and even a little bit in the early years of the Reagan presidency, Israelis would bring in bulldozers at the behest of the government and drive people off the land and implant houses on them and say, "There are Jewish settlements." In the middle of what in fact is Arab territory, the current administration calls them "an obstacle to peace." The number of settlements is now over 150. They have of course been condemned internationally across the board. In addition to which Israel has taken most of the water of the West Bank and Gaza for itself. I cite some figures, just to give you an idea of what we're referring to. It's truly astonishing. If you compare the amount of water used by the Israelis versus the amount of water used by Palestinians, you'll notice an astonishing discrepancy. Eighty-six percent of the water is consumed by Israel versus eight-to-twelve percent by Palestinians and another two-to-five percent for Israeli settlers. In other words, what you have is an absolutely crucial resource, water, which has very steadily been taken away from Palestinians who cannot get enough water to irrigate their crops and instead used for such things as swimming pools on the West Bank and Gaza and in Israel. We're talking about a stunning discrepancy here.

In addition to the water and the land, Israel has another policy which is particularly effective; they uproot trees. These are punitive measures conducted against Palestinians by the Israeli occupation army that were never done in South Africa. That is to say, in cruelty and sadism apartheid has a few lessons to learn from the Israeli occupation. Since the beginning of the intifada, they have uproot 112,000 trees. For example, a 14 year-old kid is caught throwing a stone at a jeep or an Israeli tank. An unarmed kid. This can earn the village not only the loss of some more land, but it can also result in the uprooting of fruits and vegetables which requires a permit from the military government to be replanted. You cannot plant anything on the West Bank and Gaza, nor build anything, without a permit. There was an article some years ago by an Israeli lawyer named Avigdor Feldman called "The Israeli Government Versus the Eggplant." He was talking about a particular law, in which the Israeli military governor said, "No fruit tree can be planted on the West Bank or Gaza, or vegetable, without express permission. If it was planted it would be destroyed and the person who did it would be put in jail for six months."

The second unique contribution of Israel to the annuals of persecution is the punitive demolition of a house, which means that if you are suspected of, or have in fact committed an offense against the Israeli military, whether it be a child or an adult, you are marched back to your house by the soldiers, given a few hours to pack your belongings, and the entire house is blown up. There have been over two-thousand houses blown up in the last four years.

Finally we come to two very grave measures which have to do with political prisoners and deaths. Since the intifada began, there have been over 100,000, some say close to 200,000 prisoners put in Israeli jails. By put in jails I don't mean as a result of a trial. The Israeli military occupation is entitled to bring in anyone that it wishes without charge, without trial, without lawyer and incarcerate that person for six months and then renew the incarceration for another six months. There are approximately 15,000 prisoners in Israeli jails on those grounds, and the only grounds usually given are security offenses. If you want to compare this with South Africa, you would have to say that during the years of the state of emergency in South Africa this would have meant that 234,000 prisoners would have been incarcerated. This is three times more than actually were. Israel has established a record, and it is in fact the highest number of prisoners per thousand population of any place on earth.

Then we come to the deaths. Since the intifada began there have been over 1,000 Palestinian killed by Israeli bullets. I'm not talking about accidents, I'm talking about the practice of the Israeli army killing Palestinian men, women and children who demonstrate, who try to circumvent the strictures of the occupation. And add to that the various days, months, weeks of curfew. The Gulf war, for example, serves as an interesting statistic that you might want to ponder. For the first three weeks, the entire West Bank and Gaza, two million people, were kept under 24 hour curfew. For 40 days they were not allowed to leave their houses at all. The number of people who died as a result of that was more than twice the number of Israelis who were killed during the Scud attacks; it was actually three times the number.

I'm sorry to have to recount all these figures to you, but I come to the most important figure of all: The United States, we the taxpayers, have in fact been paying for this. On Sept. 24, 1991, for the first time in a clear and consistent way, an article in the *New York Times* gave background to the discussion of the loan guarantees which Israel is requiring from the United States. The amount of money since 1967 that the United States has given to Israel is $77 billion. In 1990 alone the United States gave Israel $4 billion, and you'll recall recently in a speech the President said this amounts to $1,000 per man, woman, and Israeli child. We're talking about the largest single handout in the history of U.S. aid, relative to the population and in absolute terms. How is it that we have done this, in light of the colossal amount of violations of human rights to Palestinians that have occurred during that period? It is an irony that I find so scandalous as to be unable to understand it, that the United States every year for the last five or six years, in its own State Department annual survey of human rights, has condemned Israel for all the abuses

I've been referring to and then some; and at the same time continues to pour money into Israel, without regard for the rights of the Palestinians. There isn't a body in the world which hasn't condemned it, whether it's Amnesty International or the Red Cross or the Save the Children Fund or the Human Rights Watch, which has just published an extraordinary report on conditions in Israeli prisons. In most prisons Palestinians are crowded in the desert at the rate of something like 30 to 40 per tent in tents, without beds, without cover, without clothes, without food, without books, and without regular family visits. These are all people who have not been charged but are simply held there. We can read the ample reports. We saw them on television. And yet, the part that I cannot understand, is that until recently nobody makes the connection between the tremendous amount of support that the United States gives to Israel, the deteriorating human rights situation on the West Bank and Gaza, and the continuing oppression of Palestinians by Israel. I don't think it's enough to say Palestinians are suffering. It is not suffering made in heaven, something that takes place spontaneously. It is the result of a deliberate program in which Israeli leaders have said publicly that Palestinians, according to Rafael Eitan, who was the Israeli Chief of Staff and is now a member of the Knesset, should be turned into "drugged roaches" in a bottle. The Prime Minister of Israel, Shamir, has referred to Palestinians as "grasshoppers." Begin, the Prime Minister in 1982, when he was invading Lebanon, said Palestinians are nothing but "two-legged vermin." These are phrases that the entire world has condemned in South Africa. Why hasn't the connection been made to Palestine? You cannot say a good word about apartheid. It is impossible to say anything about South Africa without connecting South Africa to apartheid. The fact is that the same thing must be done with Israel. It has to be connected with what it is in fact doing to the Palestinians on the West Bank and has historically done to them.

When we hear that the Palestinians are bloody and violent Arabs and that they love dictatorships, and that they don't have the same attitude toward human life that we do, we should remember we used to hear the same things about the Vietnamese. We seem to be very able to talk about self-determination for the Yugoslavs, Kuwaitis, Russians, Azerbaijanis, Georgians, Lithuanians, and for the Estonians. Everybody should have self-determination. The question that I ask is why is it that it's always an exception for the Palestinians? Well, an answer might be that the Jews of Israel have suffered the Holocaust, these are the survivors of the Holocaust, and how are we to be sure that Palestinians will not wreak upon them a horrible fate? I don't accept the argument that Palestinians are inherently anti-Semitic. They're not. But it also raises the question of what it is politically that the Palestinians have put forward as an answer to that question. Now I'm not speaking as myself, not as someone who talks about the Palestinian question and gives lectures about it. I'm talking now as a student of international politics, as somebody who has something to do with the reading and writing of texts and understands political processes and of course understands recent history. The Palestinian position was put forward by the Palestine National Council, the legislative body of the Palestinian people, in 1988 (Algiers). It states: We have said that we recognize Israel. We accept the principal two U.N. Security Council resolutions 242 and 338, whose fundamental principle is that Israel has to leave the occupied territories, in return for which there will be declared secure and recognized international boundaries, and a state of peace and security will be obtained for everyone. We recognize those. We also say that we wish to end our conflict with Israel. We are the aggrieved people. We are willing to accept a political, not a military settlement with Israel and we want to negotiate an end to the conflict face to face, directly. That is the current Palestinian position. What has been the Israeli response to it? I hope you understand that in the condition of Palestinians and the historical background of Palestine since 1948, to have made those concessions, to have said all these things, certainly constitutes for people of my generation, even for people younger than I, a major compromise, an acceptance of a difficult, for many of us an awful reality, but one that we have to live with. We have accepted not only the idea of recognizing Israel but accepted a tiny state, even less than 25 percent of the land of Palestine, the West Bank and Gaza, in other words, as the territory for an independent Palestine state, so that we can live free of occupation alongside of Israel in a mutually agreed upon modality of peace and security.

This is not only my position as individual Palestinian. This is the position of the Palestine Liberation Organization (PLO), which is the representative of the Palestinians, the political authority, just as the ANC is the political representative of the black South Africans. This is the position formulated by the PNC, the Palestine National Council, and has become the policy of the PLO. To which the Israeli response is, "We don't recognize anything called Palestine. We will not deal with PLO. It's just a terrorist organization. We will not withdraw. This is the land of Israel." Recently, Mr. Shamir made a speech, not reported in this country, but in the British press. I was there. The speech was given on the 50th anniversary of the Stern gang, which was a terrorist group to which he belonged—yes, he, too, was a terrorist. Somebody said, what about the Palestinians. You always accuse them of terrorism. He said, their cause is not just. "They fight for land that is not theirs." This gives you an absolutely fantastic insight into the mentality of this gentleman from Poland who came to Palestine. He says that it's his land that was given to him 2,000 years ago, whereas the people who live there just don't count, it's not their land. They just happen to have been there. They must all go. That's his view. In that perspective, whatever the Palestinians say about peace, justice, reconciliation and recognition falls on totally deaf ears. Shamir's position is not only that he will not recognize the PLO, he won't deal with them. He will say no to a Palestinian state, no to withdrawal, and no to any kind of change in the status quo.

Enter now the peace process. In the aftermath of the Gulf War it was clear in a speech the President gave to the two Houses of Congress on March 6, 1991, that the President decided to cap off the adventure in the Persian Gulf. It was necessary to move on peace in Palestine, the Arab–Israeli struggle. The American position there has been more or less to go along with most of the Israeli conditions. We, the Palestinians, have been told that we're not allowed to be represented by our own representatives. As Abba Eban has said, Israel's positions in all of this is that is has to approve the Palestinian negotiators, which is really unique in the history of conflict. Never before has one party tried to pick the representatives of the other side. But this is going forward. The Israelis have reserved for themselves the right to veto anybody they don't want to appear. The United States position is that it's very important that Palestinians enter the process, that we have a peace conference. As the victims of the victims, the Palestinians will come forward with the enlightened, rational, humane position in which Palestinians will accept that the PLO should not participate, that only people who are not from East Jerusalem, who live only on the West Bank and Gaza will enter the process. That was our position in Madrid. We will go into a negotiating process with the Israelis and the other Arabs with I must say very little hope of anything happening.

Unless there is a determination on the part of the United States to make sure that some movement towards justice and peace be imposed upon Israel, there is no other way. The Palestinians have taken all the steps, and are already at the starting gate. The Israelis aren't even on the course yet. But the Israeli lobby has been so powerful in this country supplying Israel with 77 billion dollars over the last 20 years that very few politicians, very few elected officials, very few individuals will budge. I'm not even talking about people who have to run for office. I'm talking about people who are up front when it comes to South Africa, Vietnam, Nicaragua, and all the difficulties of Central America. You ask them about Palestine: "Well, it's a bit tricky. I'm not sure about that." That's the problem. The reason I'm making the point as strongly as I am is that it is the United States, whether we like it or not, that holds the key to the future. When we talk about the U.S., we're not talking about something out there, we're talking about our tax dollars. In the end Israel relies on the U.S. for everything. It is totally dependent upon the U.S. and has no outside support except from the U.S., to the tune of over $4 billion per year. We're talking about

$10 billon of loan guarantees. For the last several years, Israel has never repaid its loans. Some of its spokesmen on television say Israel has never defaulted on its loans. You know why it's never defaulted on its loans? Because the United States paid them. That's why. You would have a very good credit rating if your loans, your outstanding debts, were paid by the U.S. government. What Israel has been getting from the U.S. is not only current grants paid up front. Egypt gets about $2 billion a year, but Egypt gets it quarterly. Every quarter it has to certify that it's been a "good boy" and then they give them another $500 million. Egypt is approximately 20 times the size in population of Israel. Israel gets its entire grant up front, at the beginning of the fiscal year, and it can take the money, bank it and get the interest on it, which is exactly what it does. The U.S. has to borrow the money in order to make the grant to Israel, so we lose the interest and Israel earns it. And we pay the debts. Senators are very easy to forgive Israel debts and will say, as did President Bush recently, we're not going to give you the loans right away, but whatever it costs you in the delay, we will offset that too.

So the question is whether we as Americans, as concerned people who have demonstrated our concern, who have sent our children, brothers and sisters, our husbands and wives to fight in the Middle East as recently as a year ago, whether our interest is going to be commensurate with our moral sense. Whether the continued violation of the rights of an entire people will be addressed. The Palestinians are not just a miscellaneous bunch of terrorists, as they're often portrayed by the Israelis. They constitute a nation in exile, a totally dispossessed people without land and without sovereignty. Will the United States continue to collude in this and to support the continued brutalization of the population of Palestine by Israel?

I want to make two final points. One is that there can be no peace in the Middle East without settling the question of Palestine, which lies at the very core of all Middle Eastern problems, including the invasion and annexation of Kuwait by Saddam Hussein. Remember in the fall of 1990 Saddam Hussein tried to justify the annexation of Kuwait as part of the liberation of Palestine. So powerful is the symbolism of Palestine in the Arab world. But it's not only the Arab world, because Palestine is not an ordinary place. It's the most saturated—politically, culturally, historically—of any place on earth, and of great relevance to us as a people and as a culture. So the essence of peace in the Middle East is the question of Palestine, and the essence of the question of Palestine is not a political, economic, or strategic question. It is a moral question. Is there a right for a people to suffer as the Jews have suffered? Do they have a right to exact as high a price as they are exacting from the Palestinians today or not? And if not, that has to be settled. Along with that are all of the infringements on the rights to read, assemble, to political representation and self-determination, along with all the other things that are denied Palestinians. We are complicit in this as Americans, because we supply the money and we have the power. This is point number one. The essence of peace in the Middle East is the question of Palestine. To it are linked all of the other questions in the area: The cultural question, the great conflict with the West and the United States are all connected with the question of Palestine. The question of relationship between the religions of Islam and Christianity and Judaism is also connected to the question of Palestine.

A second point I want to make is that for Palestinians and for Israeli Jews there is *no* military option. They *cannot* defeat each other. There is *no* possibility for Palestinians to fight a war of any size or scope against Israel. Israel is capable of fighting a war, with one of the largest and most powerful armies in the world, much of it supplied by the United States. They can fight a war against Palestinians, but it is impossible to do. You could fight and defeat people, but you cannot exterminate them all. So I say that Palestinians and Israelis have no military option against each other. I think it's important to realize that as Palestinians, and I speak here as a Palestinian but also as an individual who firmly believes this, the answer is not exclusivism and hostility unending. It is rather reconciliation, sharing, community. We're talking about two people urgently connected to a small land in many, many ways. I say that the Palestinian vision, which is to try to accommodate, is the one in the end that's going to win. The question is how many people we can persuade of this before there is another holocaust, and it's a Palestinian holocaust that I'm talking about now. What is left to Palestinians today is the moral force of the argument that says a) there is no military option, and b) you have to live with us, we have to live together as Israelis and as Palestinians, and we have to discover modes of sharing. It's in that perspective that citizens such as ourselves, academics, people who are concerned with questions of politics and culture and history, can begin to ask questions, to say "What is this all about? Is it just a matter of giving $10 billion? Is it just a matter of sending fighter pilots and battle ships and cruisers and aircraft carriers? Or is there something simpler? Is there a moral choice here?" I think there is. I think the choice is really between life and death. The Palestinians have said, "We want to live." I think it's very important for all of us to make that choice together.

Editor's Note: This is a slightly edited transcription of a lecture given by Said at the University of Iowa on September 25, 1991.

20

Mutual Learning as an Agenda for Social Development

Tu Weiming

As we are confronted with a new world order, the exclusive dichotomy of capitalism and socialism imposed by the Cold War super powers is woefully inadequate for understanding the rich texture of the emerging global community. Intent on offering an alternative global paradigm, Francis Fukuyama and Samuel Huntington proffer two facile generalizations: "the end of history" and "the clash of civilizations." The two positions are seemingly contradictory readings of the human condition: an optimistic assertion that fundamental ideological divides no longer exist and a cautionary note that cultural, especially religious, differences are the major sources of international conflict.

It seems evident that the liberal democratic countries (Western Europe and North America), fueled by the market economy, have now set the stage for a radically new global transformation. It also seems plausible that challenges from, for example, the Confucian and the Islamic cultural zones may impede this process. Yet, should we take the trajectory of Western culture's impact as a sort of historical inevitability? Both positions evoked above are predicated on the assumption that the current working dichotomy is still "the West and the rest." Is this conceptual framework adequate for enhancing social development as an international joint venture?

If social development is seen as an aspiration and a promise for human flourishing, we need to address the fundamental ethical and spiritual issues confronting the global community. The old triumphant or confrontational Western mindset is counterproductive. The United States in particular, can take the lead in transforming itself from primarily a teaching civilization—especially in reference to East Asia since World War II—into a learning culture by considering some critical questions:

Which way is more congenial to social integration, viewing ourselves as isolated individuals or as centers of interpersonal relationships?

Even if we use quantifiable material conditions to define and measure our well-being, can we afford to cut off ourselves from the spiritual moorings of our cultures?

If success is solely measured as wealth and power to the exclusion of other goods, such as social capital, moral influence and exemplary teaching, how can we transmit cherished values to the next generation?

How can we expect others to respect our way of life, if we disregard what they themselves regard as meaningful and worthwhile?

Can our society prosper without inculcating in individuals a basic sense of duty and responsibility in addition to rights-consciousness?

Can we afford to focus our attention on the rule of law without emphasizing civility and trust in ordinary daily social intercourse?

Can liberty as an intrinsic value generate a humane society without distributive justice?

Can instrumental rationality alone right inequality without sympathy and compassion?

Should our culturally pluralistic world deliberately cultivate shared values as a common ground for organic social solidarity?

As we become more keenly aware of our earth's vulnerability and the depletion of natural resources, what steps must we take to preserve her?

Such questions suggest a much needed communal critical self-consciousness among the reflective minds of the world. We may be witnessing the very beginning of global history rather than the end of history. And, as we approach 2001, the United Nations-designated year of Dialogue Among Civilizations, this new beginning must take the desire for mutual reference as its point of departure. Our awareness of the danger of civilizational conflicts rooted in ethnicity, gender, language, land, class, age, and religion, makes the necessity of dialogue particularly compelling. If we envision development in social as well as economic terms, we recognize that globalization is not homogenization. Rather, it both intensifies and undermines various forms of localization. We should accept a plurality of models of sustainable development and emphasize the ethical and spiritual dimensions of human flourishing as integral parts of our development strategy.

A perception of development shaped by modernization as a unilinear progression and defined exclusively by quantifiable material gains is too simplistic to reflect the complexity and diversity of human flourishing. Surely, eradicating absolute poverty is one of the highest priorities of any global approach to social development, but even here, the enabling factors are political, social, cultural and legal as well as economic. This requires a more sophisticated vision of how different spheres of interests are interconnected nationally, regionally and globally.

Just as no local interests, no matter how compelling, should override national interests, regional and global interests must not be subsumed under national interests. Even if we assume that the United States alone can exert hegemonic influence in the global community, the really enduring American strength lies in "soft power"—moral persuasion—as well as military might. Social capital, the cultivation of cultural competence and the enhancement of spiritual values, is as important as economic capital, the cultivation of technical competence and the enhancement of material conditions.

The politics of domination is being replaced by the politics of communication, networking, negotiation, interaction, interfacing, and collaboration. The strong 1960's belief that "modernization would wipe out cultural, institutional, structural and mental differences and, if unimpeded, would lead to a uniform modern world" is no longer tenable. Since globalization engenders localization and indigenization as well as homogenization, cultural, institutional, structural and cognitive differences actually shape the contours of the modernizing processes. In consequence, traditions are constituent parts of modernity and modernization can assume different cultural, institutional, structural and mental forms. The thesis of convergence, meaning that the rest of the world will inevitably converge with the modern West, has been modified.

In the eighties, the thesis of reverse convergence was strongly implied, if not clearly articulated, by new modernization theorists as the result of East Asian economic dynamism. The ideas of "Asian values," "network capitalism," and "the Asia-Pacific century" were advocated as an alternative to modern Westernism. However, the observation that the engine of development had shifted from the Atlantic to the Pacific was premature. The 1997 Asian financial crisis forced a new interpretation. Authoritarianism and crony capitalism were identified as the cultural, institutional, structural and mental causes: Asian financial institutions had suffered from lack of transparency, public accountability and fair competitiveness. As the economies of the Asia-Pacific region begin to recover, East Asia will likely reemerge as the single most important reference and perhaps as a counterpoint for Western Europe and North America again.

If, instead of reverse convergence, "multiple modernities" had been presented as an explanatory model, the implications of East Asian modernity would have been far-reaching. East Asia has been deeply influenced by Western Europe and North America and its accelerating modernity is mainly the result of the Western impact. Yet, the shape of life of East Asian peoples is significantly different from that of Westerners. The possibility of being modern without being Western suggests that, under the influence of East Asia as well as West Europe and North America, Southeast Asian societies, notably Malaysia and Indonesia, may become modern without necessarily being European, American or East Asian. By implication, Latin American, South Asian and African forms of modernity are, in principle, realizable.

Is the vision of multiple modernities merely wishful thinking or practicable guide for social development? The Copenhagen Social Summit was committed to support full employment, promote social integration, achieve gender equality and equity, and attain universal and equitable access to education and primary care. If these are realizable aspirations for the global community, rather than privileges and entitlements of the First World, every country is, in both theory and practice, capable of human flourishing according to its own specific conditions. The mobilization of indigenous cultural recourses for capacity building is a precondition for such an endeavor.

East Asia is a case in point. Can East Asian political and cultural leaders be inspired by the Confucian spirit of self-cultivation, family cohesiveness, social solidarity, benevolent governance, and universal peace to practice responsibility in their domestic affairs? This question concerns us all. As Chinese, Japanese, Koreans, and Vietnamese emigrate to other parts of the world, can they share their rich cultural heritage? This question is important not only for East Asia, but for the United States, Canada, Australia, and the European Union.

The commitment to "accelerate the development of Africa and the least developed countries" is predicated on a holistic vision of human flourishing and a realistic model of interdependency. If we consider ethnic, cultural, linguistic, and religious diversity as a global asset, Africa should not be characterized by the HIV epidemic, poverty, unemployment and social disintegration alone. It should also be recognized as a rich reservoir for human spirituality and the wisdom of elders. The African Renaissance, symbolized by the geological and biological diversity of the tiny area around Capetown (said to be comparable in richness to the vast area of Canada) ought to be a source of inspiration for a changed mindset that addresses social development as a global joint venture.

The development of Africa is important for us because, without a holistic sense of human flourishing, we cannot properly anchor our sense of security, let alone well-being in the global community as a whole. The acknowledgment that there is a "multiplicity of modern societies around the globe" and that it is arrogant to proclaim our own cultural supremacy is a significant step toward mutual referencing among societies. We cannot help African societies to accelerate their development if we prematurely conclude that they have nothing to teach us. Indeed, the celebration of cultural diversity, without falling into the trap of pernicious relativism, is profoundly meaningful for global stewardship.

As the rise of Confucian East Asia suggests, traditions are present as active agents in modernity; in fact, the modernizing process has assumed a variety of cultural forms. Modernization originating in Western Europe has powerfully transformed the world in one dominant direction. In its inception, however, it was already a mixture of conflictual and even contradictory trajectories. Even if we overcome the conceptual difficulty of generalizing European cases as paradigmatic manifestations of modernity, we must sill treat North American modernity as a separate case. The story of modernization as a master narrative contains several versions of globally significant local knowledge. Now that East Asia's local knowledge is added to the story, it seems reasonable to anticipate an increasing number of normal or even exemplary modernities from other parts of the world. Fruitful comparisons across geographic, linguistic, ethnic, cultural, and religious boundaries will enrich our understanding of social development as a holistic program for human flourishing.

The common practice of "learning from the West," deemed absolutely necessary for survival by East Asian intellectuals and political leaders, will certainly continue but the need to broaden the horizons of reference cultures is obvious. As "mutual referencing" progresses, East Asia can benefit from civilizational dialogues with Latin America, South Asia, the Islamic world, and Africa. I have been advocating in Beijing and throughout Cultural China that it is in China's best interest to take India seriously as a reference society. This will significantly broaden China's symbolic resources in understanding her own indigenous traditions, such as Mahayana Buddhism and religious Daoism and help her better appreciate the modern relevance of religion. If China can recognize Tibet as an enduring spiritual tradition and a venerable cultural heritage, not only will her international reputation significantly improve but also her domestic ability to promote social integration.

In the United States and, by implication, the modern West, the need to transform America's arrogance as a teaching civilization into the humility of a learning culture is predicated on a global vision of social development. We should accept the dictum that the more powerful, wealthy and influential nations are, the more obligated they are to enlarge the well-being of the global community. Strong and rich nations, as beneficiaries of the international system, are obligated to see to it that the least developed countries benefit from their international policies. The isolationist mentality that advocates national interests as an ultimate justification for global action is, in the long run, detrimental to domestic social solidarity. The protectionist approach is self-defeating because it eventually undermines the very system that has generated and sustained its prosperity.

East Asian intellectuals have been devoted students of Western learning. In Japan, European and American tutelage has played an important role in modernization. Japan's ability to learn from the West without abandoning indigenous resources for national and cultural identity, helped this country to become one of the most developed in the world. The West, on the other hand, has not felt compelled to learn from the rest of the global community. This asymmetrical situation is particularly pronounced in United States' relationships with East Asian, notably China. To remain a strong international leader the United States needs an elite educated to be well-informed global citizens.

The time is long over due for American educators and politicians to rekindle a cosmopolitan spirit. The United States' assumption of the role of a tutor for democracy, market economy, civil society, and human rights in East Asia since World War II has been instrumental in developing an international vision. Although an implicit hegemonic mentality in this vision was unhealthy, it had the potential of evolving into true internationalism. However, as the anti-Communist ideology fades and East Asia assumes a greater role in global business and politics, a more wholesome American presence in East Asia is partnership. Implicit in partnership are recognition, understanding and appreciation. Although the obligation to address this asymmetry is mutual, the United States, as the stronger and wealthier partner has greater resources to improve the situation effectively and equitably.

America's current isolationist and protectionist mentality, a reflection of the politics of domination, cannot be transformed by top-down political will. Change can only occur through mobilization of social forces, including non-governmental organizations. Public intellectuals in government, media, business, the professions, labor, religion, and advocacy movements—for example, environmental protection, gender equality, racial harmony, or human rights—as well as the academic community should take responsibility for facilitating a new agenda to discuss the American vision of and contribution to the global community. Given America's habits of the heart and fragmented political prospects for increasing American internationalism, debates are not particularly encouraging in the short run.

At the Copenhagen Social Summit in 1995, heads of State or Government from 117 countries pledged to implement 10 commitments to alleviate poverty, promote employment and ensure social integration. This obviously newsworthy item received scant attention and was substantially overwhelmed by trivia from Los Angeles during the O. J. Simpson murder trial even in some of the nation's leading international journals. This fact alone clearly cautions against any naive optimism. Nevertheless, pragmatic idealism and a cosmopolitan spirit are also defining characteristics of the American mind. American officials as well as scholars and experts have been at the forefront in ensuring that structural adjustment programs include social development and increasing resources allocated to social development. The possibility of an authentic American internationalism is still there.

The emergence of a new communal critical self-consciousness among public intellectuals will better facilitate American participation in strengthening cooperation for social development through the UN and help realize inspiring leadership on the global scene. In the eyes of East Asian intellectuals, the strength of the United States as a model of modernity lies in vibrant market economy, functioning democratic polity, dynamic civil society, and culture of freedom. The Enlightenment values, such as liberty, rights consciousness, due process of law, and dignity of the individual, are evident in American economy, polity, society, and culture. Yet, unfortunately, American life is also plagued by inequality, litigiousness, conflict, and violence. The American people could benefit from a spirit of distributive justice in economy, an ethic of responsibility in politics, a sense of trust in society, and, above all, a culture of peace. Among the developed countries, the United States is noted for openness to change, willingness to experiment and flexibility. Somewhat liberal immigration policies, admittedly often dictated by economic need and political expediency, are clear indication of the evolution of the United States into a microcosmic "united nations." Multiculturalism and ethnic diversity are integral parts of the American way of life. The best of America is seen in a spirit of tolerance, co-existence, dialogical interaction, and mutual learning across race, gender, age, class, and religion. If the American mindset evolves to encompass responsibility, civility and compassion as well as freedom and rights and take a global perspective in defining her national interests, the United States can significantly enhance the UN agenda for social development.

Permissions

Part I Perspectives on Culture in Theory and Research

Chapter 1 was originally published in *Communication Quarterly*, 1996, Vol. 44, No. 1, pp. 70–84. Reprinted by permission of Routledge.

Chapter 2 was originally published in Josina M. Makau & Ronald C. Arnett (Eds.). (1997). *Communication ethics in an age of diversity* (pp. 73–88). Urbana, IL: University of Illinois Press. Reprinted by permission of University of Illinois Press.

Chapter 3 was originally published in Robert Shuter (Ed.), *Patterns of intracultural communication* [Special issue]. *Southern Communication Journal*, 1990, Vol. 55, No. 3, pp. 237–249, with revision for the new conclusion. Reprinted by permission of Routledge.

Part II Metatheoretical Frameworks for Future Directions

Chapter 4 was originally published in *Journal of Black Studies*, 1983, Vol. 14, No. 1, pp. 3–19. Reprinted by permission of Sage Publications.

Chapter 5 was originally published in Guo-Ming Chen & Yoshitaka Miike (Eds.), *Asian approaches to human communication* [Special issue]. *Intercultural Communication Studies*, 2003, Vol. 12, No. 4, pp. 39–63. Reprinted by permission of the International Association for Intercultural Communication Studies (IAICS).

Chapter 6 was originally published in *Communication Theory*, 1999, Vol. 9, No. 1, pp. 1–25. Reprinted by permission of Blackwell.

Part III Contextual Approaches to Culture and Communication

Chapter 7 was originally published in *Journal of Language and Social Psychology*, 1997, Vol. 16, No. 2, pp. 107–131. Reprinted by permission of Sage Publications.

Chapter 8 was originally published in *Critical Arts: A South–North Journal of Cultural and Media Studies*, 1999, Vol. 13, No. 2, pp. 24–42. Reprinted by permission of Routledge.

Chapter 9 was originally published in *Howard Journal of Communications*, 2005, Vol. 16, No. 3, pp. 149–175. Reprinted by permission of Routledge.

Chapter 10 was originally published in Judith N. Martin & Olga I. Davis (Eds.), *Ethnicity and Methodology* [special issue]. *International Journal of Intercultural Relations*, 2000, Vol. 24, No. 5, pp. 623–650. Reprinted by permission of Elsevier Science Ltd.

Part IV Impact of Globalization on Intercultural Communication

Chapter 11 was originally published in Majid Tehranian (Ed.). (1999). *Worlds apart: Human security and global governance* (pp. 153–167). London: I. B. Tauris. Reprinted by permission of I. B. Tauris.

Chapter 12 was originally published in *Women's Studies in Communication*, 1995, Vol. 18, No. 1, pp. 45–64. Reprinted by permission of *Women's Studies in Communication*.

Chapter 13 is published by permission of the author.

Part V Identity and Intercultural Communication Competence

Chapter 14 was originally published in Brant B. Burleson (Ed.). (1996). *Communication yearbook* (Vol. 19, pp. 353–383). Thousand Oaks, CA: Sage. Reprinted by permission of Sage Publications.

Chapter 15 was originally published in *International Journal of Intercultural Relations*, 2000, Vol. 24, No. 2, pp.173–201. Reprinted by permission of Elsevier Science Ltd.

Chapter 16 was originally published in *China Media Research*, 2006, Vol. 2, No. 4, pp. 9–21. Reprinted by permission of *China Media Research*.

Part VI Ethical Considerations in Intercultural Communication

Chapter 17 was originally published in Yoshitaka Miik & Guo-Ming (Eds.), *Asian contributions to communication theory* [special issue]. *China Media Research*, 2007, Vol. 3, No. 4. Reprinted by permission of *China Media Research*.

Chapter 18 was originally published in Clifford Christians & Michael Traber (Eds.). (1997). *Communication ethics and universal values* (pp. 128–158). Thousand Oaks, CA: Sage. Reprinted by permission of Sage Publications.

Chapter 19 was originally published in *Journal of Communication Inquiry*, 1992, Vol. 16, No. 1, pp. 5–19. Reprinted by permission of Sage Publications.

Chapter 20 was originally published in Jacques Baudot (Ed.). (2001). *Building a world community: Globalization and the common good* (pp. 253–260). Copenhagen, Demark: Royal Danish Ministry of Foreign Affairs and the University of Washington Press. Reprinted by permission of the University of Washington Press.

Index